AIDS

TO

ENGLISH COMPOSITION,

PREPARED FOR

STUDENTS OF ALL GRADES;

EMBRACING

SPECIMENS AND EXAMPLES OF SCHOOL AND COLLEGE EXERCISES AND MOST OF THE HIGHER DEPARTMENTS OF ENGLISH COMPOSITION, BOTH IN PROSE AND VERSE.

By RICHARD GREEN PARKER, A. M.

"Dimidium facti qui cœpit, habet."

TWENTIETH EDITION.

NEW YORK:
HARPER & BROTHERS, PUBLISHERS,
FRANKLIN SQUARE.
1863.

PREFACE.

It would be presumptuous in any author to attempt to give rules, or to lay down laws, to which all the departments of English Composition should be subjected. Genius cannot be fettered, and an original and thinking mind, replete with its own exuberance, will often burst out in spontaneous gushings, and open to itself new channels, through which the treasures of thought will flow in rich and rapid currents. Rules and suggestions, however, are not wholly useless. They encourage the diffident, and give confidence to those whose want of conversance with approved models renders it necessary for them to rely on foreign aid. In the volume to which this book is designed as a sequel, the author has attempted to render assistance in the removal of the two obstacles which beset the youthful writer in his first attempts at composition; to wit, the difficulty of obtaining ideas, or learning to think, and that of expressing them properly when obtained. There are those who profess to have been benefited by the assistance therein afforded. In this volume he has endeavored to embrace a wider range in the extensive field before him. He candidly confesses that he is not satisfied with his own labors. He would have been better contented to see the task completed by abler hands. But as his labors have been found useful, he has been encouraged to extend them, in the hope that they will prove beneficial, especially to those who have neither the leisure nor the inclination to seek in the wide fields of literature for other and deeper sources of information. If the water in the bucket drawn from the well has not the coolness and raciness of the fountain, or the spring, it will quench the thirst and cool the brow of the toiler, in his laborious ascent of the hill of science.

With regard to the manner in which this volume is to be used, the author has only to say that he has not aimed at giving a regular and systematic course of instruction. Few teachers would probably follow any path that might be pointed out. It has not been his aim to present in this volume a *progressive* course. Leaving to the judgment of those who may use the book the task of selecting such exercises as may in their opinion best promote the intellectual advancement of those whose minds they are training, he respectfully submits the volume, in the hope that it may prove a useful auxiliary in the difficult but highly useful task of Composititon.

Orange Street, Boston, January 1st, 1844.

ADVERTISEMENT TO THE SECOND EDITION.

THE Publishers having determined to stereotype this work, the Author, unwilling that it should leave his hands and be put into permanent form until he had given it a careful revision, and made it as worthy as he could of the favor with which it has been received, has made some important improvements in the plan, the arrangement, and the materials, by which he thinks its value as an Aid to Composition is greatly enhanced. The subject of Description in particular has been considerably extended and enriched, from sources not within his reach in the original preparation of the volume. The examples and exercises in various parts of the work have been much improved by the rejection of those which he had borrowed from other works, and which had long been familiar, and the substitution of others more valuable, because they are new. He now submits the work, in the hope that it will not be found unworthy of the continuance of the favor with which it has been received.

Orange Street, Boston, June 1, 1845.

INTRODUCTION.

Composition is the art of forming ideas, and expressing them in language. Its most obvious divisions, with respect to the nature of its subjects, are the Narrative, the Descriptive, the Didactic, the Persuasive, the Pathetic, and the Argumentative. With regard to its form or style, it may be considered as concise or diffuse, as nervous or feeble, as dry, plain, neat, elegant or flowery, as simple, or affected, as cold or vehement, as barren or luxuriant; and its essential requisites are clearness, unity, strength and harmony. As it is strictly a mental effort, its foundation must be laid in a disciplined and cultivated mind, in the exercise of vigorous thought, on reading and observation, and an attentive study of the meaning and the force of language. The proper preparation for its successful performance should be laid in a diligent attention to the rules of grammar, a thorough knowledge of the principles of rhetoric, and a successful application of the maxims of logic; for logic must direct us in the selection of ideas, rhetoric must clothe them in a suitable dress, and grammar must adapt the dress to the peculiar form of the idea. In the following pages an attempt is made gradually to introduce the student to the several departments of English composition by examples and exercises, with such observations and illustrations as may appear to be necessary for an intelligent comprehension of its rules and principles. The early lessons are simple and easily performed, but, in the course of the work, suggestions will be found, which, it is thought, will be useful to those by whom composition is not regarded as a task.

Of the importance of attention to the subject of composition thus much may be said; that there are few individuals, in any station of life, to whom ease and fluency in writing are not valuable acquisitions. All who are engaged in professional or commercial pursuits, and even the hardier sons of labor, whose "bread is procured by the sweat of their brow," must have correspondence to manage, or written statements to furnish, requiring at once accuracy and despatch; and therefore the facility which practice alone can impart, in the arrangement of their thoughts, and a ready and correct expression of them, is an attainment exceedingly desirable. In the language of a late transatlantic writer, then, it may boldly be asserted, that "No acquirement can equal that of composition in giving a power over the material of thought, and an aptness in all matters of arrangement, of inquest, and of argumentation." "Writing," says Lord Bacon, "makes a correct man;" and the author of the Essay on Criticism asserts, that

"True grace in writing comes from art, not chance,
As they move easiest who have learnt to dance."

"He that begins with the calf," says Mr. Locke, "may carry the ox, but he, that will go at first to take the ox, may so disable himself as not to be able to take the calf after that." On the same principle, it is recommended that an attention to the subject of composition should be commenced early in life. Exercises of a simple character prepare the mind for higher exertion; and readiness and facility in the lower departments of writing enable the student to apply himself without reluctance to those mightier efforts by which the progress of intellectual culture is most rapidly advanced.

The words of Horace may here be recommended to particular attention:

"Sumite materiam qui scribitis æquam
"Viribus."

Or, in the translation of Mr. Francis:

"Examine well, ye writers, weigh with care,
What suits your genius, what your strength will bear.

CONTENTS.

CONTENTS.

CONTENTS.

AIDS

TO

ENGLISH COMPOSITION.

I.

OBJECTS AND THEIR PARTS.

The first step to be taken in writing composition is to obtain ideas. The second is the proper expression of the idea when obtained. To acquire ideas, it is necessary to cultivate habits of observation; to use the eyes not only in noticing entire objects, but also their different parts; to consider their qualities, uses, operations, and effects; together with their relation to other things. The mind employed in such processes acquires materials for its own operations, and thoughts and ideas arise as it were spontaneously.

For the first exercise in composition, therefore, it is proposed that the student be required to enumerate the parts of some visible object, according to the following

Example.

A HOUSE.

Its parts are

The inside,	The wainscot,	The parlors or drawing rooms,
The outside,	The stairs,	The wash room,
The doors,	The fire places,	The bathing room,
The entry,	The mantel,	The inner doors,
The rooms,	The chimney,	The wood shed,
The ceiling,	The closets,	The out buildings.
The walls,	The kitchen,	

Exercises.

In a similar manner enumerate the parts of the following objects

A carriage.	A sheep.	A book.
A ship.	A cat.	A kite.
A church.	A landscape.	A cow.
A tree.	A school-room.	A goat.
A map.	A watch.	A dog.
A horse.	A clock.	A picture.

II.

OBJECTS, THEIR QUALITIES AND USES.

The parts of a visible object having been noticed, the next step to be taken is the enumeration of its qualities and uses according to the following

Example.

GLASS: It is	hard,	inodorous,	insoluble,
	solid,	colorless,	dry,
	smooth,	heavy,	fusible,
	bright,	uninflammable,	thick or thin,
	transparent,	durable,	long,
	brittle,	stiff,	short,
	cold,	inflexible,	wide,
	tasteless,	water proof,	useful.

Its uses:

For windows to admit light:
For spectacles to assist sight:
For useful vessels, such as tumblers, pitchers, decanters, wine-glasses, jelly-glasses, bottles, phials, inkstands, lamps, and lamp-glasses, chandeliers, handles of doors and drawers, vases, cups, and ornaments, such as beads, drops, prisms, &c.

Exercises.

In the same manner enumerate the qualities of the following objects.

Wood.	Sugar.	A lamp.
Iron.	Salt.	Ivory.
Lead.	Sponge.	A pin.
Silver.	A desk.	A chair.
Gold.	Wool.	A table.
A feather.	Cotton.	A penknife.
A pen.	Wax.	A quill.
Water.	Whalebone.	An inkstand.
Leather.	A horn.	Ice.
Paper.	Chalk.	Snow.

III.

OBJECTS, THEIR PARTS, QUALITIES PROPERTIES, USES AND APPENDAGES.

The parts, properties, and uses of visible objects having now been considered, the two processes may be united, in the consideration of the parts, qualities, properties, uses and appendages, as in the following

Example.

A Pen consists of the	quill,	pith,	surfaces,
	shaft,	nib,	groove,
	feather,	shoulders,	inside, and
	laminæ,	skin,	outside.
Qualities. The quill is	transparent,	smooth,	elastic,
	round or	bright,	yellowish,
	cylindrical,	hard,	horny,
	hollow,	glossy,	tough.
The shaft is	opake,	white,	hard,
	angular,	stiff,	grooved
The pith is	white,	porous.	soft,
	spongy	elastic.	light.

The use of the pen is to write down what we have seen, read, or thought, and thereby to preserve what would probably soon be lost, if intrusted to the memory alone. What is once written can be read, or preserved for future information, and thereby we can learn what our friends who are absent, and even those who are dead, have seen or said.

Exercises.

Enumerate the parts, qualities, and uses of the following objects

A book.	A work-box.	A knife.
A house.	A saw.	A wing.
A tree.	A chisel.	A fin.
A table.	A plane.	The hand.
A bureau.	A ball.	The arm.
The contents of a box.	A kite.	The foot.
A secretary.	A dressing-case.	The eye.
A plate.	A sofa.	The ear.
A barrel.	A chair.	The nose.
A lamp.	A lock.	The mouth.
A candlestick.	A key.	The human face

IV.

EVENTS.

The object of this lesson is to teach the learner to describe, in easy sentences, any circumstances which happen to himself and others.

He should be directed to write the incident just as he would relate it to his parents or a young friend; and after he has thus written it, to revise it carefully, to see whether any of his words are mis-spelt, and whether he has used the very words which he intended to use.

Example.

On returning home yesterday, I saw a man severely beating a horse. I stopped a moment to ascertain the cause; and perceived that one of the wheels of the wagon had sunk deep in the mire, and the poor animal was exerting all his strength to drag the heavy load, while the cruel driver was mercilessly beating the unfortunate creature because he could not proceed.

Exercises.

In a similar manner, the learner may describe the following events

The meeting of a beggar in the street.
The overturn of a carriage.
The passing of a procession.
The sailing of a ship.
The catching of a fish.
The capture of a bird.
The raising of a kite.
A fire.
The raising of a building.

V.

OBJECTS AND EVENTS.

The object of this lesson is to accustom the learner to combine the results of the preceding lessons.

The same directions should be given to him as are presented in the last lesson; and it will be proper to enforce the directions with regard to the spelling, and the proper use of words, in every exercise.

Example.

As my brother was riding in the country, he saw a beautiful, large house, painted white, with green blinds. In the front of the house was a small flower-garden, and the bright tulips, all in full bloom, presented a brilliant show. The rose bushes were not yet in flower; but the lily of the valley was dropping its modest head, while it perfumed the air with its delicious fragrance. At the back of the house were a number of fruit trees, in full blossom, among which was the peach tree, with its beautiful pink flowers. Some boys were seen clustering around a willow near the brook, busily engaged with their knives. One was cutting the small leaves and scions from a large branch, which he had just taken from the tree for a whip, while another was busily engaged in making a whistle. As my brother approached the house, the boys, mistaking him for the owner, immediately scampered away; some hiding themselves among the bushes, while the more active leaped over the high stone wall, to escape being caught. It appeared that these boys were truants from a neighboring school-house, and the little rogues were fearful, not only of being caught in trespassing upon private ground, but likewise lest they should be carried into the presence of their master, to be corrected for playing the truant.

Exercises.

In the same manner the learner may describe the following objects and events;

Boys fishing from a bridge.
Girls dressing their dolls.
A tree blown down by a tempest.
Boy driving cows or sheep to pasture.
Horses running at large.
A dog, in a state of madness, biting passengers in the street.
A lion, elephant, or tiger broken loose from its cage.
A menagerie, with the postures and employments of the wild animals.
A museum, with dancing puppets.
A public concert.
An exhibition of paintings and statuary.

VI.

NAMES.

The object of this exercise on names, is to prepare the student for a future exercise on definitions. How it is to be performed will be readily seen from the following

Examples.

What is the name which is applied to false or undeserved praise?

Answer. Flattery.

By what name do we call the delaying of that which we know cannot be finally escaped or avoided?

Answer. Procrastination.

By what name do we designate that animal which has two horns, a long tail, and cloven feet, and that affords beef, butter, and cheese?

Answer. The Cow.

By what name do we designate the restraint of appetite and passion?

Answer. Temperance.

Exercises.

What name is given to the reverence of God?

What name is applied to an effort of genius and art, producing an association of exalted and brilliant ideas in language harmoniously arranged?

A general coincident feeling between two persons?

Habitual inactivity both of mind and body?

That tranquil state of mind in which the agitations of anxiety and disappointment are no longer felt?

That state of mind which suffers no dismay from danger?

The dissolution of corporeal existence?

The resolution to persist in any undertaking that has been commenced?

The time after sunset?

That God is present every where, and that he knows all things?

A habit of being pleased?

VII.

SIMPLE DIALOGUE, OR CONVERSATION.

Young persons are seldom at a loss for topics of conversation, when left unrestrained to themselves. But as soon as they are required to write what is called a *composition*, they feel at a loss what to say. This arises from no inability to form ideas, nor from want of words to express them; but rather from a vague apprehension that something is required of them, which they have never done before; and to which they know not how to address themselves. The cultivation of the habits of observation, to which allusion has already been made in the first exercise, will help them wholly out of the difficulty; especially, if they be informed, that the art of writing is nothing more than the art of expressing with the hand, in signs which present themselves to the eye, that, which with their voice, they convey to the ears of others. In other words, that in their early attempts at writing composition, they may write down in letters, what they would say to their companions in their common conversations.

To cultivate the habits of observation, the following dialogue, from the pen of Dr. Aikin, is presented; with the recommendation that it be read to the young student, or that he be required to read it carefully, in order that he may learn to use his eyes aright, and attentively observe what passes before them.

THE TUTOR AND HIS PUPILS.

Eyes and no Eyes; or, the Art of Seeing.

"Well, Robert, where have you been walking this afternoon?" said a tutor to one of his pupils, at the close of a holiday.

Robert. I have been to Broom-heath, and so round by the windmill upon Camp-mount, and home through the meadows by the river side.

Tutor. Well, that is a pleasant round.

Robert. I thought it very dull, Sir; I scarcely met with a single person. I would much rather have gone along the turnpike road.

Tutor. Why, if seeing men and horses was your object, you would, indeed, have been better entertained on the high-road. But did you see William?

Robert. We set out together, but he lagged behind in the lane, so I walked on and left him.

Tutor. That was a pity. He would have been company for you.

Robert. O, he is so tedious, always stopping to look at this thing and that! I would rather walk alone. I dare say he is not got home yet.

Tutor. Here he comes. Well, William, where have you been?

William. O, the pleasantest walk! I went all over Broom-heath, and so up to the mill at the top of the hill, and then down among the green meadows by the side of the river.

Tutor. Why, that is just the round Robert has been taking, and he complains of its dulness, and prefers the high-road.

William. I wonder at that. I am sure I hardly took a step that did not delight me, and I have brought home my handkerchief full of curiosities

Tutor. Suppose, then, you give us an account of what amused you so much. I fancy it will be as new to Robert as to me.

William. I will do it readily. The lane leading to the heath, you know, is close and sandy, so I did not mind it much, but made the best of my way. However, I spied a curious thing enough in the hedge. It was an old crab-tree, out of which grew a great bunch of something green quite different from the tree itself. Here is a branch of it.

Tutor. Ah! this is a mistletoe, a plant of great fame for the use made of it by the Druids of old in their religious rites and incantations. It bears a very slimy white berry, of which birdlime may be made, whence the Latin name, *Viscus.* It is one of those plants which do not grow in the ground by a root of their own, but fix themselves upon other plants; whence they have been humorously styled *parasitical*, as being hangers on, or dependents. It was the mistletoe of the oak that the Druids particularly honored.

William. A little farther on, I saw a green woodpecker fly to a tree and run up the trunk like a cat.

Tutor. That was to seek for insects in the bark, on which they live. They bore holes with their strong bills for that purpose, and do much damage to the trees by it.

William. What beautiful birds they are!

Tutor. Yes; they have been called, from their color and size, the English parrot.

William. When I got upon the open heath, how charming it was! The air seemed so fresh, and the prospect on every side so free and unbounded! Then it was all covered with gay flowers, many of which I had never observed before. There were at least three kinds of heath, (I have got them in my handkerchief here,) and gorse, and broom, and bell-flower, and many others of all colors, of which I will beg you presently to tell me the names.

Tutor. That I will, readily.

William. I saw, too, several birds that were new to me. There was a pretty grayish one, of the size of a lark, that was hopping about some great stones; and when he flew, he showed a great deal of white above his tail.

Tutor. That was a wheat-ear. They are reckoned very delicious birds to eat, and frequent the open downs in Sussex, and some other counties, in great numbers.

William. There was a flock of lapwings upon a marshy part of the heath, that amused me much. As I came near them, some of them kept flying round and round, just over my head, and crying *pewit* so distinctly, one might almost fancy they spoke. I thought I should have caught one of them, for he flew as if one of his wings was broken, and often tumbled close to the ground; but, as I came near, he always contrived to get away.

Tutor. Ha, ha! you were finely taken in, then! This was all an artifice of the bird's, to entice you away from its nest; for they build upon the bare ground, and their nests would easily be observed, did they not draw off the attention of intruders, by their loud cries and counterfeit lameness.

William. I wish I had known that, for he led me a long chase, often over shoes in water. However, it was the cause of my falling in with an old man and a boy, who were cutting and piling up turf for fuel; and I had a good deal of talk with them, about the manner of preparing the turf, and the price it sells at. They gave me, too, a creature I never saw before — a young viper, which they had just killed, together with its dam. I have seen several common snakes, but this is thicker in proportion, and of a darker color than they are.

Tutor. True. Vipers frequent those turfy, boggy grounds pretty much, and I have known several turf-cutters bitten by them.

William. They are very venomous, are they not?

Tutor. Enough so to make their wounds painful and dangerous, though they seldom prove fatal.

William. Well — I then took my course up to the windmill on the mount. I climbed up the steps of the mill, in order to get a better view of the country round. What an extensive prospect! I counted fifteen church steeples; and I saw several gentlemen's houses peeping out from the midst of green woods and plantations; and I could trace the windings of the river all along the low grounds, till it was lost behind a ridge of hills. But I 'll tell you what I mean to do, if you will give me leave.

Tutor. What is that?

William. I will go again, and take with me Cary's country map, by which I shall probably be able to make out most of the places.

Tutor. You shall have it, and I will go with you, and take my pocket spying-glass.

William. I shall be very glad of that. Well — a thought struck me, that, as the hill is called *Camp-mount*, there might, probably, be some remains of ditches and mounds, with which I have read that camps were surrounded. And I really believe I discovered something of that sort running round one side of the mount.

Tutor. Very likely you might. I know antiquaries have described such remains as existing there, which some suppose to be Roman, others Danish. We will examine them further when we go.

William. From the hill I went straight down to the meadows below, and walked on the side of a brook that runs into the river. It was all bordered with reeds, and flags, and tall flowering plants, quite different from those I had seen on the heath. As I was getting down the bank to reach one of them, I heard something plunge into the water near me. It was a large water-rat, and I saw it swim over to the other side, and go into its hole. There were a great many dragon-flies all about the stream. I caught one of the finest, and have got him here in a leaf. But how I longed to catch a bird that I saw hovering over the water, and every now and then darting down into it! It was all over a mixture of the most beautiful green and blue, with some orange color. It was somewhat less than a thrush, and had a large head and bill, and a short tail.

Tutor. I can tell you what that bird was — a kingfisher, the celebrated halcyon of the ancients, about which so many tales are told. It lives on fish, which it catches in the manner you saw. It builds in holes in the banks; and is a shy, retired bird, never to be seen far from the stream where it inhabits.

William. I must try to get another sight at him, for I never saw a bird that pleased me so much. Well, I followed this little brook, till it entered the river, and then took the path that runs along the bank. On the opposite side, I observed several little birds running along the shore, and making a piping noise. They were brown and white and about as big as a snipe.

Tutor. I suppose they were sand-pipers, one of the numerous family of birds that get their living by wading among the shallows, and picking up worms and insects.

William. There were a great many swallows, too, sporting upon the surface of the water, that entertained me with their motions. Sometimes they dashed into the stream; sometimes they pursued one another so quickly, that the eye could scarcely follow them. In one place, where a high, steep sand-bank rose directly above the river, I observed many of them go in and out of holes, with which the bank was bored full.

Tutor. Those were sand-martins, the smallest of our four species of swallows. They are of a mouse-color above, and white beneath. They make their nests and bring up their young in these holes, which run a great depth, and by their situation are secure from all plunderers.

William. A little farther, I saw a man in a boat, who was catching eels in an odd way. He had a long pole with broad iron prongs at the end, just like Neptune's trident, only there were five instead of three. This he pushed straight down into the mud, in the deepest parts of the river, and fetched up the eels sticking between the prongs.

Tutor. I have seen this method. It is called spearing of eels.

William. While I was looking at him, a heron came flying over my head, with his large flapping wings. He alighted at the next turn of the river, and I crept softly behind the bank to watch his motions. He had waded into the water as far as his long legs would carry him, and was standing with his neck drawn in, looking intently on the stream. Presently he darted his long bill as quick as lightning into the water, and drew out a fish, which he swallowed. I saw him catch another in the same manner. He then took alarm at some noise I made, and flew away slowly to a wood at some distance, where he settled.

Tutor. Probably his nest was there, for herons build upon the loftiest tree they can find, and sometimes in society together, like rooks. Formerly, when these birds were valued for the amusement of hawking, many gentlemen had their *heronries*, and a few are still remaining.

William. I think they are the largest wild birds we have.

Tutor. They are of great length and spread of wing, but their bodies are comparatively small.

William. I then turned homeward across the meadows, where I stopped awhile to look at a large flock of starlings, which kept flying about at no great distance. I could not tell, at first, what to make of them; for they rose all together from the ground, as thick as a swarm of bees, and formed themselves into a kind of black cloud, hovering over the field. After taking a short round, they settled again, and presently rose again in the same manner. I dare say there were hundreds of them.

Tutor. Perhaps so; for, in the fenny counties, their flocks are so numerous, as to break down whole acres of reeds by settling on them. This disposition of starlings to fly in close swarms was remarked even by Homer, who compares the foe flying from one of his heroes, to a *cloud* of starlings retiring dismayed at the approach of the hawk.

William. After I had left the meadows, I crossed the cornfields in the way to our house, and passed close by a deep marl-pit. Looking into it, I saw in one of the sides a cluster of what I took to be shells; and, upon going down, I picked up a clod of marl which was quite full of them; but how sea-shells could get there I cannot imagine.

Tutor. I do not wonder at your surprise, since many philosophers have been much perplexed to account for the same appearance. It is not uncommon to find great quantities of shells and relics of marine animals even in the bowels of high mountains very remote from the sea.

William. I got to the high field next to our house just as the sun was setting, and I stood looking at it till it was quite lost. What a glorious sight! The clouds were tinged with purple and crimson, and yellow of all shades and hues, and the clear sky varied from blue to a fine green at the horizon. But how large the sun appears, just as it sets! I think it seems twice as big as when it is over head.

Tutor. It does so; and you may probably have observed the same apparent enlargement of the moon at its rising.

William. I have; but pray what is the reason of this?

Tutor. It is an optical deception, depending upon principles which I cannot well explain to you, till you know more of that branch of science. But what a number of new ideas this afternoon's walk has afforded you! I do not wonder that you found it amusing; it has been very instructive, too. Did *you* see nothing of all these sights, Robert?

Robert. I saw some of them, but I did not take particular notice of them.

Tutor. Why not?

Robert. I do not know. I did not care about them; and I made the best of my way home.

Tutor. That would have been right, if you had been sent on a message; but, as you only walked for amusement, it would have been wiser to have sought out as many sources of it as possible. But so it is; one man walks through the world with his eyes open, and another with them shut; and upon this difference depends all the superiority of knowledge the one acquires above the other. I have known sailors who had been in all the quarters of the world, and could tell you nothing but the signs of the tippling-houses they frequented in the different ports, and the price and quality of the liquor. On the other hand, a Franklin could not cross the Channel without making some observations useful to mankind. While many a vacant, thoughtless youth, is whirled throughout Europe, without gaining a single idea worth crossing a street for; the observing eye and inquiring mind find matter of improvement and delight, in every ramble in town and country. Do *you*, then, William, continue to make use of your eyes; and *you*, Robert, learn that eyes were given you to use.

The preceding dialogue, if it has been attentively read, will probably enable the young student to write simple dialogues or conversations, similar to that presented in the following

Example.

DIALOGUE BETWEEN CHARLES AND HENRY, ABOUT DOGS.

Charles. Whose dog is that, Henry, which I saw in your yard yesterday?

Henry. He belongs to my uncle, who bought him, when he was very young, of a poor boy in the street. The boy appeared very destitute, and uncle bought him rather out of compassion for the boy, than because he wanted the dog.

Charles. Is he good for any thing,—has he been trained?

Henry. O yes; he is a very valuable animal. Uncle would not sell him at any price. He is an excellent water dog, and knows more than many boys of his own age. The other morning he was sitting in a chair at the window, from which he had been accustomed to look at the boys, as they were playing in the street, and, finding that he could not see through the window, on account of the frost on the glass, he applied his warm tongue to one of the panes, and, licking the frost from the glass, attempted to look out; but, the spot which he had cleared being only large enough to admit one eye, he immediately made another, in the same manner, for the other eye, by which he was enabled to enjoy the sight as usual.

Charles. That was very remarkable. But your uncle did not teach him to do that.

Henry. No; that was rather an operation of instinct than of training. But he will carry bundles, stand on two legs, find articles that are hidden, fetch things from the water, and is also well trained for hunting.

Charles. He is a water-dog, then, is he not?

Henry. O yes. He is very fond of the water himself, but will not allow others to go into it. Uncle has a fine situation at Nahant, on the water's edge, and many of his friends go there to bathe. But uncle is obliged to tie up *Guido,* the dog, when any one wishes to bathe; for the animal will not allow any one to go into the water, if he can prevent it.

Charles. That is very selfish in him. What do you suppose is the reason that he is unwilling that others should enjoy a thing, of which, you say, he is himself so very fond?

Henry. O, he has a good reason for that, as well as for every thing else he does. The reason is, that, one day, my little brother, George, was standing on a kind of wharf, built of stones, near the bathing place, and, happening to stoop over too far to look at some eels, that were gliding through the water below, he lost his balance and fell in. Nobody was near but Guido, and he immediatety jumped into the water, and held George up by the collar till some one came to his assistance. When the servant man, John, came to help George out of the water, Guido had nearly dragged him to the shore; but he found it rather hard work, for George is very fleshy, and, of course, quite heavy; and, although Guido has a good opinion of himself, and doubts not his ability to drag any one else out of the water, yet he reasons very soundly, and thinks it much less trouble to prevent people from going into the water, than to drag them out when they have got in.

Charles. No wonder that your uncle values him; he is certainly a very valuable dog.

Henry. O, I could tell you a hundred stories about him, which would surprise you. The other day, George brought home a bundle from Miss Farrar's, for my sister Caroline, which he threw down on a chair in the entry, and then ran off to play. Caroline was in her chamber, and, hearing George come in, spoke to him from her room, not knowing that he had gone out, and requested him to bring it up stairs. Guido was lying on the rug by the fire in the parlor, and, hearing Caroline call for the bundle, immediately jumped up, and, taking the bundle in his mouth, carried it up stairs and dropped it at Caroline's feet.

Charles. I should be very happy to have such a dog, but mother is so afraid of a dog's running mad and biting us children, that she will not allow us to keep one.

Henry. Father says, that there is no fear of a dog's running mad, if he has plenty of water. He says, that the reason that we so seldom hear of a dog's running mad here in Boston is, because water is plenty here, and dogs can always get at it, if they have once found their way to the Frog Pond on the Common.

Charles. What is the name of that disease which people have who are bitten by mad dogs?

Henry. It is called *hydrophobia*, which is a Greek word, and means "fear of water." Dogs, when they are mad, cannot bear the sight of water; they will not drink; and therefore, whenever a dog *will* drink, you may be sure that he is not mad. When a person is bitten by a mad, or rabid animal, he expresses the same dread of water, and hence the disease is called, as I said, *hydrophobia.*

Charles. I thank you, Henry, for giving me all this information. I shall tell it all to mother, and as I have often heard her say, that your father is a very sensible man, per haps she may overcome her fear of hydryphobia, and allow brother James and me to keep a dog.

Examples.

In the same manner the learner may write a simple dialogue about the following subjects:

A cat.	A walk.	A Sunday School ex cursion.
A fox.	A pair of skates.	A holiday visit.
A horse.	A tree,	An evening party.
A watch.	A kite.	A wedding.
A dress.	A book.	A funeral.
A ride.	A bonnet.	A baptism.
A meeting-house,	An excursion on the water.	The celebration of an anniversary.
A school.	A lesson.	A visit to a printing office
A sled.	A new year's present.	
An evening party.	A walk about the city.	
A sleigh-ride.	An excursion into the woods.	

VIII.

WORDS.

Sentences consist of words, and words are used to express thoughts or ideas. The ideas which they express depend on their connexion with other words. Sometimes the same word will signify an action, an object, a quality, or an attribute. Thus, in the sentence "I shall *present* the book to Charles," the word "present" signifies an action. If I say "the book will then be a *present*," the word "*present*" will signify an object, and is a noun or name. But, if the sentence be, "Charles must be *present* when the book is given," the word "*present*" will signify an attribute, and is an adjective.

The proper use of words, and the correct understanding of them, constitutes one of the greatest difficulties in written language. It is therefore highly important that every writer be careful to use the proper word to express the idea which he wishes to communicate; and when he is required to use a word, that he endeavor thereby to express no other idea than that, which the word is intended to convey.

The Dictionary is however a very unsafe guide to the proper signification of words, because their meaning is so materially affected by the connexion in which they stand.

There are many words, the sound of which is exactly similar to the sound of other words that are spelt very differently. In using such words there is little danger of their being mistaken the one for the other, because, as has just been said, we are guided by the connexion in which they stand. But in writing them, many mistakes are frequently made, on account of the want of early attention to the subject of orthography. The object of this lesson is to afford an exercise in the use of such words as are both sounded and spelt alike, and of those which have the same sound and are spelt differently.

The remark may here be made that the change of a single letter, or the removal of the accent, frequently alters the entire character of a word. Thus the words *advise* and *practise*, which are verbs, expressing an action, by the change of the letter *s* to *c*, become *practice*, and *advice*, which are nouns. Again, the words comment′, increase′, are verbs; while com′ment, in′crease, &c. are nouns. In the use of such words, the student should be accustomed to note the word, in his early exercises, by the proper accent.

Example.

"I saw with some surprise that the Muses, whose business was to cheer and encourage those who were toiling up the *ascent*, would often sing in the bowers of pleasure, and accompany those who were enticed away at the call of the passions. They accompanied them, however, but a little way, and always forsook them when they lost sight of the hill. The tyrants then doubled their chains upon the unhappy captives, and led them away without resistance, and almost with their own *assent*, to the cells of Ignorance or the mansions of misery."

Johnson, slightly altered.

Example 2d.

"The bold design
Pleased highly those infernal states, and joy
Sparkled in all their eyes; with full *assent*
They rose."

Milton, Paradise Lost, B. **2d.**

"He hath deserved worthily of his country; and his *ascent (namely, to the highest honors, &c.)* is not by such easy degrees as those who have been supple and courteous to the people."
Shakspeare, Coriolanus, Act 2d, Scene 2d.

Exercises.

Air, ere, heir; devise, device; altar, alter; trans'fer, transfer'; palate, pallet, palette; fane, fain, feign; bear, bare; bore, boar; council, counsel; coarse, course; ceiling, sealing; drawer, drawer; eminent, imminent; canon, cannon; freeze, frieze, frize; gnaw, nor; hoard, horde; horse, hoarse; heal, heel; haul, hall; key, quay; lead, led; lyre, liar; manor, manner; mien, mean; meat, meet, mete; pare, pear; peas, piece; practice, practise; assent, ascent; rite, right, write, wright; rose, rows; vein, vain; rain, rein, reign; raise, rays, raze; size, sighs; slay, sleigh, slaie; their, there; vale, veil, vail; white, wight; way, weigh, whey; you, yew; fare, fair; deer, dear; hue, hew; high, hie; hole, whole; seen, scene, seine; stile, style; straight, strait; waist, waste; bell, belle; sell, cell; herd, heard; wring, ring; aught, ought; lessen, lesson; profit, prophet; choler, collar; well, *(a noun,)* well, *(an adverb)*; per'fume, perfume'; subject'; sub'ject; ob'ject, object'; im'port, import'; pres'ent, present'; absent', ab'sent; sur'vey, survey'; fer'ment, ferment'; tor'ment, torment'; insult', in'sult; com'pact, compact'; con'cert, concert'; dis'count, discount'; rec'ord, record'; ex'tract, extract';* bow, beau; berry, bury; bough, bow; capitol, capital; cask, casque; censer, censor; claws, clause; site, cite, sight; clime, climb; complement, compliment; creek, creak; flue, flew; blew, blue; fort, forte; frays, phrase; herd, heard; slight, sleight; wave, waive.

OF PHRASES, CLAUSES, AND SENTENCES.

When names, whether proper, common, or abstract, are joined to their subjects by means of connecting words, but without a verb, the collection is called *a phrase*. As, The extent of the city; The path up the mountain; The house by the side of the river.

If the connecting word be a verb, the assemblage of words

* There are about sixty words in the English language that are thus distinguished by the accent alone. *See Rice's Composition, page 21st*

is then styled *a clause*, a simple sentence, or a simple proposition, words of nearly equivalent import. As, The city is large. The path up the mountain was exceedingly steep. They are taught by a good master. *See Rice's Composition pages 7th and 65th.*

The words *phrase* and *clause* may therefore be thus defined:

A phrase is a connected assemblage of words, *without* a finite verb.

A clause is a connected assemblage of words, *with* a finite verb.*

A sentence is an assemblage of words making complete sense.

The difference between a phrase, a clause, and a sentence, may be stated as follows: A sentence *always*, a clause *some times*, but a phrase *never* makes complete sense.

There are various kinds of phrases, such as substantive phrases, participial phrases, infinitive phrases, adverbial phrases, prepositional phrases, and interjectional phrases; so named from the office which they perform, or the parts of speech which they contain.

Clauses are frequently designated neuter, active-transitive, active-intransitive, and passive; in allusion to the verbs which form them. A clause which contains a relative pronoun is called a relative clause, and one containing a verb in the subjunctive mood is called the subjunctive clause. Specimens of most of these will be found in the following sentence:

Neuter clause,	Darius was
Substantive phrase in apposition,	a King of Persia.
Active clause,	Alexander conquered Darius,
Relative clause,	who fled from the field of battle.
Passive clause,	(but) he was assassinated
Substantive phrase,	by one of his own generals,
Participial phrase,	(who) coveting the favor of Alexander,
Minor active and relative clause,	slew his unfortunate master
Infinitive phrase,	to secure his own interest
Substantive phrase.	with that monarch.

A sentence usually consists of three principal parts, the subject, the verb, and the object. As, The man struck the

* A *finite verb* is a verb that has a subject or nominative. Verbs in the infinitive mood, or the participle, as they have no nominative, are not considered *finite* verbs.

boy. Here *man* is the subject, *struck* the verb, and *boy* the object. Some verbs, however, admit no object, after them, and the sentence will then consist of only two principal parts, the subject and the verb. All the other parts of a sentence are merely adjuncts, relating to the principal parts, and designed to express some circumstance affecting their signification.

Sentences are of two kinds, simple sentences and compound sentences.

A simple sentence contains but one nominative and one finite verb. As, "Life is short."

A compound sentence contains two or more simple sentences, joined together by one or more connecting words. As, "Life is short, and art is long." The different parts of a compound sentence are called members.

Clauses are joined together to form compound sentences by conjunctions and relative pronouns; and phrases are, for the most part, united by prepositions and adverbs; the latter are also frequently employed to connect minor clauses with the other parts of a sentence.

Both the subject and the object of a verb may be expressed as follows:

First. By a single noun or pronoun. As, [John] struck [him.]

Secondly. By a series of nouns or pronouns. As, [Diligence, industry, and proper improvement of time] are material duties of the young.

Thirdly. By a substantive, or an infinitive phrase or phrases. As, [The acquisition of knowledge] is one of the most honorable occupations of youth.

Fourthly. By a noun or a pronoun, attended by a minor or relative clause. As, [The veil, which covers from our eyes the events of succeeding years] is a veil woven by the hand of mercy.

Fifthly. By an entire member of a compound sentence. As, [He who pretends to great sensibility towards men, and yet has no feeling for the high objects of religion, no heart to admire and adore the great Father of the Universe] has reason to distrust the truth and delicacy of his sensibility.

The object of this lesson is to make the student acquainted with the constituent parts and members of sentences, both simple and compound. The exercises that are subjoined, are presented that he may distinguish the phrases from the clauses, the clauses from the sentences, the imperfect sentences from the perfect, and the simple from the compound.

Exercises.

The eye of the passing traveller may mark them, or mark them not, but they stand peacefully in thousands over all the land; and most beautiful do they make it, through all its wide valleys and narrow glens, — its low holms encircled by the rocky walls of some bonny burn, — its green mounts elated with their little crowning groves of plane trees, — its yellow cornfields, — its bare pastoral hill-sides, and all its heathy moors, on whose black bosom lie shining or concealed glades of excessive verdure, inhabited by flowers, and visited only by the far-flying bees.

By arguments so strong. If we could imagine. They all agree in the belief. The fearful consequences. In spite of all admonition and reproof. Feel themselves at liberty. Such an undertaking would be vain. I am desirous of explaining. For the reasons already given. We cannot but rejoice that. Directed their attention. Attempted to prove. Make themselves accountable. The question which arises has puzzled. Has produced in our mind. Religion has its seat in the heart. Were now out in thousands. Would be expedient. Remains for us to notice. On the Sabbath morning. Overgrown with grass and moss. With somewhat diminished lustre. The daisies of a luxuriant spring had covered the spot. Opportunity of addressing each other. Had fatally infected. With indescribable pleasure. The most remote period of time. We hoped that this sight. The interior of the cavern. Very important purposes. Have a tendency to preserve. Withdraws his propitious light. However base or unworthy. Is the emblem of. How boundless. The tender assiduities of friendship. Irregular projecting rocks. Was peculiarly dear. With very great pleasure. The refulgent lamp of night. The science which treats of language is called Grammar. Writing is the art of making thoughts visible.

Now came still Evening on, and Twilight gray
Had in her sober livery all things clad.
The melancholy days have come, the saddest of the year,
Of wailing winds, and naked woods, and meadows brown and sere,
Heaped in the hollows of the grove, the withered leaves lie dead.
They rustle to the eddying gust, and to the rabbit's tread.

The lower animals, as far as we are able to judge, are entirely occupied with the objects of their present perceptions; and the case is nearly the same with the lower orders of our own species.

Diligence, industry and proper improvement of time, are material duties of the young.

Honor and shame from no condition rise;
Act well your part, there all the honor lies.

Charity, like the sun, brightens every object on which it shines.

Though I speak with the tongue of men and of angels and have not charity, I am nothing.

X.

USE OF WORDS, PHRASES, AND CLAUSES, IN THE EXPANSION OF THE IDEA.

The previous Exercise having rendered the student familiar with the parts of which a compound sentence is composed, it is now proposed that he be exercised in the construction of such sentences; as in the following

Example.

We went.

We went in a carriage.

We went in a carriage to the meeting.

We went in a carriage to the meeting last night.

We went in a carriage to the meeting in Church Street last night.

We went in a carriage to the meeting in Church Street last night, and heard an excellent sermon.

We went in a carriage to the meeting in Church Street last night, with a number of friends, and heard an excellent sermon from the Rev. Mr. Stevens.

We went in a carriage to the meeting in Church Street last night, with a number of friends from the country, and heard an excellent sermon from the Rev. Mr. Stevens, on the duties of children to their parents.

We went in a carriage to the meeting in Church Street last night, with a number of friends from the country, and heard an excellent sermon from the Rev. Mr. Stevens, on the duties of children to their parents, delivered in a very solemn and impressive manner.

Exercises.

In the same manner the student may expand the following simple sentences:

My father sailed.
John related.
If Henry had not disobeyed.
God created.
I remember.
Habitual indolence undermines.
They have done all they could.
A cat caught.
A thief was caught.
The lightning struck.
The river rolled.
The minister preached.

I heard John say.
Henry declared.
This book contains.
A horse ran away.
Gentleness corrects.
The boys took.
The servants returned.
My father keeps.
The ship sailed.
The master came.
A large number of peopled assembled.
Geography teaches.
The artist painted
I have purchased.
His parents reside.
The boy fell.
The girls rose.
A mad dog bit.
The sheriff took.
The wind blew down.
The tide overflowed.
The earthquake destroyed
The beggar came.
I heard him sing.

XI.

OF THE PARTS AND ADJUNCTS OF A SENTENCE.

The natural order of an English sentence is to place the subject with its adjuncts, if any, at the beginning of the sentence, and the verb and the objective, with their respective adjuncts after it. This order, however, it is not necessary always to preserve, but on the contrary the beauty and harmony of the sentence are often greatly increased by a departure from it. With respect to the cadence, or close of a sentence, care should be taken that it be not abrupt nor unpleasant. In order to give a sentence its proper close, the longest member and the fullest words should be reserved for the conclusion. But in the distribution of the members, and in the cadence of the period, as well as in the sentences themselves, variety must be observed; for the mind and the ear soon tire with a frequent repetition of the same tone.

In the following example the student will notice the different order in which the parts of the sentence are arranged, while they still collectively convey the same idea. The different forms of construction, which depend on the power of varying the arrangement, have a material effect upon the precision and harmony of the sentence; and therefore that arrangement is always to be preferred, which, while it sounds most harmoniously to the ear, conveys most clearly the idea intended to be expressed.

Example

The poet must study variety, above all things, not only in professed descriptions of the scenery, but in frequent allusions to natural objects, which, of course, often occur in pastorals.

Above all things, the poet, not only in professed descriptions of the scenery, but in the frequent allusions to natural objects which occur of course in pastorals, must study variety.

Not only in professed descriptions of the scenery, but in the frequent allusions to natural objects, which occur, of course, in pastorals, the poet must, above all things, study variety.*

Exercises.

[The student will notice that in the following sentences, the members are very badly arranged. It is required of him to present them in such order as will make them most harmonious and exhibit the sense to the best advantage.]

There was a feeling of strangeness, as he passed through the village, that every thing should be just as it was when he left.

In the trees, there was a melancholy gusty sound. and the night was shutting in about it, as they drew near the house.

But not only from its relation to the past night, the morning is a fit time for devotion, but considered as an introduction to a new day.

To strengthen a character, which will fit me for heaven or for hell, to perform actions which will never be forgotten, to receive impressions which may never be effaced, to that world where I have often gone astray I am to return.

Temptations which have often subdued me, this day, I am to meet; again with opportunities of usefulness, I am to help in deciding the hap-

---

* It will save much time and trouble in copying, if the student, in the preparation of his exercises, pursue the following method: placing the different members of the sentence in separate lines and numbering them, he may afterwards arrange them by their numbers, as in the following example:

1 We,
2 with the rest of our party,
3 notwithstanding the storm and darkness,
4 pursued,
5 our journey.

1, 4, 5, 3, 2,	4 1 5 2 3
1 4 5 2 3	4 1 5 3 2
1 3 4 5 2	5 1 4 2 3
2 1 4 5 3	5 1 4 3 2
2 3 1 4 5	2 4 1 5 3
3 1 2 4 5	3 2 1 4 5 &c.
3 2 1 4 5	

piness of their present and future life, in mending their characters, and to influence the minds of others.

Having on the mercy and protection of the Almighty cast ourselves, to the labor and duties which he imposes, with new confidence we should go forth.

Given in part to prayer, as of devotional topics and excitements, a va riety it furnishes, this period should be.

And gone to testify of us to our judge, and that another day has gone, at this hour, naturally a reflecting mind will remember.

Time misspent and talents wasted, defective motives and irregular de- sires, if suffered to speak plainly and inspect faithfully, conscience will recount.

Between the brothers was no deadly and deep quarrel and of this un natural estrangement the cause neither of them could tell.

In the little hollow that lay between the grave of their father, whose shroud was haply not yet still from the fall of dust to dust, and of their mother long since dead, as the brothers composedly but firmly stood, grasping each others hand, the minister said, "I must fulfill the promise which I made to your father on his death bed" and with a pleasant coun- tenance stood beside them.

On a voyage in quest of a north-west passage to India, Henry Hudson in 1609, an Englishman in the service of the Dutch, discovered the noble river that bears his name.

XII.

SENTENCES.

The following words constitute a perfect sentence. It is required to arrange them into sentences.

Example.

1.

A gratitude emotion delightful is.
Gratitude is a delightful emotion.

2.

Exclamation interesting adverse when circumstances under Mark Antony this made "have all I except lost away given have I what."

Mark Antony. when under adverse circumstances, made this interesting exclamation: "I have lost all, except what I have given away."

Exercises.

Sorrows the poor pity sufferings of the and.

To itself others heart grateful the duty at performs once its and itself grateful endears.

Beings best of God kindest the is and.

Lamented an amiable youth sincere of terms in grief parent death affectionate the of a most.

Temper even and mild remarkably a possessed Sir Isaac Newton.

Words few these in duties contained all are moral our: By do done be would as you.

To eat and drink, instead of living do as many drink and eat we should, to live in order.

Glorious the Sun how an object is; but glorious more hcw much good is great that and good Being use for our made it who.

XIII.

CAPITAL LETTERS.

Th·· first word of every book, chapter, letter, note, or any other piece of writing should begin with a capital letter.

The names of the months and the days of the week should always begin with a capital letter.

The first word after a period should begin with a capital letter.

The first word after every interrogation, or exclamation, should begin with a capital letter; unless a number of interrogative, or exclamatory sentences occur together, and are not totally independent.

The various names, or appellations of the Deity should begin with a capital letter; as, God, Jehovah, the Almighty, the Supreme Being, the Lord, Providence, the Messiah, the Holy Spirit, &c.

All proper names, such as the names of persons, places, streets, mountains, lakes, rivers, ships, &c., and adjectives derived from them, should begin with a capital letter.

The first word of a quotation after a colon, or when it is in a direct form, should begin with a capital letter.

The first word of an example, every substantative and principal word in the titles of books, and the first word of every line in poetry, should begin with a capital letter

The pronoun I, and the interjection O, are always written in capitals.

Any words, when remarkably emphatical, or when they are the principal subject of the composition, may begin with capitals.

Exercises.

when socrates Was Asked what Man Approached the Nearest to Perfect happiness, He answered, that man who Has The Fewest wants.

addison Has Remarked, with Equal piety and truth, that the Creation is a Perpetual feast To the mind of a Good man.

diligence, industry, and Proper improvement Of time, Are Material duties of the Young; but the young Often Neglect These duties.

how often shall my brother sin against me and I forgive him? till Seven Times?

but what Excuse can the englishman Plead? the custom Of duelling?

how manv lessons are there in this book? are there More Than twenty five?

why did You Not Arrive sooner? were you necessarily Detained?

daughter of faith, Awake! Arise! Illume
the Dread Unknown, The chaos of The tomb.

the lord My pasture Shall Prepare,
and Feed Me With A shepherd's care.

father of all in Every Age,
in Every Clime Adored,
by Saint, by savage, and By sage,
jehovah, jove, or lord

thou great first cause, least understood,
who All my Sense Confined (confinedst),
to Know But This, That thou Art good
and That myself Am Blind.

yet Gavest me In this Dark Estate, &c.

the language of Manv of the european nations was derived From the Ancient latin.

The english and french Fleets had a Severe Engagement.

i saw the dutch Ambassador in the Carriage of the spanish consul

Always remember this Ancient maxim, Spoken by the greek philosopher: "Know thyself."

The christian lawgiver Says, "take up Thy Cross Daily and follow me.

solomon observes, that "Pride goes Before Destruction."

johnson's dictionary has long been the standard of english orthography but the work of doctor webster seems in a Fair way to Supplant It

have you read rollin's ancient history.

thomson's seasons and cowper's task contain many Poetical Beauties

i hope You will be able to Write Correctly All that i have Written

XIV.

OF PUNCTUATION.*

Punctuation is the art of dividing a written composition into sentences, or parts of sentences; and is principally used to mark the grammatical divisions of a sentence. The marks employed in punctuation are sometimes used to note the different pauses and tones of voice, which the sense and an accurate pronunciation require.

The characters or marks, used in punctuation are:

The Comma †	,	The quotation marks	" "
The Semicolon ‡	;	The Diæresis	..
The Colon	:	Crotchets	( )
The Period §	.	Brackets	[ ]

* The importance of correct punctuation may be seen by the following extract from the London Times of September, 1818.

"The contract lately made for lighting the town of Liverpool, during the ensuing year, has been thrown void by the misplacing of a comma in the advertisement, which ran thus: 'The lamps at present are about 4050 in number, and have in general two spouts each, composed of not less than twenty threads of cotton.' The contractor would have proceeded to furnish each lamp with the said twenty threads; but, this being but half the usual quantity, the commissioner discovered that the difference arose from the comma following, instead of preceding, the word *each*. The parties agreed to annul the contract, and a new one is now ordered."

Again; the meaning of the following sentence is materially affected by the punctuation:

"I said that he is dishonest it is true and I am sorry for it."

Now the pause placed after *dishonest*, will imply that *it is true* that he is *dishonest*, thus: "I said that he is dishonest; it is true, and I am sorry for it." But, if the pause be placed after true, the sentence implies that *it is* true that I said he is dishonest, and I am sorry that I said so, thus: "I said that he is dishonest, it is true; and I am sorry for it."

The misplacing of a comma, by a Mr. Sharpe, converted an innocent remark into a piece of horrid blasphemy: "Believing Richard Brothers to be a prophet sent, by God I have engraved his portrait." Had the comma been removed two words forward, the assertion would have been innocent.

† The word *comma* is derived from the Greek language, and properly designates a segment, section, or part *cut off* from a complete sentence In its usual acceptation, it signifies the point, which marks the smaller segments, or portions of a period. It, therefore, represents the shortest pause, and consequently marks the least constructive or most dependent parts of a sentence.

‡ The word *semicolon* is derived from the Latin word *semi*, which means *half*, and the Greek word *kolon*, which signifies a member.

§ The word *period* is derived from the Greek language, and means "*a circuit*."

The Exclamation	!	The Brace	}
The Interrogation	?		
The Dash	—	The Acute Accent	´
The Ellipsis	.....	The Grave Accent	`
The Hyphen	-	The Circumflex Accent	^
The Breve	˘	The Caret	‸
The Apostrophe	’	The Cedilla	ç

To these may be added the marks of reference:

The Asterisk	*	The Section	§
The Obelisk	†	The Parallels	‖
The Double Obelisk	‡	The Paragraph	¶

RULES OF PUNCTUATION.

1. When two or more words are connected without the connecting word being expressed, the comma supplies the place of that word; as, "Alfred was a brave, pious, patriotic prince."

2. Those parts of a sentence which contain the relative pronoun, the case absolute, the nominative case independent, any parenthetical clause, and simple members of sentences, connected by words expressing a com parison, must be separated by commas; as, "The elephant, which you saw in the menagerie, took the child up with his trunk into his cage." "Shame being lost, all virtue is lost." "Peace, O Virtue, peace is all thine own." "Better is a dinner of herbs with love, than a stalled ox and hatred therewith."

3. The following words and phrases, and others similar to them, are generally separated by commas from the rest of the sentence; namely Nay, so, however, hence, besides, perhaps, finally, in short, at least, moreover, again. first, secondly, thirdly, lastly, once more, on the contrary, &c.

4. The words of another writer, not formally introduced as a quotation, and words and clauses expressing contrast or opposition, though closely connected in construction, are separated by a comma; as, "I pity the man, who can travel from Dan to Beersheba and cry, 'T is all barren."

"Though deep, yet clear; though gentle, yet not dull;
Strong, without rage; without o'erflowing, full."

5. When the absence of a word is indicated in reading or speaking by a pause, its place may be supplied by a comma; as, "From law arises security; from security, inquiry; from inquiry, knowledge."

6. Nouns in apposition, accompanied by explanatory words or phrases, are separated by commas; but if such nouns are single, or only form a proper name, they are not divided: as, "Paul the Apostle of the Gentiles was eminent for his zeal and knowledge."

7. When a sentence consists of several members, each constituting a distinct proposition, and having a dependence upon each other, or upon some common clause, they are separated by semicolons; as, "Wisdom has builded her house; she hath hewn out her seven pillars; she hath

killed her beasts; she hath mingled her wine; she hath also furnished her table."

8. The colon is used to divide a sentence into two or more parts, which, although the sense be complete in each, are not wholly independent; as, "Nature felt her inability to extricate herself from the consequences of guilt: the gospel reveals the plan of Divine interposition and aid."

9. The colon* is used when an example, a quotation, or a speech is introduced; as, "The Scriptures give us an amiable representation of the Deity in these words: God is love."

10. The period is used at the end of a complete and independent sentence. It is also placed after initial letters, when used alone; and, likewise, after all abbreviations; as, "One clear and direct path is pointed out to man." "Fear God." "Have charity towards all men." "G. W." for "George Washington." "Geo." for "George." "Benj." for "Benjamin." "O. S." for "Old Style." "F. R. S." for "Fellow of the Royal Society."

In a general view, the period separates the paragraph into sentences, the semicolon divides a compound sentence into simple ones; and the comma collects into clauses the scattered circumstances of manner time, place, relation, &c., belonging to every verb and to every noun.

The note of interrogation,† or the question, as it is sometimes called, is placed after every sentence which contains a question; as, "Who is this?" "What have you in your hand?" "The Cyprians said to me, Why do you weep?"

The exclamation point is used to express any sudden or violent emotion; such as surprise, joy, grief, love, hatred, anger, pity, anxiety, ardent wish, &c. It is also used to mark an exalted idea of the Deity; and is generally placed after the nominative case independent; and after the noun or pronoun which follows an interjection; as, "How mischievous are the effects of war!" "O blissful days! Ah me! how soon ye pass!"

The exclamation point is also used after sentences containing a question when no answer is expected; as, "What is more amiable than virtue!"

Several exclamation points are sometimes used together, either in a parenthesis or by themselves, for the purpose of expressing ridicule, or a great degree of surprise, &c.

A parenthesis ‡ is a sentence, or a part of a sentence, inserted within

---

* Some very respectable grammarians tell us, that the propriety of using a colon or semicolon is sometimes determined by the use or omission of a conjunction; as, "Do not flatter yourself with the hope of perfect happiness: there is no such thing in the world:" "Do not flatter yourselves with the hope of perfect happiness; *for* there is no such thing in the world." But many respectable writers make no use of the colon; and it may well be questioned, whether the retention of this character among the marks of punctuation adds any thing to the clearness or precision of written language.

† The word *interrogation* is derived from the Latin, and means *a question.*

‡ The word *parenthesis* is derived from the Greek language, and means *an insertion.*

another sentence, but which may be omitted without injuring the sense or construction, and is enclosed between two curved lines like these; ( ).

The curved lines between which a parenthesis is enclosed are called crotchets.

Sometimes a sentence is enclosed between marks like these, [ ] which are called brackets

The following difference is to be noticed in the use of crotchets and brackets · Crotchets are used to enclose a sentence, or part of a sentence, which is inserted between the parts of another sentence: Brackets are generally used to separate two subjects, or to enclose an explanatory note or observation standing by itself. When a parenthesis occurs within another parenthesis, brackets enclose the former and crotchets the latter; as in the following sentence from Sterne: "I know the banker I deal with, or the physician I usually call in [there is no need, cried Dr. Slop (waking), to call in any physician in this case] to be neither of them men of much religion."

It may be here remarked, that a parenthesis is frequently placed between commas, instead of crotchets, &c.; but the best writers avoid the use of parentheses as much as is possible.

The hyphen * is a small mark placed between the parts of a compound word; as, sea-water, semi-circle.

The hyphen is also used to denote the long sound of a vowel; as, Epi curēan, decō-rum, balcō-ny.

The hyphen must always be put at the end of the line when part of a word is in one line and part in another; but, in this case, the letters of a syllable must never be separated; as, extraordinary, not ext-
raordinary.

The dash is a straight mark longer than a hyphen; thus, —

The proper use of the dash is to express a sudden stop, or change of the subject; but, by modern writers, it is employed as a substitute for almost all of the other marks; being used sometimes for a comma, semi colon, colon, or period; sometimes for a question or an exclamation, and sometimes for crotchets and brackets to enclose a parenthesis.

An ellipsis † or omission of words, syllables, or letters, is indicated by various marks; sometimes by a dash; as, the k——g, for the king; sometimes by asterisks or stars, like these, * * * *; sometimes by hy phens, thus, - - - -; sometimes by small dots or periods, like these: ....

The breve (thus ◡) is placed over a vowel to indicate its short sound, as, St. Hĕlena.

The apostrophe ‡ is a comma placed above the line. It is used as the sign of the possessive case, and sometimes indicates the omission of a letter or several letters; as, John's; "'T is" for "it is"; "tho'" for "though;" "lov'd" for "loved"; "I'll" for "I will."

The quotation marks, or inverted commas, as they are sometimes

---

* The word *hyphen* is derived from the Greek language, and signifies *under one*, or *together;* and is used to imply that the words or syllables, between which it is placed, are to be taken *together* as one word.

† The word *ellipsis* is derived from the Greek language, and means *an omission.*

‡ The word *apostrophe* is derived from the Greek language, and signifies the *turning away*, or *omission*, of one letter or more.

called, consist of four commas; two inverted, or upside down, at the beginning of a word, phrase, or sentence which is quoted or transcribed from some author in his own words; and two others, in their direct position, placed at the conclusion; as, An excellent poet says:

"The proper study of mankind is man."

Sometimes the quotation is marked by single, instead of double, commas.

The diæresis * consists of two periods placed over the latter of two vowels; to show that they are to be pronounced in separate syllables; as, Laocoön, Zoönomia, coöperate.

The brace is employed to unite several lines of poetry, or to connect a number of words with one common term; and it is also used to prevent a repetition in writing or printing; thus,

"Waller was smooth; but Dryden taught to join }
The varying verse, the full-resounding line, }
The long majestic march and energy divine." }

C-e-o-u-s }
C-i-o-u-s } are pronounced like shus.
S-c-i-o-u-s }
T-i-o-u-s }

The cedilla, or cerilla, is a curve line placed under the letter *c*, to show that it has the sound of *s*. It is used principally in words derived from the French language.

Thus, garçon, in which word the ç is to be pronounced like *s*.

The accents † are marks used to signify the proper pronunciation of words.

The accents are three in number;

The grave accent thus, \`
The acute accent; thus, ´
The circumflex accent; thus, ^

The grave accent is represented by a mark placed over a letter, or syllable, to show that it must be pronounced with the falling inflection of the voice; as, Reuthàmir.

The acute accent is represented by a similar mark, pointing in the opposite direction, to show that the letter or syllable must be pronounced with the rising inflection of the voice; thus, Epicuréan, Européan.

The meaning of a sentence often depends on the kind of accent which is used; thus, the following sentence if the acute accent be used on the word *alone*, becomes a question.

"Pleased thou shalt hear, and thou alóne shalt hear?"

But, if the grave accent be placed on the word *alone*, it becomes a simple declaration; as,

---

* The word *diæresis* is derived from the Greek language, and signifies *a taking away*, or *a division*.

† The word *accent* is derived from the Latin language, and signifies *the tone of the voice*.

"Pleased thou shalt hear, and thou alòne shalt hear."

The circumflex accent is the union of the grave and acute accents, and indicates that the syllable on which it is placed should have both the rising and the falling inflection of the voice.

The caret * is a mark resembling an inverted v, placed under the line It is never used in printed books, but, in manuscripts, it shows that something has been accidentally omitted; as,

recited
"George has his lesson."

The following marks are references; and are generally used to call attention to notes on words or sentences, placed at the bottom of the page:

The Asterisk, *	The Parallels, ‖
The Obelisk, †	The Paragraph, ¶
The Double Obelisk, ‡	The Index, ☞
The Section, §	

When many notes occur on a page, and these marks are all exhausted, they are sometimes doubled. Figures and letters are also sometimes used instead of the above marks.

It is proper to remark, that, in some books the section, §, and the para graph, ¶, are used to mark the parts of a composition, which in writing or printing should be separated.

A paragraph † denotes the beginning of a new subject, or a sentence not connected with the foregoing.

A section ‡ is used for subdividing a chapter into smaller parts.

It is proper here to remark, that every composition should be divided into paragraphs, when the sense will allow the separation. Different subjects, unless they are very short, or very numerous in a small compass should be separated into paragraphs.

EXERCISES IN PUNCTUATION.

Insert Commas in their proper places in the following sentences.

Wife children servants all that could be found were savagely slaughtered.

He had been born bred and educated on a small moorland farm which he now cultivated.

Doing to others as we wish them to do to us constitutes the fundamental principle of Christian charity.

Julius Cæsar wrote in a clear natural correct flowing style.

---

* The word *caret* is derived from the Latin language, and signifies *it is wanting*.

† The word *paragraph* is derived from the Greek language, and signifies *an ascription in the margin*.

‡ The word *section* is derived from the Latin language, and signifies *a division* or *cutting*. The character which denotes a section seems to be made of *ss*, and to be an abbreviation of the words *signum sectionis*, the sign of the section.

Climate soil laws custom food and other accidental differences have produced an astonishing variety in the complexion features manners and faculties of the human race.

In our epistolary correspondence we may advise dissuade exhort request recommend discuss comfort reconcile.

Exercise ferments the humors casts them into the proper channels throws off redundancies and assists nature in her necessary operations.

A wise man will examine every thing coolly impartially accurately and rationally.

Homer the greatest poet of antiquity is reported to have been blind.

Milton the author of "Paradise Lost" and "Regained" was blind

I am my dear Sir your humble servant.

The earth like a tender mother nourishes her children.

Harold being slain the conqueror marched immediately to London

Swift says no man ever wished himself younger.

To err is human; to forgive divine.

The great Xerxes upon whom fortune had lavished all her favors not content with being master of powerful armies numerous fleets and inexhaustible treasures proposed a reward to any one who should invent a new pleasure.

You should not desire says an ancient Greek author even the thread of another man's needle.

She let concealment like a worm in the bud feed on her damask cheek.

Nature has wisely determined that man shall want an appetite in the beginning of distempers as a defence against their increase.

The whole circle of vices like shadows towards the evening of life appear enormous to a thinking person.

You are not to suppose that the fate either of single persons of empires or of the whole earth depends on the influence of the stars.

Insert the Comma, Colon, and Semicolon where they belong in the following sentences.

Green is generally considered the most refreshing color to the eye therefore Providence has made it the common dress of nature.

To err is human to forgive divine.

The aim of orators is victory of historians truth of poets admiration.

Saint Peter is painted with the keys Paul with a sword Andrew with a cross James the Greater with a pilgrim's staff and a gourd bottle James the Less with a fuller's pole John with a cup and a winged serpent Bartholomew with a knife Philip with a long staff or cross Thomas with a lance Matthew with a hatchet Matthias with a battle-axe Simon with a saw and Jude with a club.

Some place their bliss in action some in ease
Those call it pleasure and contentment these.

Most of our pleasures may be regarded as imaginary but our disquietudes may be considered as real.

Chaucer we are told by Dryden followed nature every where but that he never went beyond her.

A clownish air is but a trifling defect yet it is enough to make a man universally disagreeable.

In the New Testament as in the dignified and sober liturgy of the Church we see deep humility but not loathsome abjectness sincere repent ance but not agonizing horror steadfast faith but not presumptuous assurance lively hope but not seraphic abstraction the deep sense of human infirmity but not the unblushing profession of leprous depravity the holy and heavenly communion but not vague experiences nor the intemperate trance.

Do not flatter yourself with the idea of enjoying perfect happiness there is no such thing in the world.

Keep close to thy business it will keep thee from wickedness poverty and shame.

The path of truth is a plain and it is a safe path that of falsehood is a perplexing maze.

Do not flatter yourself with the idea of enjoying perfect happiness for there is no such thing in the world.

Were all books reduced to their quintessence many a bulky author would make his appearance in a penny paper there would be no such thing in nature as a folio the works of an age would be contained on a few shelves not to mention millions of volumes that would be utterly annihilated.

Insert the Period, Question, and Exclamation Point, where they respectively belong in the following sentences.

Honor all men Fear God Truth is the basis of every virtue Every deviation from veracity is criminal The Latin language is now called a dead language because it is not spoken as the mother tongue of any nation America was discovered in the night of Oct 11th O S A D 1492 Have you ever read its history The Rambler was written by Samuel Johnson LL D Sir Josh Reynolds F R S was a very distinguished artist

In the formation of man what wonderful proofs of the magnificence of God's works and how poor and trifling in comparison are the productions of man Why do you weave around you this web of occupation and then complain that you cannot break it How superior is the internal construction of the productions of nature to all the works of men

---

XV.

DERIVATION AND COMPOSITION OF WORDS.

Words, with regard to their origin, are divided into primitive and derivative; and, with regard to their form, into simple and compound.

A primitive word is a word which is in its original form, and is not derived from any other word; as, man, good, content.

A derivative word is that which is derived from another word; as, manful, manhood, manly, manliness; goodness, goodly, &c.; contented, contentment, contenting, contentedly, &c.; which are derived respectively from the primitive words, man, good, content.

A simple word consists of one word, not compounded; as sea, able, self.

A compound word is a word that is made up of two or more words, or of one word and some syllable added; as, sea-water, unable, myself. *

Words are found, on examination, to be reducible to groups or families, and are related to each other by identity of origin and similarity of signification. Thus the words *justly*, *justice*, *justify*, *justification*, *justiciary*, *adjust*, *readjust*, *unjust*, *injustice*, &c., are all kindred words, connected with the primitive word *just*. The primitive words of a language are generally few in number, and language is rendered copious and expressive by the formation of derivatives and compounds from the primitives.

When a syllable is added, in the composition of words, it takes its name from the position in which it is placed with regard to the word. If it is placed before the word it is called a *prefix*, if at the end of the word, it is called an *affix*.

In derivative words, there are generally three, and sometimes four things to be considered; namely, first, the *root*, from which the word is derived; secondly, the *prefix;* thirdly, the *affix;* fourthly, the letters which are added for the sake of sound, and which may be called *euphonic* letters.

The root is cometimes called the *radical letters* of a word. Thus, from the Latin word *venio*, which signifies *to come*, and its variation *ventum*, many English words are derived, in the following manner: The first three letters of the word are taken, as the radical letters, or root of the word. By adding the prefix *contra*, which signifies *against*, we have *contraven;* to which is added the euphonic letter *e*, to lengthen the last syllable, and thus is composed the word *contravene*, which means to *come against*, or *oppose*. In a similar manner, we have the words *prevent*, *invent*, *circumvent*, *convent*, and their derivatives. †

* Some compound words are formed by the union of two other words; as *sea-water*, *semi-annual*. Such words are generally recognized by the hyphen placed between the words composing the compound. Mr. Goold Brown says, that "*permanent compounds are consolidated*," that is, are written without the hyphen. But it is contended that "glass-house" is as much a permanent compound as "bookseller." The truth is, that no better reason can be given for the use or omission of the hyphen, than caprice.

† The student who wishes to study this department of etymology, will find it more fully displayed in Horne Tooke's "Diversions of Purley;" Rice's "Composition," McCulloch's "Grammar," and Towne's "Analysis of Derivative Words." In the first mentioned of these works, the "Diversions of Purley," may be found a learned and ingenious account of the derivation and meaning of many of the adverbs, conjunctions and prepositions of the English language.

Many of the prefixes used in the composition of English words are Latin or Greek prepositions; and the effect which they produce upon the meaning of the root contributes much to the copiousness of the English language.

There are so many other ways of deriving words from one another, that it would be extremely difficult and nearly impossible to enumerate them. A few instances, only, of the various modes of derivation, can be given here.

Some nouns are derived from other nouns, or from adjectives, by adding the affix *hood*, or *head*, *ship*, *ry*, *wick*, *rick*, *dom*, *ian*, *ment*, and *age*; as, from *man*, by adding the affix *hood*, comes *manhood*, from *knight*, *knighthood*, &c., from *false*, *falsehood*, &c.

Nouns ending in *hood*, or *head*, are such as signify character or quality; as, manhood, falsehood.

Nouns ending in *ship* are those that signify office, employment, state, or condition; as lordship, stewardship, hardship.

Nouns ending in *ery* signify action or habit; as, slavery, knavery, bravery.

Nouns ending in *wick*, *rick*, and *dom*, denote dominion, jurisdiction, or condition; as bailiwick, bishoprick, dukedom, kingdom, freedom.

Nouns ending in *ian* signify profession; as, physician, musician, &c.

Nouns that end in *ment* or *age* signify the act, or habit; as commandment, usage.

Nouns that end in *ard* denote character or habit; as drunkard, dotard

Nouns ending in *kin*, *ling*, *ing*, *ock*, *el*, generally signify diminution; as lamb, lambkin, duck, duckling, hill, hillock, cock, cockerel.

Nouns ending in *tude*, or *ude*, generally signify state, condition, or capacity; as plenitude, aptitude, &c.

ALPHABETICAL SYNOPSIS OF PREFIXES.

A, Ab, Abs, *from*.
Ad, Ac, Al, Ap, At, &c., *to*.
Ambi, *both*,
Amb, amphi, *round*.
Ante, *before*.
Anti, *against*.
Ana, *back*.
Apo, Aph, *from*.
Auto, *one's self*.
Be, *to make*,
Bene, *well*.
Bi, Bis, *two*, *half*.
Biblio, *book*.
Bio, *life*.
Centu, *hundred*.
Chrono, *time*.
Circum, *round*.
Co, Con, Col, Com, Cor. *with*.
Contra, *against*.
Cosmo, *the world*.
Counter, *opposite*.
De, *from*, *down*.
Deca, *ten*.
Di, Dis, &c., *separation*, *not*.
Dia, *through*.
Dys, *bad*, *difficult*, *hard*.
E, Ex, El, Em, Er, &c., *out of*
En, Em, *in*.
Epi, *upon*.
Equi, *equal*.
Extra, *beyond*.
For, *against*.
Fore, *prior*.
Geo, *the earth*.
Hetero, *of divers kinds*.
Hex, Hexa, *six*.
Homo, *of one kind*.
Hydro, *water*.
Hyper, *over*.
In, Im, Il, *not*, with an adjective, *into*, with a verb, *on*.
Inter, *among*.

Intro, *within.*
Juri, *legal.*
Juxta, *near.*
Litho, *stone.*
Male, *evil.*
Manu, *hand.*
Mis, *error.*
Mono, *one,*
Multi, *many.*
Myth, *fabulous.*
Noct, *night.*
Non, Ne, *not.*
Ob, Oc. &c., *before, against.*
Oct, *eight.*
Omni, *all.*
Ornitho, *bird.*
Ortho, *right.*
Oste, *bone.*
Out, *beyond.*
Over, *above.*
Pan, *all.*
Para, *against.*
Penta, *five.*
Per, *through.*
Peri, *around.*
Phil, *friendly.*
Physi, *nature.*
Pleni, *full.*
Poly, *many.*
Post, *after.*
Pre, *before.*
Preter, *beyond.*
Pro, *before, out.*
Pyro, *fire.*
Quad, *four.*
Re, *again.*
Retro, *back.*
Se, *separation.*
Semi. } *half.*
Demi, } *half.*
Hemi, } *half.*
Sex, *six.*
Sine, *without.*
Soli, *alone.*
Steno, *short.*
Stereo, *solid.*
Sub, Suc, &c., *under*
Subter, *under.*
Super, Supra, *above*
Sur, *over.*
Syn, Syl, &c., *with*
Tetra, *four.*
Theo, *God.*
Topo, *place.*
Trans, *across.*
Tri, *three.*
Typo, *type.*
Under, *beneath.*
Uni, *one.*
With, *opposition*
Zoo, *animal life.*

ALPHABETICAL SYNOPSIS OF AFFIXES.

Age, *rank, office.*
Ance, ancy, } *state or act of.*
Ence, ency, } *state or act of.*
Ant, ent, } *state or act of.*
Ate, ary, *having.*
Ble, *that may be.*
Bleness, *the quality of being able.*
Bly, *in a manner.*
Cy, ty, y, ity, *state, condition.*
En, *in.*
Er, or, an, ian, ex, ess, ee, eer, ist, ite, san, zen, *the person who.*
Fy, *to make.*
Ics, *science, art.*
Ion, ity, ment, *the state or act of.*
Ish, *some degree.*
Ism, *doctrine, state.*
Ive, ic, ical, ile, ine, ing, it, ial, ent ant, *pertaining to, having the quality, relating to.*
Ize, *to make.*
Less, *without.*
Ly, *like, resembling.*
Ness, *quality of.*
Oid, *resembling.*
Ous, ose, } *nature of. like, full of.*
Ory, some, } *nature of. like, full of.*
Ric, dom, *possession.*
Ship, *office.*
Ude, *state of being.*
Ure, *act of, state of being*
Ward, *in a direction.*

AFFIXES TO AFFIXES.

Ate, ated, ating, ater, ator, ately, ateness, ation, ative, atory, able, ably, ableness, ability, ty's, ties, ties'.
Ant, antly, ance, ancy, ancy's, ancies, ancies'.
Ful, fully, fulness.
Fy, fies, fiest, fied, fying, fier, fication, cative, cator.
Al, ally, alness, alism, alist, ality, ty's, &c.
Ize, ized, izing, ization, ism, ic, izable.
Ous, ously, ousness, osity, ity, y, ty.
Ive, ively, iveness, ivity.
Ile, ilely, ileness, ility.

The English language has, in many instances, two sets of derivative words, expressive of the same thing, the one of Saxon, and the other of Latin origin. Thus,

SAXON.	LATIN.	SAXON.	LATIN.
Fearful,	Timid.	Height,	Altitude.
Swiftness,	Velocity.	Lifeless,	Exanimate.
Womanish,	Effeminate.	Yearly,	Annual.
Building,	Edifice.	Watery,	Aqueous.
Fewness,	Paucity.	Hearer,	Auditor.

And, in many instances, the nouns are of Saxon origin, while the corresponding adjectives are from the Latin. Thus,

NOUNS FROM THE SAXON.	ADJECTIVES FROM THE LATIN.
Beginning,	Initial.
Body,	Corporeal.
Brother,	Fraternal.
Father,	Paternal.
Mother,	Maternal.
Cat,	Feline.
Day,	Diurnal.
Dog,	Canine.
Earth,	Terrestrial.
Flock,	Gregarious.
Flour,	Farinaceous.
Glass,	Vitreous, &c.

The student is now prepared to write a list of words derived from the proposed simple words, according to the following

Example.

From the word *press*, the following words are derived

Presser,	pressed,	pression,
pressure,	pressive,	pressingly.

depress,	uncompressed, &c.	oppressor,
depression, &c.	repress,	oppression, &c.
impress,	repressed,	suppress,
impression, &c.	repression,	suppressor,
re-impress, &c.	express,	suppression, &c.
compress,	expression,	insuppress, &c.
compression, &c.	oppress,	unsuppressed, &c.
uncompress,		

Exercises.

Write a list of words derived from the following words or roots by adding the prefixes, suffixes, &c., that have been explained.

Faith.	Jure.	Right.	Append.
Health.	Marry.	Good.	Absolve.
Pity.	Merge.	Idol.	Abridge.
Hope.	Tend.	Law.	Answer.
Mercy.	Stand.	Author.	Aspire.
Art.	Run.	Contract.	Pride.
Care.	Ply.	Present.	Blame.
Need.	Range.	Attend.	Bless.
Fear.	Create.	Moderate.	Caprice.
Shame.	Pose.	Virtue.	Censure.
Respect.	Graphic.	Use.	Caution.
Create.	Fac and	Presume.	Cite.
Fine.	Factum.*	Separate.	Commune.
Scribe.	Divide.	Critic.	Conceal.
Argue.	Improve.	False.	Correct.
Sense.	Profess.	Fire.	Reform.
Lude.	Succeed.	Full.	Defy.
Join.	Deduce.	Frolic.	Define.
Real.	Defend.	Fortune.	Discover.
Large.	Resolve.	Multiply.	Elect.
Form.	Calumny.	Note.	Elevate.
Fense.	Arm.	Conform.	Fancy.
Move.	Peace.	Hinder.	Faction.
Spect.	Love.	Book.	Fault.
Sign.	Laugh.	Apply.	Favor.

* The origin of this word is the Latin verb *facio*, and its supine *factum*, which signifies *to make*, *to do*, or *to cause*, and it enters, in some form, into the composition of more than five hundred of our English words. The word *pono*, and its supine *positum*, furnish 250 words; *plico*, 200; *fero* and *latum*, 198; *specio*, 177; *mitto* and *missum*, 174; *teneo* and *tentum*, 168; *capeo* and *captum*, 197; *tendo*, *tensum*, and *tentum*, 162; *duco* and *ductum*, 156; *logos*, (from the Greek language,) 156; *grapho*, 152. These twelve words enter, in some shape, into the composition of nearly 2500 English words. From 154 Greek and Latin primitives, nearly 13,000 English words are derived, or are affected in their signification. See Towne's *Analysis of Derivative Words.*

Figure.	Mount.	Motion.	Teach.
Form.	Open.	Rebel.	Tolerate.
Fury.	Peace.	Remark.	Tradition.
Grace.	Potent.	Represent.	Tremble.
Harm.	Prefer.	Secret.	Value.
Humor.	Presume.	Spirit.	Vapor.
Imitate.	Proper.	Subscribe.	Vivid.
Indulge.	Pure.	Suffice.	Wit.
Moral.	Reason.		

XVI.

SYNONYMES.

Synonymes are words having precisely the same meaning.

The number of words, in any language, which are strictly synonomous, are few; but, as was stated in the last lesson, in the English language there are many instances of words, derived from different sources, expressive of precisely the same idea. Thus, the words *swiftness* and *velocity*, *womanish* and *effeminate*, *building* and *edifice*, *fewness* and *paucity*, *brotherly* and *fraternal*, *fatherly* and *paternal*, *motherly* and *maternal*, *yearly* and *annual*, *height* and *altitude*, are words of precisely the same import.

Although, with exceptions of the kind just enumerated, the words strictly synonomous are few, yet it is often the case that one word of similar meaning may be substituted in a sentence for another, without materially altering the idea intended to be expressed. Thus, in the sentence, "I *design* to *show* the *difference* in these *words*," the word *design* may be changed into *intend*, *purpose*, *propose*, or *mean*; thus.

I *design* to show the difference in these words.
I *intend* to show the difference in these words.
I *purpose*, *propose*, or *mean* to show the difference, &c.

The word *show* may, in like manner, be changed into *explain*, *point out*, or *illustrate*; the word *difference* may be changed into *distinction*, and *expressions* may be substituted for *words*, without materially altering the meaning of the sentence.

Such exercises as these give a command of language to the student, and are of great use as a preparation for exercises in prose, as well as verse. But to the poet especially a familiar acquaintance with expressions of similar meaning is absolutely indispensable. Confined as he is to certain rules, it is often the case, that a long word must be substituted for a short one, or a short one for a long, in order to produce the necessary succession of syllables to constitute the measure, or the harmony, of his verses.

It has been stated, that few words are strictly synonymous. Although, in the sentence just recited, namely, "I *design* to show the difference in these words," it has been observed, that the words *intend, purpose, propose,* or *mean*, may be substituted for *design*, without materially altering the sense, yet it must be understood, that the words themselves are really different in meaning. The word *design* properly signifies *to mark out, as with a pencil; purpose* signifies *to set before one's mind as an object of pursuit; mean* signifies *to have in the mind; propose* properly implies *to offer*, and *intend* expresses *the bending of the mind toward an object.* *

The words *difficulties, embarrassments,* and *troubles*, are often used as words of precisely similar signification; but there is, in reality, considerable difference in their signification. The three terms are all applicable to a person's concerns in life, but *difficulties* relate to the *facility* of accomplishing an undertaking, and imply, that it is not *easily* done. *Embarrassments* relate to the confusion attending a state of debt, and *trouble* to the pain which is the natural consequence of not fulfilling engagements or answering demands. Of the three words, *difficulties* expresses the least, and *troubles* the most. "A young man, on his entrance into the world, will unavoidably experience *difficulties*, if not provided with ample means in the outset. But, let his means be ever so ample, if he have not prudence, and talents fitted for business, he will hardly keep himself free from *embarrassments*, which are the greatest *troubles* that can arise to disturb the peace of a man's mind."

The words *difficulty, obstacle,* and *impediment*, although frequently used as synonymous, have nice distinctions in their meanings. *Difficulty*, as has already been observed, relates to the *ease* with which a thing is *done*, *obstacle* signifies the thing which *stands in the way* between the person and the object he has in view; and *impediment* signifies the thing which *entangles the feet.* All of these terms include in their signification, that which interferes either with the actions or views of men. The *difficulty* lies most in the nature and circumstances of the thing itself; the *obstacle* and *impediment* consist of that which is *external* or *foreign;* the *difficulty* interferes with the completion of any work; the *obstacle* interferes with the attainment of any end; the *impediment* interrupts the progress and prevents the execution of one's wishes; the *difficulty* embarrasses; it suspends the powers of acting or deciding; the *obstacle* opposes itself; it is properly met in the way, and intervenes between us and our object; the *impediment* shackles and puts a stop to our proceeding; we speak of encountering a *difficulty*, surmounting an *obstacle*, and removing an *impediment;* we go *through difficulty*, *over* an *obstacle*, and pass *by impediments.* The disposition of the mind often occasions more *difficulties* in negociations, than the subjects themselves; the eloquence of Demosthenes was the greatest *obstacle* which Philip of Macedon experienced in his political career; ignorance in the language is the greatest *impediment* which a foreigner experiences in the pursuit of any object out of his own country.

---

* The student who wishes a fuller explanation of the difference between these words is referred to that very valuable work entitled, "English Synonymes explained in Alphabetical Order, with copious Illustrations and Examples drawn from the best Writers, by George Crabb, of Magdalen Hall, Oxford."

The following instances show a difference in the meaning of words reputed synonymous, and point out the use of attending, with care and strictness, to the exact import of words.

Custom, habit. Custom respects the action; habit, the actor. By custom, we mean the frequent repetition of the same act; by habit, the effect which that repetition produces on the mind or body. By the custom of walking often in the streets, one acquires a habit of idleness.

Pride, vanity. Pride makes us esteem ourselves; vanity makes us desire the esteem of others. It is just to say, that a man is too proud to be vain.

Haughtiness, disdain. Haughtiness is founded on the high opinion we entertain of ourselves; disdain, on the low opinion we have of others.

Only, alone. Only imports, that there is no other of the same kind; alone imports being accompanied by no other. An only child is one that has neither brother nor sister; a child alone is one who is left by itself. There is a difference, therefore, in precise language, between these two phrases: "Virtue only makes us happy;" and "Virtue alone makes us happy."

Wisdom, prudence. Wisdom leads us to speak and act what is most proper. Prudence prevents our speaking or acting improperly.

Entire, complete. A thing is entire when it wants none of its parts; complete when it wants none of the appendages that belong to it. A man may have an entire house to himself, and yet not have one complete apartment.

Surprised, astonished, amazed, confounded. I am surprised with what is new or unexpected; I am astonished at what is vast or great; I am amazed at what is incomprehensible; I am confounded by what is shocking or terrible.

Tranquillity, peace, calm. Tranquillity respects a situation free from trouble, considered in itself; peace, the same situation with respect to any causes that might interrupt it; calm, with regard to a disturbed situation going before or following it. A good man enjoys *tranquillity*, in himself; *peace*, with others; and *calm*, after a storm.

In a similar manner, differences can be pointed out in the words *conquer, vanquish, subdue, overcome*, and *surmount*. *Conquer* signifies to *seek or try to gain an object* *vanquish* implies the *binding of an individual; subdue* signifies to *give* or *put under; overcome* expresses the *coming over* or *getting the mastery over one; surmount* signifies to *mount over* or to *rise above any one.* Persons or things are *conquered* or *subdued;* persons, only, are *vanquished.* An enemy or a country is *conquered;* a foe is *vanquished;* people are *subdued;* prejudices and prepossessions are *overcome;* obstacles are *surmounted.* We *conquer* an enemy by whatever means we gain the mastery over him; we *vanquish* him, when by force we make him yield; we *subdue* him by whatever means we check in him the spirit of resistance. A Christian tries to conquer his enemies by kindness and generosity; a warrior tries to *vanquish* them in the field; a prudent monarch tries to *subdue* his rebel subjects by a due mixture of clemency and rigor. One may be *vanquished* in a single battle; one is *subdued* only by the most violent and persevering measures.

William the First *conquered* England by *vanquishing* his rival, Harold; after which he completely *subdued* the English.

Vanquish is used only in its proper sense; *conquer* and *subdue* are likewise employed figuratively, in which sense they are analogous to *overcome* and *surmount.* That is *conquered* and *subdued* which is in the mind; that is *overcome* and *surmounted* which is either internal or external. We *conquer* and *overcome* what makes no great resistance; we *subdue* and *surmount* what is violent and strong in its opposition. Dislikes, attachments, and feelings in general, either for or against, are *conquered;* unruly and tumultuous passions are to be *subdued:* a man *conquers* himself, he *subdues* his spirit. One *conquers* by ordinary means and efforts, one *subdues* by extraordinary means. It requires determination and force to *conquer* and *overcome;* patience and perseverance to *subdue* and *surmount.* Whoever aims at Christian perfection must strive with God's assistance to *conquer* avarice, pride, and every inordinate propensity; to *subdue* wrath, anger, lust, and every carnal appetite, to *overcome* temptations, to *vanquish* the tempter, and to *surmount* trials and impediments, which obstruct his course.

The nice distinctions which exist among some words commonly reputed synonymous having now been pointed out, the student may proceed to the exercises of this Lesson according to the following

Example.

The words *vision, way, formerly, weaken, unimportant, see,* and *think,* are proposed; and it is required to find a list of words, having a meaning similar to them respectively.

Vision, apparition, phantom, spectre ghost.

Way, manner, method, mode, course, means.

Formerly, in times past, in old times, in days of yore, anciently, in ancient times.

Weaken, enfeeble, debilitate, enervate, invalidate.

Unimportant, insignificant, immaterial, inconsiderable

See, perceive, observe, behold, look at.

Think, reflect, ponder, muse, imagine, suppose, believe deem, consider.*

In the sentences which follow, it is required to change the words as in the following examples. The student will notice that every change of words will, in most cases, produce some corresponding change in the idea; but, as the object of the exercise is to give him a command of language, it is not

* It may here be remarked that phrases, as well as words, may be expressed by appropriate synonymes. Technically speaking, the term synonyme is generally applied to simple terms. But a compound term or phrase may be sometimes expressed by a synonymous word; and a simple term may be also expressed by a synonymous *phrase*. It will be unnecessary to present in this place, any list of words for the pupil to be exercised upon, as the living teacher, or the pupil himself, may easily select them from any volume at hand. But it may here be remarked that exercises on synonymous *phrases* may be considered as more valuable than those on simple terms, because they may generally be expressed with greater precision. But the value of exercises of both kinds is clearly and forcibly set forth by Mr. Murray, in the 'Exercises' appended to his larger Grammar, in the following language:

'*On variety of Expression.* Besides the practice of transposing the parts of sentences, the compiler recommends to tutors, frequently to exercise their pupils, in exhibiting some of the various modes in which the same sentiment may be properly expressed. This practice will extend their knowledge of the language, afford a variety of expression, and habituate them to deliver their sentiments with clearness, ease, and propriety. It will likewise enable those who may be engaged in studying other languages, not only to construe them with more facility into English, but also to observe and apply more readily, many of the turns and phrases, which are best adapted to the genius of those languages.'

A few examples of this kind of exercise, will be sufficient to explain the nature of it, and to show its utility.

The brother deserved censure more than his sister.

The sister was less reprehensible than her brother.

The sister did not deserve reprehension so much as her brother.

Reproof was more due to the brother, than to the sister.

I will attend the conference, if I can do it conveniently.

I intend to be at the conference, unless it should be inconvenient.

If I can do it with convenience, I purpose to be present at the conference.

If it can be done without inconvenience, I shall not fail to attend the conference.

I shall not absent myself from the conference, unless circumstances render it necessary.

I propose to be present at the conference, if I can do so consistently with my other engagements.

I purpose to be at the conference, unless I am prevented by other avocations.

Unless I am restrained by other imperative duties, I shall certainly be at the conference.

I will be at the conference if nothing unforeseen prevents.

If I am master of my own time I will not neglect the conference.

I shall by no means absent myself from the conference if I can possibly attend it.

deemed important in these Exercises to exact strict verbal accuracy.

Example 1*st.*

He continued the work without *stopping.*
He continued the work without *resting.*
He continued the work without *cessation.*
He continued the work without *intermission.*
He continued the work without *delay.*
He continued the work without *leaving off.*
He continued the work without *interruption.*
He continued the work without *obstacle.*
He continued the work without *impediment*, &c.

Example 2*d.*

He is free from *care.*
He is free from *solicitude.*
He is *exempted* from *anxiety.*
He is *without concern*, &c.

Example 3*d.*

I found that he was an enemy.
I found that he was a foe.
I found that he was an adversary.
I found that he was an opponent.
I found that he was an antagonist.

Exercises.

Law and order are *not remembered.*

On that *elevated* ground where the *verdant* turf looks *dark* with fire, yesterday stood a noble *house.*

Thinking deeply on the nature of my *existence*, the contradictions I had *suffered* filled me with *humbleness.*

I began to *think* that there was some *deception* in the sensation conveyed by my eyes.

How loved, how valued once avails thee not,
To whom *connected* or by whom begot;
A *pile* of dust is all remains of thee,
'T is all thou art and all the *great* shall be.

The boy *translated* the book to my lodgings, and *conveyed* a *chair* to the table; and I sat down with the intention of *bringing* the first chapter, which *holds* a very interesting story from the French into the English language, in a style suitable to *fetch* the author's meaning clearly to every *intellect*

We *get up* from our *thinkings* with hearts softened and *conquered* and we *come back* into life as into a shadowy *vista* where we have "disquieted ourselves in vain."

Thus he went on until the sun *drew near* to his *mid-day* and the *augmented* heat, preyed upon his *force*. He then *cast round* about him, for some more *commodious* path.

Charity, like the sun, *rubs up* every object on which it shines.

He who is *used* to turn aside from the world, and *hold communication* with himself in retirement will sometimes at least hear the *veracities* which the world do not *speak of to him*. A more sound *teacher* will *elevate* his voice and *rouse up* within the heart those *hidden* suggestions which the world had overpowered and *put down*.

Among all our *bad* passions there is a strong and intimate *joining*. When any one of them is *taken as a child* into our family it seldom *forsakes* us until it has fathered upon us all its *relations*.

The Creator endowed man with a *lofty* countenance and directed him to look up to heaven.

In the following extracts the student may alter the words in Italic, so as to complete the rhymes; as in the following

Example.

Did sweeter sounds adorn my flowing tongue,
Than ever man pronounced or angel *chanted;*
Had I all knowledge, human and *godlike,*
That thought can reach, or science can define; &c.

Rhyme completed.

Did sweeter sounds adorn my flowing tongue,
Than ever man pronounced or angel *sung;*
Had I all knowledge, human and divine,
That thought can reach or science can define, &c.

Exercises.

A shepherd's dog, unskilled in sports,
Picked up acquaintance of all *kinds*,
Among the rest, a fox he knew;
By frequent chat their friendship *increased.*
Says Ren'ard, "'T is a cruel case,
That man should stigmatize our *generation.*
No doubt, among us, rogues you find,
As among dogs and human *sort.*
And yet, (unknown to me and you,)
There may be honest men and *not false.*
Thus slander tries, whate'er it can,
To put us on the foot with *the human race.*

Not in the solitude,
Alone, may man commune with Heaven, or *behold*,
Only in savage *forest*
And sunny vale the present Deity;
Or only hear his voice
Where the winds whisper and the waves *are glad*.

Even here do I behold
Thy steps, Almighty! here, amidst the crowd
Through the great city rolled,
With everlasting murmur, deep and *strong*—
Choking the ways that wind
'Mongst the proud piles, the work of human kind.

"Without a vain, without a grudging heart,
To him who gives us all, I yield a *portion;*
From him you came, from him accept it here—
A frank and sober, more than costly, *entertainment*."
He spoke, and bade the welcome tables spread;
Then talked of virtue till the time of *rest*,
When the grave household round his hall repair,
Warned by the bell, and close the hour with *supplication*.
At length the world, renewed by calm *sleep*,
Was strong for toil; the dappled morn arose
Before the pilgrims part, the younger crept
Near the closed cradle, where an infant *slumbered*,
And writhed his neck; the landlord's little pride—
O strange return!—grew black, and gasped, and *expired*.
Horror of horrors! what! his only son!
How looked our hermit when the deed was *completed!*
Not hell, though hell's black jaws in sunder part,
And breathe blue fire, could more assault his *breast*.
Confused, and struck with silence at the deed,
He flies; but, trembling, fails to fly with *haste*.

If all our hopes and all our *apprehensions*,
Were prisoned in life's narrow *limit;*
If, travellers through this vale of tears,
We saw no better world beyond;
Oh, what could check the rising sigh?
What earthly thing could pleasure *bestow?*
Oh, who could venture then to *expire?*
Oh, who could then endure to live?

A few examples are presented below, in which the words in Italic are improperly used for others which in some respects they resemble.

Example 1*st.*

"The lamb is *tame* in its disposition."

Here the word *tame* is incorrectly used for *gentle;* tameness is produced by discipline; gentleness belongs to the natural disposition.

Example 2d.

"Newton *discovered* the telescope, and Harvey *invented* the circulation of the blood."

In this example the words *discovered* and *invented* should change places. We discover what was hidden; we *invent* what is new.

Example 3d.

"Caius Marcus displayed *courage* when he stood unmoved with his hand in the fire; Leonidas displayed his *fortitude* at Thermopylæ when with three hundred Spartans he opposed the entire army of Xerxes."

Here also *courage* and fortitude should change places. Courage enables us to meet danger; fortitude gives us strength to endure pain

From such examples the student will learn the importance of proper attention to the exact meaning of words. A loose style of writing is the result of the careless use of words, improperly considered as synonymous.

Exercises.

I heard a *large* noise, which, though made at a *big* distance, must have been made by a very *great* animal.

The work is *capable* of great improvement, although it was written by a very *susceptible* man.

Much men were present, and their united voices caused *many* confusion.

Franklin *framed* the fact that lightning is caused by electricity. Sir Isaac Newton *discovered* the telescope. Solon *invented* a new set of laws for the city of Athens.

A wicked man *fabricates* sorrow for his sins, and often *feigns* an excuse for his crimes.

The book has many *vices*, but the *defect* is not in the author, who has sufficiently shown his abhorrence of *faults*.

I *know* the man and *am acquainted with* his faults. We are agreeably *amazed* to see our friends returning so soon. We are *surprised* that they accomplished their business so early, as well as *astonished* at the unexpected events which nearly threatened their ruin.

We often know the *spot* where a thing is, but it is not easy to find out the exact *place* where it happened.

When *dissensions* arise among neighbors, their passions often interfere to hinder accommodations; when members of a family consult interest or humor, rather than affection, there will necessarily be *variances*; and when many member of a community have an equal liberty to express their opinions, there will necessarily be *disagreements.*

A misplaced economy in people of property is *low*, but swearing and drunkenness are *meaner* vices.

We perform many duties only as the *occasion* offers, or as the *opportunity* requires.

It is the duty of a person to *govern* those who are under him in all matters wherein they are incompetent to *rule* themselves.

Fashion and caprice *regulate* the majority as the time of one clock *rules* that of many others.

Exuberance of imagination and *luxuriance* of intellect are the greatest gifts of which a poet can boast.

We may be *eminent* and *illustrious* for things good, bad, or indifferent, we may be *distinguished* for our singularities; we may be *conspicuous* for that which is the subject of vulgar discourse; but we can be *distinguished* only for that which is really good and praiseworthy.

Lovers of fame are sometimes able to render themselves *eminent* for their vices or absurdities, but nothing is more gratifying to a man than to render himself *illustrious* for his professional skill. It is the lot of few to be *noted*, and these few are seldom to be envied.

Water and snow *amass* by the continual accession of fresh quantities, the ice *accumulates* in the river until it is frozen over.

The industrious man *amasses* guineas and *accumulates* wealth.

France has long been celebrated for its *health;* and many individuals resort thither for the benefit of their *salubrity.*

The places destined for the education of youth should be *salutary;* the diet of the young *healthy* rather than delicate, and in all their disorders, care should be taken to administer the most *wholesome* remedies.

A nation may be *extravagant* of its resources, and a government may be *profuse* of the public money; but no individual should be *lavish* of what is not his own, nor *prodigal* of what he gives another.

There are but few *remarkable* things; but many things are *extraordinary.*

A man may have a *distaste* for his ordinary occupations without any apparent cause; and after long illness he will frequently take a *dislike* to the food or the amusement which before afforded him pleasure.

It is good to suppress unfounded *disgusts;* it is difficult to overcome a strong *dislike;* and it is advisable to divert our attention from objects calculated to create *distaste.**

---

* Words are sometimes similar in sound, although different in spelling and signification. Such are the words *sight, cite,* and *site; raise* and *raze aisle* and *isle; scent, cent,* and *sent,* &c. Although these are not, technically speaking, to be considered as synonymous, they may be here mentioned in order to caution the student with regard to the use of them. The verbs *lie* and *lay*, also, although entirely different in meaning, have some parts in common, which are frequently misused. The teacher who wishes for exercises of this kind, to be corrected by the pupil, will find a large collection of them in a little work recently published by a distinguished teacher of this city, entitled "The Companion to Spelling Books, in which the Orthography and Meaning of many thousand Words, most liable to be misspelled and misused, are impressed upon the Memory by a regular Series of Written Exercises." The work is by that eminent teacher, Mr. William B. Fowle. See also the exercises on words, page 17

XVII.

METHODS OF INVERSION AND TRANSPOSITION.

The same idea may be expressed in a great variety of ways by the methods of inversion and transposition suggested in the following examples.

Example 1st.

By changing active verbs into passive, and the contrary, thus, *By the active verb.* A multitude of delighted guests *soon filled* the places of those who refused to come. *By the passive verb.* The places of those who refused to come *were soon filled* by a multitude of delighted guests.

Example 2d.

By using the case absolute, instead of the nominative case and its verb, and the contrary; as, *The class having recited their lessons,* the teacher dismissed them. *The class recited their lessons* and the teacher dismissed them. Of these two sentences the former is preferable, because it preserves the unity of the sentence, which requires that the subject or nominative should be changed as little as possible during the course of the sentence. Another recommendation of the former expression is, that it throws out the conjunction, which should never be unnecessarily introduced into a sentence.

Example 3d.

Infinitive mood or substantive and participial phrases instead of nominative or objective nouns, and the reverse; as, His having been unfortunate is no disgrace; instead of, His misfortunes are no disgrace.

Diligence, industry, and proper improvement of time are material duties of the young; or, To be diligent, industrious, and properly to improve time are material duties of the young.

Example 4th.

By the negation or affirmation of the contrary; as, Solon the Athenian effected *a great change* in the government of his country. Solon, the Athenian, effected *no small* change in the government of his country.

The beauty of the earth is *as conspicuous* as the grandeur of the heavens. The beauty of the earth is *not less conspicuous* than the grandeur of the heavens.

Example 5th.

By reversing the corresponding parts of the sentence, with a negative adverb; as, The grandeur of the heavens is *not* more conspicuous than the beauty of the earth.

*The negation of the contrary.** The beauty of the earth is not less conspicuous than the grandeur of the heavens.

By a comparison. There is as much beauty in the earth, as there is grandeur in the heavens.

By an expletive cause. There is no less beauty in the earth than grandeur in the heavens.

Example 6th.

By changing the participial phrases into a personal verb with a conjunction; as, Charles, having been deprived of the help of tutors, neglected his studies. Charles was deprived of the help of tutors, and therefore he neglected his studies.

Example 7th.

Change of the nominative and verb into an infinitive phrase; as, He sacrificed his future ease and reputation *that he might enjoy* present pleasure. He sacrificed his future ease and reputation *to enjoy* present pleasure.

Example 8th.

The infinitive changed into an objective noun; as, Canst thou expect *to escape* the hand of vengeance? Canst thou expect *an escape* from the hand of vengeance?

Or into a finite verb with its nominative; as, Canst thou expect that thou *shalt escape* the hand of vengeance?

---

* The negative adjective is generally more elegant than the negative adverb. Thus, "I was *unable*," is to be preferred to the expression, '*I was not able*." "*Invisible*," rather than "*not visible*;" "*Inconsistent*," rather than "*not consistent*," &c.

Example 9th.

Participial nouns converted into common nouns, and the contrary; as, Providence alone can order *the changing* of times and seasons. Providence alone can order *the changes* of times and seasons.

Example 10th.

The change of the verb, an adjective, or an adverb, into a noun and the contrary; and the conversion of a noun into a pronoun; as, Idleness, ease, and prosperity tend to generate folly and vice. The tendency of idleness, ease, and prosperity is to generate folly and vice. Idleness, ease, and prosperity have a tendency toward the generation of folly Folly and vice are too generally the consequences of idleness, ease, and prosperity.

Simple language always pleases most. Simplicity of language always pleases most. We please most when we speak simply.

Those persons who, &c. They who, &c.

Example 11th.

The conversion of an active or a passive verb into a neuter verb with an adjective; as, Sobriety of mind *suits* the present state of man. Sobriety of mind *is suitable* to the present state of man.

Example 12th.

By the conversion of a declaration into an obligation, with a corresponding change of words.

Declaration. Man's present state renders sobriety of mind highly becoming.

Obligation. Man in his present state should be characterized by sobriety of mind.

Example 13th.

By a noun in apposition to avoid the use of the conjunction *and.* Hope is the sustainer of the mind, and supports us under many a burden. Hope, the sustainer of the mind, supports us under many a burden.

Example 14th.

By the preposition and its objective case, instead of the possessive; as, The moon's mild radiance and the sun's resplendent brightness are objects which, &c. The mild radiance of the moon and the resplendent brightness of the sun,* &c.

The repetition of and † *avoided by the use of the preposition;* as, God has given us senses to enjoy all these beautiful objects, *and* reason to guide us in the use of them. God has given us senses to enjoy all these beautiful objects, *with* reason to guide us in the use of them.

By the use of the potential mode instead of the infinitive; God has given us senses that we may enjoy all these beautiful objects, with reason, &c.

An infinitive phrase instead of a nominative noun; To do justly, to love mercy, and to walk humbly, are duties enjoined by Christianity. Justice, mercy, and humility, are duties enjoined by Christianity.

The negative adverb with the conjunction but; We can observe the exquisite skill of the Artificer in all that we see around us. We can*not but* observe the exquisite skill of the Artificer in all that we see around us.

It is to be remarked, that although some examples have been given, in which the participial noun is used, yet when there is a common noun from the same root, of similar meaning, the participial noun should be avoided. Thus, "The habit of deceiving" is not so elegant an expression as "Habits of deception."

Example 15th.

Resolution of the personal pronoun, with the conjunction and *into the relative pronoun;* thus, We can learn a lesson of resignation, *and it* will prepare us for that happy home where the weary are at rest. We can learn a lesson of resignation,

* It is deemed very inelegant to construct a sentence with many possessive nouns, or with many objectives governed by the preposition *of*. Thus, the sentence, The extent *of* the prerogative *of* the King *of* England, or, The King of England's prerogative's extent, would be better expressed thus, The extent of the King of England's prerogative.

† The use of the conjunction *and* may often be avoided by dividing long sentences into short ones.

which will prepare us for that happy home where the weary are at rest.

Example 16*th.*

By the use of the present or perfect participle instead of the verb; as, *He was called* to the exercise of the supreme power at a very early age, *and evinced* a great knowledge of government and laws, *and* was regarded by mankind with a respect which is seldom bestowed on one so young.

In this sentence the use of the participles removes one of the conjunctions, which young writers are very apt to repeat unnecessarily; thus, *Called* to the exercise of the supreme power at a very early age, and evincing a great knowledge of government and laws, he was regarded by mankind with a respect which is seldom bestowed on one so young.

By the use of the participles instead of the relative clause, as, "The smiles that encourage severity of judgement hide malice and insincerity." Smiles encouraging severity of judgement hide malice and insincerity.

For the sake of emphasis, or to gratify a taste for singularity, some writers have adopted the poetical style in prose, placing the verb before its nominative; thus, When we go, for *go we* must, &c. *Proceed we* now to the second subject of our consideration. *Recognize we* here the hand of an Almighty power.

In some instances, perhaps not strictly proper, we find the definite article placed before the relative pronoun; as, Th[illegible] things, *the which* you have seen and understood, &c.

It is to be observed, that in all the changes suggested [illegible] the foregoing models, there must be some slight change in the idea, but still the identity of the thought is sufficiently preserved in all the changes suggested. *

---

* Under the head of *variety of expression*, may be noticed some few peculiarities and improprieties, which are sometimes heard, especially in colloquial intercourse, and which, in some instances, are not noticed by any grammatical authority. And first, the improper use of *if* for *whether*, as follows: "She asked me *if* I would go with her." It should be, "She asked me *whether* I would go," &c. Again, the improper use of *me* for *my self*, and of *you* for *yourself*. As, I am going to wash *me*. Do you intend to wash *you*? It should be *myself* and *yourself*. Again, The use of *as* for *that*; as, I do not know *as* I shall go. I do not know *as* I could tell when. It should be *that*. I do not know *that* I shall go. I do not know *that* I could tell when. Again, The use of *any* and *got* with a negative; as, I have

Examples of some of the preceding methods of inversion and transposition.

Example 1*st.*

The mind is sustained by hope.
Hope sustains the mind.
Hope is the sustainer of the mind.
The sustainer of the mind is hope.

Example 2*d.*

Idleness, ease, and prosperity, tend to generate folly and vice.

The tendency of idleness, ease, and prosperity is to generate folly and vice.

Idleness, ease, and prosperity have a tendency, &c.

---

not *got any* book. It would be better to say, I have no book. Such words as *fetch* for *bring*, *sweat* for *perspiration*, and many others of a similar character, are considered, to say the least, inelegant, and are to be avoided. The word *so* is sometimes heard in use for *therefore;* as, Charles did not wish to go, *so* I did not urge him. It should be, Charles did not wish to go, *therefore* I did not urge him. *Other* is sometimes improperly followed by *but* instead of *than;* as, I saw no other *but* him. It should be, I saw no other *than* him. We sometimes hear the demonstrative pronoun improperly used for the personal pronoun; as, *Those* who hear must obey. It should be, *They* who hear must obey. We sometimes hear such expressions as this: I know of hardly [*or* scarcely] a passage, &c. It would be better to say, I know of no passage, &c. The past tenses of the word *lay* (to place) are very frequently and improperly used for the corresponding tenses of *lie* (to lie down). Thus, The water *laid* in the pool. It should be, *lay* in the pool. You have *laid* abed too long. It should be, You have *lain*, &c. Again, We frequently find a want of correspondence in the different parts of a sentence, as follows: He did not mention Leonora, nor that her father was dead. It is better to say, He did not mention Leonora, nor the death of her father. These expressions fall under grammatical rule.

In sentences where the negative adverb occurs, it should be followed by the negative conjunction. Thus, "Thou canst not tell whence it cometh *and* whither it goeth," should be, Thou canst not tell whence it cometh *nor* whither it goeth.

In the use of prepositions we find many manifest improprieties. As no certain rule can be laid down with regard to them, a few examples are presented, to show what prepositions may be properly used with certain words It may, however, be remarked that the same preposition that follows a verb or adverb, should generally follow the noun, &c., which is derived from it, as, confide *in*, confidence *in;* disposed *to* tyrannize, a disposition *to* tyranny, &c.

Accuse *of* falsehood.	Differ *from*.	Need *of*.
Accused *by* his friend.	Difficulty *in*.	Observance *of*.
Acquit *of*.	Diminution *of*.	Prejudice *against*.

Folly and vice are too frequently the consequences of idleness, ease, and prosperity.*

Exercises on the principles of the preceding methods of Inversion and Transposition.

Providence alone can order the changing of the seasons.

Can you expect to be exempted from these troubles which all must suffer?

Earth shall claim thy growth, to be resolved to earth again.

That I may convince you of my sincerity, I will repeat the assertion.

Sobriety of mind is not unsuitable to the present state of man.

He had no little difficulty in accomplishing the undertaking.

A large part of the company were pleased with his remarks.

Hope sustains the mind.

Indeed, if we could arrest time, and strike off the wheels of his chariot, and, like Joshua, bid the sun stand still, and make opportunity tarry as long as we had occasion for it, this were something to excuse our delay or at least to mitigate and abate the folly and unreasonableness of it.

---

* The word *it* commonly called the neuter pronoun, is sometimes very serviceable in enabling us to alter the arrangement. Thus, It is hope that sustains the mind. It is by hope that the mind is sustained, &c. See *Whately's Rhetoric, Part* 3*d, Chap.* 2*d, Part* 11*th.*

Adapted *to.*
Agreeable *to.*
Averse *to.*
Bestow *upon.*
Boast *or* brag *of.*
Call *on.*
Change *for.*
Confide *in.*
Conformable *to.*
Compliance *with.*
Consonant *to.*
Conversant *with** a person, *in* a thing.
Dependent *upon.*
Derogation *from.*
Die *of* or *by.*
Disappointed *in* or *of.* †
Disapprove *of.*
Discouragement *to.*
Dissent *from.*
Eager *in.*
Engaged *in.*
Exception *from.*
Expert *at* or *in.*
Fall *under.*
Free *from.*
Glad *of* or *at.* ‡
Independent *of* or *on.*
Insist *upon.*
Made *of.*
Marry *to.*
Martyr *for.*
Profit *by.*
Provide *with, for,* or *against.*
Reconcile *to.*
Replete *with.*
Resemblance *to.*
Resolve *on.*
Reduce *under* or *to.* §
Regard *to* or *for.*
Swerve *from.*
Taste *of* or *for.* ||
Think *of* or *on.*
True *to.*
Wait *on.*
Worthy *of.* **

---

* Addison has, "conversant *among* the writings," &c., and, "conversant *about* worldly affairs." Generally speaking, "conversant *with*" is preferable.

† We are disappointed *of* a thing when we do not get it; and disappointed *in* it when we have it, and find that it does not answer our expectations.

‡ "Glad *of*," when the cause of joy is something gained or possessed; and "glad *at*," when something befalls another; as, "Jonah was glad *of* the gourd;" "He that is glad *at* calamities," &c.

§ "Reduce *under*," is to conquer or subdue."

|| A taste *of* a thing, implies actual enjoyment of it; but a taste *for* it, implies only a capacity for enjoyment; as, "When we have had a taste *of* the pleasures of virtue, we can have no taste *for* those of vice."

** Many of these words sometimes take other prepositions after them, to express various meanings; thus, for example, "Fall *in*, to comply;" "Fall *off*, to forsake;" "Fall *out*, to happen;" "Fall *upon*. to attack;" "Fall *to*." to begin eagerly," &c.

The records of Scripture exhibit no character more remarkable and instructive than that of the Patriarch Joseph. He is one who is beheld by us, tried in all the vicissitudes of fortune; from the condition of a slave rising to be ruler of the land of Egypt; and in every station, favor is acquired by him with God and man, by his wisdom and virtue. When he was overseer of Potiphar's house he proved his fidelity by strong temptations, which were honorably resisted by him.

When the artifices of a false woman threw him into prison, he was soon rendered conspicuous even in that dark mansion by his integrity and prudence.

Poetry is sublime when any great and good affection, as piety or patriotism, is awakened in the mind by it.

But in this dark and bewildered state an opposite direction is taken by the aspiring tendency of our nature and a very misplaced ambition is fed by it.

The mind is sustained by hope.

Idleness, ease, and prosperity tend to generate folly and vice.

The beauty displayed in the earth equals the grandeur conspicuous in the heavens.

Solon, the Athenian, effected a great change in the government of his country.

The Spartans considered war as the great business of life. For that reason they trained their children to laborious exercise, and instilled into their minds the principles of temperance and frugality.

He sacrificed his future ease and reputation that he might enjoy present pleasure.

When virtue abandons us, and conscience reproaches us, we become terrified with imaginary evils.

Expect no more from the world than it is able to afford you.

Canst thou expect to escape the hand of vengeance?

Providence alone can order the changing of times and seasons.

She who studies her glass neglects her own heart.

It is a favorite opinion with some, that certain modes of instruction are more profitable than others, or at least that there are some branches of study which give more full and constant employment to the intellectual faculties.

While many considerations allure the young and enterprising to commercial pursuits, the amount of capital which is needed, tends to limit the number of those who thus employ themselves.

The eye could scarcely reach the lofty and noble ceiling, the sides being regularly formed with spars, and the whole place presenting the idea of a magnificent theatre, that was illuminated with a vast profusion of lights.

An endless variety of characters, dispositions, and passions, diversifies the wide circle of human affairs.

A crowd that obstructed his passage awakened him from the tranquillity of meditation. He raised his eyes and saw the chief vizier, who had returned from the divan and was entering his palace

Let us remember that of small incidents the system of human life is chiefly composed.

Her temper and her capacity were the foundation of her singular talents for government. She was endowed with a great command over herself, and she soon obtained an uncontrolled ascendancy over the people

Few sovereigns of England succeeded to the throne in more difficult circumstances, and by none was the government uniformly conducted so successfully and felicitiously.

The enemy was subdued and the garrison was silenced, and the victori ous army returned triumphing.

To be docile and attentive is required of the young.

Miss Hannah Moore's writings have produced no small influence on the morals of the people.

The elegance of her manners is as conspicuous as the beauty of her person.

He took great pains that he might obtain the reward.

Gentle manners always please us most.

Strong expressions suit only strong feelings.

Providence has furnished us with talents for performing our duties and reason to guide in their performance.

We can see the wisdom of God in all his works.

XVIII.

FORMATION OF COMPOUND SENTENCES FROM SIMPLE ONES.

In every composition there should be a due intermixture of long and short sentences. For this reason the student should understand how to form compound sentences from simple ones.* In the prosecution of this work, he must recollect that in every sentence there must be some connecting principle among the parts. Some one object must reign and be predominant. There is commonly in every well-formed sentence, some person or thing which is the governing word, and this should be continued so, if possible, from the beginning to the end of the sentence.

Another principle, which he must also bear in mind, is that

---

* Professor Newman, says, in his Rhetoric, that "Vivacity of Style is *sometimes* attained by the omission of conjunctions and the consequent division of the discourse into short sentences." The following example illustrates his remark:

"As the storm increased with the night, the sea was lashed into tremen dous confusion, and there was a fearful sullen sound of rushing waves and broken surges, while deep called unto deep."

"The storm increased with the night. The sea was lashed into tremendous confusion. There was a fearful sullen sound of rushing waves and broken surges. Deep called unto deep."

which is expressed in Dr. Blair's second rule for the preservation of the unity of a sentence, namely: "Never to crowd into one sentence, things which have so little connection, that they could bear to be divided into two or more sentences."

The violation of this rule tends so much to perplex and obscure, that it is safer to err by too many short sentences, than by one that is overloaded and embarrassed.

Example.

The Sultan was dangerously wounded.

Thy conveyed him to his tent.

Upon hearing of the defeat of his troops, they put him into a litter.

The litter transported him to a place of safety.

The place of safety was at the distance of about fifteen leagues.

Compound sentence formed from the preceding simple ones.

The Sultan being dangerously wounded, they carried him to his tent; and upon hearing of the defeat of his troops, they put him into a litter, which transported him to a place of safety, at the distance of about fifteen leagues.

This sentence will be better if it be constructed as follows so that there shall be but one governing word from the beginning to the end of the sentence. Thus:

The Sultan being dangerously wounded, was carried to his tent; and on hearing of the defeat of his troops, was put into a litter, and transported to a place of safety, about fifteen leagues distant.

The following rules for the arrangement of words should be particularly observed, in the composition of compound sentences.

Rule 1*st.* The words should be so arranged as to mark as distinctly as possible *by their location*, the relation of the several parts to each other.

This rule requires that the verb should be placed as near as possible to the nominative; that the object should follow the verb in close succession, that adverbs should be placed near the word whose signification they affect, that the preposition should be immediately followed by the word which it governs, and that pronouns should be placed in such a position as to leave no doubt in the mind, with regard to their antecedents.

Rule 2*d.* When a circumstance is thrown into the midst of a sentence it should not be placed between the capital clauses, nor so as to hang loosely, but should be distinctly determined to its connexion by the position which it occupies.

The following sentence, composed of several simple sentences, is badly arranged. The parts in Italic show what the 'circumstance' is which is thrown into the midst of the sentence.

'The minister who grows less by his elevation, *like a statue placed on a mighty pedestal*, will always have his jealousy strong about him.'

In this sentence, a beautiful simile, by its improper location, is not only deprived of its effect, but is an encumbrance. Let a slight alteration of the arrangement be made, and the simile is restored to its beauty, and becomes highly ornamental. Thus:

The minister, who, like a statue placed on a mighty pedestal, grows less by his elevation, will always have his jealousy strong about him.

Rule 3d. Every sentence should present to the mind a distinct picture, or single group of ideas. For this reason, the scene and the circumstances expressed within the compass of a sentence must not be unnecessarily changed.

In the formation of compound sentences, therefore, from simple ones, whatever cannot be grouped so as to form an harmonious picture, should be presented in a separate sentence. The following sentence shows very clearly the bad effects of a change from person to person.

'The Brittons left to shift for themselves, and daily harassed by cruel inroads from the Picts, were forced to call in the Saxons for their defence, who consequently reduced the great part of the island to their power, drove the Britons into the most remote and mountainous parts, and the rest of the country, in customs, religion and language, became wholly Saxon.'

This complicated sentence, by means of some slight alterations, and a division into several sentences, will appear clear and accurate; thus,

The Britons, left to shift for themselves, and daily harassed by the cruel inroads of the Picts, were forced to call in the Saxons for their defence. But these *(the Saxons)* soon reduced the greatest part of the island under their own power, and drove the Britons to the most remote and mountainous parts. The consequence was, that the rest of the country became inhabited by a people in language, manners and religion wholly Saxon.

Rule 4th. The too frequent repetition of the same pronouns referring to different antecedents should be avoided.

The reason for this rule is, that such words being substitutes, can be used with advantage only when that to which the pronoun refers is quite obvious. The following sentence exemplifies this remark:

'One may have an air *which* proceeds from a just sufficiency and knowledge of the matter before him, *which* may naturally produce some motions of his head and body, *which* might become the bench better than the bar.'

In this sentence the pronoun '*which*' is used three times; and each time with a different antecedent. The first time that it is used its antecedent is *air*, the second time it is *sufficiency* and *knowledge*, and the third, *motions of the head and body*. The confusion thus introduced into the sentence may be avoided by employing *this* for the second *which*, and *such as* for the third: thus,

"One may have an air which proceeds from a just sufficiency of knowledge of the matter before him, and *this* may naturally produce some motions of the head, *such as* might become the bench better than the bar.

Rule 5th. All redundant words and clauses should be avoided.

The reason for this rule is, that whatever does not add to the meaning of a sentence must be useless if not hurtful.*

In conclusion, it may be remarked in the words of Archbishop Whately, It is a useful admonition to young writers, that they should always attempt to recast a sentence that does not please; altering the arrangement and entire structure of it, instead of merely seeking to change one word for another. This will give a great advantage in point of copiousness also; for there may be, suppose *a substantive* (or noun) which, either because it does not fully express our meaning, or for some other reason, we wish to remove, but can find no other to supply its place. But the object may perhaps be easily accomplished by means of a verb, adverb, or other part of speech, the substitution of which implies an alteration in the construction. It is an exercise, accordingly, which may be commended as highly conducive to the improvement of style, to practise casting a sentence into a variety of different forms.

XIX.

OF THE ENGLISH LANGUAGE.†

The English Language consists of about thirty-eight thousand words. This includes, of course, not only radical words, but all derivatives; except the preterits and participles of verbs; to which must be added some few terms, which, though set down in the dictionaries, are either obsolete or have never ceased to be considered foreign. Of these, about twenty-three thousand, or nearly five-eighths, are of Anglo-Saxon origin. The majority of the rest, in what proportion we cannot say, are Latin and Greek; Latin, however, has the larger share. The names of the greater part of the objects of sense, in other words, the terms which occur most frequently in discourse, or which recall the most vivid conceptions, are Anglo-Saxon. Thus, for example, the names of the most striking objects in visible nature, of the chief agencies at work there, and of the changes which we pass over it, are Anglo-Saxon. This language has given names to the heavenly bodies, the sun, moon, and stars; to three out of the four elements, earth, fire, and water; three out of the four seasons, spring, summer, and winter; and, indeed, to all the natural divisions of time, except one; as, day, night, morning, evening, twilight, noon, mid-day, midnight, sunrise, sunset; some of which are amongst the most poetical terms we have. To the same language we are indebted for the names of light, heat, cold, frost, rain, snow, hail, sleet, thunder, lightning, as well as almost all those objects which form the component parts of the beautiful in external scenery, as sea and land, hill and dale, wood and stream, &c. It is from this language we derive the words which are expressive of the earliest and dearest connexions, and the strongest and most powerful feelings of nature; and which are, consequently, invested with

* See page 71, where the term Redundancy is separately considered.

† The account here given is from the "Edinburgh Review," of October 1839. See, also, pages 34 to 40, on the subject of Derivation.

our oldest and most complicated associations. It is this language which has given us names for father, mother, husband, wife, brother, sister, son, daughter, child, home, kindred, friends. It is this which has furnished us with the greater part of those metonymies, and other figurative expressions, by which we represent to the imagination, and that in a single word, the reciprocal duties and enjoyments of hospitality, friendship, or love. Such are hearth, roof, fireside. The chief emotions, too, of which we are susceptible, are expressed in the same language, as love, hope, fear, sorrow, shame; and, what is of more consequence to the orator and the poet, as well as in common life, the outward signs by which emotion is indicated are almost all Anglo-Saxon; such are tear, smile, blush, to laugh, to weep, to sigh, to groan. Most of those objects, about which the practical reason of man is employed in common life, receive their names from the Anglo-Saxon. It is the language, for the most part, of business; of the counting-house, the shop, the market, the street, the farm; and, however miserable the man who is fond of philosophy or abstract science might be, if he had no other vocabulary but this, we must recollect that language was made not for the few, but the many, and that portion of it which enables the bulk of a nation to express their wants and transact their affairs, must be considered of at least as much importance to general happiness, as that which serves the purpose of philosophical science. Nearly all our national proverbs, in which it is truly said, so much of the practical wisdom of a nation resides, and which constitute the manual and *vade mecum* of "hobnailed" philosophy, are almost wholly Anglo-Saxon. A very large proportion (and that always the strongest) of the language of invective, humor, satire, colloquial pleasantry, is Anglo Saxon. Almost all the terms and phrases by which we most energetically express anger, contempt, and indignation, are of Anglo-Saxon origin.* The Latin contributes most largely to the language of polite life, as well as to that of polite literature. Again, it is often necessary to convey ideas, which, though not truly and properly offensive in themselves, would, if clothed in the rough Saxon, appear so to the sensitive modesty of a highly refined state of society; dressed in Latin, these very same ideas shall seem decent enough. There is a large number of words, which, from the frequency with which they are used, and from their being so constantly in the mouths of the vulgar, would not be endured in polished society, though more privileged synonymes of Latin origin, or some classical circumlocution, expressing exactly the same thing, shall pass unquestioned.

There may be nothing dishonest, nothing really vulgar about the old Saxon word, yet it would be thought as uncouth in a drawing-room, as the ploughman to whose rude use it is abandoned.† Thus, the word

---

* One of the most distinguished orators and writers of the present age is remarkable for the Saxon force and purity of his language. He seldom uses an Anglicized Latin word, when a pure English expression is at hand. This will account, in some degree, for the strength of his language and the vehemence of his style. The reader scarcely needs to be informed, that reference is here made to the late Secretary of State, Hon. Daniel Webster.

† To what is here said of the Saxon, may be added a short extract from Sir Walter Scott's "Ivanhoe," in a dialogue between the jester and the swineherd. (Vol. I. p. 25. S. H. Parker's edition.)

"*stench*" is lavendered over into *unpleasant effluvia*, or *an ill odor*, "sweat," diluted into four times the number of syllables, becomes a very inoffensive thing in the shape of "perspiration."* To "squint" is softened into obliquity of vision; to be "drunk" is vulgar; but, if a man be simply intoxicated or inebriated, it is comparatively venial. Indeed, we may say of the classical names of vices, what Burke more questionably said of vices themselves, "that they lose half their deformity by losing all their grossness." In the same manner, we all know that it is very possible for a medical man to put to us questions under the seemly disguise of scientific phraseology and polite circumlocution, which, if expressed in the bare and rude vernacular, would almost be as nauseous as his draughts and pills. Lastly; there are many thoughts which gain immensely by mere novelty and variety of expression. This the judicious poet, who knows that the connexion between thoughts and words is as intimate as that between body and spirit, well understands. There are thoughts in themselves trite and common-place, when expressed in the hackneyed terms of common life, which, if adorned by some graceful or felicitous novelty of expression, shall assume an unwonted air of dignity and elegance. What was trivial, becomes striking; and what was plebeian, noble.

* See Euphemism.

XX.

PERIPHRASE, PERIPHRASIS, OR CIRCUMLOCUTION, EUPHEMISM AND ANTONOMASIA.

Periphrase, periphrasis, and circumlocution, are words all meaning the same thing, and are equivalent to what is gener-

---

"How call you these grunting brutes running about on their fore legs?" demanded Wamba.

"*Swine*, fool, *swine*," said the herd; "every fool knows that."

"And *swine* is good Saxon," said the jester. "But how call you the *sow*, when she is flayed and drawn up by the heels like a traitor?"

"*Pork*," answered the swineherd.

"I am very glad every fool knows that, too," said Wamba; "and *pork*, I think, is good Norman French; and so when the brute lives, and is in the charge of a Saxon slave, she goes by her Saxon name; but becomes a Norman and is called *pork*, when she is carried to the Castle-hall to feast among the nobles. There is old alderman *Ox*, continues to hold his Saxon epithet, while he is under the charge of serfs and bondmen; but becomes *Beef*, when he arrives before the worshipful jaws that are destined to consume him. *Calf*, too, becomes *Veal*, in the like manner; he is Saxon when he requires tendance, and takes a Norman name, when he becomes matter of enjoyment."

ally called a '*roundabout expression;*' which explanation is itself an example of the figure, because it denotes in three words what periphrase, periphrasis, or circumlocution does in one. The definitions of words, as they appear in dictionaries, are periphrases. Such circumlocutions are frequently useful, especially in poetry; and are often necessary in translations from foreign languages, when we can find no word in our own, exactly equivalent to that which we have to translate.

Periphrase* is frequently useful to avoid a repetition of the same word but periphrases of every kind require careful management; because, perhaps, more than any other figure of speech, they are apt to run into bombast.†

Under the head of periphrases may be included the figures Euphemism and Antonomasia.

Words, or phrases that call up disagreeable ideas are, in polite language, softened by means of circumlocutions. In these changes, as well as in most others, custom is the guide. It is reckoned more decorous, for example, to the memory of the departed, to say that "he perished on the scaffold," than that "he was hanged." Such softened expression is called *euphemism;* a Greek word signifying *a kind speech.*

Antonomasia is a term applied to that form of expression in which a proper name is put for a common, or a common name for a proper; or, when the title, office, dignity, profession, science, or trade, is used instead of the true name of a person. Thus, when we apply to Christ the term, "the Savior of the world," or "the Redeemer of mankind;" or to Washington, the term, "the Father of his country;" or when we say His Excellency, instead of the governor, His Honor, instead of the judge; or, His Majesty, instead of the king, the expression is called Antonomasia. So, also, when a glutton is called a Heliogabalus (from the Roman emperor distinguished for that vice,) or a tyrant is called a Nero, we have other instances of the same form of expression.

---

* Periphrase, as defined by Webster, is "The use of more words than are necessary to express the idea; as a figure of rhetoric, it is employed to avoid a common or trite manner of expression."

† Bombast is a kind of expression by which a serious attempt is made to raise a low or familiar subject above its rank, thereby never failing to make it ridiculous. *Bathos* is the reverse of bombast, and consists in degrading a subject by too low expressions. Both of these modes of writing equally excite the risible faculties of the reader.

Again, when we call Geography, "that science which describes the earth and its inhabitants," or Arithmetic is termed "the science of numbers," the antonomasia becomes apparent. It will thus be seen, that this form of expression is frequently nothing more than an instance of periphrasis, or circumlocution.

This form of expression is very common in parliamentary language and in deliberative assemblies, in which, in speaking of individual persons, they are not called by their proper names, but by their office, or some other designating appellation.* Thus, in speaking of Washington, the orator designates him, by antonomasia, as "the sage of Mount Vernon," or of Shakspeare, as "the bard of Avon," from the river on whose bank he resided.

Amplification is the expansion of a subject, by enumerating circumstances which are intended by an orator to excite more strongly in his audience the feelings of approbation or of blame. It is dwelling upon the subject longer than is actually necessary for its enunciation; and is in so far a species of circumlocution.†

---

* It is contrary to the rules of all parliamentary assemblies, to call any member by his proper name. Each individual is called by the name of the state, town, city, county, or ward, which he represents. Thus, we say, "the gentleman from Massachusetts," "the member from Virginia," "the member from Ward 10," &c.; or, from his position, "the gentleman on my right," or, "the gentleman who last spoke," &c.

The antonomasia is a figure frequently used by the most distinguished historical writers, and especially by Mr. Gibbon, the historian of the "Decline and Fall of the Roman Empire."

† The following passage is quoted by Mr. Booth from Scriblerus, "the perusal of the whole of which admirable satire," says Mr. Booth, "is indispensable to every one who would study the principles of English Composition:" —

"We may define amplification to be making the most of a thought; it is the spinning-wheel of the Bathos, which draws out and spreads it in its finest thread. There are amplifiers who can extend half a dozen thin thoughts over a whole folio; but for which, the tale of many a vast romance, and the substance of many a fair volume, might be reduced into the size of a primer.

"A passage in the 104th Psalm, 'He looks on the earth and it trembles, he touches the hills and they smoke,' is thus amplified by the same author:

'The hills forget they 're fixed, and in their fright
Cast off their weight, and ease themselves for flight;
The woods with terror winged outfly the wind,
And leave the heavy panting hills behind.'"

You here see the hills, not only trembling, but shaking off the woods from their backs, to run the faster; after this, you are presented with a foot race of mountains and woods, where the woods distance the mountains, that, like corpulent, pursy fellows, come puffing and panting a vast way behind them.

Examples of Periphrasis.

Grammar.	The science which teaches the proper use of language.
Woman.	The gentle sex; or, the female sex.
Arithmetic.	The science of numbers.
To disappoint.	To frustrate one's hopes.
The skies.	The upper deep.
Zoology.	That department of natural science which treats of the habits of animals.

Examples of Euphemism.

James worked so hard that he *sweat* very profusely.	James worked so hard that he perspired very freely; or the perspiration stood on him in drops.
The room smells badly.	There is an unpleasant effluvia in the room.
Mary is a great slut.	Mary is inattentive to her personal appearance; or, is careless in her personal habits.
He is a very dirty fellow.	He is destitute of neatness.
You lie.	You labor under a mistake.*

Examples of Antonomasia.

The Queen.	Her Majesty.
Homer.	The author of the Iliad and Odyssey.
Washington.	The Sage of Mount Vernon
Hesiod.	The earliest of the Poets.
Lord Wellington.	The Hero of Waterloo.

---

* No word of Holy Writ has in it a better turn of worldly wisdom than that from the Book of Proverbs: — "A soft answer turneth away wrath, but grievous words stir up anger." The "soft answer" is, in fact, a euphemism. No one is offended who is told that "he labors under a mistake," while, perhaps, no accusation would give greater offence, than the same idea, expressed as above, unsoftened by euphemism

Boston.	The Literary Emporium.
New York.	The Commercial Emporium.
Philadelphia.	The City of Brotherly Love.
New Orleans.	The Crescent City.
Cincinnati.	The Queen of the West.
Baltimore.	The Monumental City.
London.	The Mart of the World; or, the British Metropolis.
The King of France.	His most Christian Majesty.
Napoleon Bonaparte.	The Hero of a hundred battles.
The King of Spain.	His most Catholic Majesty.
Washington, (the capital of the United States.)	The City of magnificent distances.
St. Luke.	The beloved physician.
St. John.	The disciple that Jesus loved.
Cowper.	The author of "The Task."
The British Court.	The Court of St. James.

The following sentences present examples of Periphrasis,* Euphemism and Antonomasia, and it is required of the student to designate each.

Solomon, *(the wisest of men,)* says, "Better is a dinner of herbs, where love is, than a stalled ox and hatred therewith."

David *(The Author of the Psalms)* was one of the sweetest and most pious writers of the Old Testament.

Moses *(The Jewish Lawgiver)* was educated by the daughter of Pharaoh.

Saul *(The first king of Israel)* was a man of uncommon stature.

Methuselah *(He who lived to the greatest age recorded of man)* died before his father. †

Adam Smith *(The author of the Wealth of Nations)* says that there is in man a natural propensity to truck, barter and exchange one thing for another.

It is pleasant to relieve *(be the instrument of relieving)* distress.

Short and *(The transient day of)* sinful indulgence is followed by long and distressing (a dark and tempestuous night of) sorrow.

Christ *(He who spake as never man spoke)* says, in his sermon on the mount, "Blessed are the pure in heart, for they shall see God."

---

* The judicious use of periphrasis or circumlocution, often involves an acquaintance with figurative language, under which head it properly belongs. It is taken from that connexion in order to be applied in other exercises which precede the subject of figures.

† His father was Enoch, who never died, but was translated.

He thought the man a scoundrel (dishonest) and therefore would not pay him the money *(would place no confidence in him.)*

He behaved like a boor *(in an improper manner)* and therefore the genteel *(persons of refinement)* would have nothing to do with him.

I consider him an impudent puppy *(rude in his manners)* and shall therefore separate myself from his company.

The man was drunk *(intoxicated,* or *had indulged in liquor)* when he used *these* indecent words *(that improper language)* and although I was very mad *(was displeased)* with him, I did not scold at *(reprove)* him.

Major Andre was hanged (perished on the scaffold) although he earnestly requested that he might be fired at *(shot.)*

That man eats his victuals like a pig *(is unrefined in his manners at the table)* and guzzles down his drink like a fish *(and is too fond of his cup.)*

He has on dirty stockings *(His hose are not neat)* and muddy shoes *(his shoes are soiled.)*

A truly genteel man *(A man of refinement)* is known as well by his talk *(conversation)* as by his clothes *(dress.)* He never uses low language and vulgar expressions *(indulges in loose conversation.)* His hands and face and his whole body are well washed, he cleans his teeth, combs his hair, *(His whole person is kept neat and cleanly,)* and brushes his clothes whenever they are dirty, *(his dress never appears to be soiled,)* and he always looks well, as if he were going to a party, *(and he always looks prepared for the drawing-room.)*

Of the oldest of the English Poets, (Chaucer) as he is the father of English poetry, so I hold him in the same degree of veneration as the Greeks hold Homer *(the author of the Iliad and Odyssey)* or the Romans, hold Virgil (the author of the Æneid.) He is a perpetual fountain of good sense; learned in all sciences; and therefore he speaks properly on all subjects. As he knew what to say, so also he knows where to leave off; a continence which is practised by few writers, and scarcely by any of the ancients, excepting the authors of the Iliad, the Odyssey and the Æneid.

The author of the Essay on the Understanding *(Mr. Locke)* has advanced the opinion that moral subjects are as susceptible of demonstration as mathematical.

The Bard of Avon *(Shakspeare)* was one of the most remarkable men that the world ever produced, *(that ever appeared in the ranks of humanity.)* It may truly be said of him that he touched nothing which he did not adorn; and that he has strewed more pearls in the paths of literature than any other poet that the world has seen. His works have had more admirers than those of any other author excepting the writers of the holy Scriptures.

The science which treats of language, *(Grammar)* and the science which describes the earth and its inhabitants, *(Geography)* are branches frequently studied, but too frequently imperfectly understood.

The author of the Waverley novels *(Sir Walter Scott)* must have been a man of remarkable industry, as well as of uncommon talent.

XXI.

TAUTOLOGY AND CATACHRESIS.

Tautology is the repetition of the same meaning in different words, or the needless repetition of the same words.

Thus, in the sentence, "The nefarious wickedness of his conduct was reprobated and condemned by all," the tautology consists in the use of *nefarious* and *wickedness* together; which is the same as to say, the wicked wickedness; and *reprobated* and *condemned*, which are words of similar meaning. So, also, in the sentence, "The brilliance of the sun dazzles our eyes, and overpowers them with light," the same idea is conveyed by the word "dazzles" and the expression, "overpowers them with light;" one of them, therefore, should be omitted.

Whenever anything is represented as being the cause, condition, or consequence of itself, it may also be considered as a tautology, as in the following lines:

> "The dawn is overcast, the morning lowers,
> And heavily in clouds brings on the day."
>
> *Addison.*

Tautologies are allowable only in legal instruments, and other writings where precision is of more importance than elegance; when, therefore, it consists in the repetition of a word, it may be corrected by the use of a synonyme; but when it consists in the repetition of an idea, unless such repetition is important for clearness or for emphasis, it should be wholly suppressed.

Example.

They returned *back again* to the *same* city *from* whence they came *forth*.

In this sentence, all the words in Italic are tautologies; for the word *return* implies to *turn back*, *the city* implies *the same city*, and *from* and *forth* are both included in the word *whence*. The sentence, read without the words in Italic, is as clear and expressive as words can make it. Words which do not add to the meaning are useless, especially in prose.

Exercises.

He led a blameless and an irreproachable life, and no one could censure his conduct.

God is eternal, and his existence is without beginning and without end

Opium produces sleep, because it possesses a soporific quality.

The grass grows because of its vegetative power.

He sat on the verdant green, in the umbrageous shade of the woody forest.

How many there are by whom these tidings of good news have never been heard.

Virgil in his Æneid tells a story very similar to that which Homer tells in his Odyssey. But the one relates the adventures of a renowned Trojan hero, and the other relates the adventures of a renowned Grecian hero.

Our sight is of all faculties the most agreeable when we indulge it in seeing agreeable objects; because it is never wearied with fatigue, and it requires no exertion when it exerts itself.

He succeeded in gaining the universal love of all men.

A father, when he sees his child going to the silence and stillness of the tomb, may weep and lament when the shadow of death has fully overshaded him; and as he hears the last final departing knell sounding in his ears, may say, I will descend and go down to the grave to my son mourning in sorrow. But he turns away in the hurry and haste of business and occupation; the tear is wiped; his eyes are dried; and though when he returns and comes back to his domestic hearth and fireside at home, the playful and sportive laugh comes up to his remembrance, and is recalled to his recollection, the succeding day blunts and removes the poignancy of his grief, and it finds no permanent and lasting seat.

There is a sweetness and sacred holiness in a mother's tears, when they are dropt and fall on the face of her dying and expiring babe, which no eye can see, and no one can behold with a heart untouched and unaffected.

It is clear and obvious that religious worship and adoration should be regarded with pleasure by all men.

CATACHRESIS.

There is another fault into which careless writers are prone to fall, which is the very reverse of tautology; and to which the term *Catachresis** may not be inappropriately applied; and this is the use of the same word in different senses.

---

* The literal meaning of Catachresis is *against use*, and it is applied by rhetoricians to express *an abuse, or false use of a word*, by which it is wrested from its original application, and made to express something which is at variance with its etymology. It is a sort of blundering denomination, chiefly caused by retaining the name of an object, after the qualities from which it derived that name are changed. The thing that is made, for example, is often designated by that of the substance from which it is fabricated. Thus a vessel in which liquids are boiled is called *a copper*, because, in most cases, it is made of that material, and this figure is *a Metonomy*. But such vessels are occasionally made of other metals, still retaining the name of *coppers*, and it is this misnomer which is called *a Catachresis* From this explanation it will appear that the term as applied above, although not rigidly restricted to its rhetorical meaning, is not wholly inappropriate.

Example.

Charity expands our hearts in love to God and man; and it is by the virtue of *charity* that the rich are blessed, and the poor are supplied.

In this sentence the word *charity* is improperly applied in two different senses, namely, for the highest benevolence, and for simple alms-giving.

Exercises.

Gregory favored the undertaking for no other reason than this, that the manager in countenance favored (*i. e. resembled*) his friend.

True wit is nature to advantage dressed; and yet some works have more wit than does them good.

Honor teaches us to respect ourselves, and to violate no right nor privilege of our neighbor. It leads us to support the feeble, to relieve the distressed, and to scorn to be governed by degrading and injurious passions. And yet we see honor is the motive which urges the destroyer to take the life of his friend.

The minister proposed a plan for the support of the ministers of the church.

The professor was a professor of religion.

I expect that you have no reason to expect the arrival of your friend.*

XXII.

PLEONASM, VERBOSITY, AND REDUNDANCY.

Pleonasm consists in the use of words seemingly superfluous, in order to express a thought with greater energy: as, "I saw it *with my own eyes.*" Here the pleonasm consists in the addition of the expression, "with my own eyes.'

Pleonasms are usually considered as faults, especially in prose. But,

* It will be seen from what has been said in relation to the word *Catachresis* that it is the foundation of many witticisms, under the denomination of *paranomasia*, or *pun*. [*See Paranomasia*]

in poetry, they may be sparingly allowed as poetical licenses.* They are allowable, also, in animated discourse, to introduce abruptly an emphatic word, or to repeat an idea to impress it more strongly; as, "He that hath ears to hear, let him hear." "I know thee who thou art."

Pleonasm is nearly allied to tautology, but is occasionally a less glaring fault in a sentence; and, indeed, it may be considered justifiable, and even sometimes elegant, when we wish to present thoughts with particular perspicuity or force; but an unemphatic repetition of the same idea is one of the worst of faults in writing.

Pleonasm implies merely superfluity. Although the words do not, as in tautology, repeat the sense, they add nothing to it.

Pleonasm differs, also, from what is called verbosity. Verbosity, it is true, implies a superabundance of words; but, in a pleonasm there are words which add nothing to the sense. In the verbose manner, not only single words, but whole clauses, may have a meaning, and yet it would be better to omit them, because what they mean is unimportant.

Another difference is, that, in a pleonasm, a complete correction may be made, by simply omitting the superfluous words; but, in a verbose sentence, it will be necessary to alter, as well as to omit.

It is a good rule, always to look over what has been written, and to strike out every word and clause, which it is found will leave the sentence neither less clear, nor less forcible, than it was before.

There are many sentences which would not bear the omission of a single word, without affecting the clearness and force of the expression, and which would be very much improved, were they *recast*, and the sense expressed by fewer and more forcible words. Thus, for instance, in the following sentence, no word can be omitted without affecting the sense.

"A severe and tyrannical exercise of power must become a matter of necessary policy with kings, when their subjects are imbued with such principles as justify and authorize rebellion."

But the same sense may be much better expressed in fewer words, thus;

"Kings will be tyrants from policy, when subjects are rebels from principle."

Redundancy is another term, also employed to signify superfluity in the words and members of a sentence. Pleonasm and verbosity relate, principally, to the words in a sentence, but redundancy relates to the members as well as the words. As every word ought to present a *new idea*, so every member ought to contain a new thought. The following sentence exemplifies the fault of redundancy. "The very first discovery of it strikes the mind with inward joy, and spreads delight through all its faculties." In this example, little or nothing is added by the second member of the sentence, to what was expressed in the first.

---

* See the article on *Poetical License*.

The following sentences present examples of pleonasm, verbosity, and redundancy, which may be corrected by the learner.

Exercises.

The rain, is it not over and gone? I hear no wind, only the voice of the streams.

My banks they are furnished with bees.

It is impossible for us to behold the divine works with coldness or indifference, or to survey so many beauties, without a secret satisfaction and complacency.

Thy rod and thy staff they comfort me.

This great politician desisted from, and renounced his designs, when he found them impracticable.

He was of so high and independent a spirit, that he abhorred and detested being in debt.

Though raised to an exalted station, she was a pattern of piety, virtue, and religion.

The human body may be divided into the head, trunk, limbs, and vitals.

His end soon approached; and he died with great courage and fortitude.

He was a man of so much pride and vanity, that he despised the sentiments of others.

Poverty induces and cherishes dependence; and dependence strengthens and increases corruption.

This man, on all occasions, treated his inferiors with great haughtiness and disdain.

There can be no regularity or order in the life and conduct of that man who does not give and allot a due share of his time to retirement and reflection.

Such equivocal and ambiguous expressions, mark a formed intention to deceive and abuse us.

His cheerful, happy temper, remote from discontent, keeps up a kind of daylight in his mind, excludes every gloomy prospect, and fills it with a steady and perpetual serenity.

Being content with deserving a triumph, he refused the honor of it.

In the Attic commonwealth, it was the privilege of every citizen and poet to rail aloud in public.

XXIII.

VARIETY OF EXPRESSION.

The various modes of transposition and inversion, by which the same idea can be expressed by different inflections of the words have already been presented. In this exercise the modes are suggested by which the idea may be clothed in different language, still, for the most part preserving its identity.*

Example 1st.

The young should be diligent and industrious, and make a proper use of their time.

Diligence, industry, and proper improvement of time are material duties of the young.

Young men, be industrious; make the best use of your time; an awful responsibility rests upon you.

Young persons should be made sensible, that it is their duty to be diligent and industrious, and to employ their time in useful pursuits.

To be diligent and industrious, and to employ their time in profitable occupations, are things which we expect from young persons.

In the morning of life, when the phantoms of hope are flitting before their sight, and the visions of fancy are decorating their prospects, the young should not suffer themselves to be deluded by expectations which cannot be realized. The golden sands should not be wantonly wasted in their path, nor should the precious moments of life be suffered to take flight, without bearing on their wings some token of their value.

Duty addresses the young in an imperative tone, requiring them to apply themselves with diligence to their proper occupations, and forbidding them to pay one moment but in purchase of its worth. "And what is its worth? — Ask deathbeds; they can tell."

Young persons cannot be commended when they devote those hours to indolence, which should have been given to industry; for time is valuable, and should be properly employed.

---

* It is to be observed, that, in the practice of the principle involved in this exercise, the teacher should not be too rigid in noticing the faults of pleonasm, verbosity, or redundancy. The object of the exercise is to give a command of language, and it will be well, when this object is partially effected, to require the learner to take his own sentences and prune them on the principles explained in the preceding exercises.

The young should be diligent and industrious, and properly improve their time.*

It is not only when duty addresses them with her warning voice that the young should practise the virtues of diligence and industry; a proper improvement of their time is at all times expected from them.

Example 2d.

[The different modes of expressing the same idea give rise to the distinctions of style which have been mentioned in the Introduction. The subject of style will be more fully treated in the subsequent pages. The following sentence will exemplify to the student the effect of two of the varieties of style.]

Style of simple Narration.

Yesterday morning, as I was walking in the fields, I saw John stab James through the heart with a dagger.

Style of passionate exclamation, in which the prominent idea is brought forward, and the circumstances are cast into the shade.

James is murdered! I saw John stab him to the heart.

Exercises.

[The student must be careful to make use of his understanding and discrimination, as well as his *dictionary*, in the performance of these exercises.]

True friendship is like sound health, the value of it is seldom known until it is lost.

As no roads are so rough as those that have just been mended, so no sinners are so intolerant as those that have just turned saints.

When certain persons abuse us, let us ask ourselves what description of characters it is that they admire; we shall often find this a very consolatory question.

---

* In the Introduction to this book, notice was taken of the different *forms*, or *style*, of composition. In this model, an attempt has been made to imitate several of the diversities of style there mentioned; and it will be useful to the student, when he shall have become acquainted with the diversities of style, in the subsequent pages of this volume, to endeavor to designate them respectively by their peculiar characteristics. It may here be remarked, that the style of common conversation, called the *colloquial* style, allows the introduction of terms and expressions, which are not used in grave writing.

Contemporaries appreciate the man rather than the merit; but posterity will regard the merit rather than the man.

All beyond enough is too much; all beyond nourishment is luxury all beyond decency is extravagance.

Form your taste on the classics, and your principles on the book of all truth.

Let the first fruits of your intellect be laid before the altar of Him who breathed into your nostrils the breath of life; and with that breath, your immortal spirit.

The love of learning, though truly commendable, must never be gratified beyond a certain limit. It must not be indulged in to the injury of your health, nor to the hindrance of your virtue.

What will the fame derived from the most profound learning avail you, if you have not learned to be pious and humble, and temperate and charitable.

There is nothing more extraordinary in this country, than the transition of the seasons. The people of Moscow have no spring. Winter *vanishes*, and summer *is*. This is not the work of a week, or of a day but of one instant; and the manner of it exceeds belief.

On eagles' wings immortal scandals fly,
While virtuous actions are but born and die.

XXIV.

TRANSLATION, OR CONVERSION OF POETRY INTO PROSE.

Poetry when *literally* translated makes in general but insipid prose. Prose is the language of reason,—poetry of feeling or passion. Prose is characterized by fulness and precision. Poetry deals largely in elliptical expressions, exclamations, exaggerations, apostrophes, and other peculiarities not usually found in prose. For the purpose, also, of accommodating them to the measure of a verse, the poets frequently alter or abbreviate words, and use expressions which would not be authorized in prose. Such abbreviations and alterations, together with other changes sometimes made, are called *poetic licences*, because they are principally used by poetical writers.

The following are some of the licences used by poetical writers.

1. ELISION, or the omission of parts of a word. When the elision is from the beginning of a word, it is called *aphæresis*, and consists in cut-

ting off the initial letter or syllable of a word; as, *'squire* for *esquire* *gainst* for *against*, *'gan* for *began*, &c. When the elision is from the body of the word, it is called *syncope;* as, *list'ning* for *listening*, *thund'ring* for *thundering*, *lov'd* for *loved*, &c. When the elision is from the end of a word it is called *apocope*, and consists in the cutting off of a final vowel or syllable, or of one or more letters; as, *gi' me* for *give me*, *fro'* for *from*, *o'* for *of*, *th' evening* for *the evening*, *Philomel'* for *Philomela*.

2. SYNÆRESIS, or the contraction of two syllables into one, by rapidly pronouncing in one syllable two or more vowels which properly belong to separate syllables; as *ae* in the word *Israel*.

3. APOSTROPHE, or the contraction of two words into one; as, *'t is* f *it is*, *can't* for *cannot*, *thou 'rt* for *thou art*.

4. DIÆRESIS, or the division of one syllable into two; as, *pu-is-sant* for *puissant*.

5. PARAGOGE or the addition of an expletive letter; *withouten* for *without*, *crouchen* for *crouch*.

6. PROSTHESIS, or the prefixing of an expletive letter or syllable to word; as, *appertinent* for *pertinent*, *beloved* for *loved*.

7. ENALLAGE, or the use of one part of speech for another; as in the following lines, in which an adjective is used for an adverb; as,

> "*Blue* through the dusk the smoking currents shine."
> "The fearful hare limps *awkward*."

8. HYPERBATON, or the inversion or transposition of words, placing that first which should be last; as,

> "And though, sometimes, each dreary pause *between*."
> "*Him answered* then his loving mate and true."

9. PLEONASM, or the use of a greater number of words than are necessary to express the meaning; as,

> "My banks *they* are furnished with bees."

10. TMESIS, or the separation of the parts of a compound word; as, On *which side soever*, for, On whichsoever side.

11. ELLIPSIS, or the omission of some parts not absolutely essential to express the meaning, but necessary to complete the grammatical construction.

The poets have likewise other peculiarities which are embraced under the general name of *poetic diction*. In order to accommodate their language to the rules of melody, and that they may be relieved, in some measure, from the restraints which verse imposes on them, they are indulged in the following usages, seldom allowable in prose.

1. They abbreviate nouns, adjectives, verbs, adverbs, &c.; as, *morn* for *morning*, *amaze* for *amazement*, *fount* for *fountain*, *dread* for *dreadful*, *lone* for *lonely*, *lure* for *allure*, *list* for *listen*, *ope* for *open*, *oft* for *often*, *haply* for *happily*, &c., and use obsolete words * and obsolete meanings.

---

* Obsolete words are words which, although formerly current, are not now in common use.

2. They make use of ellipses more frequently than prose writers omitting the article, the relative pronoun, and sometimes even its antecedent; using the auxiliaries without the principal verb to which they belong; and on the contrary, they also sometimes make use of repetitions which are seldom observed in prose.

3. They use the infinitive mood for a noun; use adjectives for adverbs, and sometimes even for nouns; and nouns for adjectives; ascribe qualities to things, to which they do not literally belong; form new compound epithets; connect the word *self* with nouns, as well as pronouns; sometimes lengthen a word by an additional letter or syllable, and give to the imperative mood both the first and third persons.

4. They arbitrarly employ or omit the prefixes; use active for neuter and neuter for active verbs; employ participles and interjections more frequently than prose writers; connect words that are not in all respects similar; and use conjunctions in pairs contrary to grammatical rule.

5. They alter the regular arrangement of the words of a sentence, placing before the verb words which usually come after it, and after the verb those that usually come before it, putting adjectives after their nouns, the auxiliary after the principal verb; the preposition after the objective case which it governs; the relative before the antecedent; the infinitive mood before the word which governs it; and they also use one mood of the verb for another, employ forms of expression similar to those of other languages, and different from those which belong to the English language.

But one of the most objectionable features of poetic diction is the interjection of numerous details, between those parts of a sentence which are closely combined by the rules of Syntax. Thus, in the following extract from one of the most celebrated poets of the language, generally characterized by the simplicity of his diction, the objective case is placed before the verb which governs it, while a number of circumstances are introduced between them.

But *me*, not destined such delights to share,
My prime of life in wandering spent and care,
Impelled, with steps unceasing, to pursue
Some fleeting good, that mocks me with the view,
That, like the circle bounding earth and skies,
Allures from far, yet, as I follow, flies;
My *fortune leads* to traverse realms alone,
And find no spot of all the world my own.

Exercises.

[*In the following extracts, the student may point out the peculiarities of* POETIC DICTION, *which have now been enumerated. The words in Italic will assist him in recognizing them.*]

The cottage curs at early *pilgrim* bark.
The pipe of early *shepherd*.
Affliction's *self* deplores thy youthful doom.
What dreadful pleasure, there to stand sublime,
Like shipwrecked *mariner* on desert coast!
Ah! see! the unsightly slime and sluggish pool,
Have all the solitary *vale embrowned*

Hereditary bondmen! Know ye not
Who would be free *themselves* must strike the blow?

No *fire* the kitchen's cheerless grate *displayed.*

Efflux *divine!* nature's resplendent robe
And thou, O sun!
Soul of surrounding worlds! in whom best seen,
Shines out thy *Maker;* may I sing of thee!

Earth's meanest son, all trembling, prostrate falls,
And on the *boundless* of thy goodness calls.

In *world-rejoicing* state it moves sublime.

Oft in the *stilly* night.

For is there aught in sleep *can charm* the wise?

And *Peace,* O *Virtue!* Peace is all thy own.

Be it dapple's bray,
Or *be it* not, or be it whose it may.

Wealth heaped on wealth, *nor* truth *nor* safety buys.

And sculpture that can keep thee from *to die.*

The Muses fair, these peaceful *shades among,*
With skilful fingers sweep the trembling strings.

Behoves no more,
But sidelong to the gently waving wind,
To lay the well-tuned instrument reclined.

Had unambitious mortals minded nought
But in loose joy their time to wear away,
Rude nature's state *had been** our state to-day.

In the following exercises the learner is expected to write the ideas conveyed in the poetical extracts, in prose, varying the words and expressions, as well as the arrangement of

---

* This form of expression, where one mood of the verb is used for another, is sometimes imitated by prose writers. Thus, "Sixty summers had passed over his head without imparting one ray of warmth to his heart; without exciting one tender feeling for the sex, deprived of whose cheering presence, the paradise of the world *were* a wilderness of weeds."—*New Monthly Magazine.* In this extract, the *imperfect of the subjunctive* is used without its attendant conjunction for the pluperfect of the potential. Cowper has a similar expression in his fable entitled "The Needless Alarm," where he uses the pluperfect of the indicative for the pluperfect of the potential: thus,

"Awhile they mused; surveying every face,
Thou *hadst supposed* them of superior race.

them, so as to make clear and distinct sentences,* as in the following

Example.

Reason's whole pleasure, all the joy of sense,
Lie in three words, — health, peace and competence.

Same idea expressed in prose.

Health, peace, and competence comprise all the pleasures which this world can afford.

Example 2d.

The ploughman homeward plods his weary way.

Same line transposed in a variety of ways.

The ploughman plods his weary way homeward.
Homeward the ploughman plods his weary way.
His weary way homeward the ploughman plods.
Plods the ploughman homeward his weary way.
His weary way the ploughman plods homeward.
Homeward plods the ploughman his weary way.
The ploughman his weary way homeward plods.
Plods homeward the ploughman his weary way.
Homeward plods the ploughman his weary way.
His weary way the ploughman homeward plods, &c.

The example shows that it is not always necessary to change the language, in order to convert poetry into prose. Of the ten modes in which the above recited line has been transposed, it will be noticed that several of them are entirely *prosaic.*

It may here be remarked that in the conversion of poetry into

* Sir Walter Scott, in a letter to his son, (*See Lockhart's Life, Vol. V., p.* 54,) has the following language: "You should exercise yourself frequently in trying to make translations of the passages which most strike you, trying to invest the sense of Tacitus in as good English as you can. This will answer the double purpose of making yourself familiar with the Latin author, and giving you the command of your own language, *which no person will ever have, who does not study English Composition in early life.*" The conversion of verse into prose it is conceived will, at least in a good degree, subserve the same useful purpose of giving command of language; and for this reason the exercises in this lesson, or similar ones, cannot be too strongly recommended, especially to those whose minds have not been disciplined by an attention to the classics.

prose, the animation of the style is often endangered. Poetry admits more ornament than prose, and especially a more liberal use of that figure (Prosopopocia or Personification) by which life and action are attributed to inanimate objects. The exercises, therefore, of the pupil, in converting poetry into prose, will be deemed useful only as tending to give clear ideas and command of language.*

The learner is presumed now to be prepared to transpose simple tales and stories from verse into prose, with some additions of his own. Such exercises will be found of much use, not only in acquiring command of language, but also as an exercise of the *imagination*. In performing these exercises, the greatest latitude may be allowed, and the learner may be permitted not only to alter the language, but to substitute his own ideas, and to vary the circumstances, so as to make the exercise as nearly an *original one* as he can.

Example.

The following short tale, or story in verse, is presented to be converted into a tale in prose.

GINEVRA.

If ever you should come to Modēna,
(Where, among other relics, you may see
Tassoni's bucket, — but 't is not the true one,)
Stop at a palace near the Reggio gate,
Dwelt in of old by one of the Donati.
Its noble gardens, terrace above terrace,
And rich in fountains, statues, cypresses,
Will long detain you, — but, before you go,
Enter the house, — forget it not, I pray you, —
And look awhile upon a picture there.
'T is of a lady in her earliest youth,
The last of that illustrious family;
Done by Zampieri, — but by whom I care not.
He who observes it, ere he passes on,
Gazes his fill, and comes and comes again,
That he may call it up when far away.
She sits, inclining forward as to speak,
Her lips half open, and her finger up,
As though she said "Beware!" her vest of gold
'Broidered with flowers, and clasped from head to foot,
An emerald stone in every golden clasp;

* Any volume of poetical extracts will furnish additional exercises for the student. It is therefore deemed inexpedient to present in this volume an additional number of them.

And on her brow, fairer than alabaster,
A coronet of pearls.
But then her face,
So lovely, yet so arch, so full of mirth,
The overflowings of an innocent heart,—
It haunts me still, though many a year has fled,
Like some wild melody!
Alone it hangs
Over a mouldering heirloom, its companion,
An oaken chest, half eaten by the worms,
But richly carved by Antony of Trent
With scripture-stories from the life of Christ;
A chest that came from Venice, and had held
The ducal robes of some old ancestor;—
That by the way,—it may be true or false,—
But don't forget the picture; and you will not
When you have heard the tale they old me there
She was an only child,—her name Ginevra,
The joy, the pride of an indulgent father;
And in her fifteenth year became a bride,
Marrying an only son, Francesco Doria,
Her playmate from her birth, and her first love.
Just as she looks there in her bridal dress,
She was all gentleness, all gaiety.
Her pranks the favorite theme of every tongue.
But now the day was come, the day, the hour;
Now, frowning, smiling, for the hundredth time,
The nurse, that ancient lady, preached decorum;
And, in the lustre of her youth, she gave
Her hand, with her heart in it, to Francesco.
Great was the joy; but at the nuptial feast,
When all sate down, the bride herself was wanting
Nor was she to be found! Her father cried,
"'T is but to make a trial of our love!"
And filled his glass to all; but his hand shook,
And soon from guest to guest the panic spread.
'T was but that instant she had left Francesco,
Laughing, and looking back and flying still,
Her ivory tooth imprinted on his finger,
But now, alas, she was not to be found;
Nor from that hour could any thing be guessed,
But that she was not!
Weary of his life,
Francesco flew to Venice, and embarking,
Flung it away in battle with the Turk.
Donati lived,—and long might you have seen
An old man wandering as in quest of something,
Something he could not find,—he knew not what.
When he was gone, the house remained awhile
Silent and tenantless,—then went to strangers.
Full fifty years were past, and all forgotten,
When, on an idle day, a day of search
'Mid the old lumber in the gallery,
That mouldering chest was noticed; and 't was said
By one as young, as thoughtless as Ginevra,
"Why not remove it from its lurking-place?"
'T was done as soon as said; but on the way
It burst, it fell; and lo! a skeleton
With here and there a pearl, an emerald-stone,

A golden clasp, clasping a shred of gold.
All else had perished, — save a wedding ring,
And a small seal, her mother's legacy,
Engraven with a name, the name of both —
"Ginevra" ——
There then had she found a grave!
Within that chest had she concealed herself,
Fluttering with joy, the happiest of the happy;
When a spring-lock, that lay in ambush there,
Fastened her down for ever!

Conversion of the preceding Story into Prose.

THE LEGEND OF MODENA.*

In an elegant apartment of a palace overlooking the Reggio gate in Modena, which, about fifty years before, belonged to the noble family of Donati, but which now was occupied by a very distant branch of that illustrious race, sat the loveliest of its descendants — the beautiful Beatrice, the flower of Modena. Upon the marble table and embroidered ottomans before her, lay a variety of rich costumes, which her favorite attendant, Laura, was arranging where their rich folds fell most gracefully, and their bright tints mocked the rainbows hues of colored light; for the fair Beatrice was selecting a becoming attire for a masquerade ball, which was to be given during the gay season of the approaching Carnival. But a shadow of discontent rested on her brow, as she surveyed the splendid dresses — they were too common-place — and she turned from them with disdain. Suddenly her eye rested upon an antique picture, hanging on the tapestried wall, which represented a young and beautiful figure in the attitude of

"Inclining forward, as to speak,
Her lips half open and her finger up,
As though she said 'Beware!' her vest of gold
Broidered with flowers and clapsed from head to foot,
An emerald stone in every golden clasp,
And on her brow — a coronet of pearls."

Pushing aside the costly silks and velvets, she ran to look at the picture more closely. The lady's dress was perfect, she thought; it just suited her capricious taste, and one like it she determined to have and wear, at the approaching festival. In vain Laura expostulated, and the difficulty of obtaining such an antiquated costume was brought to her mind, and finally, the legend connected with the portrait was begun. But the wilful Beatrice would not listen, although a destiny, sad as that of the ill-fated lady of the portrait was predicted, if she persevered in her whim. Regardless of remonstrance, Beatrice proceeded to search among the finery of her ancestors for something to correspond with the dress which she determined to have, spite of all their old legends, which she

* This "Legend" was written by a young lady of about thirteen years of age, and presented as an exercise at the public school in this city, under the charge of the author.

did not believe. But she searched in vain, and she was returning through the gallery almost in despair, when her attention was attracted by an old

> "Oaken chest half eaten by the worms,
> And richly carved,"

which she thought might contain something suitable. Impatiently she waited, while her attendants lifted the mouldering cover, and then bent eagerly forward to look at its contents — she shrieked and fell into the arms of Laura, a skeleton met her eye,

> "With here and there a pearl, an emerald stone,
> A golden clasp, clasping a shred of gold."

The legend of the unfortunate lady of the portrait was indeed true — these were her remains. Beatrice was carried to her room, and a month passed before she recovered from a fever occasioned by the fright and excitement she experienced; and never again did she mingle in the dissipated circle of her native city. These scenes had lost their charms — for the skeleton and its history continually presented themselves to her mind, reminding her, that "in the midst of life we are in death," and warning her to prepare for that change which must occur in the course of our existence. After a while, Beatrice lost these gloomy sensations, and became cheerful and happy in the performance of duty, and participated in those innocent amusements of life, which she enjoyed far better than those absorbing pleasures, which she used to admire. The old chest and portrait were placed carefully together, and Beatrice ever after wore the wedding ring and the seal inscribed with the name, "Ginevra," which had been found among the other relics of the chest. She also wrote, for the perusal of her friends, the following story connected with the picture and its mouldering companion.

GINEVRA.

> "And she indeed was beautiful,
> A creature to behold with trembling 'midst our joy,
> Lest ought unseen should waft the vision from us,
> Leaving earth too dim without its brightness."

"The deep gold of eventide burned in the Italian sky," and the wind, passing through the orange groves and over the terraces which surrounded the palace of the Donati, mingled its soft, sweet sighs with the murmuring of the fountains, which sparkled in the moonbeams, occasionally sending a shower of spray over the waving foliage that shadowed them At a window, overlooking this moon-lit scene, stood Ginevra, the only child of Donati, "the joy, the pride of an indulgent father." Indeed, her gentleness and sportiveness made her loved by all, and

> "Her pranks, the favorite theme of every tongue."

She had seen but fifteen summers, and these had glided away like a fairy dream, — and then

> "Her face so lovely, yet so arch, so full of mirth,
> The overflowings of an innocent heart."

And there she stood, looking at those old familiar scenes, till a tear glittered in her dark eye, and a shade of sadness rested on her fair brow, like a cloud shadowing her "sunny skies"; — for, on the morrow, she was to part from her childhood's home, she was "to give her hand, with her heart in it," to Francesco Doria, a brave and handsome son of that noble family, whose name often occurs in the annals of Italy. Long did Ginevra linger at the window. "My only one." The voice was her father's, who, accompanied by Francesco, came to seek her; and there they remained, looking out on that lovely scene; and many were the joyous anticipations, the bright hopes, the dreams of happiness which mingled in their conversation, while Francesco plucked the white flowers from a vine which hung across the casement, and wreathed them in Ginevra's long dark curls. But a neighboring convent bell warned them to seek repose, and reluctantly they parted to dream of the morrow, which they fondly thought would bring with it the realization of their bright hopes.

"The morn is up again, the dewy morn," and sunlight and dewdrops were weaving bright rainbow webs over shrub and flower, and the fresh morning breeze blew the vines across the marble pillars of the colonnade, which echoed with the merry voices, — the gay laugh, and the light step of the proud and beautiful assemblage, collected to grace the wedding of Donati's lovely daughter. And lovely, indeed, did she appear among Italy's fairest children. Her dress of rich green velvet, clasped with emeralds, set in gold, the pearls shining among her dark curls, added to her loveliness, and made her appear the star of that bright company. Proudly and fondly her father and husband watched her graceful form, as she glided among the gay throng, receiving their congratulations as the bride of Francesco Doria. Nothing seemed wanting to complete their happiness. Mirth and festivity, the song and the dance, all lent their attractions and added to their felicity. Ah! did not that happy father and fond husband know that such happiness is not for earth?

"Fear ye the festal hour;
Ay, tremble when the cup of joy o'erflows!
Tame down the swelling heart! The bridal rose
And the rich myrtle's flower
Have veiled thee, Death!"

Gaily the hours passed by; Genevra was all gaiety, half wild with excitement. As she passed Francesco, she whispered her intention of hiding, and challenged him and her gay associates to find her. Soon were they all in search of the fair bride, and merrily they proceeded through the lofty halls, the dark closets, and secret apartments of that spacious palace, which resounded with merry voices and laughter. Long they looked, but vainly; and, as the shades of evening stole over the scene, wearied and alarmed, nearly all the now dismayed guests retired to their homes, for Genevra was nowhere to be found. Donati and Francesco, half frantic, continued the search, which grew hourly more hopeless. Week after week, months passed away, but nothing was heard of the lost one. Francesco, weary of that life which was now deprived of all that endeared it to earth, joined the army of his countrymen,

"And flung it away in battle with the Turk."

Donati still lingered around that home, so connected with the memory of her whom he idolized, who was now lost to him for ever;

"And long might you have seen,
An old man wandering, as in quest of something,
Something he could not find — he knew not what."

And where was Ginevra? Half breathless with haste, she ran to an old gallery in the upper part of the palace, fancying her pursuers had almost overtaken her. As she hastily glanced round the dimly lighted gallery, in search of a hiding place, her eye rested on an oaken chest, beautifully carved and ornamented by a celebrated sculptor of Venice, which once held the robes of a prince of her illustrious race. Quick as thought, Ginevra exerted her strength to raise the cover. The chest easily held her fragile form. Trembling with joy and excitement, she heard the loved and well-known tones of Francesco's voice, who was foremost in pursuing her; when her hand, which held the cover ajar to admit the air, slipped and it fell, "fastening her down for ever." The chest was constructed, for greater security, with a spring, which locked as it was shut, and could only be opened by one outside touching a particular part of the curious workmanship. But, before Francesco reached the gallery, the lovely and unfortunate girl had ceased to breathe in that closely shut chest. Many times they passed the gallery, but they heeded not the hiding-place of the lost bride; which, alas! was destined to be her grave. No flowers could shed their perfumes over her grave, watered by the tears of those that loved her. Her fate was a mystery, and soon her memory passed away, like all the fleeting things of earth. And Donati, — what had he to live for? In the beautiful language of Mrs. Hemans, he might have said,

"It is enough! mine eye no more of joy or splendor sees!
I go, since earth its flower hath lost, to join the bright and fair,
And call the grave a lovely place, for thou, my child, art there."

Examples for practice may be taken from any source which the teacher or the student may select.

XXV.

ANAGRAMS.

An anagram is the transposition of the letters of a word, or short sentence, so as to form another word, or phrase, with a different meaning. Thus, the letters which compose the word *stone*, may be arranged so as to form the words *tones*, *notes*, or *seton*; and, (taking *j* and *v* as duplicates of *i* and *u*,) the letters of the alphabet may be arranged so as to form the words *Styx*, *Phlegm*, *quiz*, *frown'd* and *back*.*

---

* Pilate's questi[illegible] to Jesus, "*Quid est veritas?*" (What is truth?) has

Examples.

Astronomers,	Moon-starers.
Telegraphs,	Great Helps.
Gallantries,	All great sins.
Democratical,	Comical trade.
Encyclopedia,	A nice cold pie.
Lawyers,	Sly ware.
Misanthrope,	Spare him not.
Monarch,	March on.
Old England,	Golden Land.
Presbyterian,	Best in prayer.
Punishment,	Nine Thumps.
Penitentiary,	Nay, I repent it.
Radical Reform,	Rare mad frolic.
Revolution,	To love ruin.
James Stuart,	A just master.
Charles James Stuart,	Claims Arthur's Seat.
Eleanor Davies, *	Reveal, O Daniel.
Dame Eleanor Davies,	Never so mad a Ladie.

For exercises of practice, the student may select his own words or sentences. As it is a mere literary amusement, the exercise is not considered worthy of much attention.

---

been happily converted in an anagram to the words, "*Est vir qui adest,*" (It is the man who is before you.)

Jablonski welcomed the visit of Stanislaus, King of Poland, with his noble relatives of the house of Lescinski, to the annual examination of the students under his care, at the gymnasium of Lissa, with a number of anagrams, all composed of the letters in the words *Domus Lescinia.* The recitations closed with an heroic dance, in which each youth carried a shield inscribed with a legend of the letters. After a new evolution, the boys exhibited the words *Ades incolumis;* next, *Omnis es lucida;* next, *Omne sis lucida*; fifthly, *Mane sidus loci;* sixthly, *Sis columna Dei;* and at the conclusion, *I scande solium.*

But a still more remarkable anagram than any that has been presented, will be found in the Greek inscription on the Mosque of St. Sophia, in Constantinople:

"Νίψον ανομηματα μη μοναν οψιν,"

which present the same words, whether read from left to right, or from right to left.

Sir Isaac Newton was in the habit of concealing his mathematical discoveries, by depositing the principles in the form of anagrams; by which he might afterwards claim the merit of the invention without its being stolen by others.

* This lady fancied herself a prophetess, and supposed the spirit of Daniel to be in her, because this anagram could be formed from her name. But her anagram was faulty, as it contained an *l* too much, and an *s* too little. She was completely put down by the anagram made from the name *Dame Eleanor Davies,* "Never so mad a ladie."

XXVI.

OF GRAMMATICAL PROPRIETY.

Although the details of Grammar and grammatical rule are not embraced in the plan of this work, it will be proper to present some observations, by way of review, with regard to those principles which are most frequently disregarded or forgotten by careless writers. Some remarks have already been made with regard to a few of the improprieties which are frequently observed, even in writers of respectability. The considerations now to be offered are presented in the form of directions.

Direction 1st. In determining the number of a verb, regard must be had to the *idea* which is embraced in the subject or nominative. Whenever the idea of *plurality* is conveyed, whether it be expressed by one word, or one hundred, and however connected, and in whatever number the subject may be, whether singular or plural, all verbs relating to it must be made to agree, not with the number of the *word* or *words*, but with the number of the *idea* conveyed by the words.

Direction 2d. In the use of pronouns, the same remark applies, namely, that the number of the pronoun must coincide with the *idea* contained in the word, or words, to which the pronoun relates. If it imply unity, the pronoun must be singular; if it convey plurality, the pronoun must be plural. These directions will be better understood by an example

Thus, in the sentence, "Each of them, in *their* turn, *receive* the benefits to which *they are* entitled," the verbs and pronouns are in the wrong number. The word *each*, although it includes *all*, implies but *one at a time*. The *idea*, therefore, is the idea of *unity*, and the verb and pronoun should be singular, thus, "Each of them in *his* turn *receives* the benefit to which *he* is entitled."

The same remark may be made with regard to the following sentences: "Every person, whatever be *their* (his) station, is bound by the duties of morality." "The wheel killed another man, who is the sixth that *have* (has) lost *their* (his) *lives* (life) by these means." "I do not think that any one should incur censure for being tender of *their* (his) reputation."

Direction 3d. In the use of verbs and words which express time, care must be taken that the proper tense be employed to express the time that is intended. Perhaps there is no rule more frequently violated than this, even by good writers; but young writers are very prone to the error. Thus, the author of the Waverley Novels has the following sentence: *

* See Parker's 12mo edition of the Waverley Novels, Vol. XIII. p. 14.

"'Description,' he said, '*was* (is) to the author of a romance, exactly what drawing and tinting *were* (are) to a painter; words *were* (are) his colors, and, if properly employed, they *could* (can) not fail to place the scene which he *wished* (wishes) to conjure up, as effectually before the mind's eye, as the tablet or canvass presents it to the bodily organ. The same rules,' he continued, '*applied* (apply) to both, and an exuberance of dialogue in the former case, *was* (is) a verbose and laborious mode of com position, which *went* (goes) to confound the proper art of the drama, a widely different species of composition, of which dialogue *was* (is) the very essence; because all, excepting the language to be made use of, *was* (is) presented to the eye by the dresses, and persons, and actions, of the per formers upon the stage.'"

The author was misled throughout in the tenses of the verbs in this extract, by the tense of the verb *said*, with which he introduces it.

DIRECTION 4th. Whenever several verbs belonging to one common subject occur in a sentence, the subject or nominative must be repeated whenever there is a change in the mood, tense, or form of the verb.

DIRECTION 5th. In the use of the comparative and superlative de grees of the adjective, it is to be remarked, that when two things or per sons only are compared, the comparative degree, and not the superlative, should be used. Thus, in the sentence, "Catharine and Mary are both well attired; but, in their appearance, Catharine is the neatest, Mary the most showy," the superlative degree of the adjective is improperly applied. As there are but two persons spoken of, the adjectives should be in the comparative degree namely *neater* and *more showy*.

DIRECTION 6th. Neuter and intransitive verbs should never be used in the passive form. Such expressions as *was gone*, *is grown*, *is fallen*, *is come*,* *may be relied on*, &c., although used by some good writers, are ob jectionable.

---

* Although this form of expression is sanctioned by Murray, Lowth, and other good authorities, yet reason and analogy will not justify us in assent ing to their decision; for, besides the awkwardness of the expression, it is objectionable as being an unnecessary anomaly. But the author has been influenced in his rejection of such expressions, by the very sensible and conclusive remarks of Mr. Pickbourn, in a very learned work, entitled "A Dissertation on the English Verb," published in London, 1789. Dr. Priestley, in his "Grammar," page 127, says, "It seems not to have been determined by the English grammarians, whether the passive participles of verbs neuter require the auxiliary *am* or *have* before them. The French, in this case, confine themselves strictly to the former." "This remark," says Mr. Pickbourn, "concerning the manner of using the participles of French neuter verbs is certainly not well founded; for *most of them* are conjugated with *avoir*, to have."

Such expressions as the following have recently become very common, not only in the periodical publications of the day, but are likewise finding favor with popular writers; as, "The house is being *built*." "The street is being paved." "The actions that are now being performed," &c. "The patents are being prepared." The usage of the best writers does not sanc tion these expressions; and Mr. Pickbourn, in the work just quoted, lays down the following principle, which is conclusive upon the subject. "*Whenever the participle* in *ing* is joined by an auxiliary verb to a nomina

DIRECTION 7th. In the use of irregular verbs, a proper distinction should be made in the use of the imperfect tense and the perfect participle He *done* (did) it at my request: He *run* (ran) a great risk: He has *mistook* (mistaken) his true interest: The cloth was *wove* (woven) of the finest wool: He writes as the best authors would have *wrote* (written) had they *writ* (written) on the subject: The bell has been *rang* (rung): I have *spoke* (spoken) to him upon the subject. These sentences are instances where the proper distinction between the preterite and participle has not been preserved.

DIRECTION 8th. The negative adverb must be followed by the negative conjunction; as, "The work is *not* capable of pleasing the understanding, *nor* (not *or*) the imagination." The sentence would be improved by using the conjunctions in pairs, substituting *neither* for *not*.
In the following sentences, the conjunction *but* is improperly used. "I cannot deny *but* that I was in fault." "It cannot be doubted *but* that this is a state of positive gratification," &c.

DIRECTION 9th. There must be no ellipsis of any word, when such ellipsis would occasion obscurity. Thus, when we speak of "the laws of God and man," it is uncertain whether one or two codes of laws are meant; but, in the expression, "the laws of God, and the laws of man," the obscurity vanishes. A nice distinction in sense is made by the use or omission of the articles. "A white and red house," means *but one* house but, "A white and a red house," means two houses. In the expression. "She has *a* little modesty," the meaning is positive; but, by omitting the article, "She has little modesty," the meaning becomes negative. The position of the article, also, frequently makes a great difference in the sense, as will be seen in the following examples: "As delicate a little thing;" "As a delicate little thing."

DIRECTION 10th. The adverb should always be placed as near as possible to the word which it is designed to qualify. Its proper position is generally before adjectives, after verbs, and frequently between the auxiliary and the verb. The following sentence exhibits an instance of the improper location of the adverb: "It had *almost* been his daily custom at a certain hour, to visit Admiral Priestman." The adverb *almost* should have been placed before *daily*.

DIRECTION 11th. In the use of passive and neuter verbs, care must be taken that the proper nominative is applied. That which is the object of the active verb, must in all cases be the subject or nominative of the passive verb. Thus, we say, with the active verb, "They offered him mercy" (i e. to him); and, with the passive verb, "Mercy was offered to

---

tive capable of the action, it is taken actively; but, when joined to one incapable of the action, it becomes passive. If we say, 'the men are building a house,' the participle *building* is evidently used in an active sense; because the men are capable of the action. But when we say, 'The house is building,' or 'Patents are preparing,' the participles *building* and *preparing* must necessarily be understood in a passive sense; because neither the house nor the patents are capable of action." See *Pickbourn on the English Verb*, pp. 78–80.

him;" not, "He was offered mercy," because "mercy," and not "he," is the thing which was offered. It is better to alter the expression, by substituting a synonyme with a proper nominative or subject, than to introduce such confusion of language, as must necessarily result from a change in the positive, fixed, and true significations of words, or from a useless violation of grammatical propriety.

In accordance with this direction, (see, also, Direction 6th,)

instead of	*it would be better to say*
He was prevailed on,	He was persuaded.
He was spoken to,	He was addressed.
She was listened to,	She was heard.
They were looked at,	They were seen, *or* viewed.
It is approved of,	It is liked, *or* commended.
He was spoken of,	He was named, *or* mentioned.
It is contended for,	It is maintained, *or* contested.
It was thought of,	It was remembered, *or* conceived.
He was called on by his friend,	He was visited by his friend.
These examples are commented upon with much humor,	These examples are ridiculed with much humor.
He was referred to as an oracle.	He was consulted as an oracle.

DIRECTION 12th. All the parts of a sentence should be constructed in such a manner that there shall appear to be no want of agreement or connexion among them. Thus, the following sentence, "He was more beloved, but not so much admired as Cynthio," is inaccurate, because, when it is analyzed, it will be, "He was more beloved *as* Cynthio," &c. The adverb *more* requires the conjunction *than* after it; and the sentence should be, "He was more beloved *than* Cynthio, but not so much admired."

Again; in the sentence, "If a man *have* a hundred sheep, and one of them *goes* astray," &c., the subjunctive mood, *have*, is used after the conjunction *if*, in the first part of the sentence, and the indicative, *goes*, in the second. Both of these verbs should be in the indicative, or both in the subjunctive mood.

No definite rule can be given, which will enable the learner to make the parts of a sentence agree in themselves, and with one another. They should be diligently compared, and a similarity of construction be carefully maintained; while the learner will recollect, that no sentence can be considered grammatically correct, which cannot be analyzed or parsed by the authorized rules of syntax.

[Examples for practice, under these principles, may be found in Parker and Fox's "Grammar," Part II., or in Murray's "Exercises." It has not been deemed expedient to insert them here.]

XXVII.

ON THE SELECTION OF WORDS AND EXPRESSIONS.

Besides grammatical correctness, the student who aims at being a good speaker and a good writer must pay attention to *the style*, or manner of expressing his ideas. Rules relating to this subject pertain to the science of rhetoric.

Perspicuity, (by which is meant clearness to the mind, easiness to be understood, freedom from obscurity or ambiguity) should be the fundamental quality of style; and the study of perspicuity and accuracy of expression requires attention, first, to words and phrases, and secondly, to the construction of sentences.

Of Words and Phrases.

The words and phrases employed in the expression of our ideas should have the three properties called *purity, propriety,* and *precision.*

Purity consists in the use of such words, and such constructions, as belong to the idiom of the language which we speak; in opposition to words and phrases that are taken from other languages, or that are ungrammatical, obsolete, newly coined, or used without proper authority.

Purity may be violated in three different ways. First, the words may not be English. This fault is called a *barbarism.*

Secondly, the construction of the word may not be in the English idiom. This fault is called a *solecism.*

Thirdly, the words and phrases may not be employed to express the precise meaning which custom has affixed to them. This fault is termed an *impropriety.*

Propriety of language consists in the selection of such words as the best usage has appropriated to those ideas which we intend to express by them; in opposition to low expressions, and to words and phrases which would be less significant of the ideas that we mean to convey.

There are seven principal rules for the preservation of propriety.

1. Avoid low expressions.
2. Supply words that are wanting.
3. Be careful not to use the same word in different senses.

4. Avoid the injudicious use of technical terms; that is, terms or expressions which are used in some art, occupation, or profession.
5. Avoid equivocal, or ambiguous words.
6. Avoid unintelligible and inconsistent words or phrases.
7. Avoid all such words and phrases as are not adapted to the ideas intended to be communicated.

Precision signifies the retrenching of superfluities and the pruning of the expression, so as to exhibit neither more nor less than an exact copy of the person's idea who uses it.*

The words used to express ideas may be faulty in three respects, *First*, they may not express the idea which the author intends, but some other which only resembles it; *secondly*, they may express that idea, but not fully and completely; *thirdly*, they may express it, together with something more than is intended. Precision stands opposed to these three faults, but chiefly to the last. Propriety implies a freedom from the two former faults. The words which are used may be *proper;* that is, they may express the idea intended, and they may express it fully; but to be *precise*, signifies that they express *that idea and no more.*

The great source of a loose style in opposition to precision, is the injudicious use of words termed *synonymous*. They are called synonymous because they agree in expressing one principal idea; but, for the most part, if not always, they express it with some diversity in the circumstances.†

While we are attending to precision, we must be on our guard, lest, from the desire of pruning too closely, we retrench all copiousness. To unite copiousness and precision, to be full and easy, and at the same time correct and exact in the choice of every word, is, no doubt, one of the highest and most difficult attainments in writing.

XXVIII.

OF THE CONSTRUCTION OF SENTENCES.‡

Sentences, in general, should neither be very long, nor very short; long ones require close attention to make us

---

* Precision is promoted by the omission of unnesessary words and phrases; and is opposed to Tautology, or the repetition of the same sense in different words; and to Pleonasm, or the use of superfluous words.

† See Lesson XIX The student who wishes for exercises on the subjects of purity, propriety, and precision, will find them in Parker and Fox's Grammar, Part III., pp. 78–86, or in Murray's Exercises, (Alger's Edition.)

‡ The substance of the remarks on this subject, is taken from Blair's Rhetoric. A great part of the langnage, also, is copied literally from that work.

clearly perceive the connexion of the several parts; and short ones are apt to break the sense, and weaken the connexion of thought. Yet occasionally they may both be used with force and propriety.

A train of sentences, constructed in the same manner, and with the same number of members, should never be allowed to succeed one another. A succession of either long or short sentences should also be avoided; for the ear tires of either of them when too long continued. A proper mixture of long and short periods, and of periods variously constructed, not only gratifies the ear, but imparts animation and force to style.

The properties most essential to a perfect sentence, are the four following:

1. Clearness.
2. Unity.
3. Strength.
4. Harmony.

XXIX.

OF CLEARNESS.

The first requisite of a perfect sentence is clearness. This implies that the sentence should be so constructed as to present the meaning intelligibly to the mind, and without ambiguity.

The faults in writing most destructive to clearness are two, namely: a wrong choice of words, or a wrong collocation of them.

"From the nature of our language," says Dr. Blair, "a capital rule in the arrangement of our sentences is, that words or members most nearly related should be placed as near to each other as possible, that their mutual relation may clearly appear. This rule is frequently neglected, even by good writers. Thus, Mr. Addison says,

"By greatness, I do not only mean the bulk of any single object, but the largeness of a whole view."

Here the place of the adverb *only* makes it limit the verb *mean* I do not *only mean*. The question may then be asked, "What does he more than mean?" Had it been placed after *bulk*, still it would have been wrong, for it might then be asked, "What is meant beside the bulk?" Is it the color, or any other property? Its proper place is after the word *object*.

"By greatness, I do not mean the bulk of any single object only."

For then, when it is asked — What does he mean more than the bulk of a single object? the answer comes out precisely as the author intends, 'the largeness of a whole view.'"

This extract shows the importance of giving the right position to adverbs and other qualifying words. Particular attention must be given also to the place of the pronouns *who, which, what, whose*, &c., and of all those particles which express the connexion of the parts of speech. The following sentence is faulty in this respect.

"It is folly to pretend to arm ourselves against the accidents of life, by heaping up treasures, which nothing can protect us against, but the good providence of our Heavenly Father."

Which, as it here stands, grammatically refers to the immediately preceding noun, which is *treasures*, and this would convert the whole period into nonsense. The sentence should have been constructed thus:

"It is folly to pretend, by heaping up treasures, to arm ourselves against the accidents of life, against which nothing can protect us but the good providence of our Heavenly Father."

XXX.

UNITY.

The unity of a sentence implies its *oneness*. The sentence may consist of parts; but these parts must be so closely bound together as to make an impression of one object only upon the mind.

There is generally in every sentence some person or thing which is the governing word. This should be continued so if possible from the beginning to the end.

Another direction or rule to preserve the unity of a sentence may be thus stated: Never crowd into one sentence ideas which have so little connexion that they might well be divided into two or more sentences. It is the safer extreme to err rather by too many short sentences, than by one that is overloaded or confused.

A third rule for preserving the unity of a sentence is, keep clear of parentheses in the middle of it.

In general their effect is extremely bad, being a perplexed method of disposing of some thought, which a writer has not art enough to introduce in its proper place.

The fourth rule for the unity of a sentence is, bring it to a full and perfect close.

In conformity with the first rule stated above, it may be observed, that if there are a number of nominatives, or subjects which cannot be connected by a conjunction, or thrown into some other case or form, the sentence must be divided, and the parts constructed in independent sentences.

To show the manner in which the rules now stated should be applied, the following extract is presented from "The Quarterly Review."

"The youth who had found the cavern, and had kept the secret to him self, loved this damsel; he told her the danger in time, and persuaded her to trust herself to him." In this sentence there is perfect unity. The word *youth* is the governing word, and the pronoun *he*, its representative, to prevent tautology, is substituted, to avoid the repetition of the conjunction *and*. But the writer continues, "They got into a canoe; the place of her retreat was described to her on the way to it, — these women swim like mermaids, — she dived after him, and rose in the cavern; in the widest part it is about fifty feet, and its medium height is guessed at the same, the roof hung with stalactites."

Here, every one of the rules of unity is violated. The nominative is changed six different times. Ideas having no connexion with each other, namely: Their getting into a canoe, — the description of the place of her retreat,— the swimming of the women, — her diving and rising in the cavern, — the dimensions of the cave, and the ornaments of its roof, are all crowded into one sentence. The expression, "These women swim like mermaids," is properly a parenthesis, occurring in the middle of the sentence; and the clause, "the roof hung with stalactites," does not bring the sentence to a full and perfect close. The same ideas intended to be conveyed, may be expressed as follows, without violating either of the laws of unity.

"As they got into a canoe, to proceed to the cavern, the place of her retreat was described to her. Like the rest of her countrywomen, she could swim like a mermaid, and accordingly diving after him, she rose in the cavern; a spacions apartment of about fifty feet in each of its dimensions, with a roof beautifully adorned with stalactites."

The unity of a sentence may sometimes be preserved by the use of the participle instead of the verb. Thus: "The stove stands on a platform which is raised six inches and extends the whole length of the room." This sentence is better expressed thus: "The stove stands on a platform, six inches in height, and extending the whole length of the room."

XXXI.

OF THE STRENGTH OF A SENTENCE.

The third requisite of a perfect sentence is *strength.*

By this is meant such a disposition of the several words and members as will exhibit the sense to the best advantage; as will render the impression which the period is intended to make, most full and complete, and give every word, and member its due weight and force.

To the production of this effect, perspicuity and unity are absolutely necessary; but more is requisite. For, a sentence may be clear; it may also be compact, or have the requisite unity; and yet, by some unfavorable circumstance in the structure, it may fail in that strength or liveliness of impression, which a more happy collocation would produce.

The *first* rule for promoting the strength of a sentence is, take from it all redundant words.

Thus it is better to say,

"Called to the exercise of the supreme command, he exerted his authority with moderation," &c., than "Being called to the exercise," &c.

It is a most useful exercise, on reviewing what we have written, to contract that circuitous mode of expression, and to cut off those useless excrescences, which are usually found in a first draught. Care must be taken, however, not to prune too closely. Some leaves must be left to shelter and adorn the fruit.

As sentences should be cleared of superfluous words, so also must they be of superfluous members.

Thus, speaking of beauty, one of the most elegant writers in the English language says,

"The very first discovery of it strikes the mind with inward joy *and spreads delight over the faculties.*"

In the latter member of this sentence, scarcely anything is added to what was expressed in the first.

The *second* rule for promoting the strength of a sentence is, pay particular attention to the use of copulatives, relatives, and particles employed for transition and connexion.

The separation of a preposition from the noun which it governs, is to be avoided. Thus,

Though virtue borrows no assistance *from*, yet it may often be accompanied by, the advantages of virtue."

It would be better to say,

"Though virtue borrows no assistance from the advantages of fortune in may often be accompanied by them." Or, "Though virtue may often be accompanied by the advantages of fortune, it borrows no assistance from them."

The strength of a sentence is much injured by an unnecessary multi plication of relative and demonstrative participles.

• In conversation, and in epistolary writing, the relative pronoun may be omitted; but in compositions of a serious, or dignified kind, it should always be inserted. Thus we may say, in familiar language,

"He brought the books I requested."

But in dignified discourse, the pronoun which should be inserted.

"He brought the books *which* I requested."

With regard to the conjunction *and*, it should not be unnecessarily re peated. Whenever, however, we wish objects to appear as distinct from each other as possible, the *and* may be repeated; thus,

"Such a man may fall a victim to power, but truth, and reason, and liberty, would fall with him."

[N. B. In such cases, the comma must precede each repetition of the conjunction *and*.]

The *third* rule for promoting strength is, dispose of the principal word or words in that part of the sentence, where they will make the most striking impression.

In general, the important words are placed at the beginning of a sentence. Sometimes, however, when we propose giving weight to a sen tence, it is useful to suspend the meaning a little, and then bring it out fully at the close. Thus,

"On whatever side we contemplate Homer, what principally strikes us is his wonderful invention."

The *fourth* rule for promoting the strength of a sentence is, make the members of them go on rising in importance one above another. This kind of arrangement is called a climax, and is ever regarded as a beauty in composition.

A weaker assertion should never follow a stronger one; and when a sentence consists of two members, the longer should in general be the concluding one. Thus, the following sentence admits two arrangements, of which the latter is the better, for the reasons stated above.

'We flatter ourselves with the belief that we have forsaken our passions when they have forsaken us."

"When our passions have forsaken us, we flatter ourselves with the be lief that we have forsaken them."

The *fifth* rule for constructing sentences with strength is, avoid con cluding them with an adverb, a preposition, or any insignificant word.

Sometimes, however, when words of this kind are particularly emphatical, this rule may be disregarded; as in the following sentence, and others like it in which they present an antithesis·

"In their prosperity, my friends shall never hear of me; in their adversity, *always*."

But when these inferior parts of speech are introduced as circumstances, or as qualifications of more important words, they should always be disposed of in the least conspicuous parts of the period. Thus, it is much better to say,

"Avarice is a crime *of which* wise men are often guilty," than to say, 'Avarice is a crime which wise men are often guilty of."

This latter form is a phraseology, which all correct writers shun.
Lastly, it may be observed, that any phrase which expresses a circumstance only, cannot, without great inelegance, conclude a sentence.

The *sixth* and last rule concerning the strength of a sentence is this. In the members of it, where two things are compared or contrasted; where either resemblance or opposition is to be expressed; some resemblance in the language and construction ought to be observed.
The following passage beautifully exemplifies this rule:

"Homer was the greater genius: Virgil the better artist; in the one we admire the man, in the other the work. Homer hurries as with a commanding impetuosity; Virgil leads us with an attractive majesty. Homer scatters with a generous profusion; Virgil bestows with a careful magnificence. Homer, like the Nile, pours out his riches with a sudden overflow; Virgil, like a river in its banks, with a constant stream. When we look up on their machines, Homer seems like his own Jupiter in his terrors, shaking Olympus, scattering lightnings, and firing the heavens. Virgil, like the same power in his benevolence, counselling with the gods, laying plans for empires, and ordering his whole creation."

Periods thus constructed, when introduced with propriety and not too frequently repeated, have a sensible beauty. But if such a construction be aimed at in every sentence, it betrays into a disagreeable uniformity, and produces a regular jingle in the period, which tires the ears and plainly discovers affectation.

XXXII.

OF THE HARMONY OF A SENTENCE.

Sound is a quality much inferior to sense; yet it must not be disregarded. Pleasing ideas, and forcible reasoning, lose much by being communicated to the mind by harsh and disagreeable sounds. For this reason, a sentence, besides the qualities already enumerated, under the heads of *Clearness*,

Unity, and *Strength*, should likewise, if possible, express the quality of *Harmony*.

The rules of harmony relate to the choice of words; their arrangement, the order and disposition of the members, and the cadence or close of sentences.

If we would speak forcibly and effectually, we must avoid the use of such words, — 1. As are composed of words already compounded, the several parts of which are not easily, and therefore not closely united; as, *unsuccessfulness*, *wrongheadedness*, *tenderheartedness*. 2. Such as have the syllables which immediately follow the accented syllable crowded with consonants that do not easily coalesce; as, *questionless*, *chroniclers*, *conventiclers*. 3. Such as have too many syllables following the accented syllable; as, *primarily*, *cursorily*, *summarily*, *peremptoriness*. 4. Such as have a short or unaccented syllable repeated, or followed by another short or unaccented syllable very much resembling it; as, *holily*, *sillily*, *lowlily*, *farriery*.

But let the words themselves be ever so well chosen, and well sounding, yet, if they be ill disposed, the melody of the sentence is utterly lost, or greatly impaired.

Though attention to the words and members, and the close of sentences, must not be neglected, yet, in no instance should perspicuity, precision, or strength of sentiment, be sacrificed to sound. All unmeaning words, introduced merely to round the period, or fill up the melody, are great blemishes in writing. They are childish and trivial ornaments, by which a sentence always loses more in point of weight than it can gain by such additions to its sound.

The members of a sentence should not be too long, nor disproportionate to each other. When they have a regular and proportional division they are much easier to the voice, are more clearly understood, and better remembered, than when this rule is not regarded; for whatever tires the voice and offends the ear is apt to mar the strength of the expression, and to degrade the sense of the author.

With respect to the cadence or close of a sentence, care should be taken that it be not abrupt nor unpleasant. The following examples will be sufficient to show the propriety of some attention to this part of the rule.

"Virtue, diligence, and industry, joined with good temper and prudence, are prosperous in general." It would be better thus: "Virtue, diligence, and industry, joined with good temper and prudence, have ever been found the surest road to prosperity."

An author, speaking of the Trinity, expresses himself thus:

"It is a mystery which we firmly believe the truth of, and humbly adore the depth of." How much better would it have been with this transposition: "It is a mystery, the truth of which we firmly believe, and the depth of which we humbly adore."

In the harmony of periods two things are to be considered. First, agreeable sound or modulation in general, without any particular expression. Next, the sound so ordered, as to become expressive of the sense. The first is the more common; the second the superior beauty.

The beauty of musical construction depends upon the choice and arrangement of words. Those words are most pleasing to the ear, which are composed of smooth and liquid sounds, in which there is a proper intermixture of vowels and consonants, without too many harsh consonants, or too many open vowels in succession. Long words are generally more pleasing to the ear than monosyllables; and those are the most musical, which are not wholly composed of long or short syllables, but of an intermixture of them; such as, *delight*, *amuse*, *velocity*, *celerity*, *beautiful*, *impetuosity*. If the words, however, which compose a sentence, be ever so well chosen and harmonious; yet if they be unskilfully arranged, its music is entirely lost.

There are two things on which the music of a sentence principally depends; these are, the proper distribution of the several members of it, and the close or cadence of the whole.

First, the distribution of the several members should be carefully regarded. Whatever is easy to the organs of speech, is always grateful to the ear. While a period advances, the termination of each member forms a pause in the pronunciation; and these pauses should be so distributed, as to bear a certain musical proportion to each other.

The next thing which demands attention, is the close or cadence of the period. The only important rule, which can here be given, is this, when we aim at dignity or elevation, the sound should increase to the last; the longest members of the period, and the fullest and most sonorous words, should be reserved for the conclusion.

It may be remarked, that little words in the conclusion of a sentence are as injurious to melody, as they are inconsistent with strength of expression. A musical close in our language seems in general to require either the last syllable, or the last but one, to be a long syllable. Words which consist chiefly of short syllables; as, *contrary*, *particular*, *retrospect*, seldom terminate a sentence harmoniously, unless a previous run of long syllables have rendered them pleasing to the ear.

Sentences constructed in the same manner, with the pauses at equal intervals, should never succeed each other. Short sentences must be blended with long and swelling ones, to render discourse sprightly as well as magnificent.

There is, however, a species of harmony of a higher kind than mere agreeableness to the ear; and that occurs when the sound is adapted to the sense. Of this there are two degrees. First the current of sound suited to the tenor of a discourse. Next, a peculiar resemblance effected between some object, and the sounds employed in describing it. [*See Onomatopœia.*]

The sounds of words may be employed for representing three classes of objects; first, other sounds; secondly, motions; and thirdly, the emotions and passions of the mind.

In most languages, the names of many particular sounds are so formed as to bear some resemblance to the sounds which they signify. Instances of this kind will be found under the title of Onomatopœia, on page 104. The following extracts from Milton's Paradise Lost present examples of similar words, united in sentences so happily arranged, that the sound seems almost an echo to the sense. The first represents the opening of the gates of Hell:

"On a sudden open fly,
With impetuous recoil, and jarring sounds
The infernal doors, and on their hinges grate
Harsh thunder."

The second represents the opening of the gates of Heaven

"Heaven opens wide
Her ever-during gates, harmonious sound
On golden hinges turning."

The sound of words, in the second place, is frequently employed to imitate motion.

Long syllables naturally excite an idea of slow motion; and a succession of short syllables gives the impression of quick motion. Instances of both these will be found under the title of Onomatopœia, to which reference has just been made.

The third set of objects, which the sound of words is capable of representing, consists of emotions and passions of the mind. Thus, when pleasure, joy, and agreeable objects, are described, the language should run in smooth, liquid and flowing words. The following extract presents a good example:

"But O how altered was its sprightlier tone
When Cheerfulness, a nymph of healthiest hue;
Her bow across her shoulder flung;
Her buskins gemmed with morning dew,
Blew an inspiring air that dale and thicket rang!
The hunter's call, to Fawn and Dryad known.
The oak crowned sisters, and their chaste-eyed Queen,
Satyrs and sylvan boys were seen
Peeping from forth their alleys green;
Brown Exercise rejoiced to hear,
And Sport leaped up and seized his beechen spear."

Melancholy and gloomy subjects are naturally connected with slow measure and long words. Thus:

"In those deep solitudes and awful cells
Where heavenly pensive contemplation dwells," &c.

Through glades and glooms the mingled measure stole.*

Exercises.

The student may correct the following sentences:

Want of Unity.

The successor of Henry the Second was his son Francis the Second, the first husband of Mary, afterwards Queen of Scots, who died after a reign of one year, and was succeeded by his brother Charles the Ninth, then a boy only ten years old, who had for his guardian Catharine de Medicis an ambitious and unprincipled woman.

Want of Purity.

The gardens were void of simplicity and elegance, and exhibited much that was glaring and bizarre.

Want of Propriety.

He was very dexterous in smelling out the views and designs of others.

The pretenders to polish and refine the English language have chiefly multiplied abuses and absurdities.

Want of Precision.

There can be no regularity or order in the life and conduct of that man who does not give and allot a due share of his time to retirement and reflection.

Want of Clearness.

There is a cavern in the island of Hoonga which can only be entered by diving into the sea.

Want of Strength.

The combatants encountered each other with such rage, that, being eager only to assail, and thoughtless of making any defence, they both fell dead upon the field together.

Want of Harmony.

By the means of society, our wants come to be supplied, and our lives are rendered comfortable, as well as our capacities enlarged, and our virtuous affections called forth into their proper exercise. †

---

* The teacher or student who wishes for exercises under the heads of Clearness, Unity, Strength, and Harmony, will find a good collection of them in Murray's Exercises, an appendage to his large Grammar; or an abridgement of them in Parker and Fox's Grammar, Part 3d in the appendix.

† The student who wishes a larger collection of exercises under the heads abovementioned, will find them in Parker and Fox's Grammar. Part 3d

XXXIII.

SOUND ADAPTED TO THE SENSE.

"'T is not enough no harshness gives offence,
The sound must seem an echo of the sense."

ONOMATOPŒIA.

Onomatopœia, or Onomatopy, consists in the formation of words in such a manner that the sound shall imitate the sense. Thus the words *buzz, crackle, crash, flow, rattle, roar, hiss, whistle,* are evidently formed to imitate the sounds themselves. Sometimes the word expressing an object is formed to imitate the sound produced by that object; as, *wave, cuckoo, whip-poorwill, whisper, hum.*

It is esteemed a great beauty in writing when the words selected for the expression of an idea, convey, by their sound, some resemblance to the subject which they express, as in the following lines:

The whitewashed wall, the nicely sanded floor,
The varnished clock that clicked behind the door.*

Of a similar character, and nearly of equal merit, are those sentences or expressions which in any respect imitate or represent the sense which they are employed to express. Thus Gray, in his Elegy, beautifully expresses the reluctant feeling to which he alludes in the last verse of the following stanza:

"For who, to dumb forgetfulness a prey,
This pleasing anxious being e'er resigned,
Left the warm precincts of the cheerful day,
Nor cast one *longing, lingering* look behind!"

And Pope, in his "Essays on Criticism," in a manner, though different, yet scarcely less expressive, gives a verbal representation of his idea, by the selection of his terms, in the following lines:

"These, equal syllables alone require,
Though *oft* the *ear* the *open* vowels tire,

---

* These lines will not fail to recall to the memory of the classical student those peculiarly graphic lines of Virgil, in one of which he describes the galloping of a horse:

"Quadrupedante putrem sonitu quatit ungula campum."

and in another the appearance of a hideous monster:

"Monstrum horrendum in forma ingens cui lumen ademptum."

While expletives their feeble aid *do* join,
And ten low words oft creep in one dull line."

"A needless Alexandrine ends the song,
That, like a wounded snake, drags its slow length along."

"Soft is the strain, when Zephyr gently blows,
And the *smooth stream* in *smoother numbers flows*,
But when loud surges lash the sounding shore,
The *hoarse, rough verse* should like the torrent *roar*.
When Ajax strives some rock's vast weight to throw,
The line too labors, and the words move slow.
Not so when swift Camilla scours the plain,
Flies o'er the unbending corn, and skims along the main."

As an exercise in Onomatopœia, the student may select such words as he can recall in which the sound bears a resemblance to the signification.

XXXIV.

DEFINITION, AND DISTINCTION OR DIFFERENCE

The object of this exercise is to accustom the student to acquire clear ideas of things, and to perceive distinctions and differences wherever they exist. Clear ideas of a subject must be acquired before any thing can be correctly said or written upon it.

A definition, as described by logicians, consists of two parts, which they call the *genus* and the *difference*. The genus is the name of the *class* to which the object belongs. The difference is the property or properties by which the individual thing to be defined is distinguished from other individuals of the same class. Thus, if a definition is required of the word *justice*, we may commence by saying, "Justice is that virtue which induces us to give every one his due." Here, *virtue* is the *class* to which the object belongs; but this part of the definition may be applied to *honesty*, another quality of the same class, as well as to justice; for "Honesty is also a virtue which induces us to give every one his due." Something more, therefore, must be added to our definition, by which *justice* may be distinguished from *honesty*, and this *something more*, in whatever form it may be presented, will be the *difference* which excludes honesty from the same definition.

Example.

JUSTICE.

Justice is that virtue which induces us to give to every one his due. It requires us not only to render every article of property to its right owner, but also to esteem every one according to his merit, giving credit for talents and virtues wherever they may be possessed, and withholding our approbation from every fault, how great soever the temptation that leads to it.

It will easily be seen from this definition in what the *difference* lies, which excludes honesty from the definition. Honesty, it is true, requires that we should render to every one his due. But honesty does not necessarily imply the esteeming of every one according to his merit, giving credit for talents and virtues,* &c.

A definition should generally be an analysisis of the thing defined, that is, it should comprise an enumeration of its principal qualities or attributes.

Example 2d.

A Swallow.

1. A swallow is an animal. — This definition is not correct, because it will apply also to a horse, or a cow, or a dog, or a cat, as well as to a swallow.

2. A swallow is a bird. — So also is an eagle, or a goose, and therefore this definition is not sufficiently distinct.

3. A swallow is an animal which has two legs. — And so is a man, and therefore this definition is not sufficiently exclusive.

4. A swallow is an animal that has two legs, and wings. — And so is *a bat;* and therefore this definition is faulty.

5. A swallow is an animal, that has wings, feathers, and a hard, glossy bill, with short legs, a forked tail, and large mouth, and exceeding all other birds in the untiring rapidity of its flight and evolutions. Its upper parts are steel blue, and the lower parts of a light, chestnut color. It seeks the society of man, and attaches its nest to the rafters in barns.

This definition contains the *difference*, as well as the class, and may therefore be considered as sufficiently correct for our present purpose.†

---

* See *Synonymes*, page 40.

† See Parker and Fox's Grammar, Part III., No. 387.

Example 3d.

Eternal.

The term *eternal* is properly applied to that only which always has existed and always will exist. It implies *without beginning and without end.*

This definition excludes the application of the term *eternal* from every thing that ever had a beginning, as well as from that which will ever have an end. The circumstance of *having no beginning* is the specific difference between the terms *eternal* and *infinite. Infinite*, endless, unceasing, &c., imply only *without end.*

After explaining the meaning, or giving the definition of the terms in this exercise, the student should be required to give an instance of the proper application of the word.

Exercises.

Give a definition to the following words, and point out the distinction or difference between them and other words, which in some respect resemble them.

Temperance.	To Transpose.	Amplify
Equity.	To Disregard.	Composition.
Synthesis.	Excellence.	History.
Analogy.	Activity.	Astrology.
Comparison.	To Disobey.	Literature.
Judgment.	Tautology.	Science.
Reasoning.	Narration.	Art.
Description.	Outline.	

The distinction or difference between two subjects may likewise be exhibited as in the following

Example.

Grammar, rhetoric, and logic are kindred branches of science, but each has its separate department and specific objects. Rhetoric teaches how to express an idea in proper words; grammar directs the arrangement and inflections of the words; logic relates to the truth or correctness of the idea to be expressed. Grammar addresses itself to the understanding; rhetoric, to the imagination; logic, to the judgment. Rhetoric selects the materials; grammar combines them into sentences; logic shows the agreement, or disagreement, of the sentences with one another. A sentence may be grammatically correct, but rhetorically incorrect, as in the following extract:

"To take *arms* against a *sea* of troubles, and, by opposing, end them."

Here every word is grammatically correct; but to represent a man clad in armor to *fight water*, is a mixed metaphor, violating one of the fundamental principles of rhetoric. So, also, a sentence may be both grammatically and rhetorically faultless, while it violates logical principles. Thus, "All men are bipeds, and, as birds are also bipeds, birds are to be considered as men."

Exercises.

The student may show the distinction between the following words:

Quack and charlatan.
Projector, speculator, and economist.
Bookworms and syllable hunters.
Cant, prosing, puritanical.
The word *liberal*, as applied to politicians, theologians, and philosophers; 1st, when assumed by themselves; 2dly, when applied to them by their adversaries.

The different senses in which the word *independence* is used, as applied to nations and individuals, to a man's character, opinions, and circumstances, is explained in the following

Example.

When we speak of a nation's independence, we mean, that it is not connected with any other nation, so as to be obliged to receive laws or magistrates from it, to pay a revenue into its treasury, or in any way to submit to its dictates. When we see a nation whose laws are framed by its own magistrates, whether elective or hereditary, without regard to the pleasure of any other nation; where the taxes are levied for the support of its own interest, and for the maintenance of its own magistrates; where it is not necessary that the consent of another should be obtained, before it is at liberty to make war upon a foreign state, or to enter into alliance with any foreign power that they please, — to that nation custom gives the epithet "independent."

Nor does the submission of a people to the will of a despot contradict its claim to be considered an independent nation.

The subjects are, indeed, dependent upon the caprice of a tyrant, and he has absolute power over their lives, property, and political interest; but this internal slavery does not exclude them from being considered independent as a nation, and from taking a part, as such, in the disputes of other governments, provided that their own master is not also subject to some foreign power. A subject province becomes independent, when, finding itself strong enough for its purpose, it throws off the yoke of the ruling power, and declares itself free; and it is recognized as such by other nations, if it succeeds in establishing its claim, either by arms, or the consent of the government to which it was subject.

A man is said to be independent in his character, when he does not permit the opinion of the world to influence his actions. He is independent in his opinions, when he maintains them in spite of ridicule, or the ideas of the rest of the community. If he conducts himself according to these opinions, carries into action his ideas of right and wrong, though they be contrary to what every one else thinks, he is independent in character. A man may he so subservient to another, that he will disguise his own opinions, and uphold those of the other. For some benefit conferred, or from the expectation of some advantage, he will stoop to flatter the notions of his patron, pretend to guide all his actions according to those ideas, and even regulate his conduct by rules which he knows to be wrong; and merely for the sake of being permitted to expect a slight favor. Such a man has no claim to independence of character or opinions.

When a person does not rely on the profits of his business for subsistence, but has laid up or received as an inheritance a sum of money, the income of which is sufficient for his maintenance, he is considered independent in his circumstances.

Independence is, in most cases, an excellent quality and state; but when a man's independence of character leads him to abuse, and refuse to conform to, the customs of his country, because he perceives in them something absurd, it makes him appear ridiculous.

XXXV

ANALOGY.

Analogy, as defined by Johnson, is a resemblance between two things with regard to some circumstances or effects.

Webster defines it thus: An agreement or likeness between things in some circumstances or effects, when the things are otherwise entirely different. Thus, learning is said to *enlighten* the mind, that is, it is to the mind what light is to the eye, enabling it to discover what was hidden before.*

Example.

Youth and morning resemble each other in many particulars. Youth is the first part of life. Morning is the first part of the day. Youth is the time when preparation is to be made for the business of life. In the morning, arrangements are made for the employment of the day. In youth, our spirits are light, no cares perplex, no troubles annoy us. In the morning the prospect is fair, no clouds arise, no tempest threatens, no commotion among the elements impends. In youth we form plans which the later periods of life cannot execute; and the morning, likewise, is often productive of promises which neither noon nor evening can perform.

From this example it will be seen that subjects which in reality have in themselves no actual resemblance, may be so contrasted as to present an appearance of resemblance in their effects. Many of the beauties of poetry arise from the poet's observing these similitudes, and expressing them in appropriate language. Thus darkness and adversity, comfort and light, life and the ocean, evening and old age, misfortune and a storm, a clergyman and a shepherd, smiles and sunshine, tears and rain, a guilty conscience and a defenceless body, are subjects which in themselves have no actual similitude; yet, when contrasted with their effects, points of resemblance will

* When the thing to which the analogy is supposed happens to be mentioned, analogy has after it the prepositions *to* or *with*: when both the things are mentioned after analogy, the preposition between is used. — *Johnson.*

be readily seen, which show an obvious analogy. Thus, also, in the following extract the poet in addressing the sun shows an analogy between the evaporation of water, and the flight of a bird.

> "Thou lookest on the waters, and they glow
> And take them wings and mount aloft in air," &c.

The skilful allusion to such analogies constitutes the highest art of the poet, as it forms also the most pleasing beauty of poetry. Indeed, without such allusions, poetry loses all of its charms, and verse degenerates into mere '*sing-song.*'

It will be a useful exercise for the student to prepare lists of subjects between which an analogy may be traced.

XXXVI.

FIGURATIVE LANGUAGE.

A Figure, in the science of language, is a departure from the common forms of words, from the established rules of syntax, or from the use of words according to their literal signification.

A departure from the *common form* of words is called a figure of etymology, or an etymological figure. [*See Elision, &c.*]

A departure from the established rules of syntax is called a syntactical figure. [*See Enallage, Hyperbaton, Pleonasm, &c.*]

A departure from the use of words in their literal signification is called a figure of rhetoric, or a rhetorical figure. [*See Trope, Metaphor.*]

Figurative language properly includes all of these different kinds of figures; but the term is sometimes restricted to rhetorical figures.*

---

* Holmes's "Rhetoric" enumerates a list of two hundred and fifty figures connected with the subjects of Logic, Rhetoric, and Grammar. The work is remarkable for its quaintness, and possesses some merit *as a vocabulary.* His cautions with regard to the use of figures are so characteristic, that they may afford some amusement, if not edification to the student. The follow ing is his language with regard to Tropes and Figures:

"The faults of Tropes are nine:

> "Of tropes perplext[1], harsh[2], frequent[3], swoll'n[4], fetched far[5],
> Ill representing[6], forced[7], low[8], lewd[9], beware."

Many words that are used in common discourse have two significations or rather significations of two different kinds; namely, a literal and a figurative signification.

A word is said to be used literally or to have its literal signification when it is used in a manner, which is authorized by the general consent of those who speak and write with correctness the language in which it is found.

A word is used figuratively, when though it retains its usual signification it is applied in a manner different from its common application. Thus when we speak of the *head* of an *animal*, we use the word *head* in its literal signification as implying that part of the body which contains the eyes, nose, mouth, ears, &c. But when we speak of the *head* of a class, or of a division of an army, or any thing without life, we recall to mind the analogy or resemblance between two objects, separately considering the *highest* or most prominent part of each, and apply the name of that part in the one, to the similar part in the other. In this manner the word is *turned* from its literal meaning to a figurative signification, and this turning of the word receives the rhetorical name of *a trope;* a derivation from a Greek word, which signifies *a turning*. So also, "*The dawn*," properly means the *earliest part* of the morning, or of the day; and "*twilight*" expresses the *close* or *latter part of day*. But, by a rhetorical figure, these words are used to express the *earliest* and *latest* parts of other subjects. Thus, "the *dawn* of bliss," expresses the commencement of happiness or bliss; and, "the *twilight of our woes*," is used to signify the close or termination of sorrow. "The morning of our joy," implies the earliest period of our enjoyment. "The eve of his departure," implies the *latest point of time*, previous to his departure.

The use of figures, or of figurative language, is,—

1. They render the language copious.
2. The richness of language is thereby increased.
3. They increase the power and expressiveness of language.
4. They impart animation to style.*

There is another class of figures styled *metaphors*, which so nearly resemble *tropes*, that the difference cannot always be easily described.

The literal meaning of the word metaphor is *a transferring* from one subject to another. As used in rhetoric, it implies a transferring of the

"And the faults of figures are six:

"Figures [1] unnatural, [2] senseless, [3] too fine spun,
Over [4] adorned, [5] affected, [6] copious, shun." (!!!)

"*Rhetoric made Easy*, by John Holmes. London, 1755.".

* The student who would see a beautiful illustration of this subject, is referred to Newman's Rhetoric, chap. 3d

application of a word, in its literal meaning, from one object, or class of objects, to another, founded upon some similarity, analogy, or resemblance.*

A metaphor is a simile or comparison expressed in one word. Thus: The soldiers were lions in the combat: The soldiers fought *like lions*. [*See Comparison.*]

A trope is the mere change, or turning, of a word from its original signification. Hence, if the word be changed, the figure is destroyed. Thus, when we say, The clouds *foretell* rain, we have a trope in the word *foretell*. If the sentence be read, The clouds foreshow rain, the figure disappears.

The following examples will clearly illustrate the difference between plain and figurative language:

Examples.

Figurative. She had been the pupil of the village pastor, the favorite lamb of his little flock.

Plain. She had been the pupil of the village clergyman, the favorite child of his small congregation.

Figurative. Man! thou pendulum between a smile and tear.

Plain. Man! thou who art always placed between happiness and misery, but never wholly enjoying the one, nor totally afflicted with the other.

Figurative. He found the tide of wealth flowing merely in the channels of traffic; he has diverted from it invigorating rills to refresh the garden of literature.

Plain. He saw that men of wealth were employing their riches only in the business of commerce. He set the example of appropriating a portion of wealth to the increase and diffusion of knowledge.

Figurative. A stone, perhaps, may tell some wanderer where we lie, when we came here, and when we went away; but even that will soon refuse to bear us record: Time's effacing fingers will be busy on its surface, and at length wear it smooth.

Plain. A stone, perhaps, may be erected over our graves, with an inscription bearing the date of our birth, and the day

* "Metaphore is an alteration of a worde, from the proper and naturall meaning to that which is not proper, and yet agreeth thereunto by some likenesse that appeareth to be into it."—*Wilson* — *The Arte of Rhetorique* p. 175.

of our death; but even that will not last long. In the course of time the stone will be mutilated or broken, and the inscription be entirely destroyed.

It will readily be seen from these examples that analogy is the foundation of a large proportion of figurative language. Thus in the first example, "She had been the pupil of the village pastor, the favorite *lamb* of his little flock," the analogy lies between a clergyman and a shepherd; a congregation and a flock of sheep, the little ones of the congregation and the young lambs of the flock.

It will be found a very useful exercise for the student to trace out the analogies thus presented by figurative language. The following extracts are selected, in which he may point out the subjects between which the analogy is directly or indirectly implied. Such an exercise will open his eyes to the beauties of poetry, and prepare him for the imitation of those beauties. Perhaps it will be better that this should be an *oral* exercise.

Extracts.

The meek-eyed morn appears, mother of dews,
At first faint gleaming in the dappled east.

How reverend is the face of this tall pile,
Whose ancient pillars rear their marble heads,
To bear aloft its arched and ponderous roof,
By its own weight made steadfast and immovable,
Looking tranquillity!

Youth is not rich in time; it may be poor;
Part with it, as with money, sparing; pay
No moment but in purchase of its worth;
And what its worth — ask death-beds; they can tell.

———— Enter this wild wood,
And view the haunts of nature. The calm shade
Shall bring a kindred calm, and the sweet breeze,
That makes the green leaves dance, shall waft a balm
To thy sick heart.

Throngs of insects in the glade
Try their thin wings, and dance in the warm beam
That waked them into life. Even the green trees
Partake the deep contentment; as they bend
To the soft winds, the sun from the blue sky
Looks in, and sheds a blessing on the scene.

The breath of night's destructive to the hue
Of every flower that blows.

So saying, her rash hand in evil hour
Forth reaching to the fruit, she plucked, she ate.
Earth felt the wound, and Nature from her seat,
Sighing through all her works, gave signs of woe
That all was lost.

The voice of thy brother's blood crieth unto me from the ground.

Thou 'rt purpling now, O Sun, the vines of Canaan,
And crowning with rich light the cedar tops of Lebanon.

The tempests of fortune.

The last steps of day.
The storms of adversity.

My ear is pained,
My soul is sick with every day's report
Of wrong and outrage with which earth is filled.

The superb lotus was holding up his cup to the sun. as if for a full draught of his light.

Life is a sea as fathomless,
As wide, as terrible, and yet sometimes
As calm and beautiful. The light of heaven
Smiles on it, and 'tis decked with every hue
Of glory and of joy. Anon, dark clouds
Arise, contending winds of fate go forth,
And Hope sits weeping o'er a general wreck.

XXXVII.

TRANSLATION OF PLAIN INTO FIGURATIVE LANGUAGE.

The following Examples present instances of plain language converted into figurative. This exercise will require a greater effort of imagination than the last; but the difficulty of the task must not prevent an attempt at its execution.

Examples. *

Plain. It was evening, and the sun slowly went down.
Figurative. 'T was eve: — upon his chariot throne
The sun sank lingering in the west.
Plain. Showery April.
Figurative. Tear-dropping April.

---

* For an example showing the difference in the vivacity of style in plain and figurative language, see note on pages 118 and 119.

Plain. The winds made the large trees bend.

Figurative. The giant trees leaned back from the encountering breeze.

Plain. The thunder is echoed from the tops of the mountains.

Figurative. From peak to peak leaps the live thunder.

Plain. It is again morning, a bright, fair, and pleasant morning; and the clouds have all passed away.

Figurative The morn is up again, the dewy morn,
With breath all incense, and with cheek all bloom,
Laughing the clouds away with playful scorn.

Plain. Oldest of Lakes.

Figurative. Father of Lakes.

Plain. Yonder comes the bright sun, enlightening the East.

Figurative. But yonder comes the powerful King of day,
Rejoicing in the east.

Plain. The light dew — the unpleasant storms.

Figurative. The light-footed dews: — the surly storms.

Plain. The earth is covered with snow, or
The snow covers the earth.

Figurative. The earth lies buried in a shroud of snow.

Plain. Much rain has fallen from the clouds to-day.

Figurative. The clouds have dropped their garnered fulness down.

Plain. The fair morning makes the eastern skies look bright.

Figurative. The fair morning gilds the eastern skies.

Plain. Some solitary column stands alone, while the others have been thrown down.

Figurative. Some solitary column mourns above its prostrate brethren.

Plain. If pleasant looks will not soothe your displeasure,
I shall never attempt it with tears.

Figurative. If sunshine will not dissolve thy snow,
I shall never attempt it with rain.

Plain. The love that is caused by excitement is soon destroyed by affliction.

Figurative. The love that is ordered to bathe in wine,
Would be sure to take cold in tears.

Plain. Authors of modern date write for money, not for fame.

Figurative. 'T is but to snip his locks they (modern authors) follow the golden-haired Apollo.

The conversion of plain into figurative language requires the exercise of considerable thought, and quickness of perception in tracing analogies. It is recommended to the student before he attempts an exercise of this kind, to read with attention portions of the works of some distinguished poet, with special reference to the figures he employs. Let him analyze the expressions, and point out what portions are figurative, in what the figure consists, and on what analogy the figure is founded. An exercise of this kind will bring the mind into vigorous action, and like all exercises having that tendency, cannot fail to be highly beneficial.

XXXVIII.

RULES OF METAPHORS.

The following are the rules laid down by Dr. Blair, in relation to metaphors:

First. They must be suited to the nature of the subject; neither too numerous, nor too gay, nor too elevated for it. We must neither attempt to force the subject, by the use of them, into a degree of elevation not congruous to it; nor, on the contrary, suffer it to fall below its proper dignity. Some metaphors would be beautiful in poetry, which would be unnatural in prose; some are graceful in orations, which would be highly improper in historical composition. Figures are the dress of sentiment; they should, consequently, be adapted to the ideas which they are intended to adorn.

The *second rule* respects the choice of objects whence metaphors are to be drawn. The field for figurative language is very wide. All nature opens her stores, and allows us to collect them without restraint. But we must beware of using such allusions as raise in the mind mean, low, or dirty ideas. To render a metaphor perfect, it must entertain as well as enlighten. The most pleasing metaphors are derived from the frequent occurrences of art and nature, or from the civil transactions and customs of mankind.

In the *third* place, a metaphor should be founded on a resemblance, or analogy, which is clear and striking, not far fetched, nor difficult to be discovered. Harsh or forced metaphors are always displeasing, because they perplex the reader, and, instead of illustrating the thought, they render it intricate and confused.

In the *fourth* place, we must never jumble metaphorical and plain language together; that is, never construct a period, so that part of it must be understood metaphorically, part literally.

In the *fifth* place, take care not to make two different metaphors meet on the same object. This, which is called mixed metaphor, is one of the greatest abuses of the figure. Shakspeare's expression, for example,

"To take *arms* against a *sea* of troubles," makes a most unnatural medley, and entirely confounds the imagination.*

In examining the propriety of metaphors, it is a good rule to form a picture of them, and to consider how the parts agree, and what kind of figure the whole presents, when delineated with a pencil.

Metaphors, in the *sixth* place, should not be crowded together on the same object. Though each of them be distinct, yet if they be heaped on one another, they produce confusion.

The *last* rule concerning metaphors is, they should not be too far pursued. For, when the resemblance, which is the foundation of the figure, is long dwelt upon, and carried into all its minute circumstances, an *allegory* is produced, instead of a metaphor; the reader is wearied, and the discourse becomes obscured. This is termed, straining a metaphor.

XXXIX.

PROSOPOPOEIA, OR PERSONIFICATION.

The literal meaning of prosopopoeia is, *the change of things to persons.* A fondness for life and animated beings, in preference to inanimate objects, is one of the first principles of literary taste. That figure, therefore, by which life and action are attributed to inanimate objects, is one of frequent occurrence among the best writers of prose and of poetry. To poetical writers, especially, it is of the greatest consequence, as constituting the very life and soul, as it were, of their numbers. This will easily be seen by the following example:

"The brilliant sun is rising in the east."

How tame and spiritless is this line, compared with the manner in which the same idea is expressed by the poet, thus

"But yonder comes the powerful King of Day,
Rejoicing in the east." †

---

* Mr. Steele, in his "*Prosodia Rationalis,*" has rescued the Bard of Avon from this inconsistent metaphor, by the suggestion, that it was originally written, "To take arms against assail of troubles."

† This extract, from Thomson's Seasons, operates as a temptation, that cannot be resisted, to present another from the same page, which, as a picture, remarkable alike for beauty of coloring, dignity of appearance, and sublimity of conception, is scarcely equalled in any other language. That

There are three different degrees of this figure, says Dr. Blair, which it is requisite to distinguish in order to determine the propriety of its use.

The first is, when *some of the properties* of living creatures are ascribed to inanimate objects; the second, when these inanimate objects are described as *acting like such as have life;* and the third, when they are exhibited as speaking to us, or as listening.

The first and lowest degree of this figure, which consists in *ascribing to inanimate objects some of the qualities of living creatures*, raises the style so little, that the humblest discourse admits it without any force. Thus, a *raging* storm, a *deceitful* disease, a *cruel* disaster — are familiar expressions. This, indeed, is so obscure a degree of personification, that it might, perhaps, be properly classed with simple metaphors, which almost escape our observation.

The second degree of this figure is, when we represent inanimate objects as *acting* like those that have life. Here we rise a step higher, and the personification becomes sensible. According to the nature of the action which we ascribe to those inanimate objects, and to the particularity with which we describe it, is the strength of the figure. When pursued to a considerable length, it belongs only to studied harangues; when slightly touched, it may be admitted into less elevated compositions.

---

the student may duly appreciate the skill of the poet, and the magnificence of the design, it is first presented in plain language:

"Every thing that grows depends on the light and heat of the sun, as it is passing along the ecliptic. All mankind depend upon it for their daily subsistence. The seasons, the hours, the wind and the rain, the dew and the storm, influenced as they are by the sun, are instrumental in producing herbs, fruits, and flowers, during the whole year."

From such a tame and lifeless recital, the poet has formed the following magnificent picture, which he holds up to the sun, under the name (see Onomatopœia) of "Parent of Seasons:"

"The vegetable world is also thine
Parent of Seasons! who the pomp precede,
That waits thy throne, as through thy vast domain,
Annual, along the bright ecliptic road,
In world-rejoicing state, it moves sublime.
Meantime the expecting nations, circled gay,
With all the various tribes of foodful earth,
Implore thy bounty, or send grateful up
A common hymn; while, round thy beaming car,
High seen, the Seasons lead, in sprightly dance
Harmonious knit, the rosy-fingered Hours,
The Zephyrs floating loose, the timely Rains,
Of bloom ethereal, the light-footed Dews,
And, softened into joy, the surly Storms.
These in successive turn, with lavish hand,
Shower every beauty, every fragrance shower,
Herbs, flowers, and fruits; till, kindling at thy touch,
From land to land is flushed the vernal year."

Example.

"The offended Law draws the sword from its scabbard, in vengeance against the murderer."

Here the law is beautifully personified, as reaching forth its hand to give us a sword for putting a murderer to death.

In poetry, personifications of this kind are extremely frequent, and are, indeed, the life and soul of it. In the descriptions of a poet, who has a lively fancy, every thing is animated. Homer, the father of poetry, is remarkable for the use of this figure. War, peace, darts, rivers, every thing in short, *is alive* in his writings. The same is true of Milton and Shakspeare.*

The third and highest degree of this figure is when inanimate objects are represented, not only as feeling and acting, but *as speaking to us, or listening when we address them.* This is the boldest of all rhetorical figures: it is the style of strong passion only, and therefore should never be attempted, except when the mind is considerably heated and agitated.

The following is an example of this kind:

> Must I leave thee, Paradise? thus leave
> Thee, native soil, these happy walks and shades,
> Fit haunts of gods! where I had hoped to spend,
> Quiet, though sad, the respite of that day
> That must be mortal to us both.

It is to be remarked, with regard to this degree of personification, *first*, that it should never be attempted unless when prompted by strong feeling, and should never be continued when the feeling begins to subside.

Secondly. That an object that has not some dignity in itself, or which is incapable of making a proper figure in the elevation to which we raise it, should never be personified. Thus, to address the body of a friend is not at all unnatural; but to address the several parts of the body, or the clothes which he wore, is not compatible with the dignity of grave composition.

Examples of the three degrees of personification for the student to designate:

> With other ministrations, thou, oh Nature,
> Healest thy wandering and distempered child.

> Uncomforted and friendless solitude.

> Come, funeral flower! thou shalt form my nosegay now.

---

* No personification is more striking, or introduced on a more proper occasion, than the following of Milton, upon Eve's eating the forbidden fruit:

> "So saying, her rash hand, in evil hour,
> "Forth reaching to the fruit, she plucked, she ate!
> "Earth felt the wound; and nature, from her seat,
> "Sighing, through all her works, gave signs of woe,
> "That all was lost"

Sweet scented flower, who 't wont to bloom
On January's front severe.

The meek-eyed Morn appears, mother of dews.

Young Day pours in apace,
And opens all the dawny prospect wide.

Oh! there is a charm, that morning has,
That gives the brow of age a smack of youth
And makes the lip of youth breathe perfumes exquisite.

The breath of night 's destructive to the hue
Of every flower that blows.

No arm, in the day of the conflict could wound him,
Though war launched his thunder in fury to kill.

There is no malice in this burning coal;
The breath of heaven hath blown its spirit out,
And strowed repentant ashes on his head.

Pale Autumn spreads o'er him the leaves of the forest,
The fays of the wild chant the dirge of his rest,
And thou, little brook, still the sleeper deplorest,
And moistenest the heath-bell that weeps on his breast.

No might nor greatness in mortality
Can censure 'scape; back-wounding calumny
The whitest virtue strikes.

I have marked
A thousand blushing apparitions start
Into her face; a thousand innocent shames
In angel whiteness bear away these blushes.

All delights are vain; but that most vain,
Which, with pain purchased, doth inherit pain.

Let fame, that all hunt after in their lives,
Live registered upon our broken tombs,
And then grace us in the disgrace of death;
When, spite of cormorant devouring time,
The endeavor of this present breath may bay
That honor, which shall 'bate his scythe's keen edge,
And make us heirs of all eternity.*

* Any volume of poetry will furnish exercises of this kind to the student, rendering it unnecessary to multiply them here. In personifying inanimate objects, things remarkable for power, greatness, or sublimity, are represented as *males*. Things beautiful, amiable, or prolific, or spoken of as receivers and containers, are represented as *females*.

XL.

SIMILE, OR COMPARISON.*

A simile is the likening of the subject, of which we speak, to another subject having some similarity, in order to render the description more forcible and perspicuous. In a strict sense, it differs from comparison, in which the subject may have an obvious likeness. † But many rhetoricians consider the terms as synonymous, and in this light they are presented in this connexion. This figure is extremely frequent both in prose and poetry; and it is often as necessary to the exhibition of the thought, as it is ornamental to the language in which that thought is conveyed.

In all comparisons there should be found something new or surprising, in order to please and illustrate. Consequently they must never be instituted between things of the same species. ‡

---

* Every *simile* is more or less *a comparison*, — but every *comparison* is not a *simile*; the latter compares things only as far as they are alike; but the former extends to those things which are different. In this manner there may be a *comparison* between large things and small, although there can be no good *simile.*

† The distinction between simile and comparison is, that the former has reference to the *quality*; the latter to the *quantity*. Comparison is between *more* and *less*; similitude is between *good* and *bad*. "Hannibal hung like a tempest on the declivities of the Alps" — is a likeness by *similitude*. "The sublimity of the Scriptural prophets exceeds that of Homer, as much as thunder is louder than a whisper" — is a likeness by comparison. — *J. Q. Adams*, Lec. 9.

‡ The simile, or comparison, may be considered as differing in form only from a Metaphor the resemblance being stated in the comparison, which in the metaphor is only implied. Each may be founded on actual resemblance or on analogy. Metaphors and comparisons founded on analogy are the more frequent and the more striking, because the more remote and unlike in themselves any two objects are, the more is the mind impressed and gratified by the perception of some point in which they agree. Intimately connected with Simile and Comparison is the *Emblem*; the literal meaning of which is, "*something inserted in the body of another*;" but the word is used to express "a picture, representing one thing to the eye, and another to the understanding:" or, a painting, or representation, intended to hold forth some moral, or political instruction. Thus, *a balance* is an emblem of *justice*; *a crown* is the emblem of *royalty*; a *sceptre*, of *power* or sove reignty. Any thing, which represents another thing in its predominant qualities, is also an emblem. Thus a looking glass, which shows spots, without magnifying them, is an emblem of a true friend, who will show us our faults without exaggeration. A torch, reversed and expiring, with the

All comparisons, says Dr. Blair, may be reduced under two heads, explaining, and embellishing. But embellishing comparisons are those which most frequently occur.

Resemblance, it has been observed, is the foundation of this figure, but resemblance must not be taken in too strict a sense for actual similitude. Two objects may raise a train of concordant ideas in the mind, though they resemble each other, strictly speaking, in nothing. For example, to describe the natnre of soft and melancholy music, Ossian says:

"The music of Carryl, like the memory of joys that are past, was pleasant and mournful to the soul."

This is happy and delicate; yet no kind of music bears any actual resemblance to the memory of past joys.

Comparisons should not be introduced on all occasions. As they are the language of imagination, rather than of passion, an author can hardly commit a greater fault, than in the midst of passion or strong feeling to introduce a simile. Even in poetry it should be employed with moderation; but in prose much more so.

The following rules are laid down bv Dr. Blair in the use of comparisons:

In the *first*, they must not be drawn from things which have too near and obvious a resemblance of the object with which they are compared; for the pleasure which we receive from the act of comparing arises from the discovery of likenesses among things of different species where we should not, at first sight expect, a resemblance.

In the *second* place, as comparisons ought not to be founded on likenesses too obvious, much less ought they to be founded on those which are too faint and distant. These, instead of assisting, strain the fancy to comprehend them, and throw no light upon the subject.

In the *third* place, the object from which a comparison is drawn ought never to be an unknown object, nor one of which few people can have a clear idea. Therefore similes founded on philosophical discoveries, or on any thing with which persons of a particular trade only, or a particular profession, are acquainted, produce not their proper effect. They should be drawn from those illustrious and noted objects, which most readers have either seen, or can strongly conceive.

In the *fourth* place, in compositions of a serious or elevated kind, similes should not be drawn from low or mean objects. These degrade and vilify; whereas similes are generally intended to embellish and dignify. Therefore, except in burlesque writings, or where an object is meant to be degraded, mean ideas should never be presented.

---

motto, "My nourishment is my bane," is an emblem of the improper use we are too apt to make of things, when either by using them improperly, or too freely we subvert the design for which they were at first intended.

"The oil thus feeds, thus quenches flame:
So love gives honor;—love gives shame."
Quarles' Book of Emblems.

Emblems are frequently the foundations of both Simile and Comparison. Analogy is the foundation of the three.

Examples.

1. Wit and humor are like those volatile essences, which, being too delicate to bear the open air, evaporate almost as soon as they are exposed to it.

2. Like birds whose beauties languish, half concealed,
Till mounted on the wing their glossy plumes
Expanded, shine with azure, green, and gold,
How blessings brighten as they take their flight!

3. And in the smoke the pennons flew,
As in the storm the white sea-mew.

4. Then marked they dashing broad and far
The broken billows of the war,
And plumed crests of chieftains brave,
Floating like foam upon the wave.

5. She never told her love,
But let concealment, like a worm in the bud,
Feed on her damask cheek. She pined in thought,
And with a green and yellow melancholy
She sat, like Patience on a monument,
Smiling at Grief.

6. Oh Night,
And Storm and Darkness, ye are wondrous strong,
Yet lovely in your strength as is the light
Of a dark eye in woman.

7. This quiet sail is as a noiseless wing
To waft me from distraction; once I loved
Torn ocean's roar; but thy soft murmuring
Sounds sweet as if a sister's voice reproved
That I with stern delights should e'er have been so moved.

8. They are the native courtesies of a feeling mind, showing themselves amid stern virtues and masculine energies like gleams of light on points of rocks.

9. I never tempted her with word too large;
But as a brother to a sister showed
Bashful sincerity and comely love.

10. Curses, like chickens, always come home to roost.

11. As no roads are so rough as those which have just been mended, so no sinners are so intolerant as those that have just turned saints.

12. True friendship is like sound health, the value of it is seldom known until it is lost.

Exercises.

Let the student compare a man of integrity with a rock; and show the circumstances of resemblance.

Compare Life, with the Ocean.
" Adversity, with a storm.
" Affluence, with a fountain.
" the life of man with the leaves on the tree.
" Death with the falling of the leaf.
" Youth, with Spring.
" Manhood, with Summer.
" Old age, with Autumn.
" Death, with Winter.
" The reflection of light from the water, with the sparkling of the diamond.
" Wit and Humor with a volatile essence.
" The minds of the aged, with the tombs which they are approaching.
" The style of two writers; one with a convex mirror, scattering the light, — the other with the concave speculum, concentrating the rays to a focus.
" Departing blessings to the flight of birds.

XLI.

ANTITHESIS.

Antithesis is the counterpart of comparison, and is founded on the contrast or opposition of two objects. By contrast, objects opposed to each other appear in a stronger light, and their peculiar beauties or defects appear in bold relief.

Antitheses, like comparisons, must be subjected to some rules. They must take place between things of the same species. Substantives, attributes, qualities, faculties of the same kind, must be set in opposition. To constitute an antithesis between a man and a lion, virtue and hunger, figure and color, would be to form a contrast where there is no opposition. But to contrast one man with another, virtues with virtues, figures with figures, is pertinent and proper, because in these cases there must be striking opposition.

Antithesis makes the most brilliant appearance in the delineation of characters, particularly in history. The historian, in the performance of this delicate part of his task has a good opportunity for displaying his discernment and knowledge of human nature; and of distinguishing those nice shades by which virtues and vices run into one another. It is by such colors only that a character can be strongly painted, and antithesis is necessary to denote those distinctions.

Antithesis, also, by placing subjects in contrast, prompts the judgement; and is therefore a very common figure in argumentative writing.

Antithesis is also used with great advantage in descriptions or representations of the power and extent of a quality, as follows.

"I can command the lightnings, — and am dust."

Again. In the description of the power of the steam-engine, a late writer says: "The trunk of an elephant, that can pick up a pin or rend an oak, is as nothing to it. It can engrave a seal and crush masses of obdurate metal before it, — draw out, without breaking, a thread as fine as gossamer, and lift up a ship of war like a bauble in the air. It can embroider muslin and forge anchors, — cut steel into ribands, and impel loaded vessels against the fury of the winds and waves." *

Examples.

1. Behold my servants shall *eat*, but ye shall be hungry; behold my servants shall drink, but ye shall be *thirsty;* behold my servants shall *rejoice*, but ye shall be *ashamed.*

2. *Religion and Superstition, contrasted.*

Religion is the offspring of Truth and Love, and the parent of Benevolence, Hope and Joy. Superstition is the child of

* The author of Lacon very justly remarks: "To extirpate antithesis from literature altogether, would be to destroy at one stroke about eight tenths of all the wit, ancient and modern, now existing in the world. It is a figure capable not only of the greatest wit, but sometimes of the greatest beauty, and sometimes of the greatest sublimity."

Discontent, and her children are Fear and Sorrow. The former invites us to the moderate enjoyment of the world, and all its tranquil and rational pleasures. The latter teaches us only that man was born to mourn and to be wretched. The former invites us to the contemplation of the various beauties of the globe, which heaven has destined for the seat of the human race; and proves to us that a world so exquisitely framed could not be meant for the abode of misery and pain. The latter exhorts us to retire from the world, to fly from the enchantments of social delight, and to consecrate the hours to solitary lamentation. The former teaches us that to enjoy the blessings sent by our benevolent Creator is virtue and obedience. The latter informs us that every enjoyment is an offence to the Deity, who is to be worshipped only by the mortification of every sense of pleasure, and the everlasting exercise of sighs and tears.

3. Though deep, yet clear, though gentle, yet not dull.
Strong without rage, without o'erflowing, full.

4. Knowledge and Wisdom, far from being one,
Have oft-times no connection. Knowledge dwells
In heads replete with thoughts of other men;
Wisdom in minds attentive to their own.
Knowledge, a rude, unprofitable mass,
The mere materials with which Wisdom builds,
Till smoothed and squared, and fitted to its place,
Does but encumber whom it seems to enrich.
Knowledge is proud that he has learned so much;
Wisdom is humble that he knows no more.

5. An upright minister asks *what* recommends a man; a corrupt minister asks *who* recommends him.

6. When the million applaud, you ask what *harm* you have done; when they censure you, what *good.*

7. Contemporaries appreciate the man rather than the merit; but posterity will regard the merit rather than the man.

8. Contrasted faults through all his manners reign,
Though poor, luxurious; though submissive, vain,
Though grave, yet trifling; zealous, yet untrue,
And e'en in penance planning sins anew.

The student may now write a list of subjects in pairs which can be presented in antithesis, and present one or more of them accordingly.

XLII.

PARALLEL.

A parallel, considered as a composition, is a kind of comparison made to exhibit the resemblance between two characters or writings, to show their conformity as it is continued through many particulars, or in essential points. The parallel is sometimes diversified by antitheses, to show in a strong light the points of individual distinction.

Example 1st.

PARALLEL BETWEEN POPE AND DRYDEN.

Pope professed to have learned his poetry from Dryden, whom, whenever an opportunity was presented, he praised through his whole life with unvaried liberality; and perhaps his character may receive some illustration if he be compared with his master.

Integrity of understanding, and nicety of discernment, were not allotted in a less proportion to Dryden than to Pope. The rectitude of Dryden's mind was sufficiently shown by the dismission of his poetical prejudices, and the rejection of unnatural thoughts and rugged numbers. But Dryden never desired to apply all the judgment that he had. He wrote, and professed to write, merely for the people; and when he pleased others he contented himself. He spent no time in struggles to rouse latent powers; he never attempted to make that better which was already good, nor often to mend what he must have known to be faulty. He wrote, as he tells us, with very little consideration; when occasion or necessity called upon him, he poured out what the present moment happened to supply and when once it had passed the press, ejected it from his mind; for when he had no pecuniary interest, he had no further solicitude.

Pope was not content to satisfy; he desired to excel, and therefore always endeavored to do his best; he did not court the candor, but dared the judgment of his reader, and, expecting no indulgence from others, he showed none to himself. He examined lines and words with minute and punctilious observation, and retouched every part with indefatigable diligence, till he had left nothing to be forgiven. For this reason he kept his pieces very long in his hands, while he considered and reconsidered them. The only poems which can be supposed to have been written with such regard to the times as might hasten their publication, were the two satires of Thirty-eight; of which Dodsley told me, that they were brought to him by the author, that they might be fairly copied. "Every line," said he, "was then written twice over; I gave him a clean transcript, which he sent some time afterwards to me for the press, with every line written twice over a second time."

His declaration, that his care for his works ceased at their publication, was not strictly true. His parental attention never abandoned them; what he found amiss in the first edition, he silently corrected in those that followed. He appears to have revised the Iliad, and freed it from some of its imperfections; and the Essay on Criticism received many improvements after its first appearance. It will seldom be found that he altered without adding clearness, elegance, or vigor. Pope had perhaps the judgment of Dryden; but Dryden certainly wanted the diligence of Pope.

In acquired knowledge, the superiority must be allowed to Dryden, whose education was more scholastic, and who, before he became an author, had been allowed more time for study, with better means of information. His mind has a larger range, and he collects his images and illustrations from a more extensive circumference of science. Dryden knew more of man in his general nature, and Pope in his local manners. The notions of Dryden were formed by comprehensive speculation, and those of Pope by minute attention. There is more dignity in the knowledge of Dryden, and more certainty in that of Pope. Poetry was not the sole praise of either, for both excelled likewise in prose; but Pope did not borrow his prose from his predecessor. The style of Dryden is capricious and varied; that of Pope is cautious and uniform. Dryden obeys the motions of his own mind, Pope constrains his mind to his own rules of composition. Dryden is sometimes vehement and rapid, Pope is always smooth, uniform, and gentle. Dryden's page is a natural field, rising into inequalities, and diversified by the varied exuberance of abundant vegetation; Pope's is a velvet lawn, shaven by the scythe, and levelled by the roller.

Of genius, that power which constitutes a poet; that quality without which judgment is cold, and knowledge is inert; that energy which collects, combines, amplifies, and animates; the superiority must, with some hesitation, be allowed to Dryden. It is not to be inferred, that of this poetical vigor Pope had only a little, because Dryden had more; for every other writer, since Milton, must give place to Pope; and even of Dryden it must be said, that if he has brighter paragraphs, he has not better poems. Dryden's performances were always hasty, either excited by some external occasion, or extorted by domestic necessity; he composed without consideration, and published without correction. What his mind could supply at call, or gather in one excursion, was all that he sought, and all that he gave. The dilatory caution of Pope enabled him to condense his sentiments, to multiply his images, and to accumulate all that study might produce, or chance might supply. If the flights of Dryden, therefore, are higher, Pope continues longer on the wing. If of Dryden's fire the blaze is brighter, of Pope's the heat is more regular and constant. Dryden often surpasses expectation, and Pope never falls below it. Dryden is read with frequent astonishment, and Pope with perpetual delight.

This parallel will, I hope, where it is well considered, be founa just and if the reader should suspect me, as I suspect myself, of some partial fondness for the memory of Dryden, let him not too hastily condemn me for meditation and inquiry may, perhaps, show him the reasonableness of my determination.

Example 2d.

PARALLEL BETWEEN JAY AND HAMILTON.

It were, indeed, a bold task to venture to draw into comparison the rela ve merits of Jay and Hamilton on the fame and fortunes of their country, — a bold task, — and yet, bold as it is, we feel impelled at least to venture on opening it. They were undoubtedly *par nobile fratrum*, and yet not *twin* brothers, — *pares sed impares*, — like, but unlike. In patriotic attach ment equal, for who would venture therein to assign to either the superi ority? yet was that attachment, though equal in degree, far different in kind; with Hamilton it was a sentiment, with Jay a principle; with Hamil ton, enthusiastic passion, with Jay, duty as well as love; with Hamilton, patriotism was the paramount law, with Jay, a law *sub graviori lege.* Either would have gone through fire and water to do his country service, and laid down freely his life for her safety, Hamilton with the roused cour age of a lion, Jay with the calm fearlessness of a man; or, rather, Hamil ton's courage would have been that of a soldier, Jay's, that of a Christian Of the latter it might be truly said:

> "Conscience made him firm,
> That boon companion, who her strong breastplate
> Buckles on him, that fears no guilt within,
> And bids him on, and fear not."

In intellectual power, in depth, and grasp, and versatility of mind, as well as in all the splendid and brilliant parts which captivate and adorn, Hamilton was greatly, not to say immeasurably, Jay's superior. In the calm and deeper wisdom of practical duty, in the government of others, and still more in the government of himself, in seeing clearly the right, and following it whithersoever it led firmly, patiently, self-denyingly, Jay was again greatly if not immeasurably, Hamilton's superior. In statesman-like talent, Hamil ton's mind had in it more of "constructive" power, Jay's of "executive." Hamilton had GENIUS, Jay had WISDOM. We would have taken Hamilton to plan a government, and Jay to carry it into execution; and in a court of law we would have Hamilton for our advocate, if our cause were gener ous, and Jay for judge, if our cause were just.

The fame of Hamilton, like his parts, we deem to shine brighter and far ther than Jay's, but we are not sure that it should be so, or rather we are quite sure that it should not. For, when we come to examine and compare their relative course, and its bearing on the country and its fortunes, the reputation of Hamilton we find to go as far beyond his practical share in it, as Jay's falls short of his. Hamilton's civil official life was a brief and single, though brilliant one. Jay's numbered the years of a generation, and exhausted every department of diplomatic, civil, and judicial trust. In fidelity to their country, both were pure to their heart's core; yet was Hamilton loved, perhaps, more than trusted, and Jay trusted, perhaps, more than loved.

Such were they, we deem, in differing, if not contrasted, points of char acter. Their lives, too, when viewed from a distance, stand out in equally striking but much more painful contrast. Jay's, viewed as a whole, has in it a completeness of parts such as a nicer critic demands for the perfection of an epic poem, with its beginning of promise, its heroic middle, and its peaceful end, and partaking, too, somewhat of the same cold stateliness noble, however, still, and glorious, and ever pointing, as such poem does, to the stars. *Sic itur ad astra.* The life of Hamilton, on the other hand, broken and fragmentary, begun in the darkness of romantic interest, running on into the sympathy of a high passion, and at length breaking off in the midst, like some half-told tale of sorrow, amid tears and blood, even as does the theme of the tragic poet. The name of Hamilton, therefore, was a name to conjure with; that of Jay, to swear by. Hamilton had his frailties, arising out of passion, as tragic heroes have. Jay's name was faultless, and his course passionless, as becomes the epic leader, and, in point of fact, was, while living, a name at which frailty blushed, and corruption trembled.

If we ask whence, humanly speaking, came such disparity of the fate between equals, the stricter morals, the happier life, the more peaceful death, to what can we trace it but to the healthful power of religion over the heart and conduct? Was not this, we ask, the ruling secret? Hamilton was a Christian in his youth, and a penitent Christian, we doubt not, on his dying bed; but Jay was a Christian, so far as man may judge, every day and hour of his life. He had but one rule, the gospel of Christ; in that he was nurtured, — ruled by that, through grace, he lived, — resting on that, in prayer, he died.

Admitting, then, as we do, both names to be objects of our highest sympathetic admiration, yet, with the name of Hamilton, as the master says of tragedy, the lesson is given "with pity and in fear." Not so with that of Jay; with him we walk fearless, as in the steps of one who was a CHRISTIAN as well as a PATRIOT.

Exercises.

A Parallel between the Old and New Testament.
" between the writings of St. Paul and St. John.
" The character of Napoleon and of Washington
" Lord Bacon and Sir Isaac Newton.
" The Profession of the Law and that of Divinity.
" The invention of the art of printing with the discovery of the application of steam to mechanical purposes.

XLIII.

ALLEGORY

Allegory * is a species of writing, in which one thing is ex-

* Dr. Blair says, "An allegory is a continued metaphor; as it is the representation of one thing by another that resembles it." And under the head of metaphor he says, "When the resemblance which is the foundation of this figure is long dwelt upon, and carried into all its minute circumstances, an allegory is produced instead of a metaphor."

pressed, and another is understood. The analogy is intended to be so obvious that the reader cannot miss the application; but he is left to draw the proper conclusion for his own use.

It is, for this reason, chiefly employed when a writer desires to communicate some important intelligence or advice; but is not permitted, or does not wish, to deliver it in plain terms. It is also used for ornament, or to convey instruction, so as to interest the imagination, and flatter the understanding, by giving the reader the appearance of instructing himself

Allegories are of three kinds: first, those designed for ornament; secondly, those designed for instruction; and, thirdly, those intended both to adorn and instruct. In employing allegories, care must be taken that the phraseology be all figurative, and that the attributes of the primary and secondary object be not confounded and interchanged.

Example 1*st.* *

PATIENCE, AN ALLEGORY.

Patience was the child of Forbearance and Gentleness, and they lived in the town of Perseverance. When very young, she began to exercise that virtue which was afterwards named from her. She was a very extraordinary child, and it has ever been said of her, that she could work all things. She had an aunt called Adversity, who troubled her very much, but, it was observed, that the more she was subjected to the trials of this relation, the more brightly the lustre of her character shone forth; for, while her uncle, Prosperity, was near her, she seemed to have no opportunity of exercising her graces. She had a grandmother, (on her mother's side,) named Meekness, and she seemed to imbibe many of

---

* This allegory was written by one of the pupils of the school under the charge of the author. It is presented just as it was written by the young lady, who, though but "just in her teens," has certainly sustained the figure throughout in excellent "*keeping*."

As instances of the allegory, which may be studied and imitated, may be mentioned, "The Hill of Science," and, "The Journey of a Day, a Picture of Human Life," by Johnson; "An Eastern Narrative," by Hawksworth, entitled, "No Life pleasing to God which is not useful to Man;" "The Eightieth Psalm of David;" No. 55 of the "Spectator;" and "The Pilgrim's Progress," which is, perhaps, the longest allegory ever written. To these may be added a very recent little work of Charles Dickens, entiled, "A Christmas Carol," which cannot be too highly commended for the moral lesson which it conveys.

the qualities of that excellent lady. She also had a grandfather, Goodness, whose blood seemed to run in her veins in a large degree. All who lived in her neighborhood used to say, that she was the loveliest child they ever beheld. But, although so much admired, she had no Pride about her, though Vanity, an old man living in the vicinity, used to lay a claim to relationship with her. She was very much troubled by his daughters, Selfconceit and Foolishness, but she never retorted in the least. Even they themselves could not say, that they had ever heard an angry word proceed from her lips, and, although they tried to disturb and ruffle her uniform good nature, they never could succeed so far, as even to be able to say, that she ever appeared to cherish a wrathful spirit. She had no Hatred about her, neither would she foster Spite or Malice in her innocent heart. She made rapid advances from day to day, in every good word and work, and her name even became a proverb among all who knew her. Mothers made her an example to their daughters, and fathers did not forget her when admonishing their sons. She became more beloved and respected every day of her life, by all, for no one could see her without admiring her for her many good qualities. She appeared to be compounded of all the qualities that adorn the female character, without the least mixture of anything bad. In due time she was married to a young gentleman, by the name of Longsuffering. Some of the most distinguished among her children were Faith, Hope, and Charity.

Example 2d.

THE EMPIRE OF POETRY.

BY FONTENELLE.

This empire is a very large and populous country. It is divided, like some of the countries on the continent, into the higher and lower regions. The upper region is inhabited by grave, melancholy and sullen people, who, like other mountaineers, speak a language very different from that of the inhabitants of the valleys. The trees in this part of the country are very tall, having their tops among the clouds. Their horses are superior to those of Barbary, being fleeter than the winds. Their women are so beautiful as to eclipse the star of day.

The great city which you see in the maps, beyond the lofty mountains, is the capital of this province, and is called Epic. It is built on a sandy and ungrateful soil, which few take the trouble to cultivate. The length of the city is many days' journey, and it is otherwise of a tiresome extent. On leaving its gate, we always meet with men who are killing one another; whereas, when we pass through Romance, which forms the suburbs of

Epic, and which is larger than the city itself, we meet with groups of happy people, who are hastening to the shrine of Hymen. The Mountains of Tragedy are also in the province of Upper Poetry. They are very steep, with dangerous precipices: and, in consequence, many of its people build their habitations at the bottom of the hills, and imagine themselves high enough. There have been found on these mountains some very beautiful ruins of ancient cities; and, from time to time, the materials are carried lower down to build new cities; for they now never build nearly so high as they seem to have done in former times. The Lower Poetry is very similar to the swamps of Holland. Burlesque is the capital, which is situated amidst stagnant pools. Princes speak there as if they had sprung from the dung hill, and all the inhabitants are buffoons from their birth.

Comedy is a city which is built on a pleasant spot, but it is too near to burlesque, and its trade with this place has much degraded the manners of its citizens.

I beg that you will notice, on the map, those vast solitudes which lie between High and Low Poetry, They are called the deserts of Common Sense. There is not a single city in the whole of this extensive country, and only a few cottages scattered at a distance from one another. The interior of the country is beautiful and fertile, but you need not wonder that there are so few who choose to reside in it; for the entrance is very rugged on all sides; the roads are narrow and difficult; and there are seldom any guides to be found, who are capable of conducting strangers.

Besides, this country borders on a province where every person prefers to remain, because it appears to be very agreeable, and saves the trouble of penetrating into the Deserts of Common Sense. It is the Province of False Thoughts. Here we always tread on flowers, — every thing seems enchanting. But its greatest inconvenience is, that the ground is not solid; the foot is always sinking in the mire, however careful one may be. Elegy is the Capital. Here the people do nothing but complain; but it is said that they find a pleasure in their complaints. The city is surrounded with woods and rocks, where the inhabitant walks alone, making them the confidants of his secrets; of the discovery of which he is so much afraid, that he often conjures those woods and rocks never to betray them.

The Empire of Poetry is watered by two rivers. One is the River Rhyme, which has its source at the foot of the Mountains of Reverie. The tops of some of these mountains are so elevated, that they pierce the clouds. Those are called the Points of Sublime Thought. Many climb there by extraordinary efforts; but almost the whole tumble down again, and excite, by their fall, the ridicule of those who admired them at first without knowing why. There are large platforms, almost at the bottom of these mountains, which are called the Terraces of Low Thoughts. There are always a great number of people walking upon them. At the end of these terraces are the Caverns of Deep Reverie. Those who descend into them do so insensibly; being so much enwrapt in their meditations, that they enter the caverns before they are aware. These caverns are perfect labyrinths, and the difficulty of getting out again could scarcely be believed by those who have not been there. Above the terraces we sometimes meet with men walking in easy paths, which are termed the Paths of Natural Thoughts; and these gentlemen ridicule, equally, those who try to scale the Points of Sublime Thoughts, as well as those who grovel on the terraces below. They would be in the right, if they could keep undeviatingly in the Paths of Natural Thoughts; but they fall almost instantly into a snare, by entering into a splendid palace, which is at a very little distance. It is the Palace of Badinage. Scarcely have they entered, when, in place of the natural thoughts which they formerly had, they dwell upon such only as are mean and vulgar. Those, however, who never abandon the Paths of Natural Thoughts, are the most rational of all. They aspire no higher than they ought, and their thoughts are never at variance with sound judgment.

Besides the River Rhyme, which I have described as issuing from the foot of the mountains, there is another called the River of Reason. These two rivers are at a great distance from one another, and, as they have a very different course, they could not be made to communicate, except by canals, which would cost a great deal of labor. For these canals of communication could not be formed at all places, because there is only one part of the River Rhyme which is in the neighborhood of the River Reason, and hence many cities situated on the Rhyme, such as Roundelay and Ballad, could have no commerce with the Reason, whatever pains might be taken for that purpose. Further, it would be necessary that these canals should cross the Deserts of Common Sense, as you will see by the map; and that it is almost an unknown country. The Rhyme is a large river, whose course is crooked and unequal, and, on account of its numerous falls, it is extremely difficult to navigate. On the contrary, the Reason is very straight and regular, but it does not carry vessels of every burthen.

There is, in the Land of Poetry, a very obscure forest, where the rays of the sun never enter. It is the forest of Bombast. The trees are close, spreading, and twined into each other. The forest is so ancient, that it has become a sort of sacrilege to prune its trees, and there is no probability that the ground will ever be cleared. A few steps into this forest and we lose our road without dreaming that we have gone astray. It is full of imperceptible labyrinths, from which no one ever returns. The Reason is lost in this forest.

The extensive province of Imitation is very sterile. It produces nothing. The inhabitants are extremely poor, and are obliged to glean in the richer fields of the neighboring provinces; and some even make fortunes by this beggarly occupation. The Empire of Poetry is very cold towards the north, and, consequently, this quarter is the most populous. There are the cities of Anagram and Acrostic, with several others of a similar description Finally, in that sea which bounds the States of Poetry, there is the Island of Satire, surrounded with bitter waves. The salt from the water is very strong and dark colored. The greater part of the brooks of this Island resemble the Nile in this, that their sources are unknown; but it is particularly remarkable, that there is not one of them whose waters are fresh. A part of the same sea is called the Archipelago of Trifles. The French term it L'Archipel des Bagatelles, and their voyagers are well acquainted with those islands. Nature seems to have thrown them up in sport, as she did those of the Ægean Sea. The principal islands are the Madrigal, the Song, and the Impromptu. No lands can be lighter than those islands, for they float upon the waters.

Example 3d.

A humming bird once met a butterfly, and being pleased with the beauty of its person and the glory of its wings, made an offer of perpetual friendship.

I cannot think of it, was the reply, as you once spurned me, and called me a drawling dolt.

Impossible, cried the humming bird; I always entertained the highest respect for such beautiful creatures as you. Perhaps you do now, said the other; but, when you insulted me, I was a caterpillar. So let me give you this piece of advice: Never insult the humble, as they may one day become your superiors.

Exercises.

What subject can be illustrated by an allegory with the following **hints or aids?**

Aids.—A hill with multitudes ascending.
The temptations assailing those who are endeavoring to ascend it
The temple on the top of the hill.
The failure of many who attempt to reach it.
The labors of those who do finally succeed — their success and happiness.

What subject, by an allegory with the following?

Aids. — A wide sea or ocean.
Vessels of various kinds variously decked.
Their similar destination for the same port.
The various objects of their several pursuits on the voyage
The straight and direct course kept by one single vessel.
The wreck or capture, or distress of the other vessels.
The safe arrival of the vessel which kept the direct course.

What subject by an allegory with the following?

Aids.—A foot race.
The preparations of the competitors.
The rewards offered to the victors.
The influence of those rewards on their exertions.
The course of the unsuccessful competitors.
The success of the victorious one, and the modes in which it was obtained.

XLIV.

APOLOGUE AND FABLE.

An apologue is a sort of allegorical fiction, from which a separate meaning or moral lesson may be drawn. It is, in fact, but another name for a fable, in which animals, vegetables, stocks and stones, speak and act as monitors to mankind.

An apologue, or fable, differs from a tale, in being written expressly for the sake of the moral. If there be no moral, there is no fable *

A parable is a fable, but is more generally used to denominate those allegorical tales in Scripture, which were introduced for the purpose of illustrating some truth to which they have a similitude. Such is that of "The Prodigal Son," "The Sower," "The Ten Virgins."

---

* The word *fable* is used here in a confined sense, for, generally speaking all literary fabrications are fables. There are few modern fables that are sufficiently concise. Those of Gay often lengthen into tales, or lose themselves in allegory.

An apologue differs from a parable in this: the parable is drawn from events which pass among mankind, and is therefore supported by probability; an apologue may be founded on supposed actions of brutes, or inanimate things, and therefore does not require to be supported by probability. Æsop's "Fables" are good examples of apologues.

Example.

APOLOGUE.

Sicily addressed Neptune praying to be rejoined to Italy: "You are foolish," answered the god, "if you do not know how much better it is to be a small head, than a great foot." *

Example.

FABLE.

The Belly and the Members.

In former days, when the Belly and the other parts of the body enjoyed the faculty of speech, and had separate views and designs of their own each part, it seems, in particular for himself and in the name of the whole, took exceptions at the conduct of the Belly, and were resolved to grant him supplies no longer. They said they thought it very hard, that he should lead an idle, good-for-nothing life, spending and squandering away upon his ungodly self all the fruits of their labor; and that, in short, they were resolved for the future to strike off his allowance and let him shift for himself as well as he could. The Hands protested that they would not lift up a Finger to keep him from starving; and the Mouth wished he might never speak again, if he took the least bit of nourishment for him as long as he lived; "and," said the Teeth, "may we be rotted, if ever we chew a morsel for him for the future." This solemn league and covenant was kept as long as any thing of that kind can be kept; which was until each of the rebel members pined away to skin and bone, and could hold out no longer. Then they found there was no doing without the Belly, and that, as idle and insignificant as he seemed, he contributed as much to the maintenance and welfare of the other parts, as they did to his.

Application, or Moral.

This fable was related by Menenius Agrippa to the Romans, when they revolted against their rulers. It is easy to see how the fable was applied, for, if the branches and members of a community refuse the government that aid which its necessities require, the whole must perish together. Every man's enjoyment of the products of his own daily labor depends upon the government's being maintained in a condition

* Italy, in its shape, resembles a *boot.* The point in this apologue consists in the allusion to the form of the country.

to defend and secure him in it. The fable will apply with equal force to the murmurs of the poor against the rich. If there were no rich to consume the products of the labors of the poor, none by whom public charity might "keep her channels full," the poor would derive but little fruit from their labor.

XLV.

RIDDLE, OR ENIGMA

An enigma, or riddle, is an obscure speech, or saying, in a kind of allegorical form, and written either in prose or verse, designed to exercise the mind in discovering a hidden meaning; or, it is a dark saying, in which some known thing is concealed under obscure language which is proposed to be guessed.

Example.

'T was whispered in heaven, 't was muttered in hell,
And Echo caught faintly the sound as it fell:
On the confines of earth 't was permitted to rest,
And the depths of the ocean its presence confessed,
'T will be found in the sphere, when 't is riven asunder
Be seen in the lightning, and heard in the thunder.
'T was allotted to man with his earliest breath,
Attends at his birth, and awaits him in death;
It presides o'er his happiness, honor, and health,
Is the prop of his house, and the end of his wealth.
Without it the soldier, the seaman, may roam,
But woe to the wretch who expels it from home.
In the whispers of conscience its voice will be found,
Nor e'en in the whirlwind of passion be drowned·
'T will not soften the heart, and though deaf to the ear,
'T will make it acutely and instantly hear.
But in shade let it rest, like a delicate flower,
Or breathe on it softly, — it dies in an hour. *

* The thing described or hidden in this enigma, and which is proposed

Comparisons, proverbial speeches, parables, and fables, may be easily converted the one into the other. Thus, "The miser is like the dog in the manger, who would neither eat the hay himself, nor suffer the hungry ox to eat it." This comparison may be converted into a fable as follows: "A dog was lying upon a manger full of hay. An ox, being hungry, came near, and offered to eat of the hay; but the envious, ill-natured cur, getting up and snarling at him, would not suffer him to touch it. Upon which, the ox in the bitterness of his heart, exclaimed, A curse light on thee, for a malicious wretch, who will neither eat the hay thyself, nor suffer others who are hungry to do it." A proverb may be extracted from this fable: "The envious man distresses himself in the consideration of the prosperity of others."

XLVI.

CHARADE.*

A charade is a syllabic enigma; that is, an enigma, the subject of which is a name or word, that is proposed for

---

to be guessed, is *the letter H.* The letter *M* is concealed in the following Latin enigma by an unknown author of very ancient date:

"Ego sum principium mundi et finis seculorum;
Ego sum trinus et unus, et tamen non sum Deus."

The letter *E* is thus enigmatically described:

"The beginning of eternity,
The end of time and space,
The beginning of every end,
And the end of every place."

The celebrated riddle of the Sphinx, in classic story, was this: "What animal walks on four legs in the morning, on two at noon, and on three in the evening?"

The answer is *Man*, who, in infancy or the morning of life, walks or creeps on his hands and feet, at the noon of life he walks erect, and in the evening of his days, or in old age, supports his infirmities on a staff.

* Nearly allied to the enigma and charade are the rebus, the paronomasia or pun, and the "low conundrum." [*See Catachresis.*] They are mere plays upon words, and are scarcely worthy of consideration among the departments of grave composition. The Rebus approaches, or rather is, in fact, picture writing, or a representation of words by things It is an enigmatical representation of some name, by using figures or pictures instead of words. The word is from the Latin language, and literally signifies, *by things.* Thus a gallant in love with a woman named Rose Hill, painted on the border of his gown *a rose, a hill, an eye, Cupid* or *Love*, and *a well*, which reads "*Rose Hill I love well.*" On a monumental tablet in the

discovery from an enigmatical description of its several syllables, taken separately, as so many individual words, and afterwards combined. A charade may be in prose or verse.

---

vicinity, erected for a family of the name of *Vassol*, there is the representation of a *vase* or *cup* (in Latin, *vas*), and the *sun* (in Latin, *sol*), thus forming the name "*Vassol.*" This is similar to one form of the hieroglyphics of the ancient Egyptians.

The Paronomasia, or Pun, is a verbal allusion in consequence of words of similar sound, or of the same orthography, having different meanings; or it is an expression in which two different applications of a word present an odd or ludicrous idea. It is generally esteemed a low species of wit. Thus, man having a tall wife named *Experience* observed that "He had by *long experience* proved the blessings of a married life." Another having undertaken to make a *pun* upon any given *subject*, when it was proposed that he should make one on the King, replied, that "the King is not a *subject*. That *Majesty*, if stripped of its externals, would remain *a jest.*"

Puns are sometimes expressed in verse, and appear among collections of Epigrams. (See *Epigram.*) For example,

"I cannot move," yon clamorous beggar cries,
"Nor sit, nor stand;" if he says *true*, he *lies.*

Again:

When dressed for the evening, the girls now-a-days
Scarce an atom of dress on them leave;
Nor blame them; for what is an *evening* dress
But a dress that is suited for *Eve?*

Conundrums are the lowest species of verbal witticisms, and are in general a mere play upon the *sounds* of words, without reference to their signification. They are generally expressed in the form of a question, with an answer. Thus: When is a ship not a ship? *Answer.* When it is *a-ground*, or when it is *a-float.* When is a door not a door? *Answer.* When it is *a-jar.* What part of an animal is his *elegy? Answer.* His *L E G.* If you were in an upper chamber of a house on fire, and the stairs were *a way*, how would you get down? *Answer.* By the stairs. If a demon had lost his tail, where would he go to have it replaced? *Answer.* To the place where they *retail* bad spirits. If a hungry man, on coming home to dinner, should find nothing but *a beet* on the table, what common exclamation would he utter? *Answer.* That *beat's* all.

Such plays upon the sounds of words, without reference to their signification, however they may amuse a vacant hour, or exercise the ingenuity of those to whom they are proposed, can be considered in no other light than as undignified, not to say childish diversions.

Of the same character may those witticisms be considered, commonly denominated *jests* and *jokes.* It would be futile to attempt specimens of either of these kinds of pleasantries. They are so various in their nature, that no specimens can be given, which would convey any thing like a clear idea of their general character. It may be sufficient to observe, in general, that the jest is directed at the object; the joke is practised with the person, or on the person. One attempts to make a thing laughable, or ridiculous, by jesting about it, or treating it in a jesting manner; one attempts to excite good humor in others, or indulge it in one's self by joking with them. Jests are therefore seldom harmless; jokes are frequently allowable. Nothing is more easy to be made, nor more contemptible when made, than a jest upon a serious or sacred subject. "*Ne lude cum sacris*," is a maxim which cannot be too strongly impressed on every speaker and writer.

Examples.

My *first*, if you do, will increase,
My *second* will keep you from heaven;
My *whole*, such is human caprice,
Is seldomer taken than given.

Answer, *ad-vice.*

What is that which God never sees, kings see but seldom, and which we see every day?

Answer, *an equal.*

XLVII.

HYPERBOLE.

A writer, under the influence of strong excitement, sometimes uses extravagant expressions, which he does not intend shall be taken literally. Such expressions are called hyperbole.

Example 1st.

A rescued land
Sent up a shout of victory from the field,
That rocked her ancient mountains.

Example 2d.

The iron of itself, though heat red-hot,
Approaching near these eyes, would drink my tears,
And quench its fiery indignation,
Even in the matter of mine innocence.
Nay, after that, consume away in rust,
But for containing fire to harm mine eye.

Example 3d

I found her on the floor
In all the storm of grief, yet beautiful,

Pouring out tears at such a lavish rate,
That, were the world on fire, they might have drowned
The wrath of Heaven, and quenched the mighty ruin.*

Example 4th.

There has not been a sound to-day,
To break the calm of nature,
Nor motion, I might almost say,
Of life, or living creature; —
Of waving bough, or warbling bird,
Or cattle faintly lowing;
I could have half believed *I heard*
The leaves and blossoms growing.

Example 5th.

And there are many other things which Jesus did, the which, if they should be written every one, I suppose that even the world itself would not contain the books that should be written. — [*St. John's Gospel, last verse.*]

Hyperbole or Exaggeration is a remarkable feature of Eastern poetry. Mr. Moore, in his *Lalla Rookh*, has some extravagant instances, which may be pardoned in that work, written as it was in imitation of the Eastern style, but they should not be exhibited as objects of imitation. The following is one of the instances from Lalla Rookh:

"Yet, one relief this glance of former years
Brought, mingled with its pain, tears, floods of tears,
Long frozen at her heart, but now like rills
Let loose in Spring time from the snowy hills,
And gushing warm, after a sleep of frost,
Through valleys where their flow had long been lost."

Hyperbole ought to be very carefully as well as sparingly used; for it is requisite that the mind of the hearer, as well as that of the speaker, should be strongly excited, else it degenerates into *Bombast*. It is usually the flash of an overheated imagination, and is seldom consistent with the cold canons of criticism. — [*See Booth's Principles, p.* 138.]

* The reverse of Hyperbole or Exaggeration, is Liptotes or Diminution, which is a figure by which, in seeming to lessen, we increase the force of the expression. Thus, when we say, "The man is no fool," we are understood to assert that he is wise. "I cannot praise such conduct," means that I despise it.

XLVIII.

APOSTROPHE.

Apostrophe is the *turning off* from the regular course of the subject, to address some person or thing, real or imagin ary, living or dead.

Apostrophe is generally used to address living objects that are absent, — or dead objects with which we were familiar while they were in life. Some of its boldest efforts, however, exhaust the essence of personification, and call up and address the inanimate objects of nature.

Apostrophes addressed to the *imagination* are frequently extended to a considerable length; while those addressed to the passions must be short to correspond with the frame of the mind in which they are made.

Example 1st

APOSTROPHE OF PASSION.

Oh pardon me, thou piece of bleeding earth,
That I am meek and gentle with thy butchers!
Thou art the ruins of the noblest man
That ever lived in the tide of time.

Example 2d.

APOSTROPHE OF IMAGINATION. *

O thou Parnassus! whom I now survey,
Not in the phrensy of a dreamer's eye,
Not in the fabled landscape of a lay,
But soaring, snow-clad, through thy native sky
In the wild pomp of mountain majesty!
What marvel that I thus essay to sing?
The humblest of thy pilgrims, passing by,
Would gladly woo thine Echoes with his string,
Though from thy heights no more one Muse shall wave her wing.

---

* This Apostrophe is the production of Lord Byron, who has also presented another splendid example of the same kind, in his Apostrophe to the Ocean. Our own Percival, in his Apostrophe to the Sun, affords another example, which would do honor to the literature of any age or nation.

It may be remarked, that apostrophe is, on the whole, a figure too passionate to gain much admittance into any species of composition, except poetry and oratory.

XLIX.

INTERROGATION.

The unfigured and literal use of interrogation is to ask a question; but when men are strongly moved, they naturally put into the form of a question whatever they would affirm or deny with great earnestness. Thus: Canst thou draw out Leviathan with a hook, or his tongue with a cord that thou lettest down.* — He that planted the ear, shall he not hear.

Interrogation gives life and spirit to discourse. It may be used to rouse and waken the hearers — sometimes to command with great emphasis, and sometimes to denote plaintive passion. Cicero uses it with great effect in his oration against Cataline, which he thus commences:

"How long Cataline will you abuse our patience? Do you not perceive that your designs are discovered?" &c.

Example.

Can storied urn, or animated bust,
Back to its mansion call the fleeting breath?
Can honor's voice provoke the silent dust,
Or flattery soothe the dull, cold ear of death?

L.

REPETITION.

Repetition seizes some emphatical word, or phrase, and, to mark its importance, makes it recur frequently in the same

* The book of Job abounds in beautiful instances of this figure.

sentence. It is significant of contrast and energy. It also marks passion, which wishes to dwell on the object by which it is excited.

Example 1*st.*

"Weep not, oh Love!" she cries, "to see me bleed—
Thee, Gertrude's sad survivor, thee alone—
Heaven's peace commiserate; for scarce I heed
These wounds;—yet thee to leave is death, is death indeed

Example 2*d.*

By foreign hands thy dying eyes were closed,
By foreign hands thy decent limbs composed,
By foreign hands thy humble grave adorned,
By strangers honored and by strangers mourned.

Example 3*d.*

He sung Darius, great and good,
By too severe a fate,
Fallen, fallen, fallen, fallen,
Fallen from his high estate, and weltering in his blood.

LI.

EXCLAMATION.

Exclamations are the effect of strong emotions of the mind; such as surprise, admiration, joy, grief, and the like.

Example 1*st.*

Oh Liberty! oh sound once delightful to every Roman ear Oh sacred privilege of Roman citizenship!—once sacred, now trampled upon.

Example 2d.

Oh time! time! it is fit thou shouldst thus strike thy murderer to the heart! How art thou fled forever! A month Oh for a single week! I ask not for years! though an age were too little for the much I have to do!

LII.

VISION.

Vision, another figure of speech, proper only in animated and warm compositions, is produced, when, instead of relating something that is past, we use the present tense of the verb, and describe the action or event as actually now in sight.

In tragedy, vision is the language of the most violent passion which conjures up spectres, and approaches to insanity.

Example 1st.

[Cicero, in his fourth oration against Cataline, pictures to his mind the consummation of the conspiracy, as follows:]

I seem to myself to behold this city, the ornament of the earth, and the capital of all nations, suddenly involved in one conflagration. I see before me the slaughtered heaps of citizens, lying unburied in the midst of their ruined country. The furious countenance of Cethegus rises to my view, while, with a savage joy, he is triumphing in your miseries.

Example 2d.

Methought I heard a a voice
Cry, Sleep no more! Macbeth doth murder sleep.

Example 3d.

Avaunt and quit my sight!
Let the earth hide thee; thy bones are marrowless;

Thy blood is cold ; thou hast no speculation
In those eyes which thou dost stare with.
Hence, horrible shadow ; unreal mockery, hence!

LIII.

CLIMAX.

Climax consists in an artful exaggeration of all the circumstances of some object or action, which we wish to place in a strong light. It operates by a gradual rise of one circumstance above another, till our idea is raised to the highest pitch.

A speaker makes an assertion which he feels is not strong enough for his thought;—he adds another, and another, until he reaches that point which his mind contemplates to be sufficiently expressive; and then the climax (or *climbing*) ends.

Example 1st.

Boisterous in speech, in action prompt and bold,
He buys, he sells, he steals, he kills for gold.

Example 2d.

[The following is part of an address, in the case of a woman who was accused of murdering her own child.]

Gentlemen, if one man had any how slain another; if an adversary had killed his opposer; or a woman occasioned the death of her enemy; even these criminals would have been capitally punished by the Cornelian law. But, if this guiltless infant, who could make no enemy, had been murdered by its own nurse; what punishment would not the mother have demanded? With what cries and exclamations would she have stunned your ears? What shall we say, then, when a woman, guilty of homicide; a mother, of the murder of her innocent child, hath comprised all those misdeeds in one single crime; a crime, in its own nature detestable; in a woman prodigious; in a mother incredible; and perpetrated against one, whose age called for compassion; whose near relation claimed affection and whose innocence deserved the highest favor? *

* Such regular Climaxes, however, though they have great beauty, yet

Example 3d.

The cloud-capt towers, the gorgeous palaces,
The solemn temple, the great globe itself,
Yea, all that it inhabits, shall dissolve,
And, like the baseless fabric of a vision,
Leave not a wreck behind.

Example 4th.

When we have practised good actions awhile they become easy; and when they are easy, we begin to take pleasure in them; and when they please us, we do them frequently; and by frequency of acts they grow into a habit.

Example 5th.

And besides this, giving all diligence, add to your faith, virtue; and to virtue, knowledge; and to knowledge, temperance; and to temperance, patience; and to patience, godliness; and to godliness, brotherly kindness; and to brotherly kindness, charity

Example 6th.

It is a crime to put a Roman citizen in bonds; it is the height of guilt to scourge him; little less than parricide to put him to death; what name, then, shall I give to the act of crucifying him?

---

at the same time have the appearance of art and study; and, therefore, though they may be admitted into formal harangues, yet they are not the language of passion, which seldom proceeds by steps so regular.

Climax and Antithesis are sometimes united, as in the following

Example.

Pride still is aiming at the blest abodes,
Men would be angels, angels would be gods;
Aspiring to be gods, if angels fell,
Aspiring to be angels, men rebel.

Climax is nearly related to Hyperbole, and differs from it chiefly in degree. The purpose of Hyperbole is to exalt our conceptions beyond the truth: of Climax, to elevate our ideas of the truth itself, by a series of circumstances, ascending one above another in respect of importance, and all pointing toward the same object. This figure, when properly introduced and displayed, affords a very sensible pleasure. It accords with our disposition to enlarge our conceptions of any object that we contemplate; it affords a gratification similar to what we receive on ascending an eminence, situated in the centre of a rich and varied landscape, where every step we proceed presents a grander and more extensive prospect.

LIV.

ANTICLIMAX.

The descent from great things to small is termed anticlimax. It is the opposite of climax, and is found principally in ludicrous compositions.

Examples.

1. And thou, Dalhousie, the great god of war,
   Lieutenant-colonel to the Earl of Mar.

2. Under the tropic is our language spoke,
   And part of Flanders hath received our yoke.

LV.

ALLUSION.

Allusion is that figure by which some word or phrase in a sentence calls to mind, as if accidentally, another similar or analogous subject.

Allusions, though different in form from comparisons, are of the same nature, and their introduction depends on similar principles, Like comparisons, they are illustrative, and give us pleasure from the discovery of unexpected resemblances, or coincidences of thought or expression. In making allusions, care should always be taken, that what is alluded to should be generally known.*

Examples.

1. You cannot be to them "Vich Ian Vohr," and these

* The student who would see this figure beautifully illustrated, is referred to Newman's Rhetoric.

three magic words are the only "open sesame" to their feelings and sympathies.

[Here the words "*open sesame*" recall to mind *the charm* by which the robbers' dungeon, in the Arabian tale,* was opened.]

2. There are many religionists of the present day who make it their *shibboleth* to be able to tell the precise moment when the heart was converted to God. †

3. I was surrounded with difficulties, and possessed no *clue* by which I could effect my escape. ‡

[Exercises may readily be framed by the student who attentively considers the close remblance of this figure to Simile or Comparison.]

LVI.

IRONY.

Irony is the intentional use of words which express a sense contrary to that which the writer or speaker means to convey, as when we say of one unskilled in grammar, "Admirable grammarian!"

When irony is so strong as to be termed bitter or cutting, it is Sarcasm. Irony turns things into ridicule, in a peculiar manner; it consists in laughing at an individual, under the disguise of appearing to praise or speak well of him.

The proper subjects of irony are vices and follies of all kinds; and this mode of exposing them is often more effectual than serious reasoning. The figure is, however, sometimes used on the most solemn occasions, as will be seen by the following:

Example 1st.

Cry aloud, for he is a god: either he is talking, or he is pur-

---

* The Forty Thieves.

† See the Book of Judges, chapter xii., verses 5, 6.

‡ See the story of *Ariadne*, in Lempriere's Classical Dictionary. In the use of this figure (Allusion), it may be observed that the subject to which allusion is made, should be readily perceived, and that it recompense, by its beauty or its utility, the digression necessarily made in introducing it

suing, or he is on a journey, or peradventure he sleepeth, and must be awakened.

See 1 Kings, chapter xviii., verse 27.

Example 2d.

And Job answered and said, No doubt ye are the people, and wisdom shall die with you.

Example of Sarcasm.

In the name of common sense, why should the Duke of Bedford think that none but of the House of Russell are entitled to the favor of the crown? Why should he imagine, that no king of England has been capable of judging of merit but King Henry the Eighth? Indeed, he will pardon me; he is a little mistaken: all virtue did not end in the first Earl of Bedford; all discernment did not lose its vision when his Creator closed his eyes. Let him remit his rigor on the disproportion between merit and reward in others, and they will make no inquiry into the origin of his fortune. They will regard with much more satisfaction, as he will contemplate with infinitely more advantage, whatever his pedigree has been dulcified, by an exposure to the influence of heaven in a long flow of generations, from the hard, acidulous, metallic tincture of the spring. It is little to be doubted, that several of his forefathers, in that long series, have degenerated into honor and virtue.

— —

LVIII.

ALLITERATION.

Alliteration is the repetition of the same letter at the beginning of two or more words immediately succeeding each other, or at short intervals; as, bug-bear, sea-sick, and the *f* and *g* in the following line:

Fields ever fresh, and groves for ever green.

And the *l* in the following: Love laughs at locksmiths.

The return of such sounds, if not too frequent, is agreeable to the ear because the succeeding impression is made with less effort than that which precedes.

Alliteration, as well as rhyme, is useful as an aid to the memory. Hence proverbs have generally one or the other and sometimes both of these auxiliaries. Thus:

Birds of a feather
Flock together.

Fast bind,
Fast find.

The following are remarkable instances of alliteration:

The lordly lion leaves his lonely lair.

Begot by butchers, but by bishops bred,
How high his honor holds his haughty head.

How sweetly slow the liquid lay
In holy hallelujahs rose!

Let lords and ladies laugh and sing
As loudly and as light;
We beggars, too, can dance and fling
Dull care a distant flight.

Approach, thou, like the rugged Russian bear,
The armed rhinoceros, or the Hyrcan tiger, &c.

Round rugged rocks, rude, ragged rascals ran.

Lean liquid lays, like lightly lulling lakes, &c.

These instances are not presented as models for imitation, but rather as exemplifications of the meaning of the term alliteration. It will be sufficient to observe, that alliterations at the present day have fallen into disrepute; and with good reason, lest the writer in pursuit of them should be tempted to sacrifice sense to sound. Occasionally introduced, and sparingly used, they are not perhaps obnoxious to strong objections. Kames, in his "Elements of Criticism," says: "Where two ideas are so connected as to require only a copulative, it is pleasant to find a connexion in the words that express these ideas, were it even so slight as *where both begin with the same letter*. Thus: 'The peacock, in all his pride, does not display half the color that appears in the garments of a British lady when she is dressed either for *a ball, or a birth-day*.'—*Spectator*, No. 265. Again: 'Had not my log of a steward run away as he did, without making up his accounts, I had still been immersed in *sin* and *seacoal*.'—*Ibid*, No. 530.

"'My life's companion, and my bosom friend,
One faith, one fame, one fate shall both attend.'" *

The following is presented as a literary curiosity:

ALPHABETICAL ALLITERATION.

THE BUNKER HILL MONUMENT CELEBRATION

Americans arrayed and armed attend;
Beside battalions bold, bright beauties blend.

Exercises.

The student may change the terms in the following expressions, so as to present instances of alliteration. A word of similar meaning may, in each phrase or sentence, be substituted, so as to exemplify the figure.

The royal lion.
The songs of love.
The pride of the sons of kings.
One belief, one fame, one destiny shall attend both.
The flowing lays.
How the brilliant lake shines.
His proud head shall bow.
The deceitful tiger.
The heedful cat.
He forsakes his solitary lair.
By royal prelates commended.
In sacred hallelujahs listened to.
Let noblemen and high-born ladies laugh and sing.
Birds of the same plumage assemble together.
The falling towers with curling ivy bound.
Yet would the village commend my wondrous power.

And the blithe grandsire skilled in gestic lore
Has frisked beneath the load of fourscore.

LVIII.

PARAPHRASE OR EXPLANATION.

A *paraphrase* is an *explanation* of some maxim or passage in a book in a more clear and ample manner than is ex

---

Chiefs, clergy, citizens conglomerate,—
Detesting despots,—daring deeds debate.
Each eye emblazoned ensigns entertain,—
Flourishing from far,—fan freedom's flame.
Guards greeting guards grown grey,—guest greeting uest
High-minded heroes, hither, homeward, haste;
Ingenuous juniors join in jubilee,
Kith kenning kin,—kind knowing kindred key.
Lo, lengthened lines lend Liberty liege love,
Mixed masses marshalled, *Monumentward* move.
Note noble navies near;—no novel notion;
Oft, our oppressors overawed old Ocean;
Presumptuous princes, pristine patriots, paled,
Queen's quarrel questing quotas, quondam, quailed
Rebellion roused, revolting ramparts rose,
Stout spirits, smiting servile soldiers, strove.

These thrilling themes, to thousands truly told,
Usurpers' unjust usages unfold.
Victorious vassals, vauntings vainly veiled.
Where, whilsince, Webster, warlike Warren, wailed.

'Xcuse 'xpletives 'xtraqueer 'xpressed,
Yielding Yankee yeoman zest.

pressed in the words of the author. It is in fact a translation of the author's meaning into simpler language, accompanied with such explanations as will serve to render the passage easily intelligible. The author's words, therefore, are not so strictly followed as his sense.

Maxims, proverbs,* and texts of Scripture often contain much meaning in few words. To present them in a clear light, and to explain them in all their bearings, is the province of the preacher and the didactic writer; who thus calls in the paraphrase to their aid for the benefit of illustration.

Example 1st.

"*Ne sutor ultra crepidam.*"

"Let not the shoemaker go beyond his last." These were the words of Apelles to a Crispin, (a shoemaker) who properly found fault with an ill-painted slipper in one of the pictures of Apelles; but, ascending to other parts, betrayed the grossest ignorance. The proverb implies that no man should pass his opinion in a province of art, where he is without a qualification.

Example 2d.

Dionysius, the tyrant of Sicily, stripped the statue of Jupiter of a robe of massy gold, and substituted a cloak of wool, saying, Gold is too cold in winter, and too heavy in summer,—*It behoves us to take care of Jupiter.* From this incident we see that the first consideration with a knave, is how to help himself, and the second, how to do it with an appearance of helping others.

Example 3d.

A Scottish proverb says, "Cocks are free of horse-corn." This saying implies that people are liberal or profuse of what belongs to another.

Example 4th.

Use a cat to the churn, and she will call it custom. This

* A proverb is a short sentence, expressing a well-known truth or common fact, ascertained by experience or observation. A maxim is a principle generally received or admitted as true. It may here be remarked that proverbs, parables and fables are easily converted the one into the other.—[*See Booth's Principles, p.* 161.] It will be a useful exercise for the student to attempt to convert examples 3d and 4th below into a comparison and a fable.

proverb implies that if you accustom your servants or other folks, to make too frequent use of what is yours, they will think, at last, that they have acquired a right to it.

LIX.

OUTLINES IN NARRATIVE.

A simple story is here related, with outlines of the same story in different language, which the student may fill out so as to present the same story, with all the circumstances.

Examples.

When the city of Troy was taken by the Greeks, after the first fury of plunder was over, the conquerors, pitying the misfortunes of their captives caused it to be proclaimed, that every free citizen had the liberty of taking away any one thing which he valued most: upon which Æneas, neglecting every thing else, only carried away with him his household gods. The Greeks, delighted with his piety, gave him permission to carry away with him any other thing he had the greatest regard for; and immediately he took upon his shoulders his aged father, who had grown decrepit, and was carrying him out of the town. The Greeks, struck with his filial duty, gave him leave to take every thing that belonged to him; declaring that Nature itself would not suffer them to be enemies to such as shewed so great piety to the gods, and so great reverence to their parents.

The Outline.

The city of Troy ——— thirst for plunder was ——— made proclamation ——— that every free-born citizen ——— prized the most. Æneas disregarding ——— his household gods. The Greeks pleased ——— any other thing. ——— his aged and venerable father. The Greeks admiring ——— every thing that he ——— Nature itself ——— ungenerous ——— respect ——— filial regard ———.

The outline filled out.

The city of Troy *having been captured by the Greeks, when their* thirst for plunder was *partly satiated, commiserating the misfortunes of their captives they made* proclamation *throughout the unfortunate city that every free born citizen might select from the ruins any one thing which he* prized the most. Æneas, disregarding *his houses, his goods, and valuable possessions, took only his* household gods. The Greeks pleased *with his regard for the objects of his religious worship, gave him permission to add any* other thing *among his possessions to these objects of his primary regard; upon which he immediately took* his aged and venerable father *upon his shoulders, who, from the infirmities of age, was unable to escape without assistance. While the pious son wa thus carrying his father from the ruins,* the Greeks, admiring *his disinterested filial reverence for his helpless parent, gave him permission to add to what he had already taken,* every thing that he *owned, declaring that* Nature itself *would not permit them to be* ungenerous *to one who had exhibited such respect to the dead and such* filial regard *for the being to whom he owed his existence.*

Exercises.

1.

Sir William Gascoigne was the Chief Justice of England in the reign of Henry 4th. His presence of mind and his great dignity were most nobly exhibited when the Prince of Wales determined to rescue one of his servants, who was on trial before the Judge, presumed to interrupt and even to strike the Chief Justice. Gascoigne supported the character of his station against the bold aggression, and committed the prince to prison, to await the pleasure of the King his father. The King heard of the circumstance with becoming propriety, and thanked God that he had given him a judge who knew how to administer justice, and a son who could obey it.

Outline.

One of the servants of ——— was tried before ——— and condemned, notwithstanding all the interest ——— by the King's son. The Prince of Wales was so incensed ———. The judge ——— dignity of his ——— ordered ——— and the prince ——— insult he had offered ——— of the laws ——— quietly ——— gaol. The King his father ———. Happy is the King ——— courage to execute the laws ——— a son ——— submit.

2.

A painter was desirous of drawing an elephant in an unusual attitude with his trunk erect, and his mouth open; and, in order to induce the beast to show himself to more advantage, engaged a person to stand by, and throw fruit into his mouth. The person, however, partly to deceive the unsuspecting animal, often kept in his hand the fruit which he pretended to give to the elephant; who, not liking the mockery, and supposing the innocent painter to be the cause, threw out of his trunk such a quantity of water upon his paper, as entirely spoiled his sketch, and prevented him from proceeding in his work.

Outline.

An artist ——— uncommon ——— raised ——— open ——— procured ——— and loss ——— in order to make ——— advantageous ———. The foolish ——— deceive ——— amuse ——— ——— made ——— kept the fruit ———. The sagacious ——— not relishing ——— and believing ——— collected ——— which he discharged ——— entirely spoiling ——— and preventing ——— ———.

3.

A gentleman, residing at Gosport, England, was, when visiting Portsmouth, usually accompanied by his dog, in the ferry-boat. One day, it so happened, that the dog lost his master somewhere in Portsmouth, and surmising that he had re-crossed the water for Gosport, sped his way to the house of a bookseller in High street, and by every possible means intimated his misfortune. "What," exclaimed the shopman, "you have lost your master, have you? Well, here is a penny, for your fare across the water." The dog snatched up the coin, ran directly to Point Beach, dropped the penny into the hand of the waterman, and was ferried across with the other passengers.

A resident at ——— wherever he went ——— attended ——— ——— who ——— with him. ——— It chanced ——— was missing ——— and supposing ——— returned ——— speedily ——— and by ——— that instinct ———. Have you lost ——— ——— ? Well ——— some money ——— seizing ——— made ——— and paying ——— was conveyed ———.

LX.

CONNECTED NARRATIVE, FROM SCATTERED FACTS.

The selection of incidents to be presented in a narration or a description, requires some taste as well as judgment. The union of such incidents in a connected narrative is not altogether a mechanical exertion. The order of time should be strictly observed. Subordinate to the order of time, is the order of the circumstances themselves. It is perhaps a good general rule, as in the case of the arrangement of the members of a sentence, to reserve the most important for the last. But the application of this rule must be submitted to the taste and judgment, as well as the design of the writer.

Exercises.

1.

[The following particulars are presented to be united in a connected narrative. The expressions may be changed, as it may be necessary to weave the circumstances together in one continued narration.]

History furnishes no parallel to the character of Washington.

Washington died, after a short illness, on the 14th of December, 1799

He captured Lord Cornwallis at Yorktown, in 1781.

This event established the independence of the United States.

On the 25th of December, 1776, he crossed the Delaware, and soon gained the important battles of Trenton and Princeton.

He was elected President of the United States in 1789

He was President for eight years.

He was again chosen Commander-in-chief of the American army in 1798.

His abilities were first exercised by Dinwiddie in 1753.

He was the Aid-de-camp of Gen. Braddock in 1755.

After resigning the Presidency he retired to Mount Vernon, where he devoted himself to the pursuits of agriculture.

He was born in 1732, in the county of Fairfax, in Virginia.

He was descended from an English family, which emigrated from Cheshire about 1630.

He received his education from a private tutor

2.

William Penn lost his wife in 1694, and was much afflicted by the event.

He married again in about two years, and employed himself in travelling over Ireland as a preacher of the peculiar doctrines of his sect.

In 1699 he visited America with his wife and family, and returned to England in 1701.

He died at Rushcomb, near Twyford, in Berks, July 30th, 1718.

He was buried at Jordan, near Beaconsfield, Bucks.

His character was truly benevolent and humane, and his labors were exerted for the good of mankind.

The long prosperity of Pennsylvania furnishes the best evidence of his wisdom as a legislator.

He was born in London in 1644.

He was expelled from College on account of his religious opinions.

His religious opinions differed widely from those of the Established Church.

The College was of the same religious sentiments with the Established Church.

His father left him an estate worth 1500 pounds per annum.

Charles 2d, King of England, granted him a province of North America, then called New Netherlands; but now, from William Penn, called Pennsylvania.

When he was in College, he withdrew from the national forms of worship with other students, who, like himself, had listened to the preaching of Thomas Loe, a quaker of eminence.

In 1672 he married a lady of principles similar to his own, and fixed his residence at Rickmansworth, where he labored hard to disseminate the principles of his sect both by his preachings and his writings.

In 1682 he came out to America for the first time, and laid out the city of Philadelphia, where he invited settlers from all parts of England, and held out to them a greater degree of religious liberty under his constitution than had ever before been enjoyed by any sect or people.

LXI.

NARRATION EXPANDED.*

Example.

At the battle of Philippi, Lucilius wishing to give his intimate friend Brutus an opportunity to escape, pretended himself to be Brutus, and being led before Anthony, boldly avowed the artifice. Anthony, admiring his fidelity to his friend, informed him of the death of Brutus, and offered him his friendship. Lucilius accepted the offer, and continued his faithful friend.

Same story expanded.

At the battle of Philippi, when Brutus, after the route of his army, was in danger of falling into the hands of his enemies, his bosom friend Lucilius gave him an opportunity to escape, calling out, "I am Brutus! lead me to Anthony!" Being conducted to Anthony, he spoke with great resolution: "I have employed this artifice," said he, "that Brutus might not fall alive into the hands of his enemies. The gods will never permit that fortune shall triumph so far over virtue. In spite of fortune, Brutus will always be found, dead or alive, in a situation worthy of his courage." Anthony, admiring the firmness of Lucilius, said to him, "you merit a greater recompense than it is in my power to bestow. I have been just now informed of the death of Brutus; and as your fidelity to him is now at an end, I beg earnestly to be received in his place; love me as you did him, I wish no more." Luciluis embraced the offer, engaged himself

---

* The plan in narrative writing is simply the statement of events in the order of their occurrence; and the expansion is the mention, with varying degrees of minuteness of their statement, of the different circumstances connected with these events, accompanied by incidental remarks and reflections.

to Anthony, and maintaining the same fidelity to him that he had done to Brutus, adhered to him when he was abandoned by all the world.

The same story still more expanded.

After the second battle of Philippi between Anthony and Octavius, two of the Roman triumvirs, and Brutus, which proved fatal to the latter, and indeed, to the liberty of Rome, one Lucilius Lucinus, an intimate friend of Brutus, observing a body of Thracian horse taking no notice of any other in their pursuit, but making directly towards Brutus, resolved to stop them, and save the life of his general at the hazard of his own. Accordingly, without acquainting Brutus with his design, he halted till the Thracians came up and surrendered him; then he cried out, "I am Brutus!" and begging quarter, desired they would carry him to Anthony, pretending that he feared Octavius. The Thracians, overjoyed with their prey, and thinking themselves happy, immediately detached some of their own body to acquaint Anthony with their good fortune; and, in the mean time, giving over the pursuit, returned to the field of battle with their prisoner. The report being spread in an instant, all over the army, that Brutus was taken, and that the Thracians were bringing him alive to Anthony, both soldiers and officers flocked together from all parts to see him. Some pitied his misfortunes, others accused him of a meanness unbecoming his former glory, for, suffering himself out of two much love of life, to be a prey to barbarians. As for Anthony, he was not a little concerned at this adventure, being quite at a loss in what manner he should receive, and how he should treat his illustrious captive; but he was soon delivered from his uneasiness; for as the Thracians drew near, he knew the prisoner, who had passed himself upon the Thracians for Brutus, and now addressing the Triumvir with a generous confidence: "Be assured, Anthony," said he, "that no enemy either has or ever shall take Marcus Brutus alive; forbid it, ye Gods, that fortune should ever prevail so much above virtue! But let him be discovered, dead or alive, he will certainly be found in such a state as is worthy of him. As for me, I have delivered myself up to save him, and am now ready to suffer whatever torments you think proper to inflict upon me, without demanding or expecting any quarter." Anthony, wonderfully taken with the fidelity, virtue, and generosity of Lucilius, turned to the Thracians, now sensible of, and outraged at their disappointment, and addressed them thus: "I perceive, my fellow soldiers, that you are concerned, and full of resentment for having been thus imposed upon by Lucilius; but be assured, that you have met with a booty better than that you have sought for; you have been in search of an enemy, and you have brought me a friend. I was truly at a loss how I should have treated Brutus, if you had brought him to me alive; but of this I am sure, that it is better to have such a man as Lucilius our friend, than our enemy." Having thus spoken, he embraced Lucilius and commended him to the care of one of his friends.

The student may now expand the following story or narrative:

STORY OF MEGAN.

Megan was one of a tribe of Indians, who ranged the extensive wilds about the Falls of Niagara. He was possessed of such superior personal and mental qualities as are very seldom concentrated in the same person, generous and humane, as well as brave, he knew how to conquer a foe, and how to raise him when disarmed; and, while he hastened to shed the blood of his enemies, he paused to drop the tear of sympathy with afflicted friends. By these shining qualifications he was endeared to those around him, and was looked upon as a future ornament and champion of his tribe.

From the age in which he was able to bend a bow, he was ever employed, either in pursuit of game in the forest, or in showing his skill in the management of his canoe. His nation was now involved in a war, which opened to him a field of action, and afforded frequent opportunities to display his valor. In one of his excursions, he rescued from captivity a beautiful female of his nation, who had been taken some weeks before, and for whom he had conceived a passion, previously to her being taken

Their mutual attachment was not a little strengthened by this adventure; she was conducted home in triumph, a day was appointed for the nuptial ceremonies, and Megan looked forward with fond expectation to the happy days he should spend with his beloved Alcoris. But, alas! how often are the fairest hopes we can conceive, the most deceitful! A few days only had elapsed, since his return, when he yielded to a vice, that may be called a characteristic of these people; — he drank too freely of spirit and lay down in his canoe, which was fastened to a rock on shore, and was soon lost in sleep. Impatient at his too long absence, Alcoris went in search of him, and what was her surprise and horror, as she drew near the place, to see his canoe loosened by a rival, who had made several fruitless attempts to gain her affection, and rapidly floating down the swift current towards the great falls! In vain did she cry out, in vain extend her arms towards the dearest object of her affection. He enjoyed a sweet tranquillity till roused to a sense of his danger by the noise of the cataract. Megan is now apprised of his fate. He looks back, recognizes Alcoris, and waving his cap — goes over the falls and is seen no more.*

The student may now reverse the process of expanding, and present an abridgement of the following narration.†

Many are the tales that have been repeated to us of the revolutionary struggles of our ancestors. Yet each little incident connected with those times of peril, though often listened to, becomes interesting to us, who are now enjoying the blessings of that priceless freedom for which our fathers bled.

"Proudly, O children of freedom,
The stars of your banner float high;
Bright is the halo of glory,
O'er the graves where your ancestors lie.
Cherished may every memorial be,
Of the brave ones who perished that ye might be free."

Such was the motto that my sister wrote, when I told her that, in my next composition, I should weave up a reminiscence of the Revolution, and

* This narrative is a genuine college exercise, presented some years ago at one of the colleges in this State.

† This narration is a school exercise, presented within a few weeks by one of the pupils, a young lady of about thirteen years of age, at the public school of which the author has the charge. It has been thought that models and specimens of this kind would be more useful than more finished writings; because they present to the student something within his reach. It will not be very difficult for him, after he has attained some ease in writing, to adopt as his motto the principle, "*Excelsior*"

requested her to write a sentiment to grace the commencement; but, when she glanced at the simple incident I intended to relate, she thought the motto and the sketch were not very appropriate; but, as I insisted on its appropriateness to my brave Arthur's story; and, as I also had the slip of paper in my hand on which it was pencilled, (possession being nine points of the law,) I was allowed to retain it, or rather she was obliged to yield to my whim, and, accordingly, I transferred it in triumph to the top of the page on which I commence —

A REVOLUTIONARY STORY.

Near the extremity of the beautiful peninsula on which Charlestown situated, stood a large old-fashioned house, in the year 1775, whose time-worn walls were partially concealed, in the warmer seasons, by luxuriant grape-vines, that, spreading over the latticed portico, ran across the small windows, and clambered along the gable roof. A group of horse-chestnut trees, and a hedge composed of the briery bushes of the barberry and blackberry, with here and there a sweetbrier, covered with its delicate pink blossoms, enclosed a yard overgrown with bright green grass, and which extended around the eastern and western sides of the mansion. Beneath the vine-covered windows on the west a small parterre of flowers bloomed, while beyond, a vegetable garden extended to where the bright waves of the river Charles rolled onward. The house was occupied by Mrs. Leslie, her two children, and a female domestic, — Captain Leslie being with the American army, at the neighboring town of Cambridge, where it had been stationed for nearly two months, while the British troops lay shut up in Boston.

It was the beginning of June, and, as the afternoon of a beautiful day drew near its close, Mrs. Leslie laid aside the sewing materials that had absorbed her attention during the morning, and, stepping out upon the green turf, directed her steps towards a low wooden bench beneath a large apple-tree, where a young and sweet-looking girl was sitting. As her mother approached, Anna Leslie dropped her knitting work and held forth a few simple, but fragrant, flowers. A caress was the reward which the affectionate girl expected and received for her gift. As she threw a glance so expressive of love on her mother's face, it was sad for that mother to know, that she could not perceive the smile of affection in return; for her child's dark blue eyes were sightless, — poor Anna Leslie was blind. Few persons would have thought, as they looked in the lovely child's face, as some strain of music, some loved and familiar tone, or some bright, happy thought awakened in her countenance a beautiful expression, which accorded well with her symmetrical features, — few persons would have thought that Anna had been born blind, that she never had viewed the charming scenes of nature, that her eye had never glanced over the pages of literature, or the works of art. But a mother's watchful tenderness and patient instruction had, during the twelve years of her life, somewhat supplied the deficiency which her misfortune occasioned; and her brother Arthur, two years older than herself, had, with more than a brother's usual affection, cherished and protected his helpless sister. Unlike the interesting and unfortunate Laura Bridgeman, Anna could hear the loved voices of her friends and the sweet tones of her mother's harpsichord. She could give utterance, too, in a low, clear voice, to her thoughts and feelings, and, although she *saw* not her mother's smile, she heard the whispered words of love, and returned her affectionate greeting.

Drawing her daughter's arm within her own, Mrs. Leslie returned slowly towards the house. The blushing June roses were sending forth their rich odor from the large bushes, covered with flowers, that bordered the path, and Mrs. Leslie plucked an opening bud and placed it in her daughter's nair. All around their little domain looked peacefully, but Anna echoed her mother's sigh, as the beating of the drum and other sounds of war came faintly from the hostile camps and awakened in their bosoms sorrowful thoughts of the situation of their country, and the welfare of the husband and father, whose life was so precious, yet in such peril. As they silently approached the house, Anna felt conscious that her mother was becoming absorbed in melancholy reverie, and, to divert her attention, proposed to meet Arthur. Mrs. Leslie consented, and they passed through the flower beds and proceeded to the lower parts of the grounds, where Arthur employed himself in cultivating the vegetable garden; for it was impossible to procure a man in the town for that purpose, all who were able having joined the army of their country. But Arthur, with the occasional assistance of Rachel, their faithful black servant, had managed to raise quite a respectable stock of vegetables, not only for his own family, but he sometimes found means to carry a portion to supply his father's table at the camp. Arthur, who had just completed his work and refreshed himself by a bath in the river, as his mother and sister appeared in sight, hastened to join them, and to communicate an account of an extensive depredation committed the preceding night in his garden. Naturally impetuous in his temper, Arthur now complained bitterly, and vowed vengeance on the British thief, as he persisted in calling him, for he had traced the footsteps over his delicate lettuce beds and young peas, till they terminated on the verge of the river. As his boyish imagination magnified his wrongs, Arthur's dark eye sparkled, his cheek flushed, and his red lip curled with scorn, and not till the sweet voice of his sister had communicated in a whisper a plan for watching that night, and at least ascertaining who the thief was, did his brow become unclouded, just as they entered their quiet, low-ceiled sitting-room. A very pleasant room it was, though old fashioned. Its deep window seats were nicely cushioned, its clumsy-looking mahogany tables, with dark, time-colored surfaces, highly polished, the carved boxes and stands that came from Calcutta, its fireplace, surrounded by small Dutch tiles, the antique-looking portraits, that came over in the Mayflower, it was said, and the painted screens placed around, made the apartment a favorite with Arthur and Anna. The bright flowers in the old China vases, and the white drapery of the table, now spread with their simple evening repast, enlivened the somewhat sombre aspect of the room, for the sun had just sunk below the horizon and the vines hung thickly over the windows; but Rachel pushed them aside and commenced swaying her fly-brush, as Mrs. Leslie seated herself at the table. Rachel was somewhat a privileged being in the family, as she was a faithful and trusty domestic, and she often enlivened the children at meal times by her quaint expressions and anecdotes of the olden time. This evening she began to lament, as she glanced ruefully at the plain bread, fresh strawberries, and bright water from their own cool and shaded well, that her lady could no longer preside, as formerly, over the splendid silver plate and beautiful China tea-set, that once adorned the table, covered with the delicacies of the season. But now what was the use of the plainest cups and saucers without tea, and even the strawberries must be eaten without cream, for the British foragers had stolen their last cow.

Arthur, who had been absorbed in his own thoughts, now joined in the conversation, for he generally felt interested when any thing was said respecting the injuries inflicted by the foes of his country; and, long after Mrs. Leslie had retired from the room, did the eager boy continue to listen to Rachel's tales, and even Anna at last left them, and passing out of the glass door into the large hall, for she was perfectly acquainted with every nook in her childhood's home, and could find her way without difficulty through every room of the house, she ascended the broad staircase with large wooden balustrades at the head of the hall, and entered her own chamber. Drawing the snowy curtain aside, Anna seated herself on the window seat, for though she could not look out upon the moonlit scene, it was pleasant to feel the cool fragrant breeze play over her face, and hear it rustling among the branches of the horse-chestnut trees. Long did Anna sit there, and longer she would have lingered, indulging in those waking dreams, sad and yet sometimes enchanting, that are peculiarly endeared to those, who, like her, are shut out from many of the bright realities of life, if the door communicating with her mother's apartment had not gently opened, and Mrs. Leslie entered with a mother's care to see that all was safe. "Anna, my child, nine o'clock, and you sitting here, when the damp breeze from the river is blowing directly in the window? what imprudence!" The window was closed, and Anna was carefully enveloped in flannel, and only her urgent remonstrances prevented her mother from administering some hot herb tea. After Anna had retired, Mrs. Leslie withdrew to her chamber, full of anxiety for her beloved child, whose delicate health and helplessness seemed to increase the love she felt for her.

When the old clock in the corner of the hall struck nine, Arthur lighted his candle and hastened to his room. After closing the door, he took from his chest an old fowling-piece, and carefully examined it. Placing it on the table, he repaired to the window, and, parting the waving tendrils of the vine, looked out anxiously. Light clouds had been flying across the deep blue of the sky all the evening; but now, darker and darker they gathered in huge masses, till it was impossible to discern objects with any distinctness on the river, or even in the garden below. Arthur was a brave boy, but he hesitated at the thought of descending to the garden and there watching for the thief, for the increasing darkness made it impossible to see from the window; but his hesitation vanished, for he thought he faintly heard the sound of oars on the river, and snatching up his fowling-piece, and silently opening his door, he proceeded lightly along the hall. As he passed the clock, it struck ten, and its silvery sound somewhat startled him as he felt his way in the dark. Noiselessly he opened the hall door, and stepped out into the yard. Everything around was quiet, except the rustling of the branches as a gust passed by, and the sound of oars striking the waves, which he now heard with more distinctness. Arthur bounded lightly over the hedge of sweetbrier, and made his way through the dewy shrubbery to his garden. It was very dark, and as he hid behind a group of currant bushes and awaited the coming of the depredator, he could scarcely distinguish a single object. Suddenly the noise ceased on the river, and breathlessly Arthur watched through the gloom. He started as he thought he perceived a tall form bending over near him; but, looking more closely, he saw it was a large sunflower bowing its head in the breeze. Again; did his imagination deceive him? No; a tall Highlander, his tartan and plumes shaken by the wind, crept cautiously through the bushes and proceeded to fill a large bag with all that the increasing darkness would enable him to lay his hands on. Arthur's fears, if he had any, were now dispelled, so indignant did he feel as he saw the inroads made in his fine beds of vegetables, and he sprung behind the startled Highlander, and in a voice hoarse with rage, levelling his fowling-piece close to his head, threatened him with instant death if he made the least resistance. The frightened fellow, rendered confident and more daring by his former unmolested visit, had come totally unarmed save a dirk in his belt; but the surprise and consternation which his sudden detection had occasioned, not being able to see his enemy and with death so near, his presence of mind utterly forsook him, and he followed implicitly the commands of Arthur, who ordered him to take up the bag and to walk in front whether he should direct. Tremblingly the Highlander, not daring to move his head, for the loaded gun still threatened him with instant death, obeyed; and Arthur, following closely and silently through the garden and along the road, stopped not till he arrived at the camp in Cambridge, where he delivered his prisoner into his father's hands. Proudly Captain Leslie gazed on his intrepid boy, and many were the compliments that his courage obtained from the officers and soldiers. Nothing could exceed the anger and mortification which the Highlander felt as he gazed in surprise on his youthful captor, and many were the oaths that fell from his lips, as he saw the scornful sneers and listened to the contemptuous remarks of the American soldiers as they passed him and looked upon his sturdy form, and compared it with the slight, graceful figure of Arthur Leslie. Arthur did not long remain at the camp, but hastened home to relieve the anxiety of his mother and sister, and just as the sun began to gild "tree, shrub, and flower," Arthur with one bound sprang over the thicket, shaking large pearly dew-drops from the roses, and entered the portico just as his mother was descending the stairs from his room, where the bed, which evidently had not been occupied, had dreadfully alarmed her. Her anxiety was somewhat allayed by the appearance of Arthur; and when at the breakfast table he related to her and to Anna the adventure of the night, Mrs. Leslie knew not whether to blame the temerity, or praise the courage which he undoubtedly had manifested. Rachel was delighted with her brave boy's conduct; and long afterward, when the war was ended and Captain Leslie had removed to the city, where Mrs. Leslie resumed her former station at the head of a splendid establishment, and the sweet Anna had cultivated, with her brother's assistance, the learning and accomplishments attainable by one in her situation, then did Rachel recount to her wondering hearers the story of Arthur's adventure with the Highlander.

LXII.

DESCRIPTION.

Description, as defined by Webster, is "a representation of names, natures, or properties, that give to another a view of the thing."

It is, in fine, a picture, delineated, not by lines, but by words; and it must be so presented as to convey a clear, definite, and exact semblance to the mind, such as the object described presents to the eye. Such a representation may be called a faithful description. Faithful descriptions, therefore, are faithful pictures. All definitions must be less perfect descriptions of a material thing, than a visible figure or delineation. But when a definition is expanded, so as to embrace not only all the particulars in which the object defined differs from other objects, but also those in which it resembles others of the same kind, such a definition, is, in fact, a description.

Owing to peculiar associations in the mind, and the difference in the habits of perception and observation, no two individuals would probably describe the same scene or the same object alike. This is particularly the case with young writers. Some, from a natural sluggishness of mind, will perceive few particulars worthy of notice, where others, of different temperament, will find the subject replete with interesting details, all worthy of regard.*

A few suggestions will now be presented, which will probably lead those who may use this book *to think*, and to use their eyes to some purpose, when called upon to give a written description of any sensible object These suggestions will be followed by a list of details, some one or more of which may always be noticed in a written description.

It will be noticed, that the object in presenting such a list is only, as has already been said, *to suggest ideas*, which the student himself is to mould as they may arise, and combine with what may spring spontaneously from his own mind.

To collect materials for a good description, there must be a devoted at tention to the beauties of nature and to the scenes of social life. The mind will thereby be rendered susceptible and discriminative, acquiring sources of improvement which would otherwise be lost, while variety and copiousness of expression will at the same time be secured.

There are three great classes, under one of which all the varieties of description may be arranged. Under the first class are included all those subjects which are immediately under personal notice; which are actually present before our eyes. In the second class may be arranged all those which have been noticed, but have left only their pictures in the memory. The third class includes only those subjects which are purely imaginary. In the descriptions of all these classes, the object to be effected is one and the same; namely, to present to the reader a picture, easy and natural, lively in its character, and animated in its appearance; making those de tails the most prominent which would affect the beholder as most striking, and throwing, as it were, into the shade those circumstances which are designed to produce a subordinate impression. In producing such an effect, the writer should pay particular attention to the epithets † with which he designates particular objects, that he may render the impression, which he designs that they should convey, strong and durable. For this reason he cannot be too particular in the choice of his qualifying words, for they are sometimes more expressive than the objects themselves when presented in naked simplicity.

Thus, for instance, suppose we are describing a scene in a wood or forest; the following terms would appropriately describe the appearance of the scene: Dark, obscure, deep, dreary, gloomy, overcast, indistinct, dim, cloudy, dense, lurid, livid, &c.

Or a summer's noon; the following terms will be found in most cases suitable: Bright, shining, clear, lucid, brilliant, dazzling, splendid, resplendent, sparkling, refulgent, ardent, conspicuous, clear, placid, &c.

Or a storm, or a cataract; the following terms will be found expressive: Harsh, discordant, roar, howl, hiss, crash, reverberate, dash, splash, murmur, growl, clamorous, confused, terrific, tremendous, thundering, &c.

There are many kinds of description, also, in which the following terms may not only, with considerable advantage, be interwoven, but the terms themselves, by the law of association, will suggest ideas; such as, placid, calm, tranquil, motionless, peaceful, serene, restless, lazy, unruffled,

---

* See the "Dialogue between a Tutor and his Pupils," on page 8th.

† See the article on epithets.

hushed, silent, voiceless, sleeping, breathless, transparent, clear, waveless, engulphed, unmeasured, beautiful, mingled, crystal, golden, silvery, magnificent, breezeless, kindred, &c., &c., &c.

Acquaintance with the beauties of nature, particularly with those of the earth and the sky, and with the lights and shadows of life, must be considered as a great acquisition to any mind; and consequently the command of language, so requisite to embody and depicture the same with the glow and warmth which imagination lends to description, must be regarded as an object worthy of the highest regard by all who aim at being distinguished as writers.*

In descriptions, the principal point to which to direct the attention is the selection of the circumstances. The scene, or the circumstance, should be brought with distinctness and fulness to the view. We should be placed, as it were, by the description in the midst of the group of particulars, and be made fully acquainted with all its peculiarities. That which is called *truth to nature* is effected by the skilful selection and arrangement of the circumstances, and constitutes the *amplification* of descriptive writing. In some instances, especially where it is desirable that the description should be bold and striking, the enumeration of circumstances may be less full and minute.

In describing natural scenery, the student will find some

---

* Probably no writer has ever surpassed Sir Walter Scott in the beauty fidelity, and accuracy of his descriptions. The following extract, from Mr Morritt's "Memorandum," taken from Lockhart's Life of Sir Walter, Vol. III., page 30, exhibits his views, and the pains that he took to be accurate. Speaking of the visit of the great novelist at Rokeby, Mr. Morritt says: "I had many previous opportunities of testing the almost conscientious fidelity of his local descriptions; but I could not help being singularly struck with the lights which this visit threw on that characteristic of his compositions. The morning after he arrived, he said, 'You have often given me materials for a romance; now I want a good robber's cave, and an old church of the right sort.' We rode out, and he found what he wanted in the old slate quarries of Brignal, and the ruined Abbey of Egglestone. I observed him noting down *even the peculiar little wild flowers and herbs that accidentally grew around* and on the side of a bold crag, near his intended cave of Guy Denzil; and could not help saying, that as he was not to be upon oath in his work, *daisies, violets,* and *primroses would be as poetical as any of the humbler plants he was examining.* I laughed, in short, at his scrupulousness; but I understood him when he replied, 'that in nature herself no two scenes are exactly alike; and that *whoever copied truly what was before his eyes, would possess the same variety in his descriptions, and exhibit apparently an imagination as boundless as the range of nature in the scenes he recorded;* whereas, whoever trusted to imagination, would soon find his own mind circumscribed and contracted to a few favorite images, and the repetition of these would sooner or later produce that very monotony and barrenness which had always haunted descriptive poetry in the hands of any but patient worshippers of truth. Besides which,' he said, 'local names and peculiarities make a fictitious story look so much better in the face.' In fact, from his boyish habits, he was but half satisfied with the most beautiful scenery when he could not connect with it some local legend; and when I was forced sometimes to confess, with the knife-grinder, 'Story! God bless you! I have none to tell, sir,' — he would laugh, and say, 'Then let us make one, — nothing so easy as to make a tradition.'"

aid in the following lists of particulars, which are here introduced as *suggestive* of ideas, which he himself is to mould as they may arise, and combine with what may spring spontaneously from his own mind. *

A COUNTRY.

Its principal water courses:
Its chains of mountains:
The nature of the hills, whether more or less rugged; the nature of the morasses, whether more or less practicable:
The rapidity and depth of the rivers; the nature of their fords, sluices, and piers; the state of the bridges, and their position: of the roads, and the necessary repairs; the reasons for preferring one road to another, which would lead to the same object, such as the ease of procuring subsistence, of travelling in security — the *lateral* communications opening from the great or main roads — the population of the villages, occupations of the inhabitants, the means of transportation, the chief commerce of the inhabitants, their industry, habits, and manners — the productions of the country, quantity and kind — the liquors, vinous or spirituous, with their effects on the inhabitants.

Of Rivers: Their direction — their course — the nature of their beds, their breadth — their floods and times of drought; their meadows, and the marshes that intersect them; the mills upon their banks; the breadth of their valleys — the hills and ridges which skirt them — the side on which are commanding heights — the tributary rivulets, and the ravines which open into the valley of the stream — the distance between them; of what nature are the shrubs, the gullies, the brooks, the roads, &c. — the quality of the hedges, they are thin in poor soil, but in rich land they are thick, and formidable objects to the march of troops, &c.

Canals. Their communication — the nature of the ground through which they are cut — the means of draining them, and of turning their courses; their locks — the mode of destroying and of protecting them — how their navigation may be obstructed or improved.

Mills often render water-courses fordable or not, at pleasure, by means of the water dammed up for their supply. When sand is of the ordinary

---

* These lists of particulars are taken, with slight alterations necessary to adapt them to the purposes of this work, from "Lallemand's Artillery Service," article "*Reconnoitering*." They were original in a work entitled "*L'aide memoire à l'usage des officiers d'artillerie de France*," *par le General Gassendi*.

From the dialogue between the tutor and his pupils, to which reference has already been made, the student will derive some hints upon "*the art of seeing*," or using his eyes aright. This dialogue, calculated as it is to awaken attention, and to fix habits of observation, is particularly recommended to the careful perusal of the student, who would relieve his mind from the *labors* of composition. Habits of observation, attended with careful analysis, not only aid the mind in its search after ideas, but also direct it in a judicious selection of those which are afforded by association.

color, the roads are generally good; but if the sand be black, or mixed with small white grains, the roads are impassable in winter, and often in time of rain.

CLIMATE. The physical causes which may affect health — the quality of the air, cold, hot, wet, or dry; seasons —whether inclement, and how long so — the means of protection from their effects — the customs of the inhabitants in this respect.

COASTS. The nature of the coasts — whether lined with sand-hills, covered with rocks, which render the approach more or less dangerous; or precipices, which forbid it altogether The parts which are open and uncovered, and proper for landing; the bays which form roadsteads and harbors — the points and capes fit for forts and batteries, which may defend the accessible parts; the adjacent islands, which may serve as advanced works to form barriers against the attempts of an enemy; the gulfs, the bays, the roads, the ports — the nature of the winds required to enter or leave these ports, the nature and advantages of which may be pointed out — the time of tide most favorable for entering the ports, &c. — the dangers to be met — the obstacles to be surmounted — the actual state of the forts which protect the coast — the batteries, the guard-houses, and the artillery in them; if there be rivers emptying themselves on the coasts, the tides are apt to alter their channel; an account may be given of this influence, &c.

FORESTS AND WOODS. Their situation — their extent; the kinds of trees of which they are composed, whether fit for fuel or for timber — their extent — their magnitude; is the ground of the forest level or hilly, from whence do the roads come, and whither do they lead — their quality — the nature of the ground around them — are they near fields, meadows, ravines, hills, mountains, rivers — the streams, marshes, springs, dwellings, &c., near them — the distance of all these objects from the borders of the wood or forest; the roads which intersect them, and the swamps which divide them.

HOUSES. Their situations — style of architecture — the ground which they occupy — the mode in which they are built — the materials of which they are composed — the color given them by nature or art — are they old or new — the indications of age — moss-grown, ivy-hung, black with time — appendages connected with ancient customs — their associations — the improvements of modern art — additional conveniences, &c.

LEVEL COUNTRY. Its hedges, ditches, villages, buildings, brooks, canals, marshes, roads, rivers, bridges, &c. *

MOUNTAINS. Their position — their slopes in front and rear — th means of reaching their summits — the nature of the ground — its form —are they covered with wood or with bare rocks — their height — their

* In sandy countries, and those filled with brushwood, there are many marshes covered with water during the winter, which are almost dry in summer. In the winter they are impassable, and are to be mistrusted, even in summer, after long rains.

fertility — pastures, fodder, vegetation, dwellings, towns, villages, castles workshops, roads, paths, &c.

Rivers. Do they branch off, or continue in one undivided stream * — where do they rise — whither do they flow — what is the nature of the country through which they flow — the quality of the water — clear, sparkling, transparent, thick, muddy, turbid — ruffled with eddies and counter currents — with or without falls — salt or fresh, sweet or brackish — cold or warm — safe for bathing, or dangerous — the manufactories moved by the water — the canals running from or into it — the streams, brooks rivulets, or other rivers that supply it, &c.

Villages. Their situation — the number of fires or chimneys in operation — the nature of the soil — the quantity and quality of the produce — the occupation of the inhabitants—their markets—the neighborhood which frequents them —the beasts of burden, the flocks, the beeves and poultry they possess — the architecture, or style in which the buildings, houses, barns, and sheep-cotes are built — the position of the church and burying ground — the blacksmith's shop — whether surrounded by walls, by bushes, by ditches, or palisades — the water and wind mills. †

---

* Rivers which divide into several branches, form islands and peninsulas. The rivers themselves, thus divided, are apt to change their channels at every flood.

† In the description of natural scenery, it will be well for the student to call to memory those beautiful lines of Cowper.

"Nor rural sights alone, but *rural sounds*
Exhilarate the spirits, and restore
The tone of languid nature. *Mighty winds*,
That sweep the skirt of some far-spreading wood
Of ancient growth, make music not unlike
The dash of Ocean on his winding shore,
And lull the spirit, while they fill the mind,
Unnumbered branches waving in the blast,
And all their leaves fast fluttering all at once.
Nor less composure waits upon the roar
Of *distant floods* ; or on the softer voice
Of *neighbouring fountain ;* or of *rills*, that slip
Through the cleft rock, and chiming as they fall
Upon loose pebbles, lose themselves at length
In matted grass, that with a livelier green
Betrays the secret of their silent course.
  Nature inanimate employs sweet sounds ;
But *animated nature* sweeter still,
To soothe and satisfy the human ear.
Ten thousand warblers cheer the day, and *one*
The live-long night. Nor these alone, whose notes
Nice fingered art must emulate in vain ;
But cawing rooks, and kites that swim sublime,
In still repeated circles, screaming loud :
The *jay*, the *pye*, and e'en the *boding owl*,
That hails the rising moon, have charms for me.
Sounds inharmonious in themselves, and harsh,
Yet heard in scenes where peace forever reigns,
And only there, please highly for their sake."

The particulars which have now been mentioned as suggestive of ideas, will undoubtedly aid the student, and enable him to combine what addresses itself to the eye with that which suggests itself to the imagination, in his endeavors to make *verbal* pictures of the beauties of nature. The nature and variety of such particulars must necessarily be dependent on the character of the object to be described.

If an individual sensible object is to be described, the questions which naturally arise, and which should most of them be answered in the description, are as follows:

Where is it?
Who made it?
What is it made of?
Is it old or new?
What was it made for?
How is it adapted for the purposes for which it was made?
Is it beneficial or prejudicial to the comfort and convenience of mankind?
Are its effects universal or particular?
Its divisions and parts?
Its dimensions, form, and color?
Does it produce, or is it connected with any sounds?
How is it constructed?
How does it strike the eye?
What are its resemblances or its differences?
How does it appear from different positions?

In addition to these questions, the student must call to mind what others would naturally arise in the mind of any one, desirous of exact and particular information with regard to the subject of his description, and endeavor fully to answer every such question in his written exercise.

In the description of persons, an entirely different set of questions will suggest the proper answers, to which the description should be a full reply.

What is the personal appearance, complexion, stature, figure, &c.; hands, arms, limbs, eyes, &c.?
What feature is most prominently conspicuous?
The expression of the countenance?
Is the individual remarkable for manly beauty; or illy made, awkward, and ungraceful?
What is the appearance of his chest, shoulders; length of his limbs, style of his dress?
What are his habits, his age; what graces, accomplishments, or attainments has he?
What is his moral character — his intellectual; who are his associates what influence have they wrought upon him?
For what virtues or vices is he particularly noted?

In the descriptions of persons of the other sex, such questions may be a little varied, and answered as in the following examples:

DESCRIPTION OF PERSONS.

Example 1*st.*

DESCRIPTION OF MARY QUEEN OF SCOTTS.

The turbulence of the times, the rancor of party rage, and the medium of prejudice or partiality, through which every object in those periods was beheld, render it difficult to form a just opinion of the character of Mary Her personal accomplishments and the graces which distinguished her as a woman, are admitted by all parties; respecting these, therefore, there can be no dispute. Her stature rose to the majestic, her form was elegant and her hands and arms distinguished for their delicacy and beauty. Her hair was black, though, in the fashion of the times, she frequently adorned herself in borrowed locks, and of various colors. Her eyes were dark gray, and her complexion remarkably fine. She walked, danced, and rode, with equal grace. She possessed a taste for music; she played upon the lute with skill, and sung melodiously. Towards the conclusion of her life, she began to grow corpulent, while confinement and bad accommodation brought upon her a rheumatic disorder, which deprived her of the use of her limbs. Her manners were affable and insinuating, dignified and sprightly. She spoke eloquently, and wrote with ease and elegance. Her temper was warm, and her heart affectionate. She loved flattery, and beheld the effects of her beauty with pleasure. If she had acquired the power of dissembling her sentiments in the refined and intriguing court of France, her nature was nevertheless frank and indisposed to suspicion. Her piety was fervent and sincere; her talents, if not of the highest, were undoubtedly of a superior order; and the resolution and courage which she manifested at her death, are truly worthy of admiration. A long series of successive sorrows bespeak, with few exceptions, some imprudence in the sufferer; the misfortunes of Mary, both in degree and duration, exceeded the common measure of human calamities, and even render the distresses of fiction comparatively faint. The vicissitudes of her life have afforded a fine and fruitful subject for the tragic muse. No man, says Brantome, ever beheld her without admiration and love; no one will read her history without pity and sorrow.*

---

* All writers agree in representing Mary of Scotland as distinguished for personal beauty. But on no subject, perhaps, do mankind differ so much as in their ideas of female beauty; and it seems to be wisely ordered by Providence that they should thus differ. Women in the Hottentot country are considered beautiful in proportion to the size of their ears, the flatness of their noses and the projection of their lips. In Otaheite corpulency is the constituent element of loveliness; and in China, small feet, cramped into absolute deformity, are considered an indispensable requisite for beauty. A late physiological writer, speaking of female beauty, says: "A woman of any height, from the *petite* almost to the gigantic, may be perfectly beau

Example 2d.

BERNARD DE ROHAN.

I will attempt to paint him, to the eye of the reader, as I have myself seen him, represented by the hand of an unknown artist, in one of the

---

tiful; and of any complexion, from the darkest brunette to the fairest lily. The medium height is generally preferred; but the complexion is a matter that entirely depends on individual taste — the same person, too, would be likely to waver in choice between the darkly beautiful maidens of Spain and the seraphically fair daughters of Circassia. Nevertheless, though the shades of complexion, from the Spanish olive to the Circassian white, or the varieties of altitude, from the *petite* Cleopatra to that of the towering Roxana, matters but little; there are many things arbitrarily essential to perfect beauty in woman." "I shall describe," he continues, "a beautiful woman. taking her at the medium altitude, which is generally preferred."

As such a description may be interesting to many who have not access to the original work, and as it cannot be considered wholly out of place in a volume professing to teach the art of description, the author of this volume has, with some hesitation, ventured here to present it.

"Her height is five feet five inches; her hair is of any color that agrees with her complexion; her forehead is rather low, and as free from freckle or wrinkle as a piece of Paphian marble; her brows are dark, arched, narrow, and strongly defined; her eyes are large, rather languishing than bright, and of either of the usual colors; for the grey eyes of Mary of Scotland were not less captivating than the raven orbs of the Queen of Sheba; her eye lashes are dark and long; her nose is a mitigated aquiline, — that is, an aquiline curtailed of its severity; her lips are short and small, and yet withal full and pouting; her chin is very slightly developed; her ears are small, thin, and with the tip on a line with the eyebrow; her complexion varies with the emotions of her mind, and the blush that tinges her cheek is delicate, and loses itself in her face, so as to indicate no perceptible outline; her features are exactly regular, though made to appear otherwise by the ever-varying expression of her lips and eyes, and the fluctuations of the rosy tide that ebbs and flows beneath the transparent surface of her skin; her smile indicates sweetness of disposition, blended with a gently-proud expression, dictated probably by the consciousness of her own worth and beauty; her neck is flexible, moderately slender, of medium length, and pure as alabaster; the fall from her neck to her shoulders is gradual (like that of a bird); her bust is a gentle swell, so clear that the blue veins are visible; her shoulders almost verge on broadness, and press backwards; her waist is small, but not too taper; her arms are rounded; her hands delicately small, and fingers rather long and tapered; her instep is high, to secure a good arch to the foot, which adds grace in walking, and her feet are as small as they can possibly be without subjecting them to the character of diminutive."

To this description the same author adds, that there are "three species of female beauty, of which all the rest are varieties."

No. 1. Face round, eyes soft azure; neck rather short; shoulders moderately broad and gently rounded; limbs and arms tapering and delicate; hands and feet small; complexion, rose struggling with lily; hair luxuriant, flaxen or auburn; eyes blue, and whole figure soft and easy.

No. 2. Oblong face; neck long and tapering; shoulders broad and delicate, without being angular; limbs and arms rather long and tapering; feet

15*

palaces on the banks of the Brenta. He was in person about the middle height, rather above it than below, and at this period was not more than twenty-three years of age. His forehead was broad and fine, with short dark hair curling around it; his features were small, excepting the eye and brow, the former of which was large and full, and the latter strongly marked. The mouth was very handsome, showing, when half open in speaking, the brilliant white teeth, and giving to the whole countenance a look of playful gaiety; but, when shut, there was an expression of much thoughtfulness, approaching perhaps to sternness, about it, which the rounded and somewhat prominent chin confirmed. The upper lip was very short; but on either side, divided in the middle, was a short black mustache, not overhanging the mouth, but raised above it; and the beard, which was short and black, like the hair, was only suffered to grow in such a manner as to ornament, but not to encumber the chin.

In form the cavalier was muscular, and powerfully made; his breadth of chest and shoulders giving the appearance of a more advanced period of life than that to which he had yet arrived.*—*Corse De Leon, by G. P. R. James.*

---

and hands rather small; complexion mostly dark; hair abundant, dark and strong; and the whole figure precise, striking, and brilliant.

No. 3. Oval face; high, pale, intellectual forehead; eye, expressive and full of sensibility, also indicating modesty and dignity; movements characterized by grace and elegance.

* In a note on page 172 is presented, in a quotation from a late physiological writer, the description of a beautiful woman. The same author thus describes a specimen of masculine beauty:

"A fine looking man, (the word handsome detracts from the idea of beauty in the male sex), is above the medium height, but considerably under the colossal; (about five feet ten inches is the perfection of altitude); his forehead is high and rather square; his back head is well rounded, but not too full; his eyes are dark, bright, and fairly set in their sockets—neither tending to recede nor to protrude; his hair inclines to a curl; his eyebrows are rather square than bushy, and leave a space of about three quarters of an inch between their inward extremities; his nose is a medium between Roman and aquiline; his cheek bones are not prominent, but still well defined; his cheeks neither lank nor so rounded as to indicate fatness or inflation; his mouth moderately small; his lips firm, compact, but not thin; his whiskers are well back on his cheek; his complexion is uniform, between brown and fair, with a slight tendency to a blush, but not sufficient to warrant him in being called rosy cheeked; and the whole countenance, well or even strongly marked; for a smooth, round face, where the features are all regular, and without any characteristic for a limner to fasten on, is incompatible with manly beauty. Then his neck is of moderate length and inclines to thickness; his throat is free from all protuberance commonly called '*the apple of Eve;*' his breast is fairly full; his shoulders square, but not abruptly so, and sufficiently broad to just overhang his hips; his arms are of a length to leave about eight inches between the tips of his middle fingers and his knees; there is a gradual decrease inwards from the hips and shoulder to the waist; his back is free from the least tendency to roundness, but is not thrown very much to the rear; his limbs are full, but not clumsy; his joints small; the calves of the legs so that they just touch, without pressing against each other; his shin rather slender, his ankle small; his instep high; and his foot slightly hollowed, and of a size corresponding w th his height; for, too small a foot interferes with

Example 3d.

THE ELEPHANT.

The elephant, a native of Asia and Africa, is the largest, the strongest, the most sagacious, and the most docile of all wild beasts. The usual height of this unsightly creature is from eight to twelve or fourteen feet. The color is nearly black; the eyes, which are very small, are lively, bright, and expressive; the ears are broad, and much longer, in proportion to the body, than those of the ass.

It has two long ivory tusks, thicker toward the head than a stout man's arm, and a trunk which it can contract or lengthen, as need requires. The latter is as useful to the animal as our hands are to us. With this singular organ it can take up the smallest object; it serves itself with it; and, in case of an attack, fights with it. It can also untie knots of ropes, and open and shut gates.

The legs of this stupendous quadruped are like columns of from twelve to eighteen inches in diameter, and from four to six feet high. The feet are short, and divided into five toes each, and are armed with nails of a horny substance, but which are so covered with skin, that they are scarcely visible.

The elephant, in a state of nature, is neither fierce nor mischievous. It is peaceable, mild, and brave; and exerts its powers only in its own defence, or in defence of those of its own kind, with which it is social and friendly.

Example 4th.

NATURAL SCENERY.

Long projecting reefs of rocks, extending under water, and only evincing their existence by here and there a peak entirely bare, or by the breakers which foamed over those that were partially covered, rendered Knockwinnock bay dreaded by pilots and ship-masters. The crags which rose between the beach and the main land to the height of two or three hundred feet, afforded in their crevices shelter for unnumbered sea fowl, in situations seemingly secured by their dizzy height from the rapacity of

---

that elasticity of step, and firmness of carriage, so essential in making up the perfect '*tout ensemble*' of a well-proportioned man."

In descriptions of persons the student will do well to refer to what is said on the subject of *epithets* in another page of this volume. Thus, for example, the *manners* of an individual may be insinuating, sprightly, dignified, or reserved, &c.; speech, elegant, eloquent, &c.; person, thin or spare, fleshy or corpulent; temper, warm and affectionate; nature, frank and indisposed to suspicion, &c. Notice may also be taken, as occasion requires, of such particulars as the following: resolution, courage, effects of air and exercise, or confinement and exclusion from the air, on personal appearance, — series of sorrows as causing imprudence, constant success as producing temerity, — misfortunes in degree and duration exceeding the common measure of human calamity, rendering the distresses of fiction faint, &c., &c., &c.

man. Many of these wild tribes, with the instinct which sends them to seek the land before a storm arises, were now winging towards their nests with the shrill and dissonant clang which announces fear and disquietude.

The disk of the sun became almost totally obscured ere he had altogether sunk below the horizon, and an early and lurid shade of darkness blotted the serene twilight of a summer evening. The wind began next to arise, but its wild and moaning sound was heard for some time, and its effects became more visible on the bosom of the sea, before the gale was felt on the shore. The mass of waters, now dark and threatening, began to lift itself in larger ridges, and sink in deeper furrows, forming waves that rose high in foam upon the breakers, or burst upon the beach with a sound resembling distant thunder.—*Antiquary, Vol. I. p.* 72.

Example 5th.

NATURAL SCENERY.

Citiés and villages were scattered over hill and valley, with cultivated environs blooming around them, all giving token of a dense and industrious population. In the centre of this brilliant circumference stood the Indian metropolis, with its gorgeous tiara of pyramids and temples, attracting the eye of the soldier from every other object, as he wound round the borders of the lake. Every inch of ground which the soldiers trod was familiar to them; familiar as the scenes of childhood, though with very different associations, for it had been written on their memories in characters of blood. On the right rose the hill of Montezuma, crowned by the *teocalli*, under the roof of which the shattered relics of the army had been gathered on the day following the flight from the capitol. In front lay the city of Tacuba, through whose inhospitable streets they had hurried in fear and consternation; and away to the east of it stretched the melancholy causeway.—*Prescott's Conquest of Mexico, Vol III. p.* 31.

Example 6th.

NATURAL SCENERY.

They moved cautiously forward, straining their vision to pierce the think gloom of the forests, where their wily foe might be lurking. But they saw no living thing, except only the wild inhabitants of the woods and flocks of the *zopolite*, the voracious vulture of the country, which, in anticipation of a bloody banquet, hung like a troop of evil spirits, on the march of the army.

As they descended, the Spaniards felt a sensible and most welcome change in the atmosphere. The character of the vegetation changed with it; and the funereal pine, their only companion of late, gave way to the sturdy oak, to the sycamore, and lower down, to the graceful pepper tree, mingling its red berries with the dark foliage of the forest; while in still lower depths, the gaudy-colored creepers might be seen flinging their gay blossoms over the branches, and telling of a softer and more luxurious climate.

At length, the army emerged on an open level, where the eye, unob structed by intervening wood or hill-top, could range, far and wide, over the Valley of Mexico. There it lay, bathed in the golden sunshine, stretched out, as it were, in slumber, in the arms of the giant of hills, which clustered, like a phalanx of guardian genii, around it.* — *Conquest of Mexico, Vol. II, p.* 463.

From the same source from which the preceding extract was taken, the following *personal description* has been borrowed

HERNANDO CORTÉS.

Hernando "Cortés at this time was thirty-three, or perhaps thirty-four years of age. In stature he was rather above the middle size. His complexion was pale, and his large dark eye gave an expression of gravity to his countenance, not to be expected in one of his cheerful temperament. His figure was slender, at least until later life; but his chest was deep, his shoulders broad, his frame muscular and well proportioned. It presented the union of agility and vigor, which qualified him to excel in fencing, horsemanship, and the other generous exercises of chivalry. In his diet he was temperate, careless of what he ate, and drinking little; while, to toil and privation he seemed perfectly indifferent. His dress, for he did not disdain the impression produced by such adventitious aids, was such as to set off his handsome person to advantage; neither gaudy nor striking, but rich. He wore few ornaments, and usually the same; but these were of great price. His manners frank and soldierlike, concealed a most cool and calculating spirit. With his gayest humor there mingled a settled air of resolution, which made those who approached him feel they must obey; and which infused something like awe into the attachment of his most devoted followers. Such a combination, in which love was tempered by authority, was the one probably best calculated to inspire devotion in the rough and turbulent spirits among whom his lot was to be cast."

---

* The introduction of figurative language in descriptive writing, if not too luxuriantly indulged, adds much to the beauty and animation of the style. The student will not fail to admire the beautiful figure here introduced from one of the most elegant historical writers of any age or country. Mr. Prescott, in the work from which the extract above was taken, has conferred a favor on the republic of letters, which will hand him down to posterity as the modern "*Dulcis et candidus et fusus Herodotus.*" The same remark that has been made in relation to the Father of History, may be applied with equal truth and justice to the author of "*The Conquest of Mexico.*" "His style abounds with elegance, ease, and sweetness; and if there is any of the fabulous or incredible, the author candidly informs the reader that it is introduced on the authority of others." They who are not attracted by the thrilling nature of the incidents which he relates, will be captivated by the glowing colors in which they are described, the purity and animation of his style the witchery he has woven around his subject, and the wonderful skill with which he has thrown into a connected narrative a mass of details, which with indefatigable industry he has tithed from a great variety of authors, often at variance with one another, and not unfrequently at issue with themselves. The pride with which an American peruses his works, naturally breaks forth into the apostrophe, "Perge modo, et quà te via ducit dirige gressum."

The character of Cortés seems to have undergone some change with change of circumstances; or, to speak more correctly, the new scenes in which he was placed called forth qualities which before were dormant in his bosom. There are some hardy natures that require the heats of excited action to unfold their energies; like the plants, which, closed to the mild influence of a temperate latitude, come to their full growth, and give forth their fruits only in the burning atmosphere of the tropics. Such is the portrait left to us by his contemporaries of this remarkable man.

The examples which have now been introduced are deemed sufficient, both in variety and extent, to introduce the student to descriptive writing. The attentive perusal of the examples given, with careful attention to the preliminary hints and observations, it is thought will furnish considerable aid in this department of composition.

LXIII.

NARRATION AND DESCRIPTION UNITED.

That the student may perceive how much is added to the beauty and the interest of a narration by the union of description with the narrative, the following model is presented, which is founded on the simple circumstance, that a young man in a feeble state of health is called home, after a long absence, to be present at the death-bed of his mother. The student will observe how beautifully many of the particulars presented in the list in the preceding exercises are interwoven with the narrative, and how much the union of description with the narration has added to the beauty of the story.

Example.

In looking over some papers of a deceased acquaintance, I found the following fragment. He had frequently spoken to me of the person whom it concerned, and who had been his school-fellow. I remember well his one day telling me that, thinking the character of his friend, and some circumstances in his life, were of such a kind that an interesting moral little story might be made from them, he had undertaken it; but, considering as he was going on, that bringing the private character and feelings of a deceased friend before the world, was something like sacrilege, though done under a fictitious name, he had stopped soon after beginning the tale, — that he had laid it away amongst his papers, and had never looked at it again.

As the person it concerns has been a long time dead, and no relation survives, I do not feel that there can be any impropriety in my now making it public. I give it as it was written, though evidently not revised by my friend. Though hastily put together, and beginning as abruptly as it ends, and with little of story and no novelty in the circumstances, yet there is a mournful tenderness in it, which, I trust, will interest others in some portion as it did me.

"The sun not set yet, Thomas?" "Not quite, Sir. It blazes through the trees on the hill yonder, as if their branches were all on fire."

Arthur raised himself heavily forward, and with his hat still over his brow, turned his glazed and dim eyes towards the setting sun. It was only the night before that he had heard his mother was ill, and could survive but a day or two. He had lived nearly apart from society, and, being a lad of a thoughtful, dreamy mind, had made a world to himself. His thoughts and feelings were so much in it, that, except in relation to his own home, there were the same vague and strange notions in his brain concerning the state of things surrounding him, as we have of a foreign land.

The main feeling which this self-made world excited in him was love, and, like most of his age, he had formed to himself a being suited to his own fancies. This was the romance of life, and though men, with minds like his, make imagination to stand oftentimes in the place of real existence, and to take to itself as deep feeling and concern, yet in domestic relations, which are so near, and usual, and private, they feel longer and more deeply than those who look upon their homes as only a better part of the world to which they belong. Indeed, in affectionate and good men of a visionary cast, it is in some sort only realizing their hopes and desires, to turn them homeward. Arthur felt that it was so, and he loved his household the more that they gave him an earnest of one day realizing all his hopes and attachments.

Arthur's mother was peculiarly dear to him, in having a character so much like his own. For though the cares and attachments of life had long ago taken place of a fanciful existence in her, yet her natural turn of mind was strong enough to give to these something of the romance of her disposition. This had led to a more than usual openness and intimacy between Arthur and his mother, and now brought to his remembrance the hours they had sat together by the firelight, when he listened to her mild and melancholy voice, as she spoke of what she had undergone at the loss of her parents and husband. Her gentle rebuke of his faults, her affectionate look of approval when he had done well, her care that he should be a just man, and her motherly anxiety lest the world should go hard with him, all crowded into his mind, and he thought that every worldly attachment was hereafter to be a vain thing.

He had passed the night between violent, tumultuous grief, and numb insensibility. Stepping into the carriage, with a slow, weak motion, like one who was quitting his sick chamber for the first time, he began his journey homeward. As he lifted his eyes upward, the few stars that were here and there over the sky seemed to look down in pity, and shed a religious and healing light upon him. But they soon went out, one after another, and as the last faded from his imploring sight, it was as if every thing good and holy had forsaken him. The faint tint in the east soon became a ruddy glow, and the sun, shooting upward, burst over every living thing in full glory. The sight went to Arthur's sick heart, as if it were in mockery of his misery.

Leaning back in his carriage, with his hand over his eyes, he was carried along, hardly sensible it was day. The old servant, Thomas, who was sitting by his side, went on talking in a low, monotous tone; but Arthur only heard something sounding in his ears, scarcely heeding that it was a human voice. He had a sense of wearisomeness from the motion of the carriage, but in all things else the day passed as a melancholy dream.

Almost the first words Arthur spoke were those I have mentioned. As he looked out upon the setting sun, he shuddered through his whole frame, and then became sick and pale. He thought he knew the hill near him; and, as they wound round it, some peculiar old trees appeared, and he was in a few minutes in the midst of the scenery near his home. The river before him reflecting the rich evening sky, looked as if poured out from a molten mine. The birds, gathering in, were shooting across each other, bursting into short, gay notes, or singing their evening songs in the trees. It was a bitter thing to find all so bright and cheerful, and so near his own home too. His horses' hoofs struck upon the old wooden bridge. The sound went to his heart. It was here his mother took her last leave of him, and blessed him.

As he passed through the village, there was a feeling of strangeness, that every thing should be just as it was when he left it. There was an undefined thought floating in his mind, that his mother's state should produce a visible change in all that he had been familiar with. But the boys were at their noisy games in the street, the laborers returning, talking together, from their work, and the old men sitting quietly at their doors. He concealed himself as well as he could, and bade Thomas hasten on.

As they drew near the house, the night was shutting in about it, and there was a melancholy, gusty sound in the trees. Arthur felt as if approaching his mother's tomb. He entered the parlor. All was as gloomy and still as a deserted house. Presently he heard a slow, cautious step over head. It was in his mother's chamber. His sister had seen him from the window. She hurried down and threw her arms about her brother's neck, without uttering a word. As soon as he could speak, he asked, "Is she alive?" — he could not say, my mother. 'She is sleeping," answered his sister, "and must not know to-night that you are here; she is too weak to bear it now." "I will go look at her, then, while she sleeps," said he, drawing his handkerchief from his face. His sister's sympathy had made him shed the first tears which had fallen from him that day, and he was more composed.

He entered the chamber with a deep and still awe upón him; and as he drew near his mother's bed side, and looked on her pale, placid, and motionless face, he scarcely dared breathe, lest he should disturb the secret communion that the soul was holding with the world into which it was about to enter. The loss that he was about suffering, and his heavy grief, were all forgotten in the feeling of a holy inspiration, and he was, as it were, in the midst of invisible spirits, ascending and descending. His mother's lips moved slightly, as she uttered an indistinct sound. He drew back, and his sister went near to her, and she spoke. It was the same gentle voice which he had known and felt from his childhood. The exaltation of his soul left him, — he sunk down, — and his misery went over him like a flood.

The next day, as soon as his mother became composed enough to see him, Arthur went into her chamber. She stretched out her feeble hand, and turned towards him, with a look that blessed him. It was the short struggle of a meek spirit. She covered her eyes with her hand, and the tears trickled down between her pale, thin fingers. As soon as she became tranquil, she spoke of the gratitude she felt at being spared to see him before she died.

"My dear mother," said Arthur, — but he could not go on. His voice was choked, his eyes filled with tears, and the agony of his soul was visible in his face. "Do not be so afflicted, Arthur, at the loss of me. We are not to part for ever. Remember, too, how comfortable and happy you have made my days. Heaven, I know, will bless so good a son as you have been to me. You will have that consolation, my son, which visits but a few,— you will be able to look back upon your past conduct to me, not without pain only, but with a holy joy. And think, hereafter, of the peace of mind you give me, now that I am about to die, in the thought that I am leaving your sister to your love and care. So long as you live, she will find you a father and brother to her." She paused for a moment. "I have always felt that I could meet death with composure; but I did not know," she said, with a tremulous voice, her lips quivering,—"I did not know how hard a thing it would be to leave my children, till now that the hour has come."

After a little while, she spoke of his father, and said, she had lived with the belief that he was mindful of her, and with the conviction, which grew stronger as death approached, that she should meet him in another world. She said but little more, as she grew weaker and weaker every hour. Arthur sat by in silence, holding her hand. He saw that she was sensible he was watching her countenance, for every now and then she opened her dull eye, and looked towards him, and endeavored to smile.

The day wore slowly away. The sun went down, and the melancholy and still twilight came on. Nothing was heard but the ticking of the watch, telling him with a resistless power that the hour was drawing nigh. He gasped, as if under some invisible, gigantic grasp, which it was not for human strength to struggle against.

It was now quite dark, and by the pale light of the night-lamp in the chimney corner, the furniture in the room threw huge and uncouth figures over the walls. All was unsubstantial and visionary, and the shadowy ministers of death appeared gathering round, waiting the duty of the hour appointed them. Arthur shuddered for a moment with superstitious awe; but the solemn elevation which a good man feels at the sight of the dying took possession of him, and he became calm again.

The approach of death has so much which is exalting, that our grief is, for the time, forgotten. And could one who had seen Arthur a few hours before, now have looked upon the grave and grand repose of his countenance, he would hardly have known him.

The livid hue of death was fast spreading over his mother's face. He stooped forward to catch the sound of her breathing. It grew quick and faint.—"My mother."—She opened her eyes, for the last time, upon him,—a faint flush passed over her cheek,—there was the serenity of an angel in her look,—her hand just pressed his. It was all over.

His spirit had endured to its utmost. It sunk down from its unearthly height; and with his face upon his mother's pillow, he wept like a child. He arose with a violent effort, and stepping into the adjoining chamber, spoke to his aunt. "It is past," said he. "Is my sister asleep?—Well, then, let her have rest; she needs it.' He then went to his own chamber, and shut himself in.

It is a merciful thing that the intense suffering of sensitive minds makes to itself a relief. Violent grief brings on a torpor, and an indistinctness, and dimness, as from long watching. It is not till the violence of affliction has subsided, and gentle and soothing thoughts can find room to mix with our sorrow, and holy consolations can minister to us, that we are able to know fully our loss, and see clearly what has been torn away from our affections. It was so with Arthur. Unconnected and strange thoughts, with melancholy but half-formed images, were floating in his mind, and now and then a gleam of light would pass through it, as if he had been in a troubled trance, and all was right again. His worn and tired feelings at last found rest in sleep

It is an impression, which we cannot rid ourselves of if we would, when sitting by the body of a friend, that he has still a consciousness of our presence, — that though the common concerns of the world have no more to do with him, he has still a love and care of us. The face which we had so long been familiar with, when it was all life and motion, seems only in a state of rest. We know not how to make it real to ourselves, that the body before us is not a living thing.

Arthur was in such a state of mind, as he sat alone in the room by his mother, the day after her death. It was as if her soul had been in paradise, and was now holding communion with pure spirits there, though it still abode in the body that lay before him. He felt as if sanctified by the presence of one to whom the other world had been laid open, — as if under the love and protection of one made holy. The religious reflections that his mother had early taught him, gave him strength; a spiritual composure stole over him, and he found himself prepared to perform the last offices to the dead.

It is not enough to see our friends die, and part with them for the remainder of our days, — to reflect that we shall hear their voices no more, and that they will never look on us again, — to see that turning to corruption which was but just now alive, and eloquent, and beautiful with all the sensations of the soul. Are our sorrows so sacred and peculiar as to make the world as vanity to us, and the men of it as strangers, and shall we not be left to our afflictions for a few hours? Must we be brought out at such a time to the concerned or careless gaze of those we know not, or be made to bear the formal proffers of consolation from acquaintances who will go away and forget it all? Shall we not be suffered a little while a holy and healing communion with the dead? Must the kindred stillness and gloom of our dwelling be changed for the solemn show of the pall, the talk of the passers-by, and the broad and piercing light of the common sun? Must the ceremonies of the world wait on us even to the open graves of our friends?

When the hour came, Arthur rose with a firm step and fixed eye, though his whole face was tremulous with the struggle within him. He went to his sister, and took her arm within his. The bell struck. Its heavy, undulating sound rolled forward like a sea. He felt a violent beating through his whole frame, which shook him that he reeled. It was but a momentary weakness. He moved on, passing those who surrounded him, as if they had been shadows. While he followed the slow hearse, there was a vacancy in his eye as it rested on the coffin, which showed him hardly conscious of what was before him. His spirit was with his mother's. As he reached the grave, he shrunk back and turned deadly pale; but sinking his head upon his breast, and drawing his hat over his face, he stood motionless as a statue till the service was over.

He had gone through all that the forms of society required of him. For, as painful as the effort was, and as little suited as such forms were to his own thoughts upon the subject, yet he could not do any thing that might appear to the world like a want of reverence and respect for his mother. The scene was ended, and the inward struggle over; and now that he was left to himself, the greatness of his loss came up full and distinctly before him.

It was a dreary and chilly evening when he returned home. When he entered the house from which his mother had gone for ever, a sense of dreary emptiness oppressed him, as if his very abode had been deserted by every living thing. He walked into his mother's chamber. The naked bedstead, and the chair in which she used to sit, were all that was left in the room. As he threw himself back into the chair, he groaned in the bitterness of his spirit. A feeling of forlornness came over him, which was not to be relieved by tears. She, whom he had watched over in her dying hour and whom he had talked to as she lay before him in death, as if she could hear and answer him, had gone from him. Nothing was left for the senses to fasten fondly on, and time had not yet taught him to think of her only as a spirit. But time and holy endeavors brought this consolation; and the little of life that a wasting disease left him, was passed by him, when alone, in thoughtful tranquillity; and amongst his friends he appeared with that gentle cheerfulness, which, before his mother's death, had been a part of his nature.*

Exercises.

Narration and Description may now be united in the history of

Moses	Elizabeth of England
Saul	Arabella Stewart
Elijah	Arabella Johnson
Elisha	Washington
Daniel	Jay
Judith	Marshall
Joshua	Franklin
Jepthah	Montezuma.

To the historical data which can be gleaned from any authentic source, the student may be permitted to add fictitious circumstances of his own invention.

In the same manner, he may present notices of any other character which may occur in the course of his reading or observation. He may also reverse the process of amplifying, and present an abridgement of the example.

LXIV.

EPISTOLARY CORRESPONDENCE, OR LETTER WRITING.†

A Letter is, perhaps, one of the most common, as well as one of the most useful forms of composition, and there are few, who can read or write at all, who are not frequently called

---

* It is recommended that the student be required to analyze this beautiful specimen of narration united with description, by presenting a list of the particulars which enter into the narrative and descriptive parts respectively.

† It is generally allowed, that epistolary writing, if not one of the highest, is one of the most difficult branches of composition. An *elegant* letter is much more rare than an elegant specimen of any other kind of writing. It is for this reason, that the author has deviated from the usual order practised by respectable teachers who give epistolary writing the first place in

upon to perform it. Under the head of Letter Writing, it is intended in this exercise to include all the forms of epistolary correspondence, whether in the shape of billets, notes, formal letters, or ceremonious cards, &c. It is proper to premise, that, whenever a letter is to be written, regard should be had to the usual forms of complimentary address, to the date, the superscription, and the closing. The folding, also, of the letter should not be disregarded. If it be true, that "trifles form the principal distinction between the refined and the unrefined," surely those trifles deserve some sort of consideration.

And, first, it is to be observed, that, whenever a *written* communication is made by one individual to another, the usages of society require that the *reply* should also be *written;* and that the same style of address should be preserved in both the communication and the reply. A different style, or form, seems to express a want of respect, or an arrogance of superior knowledge, — faults equally to be avoided in the intercourse of polished society.

If the letter is written in the *first* person, the reply should also be in the *first* person. Thus, when the letter begins:

"Dear Sir,
"I write to inform you," &c.,

the answer should be in the *first* person also; thus:

"Dear Sir,
"I have received your letter," &c., or "Your letter informing me, &c., has been received, and I hasten to say," &c.

If the letter is written in the *third* person, thus:

"Mr. Parker has the honor of informing the Hon. Mr Brimmer," &c.,

the answer should also be in the *third* person; thus:

"Mr. Brimmer has received the letter of Mr. Parker," &c.

---

the attention of the student. He has deemed it expedient to reserve the subject for this part of the volume, and for the practice of the student who has been previously exercised in other attempts. At this stage of his progress, he may be profitably exercised in the writing of letters. The teacher may now require him to write notes, billets, and letters addressed to a real or fictitious person, announcing some event, or on some formal subject. The teacher cannot be too particular in his directions with regard to folding, sealing, &c., for early habits of negligence, or want of neatness, are with difficulty eradicated.

The name of the writer should always be subscribed to the letter when it is written in the *first* person, but never when it is written in the third. The date of the letter should also be written *at the beginning*, when the letter is written in the first person, and *at the end*, when it is written in the third. The address of the letter should be written under the signature, and towards the left side of the letter, when it is written in the first person, but not when it is written in the third.

A neat and well-written letter is a much moie rare production than it ought to be. Few directions can be given with regard to the composition of a letter; but it is intended in this exercise to give some general directions with regard to the mechanical execution of letters, notes, and billets. And, first, with regard to Letters.

A letter should embrace the following particulars, namely. 1st. The date. 2d. The complimentary address. 3d. The body of the letter. 4th. The style, or complimentary closing. 5th. The signature; and, 6th. The address, with the title, if any.

The date should be written near the right hand upper corner of the sheet. The complimentary address follows, a little lower down, near the left hand side of the sheet. The body of the letter should be commenced very nearly under the last letter of the complimentary address. The style, or complimentary closing, should stand very nearly under the last letter of the body; the signature very nearly under the last letter of the style; and the address should be placed a little below the signature, and towards the left hand side of the sheet.

Example 1*st.*

FORM OF A LETTER.

Date.

Complimentary address.

Body of the Letter.

Style, or Complimentary Closing.

Signature.

Address, or Superscription.

Title, if any.

Example 2d.

A LETTER, WITH ITS PARTS.

(date.)
Boston, May 2d, 1843.

(complimentary address.)
Dear Sir,

(body of the letter.)
I have endeavored to present a few plain directions for letter-writing, which, I hope, will be sufficiently intelligible, without much labored explanation. If, however, I have unfortunately neglected any material point, I shall very gladly supply the deficiency, if you will have the kindness to mention it, either personally, or by note.

(style, or complimentary closing.)
Yours respectfully,

(signature.)
George C. S. Parker.

(the address, or superscription.)
Hon. James Harper.

(title.)
Mayor of New York.

In very formal letters, the address should precede the letter and the signature, so that the individual addressed may, at first sight, perceive that the communication is intended for him, before he has taken the trouble to read it through. In this case, also, the date should be written below, in the place of the address.

Example 3d.

A FORMAL LETTER.

To the Hon. Mr. Brimmer,
Mayor of Boston.
Sir,
The public schools of this commonwealth are under great obligations to you for your late munificent benefaction. That you may long live to witness, and to rejoice in the widely extended influences of that benefaction is the ardent wish of,
Sir,
Yours very respectfully,
Rich'd. G. Parker.
Boston, Aug. 3d, 1843.

The folding * of a letter, though in itself a thing of apparently trivial importance, is still deserving of attention. The following will be more intelligible than written directions.

* Official documents and very formal letters have, sometimes, but two folds; and these are made by doubling over the top and bottom parts of the whole sheet, or open letter, in the manner in which papers are generally kept on file. The whole is then enclosed in an envelope.

Example 4th.

This Cut represents the folding of a Letter.

No. 1. The Letter before it is folded.

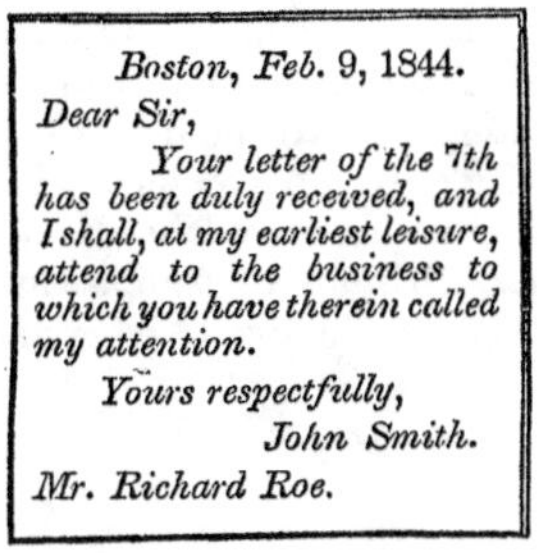

Boston, Feb. 9, 1844.
Dear Sir,
Your letter of the 7th has been duly received, and I shall, at my earliest leisure, attend to the business to which you have therein called my attention.
Yours respectfully,
John Smith.
Mr. Richard Roe.

No. 2. The first fold, one fourth part of the first leaf turned over.

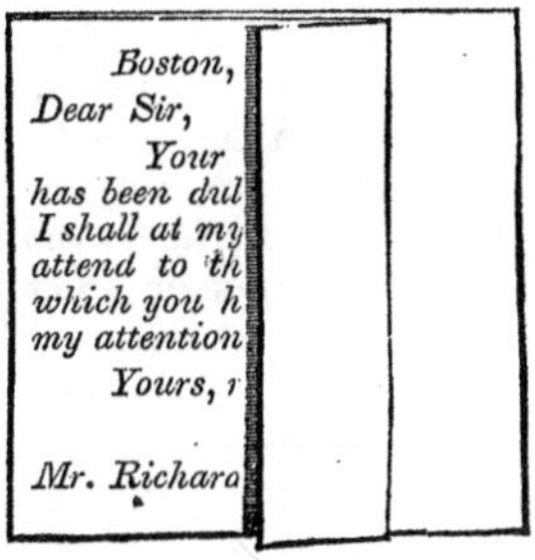

Boston,
Dear Sir,
Your
has been dul
I shall at my
attend to th
which you h
my attention
Yours, r
Mr. Richard

No. 3. The second fold; the folded part turned over so as to meet the left side of the sheet.

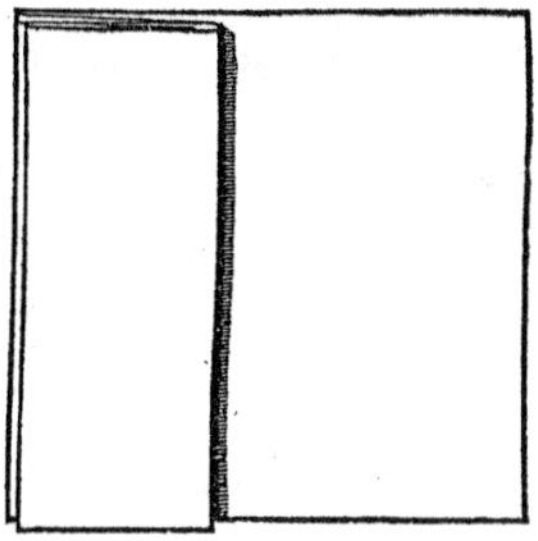

No. 4. The third fold.

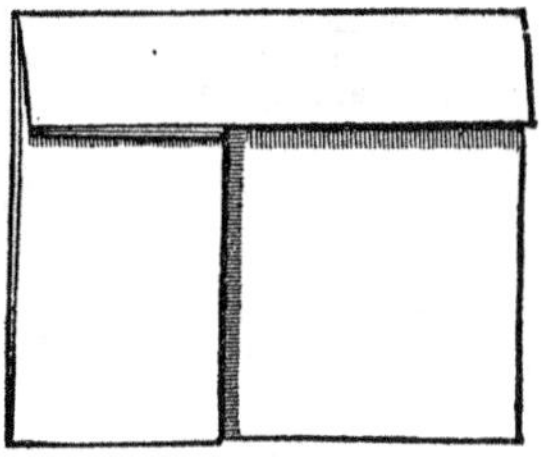

No. 5. The fourth fold

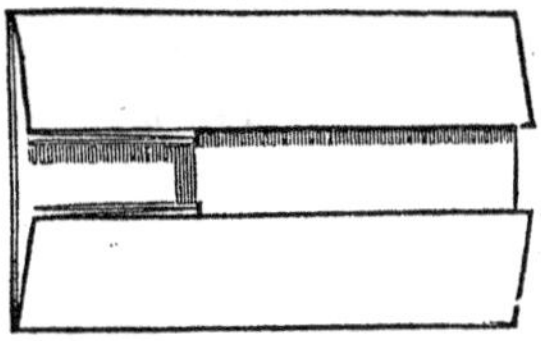

No. 6. The fifth fold.

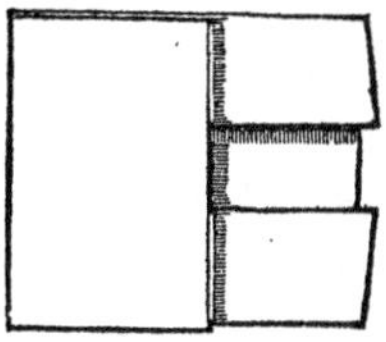

No. 7. The letter closed.

No. 8. The letter sealed.

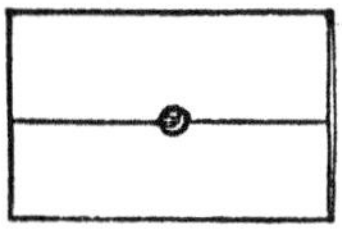

No. 9. The letter directed.

Richard Roe,
Boston.

TITLES.

In the superscription of a letter, the title of Honourable is generally given by courtesy to the Vice-President of the United States; to the Lieutenant-Governor of a State; to the Senators and Representatives of the United States; to the Senators of the respective States, and to the Judges of all the courts; to the Mayor of a city; to the Heads of Departments, &c. In addressing the President of the United States, the Governor of a Commonwealth, or an Ambassador of the United States, the title "His Excellency" * is generally used. †

---

* See *Antonomasia*, page 82.

† No titles are formally recognized by law in this country, except in Massachusetts, where the legal title of the Governor is "His Excellency," and that of the Lieutenant-Governor, "His Honor;" and, therefore, as it is stated above, it is *by courtesy* only, that the usage has obtained. As it is possible that this volume may fall into the hands of some individuals who are curious to know something of the forms of address in the mother country, the following directions are extracted from the grammar of Mr. Lennie, published in Edinburgh a few years ago.

"*Directions for Superscriptions and Forms of Address to Persons of every Rank.*

[The *superscription*, or what is put on the *outside* of a letter, is printed in Roman characters, and begins with *To*. The terms of *address* used in *beginning* either a letter, a petition, or verbal address, are printed in Italic letters, immediately after the superscription. The *blanks* are to be filled up with the *real* name and title.]

"To the King's Most Excellent Majesty, — *Sire*, or *May it please your Majesty*. Conclude a petition, or speech, with, — Your Majesty's most Loyal and Dutiful Subject.

To the Queen's Most Excellent Majesty, — *Madam*, or, *May it please your Majesty*.

To his Royal Highness, Frederick, Duke of York, — *May it please your Royal Highness*.

In the same manner address every other member of the Royal Family, *male* or *female*.

Nobility. To his Grace the Duke of ——, *My Lord Duke, Your Grace*, or, *May it please your Grace*.

To the Most Noble the Marquis of ——, *My Lord Marquis, Your Lordship*

To the Right Honorable ——, Earl of ——, *My Lord, Your Lordship*.

To the Right Honorable Lord Viscount ——, *My Lord, May it please your Lordship*.

To the Right Honorable Baron ——, *My Lord, May it please your Lordship*.

The wives of noblemen have the same Titles with their husbands, thus:

To her Grace the Duchess of ——, *May it please your Grace*.

To the Right Honorable Lady Ann Rose, — *My Lady, May it please your Ladyship*.——

The titles of *Lord* and *Right Honorable* are given to all the sons of Dukes

The members of a house of representatives, or of a board of aldermen, taken collectively, should be addressed as "The Honorable," &c.

The title of Esquire is also given by courtesy in the superscription of a letter, to all gentlemen to whom we wish to show respect; but, when the title of Hon. or Honorable is

---

and Marquises, and to the eldest sons of Earls; and the title of *Lady* and *Right Honorable* to all their daughters. The younger sons of Earls are all *Honorables* and *Esquires*.

Right Honorable is due to Earls, Viscounts, and Barons, and to all the members of Her Majesty's Most* Honorable Privy Council, to the Lord Mayors of *London*, *York*, and *Dublin*, and to the Lord Provost of *Edinburgh*, during the time they are in office; to the Speaker of the House of Commons; to the Lords Commissioners of the Treasury, Admiralty, Trade, and Plantations, &c.

The House of Peers is addressed thus,—To the Right Honorable the Lords Spiritual and Temporal of the United Kingdom of Great Britain and Ireland in Parliament assembled. *My Lords, May it please your Lordships.*

The House of Commons is addressed thus,—To the Honorable the Knights, Citizens, and Burgesses of the United Kingdom of Great Britain and Ireland in Parliament assembled. *Gentlemen*, or, *May it please your Honors.*

The sons of Viscounts and Barons are styled Honorable and Esquire; and their daughters have their letters addressed thus,—to the Honorable Miss or Mrs. D. B.

The king's commission confers the title of *Honorable* on any gentleman in a place of honor or trust; such as, the Commissioners of Excise, His Majesty's Customs, Board of Control, &c., Admirals of the Navy, Generals, Lieutenant-Generals, and Colonels in the Army.

All noblemen, or men of title, in the army and navy, use their title by *right*, such as *Honorable*, before their title of rank, such as *Captain*, &c.; thus the *Honorable Captain* James James of the ——, *Sir*, or *Your Honor*.

Honorable is due, also, to the Court of Directors of the East India Company, the Governors and Deputy-Governors of the Bank of England.

The title *Excellency* is given to all Ambassadors, Plenipotentiaries, Governors in foreign countries, to the Lord-Lieutenant, and to the Lords Justices of the Kingdom of Ireland. Address such thus,—

To his Excellency Sir ——, Bart., Her Britannic Majesty's Envoy Extraordinary, and Plenipotentiary to the Court of Rome,—*Your Excellency May it please your Excellency.*

The title *Right Worshipful*, is given to the Sheriffs, Aldermen, and Recorder of London; and *Worshipful*, to the Aldermen and Recorders of other Corporations, and to Justices of the Peace in England,—*Sir*, or *Your Worship.*

The Clergy are all styled *Reverend*, except the Archbishops and Bishops, who have something additional; thus,—

To his Grace the Archbishop of Canterbury, or, To the *Most* Reverend Father in God, Charles, Lord Archbishop of Canterbury,—*My Lord*, or, *Your Grace.*

To the *Right* Reverend Father in God, John, Lord Bishop of ——, *My Lord*, or, *Your Lordship.*

* The Privy Counsellors, taken collectively, are styled his Majesty's *Most* Honorable Privy Council.

used, that of Esquire is always to be omitted, on the principle that the greater contains the less. For the same reason, the title Mr. should never precede that of Esquire.*

OF NOTES OF INVITATION.

Notes of invitation, except where a great degree of familiarity is used, are generally written in the third person, and on paper of smaller size, called billet paper. The answers should also be written in the third person, and the same forms of expression should be used, as those employed in the invitation. A departure from the form seems like arrogance of superior knowledge of propriety; but where an expression is manifestly out of place, or improper, the writer of the reply is by no means bound to sacrifice his own sense of propriety to the carelessness or the ignorance of the one who addresses him.

The same observations that were made with regard to the date of a letter addressed in the third person, apply also to

* In the address on the outside of a letter, note, &c., when the residence of the person addressed is unknown, but it is known that he is an inhabitant of the town or city in which we write, the word "*Present*" is frequently introduced to supply the place of the residence.

To the very Rev. Dr. A. B., Dean of ——, *Sir.*

To the Rev. Mr. Desk, or, To the Rev. John Desk. *

The general address to clergymen is, *Sir*, and when written to, *Reverend Sir*. Deans and Archdeacons are usually called *Mr. Dean*, *Mr. Archdeacon*.

Address the Principal of the University of Edinburgh thus, — To the Very Rev. Dr. B., Principal of the University of Edinburgh, — *Doctor;* when written to, *Very Rev. Doctor*. The other Professors thus, — To Dr. D. R., Professor of Logic in the University of E., — *Doctor*. If a Clergyman say, — To the Rev. Dr. J. M., Professor of, &c., — *Reverend Doctor*.

Those who are not Drs. are styled *Esquire*, but not Mr. too; thus, — To J. P., Esq., Professor of Humanity in the University of Edinburgh, — *Sir* If he has a literary title, it may be added. Thus, To J. P., Esq., A. M. Professor of, &c.

Magistrates, Barristers at Law, or Advocates, and Members of Parliament, viz. of the House of Commons (these last have *M. P.* after Esq.,) and all gentlemen in independent circumstances, are styled *Esquire*, and their wives Mrs."

* It seems to be unsettled whether *Mr.* should be used after *Reverend*, or not. In my opinion (says Mr. Lennie) it should, because it gives a clergyman his own honorary title over and above the common one. May we not use the Rev. *Mr.* as well as the Rev. *Dr.*? Besides, we do not always recollect whether his name is *James*, or *John*, &c. Mr., in such a case, would look better on the back of a letter than a long, ill-drawn dash, thus, *The Rev.* —— *Desk.* In short, *Mr.* is used by our best writers after Reverend, but not uniformly. The words *To the*, not being necessary on the *back* of a letter, are seldom used; but, in addressing it in the *inside*, left hand corner, at the bottom, they are generally used.

notes of invitation. The date should be at the bottom of the note, and at the left hand. *

Example 5th.

FORM OF NOTES OF INVITATION, WITH THE REPLY.

INVITATION FOR THE EVENING.

Mrs. Smith† requests the pleasure of Mr. and Mrs. Chapman's company on Thursday Eve'g, the 5th inst.
Beacon St.
Aug. 2d.

Example 6th.

THE REPLY.

Mr. and Mrs. Chapman accept with pleasure Mrs. Smith's invitation for Thursday Evening, the 5th inst.‡
Chestnut St.
Feb. 12th.

* When notes or letters are addressed to gentlemen of the same name, they should be addressed, "The Messrs.," or, "Messrs.;" if to two single ladies, "The Misses," not the "Miss." Thus, "The Misses Smith, or, "The Misses Davies," not, "The Miss Smiths," nor "The Miss Davises."

† As the lady is generally considered the head of the tea-table, there seems to be a propriety in the invitation to tea, or the evening, coming from the lady of the house alone.

‡ Or, *Mr. and Mrs Chapman regret that a previous engagement will de*

Example 7th.

INVITATION TO DINNER.

Mr. Tyler requests the pleasure of the Hon. Mr. Otis' company at dinner on Saturday next, at 5 o'clock.

Bowdoin Square,

Wednesday, 13th July.

Example 8th.

THE REPLY *

Mr. Otis accepts with pleasure Mr. Tyler's invitation to dinner on Saturday next, at 5 o'clock.

Beacon Street,

Thursday, 14th July.

prive them of the pleasure of accepting Mrs. Smith's polite invitation for Thursday evening, the 5th inst.

The address of a gentleman to a lady's invitation may be : *Mr. Chapman has the honor of accepting*, &c., or, *regrets that a previous engagement will vrevent his having the honor*, &c.

* The latest and most approved style of folding notes, is to enclose them in an envelope, in the manner explained in reference to official docu ments, in the note on page 188th. The envelopes, ready made, are fur nished by the stationer. If not enclosed, they generally have two folds only ; and in directing them, the open part, or leaves, of the note should be *on the left side.* When enclosed, but one fold is necessarw

With regard to the sealing of a letter, if a wafer is to be used, care should be taken that it be not made too moist, for, in that case, it will not receive a good impression from the seal; and, moreover, is apt to give the letter a soiled appearance. But they who are particular about these matters always use wax in preference to wafers. *

FORMS OF CARDS.

Under the head of epistolary correspondence, may also be embraced the different forms of ceremonious cards, designed for morning calls, nuptial ceremonies, &c. As these are all supposed to be written or dictated by the individual who uses them, no title conceded by *courtesy* alone should ever be seen on them. Even the prefix of Mr. on a gentleman's card, savors of arrogance, for the literal meaning of the prefix is "Master." But the case is different on the card of a lady, and the prefix Mrs. (although it means "Mistress") is to be used, in order to distinguish her name from that of her husband. The question may arise, whether the residence should be inserted on the card. To this question a decided affirmative reply is given, although it is known to be at variance with not unfrequent usage. The omission of the residence seems to imply the belief, that the individual is a person of such distinction, that the knowledge of the residence is a matter of notoriety, and needs not to be mentioned. Now, in all the courtesies of life, the individual speaking of himself, should speak modestly and with humility; and, however distinguished he may be, he should be guilty of no arrogance of distinction. The insertion of the residence, therefore, is to be recommended on this ground alone, to say nothing of the possibility of mistake, arising from the bearing of the same name by two different families or by two different individuals.

In the cards of the young ladies of a family, the family name, with the

* Lord Chesterfield, having received a letter sealed with a wafer, is said to have expressed strong disapprobation, saying, "What does the fellow mean by sending me his own *spittle!*" It is related, also, of Lord Nelson, that, in the very midst of the battle of Copenhagen, when the work of carnage and destruction was the hottest around him, and he judged it expedient to propose a cessation of hostilities, a wafer being brought to him to seal his communication to the Danish authorities, he rejected it, directing the wax and a taper to be brought, saying, "What! shall I send my own *spittle* to the Crown Prince?" In this latter case, however, *policy* might have been mingled with refinement; for a wafer seems to imply haste, and the sealing of his letter with a wafer would have implied a desire for a speedy cessation of hostilities, which would have been construed into a necessity of the same, and have rendered his enemies confident of success, and unwilling to accede to the proposal. The coolness and deliberation implied in the sealing with wax, concealed from his enemies the knowledge of the condition of his fleet, and disposed them to comply with his wishes.

There is a kind of transparent glazed wafer very much in use at the present day; but even this seems to be obnoxious to the same objections, —it implies haste, which is inconsistent with the studied courtesies of polished life, and, moreover, involves the necessity of sending one's ow "*spittle.*"

prefix of "*Miss*," is proper to be used *without the "Christian name*," by the eldest of the single daughters. The Christian names of the younger daughters should be inserted. To illustrate by an example, suppose a gentleman, by the name of *Arthur S. Wellington*, resides with his family, a wife, and three daughters, *Caroline M.*, *Catharine S.*, and *Augusta P.* in *Tremont Street*. His card should be:

Arthur S. Wellington,
Tremont Street.

that of his wife,

Mrs. Arthur S. Wellington,
Tremont Street.

his eldest daughter's,

Miss Wellington,
Tremont Street.

his second daughter's,

Miss Catharine S. Wellington,
Tremont Street.

his third daughter's,

Miss Augusta P. Wellington,
Tremont Street.

On the death, or marriage, of the eldest daughter, the second daughter becomes *Miss Wellington*,* &c.

---

* On wedding cards, or cards preceding a wedding, there is considerable diversity of opinion, whether the name of both the gentleman and the lady should be inserted, or whether that of the lady alone should be expressed. A decided opinion is, however, expressed, that the name *of the lady alone* belongs on the card. She is to be the future mistress of the house; over its internal arrangements she alone has (or should have) any control, and to her alone also, all visits of ceremony are directed. The same reasons, therefore, which exclude the name of the husband from the notes of invitation, seem to apply with equal force to the exclusion of the name of the future husband from the wedding cards. Thus, supposing that Mr. John Singleton and Miss Sarah Greenwood intend marriage, the wedding card should be expressed thus:

Miss Sarah Greenwood,
At home on Tuesday Eve'g, at 8 o'clock.
48 Winter Street

Another class of cards,* called business cards, form a convenient mode of advertising, and are much used at the present day. Of these it will be sufficient to say, that they should be short, comprehensive, clear, and distinct. The card of an attorney or a counsellor at law will read thus:

William Blackstone,
Counsellor, (or Attorney,) at Law
47 Court Street,
Boston.

Reference:
Hon. John Dane,
Nath'l Royall, Esq

The card of a physician may be expressed in the following form.

William Danforth, M. D., M. M. S.,
57 Winter Street,
Boston.

Reference:
Dr. William Rand,
" John Warren.

---

* There are some portions of this article, particularly those relating to ceremonious observances in epistolary correspondence, which may be deemed out of place in a volume professing to treat of grave composition. The author's apology for their introduction is the want he has long felt of something of the kind for the use of his own pupils. He confesses that he is alone responsible for *all* the directions and the suggestions in the introduction to the Exercise; and, while he is conscious that the attitude of a learner would become him better than that of a teacher in these points, he apologizes for his presumption by the statement, that he knows no source in print to which he can refer those who are desirous of information upon these topics. How he has thus supplied the deficiency, he leaves for others to judge. To those who have any thing to object to what he has advanced, he respectfully addresses the words of the Venusian poet:

—— "Si quid novisti rectius istis,
"Candidus imperti; si non, his utere mecum."

That the whole subject is important in an enlightened community, needs no stronger corroboration than the assertion of the author of Waverley, (see "*Ivanhoe*," Parker's edition, Vol. 1st, p. 169,) that "a man may with more impunity be guilty of an actual breach of good breeding or of good morals, than appear ignorant of the most minute point of fashionable etiquette."

The card of a commission merchant is as follows:

Horatio Gates,
Commission Merchant,
49 Water Street,
New York.

Reference:
Samuel Good,
Fiske & Rand,
George W. Lawrence, } *Esquires.*

Example 9th.

A LETTER OF INTRODUCTION.

[N. B. It will be noticed, that it is not customary to seal a Letter of Introduction.]

Boston, April 19th, 1845

Dear Sir,

This will be handed to you by my friend, Mr. John Smith, who visits your city on business connected with his profession. Mr. Smith is one of the most distinguished members of the Suffolk Bar, and you will not fail to discover that he is as remarkable for his general scholarship, and the polish of his manners, as for his eminence in the legal profession. The attentions which you may please to show him for my sake, I have no doubt that you will be happy to continue for his own,—all of which shall be gratefully acknowledged and heartily reciprocated by

Yours respectfully,
Rich'd Roe.

John Doe, Esq.

Example 10*th*.

A LETTER OF CONDOLENCE.

BOSTON, *April* 19*th*, 1845.

Dear Friend,

I write this under the utmost oppression of sorrow; the youngest daughter of our friend Jones is dead! Never, surely, was there a more agreeable, and more amiable young person; or one who better deserved to have enjoyed a long, I had almost said, an immortal life! She had all the wisdom of age, and the discretion of a matron, joined with youthful sweetness and virgin modesty.

With what an engaging fondness did she behave to her father! How kindly and respectfully receive his friends! How affectionately treat all those, who, in their respective offices, had the care and education of her! She employed much of her time in reading, in which she discovered great strength of judgment; she indulged herself in few diversions, and those with much caution. With what forbearance, with what patience, with what courage, did she endure her last illness!

She complied with all the directions of her physicians; she encouraged her sister, and her father; and when all her strength of body was exhausted, supported herself by the single vigor of her mind. That, indeed, continued even to her last moments, unbroken by the pain of a long illness, or the terrors of approaching death; and it is a reflection which makes the loss of her so much the more to be lamented. A loss infinitely severe! more severe by the particular conjuncture in which it happened!

She was contracted to a most worthy youth; the wedding day was fixed, and we were all invited. How sad a change from the highest joy, to the deepest sorrow! How shall I express the wound that pierced my heart, when I heard Jones himself, (as grief is ever finding out circumstances to aggravate its affliction,) ordering the money he had designed to lay out upon clothes and jewels for her marriage, to be employed in defraying the expenses of her funeral!

He is a man of great learning and good sense, who has applied himself, from his earliest youth, to the noblest and most elevating studies: but all the maxims of fortitude which he has received from books, or advanced himself, he now absolutely rejects; and every other virtue of his heart gives place to all a parent's tenderness. We shall excuse, we shall even approve his sorrow, when we consider what he has lost. He has lost a daughter who resembled him in his manners, as well as his person; and exactly copied out all her father.

If you shall think proper to write to him upon the subject of so reasonable a grief, let me remind you not to use the rougher arguments of consolation, and such as seem to carry a sort of reproof with them; but those of kind and sympathizing humanity. Time will render him more open to the dictates of reason; for, as a fresh wound shrinks back from the hand of the surgeon, but by degrees submits to, and even requires the means of its cure, so a mind, under the first impressions of a misfortune, shuns and rejects all arguments of consolation; but at length, if applied with tenderness, calmly and willingly acquiesces in them.*

Very truly yours,
GEORGE C. S. PARKER

Henry Dix, Esq.

Exercises in Epistolary Writing.

A Letter to a friend announcing any event, real or imaginary.
" " the inhabitants of the moon, or the stars, or a comet
" " any character in history.
" " any one in a foreign country.
" containing a journal of occurrences.
" " criticisms on works that have been read.
" " opinions on subjects discussed at any seminary
" " suggestions caused by daily studies.
" " requesting the acceptance of some present
" describing a sunrise at sea.
" " sunset "
" from Palestine, describing the country, &c.
" " England, " " "
" " France, " " "
" " Italy, " " "
" " Greece, " " "
" describing the personal appearance and style of preaching of some eminent divine.
" " the Falls of Niagara.
" " the White Mountains.
" " Lake Erie, &c.
" " the Pyramids of Egypt.
" " Mount Vesuvius.

LXV.

REGULAR SUBJECTS.

ON A SUBJECT, AND THE METHOD OF TREATING IT.

In writing on a regular subject, the following directions are given by Mr. Walker, as suggestions for the different divisions, as well as for the systematic train of reflections.

* This letter is an original of Pliny the Younger to Marcellinus, translated by Melmoth. The address, &c. has been altered to accommodate it to the purposes of this volume.

The definition; the cause; the antiquity, or novelty; the universality or locality; the effects; namely, the goodness or badness, or the advantages or disadvantages.

1st. If your subject require explanation, define it or explain it at large.

2nd. Show what is the cause of your subject; that is, what is the occasion of it, or what it is derived from.

3d. Show whether your subject be ancient or modern; that is, what was in ancient times, and what it is at present.

4th. Show whether your subject relates to the whole world, or only to a particular part of it.

5th. Examine whether your subject be good or bad; show wherein its goodness or badness consists, and what are the advantages or disadvantages that arise from it.*

Example.

ON GOVERNMENT.

Definition. Government is the direction and restraint exercised over the actions of men in communities, societies, or states. It controls the administration of public affairs, according to the principles of an established constitution, a code of written laws, or by well-known usages; or it may be administered, as in some countries, by the arbitrary edicts of the sovereign. Government is the soul of society: it is that order among rational creatures which produces almost all the benefits they enjoy. A nation may be considered as a large family;—all the inhabitants are, as it were, relations; and the supreme power, wherever it is lodged, is the common parent of every individual.

Cause. The necessity of government lies in the nature of man. Interest and selfishness, unrestrained by salutary laws and restrictions, would be the controlling principle of every man's actions, uninfluenced by a proper regard for the rights of others. It is necessary, therefore, to have some restraint laid upon every man—some power which shall control him, and impel him to what is right, and deter him from what is wrong, and this power is government. To this restraint every one must submit; and if in such submission any one finds it necessary to give up

* These directions are thus versified by Mr. Walker:

If first your subject definition need,
Define your subject first, and then proceed;
Next, if you can, find out your subject's cause,
And show from whence its origin it draws:
Ancient or modern may your subject be,
Pursue it, therefore, to antiquity;
Your subject may to distant nations roam,
Or else relate to objects nearer home:
The subject which you treat is good, or ill
Or else a mixture of each principle:
And ere your subject a conclusion know,
The advantage or the disadvantage show.

a portion of the rights with which he fancies that God and nature endowed him, he will be consoled by the reflection that all have to make the sacrifice, and that the concession is made for the protection of his property and his life, for without government neither would be safe.

Antiquity. Accordingly, we find, so deeply seated is the necessity for government, that in the earliest ages of the world a kind of government was existing among all tribes and nations; and so remarkable is this fact, that almost all that history records of the earliest people is the history of these kings.

Universality. In every part of the world, also, at the present day, where human creatures are to be seen, there also some kind of government is found among them. Even the rudest among the savage nations have their kings and chiefs, whose word is law, and whose power is seldom disputed.

Locality. But government, in its most perfect form, is generally found among the most civilized and enlightened people. Almost all the different kinds of government now existing, or that ever did exist, may be reduced to three, namely, Monarchy, Aristocracy, and Democracy. Under one of these forms every nation now known to exist is regulated and controlled. The painted Indian, whose life and death are at the mercy of his sachem, the naked African, who looks in terror at his king, and the wild Arab, whose chief is the sovereign arbiter in the division of the plunder obtained by the horde, all are in fact the subjects of a monarch. Rome, under the decemvirs, and Venice and Genoa under their nobles, presented the spectacle of an Aristocracy; while Athens, luxurious Athens, invested the chief power in an assembly of the people, and presented to the world a splendid example of a Democracy. Each of these different forms is attended by its own peculiar advantages and disadvantages which the unity of our subject does not permit us now to discuss. But the advantages of some form of government remains yet to be presented.

Advantages. Order is said to be the first law of heaven. But among men it is essentially necessary for their very existence. Man, uncontrolled and unrestrained, would ever be invading his brother's rights Nothing would be safe. Might would be right, and the strongest might revel in the possession of that which the weaker had no power to keep from him. Laws emanate from government. Without government there could be no laws. It is the laws which protect every man in the enjoyment of his life, his liberty, and his possessions. Without laws, property would not be respected; the weak would be the slave of the strong, and the strong could enjoy their ill-gotton possessions only so long as they could maintain their ascendancy. It is government, therefore, that secures to every one the enjoyment of what he possesses, and restrains the strong from encroaching on the rights of the weak.

Disadvantages. Every form of government is liable to abuse. They who are in power are engaged in a constant struggle to maintain that power, while the ambitious and the aspiring are eagerly watching their opportunity to supplant them. This gives rise to parties and cabals, to plots and intrigues, to treachery, to treason and rebellion, to civil wars and family feuds, in which the innocent often share the punishment prepared for the guilty. But these evils are light in comparison with those which spring from anarchy, or want of government. It becomes every one, therefore, to lend his aid in support of the government under which it has pleased providence to place him, until that government shows by its actions that the good of the people for whom it was instituted is not its aim, and thereby renders rebellion a palliated evil, if not a virtue.

Exercises.

On Time.	On Justice.	On Joy.
Temperance.	The Mind.	Gaming.
Modesty.	The corporeal faculties.	Industry.
Sculpture.	Forgiveness.	Luxury.
Clemency.	Affection filial.	Patience.
Religion.	Affection parental, &c.	Pride.
Morning.	Cruelty.	Perseverance.
Evening.	Faith.	Conscience.
Day.	Happiness.	Compassion.
Night.	Flattery.	Equity.
Ambition.	Indolence.	Generosity.
Revenge.	Justice.	Melancholy.
Honor.	Magnanimity.	Humanity.
Virtue.	Politeness.	Ingratitude.
Education.	Prudence.	Frugality.
Truth.	Courage.	Patriotism.
The World.	Fortitude.	Prodigality.
Anger.	Disinterestedness.	Poverty.
Knowledge.	Fidelity.	

LXVI.

THEMES.

Themes are subjects, or topics, on which a person writes or speaks.

A theme, as defined by Mr. Walker, is the proving of some truth.

Themes are divided into two classes, the simple and the complex.

Simple themes comprehend such as may be expressed by one term or more, without conveying either an affirmation or a negation. Such as Logic, Education, Habit, The Fall of the Roman Empire, The Institution of Chivalry. *

* Such, also, are the subjects of the last Exercises under the head of Regular Subjects.

Complex themes comprehend such propositions as admit of proof or illustration; expressing a judgment which of course may be denied without invoking any positive contradiction in the meaning of the terms. The following are examples: "Logic is a useful study." "Youth is the season of improvement." "Wisdom is better than riches." "A public is preferable to a private education."

In the last set of exercises the course was laid down for the management of "a regular subject," which is prescribed by Mr. Walker in his "Teacher's Assistant." What he calls "regular subjects" are designed for simple themes. The course prescribed by Mr. Jardine, in his Outlines of a Philosophical Education, is less mechanical, and is to be preferred, because the mind of the student is less fettered by "leading strings," and left more to its own resources. The following are his preliminary remarks:

"To give an illustration of a simple theme I shall suppose the subject to be Logic, and shall shortly apply the scholastic rules to the structure of the essay which should be composed upon it."

"The first rule directs the student to begin by fixing exactly the meaning of the term, which is the subject of the theme, removing every thing that is doubtful or equivocal in its signification; and, when difficulties of that kind occur, the true import of the word must be determined by the canons of etymology, or by the practice of the best writers."

"By the second rule, which is the principle one, he is required to explain the essential and accidental qualities of the subject, here supposed to be *logic;* and to enumerate them, according to their order and importance, and with a reference to the end which is contemplated by the logician. That end is the establishment of truth or the refutation of error, and it is accomplished by the application of those rules of right reasoning, in which the art of *logic* may be said to consist. In these rules are included definition, division, classification, as well as those general directions relative to propositions which are derived from the ancient dialectics. But it is unnecessary here to enlarge; for the most important of the rules, for both kinds of themes, are the same, in so far, at least, as the object of both is the attainment of clear notions, lucid arrangement, and perspicuous expression."

"The special rules which relate to the management of complex themes, may be shortly enumerated. That no propositions, advanced as the ground of inference and deduction should be admitted, but upon the best and most solid evidence, arising from sense, from consciousness, or experience, or from undeniable truths, such as axioms and intuitive propositions; or lastly, upon testimony, analogy, facts already proved, the undeviating laws of nature, &c. — that the meaning of the subject, and predicates of the radical proposition be accurately fixed — that the extent of the affirmation or negation be exactly ascertained, so that the proposition may be stated in the most intelligible manner, and the logical rules of division be applied — that the attention be next directed to the kind of evidence by which the proposition is established — and the arguments to be introduced in such order, that those which precede shall throw light on those that follow, and form a connected chain of comparisons, by which ultimately the agreement or disagreement, expressed in the proposition, shall be made manifest; and finally that all objections against the proposition be candidly and explicitly answered. The proof, when it is long, may be concluded with a recapitulation, containing the united strength of all the arguments which have been brought to confirm it."

"It is impossible to prescribe rules which shall exactly accord with the variety of subjects which may come under this order of themes, and, therefore, much must be left to the judgment and experience of the teacher. It is not every theme that requires the application of all the rules. The first rule may be sometimes necessary; the second is indispensable on all subjects; the other rules are only occasionally required;—a rigid adherence to these rules might render composition stiff and formal; but that would, in a great measure, be prevented, by frequent use and judicious application."

"Though, in the management of complex themes, the rules of demonstration cannot be always followed, yet the clearness, certainty, and progress of that kind of reasoning, ought to be the standard, as the best and most effectual mode of procuring the assent of the mind. Let the young composer imitate the geometrician, in first attempting to establish clearly the datum on which the deduction rests, and then proceed, with gradual and increasing strength, to the conclusion." *

---

* It may, perhaps, be objected that the course here prescribed by Mr. Jardine is too difficult for the young student. If perfect or finished compositions were required, there might be good grounds for such an opinion. In all cases, perfect specimens must be preceded by many unsuccessful efforts. An eminent writer has candidly acknowledged that he would be ashamed to disclose the many unsuccessful attempts he had made, before he could produce any thing worthy of public attention. Imperfect, then, as the first essays of the student may be, they constitute the natural and indispensable steps which lead to higher degrees of perfection.

The following extract from one of Mrs. Sherwood's "Social Tales" is so pertinent to the subject, that it is thought that it will be useful to the student to present it in this place. The tale from which it is extracted is entitled "*Hoc Age.*"

"It was the custom of my father, when I was a girl, to require of me every Saturday, a few pages written upon a given subject. Well do I remember the hours which I sometimes used to spend on these unfortunate Saturday mornings, in endeavoring to elicit sparks of genius from the cold iron of my brain; and how pleased I was wont to be, when any thing like a bright idea presented itself to my imagination: such were welcome to me as angel's visits, which are said to be few and far between.

"Much of my success, however, I found, depended upon the subject which was given me. When these subjects were fruitfnl and congenial to my feelings, the task was comparatively easy; but when they were new and strange to me, my labor was greatly increased, and so far from being able to put my ideas into any new form, I seemed to lose the power of expressing them, even in the most ordinary way.

"Judge, then, what must have been my despair, when on a certain Saturday, having stolen up into my father's study, with that sort of quiet pace which children use when they are going about any thing they do not much relish, (for the motion of the foot is a never-varying index in a simple mind, of the feelings of the heart.) I stood behind his chair as he sat writing, and said, 'Papa, please for the subject of my theme, to day?'

'*Hoc age*,' he replied, still writing on.

18

"Of one thing," continues Mr. Jardine, "the youngest student must be made sensible, from the evidence of his own consciousness, *that he cannot expect to compose even the simplest theme without directing and continuing his power of thinking upon it.*"

"Instructions cannot be too plain nor too minute, when directed to young persons entering upon a new and difficult course of study. The experience of the perplexities which assail the juvenile mind, in its first endeavors to discover materials and to find expressions, has induced me to lay aside the authority of the teacher, and to place myself as the companion or friend of the student, in those moments when his difficulties are most formidable."

"I suppose, then, 'Emulation' chosen as the subject of a simple theme, which the student is required to explain and illustrate, from lectures, books

---

"'What, papa?' I said.

"'Hoc age, child,' he answered; '*Hoc age* — go and make the best of it, but do n't disturb me.'

"'Hoc age,' I repeated, as I went down stairs. 'Hoc age — it is Latin; I know it is Latin. *Hoc* is *this*, and it is neuter, and the word *thing* is understood; and *age* is *do;* I know enough of Latin for this; therefore, *Hoc age* means, Do this thing.'

"So I mended a pen, and took a sheet of paper, and wrote 'Hoc age' in a fair hand at the top of the paper; and then I added the translation; and then wrote my own name in one corner, and the date at another; and then looked out of the window, and up to the ceiling, and wrote again, and actually made out a sentence to this effect: 'It is our duty, under every circumstance of life, to attend to this admonition;' and there I stopped, for the question suggested itself, to wit, what admonition? Further, therefore, I could not get, and when my father called me to dinner, I had not advanced an inch beyond the full round stop after the word admonition.

"My father was one of the kindest and gentlest of parents, and when I presented my vacant sheet to him, he smiled, and said, ''T is as much as I expected; but I am perfectly satisfied, nevertheless. If you have spent your morning in considering the nature of the injunction meant to be expressed in the words 'Hoc age,' you have not lost your time." My father then entered into an explanation of the subject, and pointed out to me that these two words were equivalent to the Scripture injunction, 'Whatsoever thine hand findeth to do, do it with thy might.' And then he showed me that the world abounded with persons who never seemed to give their full and undivided attention to any thing which they had to do, and in consequence, when suddenly called upon to act or speak with promptitude, were never ready and never had their words or their actions at command. 'Hence,' continued he, 'on smaller occasions, they are for ever wasting their time, and on more important ones losing advantages and opportunities never to be recovered.' My father added much more to me on this subject; but as I shall hope, in what follows, to elucidate what he said by a very appropriate example, I shall cite no more of his valuable discourse, with the exception of one remark only, which was most important; it was to this effect: that the salvation of the soul is the thing to be done in the first instance; the 'Hoc age' to which every human creature should principally attend — all other concerns being made subordinate to this one object, and all other efforts or exertions being in the end wholly inefficient in producing the happiness of any individual, when this one thing needful is neglected."

The whole of the tale, of which the above extract is merely the introduction, may well be recommended to the perusal of both teachers and students.

and observations, in such a way as to communicate a distinct account of emulation to all who shall read his essay. Where are the materials to be found? His first recourse would probably be to authors who have treated of emulation, from whom he might take what serves his purpose. But he is instructed that there is a nearer and much more fertile source, which will furnish him with materials, providing he seek for them in the proper way. And what is that source? His own mind, working upon the materials which he already possesses. Let him put the question to himself, What is emulation? Here let him recollect the early scenes in which this feeling was first excited. On the verge of childhood, he must remember the language used in amusements, 'I can do this, and you cannot,' 'I shall be at that mark before you.' He may have, perhaps, read the beautiful description of Gray, in the distant prospect of Eton College:

> Who, foremost, now delights to cleave
> With pliant arms, the glassy wave, &c.

Or the description of the Trojan games, in the sixth book of the Æneid. He may recollect that, when at school, he contended for the first place in his class, or may be now contending for the first prize at college. Upon the recollection of these scenes, and from associated feelings which exist in his mind, he is in some sort prepared to answer the question, What is 'emulation?' A desire and endeavor to excel others, — to be the first in any competition."

"From whence proceeds, or what excites this desire and endeavor? From obtaining an object first, which other competitors wish to possess. Is it the intrinsic value of the object of competition? No; — it may be a sprig of laurel, — a palm-branch, — a fox's tail, — a medal of little value, — a book, a seat of preferment or of honor. From what, then, does the object receive its value? It is the circumstance of obtaining it before other competitors. And what is it that gives such value to the being first in the competition? It is the presence of many spectators and admirers It is their reflected praise, which animates the competitors, — which makes the breast of the student palpitate when he receives the prize. Let the competition take place in a desert, where there are no spectators, the charm is dissolved, and the competitors walk over the course without pleasure or expectation."

"Again, what are the effects of emulation? When this principle operates with full effect, and under control of virtue and honor, it produces vigorous conflict, persevering exertion, contempt of difficulties and dangers, increasing hopes, eager expectations, and, in the moments of success, exquisite delight. The student may have a clearer view of this generous and energetic feeling, by turning his attention to the histories of great characters and great events, and distinguishing emulation from the effects of other feelings not unfrequently associated with it. He will thus be enabled to draw a line of distinction between it and its collaterals, ambition and fame. These fix upon the possession of their objects without any view of competition, or of the means by which they may be obtained, whereas the pleasures of emulation spring from the love of excellence and superiority."

"The experience of competitions, in which the student has been engaged, or of those which he has observed, will suggest to him, that emulation in its purest form can only take place where the prize is won by the personal exertions of the individual. When any undue means are used to obtain it, or any obstacle indirectly thrown in the way of a rival competitor, the generous flame of emulation is extinguished, and a mean degrading spirit is substituted in its place. One would think that the mortification which the student must suffer, when he receives a prize which he is conscious he did not deserve, should dispose him to reject it as altogether unworthy of his acceptance. The student cannot have forgotten the manner in which the friendly stratagem of Nisus, in favor of Euryalus, was received by the other competitors at the celebration of the Trojan games."

"An enlarged view should be taken of the field of competition. That field may be called up by the imagination. The person in whom the true spark of emulation is kindled, may imagine himself placed upon the same arena with the competitors of other centuries and other ages. Virgil endeavored to rival the fame of Homer, and Cicero that of Demosthenes When Cæsar passed the statue of Alexander, he is said to have burst into tears, because the Macedonian had surpassed him in military achievements. When ambition and emulation are conjoined in the same character occupied in similar exploits, it requires some discrimination to determine what belongs to each."

This sketch, of course, is not intended as a specimen of a simple theme on emulation, but merely as a general outline of the materials, with the view of pointing out to the student the course he should take to find them. He has only to embrace the subject of the theme closely, — to apply to his own mind for light and knowledge, — to press himself with interrogatories relative to his demands, — to follow the natural associations of things, and he will soon find materials enough, and arrive at much information which he could not otherwise have conceived to be within his reach. The concluding step is to select from these materials, and to arrange them according to the particular end he has in view. If this part of his work be rightly performed, he will not find much difficulty in suitably expressing what he clearly and distinctly knows."

[A list of subjects for Exercises will be found in the last article, under the head of Regular Subjects.]

If the course thus laid down by Mr. Jardine for the management of themes, be found too loose or too difficult, the student may follow the more mechanical one of Mr. Walker. His course for regular subjects or simple themes has already been given. The following is his course, with regard to themes in general: *

After the Theme or Truth is laid down, the Proof consists of the following parts:

1st. The Proposition or Narrative; where we show the meaning of the Theme, by amplifying, paraphrasing, or explaining it more at large.

---

* It will be noticed that Mr. Walker designates *simple themes* as *Regular Subjects;* while he embraces, under the term of Theme, those only which in general are called *complex* themes. This accords with his definition of a theme, which he says is the "proving of some truth."

2d. The Reason; where we prove the truth of the Theme by some reason or argument.

3d. The Confirmation; where we show the unreasonableness of the contrary opinion; or, if we cannot do that, we try to bring some other reason in support of the former.

4th. The Simile; where we bring in something in nature or art, similar to what is affirmed in our Theme, for illustrating the truth of it.

5th. The Example; where we bring instances from History to corroborate the truth of our Theme.

6th. The testimony or Quotation; where we bring in proverbial sentences or passages frcm good authors, which show that others think as we do.

7th. The Conclusion; when we sum up the whole and show the practical use of the Theme, by concluding with some pertinent observations.*

Example.

TOO MUCH FAMILIARITY GENERALLY BREEDS CONTEMPT.

Proposition. There is no observation more generally true than that our esteem of a person seldom rises in proportion to our intimacy with him.

Reason. Such is the general disguise men wear, that their good qualities commonly appear at first, and their bad ones are discovered by degrees; and this gradual discovery of their

---

* The rules are thus versified by Mr. Walker

The Proposition, the Reason, the Confirmation, tne Simile, the Example he Testimony, and the Conclusion.

The Theme at large the Proposition gives,
And the same thought in other words conceives
The Reason shows the Proposition true,
By bringing arguments and proofs to view;
The Confirmation proves th' opinion right,
By showing how absurd 's the opposite.
If that 's not to be done, it tries to explore
Some proof in aid of what was given before.
The Simile an apt resemblance brings,
Which shows the theme is true in other things;
The Example instances from History draws,
That by mankind's experience prove our cause:
The Testimony to the wise appeals,
And by their suffrage our opinion seals.
Some useful observations come at last,
As a conclusion drawn from what is past.

failings and weaknesses, must necessarily lessen our opinion of them.

Confirmation. It is the nature of man to have a high opinion of any excellence he is not fully acquainted with: he is prone to imagine it much greater than it really is; and therefore when it becomes thoroughly known, the expectation is at an end, and the good qualities which we at first admired, having no longer the recommendation of novelty, become not only less striking, but often produce indifference and contempt.

Simile. As the frogs in the fable were at first terrified by the noise of the falling of the log which Jupiter threw down into the lake for their king, but by degrees became so familiar with their wooden monarch as to despise it; so kings have often found by mixing too familiarly with their subjects, and masters by being too free with their servants, that they have lost their importance in proportion to their condescension.

Example. James the First, King of England, was a man of considerable learning, and had as few bad qualities as the generality of his subjects; but, by jesting with his attendants, and descending to childish familiarity with them, scarcely any King of England was held in greater contempt.

Testimony. A celebrated teacher has said that young people cannot be too much on their guard against falling into too great familiarity with their companions; for they are sure to lose the good opinion of those with whom they are familiar.

Conclusion. It may, therefore, be laid down, as confirmed by reason and experience, that nothing requires greater caution in our conduct, than our behaviour to those with whom we are most intimate.

Exercises.

The necessity of Exercise.
The proper use of Amusements.
On Laudable Exertion.
The importance of a good character.
The Folly of Dissipation.
Want of Piety arises from the want of sensibility.
The importance of Hospitality and the civilities of common life.
Religion consistent with true politeness.
On the pleasures of Conversation.
The dignity of virtue amid corrupt examples.
The duties and pleasures of Reflection.
The obligations of Learning to the Christian Religion.
On Decency as the only motive of our apparent virtues.

The importance of the government of temper.
The value of the art of printing.
The baneful effects of Indulgence.
The influence of the Great.
The Beauty and Happiness of an open behaviour and an ingenuous Disposition.
The utility of religious ceremonies.
A good heart necessary to enjoy the beauties of nature.
The wisdom of aiming at perfection.
Family Disagreements the frequent cause of immoral conduct.
The selfishness of men of the world.
The necessity of Temperance to the health of the mind.
Advantages of music as a recreation.
Necessity of attention to things as well as books.
The influence of fashion.
An honorable death preferable to a degraded life.

LXVII.

ABSTRACTS.

An abstract is a summary, or epitome, containing the substance, a general view, or the principal heads of a treatise or writing.

The taking of abstracts from sermons, speeches, essays, &c. is an exercise which the student will find exceedingly useful in the cultivation of habits of attention, as well as of analysis. In writing abstracts, it is not necessary to endeavor to recall the exact language of the original, the purpose of the exercise is fully subserved, if the principal idea be recorded

Example.

ON DIVERSIONS.

It is generally taken for granted, by most young people of fortune, that diversion is the principle object of life; and this opinion is often carried to such an excess, that pleasure seems to be the great ruling principle which directs all their thoughts, words, and actions, and which makes all the serious duties of life heavy and disgusting. This opinion, however, is no less absurd than unhappy, as may be shown by taking the other side of the question, and proving that there is no pleasure and enjoyment of life without labor.

The words commonly used to signify diversion are these three, namely, relaxation, amusement, and recreation; and the precise meaning of these words may lead us to very useful instruction. The idea of relaxation is taken from a bow, which must be *unbent* when it is not wanted to be used.

that its elasticity may be preserved. Amusement literally means an occasional forsaking of the *Muses*, or the laying aside our books when we are weary with study; and recreation is the refreshing or recreating of our spirits when they are exhausted with labor, that they may be ready, in due time, to resume it again.

From these considerations it follows that the idle man who has no work can have no play; for, how can he be relaxed who is never bent? How can he leave the Muses who is never with them? How can play refresh him who is never exhausted with business?

When diversion becomes the business of life, its nature is changed all rest presupposes labor. He that has no variety can have no enjoyment; he is surfeited with pleasure, and in the better hours of reflection would find a refuge in labor itself. And, indeed, it may be observed, that there is not a more miserable, as well as a more worthless being, than a young person of fortune, who has nothing to do but find out some new way of doing nothing.

A sentence is passed upon all poor men, that if they will not work, they shall not eat; and a similar sentence seems passed upon the rich, who, if they are not in some respect useful to the public, are almost sure to become burthensome to themselves. This blessing goes along with every useful employment; it keeps a man on good terms with himself, and consequently in good spirits, and in a capacity of pleasing and being pleased with every innocent gratification.

As labor is necessary to procure an appetite to the body, there must also be some previous exercise of the mind to prepare it for enjoyment; indulgence on any other terms is false in itself, and ruinous in its consequences. Mirth degenerates into senseless riot, and gratification soon terminates in satiety and disgust.

Abstract of the above.

1. It is a common error to suppose that diversion should form the business of life, the contrary being true.
2. This is proved by the derivation of the words used to express diversion — viz., relaxation, amusement, and recreation.
3. They who have no labor can have no diversion.
4. When diversion becomes labor, it is no longer diversion.
5. All men must have occupation, or be miserable.
6. There must be labor of mind as well as labor of the body, for the well being of both.

Exercises.

Exercises in the practice of taking abstracts are frequently presented by the preacher. They may also be found in volumes of sermons, in periodical papers and essays, in common text-books in literary institutions, and in the wide circle of English literature. It is not, therefore, deemed important to present them in detail in this volume.

LXVIII.

The faculty of invention, it is thought, has been sufficiently exercised in the preceding principles to enable the student now to fill out an essay from heads, outlines, or abstracts, as in the following

Example.

ON INDEPENDENCE.

HEADS.

1. No being perfectly independent but God.
2. The dependence created by trade and commerce is, in fact, a kind of independence.
3. Pecuniary dependence the most humiliating of any.
4. Pecuniary dependence naturally degrades the mind and depraves the heart.
5. Young people ought to be particularly careful to avoid pecuniary dependence.

The Essay founded on the above heads.

Independence, in the largest and most unlimited sense, is to created beings, a state impossible. No being is perfectly independent, but the One Supreme Being: all other beings, by their very nature, are dependent, in the first place, on their Creator, and in the second, on their fellow-creatures; from whose good-will and assistance they derive their chief happiness.

This dependence, however, consists in a mutual interchange of good offices; in such a suitable return of favors received, as makes each party obliged to the other, and at the same time leaves each other independent. This kind of dependence we find in different countries, that trade in commodities which are necessary to both; by which means, they become useful, but not indebted to each other.

But the most general sense of independence is that of property. The circulating medium, called money, and which is the representative of almost every thing that we wish, has in it something so sacred, that we can never receive it gratuitously, without losing our dignity and becoming dependent. We may ask for favors of another kind, and though they are granted to us, we are not degraded; but if once we ask a pecuniary favor we lose our independence, and become enslaved. No more can we converse with our creditor on the same equal terms that we did before. No more can we controvert his opinion, and assert our own: a conscious in feriority has deprived us of freedom, and we are the slave of him who was formerly our equal.

But the most deplorable part of this picture is, that dependence not only enslaves the mind, but tends to deprave the heart. We feel ourselves degraded by receiving pecuniary favors, and conscious of what our creditor must think of us, when we cannot return them, we are apt to view him with an eye of jealousy and distaste; and thus become guilty of one of the worst of crimes, the crime of ingratitude.

Young people, who know but little either of themselves or of the world, are apt to think such pictures of human nature misanthropical. They are, however, such as have been drawn by the experience of all ages and nations; and concur with several other traits to show us the natural depravity of man. If, therefore, we wish to preserve ourselves independent, — if we wish to maintain a proper dignity of character and freedom of opinion, — if we desire, above all things, to preserve ourselves from that depravity of heart, which we are so apt to slide into when we cannot pay our debts, — let us beware of borrowing money; for, as our immortal Shakspeare says,

> "A loan oft loseth both itself and friend,
> And borrowing dulls the edge of husbandry."

Exercises.

On the Multiplication of Books.

1. No amusements more attainable, or attended with more satisfaction, than those derived from literary subjects.
2. The student can enjoy in his library all that has employed the active mind of man.
3. Reading especially gratifying to those who are confined by profession or by circumstances.
4. Much of the student's time necessarily employed in retracing the progress of those who have gone before him.
5. Modern authors justify to themselves and others the addition which they make to the number of books.

2.

On the means of rendering old age honorable and comfortable.

1. Man degenerates in his nature as he advances in life.
2. That state is wretched, when the heart loses its sensibility.
3. Old age, though insensible to many pleasures, has a keen perception of pain.
4. Old age not always attended with natural infirmity.
5. A life of temperance preserves the equanimity of the mind.
6. A devotional spirit will afford the most lively enjoyments.
7. These enjoyments increase with the nearness of the approach of fruition.
8. That life honorable which affords the most useful lessons of virtue.
9. That life comfortable, which, although unattended with absolute enjoyment, has a solace for pain and a prospect of enjoyment near.

3.

Moderation in our wishes necessary.

1. Man's active mind seldom satisfied with its present condition.
2. Restlessness and excitement prevalent.
3. Ambition and hope constantly deceive us with delusive dreams.
4. If we dwell with satisfaction on the ideal, the real can never fulfil our expectations.
5. Few have realized their expectations. Many have been disappointed and deceived.
6. What is rational and attainable, should, therefore, be the only objects of desire.

4.

Wealth and fortune afford no ground for envy.

1. Envy most generally excited against wealth and fortune.
2. The rich and fortunate are not always happy.
3. We are deceived by appearances.
4. The poor are exempted from many evils to which the rich are subjected.
5. The rich have troubles from which the poor are exempted.
6. The real wants and enjoyments of life are few, and are common to almost all classes.
7. If the balance of happiness be adjusted fairly, it will be found that all conditions of life fare equally well.

LXIX.

DIVISIONS OF A SUBJECT.

One of the most difficult of the departments of composition consists in methodizing, or arranging, a subject; laying it out, as it were, and forming a sort of plan on which to treat it. The writer may be figuratively said to make a map of it in his own mind, ascertaining its boundaries, that is to say, the collateral subjects with which it is connected, its dependencies, influences, and prominent traits. And as no two geographers would probably lay down the same country exactly in the same way — some giving special attention to the mountains, others to the rivers, others to the sea-coast, others to the chief towns, &c., so no two writers would probably "*map out*" a subject in the same way. On this subject the following directions will probably be useful to the student:

Having before his mind the precise object of inquiry, and having also stated, either in a formal manner or by implication, the proposition to be supported, the writer now should turn his attention to the formation of his plan; or, in other words, he should determine in what order and connection his thoughts should be presented. Thus are formed *the heads* or divisions of a composition. These must correspond in their nature to the leading design and character of the performance.

In argumentative discussions, *the heads* are distinct propositions or arguments, designed to support and establish the leading proposition.

In persuasive writings, *the heads* are the different considerations which the writer would place before his readers, to influence their minds, and induce them to adopt the opinions and pursue the course which he recommends.

In didactic writings, they are the different points of instruction.

In narrative and descriptive writings, they are the different events and scenes which are successively brought before the mind.

No rules of universal application can be given to aid the writer in forming the plan, or *methodizing* his subject. His plan must vary with the subject and the occasion, Room is also left for the exercise of the taste and judgment of the writer. But although no special rules can be applied, the following general directions may be serviceable, so far, at least, as they may prevent or correct a faulty division:

First. Every division should lead directly to the purpose which the writer has in view, and be strictly subservient to the rules of unity.

Second. One division must not include another, but be distinct and independent in itself.

Third. The different divisions should, so far as may be, be so comprehensive, as to include all that can with propriety be said in relation to the subject, and, when taken together, present the idea of one whole.

In illustration of these rules, let us suppose that it is proposed to write an essay on *Filial Duties.* The writer designs to show, as the object of the essay, that children should render to their parents obedience and love. His division is as follows: — Children should render obedience and love to their parents.

1. Because they are under obligations to their parents for benefits received from them.
2. Because in this way they secure their own happiness.
3. Because God has commanded them to honor their parents.

In this division there is a manifest reference to the object of the writer The different heads are also distinct from each other, and, taken together, give a sufficiently full view of the subject. It is in accordance, then, with the preceding directions. Let us now suppose that the following division had been made: — Children should render love and obedience to their parents.

1. Because they are under obligations to them for benefits received from them.
2. Because their parents furnish them with food and clothing.
3. Because in this way they secure their own happiness.
4. Because there is a satisfaction and peace of conscience in the discharge of filial duties.

This division is faulty, since the different parts are not distinct from each other. The second head is included under the first, and the fourth under the third.

A third division might be made as follows:— Children should render obedience and love to their parents.

1. Because they should do what is right.
2. Because in this way they secure their own happiness.
3. Because God has commanded them to love their parents.

It may be said of the first part of this division, that it has no particular reference to the object of the writer. It is a truth of general application, and may with equal propriety be assigned in enforcing any other duty, as well as that of filial obedience. It is also implied in the other heads, since children do what is right, when, in obedience to God's command, they seek to secure their own happiness.*

In the divisions made in the mind of the writer in forming his plan, he may present them as independent topics, to be united by the reasoning which he employs in support of each; or as distinct propositions, each of which has a particular bearing on what he purposes to prove or to advance

Example of Independent Topics.

ON CHARITY.

Senses in which it is used in Scripture.
The kindred virtues with which it is allied.
Its operation on individuals.
On Society.
Field of action extended by Christianity.

Example of Distinct Propositions.

1. Charity employed in the Scriptures to denote all the good affections which we should bear to one another.
2. Charity the most important duty enjoined in Holy Writ.
3. Charity is an active principle.
4. Charity does not give every man an equal title to our love.
5. Charity produces peculiar and important effects on individual character.

Exercises.

The importance of a good education.
Happiness founded on rectitude of conduct.
Virtue man's highest interest.
The misfortunes of men mostly chargeable on themselves.

---

* The question may arise, says Mr. Newman, from whose valuable treatise on Rhetoric the above directions are principally derived, Is it of importance distinctly to state the plan which is pursued in treating any subject? To this question he replies, that in the treatment of intricate subjects, where there are many divisions, and where it is of importance that the order and connection of each part should be carefully observed, to state the divisions is the better course. But it is far from being essential. Though we never should write without forming a distinct plan for our own use yet it may often be best to let others gather this plan from reading our productions. A plan is a species of scaffolding to aid us in erecting the building. When the edifice is finished, we may let the scaffolding fall.

The soul is immortal.
God is eternal.
Omniscience and omnipresence of the Deity.
Diffidence of our abilities a mark of wisdom.
The importance of order in the distribution of time.
Change of external condition often adverse to virtue.
The mortifications of vice greater than those of virtue.
Fortitude of mind.
The influence of devotion on the happiness of mankind.
The power of custom.
The real and solid enjoyments of life.
The vanity of wealth.
Nothing formed in vain.

Remark. The plan, or the right division of a composition, should be a prominent object of attention and study. The young writer will find it a very useful exercise, in all his compositions, to lay down his plan first, before writing. In this way habits of consecutive thinking will be formed and a principle of order established in the mind, which will be imparted to every subject of its contemplation.

LXX.

AMPLIFICATION.

Amplification may be defined an enlargement, by variou examples and proofs.

Various are the ways in which writers amplify, or enlarge, upon the propositions which they advance. The ingenuity of the writer may here have full play, providing that he do not violate the unity of his subject. There are, however, some general principles which the student should have in view in the performance of such an exercise.

The principal object of amplification is to exhibit more fully the meaning of what has been advanced. This may be done as follows:

1. By formal definitions and paraphrases of the propositions forming the heads of a subject. This is particularly requisite when the words employed in the proposition are ambiguous, new, or employed differently from their common acceptation.

2. By presenting the proposition in various forms of expression, avoid ing absolute tautology, and showing in what general or restricted sense the words employed should be received, explaining the manner, also, in which to guard against mistakes.

3. By giving individual instances, explanatory of the general proposi tion.

4. By similes, comparisons, antitheses, and historical allusions.

Writings which are designed to excite emotions, and to influence the will, require a more extended amplification than those which are argumentative, or those addressed directly to the understanding. In the former case, it is desirable that the mind should be led to dwell on what is presented to it, and to notice whatever is fitted and designed to excite the desired emotion. Hence, copiousness of detail, and a full and minute statement of attending circumstances, are required. But an argument should be stated concisely and simply, excepting only when it is in itself abstruse and complex, and when it is addressed to minds uncultivated and unaccustomed to connected reasonings. In such cases, even an argument may, with propriety, be amplified or enlarged.

The successful exercise of amplification depends,

1 Upon extent and command of knowledge;
2. On the power of illustration;
3. On definiteness of thought in our reasonings;
4. On copiousness of expression.

[The subjects of the Exercises, in various parts of this volume, will present a sufficient opportunity for the student to practise the art of amplification.]

LXXI.

ILLUSTRATION OF A SUBJECT.

Illustration properly signifies the rendering clear what is obscure or abstruse.

It is often the case, that subjects for consideration are presented which at first view appear to afford no avenue by which they may be approached. All appears dark around them; the subjects themselves appear isolated and distinct from any form of close examination. But as they are revolved in the mind, some connecting point is discovered, in which they may at last be seen to be united or closely allied to other subjects, and plain and clear deductions and inferences may be drawn from them. The process by which the illustration of such subjects may be effected, is thus explained by Mr. Jardine, in his remarks on what he calls "The Fourth Order of Themes." *

"To investigate, is, in the original sense of the word, to search out for an absent object, by discovering and following out the traces which it has left

* Jardine's "Outlines of a Philosophical Education," page 322.

in the path over which it has passed. Thus, we attempt to discover a person who has concealed himself, by *marking his footsteps* towards the place of his retreat; and on the same principle, the hound may be literally said to investigate the track of the fox, by pursuing the scent, which remains on the line along which the latter had directed his flight.*

"To these familiar processes may be compared the keen and earnest search of the mind, in its endeavors to ascertain the unknown causes and principles of things. Indeed, the perplexed anxiety which the set-dog often exhibits in the search of game, affords a striking example of the careful, anxious, and occasionally disappointed state of mind which the philosopher frequently experiences in his researches after truth. Trusting to a persuasion, natural to the human mind, that every effect must have a cause, and that the connection between causes and their effects is constant and uniform, the student of nature proceeds through the labyrinth of phenomena, guided by the chain which associates every event he witnesses with some prior event, which he infers must have preceded it, until at length he arrives at that ultimate point, which marks the boundary of physical causation, and limits the researches of philosophy.

"Suppose, for example, he proposes, as an object of investigation, to discover the state of Egypt in respect to government, science, and art, in the time of Moses, and the only *datum* given, is this single fact — that fine linen existed in Egypt at that period. In what manner should the student be directed to proceed? He must begin with directing his attention closely to this fact as an effect, and then consider that fine linen — that is, fine comparatively to other fabrics at that time — must be formed of fine threads, which can only be made of fine flax, which must also have gone through various acts of preparation, in which many workmen are employed, before the threads could be made into fine linen.

The production of *fine flax* supposes an improved state of agriculture, and the raising of many other kinds of grain, — wheat, barley, &c., — to support the cultivators of flax, and the artists who form it into cloth. In no country can flax be the sole article of cultivation. It may be, then, certainly inferred, that, in the time of Moses, the art of agriculture, and the arts connected with it, had arrived at considerable perfection.

Returning again to the *datum*, fine linen can be woven only in a fine loom, which must be accommodated to the fine texture of the threads; and a fine loom cannot be made without much skill in the arts of working metal and wood. The former is extracted, with great labor, from ores, dug from the bowels of the earth, and must go through many difficult and laborious

---

* The following remarkable instance of the wonderful powers of reasoning possessed by the aborigines of this country, is presented to the student, to enable him to prosecute similar inquiries to a satisfactory result. The extract is from "Thatcher's Lives of the Indians."

"Owing partly to his organization, doubtless, as well as to his mode of living from childhood up, the senses of the Indian are extremely acute. It is related, in modern times, that a hunter, belonging to one of the western tribes, on his return home to his hut one day, discovered that his venison, which had been hung up to dry, had been stolen. After taking observations on the spot, he set off in pursuit of the thief, whom he traced through the woods. Having gone a little distance, he met some persons, of whom he inquired, whether they had seen *a little, old white man*, with a *short gun*, accompanied by a *small dog*, with a *short tail*. They replied in the affirmative; and upon the Indian assuring them that the man thus described had stolen his venison, they desired to be informed how he was able to give such a minute description of a person he had never seen. The Indian replied thus: The thief is a *little man*, I know by his having made a pile of stones to stand upon, in order to reach the venison from the height I hung it, standing on the ground. That he is *an old man*, I know by his short steps, which I have traced over the dead leaves in the woods; that he is a *white man*, I know by his turning *out* his toes when he walks, which an Indian never does; his gun, I know to be *short*, by the mark the muzzle made in rubbing the bark of the tree where it leaned; that his dog is *small*, I know by his tracks, and that he has *a short tail*, I discovered by the mark it made in the dust where he was sitting, at the time that his master was taking down the venison."

processes before it becomes malleable. The latter, also, must undergo much preparation before it can go into the hands of the carpenter; and the loom itself is a complex machine, supposing great skill and progress of the mechanical arts in Egypt at the time of Moses.

The weaving of fine linen, too, supposes that artists, by imitation and example, have acquired skill and dexterity in that art; and such perfection cannot be expected in any country, till a division of labor — the greatest instrument of improvement in all the arts — be in some degree established.

The skilful weaver must be wholly occupied in making fine linen; and, therefore, there must exist many other artists employed in providing food, clothes, and lodging, — the necessaries and conveniences of life.

Before the arts could have made such progress in any country, men must have acquired much knowledge of facts and events, by observation and experience; and have laid the foundation of general knowledge, by speculating on means of improving the arts; on removing the obstacles which retard their progress, and in opening up prospects of higher degrees of perfection.

Farther, without taking up time to follow the natural and connected progress of the arts from their rude to their more perfect state, — I conclude this process of investigation with observing, that there can be little progress either in art or science in any country, without the existence of a supreme, controlling power, in some or other of its forms; by which men are compelled to live in peace and tranquillity, and the different orders of society are prevented from encroaching on each other, by every individual being kept in his proper station. No arts or division of labor, — no fine linen or fine workmanship of any kind, can be found in those nations which live in continual warfare, either among themselves, or with their neighbors. Thus, by such a continued chain of regular and progressive deductions, proceeding from the *datum* with which it began, and without information from any other quarter, we have sufficient reason to believe, that, at the time of Moses, Egypt was a great and populous country; that the arts and sciences had made considerable progress, and that government and laws were established.

Subjects for illustration.

What may be learned of the state of Greece, and of the character of that nation at the time when Homer wrote the Iliad, without drawing information from any other source than from the Iliad itself?

What was the state of the Highlands of Scotland, as indicated by the poems of Ossian? Are there any marks in these poems of a later origin than that generally assigned to them?

What were the causes which produced an absolute government at Rome under Augustus?

What occasioned the conspiracy of Catiline?

Is the character of Hannibal, in Livy, supported by the narrative he has given of his transactions?

What were the grounds upon which the Trojans trusted to Simon's account of the wooden horse?

What are the difficulties which occur in forming a standard of taste?

In what sense is poetry called an imitative art?

What are the proofs by which Horne Tooke confirms his theory of the origin of prepositions and conjunctions in the English language?

What are the standards by which we judge of the perfection of one language above another?

What are the causes which render it difficult for the student to acquire habit of attention?

What was the origin of the present political parties in the United States?

LXXII.

ON THE TREATMENT OF A SUBJECT

The first and leading object of attention in every composition is, to determine the precise point of inquiry, — the proposition which is to be laid down and supported, or the subject which is to be explained or described. Unless the writer has steadily before him some fixed purpose which he would obtain, or some point which he would reach, he will be liable to go astray, — to lose himself and his readers. It is not until he has determined on the definite object that he proposes to accomplish, that he can know what views to present, and how to dwell on the different topics he may discuss.

Let us suppose, in illustrating the views now to be presented, that the thoughts of the writer have been turned towards the manifestations of wisdom, goodness, and power, in the works of creation around him, and he wishes his readers to be mindful of these things. By asking himself the three following questions with regard to the train of thought in his mind, his ideas will immediately assume some definite form, and he will be enabled to present them in a lucid and systematic manner.

1st. What is the fact?

2d. Why is it so?

3d. What consequences result from it?

And with regard to the first point of inquiry, namely, 'What is the fact?' in reply it may be said, — that, in the material world, there are numerous indications of infinite wisdom and benevolence, and of Almighty power.

2. 'Why is it so?' or, How is the existence of these works to be accounted for? What is the cause? To which it may be replied, that God created them.

3. Again; 'What consequences result from it?' To this the answer may be given, that — Men should live mindful of God.

By embodying the results of these inquiries, he will obtain the following conclusion or point at which he aimed, namely, — Men who live in the midst of objects which show forth the perfections of the great Creator should live mindful of him.

It is not necessary, that the proposition to be supported should always be thus formally stated, though this is usually done in writings of an argumentative nature. Sometimes it is elegantly implied, or left to be inferred from the introductory remarks.

It is a common impression with young writers, that the wider the field of inquiry on which they enter, the more abundant and obvious will be the thoughts which will offer themselves for their use. Hence, by selecting some general subject, they hope to secure copiousness of matter, and thus to find an easier task. Experience, however, shows that the reverse is true, — that, as the field of inquiry is narrowed, questions arise more exciting to the mind, and thoughts are suggested of greater value and interest to the readers. Suppose, as an illustration, that a writer proposes to himself to write an essay on 'Literature.' Amidst the numerous topics which might be treated upon under this term, no *unity* could be preserved. The thoughts advanced would be common-place and uninteresting. But let some distinct inquiry be proposed, or some assertion be made and supported, and there will be an influx of interesting thoughts presented in a distinct and connected manner.

Instead, therefore, of the *general* subject '*Literature*,' let us suppose a particular subject, namely, a 'Defence of literary studies in men of business' is proposed. It will be seen by the following model how spontaneously, as it were, ideas will present themselves, and with what ease they can be arranged with the strictest regard to unity.

Example.

A DEFENCE OF LITERARY STUDIES IN MEN OF BUSINESS.

Among the cautions which prudence and worldly wisdom inculcate on the young, or at least among those sober truths which experience often pretends to have acquired, is that danger, which is said to result from the pursuit of letters and of science, in men destined for the labors of business, for the active exertions of professional life. The abstraction of learning, the speculations of science, and the visionary excursions of fancy are fatal, it is said, to the steady pursuit of common objects, to the habits of plodding industry, which ordinary business demands. The fineness of mind which is created or increased by the study of letters, or the admiration of the arts, is supposed to incapacitate a man for the drudgery by which professional eminence is gained; as a nicely tempered edge, applied to a coarse and rugged material, is unable to perform what a more common instrument would have successfully achieved. A young man, destined for law or commerce, is advised to look only into his folio of precedents, or his method of book-keeping; and dulness is pointed to his homage, as that benevolent goddess, under whose protection the honors of station and the blessings of opulence are to be obtained; while learning and genius are proscribed, as leading their votaries to barren indigence and merited neglect.

In doubting the truth of these assertions, I think I shall not entertain any hurtful degree of skepticism, because the general current of opinion seems, of late years, to have set too strongly in the contrary direction, and one may endeavor to prop the falling cause of literature, without being accused of blameable or dangerous partiality.

In the examples which memory and experience produce of idleness, of dissipation, and of poverty, brought on by indulgence of literary or poetical enthusiasm, the evidence must necessarily be on one side of the question only. Of the few whom learning or genius has led astray, the ill success or the ruin is marked by the celebrity of the sufferer. Of the many who have been as dull as they were profligate, and as ignorant as they were poor, the fate is unknown, from the insignificance of those by whom it was endured. If we may reason *a priori* on the matter, the chance, I think, should be on the side of literature. In young minds of any vivacity, there is a natural aversion to the drudgery of business, which is seldom overcome, till the effervescence of youth is allayed by the progress of time and habit, or till that very warmth is enlisted on the side of their profession, by the opening prospects of ambition or emolument. From this tyranny, as youth conceives it, of attention and of labor, relief is commonly sought from some favorite avocation or amusement, for which a young man either finds or steals a portion of his time, either patiently plods through his task, in expectation of its approach, or anticipates its arrival by deserting his work before the legal period for amusement is arrived. It may fairly be questioned, whether the most innocent of these amusements is either so honorable or so safe as the avocation of learning or of science. Of minds uninformed and gross, whom youthful spirits agitate, but fancy and feeling have no power to impel, the amusement will generally be boisterous or effeminate, will either dissipate their attention, or weaken their force. The employment of a young man's vacant hours is often too little attended to by those rigid masters, who exact the most scrupulous observance of the periods destined for business. The waste of time is, undoubtedly, a very calculable loss; but the waste or the depravation of mind is a loss of a much higher denomination. The votary of study, or the enthusiast of fancy, may incur the first, but the latter will be suffered chiefly by him whose ignorance or want of imagination has left him to the grossness of mere sensual enjoyments.

In this, as in other respects, the love of letters is friendly to sober manners and virtuous conduct, which, in every profession, is the road to success and to respect. Without adopting the common-place reflections against some particular departments, it must be allowed, that, in mere men of business, there is a certain professional rule of right, which is not always honorable, and, though meant to be selfish, very seldom profits. A superior education generally corrects this, by opening the mind to different motives of action, to the feelings of delicacy, the sense of honor, and a contempt of wealth, when earned by a desertion of those principles.

To the improvement of our faculties as well as of our principles, the love of letters appears to be favorable. Letters require a certain sort of application, though of a kind, perhaps, very different from that which business would recommend. Granting that they are unprofitable in themselves, as that word is used in the language of the world, yet, as developing the powers of thought and reflection, they may be an amusement of some use, as those sports of children, in which numbers are used to familiarize them to the elements of arithmetic. They give room for the exercise of that discernment, that comparison of objects, that distinction of causes, which is to increase the skill of the physician, to guide the speculations of the merchant, and to prompt the arguments of the lawyer; and, though some professions employ but very few faculties of the mind, yet there is scarcely any branch of business in which a man who can think will not excel him who can only labor. We shall accordingly find, in many departments where learned information seemed of all qualities the least necessary, that those who possessed it, in a degree above their fellows, have found, from that very circumstance, the road to eminence and wealth.

But I must often repeat, that wealth does not necessarily create happiness, nor confer dignity; a truth which it may be thought declamation to insist on, but which the present time seems particularly to require being told.

The love of letters is connected with an independence and delicacy of mind, which is a great preservative against that servile homage, which abject men pay to fortune; and there is a certain classical pride, which, from the society of Socrates and Plato, Cicero and Atticus, looks down with an honest disdain on the wealth-blown insects of modern times, neither enlightened by knowledge, nor ennobled by virtue.

In the possession, indeed, of what he has attained, in that rest and retirement from his labors, with the hopes of which his fatigues were lightened and his cares were smoothed, the mere man of business frequently undergoes suffering, instead of finding enjoyment. To be busy as one ought is an easy art; but to know how to be idle is a very superior accomplishment. This difficulty is much increased with persons to whom the habit of employment has made some active exertion necessary; who cannot sleep contented in the torpor of indolence, or amuse themselves with those lighter trifles in which he, who inherited idleness as he did fortune, from his ancestors, has been accustomed to find amusement. The miseries and misfortunes of the 'retired pleasures' of men of business, have been frequently matter of speculation to the moralist, and of ridicule to the wit. But he who has mixed general knowledge with professional skill, and literary amusements with professional labor, will have some stock wherewith to support him in idleness, some spring for his mind when unbent from business, some employment for those hours, which retirement and solitude has left vacant and unoccupied. Independence in the use of one's time is not the least valuable species of freedom. This liberty the man of letters enjoys, while the ignorant and the illiterate often retire from the thraldom of business, only to become the slaves of languor, intemperance, or vice. But the situation in which the advantages of that endowment of mind, which letters bestow, are chiefly conspicuous, is old age, when a man's society is necessarily circumscribed, and his powers of active enjoyment are unavoidably diminished. Unfit for the bustle of affairs, and the amusements of his youth, an old man, if he has no source of mental exertion or employment, often settles into the gloom of melancholy and peevishness, or petrifies his feelings by habitual intoxication. From an old man, whose gratifications were solely derived from those sensual appetites which time has blunted, or from those trivial amusements which youth only can share, age has cut off almost every source of enjoyment. But to him who has stored his mind with the information, and can still employ it in the amusement of letters, this blank of life is admirably filled up. He acts, he thinks, and he feels with that literary world, whose society he can at all times enjoy. There is, perhaps, no state more capable of comfort to ourselves, or more attractive of veneration from others, than that which such an old age affords; it is then the twilight of the passions, when they are mitigated, but not extinguished, and spread their gentle influence over the evening of our day, in alliance with reason and in amity with virtue.

REMARKS AND ANALYSIS.

In examining the preceding example of argumentative writing, the principal object of attention will be, the plan or management of the subject.

The introduction consists of an indirect statement of the question to be agitated. We are told how those have thought and reasoned, whose opinions are opposed to the opinions of the writer. This statement is distinctly, and fairly, and skilfully made. Our literary taste is gratified by the illustrations and ornaments of language which are found. Our curiosity is roused, and we are ready to enter with interest on the proposed investigation. It should be noticed, that there is no formal statement of the proposition which is to be supported, but that it is clearly and happily implied in the introductory paragraphs.

After the introduction, follows the refutation of an objection. That this is the proper place for considering the objection stated, is evident, since, had it been unnoticed, or its refutation deferred to the close of the essay, the minds of readers might have been prevented by its influence from giving due weight to the arguments adduced. There are two modes of refuting objections; one, by denying the premises from which a conclusion is drawn, — the other, by showing that the conclusion does not truly follow from the premises. The objection here considered is, that facts establish the opposite of the opinion advanced by the writer; of course, the opinion can have no good foundation. To refute the objection, the premise is denied. Facts are otherwise, says the writer, and a satisfactory reason is assigned why a different impression as to the bearing of facts on the case has prevailed. Having assigned this reason, the writer leaves the point at issue, as to facts in the case, to be determined by the observation and the good sense of his readers. Having thus introduced his subject to our attention, stating by implication the proposition to be examined, and having removed an objection which presented itself at the threshold, the writer now enters on the direct examination of his subject.

The following proposition is supported: Men of business may advantageously devote a portion of their time to literary pursuits.

1st Argument. Young men of business should engage in literary studies, since in them is found a pleasant relaxation and security against hurtful indulgences.

2d Argument. Young men of business should engage in literary studies, because in this way they acquire a refinement and exaltation of mind, which raises them above grovelling and selfish principles and conduct.

3d Argument. Young men of business should engage in literary studies, because the cultivation of letters is favorable to the improvement of the mind.

4th Argument. A man of business should engage in literary pursuits, because in this way he acquires an independence of feeling, which prepares him to enjoy his wealth. Without cultivation of mind and literary taste, the retirement of the man of wealth is wearisome and disgusting to him

5th Argument. Men of business should cultivate letters, that they may find in them grateful employment for old age.

This is the plan. Upon examination, we find that it conforms to the general directions given. The several heads are distinct from each other. They have a similar bearing on the leading proposition to be supported, and taken together they give a *unity* to the subject.

The kind of argument here used, is the argument from cause to effect. Different reasons are stated, which account for and support the assertion that is made, and which forms the leading proposition. Let us now take a nearer view of these different arguments, and see in what way they are supported. Under the first argument, the reasoning is as follows: 1. Young men in business *will have* relaxation and amusement. 2. Unless those of a salutary kind are provided, they will fall into such as are hurtful. Hence the importance of their being directed to literary pursuits, which may interest and benefit them. It may be asked, on what authority do these assertions of the writer rest? How do we know that young men thus *will have* relaxation and amusement? and that, unless those of a salutary kind are provided, they will fall into such as are hurtful? I answer, that these assertions rest on the common observation and experience of men. Hence the writer takes it for granted, that those whom he addresses will yield their assent to his premises, and, consequently, if his conclusion is correctly drawn, will acknowledge the validity of his argument.

In analyzing the second argument, the inquiry arises, How is it known, that literary studies give refinement and elevation to the mind, raising it above mean and grovelling pursuits? Here the appeal is to consciousness Men who have thus cultivated their intellectual powers, are conscious, when they look in upon the operations of their own minds, that these salutary influences have been exerted upon them. The third argument, which asserts that the love of letters is favorable to the cultivation of the intellectual powers, rests principally upon experience and observation.

There is also found an illustration, which is of an analogical kind. It is where the writer refers to the sports of children, which familiarize them with the elements of arithmetic. This argument from analogy may be regarded as an appeal to the common sense of the readers. The remaining argument rests in like manner on appeals to experience, observation, common sense, and consciousness, and it is not necessary to analyze them. The student, in the analysis which has been made, has had an opportunity of seeing some of the grounds on which assertions and reasonings are founded.

LXXIII.

GENERALIZATION OF A SUBJECT.

Generalization is the act of extending from particulars to generals, or the act of making general.

In the treatment of all subjects there is a tendency in young writers to dwell too much on isolated particulars, without reference to their general application. The object of all investigations, whether literary, physical, or intellectual, and the purport of all inquiries, should be, the establishment of general principles; and every thought, which may tend to their elucidation, and every idea which may contribute to their discovery, must be reckoned among the most valuable of all literary labors. Hence, the efforts of the student should be directed towards the attainment of so valuable an end, and in the training of his mind, on the part of the teacher, there should always be a distinct reference to this consideration.

In the study, therefore, which the writer should always employ in his preparation for his work, it should be his aim to discover some *general* principle, with which his subject is directly or remotely connected, and endeavor to follow out that principle in all its consequences, — to show how his subject affects, or is affected, by this general principle, and how that principle influences the interest of learning and science, or contributes to the well-being of society, and the moral, physical, and intellectual condition of the world. Let us suppose, for instance, that the teacher has assigned to a class in composition, *Truth*, as the subject of a theme. The young writer, who is too much in haste to finish his task, would, perhaps, commence his exercise with some hackneyed observations on its importance, and dwell with considerable prolixity on its influence on a particular individual.

Individual instances, it is true, may have their influence in establishing the importance, or illustrating the effects of a general principle; but to confine an exercise upon a general subject to individual instances, is to present but narrow views of its importance. So far as the example introduced into the exercise of the student may serve to show the importance of a general principle, that example may be valuable, but it should by no means form the body of his work. It may be introduced into the exercise, as an illustration, or as a subsidiary portion of his labor, but it should not be dwelt upon to the exclusion of the principle which it is designed to illustrate. Thus, in the subject to which reference has already been made, namely, "Truth," the well-known story of Petrarch may incidentally be mentioned, to show the dignity which attends the strictest observance of veracity; but, an exhibition of the effects on society in general of the presence or absence of the subject itself, would be a more useful and, of course, a more valuable mode of considering the subject, than any attempts to show its importance in individual cases. It should be the constant endeavor of the teacher to lead the student to the consideration of causes and effects, their operations and their tendencies, and, by the method of reasoning from particulars to generals, to show how general truths are inferred from particular instances, and general principles are established by the consideration of the effects of particular causes.

The student who is thus led to perceive the general bearings of a subject, will not take partial views, — he will go out into the world, — on board ship, — into factories and other large establishments, and view the operations of general principles; will have the sphere of intellectual vision enlarged, and insensibly acquire a comprehensiveness of mental perception, which will release him from the shackles of a narrow education, and enable him to take in, as it were at a glance, the grand theatre of the moral world, with all the stupendous machinery by which the changes in its scenery are effected.

As an exercise in generalization, the student may fill out some one or more of the following models from the outline presented.

Example.

1. Time. Definition of; its divisions; mode of marking them; mode of ascertaining; meridian; the sun; parallel between time and space, finite and infinite.

2. The Feudal System. Its nature and origin, including a clear definition of the meaning of the term; the countries where it existed; the relations which it caused among the inhabitants of a feudal country; its effects upon the morals and the happiness of the respective nations where it existed; the virtues and vices which it encouraged and engendered, and a consideration of the causes of its gradual overthrow.

3. The Grecian Lawgivers, Draco, Solon, and Lycurgus. The different character of their respective laws; the effect which they produced on the people their duration, and the probable cause of their alteration and abrogation the consequences which they produced; and their comparative effects on the morals and happiness of the people.

4. The Crusades. What were they? their object; the manner in which they originated; the superstitions to which they gave rise; their effect on the religion, manners, and morals of the age; the vices and profligacy which they engendered; their influence on the moral condition of the world, and the balance of power in Europe; the sacrifices of blood and treasure which they occasioned; the benefits which they have produced.

5. Chivalry. What was it? give a clear definition or description of it; how it arose; the manner in which candidates were admitted to its orders; the most eminent of its orders; the effects of the institution on the morals and prevalent habits of the age; its particular effect on the female character; the virtues and vices which it would naturally engender or encourage; and the good or bad consequence of its universal prevalence at the present day.

6. The ancient Sects of Philosophy. Describe the various sects; their doctrines; the manner in which they were taught; the character of the respective founders; their influence; the remarkable individuals who have embraced the principles of the respective sects; and the effect of their writings and example on mankind, &c.

7. The Public Games of Greece. Their origin; the nature of these games, or in what they consisted; the places where they were celebrated; the rewards bestowed upon the victors; the estimation in which these honors were held; the effects of these games upon the victors, and upon the nation to which they belonged, by encouraging athletic exercises and spirit of emulation; did the encouragement of physical exertion influence literary or intellectual effort for the better or the worse? the probable effects of the institution of similar games at the present day.

8. The Grecian Oracles. What they were; where situated; by whom, and on what occasions, were they consulted; the superstitions which they encouraged; their probable nature; their effects upon the religious character of the people; their duration; probable cause of their falling into disuse; the wisdom of Providence in concealing from mankind the knowledge of future events; fatalism.

The following subjects are suggested for the unaided efforts of the students

9. The Reformation.
10. The Invention of the Art of Printing.
11. The Invention of the Mariner's Compass.
12. The Telescope.

LXXIV.

POETRY AND VERSIFICATION.

Poetry may properly be defined the language of the imagination. Its usual form is in verse,* and it is sometimes, and indeed most generally, adorned with rhyme. But true poetry consists in the idea, not in the harmonious arrangement of words in sentences, nor in the division of a composition into lines containing a certain succession of long and short syllables.

Poetry † deals largely in figurative language, especially in tropes, metaphors, personifications, similes, and comparisons. It is also exceedingly partial to compound epithets, and new combinations employed for the purposes of illustration and description.

Versification is the art of making verses. A verse is a line consisting of a certain succession of long and short syllables. A hemistich is a half of a verse. A distich, or couplet, consists of two verses.

Metre ‡ is the measure by which verses are composed.

---

* The word *verse* is frequently incorrectly used for *stanza*. A verse consists of a single line only. A stanza, sometimes called *a stave*, consists of a number of lines regularly adjusted to each other. The word verse is derived from the Latin language, and signifies *a turning*. The propriety of the name will be seen in the fact, that when we have finished a line we *turn* to the other side of the page to commence another.

† There are few words in the English language, the true signification of which is more frequently mistaken than the word Poetry. It is generally thought to consist in the harmonious arrangement of words in sentences, and the division of a composition into lines containing a certain succession of long or short syllables. This is a mistaking of the dress for the substance which the dress should cover. True poetry consists in the idea that it may be presented even in the form of prose. It addresses itself to the imagination and to the feelings. Thus the scriptural adage, "Love your enemies," although in prose, becomes highly poetical, when presented with the beautiful illustration of Menon: "Like the sandal tree which sheds a perfume on the axe which fells it, we should love our enemies." This distinction between the idea and the dress which it assumes, must be carefully noticed by all who aspire to poetical fame.

Perhaps there is in no language a more beautiful exhibition of poetical beauties in the form of prose, than in the beautiful tale called "The Epicurean," by Thomas Moore, Esq.

‡ It may perhaps be useful, although not properly connected with the subject of English versification, to explain what is meant in psalmody by

This measure depends on the number of the syllables and the position of the accents.

The divisions made in a verse to regulate the proper succession of long and short syllables are called *feet*. They are called feet, because the voice, as it were, *steps* along through the verse in a measured pace. The divisions of a verse into *feet* depend entirely upon what is called the *quantity* of the syllables, that is, whether they are *long* or *short*, without reference to the words.

Sometimes a foot consists of a single word, but it also sometimes embraces two or three different words, and sometimes is composed of parts of different words.

There are eight kinds of feet, four of which are feet of two syllables, and four are feet of three syllables.

The feet consisting of two syllables are the Trochee, the Iambus, the Spondee, and the Pyrrhic.

The feet of three syllables are the Dactyle, the Amphibrach, the Anapæst, and the Tribrach.

The Trochee consists of one long and one short syllable; as, hātefŭl.

The Iambus consists of a short syllable and a long one; as, bĕtrāy

The Spondee consists of two long syllables; as, Pāle mōrn.

The Pyrrhic consists of two short syllables; as, ŏn thĕ tall tree.

The Dactyle consists of one long syllable and two short ones; as, hōlĭnĕss, thūndĕrĭng.

The Amphibrach consists of a short, a long, and a short syllable; as dĕlīghtfŭl, rĕmōvăl, cŏēvăl.

The Anapæst consists of two short syllables and one long one; as, cŏntrăvēne.

The Tribrach consists of three short syllables; as, *-rĭtŭăl* in the word *spiritual.*

Of these eight different kinds of feet, the Iambus, the Trochee, the Anapæst, and the Dactyle are most frequently used, and verses may be wholly or chiefly composed of them. The others may be termed secondary feet, because their use is to diversify the harmony of the verse.

English verses may be divided into three classes, from the feet of which they are principally composed; namely, the Iambic, the Trochaic, and the Anapæstic. To these some authors add the Dactylic as a fourth division; but an attentive consideration of what is called the Dactylic verse will

---

Long, *Common*, *Short*, and *Particular* metre. When each line of a stanza has eight syllables, it is called *Long Metre*. When the first and third lines have eight syllables, and he second and fourth have six syllables, it is called *Common Metre*. When the third line has eight, and the rest have six syllables, it is called *Short Metre*. Stanzas in *Particular Metre* are of various kinds, and are not subject to definite rules

show that it is nothing more than the Anapæstic, with the omission of the first two unaccented syllables.

Every species of English verse *regularly* terminates with an accented syllable; but every species also *admits* at the end an additional unaccented syllable, producing (if the verse be in rhyme) a double rhyme, that is, a rhyme extending to two syllables, as *the rhyme must always commence on the accented syllable.* This additional syllable often changes the character of the verse from grave to gay, from serious to jocose; but it does not affect the measure or rhyme of the preceding part of the verse A verse thus lengthened is called hypermeter, or *over measure.*

Pure Iambic verses contain no other foot than the Iambus, and are uniformly accented on the *even* syllables.

Trochaic verses are accented on the *odd* syllables.

There are seven forms of Iambic verse, named from the number of feet which they contain. The following line of fourteen syllables contains all the seven forms of pure Iambic verse.

1. Hŏw blīthe | whĕn fīrst | frŏm fār | I cāme | tŏ wōō | ănd wīn | thĕ māid.*
2. When first | from far | I came | to woo | and win | the maid.
3. From far | I came | to woo | and win | the maid.
4. I came | to woo | and win | the maid.
5. To woo and win | the maid.
6. And win | the maid.
7. The maid.

The additional syllable *en* at the end of each line, to convert *maid* into *maiden,* will furnish seven *hypermeters,* and the line will thereby be made to exemplify fourteen different forms of the Iambic verse.†

Trochaic verse is in reality only defective Iambic; that is to say, Iambic wanting the first syllable.‡

The following line is an example of Trochaic verse:

Vītăl | spārk ŏf | heāvenly̆ | flāme.§

---

* This measure is sometimes broken into two lines, thus:

How blithe when first I came from far
To woo and win the maid.

† The fifth form of Iambic verse, consisting of five Iambuses, is called the Heroic measure. The following lines exemplify it:

Hŏw lōved, | hŏw vāl | ŭed ōnce | ăvāils | thĕĕ nōt,
To whom related, or by whom begot, &c.

The sixth form of Iambic verse is called the Alexandrine measure:

A needless Alexandrine ends the song,
. Whĭch lĭke | ă woūnd | ĕd snāke | drāgs ĭts | slŏw lēngth | ălōng.

‡ See Carey's English Prosody, London edition of 1816. pp. 25 and 27

§ This line, scanned as Iambic, has a broken foot at the beginning:

Vī | tăl spārk | ŏf heāven | ly flāme.

Scanned as Trochaic, it has the broken foot at the end.

Anapæstic verse properly consists of anapæsts alone; as,

At thĕ clōse | ŏf thĕ dāy | whĕn thē hām | lĕt ĭs stĭll.

The first foot, however, in all the different forms of Anapæstic metre, may be a foot of two syllables, provided that the latter syllable of the foot be accented. Such are the Iambus and the Spondee. But the Pyrrhic and the Trochee, which have not the second syllable accented, are on that account inadmissible.*

Different kinds of feet frequently occur in all the different kinds of verse. But it is not always that they can be exactly discriminated. Concerning the Trochee, the Spondee, and the Pyrrhic, there can be little doubt; but with respect to the Dactyle, the Anapæst, and the Tribrach, the case is different;

Vĭtăl | spărk ŏf | heăvenly | flāme.

In like manner, if we cut off the first syllable from any form of the Iambic, we shall find that it may be scanned both ways, with the deficiency of a semi foot at the beginning of the end, according as we scan it in Iambuses or Trochees.

Thus, the line given as an exemplification of the Iambic metre, on the preceding page, if deprived in each form of its first syllable, becomes Trochaic:

how)	Blīthe whĕn	fĭrst frŏm	fār I	cāme tŏ	wōō ănd	wĭn thĕ	māid.
	when)	First from	far I	came to	woo and	win the	maid.
		from)	Far I	came to	woo and	win the	maid.
			I)	Came to	woo and	win the	maid.
				to)	Woo and	win the	maid.
					and)	Win the	maid

And thus we see, that what we call Trochaics *regularly* terminate in an accented syllable, as is the case in every other form of English metre; though, like every other form, they also admit an additional unaccented syllable at the end, producing a double rhyme; so that by changing maid for maiden in each of the preceding lines, (as directed under Iambic verse,) we shall have twelve forms of Trochaic verse. But it may be remarked, that of the six regular forms of Trochaic verse, and the six hypermeter related to them, the first three in each class are very seldom used.

* The following stanza is given by some authorities as an instance of Dactylic verse:

Hōly ănd | pūre ăre thĕ | pleăsūres ŏf | pīĕty,
Drāwn frŏm thĕ | foūntaīn ŏf | mērcy ănd | lōve;
Endlĕss, ĕx | haūstlĕss, ĕx | ēmpt frŏm să | tīĕty,
Rīsīng ŭn | eārthly ănd | sōarīng ă | bōve.

An attentive consideration of these lines will show that they are legitimate Anapæstic lines with the omission of the first two unaccented syllables in each line. When scanned as Dactylic measure, the two unaccented syllables are omitted at the end of the even lines. By supplying the two unaccented syllables at the beginning of each line, they may thus be shown to be Anapæstic:

Oh hŏw hō | ly ănd pūre | ăre thĕ pleās | ŭres ŏf pī | ĕty
As thĕy 're drāwn | frŏm thĕ foūn | taīn ŏf mēr | cy ănd lōve, &c.

And thus it appears, that when scanned as Anapæstic they want the accented syllable at the end of the odd lines.

because, by a poetic license, the writer may make the foot in question a Trochee, a Spondee, or a Pyrrhic. *

It remains to be observed, that if from any verse of ordinary construction, we remove any number of syllables, and substitute an equal number of others, exactly corresponding with them in accent, the metre will still be perfect, although the sense may be altered. Thus,

Pēlīdēs' wrāth, tŏ Grēēce the direful spring
Of wōes ŭnnūmbĕred, heavenly goddess, sing.

Altered thus:

Thĕ Frēnchmăn's ārts, tŏ Spāin the direful spring
Of feuds and carnage, heavenly goddess, sing.

Hark! the *numbers, soft* and clear,
Gently steal upon the ear.

Altered thus:

Hark! the *thunders, loud* and clear,
Rudely burst upon the ear.

The Cæsura (which word means a division) is the separation, or pause, which is made in the body of a verse in utterance; dividing the line, as it were, into two members.

In different species of verse, and in different verses of the same species, this pause occurs in different parts of the verse; and serves to give variety to the line. Its position is, for the most part, easily ascertained, by the grammatical construction and the punctuation, which naturally indicate the place where the sense either requires or admits a pause.

The most advantageous position for the Cæsura is generally after the fourth, fifth, or sixth syllable; although it occasionally takes place after the third or the seventh.

In the following lines the figures denote the number of the syllable where the *cæsura* belongs.

The Saviour comes 4 || by ancient bards foretold.
From storms a shelter 5 || and from heat a shade.
Exalt thy towering head 6 || and lift thy eyes.
Exploring 3 || till they find their native deep.
Within that mystic circle 7 || safely seek.

Sometimes, though rarely, the cæsura occurs after the second or the eighth syllable: as,

Happy 2 || without the privilege of will.
In different individuals 8 || we find.

Sometimes the line requires or admits two pauses or cæsuras. This double pause is by some writers called the cæsura and the demi-cæsura as,

Cæsar, 2 || the world's great master, 7 || and his own.
And goodness 3 || like the sun 6 || enlightens all.

---

* See Carey's English Prosody, p. 49.

There are few more melodious instances of these pauses to be found than in the following lines from one of the most polished poets which the English language has produced.

> Warms || in the sun, 4 || refreshes 6 || in the breeze,
> Glows || in the stars, || and blossoms || in the trees;
> Lives || through all life, || extends || through all extent,
> Spreads || undivided, operates || unspent.

It remains to be observed, that in poetry, as well as in prose, but more especially in poetry, it is esteemed a great beauty when the sound of the verse, or of the feet of which it is composed, corresponds with the signification. Instances of this kind will be found under the head of Onomatopœia. A similar beauty appears in the following lines:

> "On the ear
> *Drops* the light *drip* of the suspended oar."

> "The string let fly
> Twanged short and sharp, like the shrill swallow's cry."

SPECIMENS OF DIFFERENT KINDS OF ENGLISH VERSE.

Iambic of the shortest form, consisting of an Iambus with an additional syllable; thus coinciding with the amphidrach.

> Disdaining. Consenting.
> Complaining. Repenting.

This form may be found in stanzas of other measure, but is not used alone.

Second form of the Iambic, consisting of two Iambuses.

> With ravished ears
> The monarch hears,
> Assumes the god,
> Affects to nod.

Hypermeter of the same kind.

> Upon a mountain,
> Beneath a fountain.

Three Iambuses, with hypermeter of the same kind.

> 'T was when the seas were roaring
> With hollow blasts of wind,
> A damsel lay deploring,
> All on a rock reclined.

Four Iambuses.

> And may at last my weary age
> Find out the peaceful hermitage.

Five Iambuses, or the Heroic measure.

Be wise to-day, 't is madness to defer

How loved, how valued once, avails thee not,
To whom related, or by whom begot:
A heap of dust alone remains of thee,
'T is all thou art, and all the proud shall be.

Six Iambuses, or the Alexandrine measure.

For thou art but of dust; be humble and be wise.

(*The latter of the two following is an Alexandrine.*)

A needless Alexandrine ends the song,
That, like a wounded snake, drags its slow length along.

Seven Iambuses.

The melancholy days have come, the saddest of the year,
Of wailing winds, and naked woods, and meadows brown and sere.
The robin and the wren have flown, and from the shrub the jay,
And from the wood top caws * the crow, through all the gloomy day.

This measure is sometimes broken into two lines, thus:

When all thy mercies, O my God!
My rising soul surveys,
Transported with the view, I 'm lost
In wonder, love, and praise.

Trochaic verse of one Trochee and a long syllable.

Tumult cease
Sink to peace.
See him stride,
Valleys wide,
Over woods,
Over floods.

Two Trochees.

Rich the treasure,
Sweet the pleasure.
Soft denials
Are but trials.

---

* This alteration in a line of one of the sweetest pieces of poetry ever written in any language, was suggested by the lamented Mr. Bailey, of the High School for Girls, in this city. In compiling "The Young Ladies' Class Book," he expressed a wish to the author to take this liberty, but he deemed it unwarrantable. The reading is adopted here as a beautiful exemplification of what is stated under Onomatopœia; and, indeed, when we consider how easily the printer might mistake in manuscript a *w* for a double *l*, it would not be surprising if it should hereafter appear that our gifted countryman originally wrote it *caws*, and not *calls*, as it is generally written.

Two Trochees, with an additional long syllable.

In the days of old
Fables plainly told.

Three Trochees.

Go where glory waits thee.

Three Trochees, with an additional syllable.

Restless mortals toil for nought;
Bliss in vain from earth is sought.

Four Trochees.

Round us wars the tempest louder.

With an additional syllable.

Idle after dinner in his chair.

Five Trochees.

All that walk on foot or ride in chariots.

Six Trochees.

On a mountain, stretched beneath a hoary willow.

Anapæstic verse consisting of one Anapæst

But in vain
They complain.*

Two Anapæsts.

But his courage 'gan fail,
For no arts could avail.

With an additional syllable.

But his courage 'gan fail him,
For no arts could avail him.

Three Anapæsts.

I am monarch of all I survey,
My right there is none to dispute,
From the centre all round to the sea,
I am lord of the fowl and the brute.

Four Anapæsts.

At the close of the day when the hamlet is still.

Hypermeter of four Anapæsts.

On the warm cheek of youth, smiles and roses are blending.

VERSES IN WHICH THE SECONDARY FEET ARE ADMITTED TO GIVE VARIETY TO THE MELODY.

The student will observe, by the marks on the vowels, what the secondary feet are, which are introduced in the following lines; the first foot is a spondee

Thēre sōōn the sufferer sinks to rest.
Thēre tōō was he, who nobly stemmed the tide.
Thăt breăst the seat of sentimĕnt refined.
Hāil, lōng lost Peace! hāil, dōve-eyed māid divine

* This measure is ambiguous, for by accenting the first and third syllables we may make it *Trochaic*.

A Pyrrhic occurs in the following.

If aught be welcŏme tŏ our sylvan shed,
Bē ĭt the the trav llĕr whŏ has lost his way.
I sought the beautĭes ŏf the painted vale,
The flowers I often watĕred wĭth my tears.
And loadĕd wĭth my sighs the passing gale

Spondees and Pyrrhics with Iambuses.

Gō pīous offsprĭng ănd restrain those tears;
I fly to regiŏns ŏf eternal bliss.
Hēaven ĭn your favor hears my dying prayers;
Tāke my lāst blĕssĭng ĭn this clay cold kiss.

A Dactyl with Iambuses.

Mūrmŭrĭng, and with him fled the shades of night.

Amphibrachs mixed with Iambuses.

O'ĕr māny a frozĕn, māny a fiĕry ălp.

A Spondee and a Tribrach, with Iambuses.

Innumerable before th' Almighty throne.

It will thus be perceived, that by the mixture of different kinds of feet, all that variety is produced, which renders poetry agreeable to the ear. To constitute verse, it is not sufficient that a number of jarring syllables should be ranged in uncouth lines, with rhyme at the end. Order, regularity, symmetry, and harmony are requisite, while the taste and judgment of the poet are displayed by the proper mixture of accented and unac cented syllables to form an harmonious line.*

The student, having now been made acquainted with the different kinds of verse, may be required to compose verses himself in all the different kinds of measure. As a first exercise in versification, he may be permitted to write words in verses *without regard to their signification*, making what may be called *nonsense* verses, as in the following

Example.

Five foot Iambus or Heroic Verse.

Thus man attempts some nobler end to scan.
Bestrides the flood in horror at the plan.

---

* The harmony of a verse may sometimes be utterly destroyed by the misplacing of a single monosyllable; thus,

"Thrice is he armed that hath his quarrel just,
And he but naked, though locked up in steel,
Whose conscience *is* with injustice corrupted."

In this extract, the measure of the third line is utterly destroyed by the misplacing of the word *is*. It should be,

"Whose conscience with injustice is corrupted."

Trochaic.

Boiling in the troubled sea.
Full of mirthful hope to be.

Anapæstic.

From the brow of the hill see the hermit appear,
And with joy in his face mark the waters so clear, &c.

Exercises.

Having previously attempted to form verses in all the different sorts of measure that have been described, with words without reference to sense, the student may arrange the following lines in regular order. The lines themselves contain all the words necessary both for the harmonious construction and the expression of the sense. The order of them is, how ever, disturbed, as will be seen by the following

Example.

Adieu to the woodlands, where, gay and sportive,
The cattle play so frolicsome, light bounding.
Adieu to the woodlands where I have roved oft,
And, with the friend that I loved, conversed so sweetly

Same words properly arranged.

Adieu to the woodlands, where, sportive and gay,
The cattle light bounding so frolicsome play.
Adieu to the woodlands where oft I have roved,
And sweetly conversed with the friend I have loved.

Exercises.

*Verses to be arranged by the Student in Anapæstic * lines of four feet*

Content and joy are now fled from our dwellings,
And, instead, disease and want are our inmates.

---

* Dr. Carey, in his English Prosody, says, "If, like Tertæus of old, I had to awake dormant valor with the voice of song, I would in preference to every other form of English metre, choose the Anapæstic, of four feet in couplets, which, if well written, in real anapæsts, unincumbered with an undue weight of heavy syllables, and judiciously aided by appropriate music, could hardly fail to martialize even shivering cowards, and warm them into heroes; the brisk, animating march of the verse having the same effect on the soul, as the body experiences from the quick, lively step, which, by accelerating the circulation of the blood, at once warms and dilates the heart, and renders the warrior more prompt to deeds of prowess." If any one would test the justness of Dr. Carey's opinion, as thus expressed, his doubts will be resolved by the perusal of Campbell's beautiful piece, entitled "Lochiel's Warning."

Now chivalry is dead, and Gallia ruined,
And the glory of Europe is fled for ever.

'T is woman, whose charms impart every rapture,
And to the pulse of the heart add a soft spring.
Her sway is so supreme, the miser himself
Resigns her his key, and to love grows a convert.
Sorrow lifts up his head at the sound of her voice
And, from his shed, Poverty well pleased listens.
Even age, hobbling along, in an ecstasy
Beats time to the tune of her song with her crutch.

How sweet is the thought of to-morrow to the heart,
When Hope's fairy pictures display bright colors,
How sweet when we can borrow from futurity
A balm for the griefs that to-day afflict us.

To be made into Iambic verses with four feet.

And while I feel thy gracious gifts
My song shall reveal all thy praise.

The search shall teach thee to prize life,
And make thee good, wise, and grateful.

With ease you wear a thousand shapes,
And still you please in every shape.

Neither wealth I pursue, nor power,
Nor hold in view forbidden joys.

The prudent nymph, whose cheeks disclose
The blushing rose and the lily,
Will screen her charms from public view,
And rarely be seen in the crowd.

*Iambic verses of five feet, or the Heroic * measure.*

As Orpheus tunes his song in Thracian wilds,
The raptured beasts throng around him in crowds.

Seek not thou to find, with vain endeavor,
Of Almighty mind the secret counsels;
The great decree lies involved in darkness;
Nor can the depths of fate by thee be pierced.

O could some poet rise, bold in wisdom,
And unfold half thy beauties to the world,
Roving on fancy's wing, impart thy fire,
And feel thy genius beaming on his heart, —
I 'd wish humbly, though the wish would be vain,
That on me some small portion might alight.

---

* This is the principal metre of our language, and it is happily adapted to every kind of subject, from the most exalted to the most humble and familiar, and it may be used with or without rhyme.

Trochaic verses.

Where spreads the rising forest,
For the lordly dome shelter,
To their airy beds high built,
See returning home the rooks.

Now battle glows with fury
In torrents flows hostile blood.

Here you 'll find mental pleasures,
Pleasures that the mind adorn.
The joys of sense are transient,
They dispense no solid bliss.

The shepherd dines by the brook
Heat the fierce meridian from
By the branching pines sheltered
O'er his grassy seat pendent.

But from stream, dell, or mountain
Springs not a fluttering zephyr,
Lest the noontide beam, fearful
His silken, his soft wings scorch.

RHYME.

Rhyme is a similarity, or agreement, in the sound of final syllables.

Verse without rhyme is called *blank verse.**

It is a general rule in poetry, with regard to rhymes, that they should begin on the accented syllable.

In the forming of verses with rhyme, it is a good rule to let the weaker line stand first.†

* Rhyme is by no means to be considered as an essential constituent in English poetry. Much poetry has been written, and that, too, of the choicest description, in which rhyme has no part. The poetry of Milton, Shakspeare, Thomson, Young, and a host of others, whose writings have contributed so much to the literature of the language, seldom admits this "*meretricious*" ornament, as it has been called. But it has been said, that, although, in the five feet Iambic measure, the measured dignity of the verse supplies the place of rhyme, in the other forms of English versification it is absolutely essential. Whoever will be at the pains to convince himself that this is an erroneous opinion, may easily do so by the perusal of the works of Dr. Southey, especially, his "Thalaba, or the Destroyer."

† The student, in his first attempts at versification, should be cautioned against the injudicious use of *expletives*. An expletive is a word introduced merely to fill out the line, while it not only contributes nothing to the sense, but absolutely weakens it. Pope, in his Essay on Criticism, exemplifies, while he condemns this fault.

"While expletives their feeble aid *do* join,
And ten low words oft creep in one dull line."

Rhymes may occur in consecutive, or alternate lines, or in any other regular order, at the pleasure of the writer.

Rhymes are of two kinds, perfect rhymes and allowable rhymes. The difference between the two kinds will readily be seen by the following Vocabulary, taken from Walker's "Rhyming Dictionary." *

---

* On the same principle of association, on which some of the earlier lessons in this volume are founded, it is thought that this vocabulary will aid the student, not only in finding a rhyme, but likewise in suggesting ideas. Dr. Carey, in the Preface to his "English Prosody," says: "It is not with the view of making poets and poetesses that I send forth this publication. That must be the work of nature alone: it is not in my power to create them; and if it were, I might be accused of doing more harm than good, in tempting many of my young readers to quit a gainful calling for the ungainful trade. My aims are more humble; — 1. To teach the learner to read poetry with propriety and grace; 2. To improve and polish his style for prose composition." And, further on, he adds; "Indeed, every person, whether poet or not, who has received any tolerable education, and pretends to write decent prose, ought likewise to be qualified for the occasional production of a few verses, smooth, at least, and metrically correct, whatever may be their merit or demerit in other respects. That the practice of versification materially improves the style for prose composition, there cannot be a doubt. The ear which is acutely sensible to the harmonies of verse, will naturally revolt against inharmonious harshness in prose; and the pains bestowed in searching for a variety of words of different lengths, quantities, and *terminations*, to suit the exigencies of the metre, —

'the shifts and turns,
Th' expedients and inventions multiform,
To which the mind resorts in chase of terms,
T' arrest the fleeting images, that fill
The mirror of the mind.'

will copiously enlarge the writer's stock of expressions, — will enable him to array his thoughts in a more elegant and attractive garb, and to vary that garb at pleasure, by the ready aid of a diversified phraseology. It will, at the same time, produce a more important and beautiful effect, — it will enrich the intellectual store of thought; for, while in search for an *epithet*, for an example, or a periphrase, he is obliged to view the subject in all its possible bearings and relations, that he may choose such particular word or phrase, as shall exhibit it in the most advantageous light. And what study more effectual to call into action the powers of the mind, to exercise the judgment, to whet the sagacity, *and give birth to a variety of ideas*, which might otherwise have lain for ever dormant? For these weighty considerations, the practice of verse-making has been recommended by Locke, Chesterfield, Franklin, &c., &c."

The teacher will find the following exercise, called by the French "*Bouts Rimes*," interesting to the *young* student, and, like all other inducements to thought, auxiliary to the subject of composition.

"One of a party writes down the rhyming words for a short poem; which another undertakes to complete, by filling up the several verses, on a subject either chosen at pleasure, or prescribed, as the case may be. The following stanza, in which the words in italic are the rhyming words previously assigned, will be sufficiently explanatory of the practice:

LXXV.

VOCABULARY OF RHYMES.

Directions for finding Rhymes.

1. In looking for a word in the following vocabulary, consider the five vowels, *A*, *E*, *I*, *O*, *U*, and begin at the vowel that precedes the last consonant of the word; for example, to find *persuade*, and the words that rhyme to it, *D* is the last consonant, *A* the vowel that precedes it; look for *ADE*, and you will find *made*, *fade*, *invade*, and all the other words of that rhyme.

'To Hope.

Down, down, vain hope, to me no . . . . . *more*
Can spring return, with blossoms . . . . . *crowned*,
Nor Summer ripen Autumn's . . . . . *store*,
Which now lies withering on the . . . . . *ground*.

Fade, fade, vain Hope! all else has . . . . . *faded;*
Why should I dream and cherish . . . . . *thee?*
Since dark Despair, that sun has . . . . . *shaded*,
Which once gave light and joy to . . . . . *me*.

Go, flatterer, go! thy hour is . . . . . *past;*
Thy promised pleasures all are . . . . . *vain:*
I know they are not meant to . . . . . *last*
And ne'er will trust to thee . . . . . *again*.'

Another sort of poetical amusement has the name of *Echo Verses*. In these the repetition of the last word or syllable of a verse gives an answer to a question, or explains some subject, which that verse contains. The following echo verses allude to the Roundheads in the reign of Charles the First.

Now, Echo, on what 's religion grounded?
Roundhead.
Who 's its professor most considerable?
Rabble.
How do these prove themselves to be the godly?
Oddly.
But they in life are known to be the holy.
O lie!
Do they not learning from their doctrine sever?
Ever!
Yet they pretend, that they do edify;
O fie!
What church have they, and what pulpits?
Pitts.
Are crosses, images, and ornaments their scandal?
All!
How do they stand affected to the government civil?
Evil.

2. In like manner, if a word end in two or more consonants, begin at the vowel that immediately precedes the first of them; for example, *land*, *N* is first of the final consonants, *A* the vowel that precedes it; see *AND*, and you will find *band*, *stand*, *command*, &c.

3. But if a diphthong, that is to say, two or more vowels together, precedes the last consonant or consonants of a word, begin at the first of these two vowels; thus, to find the rhymes to *disdain*, look not for *IN* but for *AIN*, and you will find *brain*, *chain*, *gain*, &c.

4. To find a word that ends in a diphthong preceded by a consonant, begin only at the first vowel of the diphthong; for example, to find the rhymes to *subdue*, look for *UE*, and you will find *clue*, *due*, *ensue*, &c.

5. All the words that end in a single vowel, preceded by a consonant, are found by looking for that vowel only, except always the words that end in mute *E*, which are constantly found by the same method that has been already prescribed for finding the rhymes to *persuade*, whose final *E* is silent, and serves only to lengthen the sound of the *A* in the last syllable.

AB.

Bab, cab, dab, mab, nab, blab, crab, drab, scab stab. *Allowable rhymes* babe, astrolabe, &c. See *Direction* 3.

ACE.

Ace, dace, pace, face, lace, mace, race, brace, chace, grace, place, space, trace, apace, deface, efface, disgrace, displace, misplace, embrace, grimace, interlace, retrace, populace, &c. *Perfect rhymes*, base, case, abase, debase, &c. *Allowable rhymes*, grass, glass, &c., peace, cease, &c., dress, less, &c

ACH.

Attach, detach, &c. *Perfect rhymes*, batch, match, &c. *Allowable rhymes*, fetch, wretch, &c. See *Direction* 3.

ACK.

Back, cack, hack, jack, lack, pack, quack, tack, sack, rack, black, clack, crack, knack, slack, snack, stack, track, wrack, attack, zodiac, demoniac symposiac, almanac. *Allowable rhymes*, bake, take, &c., neck, speck, &c.

ACT.

Act, fact, pact, tract, attract, abstract, extract, compact, contract, detract, distract, exact, protract, enact, infract, subtract, transact, cataract, *with the preterits and participles of verbs in* ack, *as* backed, hacked, &c. *Allowable rhymes, the preterits and participles of verbs in* ake, *as* baked, caked, &c. See *Direction* 3.

But to the King they say they are most loyal.
Lie all.
Then God keep King and state from these same men.
Amen.

It remains to be observed: 1. That the two corresponding syllables of a rhyme must not only begin their consonance with the accented vowel, but must preserve it through the remaining letters; thus, *text* and *vext*, *song* and *long* echo with one another respectively, in the sounds *ext* and *ong*.

2. The *sounds*, and not the letters, constitute the rhyme. Thus, *muff* and *rough*, *blew* and *grew*, though different to the eye, form an unobjectionable rhyme; but *bough* and *tough*, though similar to the eye, have no similarity in sound.

3. The letter or letters in the syllable which precede the accented vowel, must be different in form and sound, otherwise the consonance will be disagreeable to the ear. Hence, *tend* and the last syllable in *contend*, *sent* and *scent* are not allowable rhymes.

AD.

Add, bad, dad, gad, had, lad, mad, pad, sad, brad, clad, glad, plad, chad, &c. *Allowable rhymes*, cade, fade, &c., glede, bead, read, &c. See *Direction* 3.

ADE.

Cade, fade, made, jade, lade, wade, blade, glade, shade, spade, trade, degrade, evade, dissuade, invade, persuade, blockade, brigade, esplanade cavalcade, masquerade, renegade, retrograde, serenade, ambuscade, cannonade, pallisade, &c. *Perfect rhymes*, aid, maid, braid, afraid, upbraid, &c., *and the preterits and participles of verbs in* ay, ey, and eigh, *as* played, obeyed, weighed, &c. *Allowable rhymes*, add, bad, &c., bed, dead, &c., bead, mead, &c., heed, need, &c. See *Direction* 3.

AFE.

Safe, chafe, vouchsafe, &c. *Allowable rhymes*, leaf, sheaf, &c., deaf, &c., laugh, staff, &c.

AFF.

Gaff, chaff, draff, quaff, staff, engraff, epitaph, cenotaph, paragraph, &c. *Perfect rhyme*, laugh. *Allowable rhymes*, safe, chafe, &c.

AFT.

Aft, haft, raft, waft, craft, shaft, abaft, graft, draft, ingraft, handicraft. *Perfect rhymes*, draught, *and the preterits and participles of verbs in* aff *and* augh, *as* quaffed, laughed, &c. *Allowable rhymes*, *the preterits and participles of verbs in* afe, *as* chafed, vouchsafed, &c.

AG.

Bag, cag, fag, gag, nag, quag, rag, tag, wag, brag, crag, drag, flag, knag shag, snag, stag, wrag, scrag, Brobdignag.

AGE.

Age, cage gage, page, rage, sage, wage, stage, swage, assuage, engage disengage, enrage, presage, appenage, concubinage, heritage, hermitage parentage, parsonage, personage, pasturage, patronage, pilgrimage, villanage, equipage. *Allowable rhymes*, edge, wedge, &c., liege, siege, oblige &c.

AID, see ADE.

AIGHT, see ATE.

AIGN, see ANE.

AIL.

Ail, bail, fail, hail, jail, mail, nail, pail, quail, rail, sail, tail, wail, flail frail, snail, trail, assail, avail, detail, bewail, entail, prevail, retail, countervail, &c. *Perfect rhymes*, ale, bale, dale, gale, hale, male, pale, sale, tale vale, wale, scale, stale, swale, whale, impale, exhale, regale, veil, nightingale, &c. *Allowable rhymes*, peal, steal, &c., bell, cell, &c.

AIM, see AME.

AIN.

Cain, blain, brain, chain, fain, gain, grain, lain, main, pain, rain, vain, wain, drain, plain, slain, Spain, stain, swain, train, twain, sprain, strain, abstain, amain, attain, complain, contain, constrain, detain, disdain, distrain, enchain, entertain, explain, maintain, ordain, pertain, obtain, refrain, regain, remain, restrain, retain, sustain, appertain. *Perfect rhymes*, bane, cane, dane, crane, fane, jane, lane, mane, plane, vane, wane, profane, hurricane, &c., deign, arraign, campaign, &c., feign, reign, &c., vein, rein, &c. *Allowable rhymes* lean, mean, &c., queen, seen, &c., ban, can, &c., den, pen, &c.

AINT.

Faint, paint, plaint, quaint, saint, taint, acquaint, attaint, complaint, con

21*

straint, restraint, &c. *Perfect rhyme*, feint. *Allowable rhymes*, cant, pant &c., lent, rent, &c.

AIR, see ARE.

AISE, see AZE.

AIT, see ATE.

AITH, see ATH.

AIZE, see AZE.

AKE.

Ake, bake, cake, lake, make, quake, rake, sake, take, wake, brake, drake, flake, shake, snake, stake, strake, spake, awake, betake, forsake, mistake, partake, overtake, undertake, bespake. *Perfect rhymes*, break, steak, &c. *Allowable rhymes*, back, rack, &c., beck, deck, &c., speak, weak, &c.

AL.

Cabal, canal, animal, admiral, cannibal, capital, cardinal, comical, conjugal, corporal, criminal, critical, festival, funeral, general, hospital, interval, liberal, madrigal, literal, magical, mineral, mystical, musical, natural, original, pastoral, pedestal, personal, physical, poetical, political, principal, prodigal, prophetical, rational, satrical, reciprocal, rhetorical, several, temporal, tragical, tyrannical, carnival, schismatical, whimsical, arsenal. *Allowable rhymes*, all, ball, &c., ail, mail, &c., ale, pale, &c.

ALD.

Bald, scald, emerald, &c. *Perfect rhymes, the preterits and participles of verbs in* all, aul, *and* awl, *as* called, mauled, crawled, &c.

ALE, see AIL.

ALF.

Calf, half, behalf, &c. *Allowable rhymes*, staff, laugh, &c.

ALK.

Balk, chalk, stalk, talk, walk, calk, &c. *Perfect rhyme*, hawk. *Allowable rhymes*, sock, clock, &c.

ALL.

All, ball, call, &c. *Perfect rhymes*, awl, bawl, brawl, crawl, scrawl, sprawl, squall. *Allowable rhymes*, cabal, equivocal, &c. See AL.

ALM.

Calm, balm, becalm, psalm, palm, embalm, &c., *whose plurals and third persons singular rhyme with* alms, *as* calms, becalms, &c.

ALT.

Halt, malt, exalt, salt, vault, assault, default, *and* fault, *the last of which is by Pope rhymed with* thought, bought, &c.

ALVE.

Calve, halve, salve, valve.

AM.

Am, dam, ham, pam, ram, sam, cram, dram, flam, sham, swam, epigram, anagram, &c. *Perfect rhymes*, damn, lamb. *Allowable rhymes*, dame, lame, &c.

AME.

Blame, came, dame, same, flame, fame, frame, game, lame, name, tame shame, inflame, became, defame, misname, misbecame, overcame, &c. *Perfect rhymes*, aim, claim, maim, acclaim, declaim, exclaim, proclaim, reclaim. *Allowable rhymes*, dam, ham, &c., hem, them, &c., theme, scheme &c., dream, gleam, &c.

AMP.

Camp, champ cramp, damp, stamp, vamp, lamp, clamp, decamp, encamp, &c.

AN.

Bar an, dan, man, nan, pan, ran, tan, van, bran, plan, scan, span, than, unman, fore-ran, began, trepan, courtesan, partisan, artisan, pelican, caravan, &c. *Allowable rhymes*, bane, cane, plain, mane, &c., bean, lean, wan, swan, &c., gone, upon, &c.

ANCE.

Chance, dance, glance, lance, trance, prance, entrance, romance, advance, mischance, complaisance, circumstance, countenance, deliverance, consonance, dissonance, extravagance, ignorance, inheritance, maintenance, temperance, intemperance, exhorbitance, ordinance, concordance, sufferance, sustenance, utterance, arrogance, vigilance, expanse, enhance.

ANCH.

Branch, stanch, lanch, blanch, ranch, hanch. *Perfect rhymes*, launch paunch.

AND.

And, band, hand, land, rand, sand, brand, bland, grand, gland, stand, strand, command, demand, countermand, disband, expand, withstand, understand, reprimand, contraband, &c. *Allowable rhymes*, wand, fond bond, &c., *and the preterits and participles of verbs in* ain *and* ean, *as* remained, leaned, &c

ANE, see AIN.

ANG.

Bang, fang, gang, hang, pang, tang, twang, sang, rang, harangue, clang. *Allowable rhymes*, song, long, &c.

ANGE.

Change, grange, range, strange, estrange, arrange, exchange, interchange. *Allowable rhymes*, revenge, avenge, &c.

ANK.

Rank, blank, shank, clank, dank, drank, slank, frank, spank, stank, lank plank, prank, rank, thank, disrank, mountebank, &c.

ANSE, see ANCE.

ANT.

Ant, cant, chant, grant, pant, plant, rant, slant, aslant, complaisant, dis plant, enchant, gallant, implant, recant, supplant, transplant, absonant, adamant, arrogant, combatant, consonant, cormorant, protestant, significant, visitant, covenant, dissonant, disputant, elegant, elephant exhorbitant, con versant, extravagant, ignorant, insignificant, inhabitant, militant, predomi nant, sycophant, vigilant, petulant, &c. *Allowable rhymes*, faint, paint, &c. See AINT and ENT.

AP.

Cap, gap, hap, lap, map, nap, pap, rap, sap, tap, chap, clap, trap, flap, knap, slap, snap, wrap, scrap, strap, enwrap, entrap, mishap, &c. *Allowable rhymes*, cape, tape, &c., cheap, heap, *and* swap.

APE.

Ape, cape, chape, grape, rape, scrape, shape, escape, mape, crape, tape, &c. *Allowable rhymes*, heap, keep, &c.

APH, see AFF.

APSE.

Lapse, elapse, relapse, perhaps, *and the plurals of nouns and third persons singular of the present tense in* ap, *as* caps, maps, &c., he saps, he laps, &c. *Allowable rhymes, the plurals of nouns and third persons singular of verbs in* ape *and* eap, *as* apes, he apes, heaps, he heaps, &c.

APT.

Apt, adapt, &c., *rhymes, the preterits and participles of the verbs in* ap, *as* tapped, slapped, &c. *Allowable rhymes, the preterits and participles of the verbs in* ape, *as* aped, escaped, &c

AR.

Bar, car, far, jar, mar, par, tar, spar, scar, star, chair, afar, debar, unbar catarrh, particular, perpendicular, secular, angular, regular, popular, singular, titular, vinegar, scimeter, calendar, colander. *Perfect rhyme, the plural verb* are. *Allowable rhymes,* bare, prepare, &c., pair, repair, wear, tear, war, &c., *and words ending in* er *or* or, *having the accent on the last syllable, or last but two.*

ARB.

Barb, garb, &c.

ARCE.

Farce, parse, Mars, &c. *Allowable rhyme,* scarce.

ARCH.

Arch, march, parch, starch, countermarch, &c.

ARD.

Bard, card, guard, hard, lard, nard, shard, yard, bombard, discard, regard, interlard, retard, disregard, &c., *and the preterits and participles of verbs in* ar, *as* barred, scarred, &c. *Allowable rhymes,* cord, reward, &c

ARD.

Ward, award, reward, &c. *Allowable rhymes,* hard, card, *see the last article,* hoard, lord, bird, curd, *and the preterits and participles of the verbs in* ar, or, *and* ur, *as* barred, abhorred, incurred, &c.

ARE.

Bare, care, dare, fare, hare, mare, pare, tare, rare, ware, flare, glare, scare, share, snare, spare, square, stare, sware, prepare, aware, beware, compare, declare, ensnare. *Perfect rhymes,* air, fair, hair, lair, pair, chair, stair, affair debonnair, despair, impair, repair, &c., bear, pear, swear, tear, wear, forbear, forswear, &c., there, were, where, ere, e'er, ne'er, elsewhere, whate'er, nowe'er, howsoe'er, whene'er, where'er, &c., heir, coheir, their. *Allowable rhymes,* bar, car, &c., err, prefer, *and* here, hear, &c., regular, singular war, &c.

ARES.

Unawares. *Rhymes,* theirs, *and the plurals of nouns and third persons singular of verbs in* are, air, eir, ear, *as* care, he cares, pair, he pairs, heirs bear, he bears, &c. *The allowable rhymes are the plurals of nouns and the third persons singular of verbs which are allowed to rhyme with the termination* ars, *as* bars, cars, errs, prefers, &c.

ARF.

Scarf. *Allowable rhymes,* dwarf, wharf.

ARGE.

Barge, charge, large, targe, discharge, o'ercharge, surcharge, enlarge *Allowable rhymes,* verge, emerge, gorge, forge, urge, &c.

ARK.

Bark, cark, clark, dark, lark, mark, park, shark, spark, stark, embark remark, &c. *Allowable rhymes,* cork, fork, &c.

ARL.

Snarl, marl, parl. *Allowable rhymes,* curl, furl, &c.

ARM.

Arm, barm, charm, farm, harm, alarm, disarm. *Allowable rhymes* warm swarm, storm, &c.

ARN.

Barn, yarn, &c. *Allowable rhymes,* warn, forewarn, &c., horn, morn, &c

ARN.

Warn, forwarn. *Perfect rhymes,* horn morn, &c. *Allowable rhymes* barn, yarn, &c.

ARP.

Carp, harp, sharp, counterscarp, &c. *Allowable rhyme*, warp

ARSH.

Harsh, marsh, &c.

ART.

Art, cart, dart, hart, mart, part, smart, tart, start, apart, depart, impart dispart, counterpart. *Perfect rhymes*, heart, &c. *Allowable rhymes*, wart thwart, &c., hurt, &c., dirt, flirt, &c., pert, &c.

ART (sounded ORT).

Wart, thwart, &c. *Perfect rhymes*, short, retort, &c. *Allowable rhymes* art, sport, court, &c.

ARTH, see EARTH.

ARVE.

Carve, starve, &c. *Allowable rhymes*, nerve, deserve, &c.

AS.

Was. *Allowable rhymes*, has as.

ASS.

Ass, brass, class, grass, lass, mass, pass, alas, amass, cuirass, repass, surpass, morass, &c. *Allowable rhymes*, base, face, deface, &c., loss, toss, &c

ASE, see ACE.

ASH.

Ash, cash, dash, clash, crash, flash, gash, gnash, hash, lash, plash, rash, thrash, slash, trash, abash, &c. *Allowable rhymes*, wash, quash, &c., leash &c.

ASH.

Wash, quash, &c. *Allowable rhymes*, cash, dash, &c.

ASK.

Ask, task, bask, cask, flask, mask.

ASP.

Asp, clasp, gasp, grasp, hasp. *Allowable rhymes*, wasp, &c.

AST.

Cast, last, blast, mast, past, vast, fast, aghast, avast, forecast, overcast, outcast, repast. *Perfect rhymes, the preterits and participles of verbs in* ass, *as* classed, amassed, &c. *Allowable rhymes, the preterits and participles of verbs in* ace, *as* placed, &c. *Nouns and verbs in* aste, *as* taste, waste, &c.

ASTE.

Baste, chaste, haste, paste, taste, waste, distaste. *Perfect rhymes*, waist, *and the preterits and participles of verbs in* ace, *as* faced, placed, &c. *Allowable rhymes*, cast, fast, &c., best, nest, &c., *and the preterits and participles of verbs in* ess, *as* messed, dressed, &c.

AT.

At, bat, cat, hat, fat, mat, pat, rat, sat, tat, vat, brat, chat, flat, plat, sprat, that, gnat. *Allowable rhymes*, bate, hate, &c.

ATCH.

Catch, match, hatch, latch, patch, scratch, smatch, snatch, despatch.

ATE.

Bate, date, fate, gate, grate, hate, tate, mate, pate, plate, prate, rate, sate, state, scate, slate, abate, belate, collate, create, debate, elate, dilate, estate, ingrate, innate, rebate, relate, sedate, translate, abdicate, abominate, abrogate, accelerate, accommodate, accumulate, accurate, adequate, affectionate, advocate, adulterate, aggravate, agitate, alienate, animate, annihilate, antedate, anticipate, antiquate, arbitrate, arrogate, articulate, assassinate, calculate, capitulate, captivate, celebrate, circulate, coagulate, commemorate, commiserate, communicate, compassionate, confederate, congratulate, congregate, consecrate, contaminate, corroborate, cultivate, candidate, coöp erate, celebrate, considerate, consulate, capacitate, debilitate, dedicate, degenerate, delegate, deliberate, denominate, depopulate, dislocate, deprecate discriminate, derogate, dissipate, delicate, disconsolate, desperate, deprecate, educate, effeminate, elevate, emulate, estimate, elaborate, equivocate, eradicate, evaporate, exaggerate, exasperate, expostulate, exterminate, extricate, facilitate, fortunate, generate, gratulate, hesitate, illiterate, illuminate, irritate, imitate, immoderate, impetrate, importunate, imprecate, inanimate, innovate, instigate, intemperate, intimate, intimidate, intoxicate, intricate, invalidate, inveterate, inviolate, legitimate, magistrate, meditate, mitigate, moderate, necessitate, nominate, obstinate, participate, passionate, penetrate, perpetrate, personate, potentate, precipitate, predestinate, predominate, premeditate, prevaricate, procrastinate, profligate, prognosticate, propagate, recriminate, regenerate, regulate, reiterate, reprobate, reverberate, ruminate, separate, sophisticate, stipulate, subjugate, subordinate, suffocate, terminate, tolerate, temperate, vindicate, violate, unfortunate. *Perfect rhymes*, bait, plait, strait, wait, await, great. *Nearly perfect rhymes*, eight, weight, height, straight. *Allowable rhymes*, beat, heat, &c., bat, cat, &c., bet, wet, &c.

ATH.

Bath, path, &c. *Allowable rhymes*, hath, faith, &c.

ATHE.

Bathe, swathe, lathe, rathe.

AUB, see OB.

AUCE, see AUSE.

AUCH, see OACH.

AUD.

Fraud, laud, applaud, defraud. *Perfect rhymes*, broad, abroad, bawd; *and the preterits and participles of verbs in* aw, *as* gnawed, sawed, &c. *Allowable rhymes*, odd, nod, &c., ode, bode, &c.; *also the word* load.

AVE.

Cave, brave, gave, grave, crave, lave, nave, knave, pave, rave, save, shave, slave, stave, wave, behave, deprave, engrave, outbrave, forgave, misgave architrave. *Allowable rhyme, the auxiliary verb* have.

AUGH, see AFF.

AUGHT, see OUGHT.

AULT, see ALT.

AUNCH.

Launch, paunch, haunch, staunch, &c.

AUNCE, see ONSE.

AUNT.

Aunt, daunt, gaunt, haunt, jaunt, taunt, vaunt, avaunt. *Perfect rhymes* slant, aslant. *Allowable rhymes*, want, &c., pant, cant, &c

AUSE.

Cause, pause, clause, applause, because. *Perfect rhymes, the plurals of nouns, and third persons singular of verbs in* aw, *as* laws, he draws, &c. *Allowable rhyme*, was.

AUST, see OST,

AW.

Craw, daw, law, chaw, claw, draw, flaw, gnaw, jaw, law, maw, paw, raw, saw, straw, thaw, withdraw, foresaw.

AWD, see AUD.

AWK, see ALK.

AWL.

Bawl, brawl, drawl, crawl, scrawl, sprawl, squall. *Perfect rhymes*, ball, call, fall, gall, small, hall, pall, tall, wall, stall, install, forestall, thrall, inthrall

AWN.

Dawn, brawn, fawn, pawn, spawn, drawn, yawn, lawn, withdrawn.

AX.

Ax, tax, wax, relax, flax. *Perfect rhymes, the plurals of nouns, and third persons singular of verbs in* ack, *as* backs, sacks, &c., he lacks, he packs, &c. *Allowable rhymes, the plurals of nouns, and third persons singular of verbs in* ake, *as* cakes, lakes, &c., he makes, he takes, &c.

AY.

Bray, clay, day, dray, tray, flay, fray, gay, hay, jay, lay, may, nay, pay, play, ray, say, way, pray, spray, slay, spay, stay, stray, sway, affray, allay, array, astray, away, belay, bewray, betray, decay, defray, delay, disarray, display, dismay, essay, forelay, gainsay, inlay, relay, repay, roundelay, virelay. *Perfect rhymes*, neigh, weigh, inveigh, &c., prey, they, convey, obey, purvey, survey, disobey, grey. *Allowable rhymes*, tea, sea, fee, see, glee, &c.

AZE.

Craze, daze, blaze, gaze, glaze, maze, raze, amaze, graze. *Perfect rhymes*, raise, praise, dispraise, &c., phrase, paraphrase, &c., *and the nouns plural, and third persons singular of the present tense of verbs in* ay, eigh, *and* ey; *as* days, he inveighs, he obeys, &c. *Allowable rhymes*, ease, tease, seize, &c *and* keys, *the plural of* key; *also the auxiliaries* has *and* was.

E and EA, see EE.

EACE, see EASE.

EACH.

Beach, breach, bleach, each, peach, preach, teach, impeach. *Nearly perfect rhymes*, beech, leech, speech, beseech. *Allowable rhymes*, fetch, wretch, &c.

EAD, see EDE and EED.

EAF, see IEF.

EAGUE.

League, teague, &c. *Perfect rhymes*, intrigue, fatigue, &c. *Allowable rhymes*, Hague, vague, &c., leg, beg, &c., bag, rag, &c.

EAK, see AKE.

Beak, speak, bleak, creak, freak, leak, peak, sneak, squeak, streak, weak, tweak, wreak, bespeak. *Nearly perfect rhymes*, cheek, leek, creek, meek, reek, seek, sleek, pique, week, shriek. *Allowable rhymes*, beck, speck, &c., lake, take, thick, lick, &c.

EAL.

Deal, heal, reveal, meal, peal, seal, steal, teal, veal, weal, zeal, squeal, repeal, conceal, congeal, anneal, appeal. *Nearly perfect rhymes*, eel, heel, feel, keel, kneel, peel, reel, steel, wheel. *Allowable rhymes*, bell, tell, &c., pale, tale, &c., bill, fill, &c., ail, fail, &c.

EALM, see ELM.

EALTH.

Health, wealth, stealth, commonwealth, &c,

EAM.

Bream, cream, gleam, seam, scream, steam, stream, team, beam, dream. *Perfect rhymes*, phlegm, scheme, theme, blaspheme, extreme, supreme. *Nearly perfect rhymes*, deem, teem, beseem, misdeem, esteem, disesteem, redeem, seem, &c. *Allowable rhymes*, dame, lame, &c., limb, him, &c., them, hem, &c., lamb, dam, &c. See AME.

EAN.

Bean, clean, dean, glean, lean, mean, wean, yean, demean, unclean. *Perfect rhymes*, convene, demesne, intervene, mien. *Nearly perfect rhymes*, machine, keen, screen, seen, green, spleen, between, careen, foreseen, serene, obscene, terrene, &c., queen, spleen, &c. *Allowable rhymes*, bane, mane &c ban, man, &c., bin, thin, begin, &c.

EANS, see ENSE.

EANT, see ENT.

EAP, see EEP and EP.

EAR, see EER.

EARD.

Heard, herd, sherd, &c. *Perfect rhymes, the preterits and participles of verbs in* er, *as* erred, preferred, &c. *Allowable rhyme*, beard, *the preterit and participles of verbs in* ere, ear, *and* ar, *as* revered, feared, barred.

EARCH.

Search, perch, research. *Allowable rhymes*, church, smirch, lurch, parch march, &c.

EARL.

Earl, pearl. *Perfect rhyme*, girl, &c. *Allowable rhymes*, snarl, marl, churl furl, &c.

EARN, see ERN.

EARSE, see ERSE.

EART, see ART.

EARTH.

Earth, dearth. *Perfect rhymes*, birth, mirth, &c. *Allowable rhymes* hearth, &c.

EASE, sounded EACE.

Cease, lease, release, grease, decease, decrease, increase, release, surcease *Perfect rhyme*, peace. *Nearly perfect rhymes*, piece, niece, fleece, geese frontispiece, apiece, &c. *Allowable rhymes*, less, mess, &c., lace, mace, &c miss, hiss, &c., nice, vice, &c.

EASH, see ESH.

EAST.

East, feast, least, beast. *Perfect rhymes, and preterits and participles of verbs in* ease, *as* ceased, increased, &c. *Nearly perfect rhyme*, priest. *Allowable rhymes*, haste, taste, &c., best, chest, &c., fist, list, &c., *and the preterits and participles of verbs in* esse *and* iss, *as* dressed, hissed, &c.

EAT.

Bleat, eat, feat, heat, meat, neat, seat, treat, wheat, beat, cheat, defeat, estreat, escheat, entreat, retreat, *Perfect rhymes*, obsolete, replete, concrete, complete. *Nearly perfect rhymes*, feet, fleet, gleet, greet, meet, sheet, sleet, street, sweet, discreet. *Allowable rhymes*, bate, grate, hate, &c., get, met, &c bit, hit, &c. See ATE.

EATH.

Breath, death, &c, *Allowable rhymes*, heath, sheath, teeth.

EATHE.

Breathe, sheathe, &c. *Perfect rhymes*, wreath, inwreath, bequeath, beneath, underneath, &c. *Nearly perfect rhymes*, seethe, &c.

EAVE.

Cleave, heave, interweave, leave, weave, bereave, inweave. *Perfect rhymes*, receive, conceive, deceive, perceive. *Nearly perfect rhymes*, eve, grieve, thieve, aggrieve, achieve, believe, disbelieve, relieve, reprieve, retrieve. *Allowable rhymes*, give, live, &c., lave, cave, &c., *and* have.

EBB.

Ebb, web, &c. *Allowable rhymes*, babe, astrolabe, &c., glebe, &c.

ECK.

Beck, neck, check, deck, speck, wreck. *Allowable rhymes*, break, take &c., beak, sneak &c

ECT.

Sect, abject, affect, correct, incorrect, collect, deject, detect, direct, disrespect, disaffect, dissect, effect, elect, eject, erect, expect, indirect, infect, inspect, neglect, object, project, protect, recollect, reflect, reject, respect, select, subject, suspect, architect, circumspect, dialect, intellect. *Perfect rhymes, the preterits and participles of verbs in* eck, *as* decked, checked, &c. *Allowable rhymes, the preterits and participles of verbs in* ake, *and* eak, *as* baked, leaked.

ED.

Bed, bled, fed, fled, bred, led, red, shred, shed, sped, wed, abed, inbred misled. *Perfect rhymes,* said, bread, dread, dead, head, lead, read, spread, thread, tread, behead, o'erspread. *Allowable rhymes,* bead, mead, &c., blade, fade, &c., maid, paid, &c., *and the preterits and participles of verbs in* ay, ey, *and* eigh, *as* bayed, obeyed, veighed, &c.

EDE, see EED.

EDGE.

Edge, wedge, fledge, hedge, ledge, pledge, sedge, allege. *Allowable rhymes* age, page, &c., siege, oblige, &c., privilege, sacrilege, sortilege.

EE.

Bee, free, glee, knee, see, three, thee, tree, agree, decree, degree, disagree, foresee, o'ersee, pedigree, he, me, we, she, be, jubilee, lee. *Nearly perfect rhymes,* sea, plea, flea, tea, key. *Allowable rhymes, all words of one syllable ending in* y, ye, *or* ie, *or polysyllables of these terminations having the accent on the ultimate or antepenultimate syllable.*

EECE, see EASE.

EECH, see EACH.

EED.

Creed, deed, indeed, bleed, breed, feed, heed, meed, need, reed, speed seed, steed, weed, proceed, succeed, exceed. *Perfect rhymes,* knead, read intercede, precede, recede, concede, impede, supersede, &c., bead, lead mead, plead, &c. *Allowable rhymes,* bed, dead, &c., bid, hid, &c., made blade, &c.

EEF, see IEF.

EEK, see EAK

EEL, see EAL

EEM, see EAM

EEN, see EAN.

EEP.

Creep, deep, sleep, keep, peep, sheep, steep, sweep, weep, asleep. *Nearly perfect rhymes,* cheap, heap, neap, &c. *Allowable rhymes,* ape, rape, &c. step, nep, &c., hip, lip, &c.

EER.

Beer, deer, fleer, geer, jeer, peer, meer, leer, sheer, steer, sneer, cheer, veer, picker, domineer, cannoneer, compeer, engineer, mutineer, pioneer, privateer, charioteer, chanticleer, career, mountaineer. *Perfect rhymes* here, sphere, adhere, cohere, interfere, persevere, revere, austere, severe, sincere, hemisphere, &c., ear, clear, dear, fear, hear, near, sear, smear spear, tear, rear, year, appear, besmear, disappear, endear, auctioneer. *Allowable rhymes,* bare, dare, &c , prefer, deter, character, &c.

EESE, see EEZE.

EET, see EAT.

EETH, see EATH.

EEVE, see EAVE.

EEZE.

Breeze, freeze, wheeze, sneeze, squeeze, *and the plurals of nouns and third persons singular, present tense, of verbs in* ee, *as* bees, he sees. *Perfect rhymes*, cheese, these, &c. *Nearly perfect rhymes*, ease, appease, disease, displease, tease, seize, &c., *and the plurals of nouns in* ea, *as* teas, pleas, &c., *and the polysyllables ending in* es, *having the accent on the antepenultimate, as* images, monarchies, &c.

EFT.

Cleft, left, theft, weft, bereft, &c. *Allowable rhymes*, lift, sift, &c., *and the third persons singular, present tense, of verbs in* afe, aff, augh, *and* iff, *as* chafed, quaffed, laughed, whiffed, &c.

EG.

Egg, leg, beg, peg. *Allowable rhymes*, vague, plague, &c., league, teague, &c.

EIGH, see AY.

EIGHT, see ATE.

EIGN, see AIN.

EIL, see AIL.

EIN, see AIN.

EINT, see AINT.

EIR, see ARE.

EIT, see EAT.

EIVE, see EAVE.

EIZE, see EEZE.

ELL.

Ell, dwell, fell, hell, knell, quell, sell, bell, cell, dispel, foretell, excel, compel, befell, yell, well, tell, swell, spell, smell, shell, parallel, sentinel, infidel, citadel, refel, repel, rebel, impel, expel. *Allowable rhymes*, bale, sale, &c., heal, peal, &c., eel, steel, &c.

ELD.

Held, geld, withheld, upheld, beheld, &c. *Perfect rhymes, the preterits and participles of verbs in* ell, *as* swelled, felled, &c. *Allowable rhymes, the preterits and participles of verbs in* ale, ail, &c., heal, seal, &c., *as* empaled, wailed, &c., healed, sealed, &c.

ELF.

Elf, pelf, self, shelf, himself, &c.

ELK.

Elk, whelk, &c.

ELM.

Elm, helm, realm, whelm, overwhelm, &c. *Allowable rhymes* palm, film, &c.

ELP.

Help, whelp, yelp, &c.

ELT.

Belt, gelt, melt, felt, welt, smelt, pelt, dwelt. *Perfect rhyme*, dealt.

ELVE.

Delve, helve, twelve, &c.

ELVES.

Elves, themselves, &c. *Perfect rhymes, the plurals of nouns and third persons singular of verbs in* elf *and* elve, *as* twelves, delves, shelves, &c.

EM.

Gem, hem, stem, them, diadem, stratagem, &c. *Perfect rhymes*, condemn, contemn, &c. *Allowable rhymes*, lame, tame, &c., team, seam, theme, phlegm, &c.

EME, see EAM.

EMN.

Condemn, contemn, &c. *Perfect rhymes*, gem, hem, &c. *Allowable rymes*, lame, tame, &c., team, seam, &c.

EMPT.

Tempt, exempt, attempt, contempt.

EN.

Den, hen, fen, ken, men, pen, ten, then, when, wren, denizen. *Allowable rhymes*, bane, fane, &c., mean, bean, &c.

ENCE.

Fence, hence, pence, thence, whence, defence, expense, offence, pretence, commence, abstinence, circumference, conference, confidence, consequence, continence, benevolence, concupiscence, difference, diffidence, diligence, eloquence, eminence, evidence, excellence, impenitence, impertinence, impotence, impudence, improvidence, incontinence, indifference, indigence, indolence, inference, intelligence, innocence, magnificence, munificence, negligence, omnipotence, penitence, preference, providence, recompense, reference, residence, reverence, vehemence, violence. *Perfect rhymes*, sense, dense, cense, condense, immense, intense, propense, dispense, suspense, prepense, incense, frankincense.

ENCH.

Bench, drench, retrench, quench, clench, stench, tench, trench, wench, wrench, intrench.

END.

Bend, mend, blend, end, fend, lend, rend, send, spend, tend, vend, amend, attend, ascend, commend, contend, defend, depend, descend, distend, expend, extend, forefend, impend, misspend, obtend, offend, portend, pretend, protend, suspend, transcend, unbend, apprehend, comprehend, condescend, discommend, recommend, reprehend, dividend, reverend. *Perfect rhymes*, friend, befriend, *and the preterits and participles of verbs in* en, *as* penned, kenned, &c. *Allowable rhymes, the preterits and participles of verbs in* ean, *as* gleaned, yeaned, &c.

ENDS.

Amends. *Perfect rhymes, the plurals of nouns, and third persons singular, present tense, of verbs in* end, *as* ends, friends, he mends, &c.

ENE, see EAN.

ENGE.

Avenge, revenge, &c.

ENGTH.

Length, strength, &c.

ENSE, sounded ENZE.

Cleanse. *Perfect rhymes, the plurals of nouns, and third persons singular, present tense, of verbs in* en, *as* hens, fens, he pens, he kens, &c.

ENT.

Bent, lent, rent, pent, scent, sent, shent, spent, tent, vent, went, absent, meant, ascent, assent, attent, augment, cement, content, consent, descent, dissent, event, extent, foment, frequent, indent, intent, invent, lament, misspent, o'erspent, present, prevent, relent, repent, resent, ostent, ferment, outwent, underwent, discontent, unbent, circumvent, represent, abstinent, accident, accomplishment, admonishment, acknowledgment, aliment, arbitrement, argument, banishment, battlement, blandishment, astonishment, armipotent, bellipotent, benevolent, chastisement, competent, compliment, complement, confident, continent, corpulent, detriment, different, diffident, diligent, disparagement, document, element, eloquent, eminent, equivalent, establishment, evident, excellent, excrement, exigent, experiment, firmament, frandulent, government, embellishment, imminent, impenitent, im pertinent, implement, impotent, imprisonment, improvident, impudent, incident, incompetent, incontinent, indifferent, indigent, innocent, insolent, instrument, irreverent, languishment, ligament, lineament, magnificent, management, medicament, malecontent, monument, negligent, nourishment, nutriment, occident, omnipotent, opulent, ornament, parliament, penitent, permanent, pertinent, president, precedent, prevalent, provident, punishment, ravishment, regiment, resident, redolent. rudiment, sacrament, sediment, sentiment, settlement, subsequent, supplement, intelligent, tenement, temperament, testament, tournament, turbulent, vehement, violent, virulent reverent. *Allowable rhymes*, paint, saint, &c.

ENTS.

Accoutrements. *Perfect rhymes, the plurals of nouns, and third persons singular, present tense, of verbs in* ent, *as* scents, he assents, &c.

EP.

Step, nep, &c. *Allowable rhymes*, leap, reap, &c., rape, tape, &c.

EPT.

Accept, adept, except, intercept, &c. *Perfect rhymes*, crept, slept, wept, kept. *Allowable rhymes, the preterits and particles of verbs in* ape, eep, *and* eap, *as* peeped, reaped, shaped, &c.

ERR.

Err, aver, defer, infer, deter, inter, refer, transfer, confer, prefer, parterre, administer, wagoner, islander, arbiter, character, villager, cottager, dowager, forager, pillager, voyager, massacre, gardener, slanderer, flatterer, idolater, provender, theatre, amphitheatre, foreigner, lavender, messenger, passenger, sorcerer, interpreter, officer, mariner, harbinger, minister, register, canister, chorister, sophister, presbyter, lawgiver, philosopher, astrologer, loiterer, prisoner, grasshopper, astronomer, sepulchre, thunderer, traveller, murderer, usurer. *Allowable rhymes*, bare, care, &c., ear, fear, &c., bar, car, &c., sir, fir, her, &c.

ERCH, see EARCH.

ERCE, see ERSE.

ERD, see EARD.

ERE, see EER.

ERGE.

Verge, absterge, emerge, immerge. *Perfect rhyme*, dirge. *Nearly perfect rhyme*, urge, purge, surge. *Allowable rhymes*, barge, large, &c.

ERN.

Fern, stern, discern, concern. *Perfect rhymes*, learn, earn, yearn, &c. *Allowable rhymes*, barn, yarn, &c., burn, turn, &c.

ERSE.

Verse, herse, absterse, adverse, averse, converse, disperse, immerse, perverse, reverse, traverse, asperse, intersperse, universe. *Perfect rhymes*, amerce, coerce, &c., fierce, tierce, pierce, &c. *Allowable rhymes*, farce, parce, Mars, &c., purse, curse, &c.

ERT.

Wert, advert, assert, avert, concert, convert, controvert, desert, divert, exert, expert, insert, invert, pervert, subvert. *Allowable rhymes*, heart, part, &c., shirt, dirt, &c., hurt, spurt, &c.

ERVE.

Serve, nerve, swerve, preserve, deserve, conserve, observe, reserve disserve, subserve. *Allowable rhymes*, starve, carve, &c., curve, &c.

ESS.

Bless, dress, cess, chess, guess, less, mess, press, stress, acquiesce, access address, assess, compress, confess. caress, depress, digress, dispossess, dis tress, excess, express, impress, oppress, possess, profess, recess, repress, re dress, success, transgress, adulteress, bashfulness, bitterness, cheerfulness, comfortless, comeliness, dizziness, diocese, drowsiness, eagerness, easiness, embassadress, emptiness, evenness, fatherless, filthiness, foolishness, forgetfulness, forwardness, frowardness, fruitfulness, fulsomeness, giddiness, greediness, gentleness, governess, happiness, haughtiness, heaviness, idle ness, heinousness, hoaryness, hollowness, holiness, lasciviousness, lawful ness, laziness, littleness, liveliness, loftiness, lioness, lowliness, manliness, masterless, mightiness, motherless, motionless, nakedness, neediness, nois omeness, numberless, patroness, peevishness, perfidiousness, pitiless, poetess, prophetess, ransomless, readiness, righteousness, shepherdess, sorceress, sordidness, spiritless, sprightliness, stubbornness, sturdiness, surliness, steadiness, tenderness, thoughtfulness, ugliness, uneasiness, unhappiness, vota ress, usefulness, wakefulness, wantonness, weaponless, wariness, willing ness, wilfulness, weariness, wickedness, wilderness, wretchedness, drunken ness, childishness. *Allowable rhymes*, mass, pass, &c., mace, place, &c.

ESE, see EEZE.

ESH.

Flesh, fresh, refresh, thresh, afresh, mesh. *Allowable rhymes*, mash, flash, &c.

ESK.

Desk. *Perfect Rhymes*, grotesque, burlesque, &c. *Allowable Rhymes*, mask, ask.

EST.

Best, chest, crest, guest, jest, nest, pest, quest, rest, test, vest, west, arrest, attest, bequest, contest, detest, digest, divest, invest, infest, molest, obtest, protest, request, suggest, unrest, interest, manifest, &c. *Perfect rhymes*, breast, abreast, &c., *and the preterits and participles of verbs in* ess, *as* dressed, abreast, expressed, &c. *Allowable rhymes*, cast, fast, &c., haste, waste, &c., beast, least, &c. See EAST.

ET.

Bet, jet, fret, get, let, met, net, set, wet, whet, yet, debt, abet, beget, be set, forget, regret, alphabet, amulet, anchoret, cabinet, epithet, parapet, rivulet, violet, counterfeit, coronet, &c. *Perfect rhymes*, sweat, threat, &c *Allowable rhymes*, bate, hate, &c., beat, heat, &c.

ETCH.

Fetch, stretch, wretch, sketch, &c. *Allowable rhymes*, match, latch, &c peach, bleach, &c.

ETE, see EAT.

EVE, see EAVE.

EUM, see UME.

EW.

Blew, chew, dew, brew, drew, flew, few, grew, new, knew, hew, few, mew, view, threw, yew, crew, slew, anew, askew, bedew, eschew, renew review, withdrew, screw, interview, &c. *Perfect rhymes*, blew, clue, due, one, glue, hue, rue, sue, true, accrue, ensue, endue, imbue, imbrue, pursue, subdue, adieu, purlieu, perdue, residue, avenue, revenue, retinue.

EWD, see EUD.

EWN, see UNE.

EX.

Sex, vex, annex, convex, complex, perplex, circumflex, *and the plurals of nouns and third persons singular of verbs in* eck, *as* checks, he checks, &c. *Allowable rhymes*, ax, wax, &c., *and the plurals of nouns and third persons singular of verbs in* ake, ack, eak, eke, ique, ike, &c., breaks, rakes he takes, he breaks, racks, he ekes, pikes, he likes, he pipes, &c.

EXT.

Next, pretext, *and the preterits and participles of verbs in* ex, *as* vexed, perplexed, &c. *Allowable rhymes, the preterits and participles of verbs in* ax, *as* waxed, &c.

EY, see AY.

IB.

Bib, crib, squib, drib, glib, nib, rib. *Allowable rhymes,* bribe, tribe, &c

IBE.

Bribe, tribe, scribe, ascribe, describe, superscribe, prescribe, proscribe subscribe, transcribe, inscribe. *Allowable rhymes,* bib, crib, &c.

ICE.

Ice, dice, mice, nice, price, rice, spice, slice, thrice, trice, advice, entice vice, device. *Perfect rhymes, the nouns,* rise, concise, precise, paradise, &c. *Allowable rhymes* miss, kiss, hiss, artifice, avarice, cockatrice, benefice, cicatrice, edifice, orifice, prejudice, precipice, sacrifice, &c., piece, fleece, &c.

ICH, see ITCH.

ICK.

Brick, sick, chick, kick, lick, nick, pick, quick, stick, thick, trick, arithmetic, asthmatic, choleric, catholic, phlegmatic, heretic, rhetoric, schismatic, splenetic, lunatic, asteric, politic, empiric. *Allowable rhymes,* like, pike, &c., weak, speak, &c.

ICT.

Strict, addict, afflict, convict, inflict, contradict, &c. *Perfect rhymes, the preterits and participles of verbs in* ick, *as* licked, kicked, &c. *Allowable rhymes the preterits and participles of verbs in* ike, eak, *as* liked, leaked, &c.

ID.

Bid, chid, hid, kid, lid, slid, rid, bestrid, pyramid, forbid. *Allowable rhymes,* bide, chide, parricide, &c., *and the preterits and participles of the verbs in* y *or* ie, *as* died, replied, &c., lead, bead, mead, deed, need, &c., *and the preterits and participles of verbs in* ee, *as* freed, agreed, &c.

IDE.

Bide, chide, hide, glide, pride, ride, slide, side, stride, tide, wide, bride, abide, guide, aside, astride, beside, bestride, betide, confide, decide, deride, divide, preside, provide, subside, misguide, subdivide, &c. *Perfect rhymes, the preterits and participles of verbs in* ie *and* y, *as* died, replied, &c., *and the participle* sighed. *Allowable rhymes,* bead, mead, &c., bid, hid, &c.

IDES.

Ides, besides. *Perfect rhymes, the plurals of nouns and third persons singular of verbs in* ide, *as* tides, he rides. *Allowable rhymes, the plurals of nouns and third persons singular of verbs in* ead, id, *as* beads, he leads, &c., kids, he bids, &c.

IDGE.

Bridge, ridge, abridge, &c.

IDST.

Midst, amidst, &c. *Perfect rhymes the second person singular of the present tense of verbs in* id, *as* thou biddest, thou hiddest, &c. *Allowable rhymes, the second persons singular of the present tense of verbs in* ide, *as* thou hiddest, thou readest, &c.

IE or Y.

By, buy, cry, die, dry, eye, fly, fry, fie, hie, lie, pie, ply, pry, rye, shy, sly, spry, sky, sty, tie, try, vie, why, ally, apply, awry, bely, comply, decry, defy, descry, deny, imply, espy, outvie, outfly, rely, reply, supply, untie, amplify, beautify, certify, crucify, deify, dignify, edify, falsify, fortify, gratify, glorify, indemnify, justify, magnify, modify, mollify, mortify, pacify, petrify, purify, putrify, qualify, ratify, rectify, sanctify, satisfy scarify, signify, specify, stupify, terrify, testify, verify, villify, vitrify, vivify prophesy. *Perfect rhymes*, high, nigh, sigh, thigh. *Allowable rhymes*, bee, she, tea, sea, &c., pleurisy, chemistry, academy, apostasy, conspiracy, confederacy, ecstasy, democracy, embassy, fallacy, legacy, supremacy, lunacy, privacy, piracy, malady, remedy, tragedy, comedy, cosmography, geography, geometry, &c., elegy, certainty, sovereignty, loyalty, disloyalty, penalty, casualty, ribaldry, chivalry, infamy, constancy, fealty, cavalry, bigamy, polygamy, vacancy, inconstancy, infancy, company, accompany, dittany, tyranny, villany, anarchy, monarchy, lethargy, incendiary, infirmary, library, salary, sanctuary, votary, auxiliary, contrary, diary, granary, rosemary, urgency, infantry, knavery, livery, recovery, robbery, novelty antipathy, apathy, sympathy, idolatry, galaxy, husbandry, cruelty, enemy blasphemy, prophecy, clemency, decency, inclemency, emergency, regency, progeny, energy, poverty, liberty, property, adultery, artery, artillery, battery, beggary, bribery, bravery, delivery, drudgery, flattery, gallery, imagery, lottery, misery, mystery, nursery, raillery, slavery, sorcery, treachery, discovery, tapestry, majesty, modesty, immodesty, honesty, dishonesty, courtesy, heresy, poesy, poetry, secresy, leprosy, perfidy, subsidy, drapery, symmetry, drollery, prodigy, policy, mutiny, destiny, scrutiny hypocrisy, family, ability, activity, avidity, assiduity, civility, community, concavity, consanguinity, conformity, congruity, diuturnity, facility, fal sity, familiarity, formality, generosity, gratuity, humidity, absurity, activity, adversity, affability, affinity, agility, alacrity, ambiguity, animosity, antiquity, austerity, authority, brevity, calamity, capacity, captivity, charity, chastity, civility, credulity, curiosity, finery, declivity, deformity, duty, dexterity, dignity, disparity, diversity, divinity, enmity, enormity, equality, equanimity, equity, eternity, extremity, fatality, felicity, fertility, fidelity, frugality, futurity, gravity, hostility, humanity, humility, imman ity, immaturity, immensity, immorality, immortality, immunity, immuta bility, impartiality, impossibility, impetuosity, improbity, inanity, incapacity, incivility, incongruity, inequality, indemnity, infinity, inflexibility, instability, invalidity, jollity, lenity, lubricity, magnanimity, majority, mediocrity, minority, mutability, nicety, perversity, perplexity, perspicuity, prosperity, privity, probalility, probity, propensity, rarity, rapidity, saga city, sanctity, sensibility, sensuality, solidity, temerity, timidity, tranquil ity, virginity, visibility, university, trumpery, apology, genealogy, ety mology, simony, symphony, soliloquy, allegory, armory, factory, pillory, faculty, treasury, usury, augury, importunity, impunity, impurity, inaccuracy, inability, incredulity, indignity, infidelity, infirmity, iniquity, integrity, laity, liberality, malignity, maturity, morality, mortality, nativity, necessity, neutrality, nobility, obscurity, opportunity, partiality, perpetuity, prosperity, priority, prodigality, purity, quality, quantity, scarcity, security, severity, simplicity, sincerity, solemnity, sterility, stupidity, Trinity, vacuity, validity, vanity, vivacity, unanimity, uniformity, unity, anxiety, gaiety, impiety, piety, satiety, sobriety, society, variety, customary, melody, philosophy, astronomy, anatomy, colony, gluttony, harmony, agony, gallantry, canopy, history, memory, victory, calumny, injury, luxury penury, perjury, usury, industry.

IECE, see EASE.

IEF.

Grief, chief, fief, thief, brief, belief, relief, &c. *Perfect rhymes*, reef, beef, &c. *Nearly perfect rhymes*, leaf, sheaf, &c.

IEGE.

Liege, siege, oblige, disoblige, asseige, besiege.

IELD.

Field, yield, shield, wield, afield. *Nearly perfect rhymes, the presents and participles of verbs in* eal, *as* healed, repealed, &c.

IEN, see EEN.

IEND, see END.

IERCE, see ERSE.

IEST, see EAST.

IEVE, see EAVE.

IFE.

Rife, fife, knife, wife, strife, life. *Allowable rhymes*, cliff, skiff, stiff, whiff &c.

IFF, see IFE.

IFT.

Gift, drift, shift, lift, rift, sift, thrift, adrift, &c., *and the preterits and participles of verbs in* iff, *as* whiffed, &c.

IG.

Big, dig, gig, fig, pig, rig, sprig, twig, swig. *Allowable rhymes*, league. teague, fatigue, &c.

IGE, see IEGE.

IGH, see IE.

IGHT, see ITE.

IGN, see INE.

IGUE, see EAGUE.

IKE.

Dike, like, pike, spike, strike, alike, dislike, oblique. *Allowable rhymes*, leak, speak, antique, &c., lick, pick, &c.

ILL.

Bill, chill, fill, drill, gill, hill, ill, kill, mill, pill, quill, rill, shrill, fill, skill, spill, still, swill, thrill, till, trill, will, distil, fulful, instil, codicil, daffodil, utensil. *Perfect rhymes, all words ending in* ile, *with the accent on the antepenultimate syllable, as* volatile, &c. *Allowable rhymes*, byle, chyle, file, feel, reel, &c., meal, peal, seal, &c., *and words in* ble, *having the accent on the antepenultimate, as* suitable, &c.

ILD.

Child, mild, wild, &c. *Perfect rhymes, the preterits and participles of verbs of one syllables, in* ile, *or of more syllables, provided the accent is on the last, as* piled, reviled, &c. *Allowable rhymes, the preterits and participles of verbs in* ill, *as* filled, willed, &c., *in* oil, as oiled, boiled, foiled, &c.

ILD.

Gild, build, rebuild, &c. *Perfect rhymes, the preterits and participles of verbs in* illed, *as* filled, willed, &c. *Allowable rhymes*, child, mild, *and their allowable rhymes, which see.*

ILE.

Bile, chyle, file, guile, isle, mile, pile, smile, stile, style, tile, vile, while awhile, compile, revile, defile, exile, erewhile, reconcile, beguile. *Allowable rhymes*, oil, boil, &c., bill, fill, &c.

ILK.

Milk, silk, bilk, &c.

ILT.

Gilt, jilt, built, quilt, guilt, hilt, spilt, stilt, tilt.

ILTH.

Filth, tilth, &c.

IM.

Brim, dim, grim, him, rim, skim, slim, trim, whim, prim. *Perfect rhymes*, limb, hymn, limn. *Allowable rhymes*, lime, time, climb, &c., team, gleam, &c.

IMB, see IM.

IME.

Chime, time, grime, climb, clime, crime, prime, mime, rhyme, slime, thyme, lime, sublime. *Allowable rhymes*, brim, dim, maritime, &c.

IMES.

Betimes, sometimes, &c. *Perfect rhymes, the plurals of nouns and third persons singular, present tense, of verbs in* ime, *as* chimes, he rhymes, &c. *Allowable rhymes, the plurals of nouns and third persons singular, present tense, of verbs in* eam *and* im, *as* dreams, brims, he swims, &c.

IMN, see IM.

IMP.

Imp, pimp, limp, gimp.

IMPSE.

Glimpse. *Rhymes, the plurals of nouns and third persons present of verbs in* imp, *as* imps, he limps, &c.

IN.

Chin, din, fin, gin, grin, in, inn, kin, pin, shin, sin, spin, skin, thin, tin, win, within, assassin, javelin, begin. *Allowable rhymes*, chine, dine, &c.; lean, bean, &c., machine, magazine, &c.

INCE.

Mince, prince, since, quince, rince, wince, convince, evince.

INCH.

Clinch, finch, winch, pinch, inch.

INCT

Instinct, distinct, extinct, precinct, succinct, &c., *and the preterits and participles af verbs in* ink, *as* linked, pinked, &c

IND.

Bind, find, mind, blind, hind, kind, grind, rind, wind, behind, unkind, remind, &c., *and the preterits and participles of verbs in* ine, *as* refined. *Allowable rhymes*, rescind, prescind, *and the noun* wind, *as it is frequently pronounced, also the participles of verbs in* oin, *as* joined.

INE.

Dine, brine, mine, chine, fine, line, nine, pine, shine, shrine, kine, thine, trine, twine, vine, wine, whine, combine, confine, decline, define, incline, inshrine, intwine, opine, calcine, recline, refine, repine, superfine, interline, countermine, undermine, supine, concubine, porcupine, divine. *Perfect rhymes*, sign, assign, consign, design, &c. *Allowable rhymes*, bin, thin, tin, origin, join, loin, &c., *and polysyllables ending in* ine, *pronounced* in, *as* masculine, feminine, discipline, libertine, heroine, &c.

ING.

Bring, sing, cling, fling, king, ring, sling, spring, sting, string, swing, wing, wring, thing, &c., *and the participles of the present tense in* ing, *with the accent on the antepenultimate, as* recovering, altering, &c.

INGE.

Cringe, fringe, hinge, singe, springe, swinge, tinge, twinge, infringe.

INK.

Ink, think, wink, drink, blink, brink, chink, clink, link, pink, shrink, sink, slink, stink, bethink, forethink.

INT.

Dint, mint, hint, flint, lint print, squint, asquint, imprint.

IP.

Chip, lip, hip, clip, dip, drip, lip, nip, sip, rip, scrip, ship, skip, slip, snip, strip, tip, trip, whip, equip, eldership, fellowship, workmanship, rivalship, *and all words in* ship, *with the accent on the antepenultimate. Allowable rhymes*, wipe, gripe, &c., leap, heap, &c.

IPE.

Gripe, pipe, ripe, snipe, type, stripe, wipe, archetype, prototype *Allow able rhymes*, chip, lip, workmanship, &c.

IPSE.

Eclipse. *Rhymes, the plurals of nouns and third persons singular, present tense, in* ip, *as* lips, strips, &c. *Allowable rhymes, the plurals of nouns and third persons singular, present tense, of verbs in* ipe, *as* gripes, wipes, &c.

IR, see UR.

IRCH, see URCH.

IRD, see URD.

IRE.

Fire, dire, hire, ire, lyre, mire, quire, sire, spire, squire, hire, wire, tire attire, acquire, admire, aspire, conspire, desire, inquire, entire, expire, in spire, require, retire, transpire, Tyre. *Perfect rhymes*, friar, liar, brier, *and nouns formed from verbs ending in* ie *or* y, as crier, dier, *as also the comparative of adjectives of the same sounding terminations, as* nigher, shier, &c.

IRGE, see ERGE.

IRL.

Girl, whirl, twirl. *Nearly perfect rhymes*, curl, furl, churl, &c.

IRM.

Firm, affirm, confirm, infirm. *Nearly perfect rhymes*, worm, term, &c

IRST, see URST.

IRT, see URT.

IRTH.

Birth, mirth. *Perfect rhymes*, earth, dearth, *which see.*

ISS.

Bliss, miss, hiss, kiss, this, abyss, amiss, submiss, dismiss, remiss. *Allow able rhymes*, mice, spice, &c., peace, lease, &c.

IS, pronounced like IZ.

Is, his, whiz.

ISE, see ICE and IZE.

ISH.

Dish, wish, fish, cuish, pish.

ISK.

Brisk, frisk, disk, risk, whisk, basilisk, tamarisk.

ISP.

Crisp, wisp, lisp.

IST.

Fist, list, mist, twist, wrist, assist, consist, desist, exist, insist, persist, re sist, subsist, alchemist, amethyst, anatomist, antagonist, annalist, evangelist, eucharist, exorcist, herbalist, humorist, oculist, organist, satirist, &c., *and the preterits and participles of verbs* iss, *as* missed, hissed, &c. *Allowable rhymes, the preterits and participles of verbs in* ice, *as* spiced, sliced, &c.

IT.

Bit, cit, hit, fit, grit, flit, knit, nit, pit, quit, sit, split, twit, wit, whit, writ, admit, acquit, commit, emit, omit, outwit, permit, remit, submit, transmit, refit, benefit, perquisite. *Allowable rhymes*, beat, heat, &c., bite, mite light, &c.

ITCH and HITCH.

Ditch, pitch, rich, which, fitch, bitch, flitch, hitch, itch, stitch, switch twitch, witch, bewitch, nich, enrich.

ITE and IGHT.

Bite, cite, kite, bite, mite, quite, rite, smite, spite, trite, white, write, contrite, disunite, despite, indite, invite, excite, incite, polite, requite, recite unite, reunite, aconite, appetite, parasite, proselyte, expedite. *Perfect rhymes*, blight, benight, bright, fight, flight, fright, height, light, knight, night, might, plight, right, tight, slight, sight, spright, wight, affright, alight, aright, foresight, delight, despite, unsight, upright, benight, bedight, over sight. *Allowable rhymes*, eight, height, weight, &c., bit, hit, &c., favorite, hypocrite, infinite, requisite, opposite, apposite, exquisite, &c.

ITH.

Pith, smith, frith.

ITHE.

Hithe, blithe, tithe, scythe, writhe, lithe. *Allowable rhyms*, with.

IVE.

Five, dive, alive, gyve, hive, drive, rive, shrive, strive, thrive, arrive, connive, contrive, deprive, derive, revive, survive. *Allowable rhymes*, give, live, sieve, forgive, outlive, fugitive, laxative, narrative, prerogative, primitive, sensitive, vegetive, affirmative, alternative, contemplative, demonstrative, diminutive, distributive, donative, inquisitive, lenitive, negative, perspective, positive, preparative, provocative, purgative, restorative.

IX.

Fix, six, flix, mix, affix, infix, prefix, transfix, intermix, crucifix, &c., *and the plurals of nouns and third persons of verbs in* ick, *as* wicks, licks, &c. *Allowable rhymes, the plurals of nouns and third persons singular of verbs in* ike, *as* pikes, likes, &c.

IXT.

Betwixt. *Rhymes, the preterits and participles of verbs in* ix, *as* fixed mixed, &c.

ISE and IZE.

Prize, wise, rise, size, guise, disguise, advise, authorize, canonize, chastise, civilize, comprise, criticise, despise, devise, enterprise, excise, exercise, idolize, immortalize, premise, revise, signalize, solemnize, surprise, surmise, suffice, sacrifice, sympathize, tyrannize, *and the plurals of nouns and third persons singular, present tense, of verbs ending in* ie *or* y, *as* pies, lies, he replies, &c. *Allowable rhymes*, miss, hiss, precipice, &c.

O, see OO and OW.

OACH.

Broach, croach, poach, abroach, approach, encroach, reproach. *Perfect rhyme*, loach. *Allowable rhymes*, botch, notch, &c., mutch, hutch, &c

OAD, see AUD and ODE.

OAF, see OFF.

OAK, see OKE.

OAL, see OLE.

OAM, see OME

OAN, see ONE.

OAP, see OPE.

OAR, see ORE.

OARD, see ORD.

OAST, see OST.

OAT, see OTE.

OATH, see OTH.

OB.

Fob, bob, mob, knob, sob, rob, throb. *Perfect rhymes*, swab, squab *Allowable rhymes*, daub, globe, robe, dub, &c.

OBE.

Globe, lobe, probe, robe, conglobe. *Allowable rhymes*, rob, mob, &c., rub dub, &c., daub, &c.

OCE, see OSE.

OCK.

Block, lock, cock, clock, crock, dock, frock, flock, knock, mock, rock, shock, stock, sock. *Allowable rhymes*, oak, poke, cloke, &c., look, took, &c., buck, suck, &c.

OCT.

Concoct. *Rhymes, the preterits and participles of verbs in* ock, *as* blocked, locked, &c. *Allowable rhymes, the preterits and participles of verbs in* oak *and* oke, *as* croaked, soaked, yoked, &c.

OD.

Clod, God, rod, sod, trod, nod, plod, odd, rod, shod. *Allowable rhymes*, ode, code, mode, &c., *and the preterits and participles of verbs in* ow, *as* sowed, did sow, &c.

ODE and OAD.

Bode, ode, code, mode, rode, abode, corrode, explode, forebode, commode, incommode, episode, &c. *Perfect rhymes*, road, toad, goad, load, &c., *and the preterits and participles of verbs in* ow, *as* owed, showed, &c. *Allowable rhymes*, blood, flood, clod, hod, nod, broad, fraud, &c. See OOD.

OE, see OW.

OFF and OUGH.

Off, scoff, &c. *Perfect rhymes*, cough, trough, &c. *Allowable rhymes*, oaf, loaf, &c., proof, roof, &c. See OOF.

OFT.

Oft, croft, soft, aloft, &c., *and the preterits and participles of verbs in* off *and* uff, *as* uff, scoffed, &c.

OG.

Hog, bog, cog, dog, clog, fog, frog, log, jog, &c. *Perfect rhymes*, dialogue, epilogue, agog, synagogue, catalogue, pedagogue. *Allowable rhymes*, rogue, vogue, &c.

OGUE.

Rogue, vogue, prorogue, collogue, disembogue. *Allowable rhymes*, bog, log, dialogue, &c.

OICE.

Choice, voice, rejoice. *Allowable rhymes*, nice, vice, rice, &c.

OID.

Void, avoid, devoid, &c., *and the preterits and participles of verbs in* oy, *as* buoyed, cloyed, &c. *Allowable rhymes*, hide, bide, ride, &c.

OIL.

Oil, boil, coil, moil, soil, spoil, toil, despoil, embroil, recoil, turmoil, disembroil. *Allowable rhymes*, isle, while, tile, &c.

OIN.

Coin, join, subjoin, groan, loin, adjoin, conjoin, disjoin, enjoin, purloin, rejoin. *Allowable rhymes*, whine, wine, fine, &c. See INE.

OINT.

Oint, joint, point, disjoint, anoint, appoint, disappoint, counterpoint. *Allowable rhyme*, pint.

OISE.

Poise, noise, counterpoise, equipoise, &c., *and the plurals of nouns, and third persons singular, present tense, of verbs in* oy, *as* boys, cloys, &c. *Allowable rhymes*, wise, size, prize, *and the plurals of nouns, and third persons singular, present tense, of verbs in* ie *or* y, *as* pies, tries, &c.

OIST.

Hoist, moist, foist. *Perfect rhymes, the preterits and participles of verbs in* oice, *as* rejoiced. *Allowable rhymes, the preterits and participles of verbs in* ice, *as* spiced.

OIT.

Coit, exploit, adroit, &c. *Allowable rhymes,* white, light, might, sight, mite, &c.

OKE.

Broke, choke, smoke, spoke, stroke, yoke, bespoke, invoke, provoke, revoke, &c. *Perfect rhymes,* choak, cloak, oak, soak, stroak. *Allowable rhymes,* stock, mock, &c., buck, luck, &c., talk, walk, &c., look, book &c. See OCK and OOK.

OL.

Loll, doll, droll, extol, capitol, &c. *Allowable rhymes,* all, ball, &c., awl, bawl, &c., hole, mole, &c., dull, mull, &c.

OLD.

Old, bold, cold, gold, hold, mold, scold, sold, told, behold, enfold, unfold, uphold, withhold, foretold, manifold, marigold. *Perfect rhymes, preterits and participles of verbs in* oll, owl, ole, *and* oal, *as* rolled, cajoled, foaled, bowled, &c.

OLE.

Bole, dole, jole, hole, mole, pole, sole, stole, whole, shole, cajole, condole, parole, patrole, pistole, &c. *Perfect rhymes,* coal, foal, goal, soal, bowl, droll, prowl, roll, scroll, toll, troll, control, enroll, &c., soul, &c., to roll, &c. *Allowable rhymes,* gull, dull, &c., bull, full, &c., loll, doll, &c., fool, cool, &c

OLIN.

Stolen, swollen.

OLT.

Bolt, colt, jolt, holt, dolt, molt, revolt, thunderbolt. *Allowable rhymes*, vault, fault, salt, &c.

OLVE.

Solve, absolve, resolve, convolve, involve, devolve, dissolve, revolve.

OM, see UM.

OME.

Lome, dome, home, tome. *Perfect rhymes,* foam, roam, comb. *Allowable rhymes,* dumb, hum, come, bomb, &c., troublesome, &c. See OOM

OMB, see OOM.

OMPT, see OUNT

ON, see UN.

ON.

Don, on, con, upon, anon, &c. *Perfect rhymes,* gone, undergone, &c. *Allowable rhymes,* dun, run, won, &c., own, moan, &c., lone, bone, &c. Amazon, cinnamon, comparison, caparison, garrison, skeleton, union, juppon

OND.

Pond, bond, fond, beyond, abscond, correspond, despond, diamond, vagabond, &c., *and the preterits and participles of verbs in* on, *as* donned, conned, &c. *Allowable rhymes, the preterits and participles of verbs in* one, oan, *and* un, *as* stoned, moaned, stunned, &c.

ONCE, see UNCE.

ONE.

Prone, bone, drone, throne, alone, stone, tone, lone, zone, atone, enthrone dethrone, postpone, &c. *Perfect rhymes,* grown, flown, disown, thrown, sown, own, loan, shown, overthrown, groan, blown, moan, known. *Allowable rhymes,* dawn, lawn, &c., on, con, &c., none, bun, dun, &c., moon boon, &c

ONG.

Long, prong, song, thong, strong, throng wrong, along, belong, **prolong** *Allowable rhymes*, bung, among, hung, &c.

ONGUE, see UNG.

ONK, see UNK.

ONSE.

Sconce, ensconce, &c. *Allowable rhymes*, once, nonce, askaunce, &c.

ONT.

Font. *Perfect rhyme*, want. *Allowable rhymes*, front, affront, &c., con front, punt, runt, &c., *the abbreviated negatives*, won't, don't, &c.

OO.

Coo, woo. *Nearly perfect rhymes*, shoe, two, too, who, &c., do, ado, undo, through, you, true, blue, flew, strew, &c. *Allowable rhymes*, know, blow go, toe, &c. See *Direction* 3.

OOD.

Brood, mood, food, rood, &c. *Nearly perfect rhymes, the preterits and participles of verbs in* oo, *as* cooed, wooed, &c. *Allowable rhymes*, wood, good, hood, stood, withstood, understood, brotherhood, livelihood, likelihood, neighborhood, widowhood, &c., blood, flood, &c., feud, illude, habitude, &c., *the preterits and participles of verbs in* ue, *and* ew, *as* brewed, strewed, &c., imbued, subdued, &c., bud, mud, &c., *and the three apostrophized auxilia ries*, would, could, should, *pronounced* wou'd, cou'd, shou'd, &c., ode, code, *and the preterits and participles of verbs in* ow, *as* crowed, rowed, &c., *also* nod, hod, &c.

OOF.

Hoof, proof, roof, woof, aloof, disproof, reproof, behoof. *Allowable rhymes* huff, ruff, rough, enough, &c., off, scoff, &c.

OOK.

Book, brook, cook, crook, hook, look, rook, shook, took, mistook, under took, forsook, betook. *Allowable rhymes*, puke, fluke, &c., duck, luck, &c., broke, spoke, &c.

OOL.

Cool, fool, pool, school, stool, tool, befool. *Allowable rhymes*, pule, rule, &c., dull, gull, &c., bull, pull, &c., pole, hole, &c.

OOM.

Gloom, groom, loom, room, spoom, bloom, doom, &c. *Perfect rhymes*, tomb, entomb, *and the city* Rome. *Nearly perfect rhymes*, whom, womb, &c. *Allowable rhymes*, come, drum, &c., bomb, thumb, clomb, &c., plume, spume, &c., *and* from, home, comb, &c.

OON.

Boon, soon, moon, noon, spoon, swoon, buffoon, lampoon, poltroon. *Al lowable rhymes*, tune, prune, &c., bun, dun, &c., gone, don, &c., bone, alone, &c., moan, roan, &c. See ONE.

OOP.

Loop, poop, scoop, stoop, troop, droop, whoop, coop, hoop, &c. *Perfect rhymes*, soup, group, &c. *Allowable rhymes*, dupe, up, sup, tup, &c., cop, top, &c., cope, hope, &c.

OOR.

Boor, poor, moor, &c. *Perfect rhymes*, tour, amour, paramour, contour. *Allowable rhymes*, bore, pore, &c., pure, sure, &c., your, pour, &c., door floor, &c., bur, cur, &c., sir, stir, &c.

OOSE.

Goose, loose, &c. *Nearly perfect rhymes, the nouns* deuce, use, &c., pro fuse, seduce. *Allowable rhymes*, dose, jocose, globose, &c., moss, toss. &c., us, pus, thus, &c.

OOT.

Root, boot, coot, hoot, shoot. *Nearly perfect rhymes* suit, fruit, &c., lute, impute, &c. *Allowable rhymes*, rote, vote, &c., goat, coat, &c., but, hut, soot, &c., foot, put, &c., hot, got, &c.

OOTH.

Booth, sooth, smooth. *Allowable rhymes*, tooth, youth, sooth, uncouth, forsooth, &c. *Though these are frequent, they are very improper rhymes the* th *in one class being flat, and in the other sharp.*

OOZE.

Ooze, nooze. *Perfect rhymes*, whose, choose, lose. *Nearly perfect rhymes, the verbs*, to use, abuse, &c. *Allowable rhymes*, doze, hose, &c., buzz *and* does, *the third persons singular of* do, *with the plurals of nouns, and third persons singular, present tense, of verbs in* ow, o, oe, ew, ue, *as* foes, goes, throws, views, imbues, flues, &c.

OP.

Chop, hop, drop, crop, fop, top, prop, flop, shop, slop, sop, stop, swop, top, underprop. *Allowable rhymes*, cope, trope, hope, &c., tup, sup, &c., coop, &c.

OPE.

Sope, hope, cope, mope, grope, pope, rope, scope, slope, tope, trope, aslope, elope, interlope, telescope, heliotrope, horoscope, antelope, &c., *and* ope *contracted in poetry for* open. *Allowable rhymes*, hoop, coop, &c., lop, top &c., tup, sup, &c.

OPT.

Adopt *rhymes perfectly with the preterits and participles of verbs in* op, *as* hopped, lopped, &c. *Allowable rhymes, the preterits and participles of verbs in* ope, upe, oop, *and* up, *as* coped, duped, hooped, cupped, &c.

OR.

Or, for, creditor, counsellor, confessor, competitor, emperor, ancestor, ambassador, progenitor, conspirator, successor, conqueror, governor, abhor, metaphor, bachelor, senator, &c., *and every word in* or, *having the accent on the last, or last syllable but two, as* abhor, orator, &c. *Allowable rhymes*, bore, tore, &c., boar, hoar, &c., pure, endure, &c., pur, demur, &c., stir, sir, &c.

ORCH.

Scorch, torch, &c. *Allowable rhymes*, birch, smirch, church, &c., porch, &c.

ORCE.

Force, divorce, enforce, perforce, &c. *Perfect rhymes*, corse, coarse, hoarse, course, discourse, recourse, intercourse, source, resource, &c. *Allowable rhymes*, worse, purse, &c., horse, endorse, &c.

ORD.

Cord, lord, record, accord, abhorred. *Allowable rhymes*, hoard, board, aboard, ford, afford, sword, &c., word, surd, bird, &c., *and the preterits and participles of verbs in* ore, ur, *and* ir, *as* bored, incurred, stirred, &c.

ORE.

Bore, core, gore, lore, more, ore, pore, score, shore, snore, sore, store, swore, tore, wore, adore, afore, ashore, deplore, explore, implore, restore, forbore, forswore, heretofore, hellebore, sycamore. *Perfect rhymes*, boar, gore, oar, roar, soar, four, door, floor, *and* o'er, *for* over. *Allowable rhymes*, hour, sour, &c., pow'r, *for* power; show'r, *for* shower, &c., bur, cur, &c., poor, your, &c., abhor orator, senator, &c. See OOR *and* OR.

ORGE.

Gorge, disgorge, regorge, &c. *Allowable rhymes*, forge, urge, dirge &c.

ORK.

Ork, cork, fork, stork, &c. *Allowable rhymes*, pork, work

ORLD.

World *rhymes perfectly with the preterits and participles of verbs in* url *as* hurled, curled, &c.

ORM, see ARM.

Form, storm, conform, deform, inform, perform, reform, misinform, uniform, multiform, transform. *Allowable rhymes,* form (*a seat*), *and* worm.

ORN, rhyming with HORN.

Born, corn, morn, horn, scorn, thorn, adorn, suborn, unicorn, capricorn. *Allowable rhymes, the participles* borne (*suffered*), shorn, &c., *the verb* mourn, *the nouns* urn, turn, &c.

ORN, rhyming with MORN.

Born, shorn, torn, worn, lorn, forlorn, love-lorn, sworn, forsworn, overborn, forlorn. *Perfect rhyme,* mourn. *Allowable rhymes,* born, corn, &c., urn, turn, &c.

ORSE, see ORCE.

Horse, endorse, unhorse. *Allowable rhymes,* worse, curse, &c., remorse, coarse, course, corse, &c.

ORST, see URST.

ORT, see ART.

ORT, rhyming with WART.

Short, sort, exhort, consort, distort, extort, resort, retort, snort. *Allowable rhymes,* fort, court, port, report, &c., dirt, shirt, &c., wort, hurt, &c.

ORT, rhyming with COURT.

Fort, port, sport, comport, disport, export, import, support, transport, report. *Allowable rhymes,* short, sort, &c., dirt, hurt, &c.

ORTH.

Forth, fourth. *Allowable rhymes,* north, worth, birth, earth, &c.

OSE, sounded OCE.

Close, dose, jocose. *Perfect rhymes,* morose, gross, engross, verbose. *Allowable rhymes,* moss, cross, &c., us, thus, &c.

OSE, sounded OZE.

Close, dose, hose, pose, chose, glose, froze, nose, prose, those, rose, compose, depose, disclose, dispose, discompose, expose, impose, inclose, interpose, oppose, propose, recompose, repose, suppose, transpose, arose, presuppose, foreclose, &c., *and the plurals of nouns and apostrophized preterits and participles of verbs in* ow, oe, o, &c., *as* rows, glows, foes, goes, &c. *Allowable rhymes, the verbs* choose, lose, &c., *and the plurals of nouns and third persons singular of verbs in* ow, *rhyming with* now, *as* cows, *and the word* buzz.

OST.

Boss, loss, cross, dross, moss, toss, across, emboss. *Allowable rhymes, the nouns* close, dose, jocose, &c., *and* us, thus, &c.

OST.

Cost, frost, lost, accost, &c., *and the preterits and participles of words in* oss, *as* mossed, embossed, &c., *the verb* exhaust, *and the noun* holocaust. *Allowable rhymes,* ghost, host, post, compost, most, &c., coast, boast, toast, &c., bust, must, &c., roost, *and the preterits and participles of verbs in* oose, *as* loosed, &c.

OT, see AT.

Clot, cot, blot, got, hot, jot, lot, knot, not, plot, pot, scot, shot, sot, spot, apricot, trot, rot, grot, begot, forgot, allot, besot, complot, counterplot. *Allowable rhymes,* note, vote, &c., boat, coat, &c., but, cut, &c.

OTCH.

Botch, notch, &c. *Perfect rhyme,* watch. *Allowable rhymes,* much such, &c.

OTE.

Note, vote, mote, quote, rote, wrote, smote, denote, promote, remote, devote, anecdote, antidote, &c. *Perfect rhymes*, boat, coat, bloat, doat, float, gloat, goat, oat, overfloat, afloat, throat, moat. *Allowable rhymes* bout, flout, &c., hot, cot, &c., but, cut, &c., boot, hoot, &c.

OTH.

Broth, cloth, froth, moth, troth, betroth. *Perfect rhyme*, wrath. *Allowable rhymes*, both, loth, sloth, oath, growth, &c., forsooth, *the noun* mouth, *and the solemn auxiliary* doth, *to which some poets add* loathe, clothe, *but I think improperly*. See OOTH.

OU, see OO and OW.

OUBT, see OUT.

OUCH.

Couch, pouch, vouch, slouch, avouch, crouch. *Allowable rhymes*, much, such, &c., coach, roach, &c.

OUD.

Shroud, cloud, proud, loud, aloud, croud, overshroud, &c., *and the preterits and participles of verbs in* ow, *as* he bowed, vowed, &c. *Allowable rhymes, the preterits and participles of verbs in* ow, *as* owed, flowed, &c., blood, flood, bud, much, &c.

OVE.

Wove, inwove, interwove, alcove, clove, grove, rove, stove, strove, throve, drove. *Allowable rhymes*, dove, love, shove, glove, above, &c., move, behove, approve, disprove, disapprove, improve, groove, prove, reprove, &c.

OUGH, see OFF, OW, and UFF.

OUGHT.

Bought, thought, ought, brought, forethought, fought, nought, sought, wrought, besought, bethought, methought, &c. *Perfect rhymes*, aught, naught, caught, taught, &c., *sometimes* draught. *Allowable rhymes*, not, yacht, &c., note, vote, &c., butt, hut, &c., hoot, root, &c.

OUL, see OLE and OWL.

OULD.

Mould. *Perfect rhymes*, fold, old, cold, &c., *and the preterits and participles of verbs in* owl, ol, *and* ole, *as* bowled, tolled, cajoled, &c. *Allowable rhymes, the preterits and participles of verbs in* ull, *as* gulled, pulled, &c.

OUNCE.

Bounce, flounce, renounce, pounce, ounce, denounce, pronounce.

OUND.

Bound, found, mound, ground, hound, pound, round, sound, wound, abound, aground, around, confound, compound, expound, profound, rebound, redound, resound, propound, surround, &c., *and the preterits and participles of the verbs in* own, *as* frowned, renowned, &c. *Allowable rhymes, the preterits and participles of verbs in* one, oan, *and* un, *as* toned, moaned, sunned, &c., *consequently* fund, refund, &c., *and* wound (*a hurt*) *pron* woond.

OUMG, see UNG.

OUNT.

Count, mount, fount, amount, dismount, remount, surmount, account, discount, miscount. *Allowable rhymes*, want, font, don't, wont, &c.

OUP, see OOP.

OUR.

Hour, lour, sour, our, scour, deflour, devour, &c., *rhymes perfectly with* bower, cower, flower power, shower, tower, &c., *pronounced* bow'r, tow'r

&c. *Allowable rhymes*, bore, more, roar, pour, tour, moor, poor, &c., pure sure, &c., sir, stir, bur, cur, &c.

OURGE, see URGE.

OURNE, see ORN and URN.

OURS.

Ours *rhymes perfectly with the plurals of nouns and third persons present of verbs in* our, *and* ower, *as* hours, scours, deflours, bowers, showers, &c. *Allowable rhymes the plurals of nouns and third persons present of verbs in* oor *and* ure, *as* boors, moors, &c., cures, endures, &c.

OURS.

Yours *rhymes perfectly with the plurals of nouns, and third persons present of verbs in* ure, as cures, endures, &c. *Allowable rhyme*, ours, *and its perfect rhymes and the plurals of nouns and third persons present of verbs in* oor, ore, *and* ur, *as* boors, moors, &c., shores, pores, &c., burs, slurs, stirs, &c.

OURSE, see ORCE.

OURT, see ORT.

OURTH, see ORTH.

OUS, see US.

OUS, pronounced OUCE.

House, mouse, chouse, &c. *Allowable rhymes, the nouns* close, dose, jocose, &c., deuce, use, produce, &c., us, thus, &c., moose, *and the noun* noose.

OUSE, pron. OUZE, see OWZE.

OUT.

Bout, stout, out, clout, pout, gout, grout, rout, scout, shout, snout, spout, stout, sprout, trout, about, devout, without, throughout, &c., *rhymes perfectly with* doubt, redoubt, misdoubt, drought, &c. *Allowable rhymes*, note, vote, &c., boat, coat, &c., lute, suit, &c., got, not, &c., nut, shut, hoot, boot, &c.

OUTH.

Mouth, south, *when nouns have the* th *sharp. The verbs* to mouth, to south, &c., *may allowably rhyme with* booth, smooth, &c., *which see.*

OW, sounded OU.

Now, bow, how, mow, cow, brow, plow, sow, vow, prow, avow, allow, disallow, endow, &c. *Perfect rhymes*, bough, plough, slough (*mire*), &c., thou. *Allowable rhymes*, go, no, blow, sow, &c.

OW, sounded OWE.

Blow, stow, crow, bow, flow, glow, grow, know, low, mow, row, show, sow, strow, stow, slow, snow, throw, trow, below, bestow, foreknow, outgrow, overgrow, overflow, overthrow, reflow, foreshow, &c. *Perfect rhymes* go, no, toe, foe, owe, wo, oh, so, lo, though, hoe, ho, ago, forego, undergo, dough, roe, sloe, *and the verb to* sew (*with the needle.*) *Allowable rhymes*, now, cow, vow, do, &c. *See the last article.*

OWL, see OLE.

Cowl, growl, owl, fowl, howl, prowl, &c. *Perfect rhymes*, scoul, foul, &c. *Allowable rhymes*, bowl, soul, hoal, goal, &c., dull, gull, &c.

OWN, see ONE.

Brown, town, clown, crown, down, drown, frown, grown, adown, renown, embrown, &c. *Perfect rhyme*, noun. *Allowable rhymes*, tone, bone, moan, own, *and the participles*, thrown, shown, blown, &c.

OWSE, see OUSE.

Blowse. *Perfect rhymes*, browse, trouse, rouse, spouse, carouse, souse, espouse, *the verbs* to house, mouse, &c., *and the plurals of nouns and third persons present tense of verbs in* ow, *as* brows, allows, &c. *Allowable rhymes,* hose, those, to dose, &c.

OX.

Ox, box, fox, equinox, orthodox, heterodox, &c. *Perfect rhymes, the plurals of nouns and third persons present of verbs in* ock, *as* locks, stocks, &c. *Allowable rhymes, the plurals of nouns, and third persons present of verbs in* oke, oak, *and* uck, *as* strokes, oaks, cloaks, sucks, &c.

OY.

Boy, buoy, coy, employ, cloy, joy, toy, alloy, annoy, convoy, decoy, destroy, enjoy, employ.

OZE, see OSE.

UB.

Cub club, dub, chub, drub, grub, rub, snub, shrub, tub. *Allowable rhymes,* cube, tube, &c., cob, rob, &c.

UBE.

Cube, tube. *Allowable rhymes,* club, cub, &c.

UCE.

Truce, sluce, spruce, deuce, conduce, deduce, induce, introduce, produce, seduce, traduce, juice, reduce, &c., *rhymes perfectly with the nouns* use, abuse, profuse, abstruse, disuse, excuse, misuse, obtuse, recluse.

UCH, see UTCH.

UCK.

Buck, luck, pluck, suck, struck, tuck, truck, duck. *Allowable rhymes,* puke, duke, &c., look, took, &c.

UCT.

Conduct, deduct, instruct, abstruct, aqueduct. *Perfect rhymes, the preterits and participles of verbs in* uck, *as* ducked, sucked, &c. *Allowable rhymes, the preterits and participles of verbs in* uke *and* ook, *as* puked, hooked, &c.

UD.

Bud, scud, stud, mud, cud, *rhymes perfectly with* blood *and* flood. *Allowable rhymes,* good, hood, &c., rood, food, &c., beatitude, latitude, &c.

UDE.

Rude, crude, prude, allude, conclude, delude, elude, exclude, exude, include, intrude, obtrude, seclude, altitude, fortitude, gratitude, interlude, latitude, longitude, magnitude, multitude, solicitude, solitude, vicissitude, aptitude, habitude, ingratitude, inaptitude, lassitude, plenitude, promptitude, servitude, similitude, &c. *Perfect rhymes,* leud, feud, &c., *and the preterits and participles of verbs in* ew, *as* stewed, viewed, &c. *Allowable rhymes,* bud, cud, &c., good, hood, blood, flood, &c.

UDGE.

Judge, drudge, grudge, trudge, adjudge, prejudge.

UE, see EW.

UFF.

Buff, cuff, bluff, huff, gruff, luff, puff, snuff, stuff, ruff, rebuff, counterbuff, &c. *Perfect rhymes,* rough, tough, enough, slough, (*cast skin*), chough, &c. *Allowable rhymes,* loaf, oaf, &c.

UFT.

Tuft. *Perfect rhymes, the preterits and participles of verbs in* uff, *as* cuffed, stuffed, &c.

UG.

Lug, bug, dug, drug, hug, rug, slug, snug, mug, shrug, pug. *Allowable rhymes,* vogue rogue, &c.

UICE, see USE.

UISE, see ISE and USE.

UIE, see IE.

UKE.

Duke, puke, rebuke, &c. *Nearly perfect rhymes*, cook, look, book, &c. *Allowable rhymes*, duck, buck, &c.

UL and ULL.

Cull, dull, gull, hull, lull, mull, null, trull, skull, annul, disannul. *Allowable rhymes*, fool, tool, &c., wool, bull, pull, full, bountiful, fanciful, sorrowful, dutiful, merciful, wonderful, worshipful, *and every word ending in* ful *having the accent on the antepenultimate syllable.*

ULE.

Mule, pule, yule, rule, overrule, ridicule, misrule. *Allowable rhymes*, cull, dull, wool, full, bountiful, &c. See the last article.

ULGE.

Bulge, indulge, divulge, &c.

ULK.

Bulk, hulk, skulk.

ULSE.

Pulse, repulse, impulse, expulse, convulse.

ULT.

Result, adult, exult, consult, indult, occult, insult, difficult, &c. *Allowable rhymes*, colt, bolt, &c.

UM.

Crum, drum, grum, gum, hum, mum, scum, plum, stum, sum, swum, thrum. *Perfect rhymes*, thumb, dumb, succumb, come, become, overcome, burthensome, cumbersome, frolicsome, humorsome, quarrelsome, troublesome, martyrdom, christendom. *Allowable rhymes*, fume, plume, rheum, *and* room, doom, tomb, hecatomb.

UME.

Pume, plume, assume, consume, perfume, resume, presume, deplume.

UMP.

Bump, pump, jump, lump, plump, rump, stump, trump, thump. *Perfect rhyme*, clomp.

UN.

Dun, gun, nun, pun, run, sun, shun, tun, stun, spun, begun. *Perfect rhymes*, son, won, ton, done, one, none, undone. *Allowable rhymes*, on gone, &c., tune, prune, &c. See ON.

UNCE.

Dunce, once, &c. *Allowable rhymes*, sconce.

UNCH.

Bunch, punch, hunch, lunch, munch.

UND.

Fund, refund. *Perfect rhymes the preterits and participles of verbs in* un, *as* shunned, &c.

UNE.

June, tune, untune, jejune, prune, importune, &c. *Nearly perfect rhymes* moon, soon, &c. *Allowable rhymes*, bun, dun, &c.

UNG.

Clung, dung, flung, hung, rung, strung, sung, sprung, slung, stung, swung rung, unsung. *Perfect rhymes*, young, tongue, among. *Allowable rhymes* song, long, &c.

UNGE.

Plunge, spunge, expunge, &c.

UNK.

Drunk, sunk, shrunk, stunk, spunk, punk, trunk, slunk. *Perfect rhyme* monk.

UNT.

Brunt, blunt, hunt, runt, grunt. *Perfect rhyme,* wont (*to be accustomed*)

UP.

Cup, sup, up. *Allowable rhymes,* cope, scope, *and* dupe, group, &c.

UPT.

Abrupt, corrupt, interrupt. *Perfect rhymes, the participles of verbs in* up, *as* supped, &c.

UR

Blur, cur, bur, fur, slur, spur, concur, demur, incur. *Perfect rhymes,* sir, stir. *Nearly perfect rhyme,* fir, &c. *Allowable rhymes,* pore, oar, &c.

URB.

Curb, disturb. *Nearly perfect rhymes,* verb, herb, &c. *Allowable rhyme,* orb.

URCH.

Church, lurch, birch. *Nearly perfect rhymes,* perch. search. *Allowable rhyme,* porch.

URD.

Curd, absurd. *Perfect rhymes,* bird, word, *and the preterits and participles of verbs in* ur, *as* spurred. *Allowable rhymes,* board, ford, cord, lord, &c., *and the preterits and participles of verbs in* ore, oar, *and* or, *as* gored, oared, abhorred, &c., *also the preterits and participles of verbs in* ure, *as* cured, immured, &c. See ORD.

URE.

Cure, pure, dure, lure, sure, adjure, allure, assure, demure, conjure, endure, manure, enure, insure, immature, immure, mature, obscure, procure, secure adjure, calenture, coverture, epicure, investiture, forfeiture, furniture, miniature, nouriture, overture, portraiture, primogeniture, temperature. *Allowable rhymes,* poor, moor, power, sour, &c., cur, bur, &c.

URF.

Turf, scurf, &c.

URGE.

Purge, urge, surge, scourge. *Perfect rhymes,* verge, diverge, &c. *Allowable rhymes,* gorge, George, &c., forge, &c.

URK.

Lurk, Turk. *Perfect rhyme,* work. *Nearly perfect rhymes,* irk, jerk, perk

URL, see IRL,

Churl, curl, furl, hurl, purl, uncurl, unfurl. *Nearly perfect rhymes,* girl, twirl, &c., pearl, &c.

URN.

Burn, churn, spurn, turn, urn, return, overturn. *Perfect rhymes,* sojourn, adjourn, rejourn.

URSE.

Nurse, curse, purse, accurse, disburse, imburse, reimburse. *Perfect rnyme,* worse. *Allowable rhymes,* coarse, corse, force, verse, disperse, horse, &c.

URST.

Burst, curst, durst, accurst, &c. *Perfect rhymes,* thirst, worst, first.

URT.

Blurt, hurt, spurt. *Perfect rhymes,* dirt, shirt, flirt, squirt, &c. *Allowable rhymes,* port, court, short, snort, &c.

US.

Us, thus, buss, truss, discuss, incubus, overplus, amorous, boisterous, clamorous, credulous, dangerous, degenerous, generous, emulous, fabulous frivolous, hazardous, idolatrous, infamous, miraculous, mischievous, mountainous, mutinous, necessitous, numerous, ominous, perilous, poisonous populous, properous, ridiculous, riotous, ruinous, scandalous, scrupulous sedulous, traitorous, treachous, tyrannous, venomous, vigorous, villainous, adventurous, adulterous, ambiguous, blasphemous, dolorous, fortuitous, sonorous, gluttonous, gratuitous, incredulous, lecherous, libidinous, mag nanimous, obstreperous, odoriferous, ponderous, ravenous, rigorous, slan derous, solicitous, timorous, valorous, unanimous, calamitous. *Allowable rhymes, the nouns* use, abuse, diffuse, excuse, *the verb* to loose, *and the nouns*, goose, deuce, juice, truce, &c., close, dose, house, mouse, &c.

USE, with the *s* pure.

The nouns use, disuse, abuse, deuce, truce. *Perfect rhymes, the verb* to loose, *the nouns*, goose, noose, moose. *Allowable rhymes*, us, thus, buss, &c.

USE, sounded UZE.

Muse, *the verbs* to use, abuse, amuse, diffuse, excuse, infuse, misuse, peruse, refuse, suffuse, transfuse, accuse. *Perfect rhymes*, bruise, *and the plurals of nouns and third persons singular of verbs in* ew, *and* ue, *as* dews, imbues, &c. *Allowable rhymes*, buzz, does, &c.

USH.

Blush, brush, crush, gush, flush, rush, hush. *Allowable rhymes*, bush, push.

USK.

Busk, tusk, dusk, husk, musk.

UST.

Bust, crust, dust, just, must, lust, rust, thrust, trust, adjust, adust, disgust, distrust, intrust, mistrust, robust, unjust. *Perfect rhymes, the preterits and participles of verbs in* uss, *as* trussed, discussed, &c.

UT.

But, butt, cut, hut, gut, glut, jut, nut, shut, strut, englut, rut, scut, slut smut, abut. *Perfect rhyme*, soot. *Allowable rhymes*, boot, &c., dispute, &c. boat, &c.

UTCH.

Hutch, crutch, Dutch. *Perfect rhymes*, much, such, touch, &c.

UTE.

Brute, lute, flute, mute, acute, compute, confute, dispute, dilute, depute, impute, miuute, pollute, refute, repute, salute, absolute, attribute, constitute, destitute, dissolute, execute, institute, irresolute, persecute, prosecute, pros titute, resolute, substitute. *Perfect rhymes*, fruit, recruit, &c. *Allowable rhymes*, boot, &c., boat, &c., note, &c., hut, &c.

UX.

Flux, reflux, &c. *Perfect rhymes, the plurals of nouns and third persons of verbs in* uck, *as* ducks, trucks, &c. *Allowable rhymes, the plurals of nouns and third persons of verbs in* ook, uke, oak, &c., *as* cooks, pukes, oaks, &c.

Y, see IE.

[It is suggested here, that the student be exercised in finding rhymes to a few words proposed by the teacher, and in his presence; and that this be done without the aid of the preceding vocabulary. After the student has exercised his own inventive powers, he may then be permitted to inspect the vocabulary. Such an exercise, if it subserve no other purpose will be found useful in giving command of language.]

In humorous pieces, the poet sometimes takes great liberties in his rhymes; aiming at drollery in the form, as well as the matter of his verse. The following tale exemplifies this remark, particularly in the 33d and 36th lines, where the expression "*paws off, he*" is made to rhyme with the word "*philosophy*"; and below, "*weeping*" and "*deep in*"; "*fitting*" and "*bit in*"; "*divine as*" and "*Aquinas*"; "*sully verse*" and "*Gullivers*"; "*few so*" and "*Crusoe*"; "*said he*" and "*ready*"; "*home as*" and "*Thomas*"; "*me as*" "*ideas*"; "*suffice it her*" and "*eyes at her*" "*matter he*" and "*battery*"; "*brought her*" and "*water*," &c.

Although the tale is rather long, it is thought that the introduction of the whole of it may afford instruction as well as amusement, as an example of this peculiar style.

THE KNIGHT AND THE LADY.

A DOMESTIC LEGEND OF THE REIGN OF QUEEN ANNE.

BY THOMAS INGOLDSBY, ESQ.

"Hail! wedded love! mysterious tie!"
Thomson—or Somebody.

The Lady Jane was tall and slim,
The Lady Jane was fair,
And Sir Thomas, her lord, was stout of limb,
But his cough was short, and his eyes were dim,
And he wore green "specs," with a tortoise-shell rim,
And his hat was remarkably broad in the brim,
And she was uncommonly fond of him,
And they were a loving pair!—
And the name and the fame
Of the Knight and his Dame,
Were ev'ry where hail'd with the loudest acclaim;
And wherever they went, or wherever they came,
Far and wide,
The people cried
Huzza! for the lord of this noble domain—
Huzza! Huzza! Huzza!—once again!—
Encore!—Encore!
One cheer more!
All sorts of pleasure, and no sort of pain
To Sir Thomas the Good and the fair Lady Jane!

Now, Sir Thomas the Good,
Be it well understood,
Was a man of a very contemplative mood—
He would pore by the hour
O'er a weed or a flower,
Or the slugs that come crawling out after a shower;
Black-beetles, and Bumble-bees,—Blue-bottle Flies,
And Moths were of no small account in his eyes;
An "Industrious Flea" he'd by no means despise,
While an "Old Daddy-long-legs," whose "long legs" and thighs
Pass'd the common in shape, or in color, or size,
He was wont to consider an absolute prize.
Nay, a hornet or wasp he could scarce "keep his paws off"—he
Gave up, in short,
Both business and sport,

And abandoned himself, *tout entier*, to Philosophy.
Now, as Lady Jane was tall and slim,
And Lady Jane was fair,
And a good many years the junior of him, —
And as she,
All agree,
Look'd less like her *Mari*,
As he walked by her side, than her *Pere*,*
There are some might be found entertaining a notion
That such an entire and exclusive devotion
To that part of science folks call Entomology,
Was a positive shame,
And to such a fair Dame,
Really demanded some sort of apology;
No doubt it *would* vex
One half of the sex
To see their own husband, in horrid green "specs,"
Instead of enjoying a sociable chat,
Still poking his nose into this and to that,
At a gnat, or a bat, or a cat, or a rat,
Or great ugly things,
All legs and wings,
With nasty long tails arm'd with nasty long stings;
And they'd join such a log of a spouse to condemn,
One eternally thinking,
And blinking, and winking
At grubs, — when he ought to be winking at them
But no! — oh no!
'Twas by no means so
With the Lady Jane Ingoldsby — she, far discreeter,
And, having a temper more even, and sweeter,
Would never object to
Her spouse, in respect to
His poking and peeping
After "things creeping;"
Much less be still keeping lamenting and weeping
Or scolding, at what she perceived him so deep in.
Tout au contraire,
No lady so fair
Was e'er known to wear more contented an air;
And, — let who would call, — every day she was there,
Propounding receipts for some delicate fare,
Some toothsome conserve, of quince, apple, or pear,
Or distilling strong waters, — or potting a hare, —
Or counting her spoons, and her crockery-ware
Or else, her tambour-frame before her, with care
Embroidering a stool, or a back for a chair,
With needle-work roses, most cunning and rare,
Enough to make less gifted visters stare,
And declare, where'er
They had been, that "they ne'er
In their lives had seen ought that at all could compare
With dear Lady Jane's housewifery — that they would swear."

---

* My friend, Mr. Hood,
In his comical mood,
Would have probably styled the good Knight and his Lady
Him—"Stern-old and Hop-kins," and her "Tete and Brady."

Nay more; don't suppose
With such doings as those
This account of her merits must come to a close;
No; — examine her conduct more closely, you'll find
She by no means neglected improving her mind;
For there, all the while, with air quite bewitching,
She sat herring-boning, tambouring, or stitching,
Or having an eye to affairs of the kitchen,
Close by her side,
Sat her kinsman M'Bride,
Her cousin, fourteen times removed — as you'll see
If you look at the Ingoldsby family tree,
In "Burke's Commoners," vol. 20, page 53.
All the papers I've read agree,
Too, with the pedigree,
Where, among the collateral branches, appears,
'Captain Dugald MacBride, Royal Scots-Fusileers;"
And I doubt if you'd find in the whole of his clan
A more highly intelligent, worthy young man, —
And there he'd be sitting,
While she was a knitting,
Or hemming, or stitching, or darning and fitting,
Or putting a "gore" or a "gusset," or "bit" in,
Reading aloud, with a very grave look,
Some very "wise saw" from some very good book, —
Some such pious divine as
St. Thomas Aquinas;
Or, Equally charming
The works of Bellarmine;
Or else he unravels
The "voyages and travels"
Of Hackluytz — how sadly these Dutch names *do* sully verse
Purchas's, Hawksworth's or Lemuel Gulliver's —
Not to name others 'mongst whom are few so
Admired as John Bunyan, and Robinson Crusoe, —
No matter who came
It was always the same,
The Captain was reading aloud to the dame,
Till, from having gone through half the books on the shelf,
They were almost as wise as Sir Thomas himself.

Well, — it happened one day,
I really can't say
The particular month — but I *think* 'twas in May, —
'Twas, I *know*, in the Spring time, — when "Nature looks gay,"
As the poet observes, — and on treetop and spray
The dear little dickey birds carol away;
When the grass is so green, and the sun is so bright,
And all things are teeming with life and with light, —
That the whole of the house was thrown into affright,
For no soul could conceive what had gone with the Knight
It seems he had taken,
A light breakfast — bacon,
An egg — with a little broiled haddock — at most
A round and a half of some hot butter'd toast,
With a slice of cold sirloin from yesterday's roast,
And then — let me see! —
He had two — perhaps three

Cups (with sugar and cream) of strong Gunpowder tea,
With a spoonful in each of some choice *eau de vie*,
Which with nine out of ten would perhaps disagree.
In fact, I and my son
Mix "black" with our "Hyson,"
Neither having the nerves of a bull or a bison,
And both hating brandy like what some call "pison."
No matter for that —
He had called for his hat,
With the brim that I've said was so broad and so flat,
And his "specs" with the tortoise-shell rim, and his cane,
With the crutch-handled top, which he used to sustain
His steps in his walks, and to poke in the shrubs
And the grass, when unearthing his worms and his grubs —
Thus armed, he set out on a ramble — alack!
He *set out*, poor dear Soul! — but he never came back!
"First" dinner-bell rang
Out its euphonious clang
At five — folks kept early hours then — and the "Last"
Ding-dong'd, as it ever was wont, at half-past.
While Betsey, and Sally,
And Thompson, the *Valet*,
And every one else was beginning to bless himself,
Wondering the Knight had not come in to dress himself. —
— Quoth Betsey, "Dear me! why the fish will be cold!"
Quoth Sally, "Good gracious! how 'Missis' *will* scold!" —
Thompson, the *Valet*,
Looked gravely at Sally,
As who should say, "Truth must not always be told!"
Then expressing a fear lest the Knight might take cold.
Thus exposed to the dews,
Lambs'-wool stockings, and shoes,
Of each a fresh pair,
He put down to air,
And hung a clean shirt to the fire on a chair —

Still the Master was absent — the Cook came and said "he
Much fear'd, as the dinner had been so long ready,
The roast and the boil'd
Would be all of it spoil'd,
And the puddings, her Ladyship thought such a treat,
He was morally sure, would be scarce fit to eat!"
This closed the debate —
"'T would be folly to wait,"
Said the Lady, "Dish up! — Let the meal be served straight;
And let two or three slices be put in a plate,
And kept hot for Sir Thomas, — He 's lost, sure as fate!
And, a hundred to one, won't be home till it 's late!"
— Captain Dugald MacBride then proceeded to face
The Lady at table, — stood up, and said grace, —
Then set himself down in Sir Thomas's place.

Wearily, wearily, all that night,
That live-long night, did the hours go by;
And the Lady Jane,
In grief and in pain,
She sat herself down to cry! —
And Captain M'Bride
Who sat by her side

Though I really can't say that he actually cried,
At least had a tear in his eye!
As much as can well be expected, perhaps,
From very "young fellows" to very "old chaps;"
And if he had said
What he 'd got in his head,
'T would have been "Poor old Buffer! he 's certainly dead!"
The morning dawn'd, — and the next, — and the next,
And all the mansion were still perplex'd;
No watch dog "bay'd a welcome home," as
A watch dog should, to the "Good Sir Thomas;"
No knocker fell
His approach to tell,
Not so much as a runaway ring at the bell —
The Hall was as silent as a Hermit's cell.
Yet the Sun shone bright upon tower and tree,
And the meads smiled green as green may be,
And the dear little dickey birds caroll'd with glee,
And the lambs in the park skipp'd merry and free —
— Without, all was joy and harmony!
"And thus 't will be, — nor long the day, —
Ere we, like him, shall pass away!
Yon sun that now *our* bosom warms,
Shall shine, — but shine on other forms; —
Yon Grove, whose choir so sweetly cheers
Us now, shall sound on other ears, —
The joyous Lamb, as now, shall play,
But other eyes its sports survey —
The stream we loved shall roll as fair,
The flowery sweets, the trim Parterre,
Shall scent, as now, the ambient air, —
The Tree, whose bending branches bear
The one loved name — shall yet be there; —
But where the hand that carved it? — Where?"
These were hinted to me as
The very ideas
Which passed through the mind of the fair Lady Jane.
Her thoughts having taken a sombre-ish train
As she walked on the esplanade, to and again,
With Captain M'Bride,
Of course at her side,
Who could not look quite so forlorn, though he tried.
— An "idea," in fact, had got into HIS head,
That if "poor dear Sir Thomas" should really be dead,
It might be no bad "spec." to be there in his stead,
And, by simply contriving, in due time to wed
A lady who was young and fair,
A lady slim and tall,
To set himself down in comfort there
The Lord of Tapton* Hall. —
Thinks he, "We have sent
Half over Kent,
And nobody knows how much money 's been spent,
Yet no one 's been found to say which way he went!

* The familiar abbreviation for Tappington Everard still in use among the tenantry. — *Vide Prefatory Introduction to the Ingoldsby Legends.*

The groom, who 's been over
To Folkstone and Dover,
Can't get any tidings at all of the rover.
— Here 's a fortnight and more has gone by, and we 've tried
Every plan we could hit on — the whole country-side,
Upon all its dead walls, with placards we 've supplied, —
And we 've sent out the Crier, and had him well cried —
MISSING !!
Stolen or strayed,
Lost or mislaid,
A GENTLEMAN ; middle-aged, sober, and staid;
Stoops slightly — and when he left home was arrayed
In a sad-colored suit, somewhat dingy and fray'd ; —
Had spectacles on with a tortoise-shell rim,
And a hat rather lower-crown'd, and broad in the brim,
Whoe'er
Shall bear
Or send him, with care,
(Right side uppermost) home ; — or shall give notice where
The said middle-aged Gentleman is ; — or shall state
Any fact that may tend to throw light on his fate,
To the man at the turnpike called TAPPINGTON-GATE,
Shall receive a REWARD OF FIVE POUNDS for his trouble —
☞ N. B. If defunct, the reward shall be double! ☜
Had he been above ground
He MUST have been found.
No — doubtless he 's shot — or he 's hang'd — or he 's drown'd ! —
Then his Widow — aye ! aye ! —
But, what will folks say ? —
To address her at once — at so early a day ?
Well — what then ? — who cares ? — let 'em say what they may —
A fig for their nonsense and chatter ! — suffice it, her
Charms will excuse one for casting sheep's eyes at her ! "
When a man has decided,
As Captain M'Bride did,
And once fully made up his mind on the matter, he
Can't be too prompt in unmasking his battery.
He began on the instant, and vow'd that "her eyes
Far exceeded in brilliance the stars in the skies, —
That her lips were like roses — her cheeks were like lilies —
Her breath had the odor of daffy-down dillies ! "
With a thousand more compliments equally true,
And expressed in similitudes equally new !
Then his left arm he placed
Round her jimp, taper waist —
Ere she fix'd to repulse, or return his embrace,
Up came running a man at a deuce of a pace,
With that very peculiar expression of face
Which always betokens dismay or disaster,
Crying out—'T was the Gardener— "Oh, ma'm ! we 've found master ! !"
— "Where ? where ?" scream'd the lady ; and Echo scream'd "Where?"
The man couldn't say "There ! "
He had no breath to spare,
But, gasping for air, he could only respond
By pointing — he pointed, alas ! — TO THE POND !
—'T was e'en so ! — poor dear Knight ! — with his 'specs" and his hat
He'd gone poking his nose into this and that ;
When, close to the side
Of the bank, he espied
An "uncommon fine" tadpole, remarkably fat ;

He stooped; — and he thought her
His own; — he had caught her!
Got hold of her tail, — and to land almost brought her,
When — he plump'd head and heels into fifteen feet water!

The Lady Jane was tall and slim,
The Lady Jane was fair —
Alas, for Sir Thomas! she grieved for him,
As she saw two serving-men, sturdy of limb,
His body between them bear.
She sobbed, and she sighed; she lamented, and cried,
For of sorrow brimful was her cup;
She swooned, and I think she'd have fallen down and died
If Captain MacBride
Had not been by her side,
With the Gardener; they both their assistance supplied,
And managed to hold her up —
But, when she "comes to,"
Oh! 'tis shocking to view
The sight which the corpse reveals!
Sir Thomas's body,
It looked so odd — he
Was half eaten up by the eels!
His waistcoat and hose, and the rest of his clothes,
Were all gnawed through and through;
And out of each shoe
An eel they drew,
And from each of his pockets they pulled out two!
And the gardener himself had secreted a few,
As well we may suppose;
For, when he came running to give the alarm,
He had six in the basket that hung on his arm.

Good Father John *
Was summoned anon;
Holy water was sprinkled,
And little bells tinkled,
And tapers were lighted,
And incense ignited,
And masses were sung and masses were said,
All day, for the quiet repose of the dead,
And all night — no one thought of going to bed.

But Lady Jane was tall and slim,
And Lady Jane was fair, —
And, ere morning came, that winsome dame
Had made up her mind — or, what's much the same,
Had *thought about* — once more "changing her name,"
And she said, with a pensive air,
To Thompson, the valet, while taking away,
When supper was over, the cloth and the tray, —
"Eels a many
I've ate; but any
So good ne'er tasted before! —

* For some account of Father John Ingoldsby, to whose papers I am so much beholden, see *Ingoldsby's Legends, first series*, p. 216, (2d Edit.) This was the last ecclesiastical act of his long and valuable life.

24*

They 're a fish, too, of which I 'm remarkably fond.—
Go — pop Sir Thomas again in the pond—
'Poor dear!' — HE 'LL CATCH US SOME MORE!!"

MORAL.

All middle-aged gentlemen let me advise,
If you 're married, and have not got very good eyes,
Don't go poking about after blue-bottled flies! —
If you 've spectacles, don't have a tortoiseshell rim,
And don't go near the water, — unless you can swim!

Married ladies, especially such as are fair,
Tall, and slim, I would next recommend to beware,
How, on losing *one* spouse, they give way to despair;
But let them reflect, "There are fish, and no doubt on 't —
As good *in* the river as ever came *out* on 't!"

Should they light on a spouse who is given to roaming
In solitude — *raison de plus*, in the "gloaming,"—
Let them have a fixed time for said spouse to come home in
And if, when "last dinner-bell" 's rung, he is late,
To insure better manners in future — Do n't wait!

If of husband or children they chance to be fond,
Have a stout wire fence put all round the pond!
One more piece of advice, and I close my appeals —
That is — if you chance to be partial to eels,
Then — *Crede experto* — trust one who has tried,
Have them spitch-cock'd, — or stewed — they're too oily when fried.

LXXVI.

EPITHETS.

The rules of rhyme have now been presented, together with a full vocabulary, by which the appropriate rhyme to any word may be found. The use of appropriate epithets by which animated descriptions may be given, or the measure of the verse filled out, comes now to be considered.*

An epithet is an adjective, expressing some real quality of the subject to which it is applied, or an attributive, expressing some quality ascribed to it; as a *verdant* lawn, a *brilliant* appearance, a *just* man, an *accurate* description.

---

* See page 166, under Description, for some remarks and suggestions with regard to epithets.

Epithets are of two kinds, simple and compound.

Simple epithets are single words, as, *joyous* youth, *decrepit* age, *thoughtless* infancy.

Compound epithets consist of compound words, and are frequently composed of nouns and other parts of speech, in connexion with adjectives, participles, &c., as, The *meek-eyed* morn, *Tear-dropping* April, The *laughter-loving* goddess, The *dew-dropping* morn, In *world-rejoicing* state it moves along, &c.

The judicious application of epithets constitutes one of the greatest beauties of composition; and in poetry, especially, the melody of the verse, and the animation of the style is, in great measure, dependent upon it.

Figurative language (*see page* **111**) presents a wide and extensive field for the supply of rich and expressive epithets; and the poet is indulged, by his peculiar license, in the formation of new and original compound epithets. (*See page* **166**.)

Alliteration, also, (*see page* 151) if not profusely applied, and expressions in which the sound is adapted to the sense, when introduced with simple or compound epithets, contribute in a good degree to the beauty and harmony of verse. The following couplet, from Goldsmith's Deserted Village, presents an exemplification of this remark:

"The *white-washed wall*, the *nicely-sanded* floor,
The varnished *clock* that *clicked* behind the door."

[*See Onomatopœia.*]

Example.

The word *anger* is suggested for the application of epithets, and the following terms will be found respectively applicable to it:

Violent, impetuous, threatening, menacing, unbridled, untamed, mistaking, boiling, swelling, frantic, raging, flaming, burning, passionate, roaring, secret, waspish, impatient, red-looking, red-glaring, inflaming, bloody, blood-spilling, incensed, stormy, scarlet, blood-dyed, moody, choleric, wrathful, revengeful, vengeful, chafing, foaming, hot-headed, heating, sparkling, rash, blind, heady, head-strong, disordered, stern-visaged, giddy, flame-eyed, ghostly, distempered, transporting, tempestuous, blustering, fierce, cruel, truculent, overseeing, frothy, implacable, pettish, bitter, rough, wild, stubborn, unruly, litigious, austere, dreadful, peace-destroying joy-killing, soul-troubling, blasting, death-dealing, fury-kindled, mortal hellish, heaven-rejected.

Example 2d.

FOUNTAIN.

Chrystal, gushing, rustling, silver, gently-gliding, parting, pearly, weeping, bubbling, gurgling, chiding, clear, grass-fringed, moss-fringed, pebble-paved verdant, sacred, grass-margined, moss-margined, trickling, soft dew-sprinkled, fast-flowing, delicate, delicious, clean, straggling, dancing vaulting, deep-embosomed, leaping, murmuring, muttering, whispering, prattling, twaddling, swelling, sweet-rolling, gently-flowing, rising, sparkling, flowing, frothy, dew-distilling, dew-born, exhaustless, inexhaustible, never-decreasing, never-failing, heaven-born, earth-born, deep-divulging, drought-dispelling, thirst-allaying, refreshing, soul-refreshing, earth refreshing, laving, lavish, plant-nourishing.

Examples for Practice.

Apply epithets to the following names:

Friend, friendship, love, joy, sorrow, revenge, mirth, justice, a forest, a wood, a mountain, billow, wave, ripple, bloom, blossom, bud, banquet, adversity, affection, affliction, sorrow, despair, allurement, ambition, anguish, appetite, avarice, autumn, beauty, bee, beggar, bird, bride, cave, cloud, clown, cold, countenance, critic, death, deceit, delight, destroy, disease, discord, dog, dream, eagle, earth, eye, envy, eloquence, countenance. fear, fire, firmament, flame, flatter, flower, gift, glory, gold, grove, grief, hair, hand, honor, hour, hope, jealousy, ignorance, innocence, lay, law, liberty, light, maid, majesty, malice, mead, meadow, minute, monarch, mist, multitude, night, pain, peace, pleasure, poetry, poverty, pride, prosperity, providence, rage, rebellion, remorse, rock, sea, shore, skin, sleep, snake, snow, stream, sun, swain, tail, tear, tempest, temple, throne, thunder, time, tongue, tree, vale, vengeance, verse, vine, want, water, war, wine, woman, wit, wind, wing, winter, wood, woe, year, youth, zeal.

LXXVII.

LYRIC POETRY.

Lyric poetry literally implies that kind of poetry which is written to accompany *the lyre*, or other musical instrument. The versification may either be regular, or united in fanciful combinations, in correspondence with the strain for which it is composed.

Example 1st.

THE WINGED WORSHIPPERS.

Addressed to two Swallows that flew into Church during Divine Service

Gay, guiltless pair,
What seek ye from the fields of heaven?
Ye have no need of prayer,
Ye have no sins to be forgiven.

Why perch ye here,
Where mortals to their Maker bend?
Can your pure spirits fear
The God you never could offend?

Ye never knew
The crimes for which we come to weep;
Penance is not for you,
Blessed wanderers of the upper deep.

To you 't is given
To make sweet nature's untaught lays;
Beneath the arch of heaven
To chirp away a life of praise.

Then spread each wing,
Far, far above, o'er lakes and lands,
And join the choirs that sing
In yon blue dome not reared with hands.

Or, if ye stay,
To note the consecrated hour,
Teach me the airy way,
And let me try your envied power.

Above the crowd,
On upward wings could I but fly,
I 'd bathe in yon bright cloud,
And seek the stars that gem the sky.

'T were heaven indeed
Through fields of trackless light to soar,
On nature's charms to feed,
And nature's own great God adore.

Example 2d.

LINES ADDRESSED TO LADY BYRON.

There is a mystic thread of life
So dearly wreathed with mine alone,
That destiny's relentless knife
At once must sever both or none.

There is a form on which these eyes
Have often gazed with fond delight;
By day that form their joy supplies,
And dreams restore it through the night.

There is a voice whose tones inspire
Such thrills of rapture through my breast;
I would not hear a seraph choir,
Unless that voice could join the rest.

There is a face whose blushes tell
  Affection's tale upon the cheek;
But, pallid at one fond farewell,
  Proclaims more love than words can speak.

There is a lip which mine has pressed,
  And none had ever pressed before;
It vowed to make me sweetly blessed,
  And mine, — mine only, pressed it more.

There is a bosom, — all my own, —
  Hath pillowed oft this aching head;
A mouth which smiles on me alone,
  An eye whose tears with mine are shed.

There are two hearts whose movements thrill
  In unison so closely sweet!
That, pulse to pulse, responsive still,
  That both must heave, — or cease to beat.

There are two souls whose equal flow
  In gentle streams so calmly run,
That when they part — they part! — ah, no!
  They cannot part, — those souls are one.

The highest of the modern lyric compositions is the Ode The word *ode* is from the Greek, and is generally translated *a song*, but it is not *a song*, as we use the term in our language. The ode was the result of strong excitement, a poetical attempt to fill the hearts of the auditors with feelings of the sublime. Odes that were sung in honor of the gods were termed *Hymns*, from a Greek word *hymneo*, which signifies *to celebrate.* The name is now applied to those sacred songs that are sung in churches. The Hebrew hymns which bear the name of King David are termed *Psalms,* from the Greek word *psallo,* which signifies *to sing.*

The Greek Ode, when complete, was composed of three parts, the Strophe, the Antistrope, and the Epode. The two former terms indicated the turnings of the priests round and about the altar. The Epode was the *end of the song*, and was repeated standing still, before the altar.

Pæans were songs of triumph sung in procession in honor of Apollo, on occasions of a victory, &c., or to the other gods as thanksgivings for the cessation or *cure* of an evil. The word is derived from a word signifying to heal or *cure.*

For examples of the English ode, the student is referred to the well-known pieces, "Alexander's Feast," by Dryden, and the "Ode on the Passions," by Collins.

A Ballad is a rhyming record of some adventure or transaction which is amusing or interesting to the populace, and written in easy and uniform verse, so that it may easily be sung by those who have little acquaintance with music.

A Sonnet is a species of poetical composition, consisting of fourteen lines or verses of equal length. It properly consists of fourteen iambic verses, of eleven syllables, and is divided into two chief parts; — the first consists of two divisions, each of four lines, called *quatrains;* the second of two divisions of three lines each, called *terzines.* The rhymes in these parts respectively were managed according to regular rules. But these rules have been seldom regarded in modern compositions. The sonnet generally contains one principal idea, pursued through the various antitheses of the different strophes, and adorned with the charm of rhyme.

Example of the Sonnet.

SONNET TO ONE BELOVED.

Deep in my heart thy cherished secret lies
  Deep as a pearl on ocean's soundless floor,
  Where the bold diver never can explore
The realms o'er which the mighty billows rise.
It rests far hidden from all mortal eyes,
  Not e'en discovered when the piercing light
Of morn illumines the uncurtained skies,
  And fills with sunshine the dark vaults of night.
Repose in me thy heart's most sacred trust,
  And nothing shall betray it; I will bend
This human fabric to its native dust,
  But nothing from me shall that secret rend,
Which to my soul is brighter, dearer far,
Than any lustre of sun, moon, or star.

A Cantata is a composition or song intermixed with recitatives and airs, chiefly intended for a single voice.

A Canzonet is a short song in one, two, or three parts.*

Example.

BLACK EYES AND BLUE.

Black eyes most dazzle in a hall;
Blue eyes most please at evening fall;
The black a conquest soonest gain;
The blue a conquest most retain;

* In musical compositions, a song consisting of two parts is called a ***Duet*** if in three parts, a *Trio*, if in four, a *Quartette*, &c.

The black bespeaks a lively heart,
Whose soft emotions soon depart;
The blue a steadier flame betray,
That burns and lives beyond a day;
The black may features best disclose;
In blue may feelings all repose.
Then let each reign without control,
The black all MIND,—the blue all SOUL!

A Logogriph is a kind of riddle.

Charades (which are frequently in verse) are compositions, in which the subject must be a word of two syllables, each forming a distinct word, and these syllables are to be concealed in an enigmatical description, first separately and then together.

Madrigals are short lyric poems adapted to express ingenious and pleasing thoughts, commonly on amatory subjects, and containing not less than four, nor more than sixteen verses, of eleven syllables, with shorter verses interspersed, or of verses of eight syllables irregularly rhymed. The madrigal is not confined to the regularity of the sonnet, but contains some tender and delicate, though simple thought, suitably expressed.

Example of the Madrigal.

TO A LADY OF THE COUNTY OF LANCASTER, WITH A WHITE ROSE.

If this fair rose offend thy sight,
It in thy bosom wear;
'T will blush to find itself less white,
And turn Lancastrian there.

The Rondeau or rondo, roundo, roundel or roundelay, all mean precisely the same thing. It commonly consists of thirteen lines or verses, of which eight have one rhyme, and five another. It is divided into three couplets, and at the end of the second and third, the beginning of the rondeau is repeated, if possible, in an equivocal or punning sense.

The Epigram is a short poem, treating only of one thing, and ending with some lively, ingenious, and natural thought, rendered interesting by being unexpected. Conciseness is one of the principal characteristics of the epigram. Its point often rests on a witticism or verbal pun; but the higher species of the epigram should be marked by fineness and delicacy, rather than by smartness or repartee.

Example.

WRITTEN ON A GLASS WITH A DIAMOND PENCIL BELONGING TO LORD STANHOPE

Accept a miracle in place of wit;—
See two dull lines by Stanhope's pencil writ.

An Impromptu is an extemporaneous composition, that is, one made at the moment, or without previous study.

An Acrostic is a composition in verse, in which the initial letters of each line, taken in order from the top to the bottom, make up a word or phrase, generally a person's name, or a motto

Example of the Acrostic.

F riendship, thou 'rt false! I hate thy flattering smile!
R eturn to me those years I spent in vain.
I n early youth the victim of thy guile,
E ach joy took wing ne'er to return again,—
N e'er to return; for, chilled by hopes deceived,
D ully the slow paced hours now move along;
S o changed the time, when, thoughtless, I believed
H er honeyed words, and heard her syren song.
I f e'er, as me, she lure some youth to stray,
P erhaps, before too late, he 'll listen to my lay.

An Epithalamium is a nuptial song or poem, in praise of the bride and bridegroom, and praying for their prosperity.*

LXXVIII.

PASTORAL AND ELEGIAC POETRY.

Pastorals or bucolics are the narratives, songs, and dramas, which are supposed to have been recited, sung, or acted by shepherds.

The ancient pastorals were either dialogues or monologues. A monologue is a poetical piece, where there is only a single speaker.

* The forty fifth Psalm is an epithalamium to Christ and the Church.

An Idyl, Idillion or Idyllium is a short pastoral of the narrative or descriptive kind.

An Eclogue is the conversation of shepherds. The word literally means *a select piece*, and the art of the poet lies in *selecting* the beauties without the grossness of rural life. The eclogue differs from the idyl, in being appropriated to pieces in which shepherds themselves are introduced.

ELEGY AND EPITAPH.

An Elegy is a poem or a song expressive of sorrow and lamentation

An Epitaph is, literally, an inscription on a tomb. When written in verse, and expressive of the sorrow of the survivors, epitaphs are short elegies.*

---

* The following remarks on the subject of epitaphs, were originally presented by a young friend, as a college exercise. They appear to be so much to the purpose, that they are presented entire:—

"'Nature and Nature's laws lay hid in night
God said, Let Newton be! and all was light."

"One common fault in epitaphs is their too great length. Not being easily read upon stone, few trouble themselves to peruse them, if they are long; and in a churchyard so many solicit our attention, that we prefer to examine those which are concise, rather than spend our time on a few long ones. Every one, too, soon discovers, that those which *cover* the stones on which they are inscribed, are, for the most part, feebly expressed, and hardly recompense one for the trouble of deciphering them; while a concise inscription immediately attracts notice, and is generally found to be pointed. We can frequently perceive the description of character to be untrue, because it is coldly worded, and expressed in very general terms; in short, a character which would apply to one man as well as another, and such as is frequently given to a person whom we care nothing about. Such epitaphs I consider faulty. After the death of an acquaintance, all our feelings of dislike, caused by his presence, are dispelled; all the animosity, growing out of the clashing of our interests with his, vanishes with the man; and, perhaps, being in some degree reproved by our consciences for our uncharitable feelings during his life, we endeavor to make amends by inscribing to his memory a eulogy, which, if he still lived, we should pronounce undeserved flattery, if spoken by others, and which would never have proceeded from our own lips, except in irony. In such a case, an epitaph usually begins by gravely telling the reader that we are all mortal, and ends by commending the soul of the defunct to heaven!

"But, though epitaphs give us, generally, exaggerated characters, yet I would not have it otherwise. Our churchyards should be schools of morality and religion. Every thing we see there, of course, reminds us of death; and it would appear to us sacrilege, if we should behold any record of vice. Since everywhere we find virtue ascribed to the tenants of the place, their death, and death in general, will not be to us so terrible and gloomy a subject of reflection; yet will produce such a serious turn of mind as will lead to religious meditation, which always has the effect of calming the passions

Example.

ELEGY WRITTEN IN A COUNTRY CHURCHYARD.

The curfew tolls the knell of parting day;
  The lowing herd winds slowly o'er the lea;
The ploughman homeward plods his weary way,
  And leaves the world to darkness and to me.

Now fades the glimmering landscape on the sight,
  And all the air a solemn stillness holds;
Save where the beetle wheels his droning flight,
  And drowsy tinklings lull the distant folds.

Save that, from yonder ivy-mantled tower,
  The moping owl does to the moon complain
Of such as, wandering near her secret bower,
  Molest her ancient solitary reign.

---

and facilitates, in a great degree, our conquest over them, and the infrequency of which is the cause of most of our transgressions.

"Eulogizing epitaphs give us a more exalted idea of the power of religion, to which they chiefly have reference; and therefore have, in some measure, the force of examples. When a person has not been known to the world as a philosopher and a scholar, or in any other way a distinguished man, it is sufficient that his epitaph should be calculated to excite tender and serious feelings. In such a case, elegiac poetry should be congenial to those feelings. This, Stewart says, may be effected by the smoothness of the verse, and the apparently easy recurrence of the rhymes. Blank verse would be peculiarly inappropriate to this species of poetical composition. When, on the other hand, a person has been conspicuous, as a philosopher, for instance, his epitaph should convey a different lesson; by a description of his discoveries, it should remind us of what is due from us to science and our fellow creatures, besides suggesting the reflection that the greatest men must perish.

"Considering this quality desirable in an epitaph on a philosopher, we should praise an epitaph on Newton, which represented him as the greatest philosopher the world has ever seen, and is expressive also of the gratitude which is due to him, for the improvement he has made in the condition of the human race by his discoveries. I think that the above epitaph, by Pope, conveys all this; for the observation, that 'Nature and nature's laws lay hid in night,' implies that information on the subject of those laws would be beneficial to mankind, inasmuch as an idea of disadvantage is associated with the word 'night;' and the second line expresses that Newton alone made the whole subject clear to our minds; an exaggerated expression, but one that certainly describes an exalted genius. I do not think, that the epitaph redounds much to the honor of Pope, except for the felicity of the expression; for the *idea* would occur to many minds. We should not, in judging of this couplet, consider it alone, for united with the rest of the epitaph, of which it is but a part, the whole together deserves much greater praise than is due to either part taken separately. A complete eulogy on Newton should not be expected in the inscription on his tomb, and therefore we should not consider its merits in that character. I think that the conciseness of the epitaph, which is a great recommendation, will compensate and account for whatever defect it may have in giving us a just and exact idea of Newton."

Beneath those rugged elms, that yew-tree's shade.
  Where heaves the turf in many a mouldering heap,
Each in his narrow cell for ever laid,
  The rude forefathers of the hamlet sleep.

The breezy call of incense-breathing morn,
  The swallow twittering from the straw-built shed,
The cock's shrill clarion, or the echoing horn,
  No more shall rouse them from their lowly bed.

For them no more the blazing hearth shall burn,
  Nor busy housewife ply her evening care;
No children run to lisp their sire's return,
  Or climb his knees the envied kiss to share.

Oft did the harvest to their sickle yield;
  Their furrow oft the stubborn glebe has broke;
How jocund did they drive their team afield!
  How bowed the woods beneath their sturdy stroke.

Let not Ambition mock their useful toil,
  Their homely joys and destiny obscure;
Nor Grandeur hear, with a disdainful smile,
  The short and simple annals of the poor.

The boast of heraldry, the pomp of power.
  And all that beauty, all that wealth e'er gave,
Await, alike, the inevitable hour;—
  The paths of glory lead but to the grave.

Nor you, ye proud, impute to these the fault,
  If memory o'er their tomb no trophies raise,
Where, through the long-drawn aisle and fretted vault,
  The pealing anthem swells the note of praise.

Can storied urn, or animated bust,
  Back to its mansion call the fleeting breath?
Can Honor's voice provoke the silent dust,
  Or Flattery soothe the dull cold ear of death?

Perhaps, in this neglected spot, is laid
  Some heart, once pregnant with celestial fire;
Hands, that the rod of empire might have swayed,
  Or waked to ecstasy the living lyre:

But Knowledge to their eyes her ample page,
  Rich with the spoils of time, did ne'er unroll;
Chill Penury repressed their noble rage,
  And froze the genial current of the soul.

Full many a gem, of purest ray serene,
  The dark, unfathomed caves of ocean bear;
Full many a flower is born to blush unseen,
  And waste its sweetness on the desert air.

Some village Hampden, that, with dauntless breast,
  The little tyrant of his fields withstood;
Some mute, inglorious Milton here may rest;
  Some Cromwell, guiltless of his country's blood.

The applause of listening senates to command,
  The threats of pain and ruin to despise,
To scatter plenty o'er a smiling land,
  And read their history in a nation's eyes,

Their lot forbade: nor circumscribed alone,
  Their growing virtues, but their crimes confined;—
Forbade to wade through slaughter to a throne,
  And shut the gates of mercy on mankind;

The struggling pangs of conscious Truth to hide,
  To quench the blushes of ingenuous Shame;
Or heap the shrine of Luxury and Pride
  With incense kindled at the muse's flame.

Far from the maddening crowd's ignoble strife,
  Their sober wishes never learnt to stray:
Along the cool, sequestered vale of life
  They kept the noiseless tenor of their way.

Yet even these bones from insult to protect,
  Some frail memorial, still erected nigh,
With uncouth rhymes and shapeless sculpture decked,
  Implores the passing tribute of a sigh.

Their names, their years, spelled by the unlettered Muse,
  The place of fame and elegy supply;
And many a holy text around she strews,
  That teach the rustic moralist to die.

For who, to dumb forgetfulness a prey,
  This pleasing, anxious being e'er resigned;—
Left the warm precincts of the cheerful day,—
  Nor cast one longing, lingering look behind?

On some fond breast the parting soul relies;
  Some pious drops the closing eye requires;
Even from the tomb the voice of Nature cries·
  Even in our ashes live their wonted fires.

For thee, who, mindful of the unhonored dead
  Dost in these lines their artless tale relate
If, chance, by lonely contemplation led,
  Some kindred spirit shall inquire thy fate,

Haply, some hoary-headed swain may say,
  "Oft have we seen him, at the peep of dawn,
Brushing, with hasty steps, the dews away,
  To meet the sun upon the upland lawn.

"There, at the foot of yonder nodding beech,
That wreathes its old fantastic roots so high,
His listless length at noontide would he stretch,
And pore upon the brook that babbles by.

"Hard by yon wood, now smiling, as in scorn,
Muttering his wayward fancies, he would rove,
Now drooping, woful wan, like one forlorn,
Or crazed with care, or crossed with hopeless love.

"One morn I missed him on the accustomed hill,
Along the heath, and near his favorite tree;
Another came; nor yet beside the rill,
Nor up the lawn, nor at the wood was he:

"The next with dirges due, in sad array,
Slow through the church-way path we saw him borne.
Approach and read, (for thou canst read,) the lay,
Graved on the stone beneath yon aged thorn."

EPITAPH.

Here rests his head upon the lap of earth,
A youth, to fortune and to fame unknown:
Fair Science frowned not on his humble birth,
And Melancholy marked him for her own.

Large was his bounty, and his soul sincere;
Heaven did a recompense as largely send:—
He gave to misery all he had,—a tear;
He gained from Heaven—'twas all he wished—a friend.

No farther seek his merits to disclose,
Nor draw his frailties from their dread abode,—
(There they, alike, in trembling hope repose,)
The bosom of his Father and his God.

LXXIX.

OF THE HIGHER SPECIES OF POETRY.

The higher species of poetry embraces the three following divisions, namely:

1. Tales and Romances.
2. Epic and Dramatic Poetry.

3. Didactic and Descriptive Poetry.*

A Tale is, literally, any thing that is *told*, and may relate either real or fictitious events. When the events related in a tale are believed really to have happened, the tale is termed *history*.

A Romance is a tale of interesting, or wonderful adventures; and has its name from those that were recited by the Troubadours, (that is, *inventors*,) or wandering minstrels, of the twelfth and thirteenth centuries.

The tales of the Troubadours related principally to the military achievements of the crusading knights, their gallantry, and fidelity They were delivered in a corrupted Latin dialect, called Provençal, or Provincial, by the inhabitants of Rome, and *Romanzo*, or Romish, by the Gothic nations, and hence the tale itself was called a *Romance*. Some of them were prose, some in verse, and some in a miscellaneous union of prose narrative and song. But in neither form were they in all cases worthy of the name of poems.

Novels, (literally, something *new*,) are the adventures of imaginary persons, in which supernatural beings are not introduced. The novel is generally also *in prose*. Whenever a power is introduced superior to that of mortals, the novel is properly a romance. "The Epicurean," by Moore, is an example of this kind, which, although in the form of prose, is highly poetical in its character. It is full of imaginative power, and abounds in figures of the most beautiful kind, dressed in the most glowing colors.

That power, which the poet introduces, whatever it may be, to accom plish what mere human agency cannot effect, is called the *machinery* of the poem.

An Epic poem is a poetical, romantic tale, embracing many personages and many incidents. One general and important design must be apparent in its construction, to which every separate actor and action must be subservient. The accounts of these subordinate actions are called *episodes*, and should not be extended to a great length.

Examples of epic poems may be seen in the "Iliad," and "Odyssey," of Homer, (translated by Pope,) the "Æneid," of Virgil, (translated by Dryden,) the "Pharsalia," of Lucan, (translated by Rowe,) and the "Paradise Lost" of Milton. Epic poems are rare productions, and scarcely any nation can boast of more than one.

The word *epic* literally means nothing more than a tale. It is, however, a tale concerning a hero or heroes, and hence epic poetry is also

---

* See the piece entitled "The Empire of Poetry," by Fontenelle, page 133, under the head of *Allegory*.

called *heroic verse.* Epopea, or Epopœia, is merely a learned name for epic poem.

A Drama is a poem of the epic kind, but so compressed and adapted, that the whole tale, instead of requiring to be read or recited at intervals, by an individual, may be exhibited as actually passing before our eyes. Every actor in the poem has his representative on the stage, who speaks the language of the poet, as if it were his own; and every action is literally performed or imitated, as if it were of natural occurrence.

As a dramatic writer, Shakspeare stands unrivalled, among English authors, and it may well be questioned, whether any nation has produced his superior.

In the construction of a Drama, rules have been laid down by critics, the principal of which relate to the *three Unities*, as they are called, of action, of time, and of place. Unity of action requires, that a single object should be kept in view. No underplot, or secondary action is allowable unless it tend to advance the prominent purpose. Unity of time requires, that the events should be limited to a short period; seldom if ever more than a single day. Unity of place requires the confinement of the actions represented within narrow geographical limits. Another rule of dramatic criticism is termed *poetical justice;* by which it is understood, that the personages shall be rewarded or punished, according to their respective desert. A regular drama is an historical picture, in which we perceive unity of design, and compare every portion of the composition, as harmonizing with the whole.

Dramatic compositions are of two kinds, Tragedy and Comedy. Tragedy is designed to fill the mind of the spectators with pity and terror; comedy to represent some amusing and connected tale. The muse of tragedy, therefore, deals in desolation and death, — that of comedy is surrounded by the humorous, the witty, and the gay. It is to tragedy that we chiefly look for poetical embellishment, and it is there only that we look for the sublime. Accordingly, it is, with few exceptions, still composed of measured lines, while comedy is now written wholly in prose.

A Prologue is a short poem, designed as an introduction to a discourse or performance, chiefly the discourse or poem spoken before a dramatic performance or play begins.

An Epilogue is a speech, or short poem, addressed to the spectators by one of the actors, after the conclusion of a dramatic performance. Sometimes it contains a recapitulation of the chief incidents of the play.

Farce is the caricature of comedy, and is restrained by no law, not even those of probability and nature. Its object is to excite mirth and uproarous laughter. But, in some of its forms, such as personal satire, occasional grossness, and vulgarity, it has rendered itself so obnoxious to reprobation, that the very name is an abomination. It is commonly in prose.

Those compositions in which the language is so little in unison with the subject as to impress the mind with a feeling of the ridiculous, are called Burlesques.

The Burletta is a species of composition in which persons and actions of no value are made to assume an air of importance. Or, it is that by which things of real consequence are degraded, so as to seem objects of derision.

Parodies, Travesties, and Mock Heroics are ludicrous imitations of serious subjects. They belong to the burlesque.*

---

* As a happy illustration of burlesque writing in several different styles, the following are presented from Bentley's Miscellany, with the facetious introduction with which they are prefaced:

" But another class of persons claims our attention. We mean those who are, for some cause or other, constantly called upon to write verses. Now, many of these, when suddenly required to make a song to a given tune, to scribble a chorus for the end of a farce, or to jot down an impromptu on the blue leaf of an album, suddenly find themselves at a nonplus, — not because they are not masters of rhyme and metre, but simply because they cannot get a subject. We propose to show, that, far from this want being a just cause for embarrassment, it is absolutely impossible *not* to find a subject The first thing that catches the eye, or comes into the head, will do, and may be treated in every manner. In this age, although a chosen few can fill the post of fiddler, opera-dancer, juggler, or clown to the ring, these occupations requiring innate genius, he who cannot become a poet is a very poor creature. But, to our task. We take the Dodo, that ugly bird, which every child knows from its picture in the books on natural history, as a subject that seems of all others the least promising, and we shall show our readers how artistically we can manage it in all sorts of styles.

I. The Descriptive. — For this we must go to our encyclopedias, cram for the occasion, and attentively observe the picture. ' Our Rees ' tells us that the Latin name for the bird is ' Didus,' that the Dutch are said to have found it in the Mauritius, and called it ' Dodaerts ; ' while the French termed it ' Cygne a Capuchon ; ' and the Portuguese, ' Dodo. Its existence, it seems, has been doubted, and at all events it is now supposed to be extinct.

In the island of Mauritius once a sturdy Dutchman found
Such a curious bird as ne'er before was seen to tread the ground;
Straight he called it ' Dodaerts ; ' when a Frenchman gazed upon
Its hood of down, and said it was a ' Cygne a Capuchon.'

French and Dutch might be content with making sorry names like these
But they would not satisfy the proud and high-souléd Portuguesé;
He proclaimed the bird a ' Dodo.' ' Dodo ' now each infant cries.
Pedants, they may call it ' Didus ; ' but such pedants we despise.

'T was a mighty bird ; those short, strong legs were never known to fail,
And he felt a glow of pride when thinking of that little tail;
And his beak was marked with vigor, curving like a wondrous hook,
Thick and ugly was his body, — such a form as made one look.

Didactic poetry is that which is written professedly for the purpose of instruction. Descriptive poetry merely describes the person or the object.

Didactic poetry should be replete with ornament, especially, where it can be done, with figurative language. This rule should be preserved in order to keep up the interest in the subject, which is usually *dry*. Not even the epic demands such glowing and picturesque epithets, such daring and forcible metaphors, such pomp of numbers and dignity of expression, as the didactic; for, the lower or more familiar the object described is, the greater must be the power of language to preserve it from debasement. Didactic and descriptive poetry are so intimately allied, that the two kinds can rarely be found asunder, and we give a poem this or that denomination, according as the one or the other of these characteristics appears to predominate.

No one now can see the dodo, which the sturdy Dutchman found;
Long ago those wondrous stumps of legs have ceased to tread the ground.
If, perchance, his bones we find, oh, let us gently turn them o'er,
Saying, ''T was a gallant world when dodos lived in days of yore.'

II. The Melancholy Sentimental. — We need only recollect, that when the dodo lived, somebody else lived, who is not living now, and we have our cue at once.

Oh, when the dodo's feet
His native island pressed,
How many a warm heart beat
Within a living breast,
Which now can beat no more,
But crumbles into dust,
And finds its turn is o'er,
As all things earthly must!

He 's dead that nam'd the bird,
That gallant Portuguese;
Who weeps not, having heard
Of changes such as these?
The Dutchman, too, is gone:
The dodo 's gone beside;
They teach us every one
How vain is earthly pride!

III. Impromptu *for a lady's album.*

The dodo vanished, as we must confess,
Being unfit to live from ugliness;
Surely, methinks, it will not be too bold
To hope the converse of the rule will hold.
If lovely things no power from earth can sever,
Celia, we all may swear, will live forever.

IV Bacchanalian, with full chorus.

The dodo once lived, and he does n't live now;
Yet, why should a cloud overshadow our brow?
The loss of that bird ne'er should trouble our brains,
For, though he is gone, still our claret remains.
Sing dodo — dodo — jolly dodo!
Hurrah! in his name let our cups overflow!

As examples of didactic poetry, the student is referred to Pope's "Moral Essays;" and, for instances of descriptive poetry, to his "Windsor Forest," to Milton's "L'Allegro," and "Il Penseroso," and to Thomson's "Seasons."

Among the examples of didactic poetry, Akenside's "Pleasures of the Imagination," and Young's "Night Thoughts," should not be forgotten.* In the opinion of Johnson, the versification of the former work is considered equal, if not superior, to that of any other specimen of blank verse in the language. Of Young's "Night Thoughts" it may be said, although it has been stigmatized as a long, lugubrious poem, opposed in its composition to every rule of sound criticism, full of extravagant metaphors, astounding hyperboles, and never-ending antitheses, that few poems in any language present such a concentration of thought, such a rich fund of poetical beauties, so numerous and brilliant corruscations of genius, and so frequent occurrence of passages of the pathetic and the sublime.†

* Another class of poems, uniting the didactic and the descriptive classes, may be mentioned, which are called the Sentimental. "The Pleasures of Memory," by Rogers, "The Pleasures of Hope," by Campbell, belong to this class. "The Deserted Village," and "The Traveller," by Goldsmith, are of the same class, and can scarcely be too highly estimated.

† The author has here, as in some other parts of the preceding remarks, departed from the expressions of Mr. Booth, to whose excellent work on the principles of English Composition he is largely indebted, here as elsewhere, in this volume.

We know that he perished; yet why shed a tear!
This generous bowl all our bosoms can cheer.
The dodo is gone, and, no doubt, in his day,
He delighted, as we do, to moisten his clay.
Sing dodo — dodo — jolly dodo!
Hurrah! in his name let our cups overflow!

V. The Remonstrative, addressed to those who do not believe there ever was a dodo.

What! disbelieve the dodo!
The like was never heard!
Deprive the face of nature
Of such a wondrous bird!
I always loved the dodo,
When quite a little boy,
I saw it in my "Goldsmith,"
My heart beat high with joy.

I think now how my uncle
One morning went to town
He brought me home a "Goldsmith,"
Which cost him half a crown.
No picture like the dodo
Such rapture could impart;
Then don't deny the dodo,
It wounds my inmost heart."

Satires are discourses or poems in which wickedness and folly are exposed with severity, or held up to ridicule. They differ from *Lampoons* and Pasquinades, in being *general*, rather than personal, and from sarcasm, in not expressing contempt or scorn.

Satires are usually included under the head of didactic poems, but every class of poems may include the satirical. In satires it is the class, the crime, or the folly, which is the proper object of attack, and not the individual.

A Lampoon, or Pasquinade, is a personal satire, written with the intention of reproaching, irritating, or vexing the individual, rather than to reform him. It is satisfied with low abuse and vituperation, rather than with proof or argument.

An Apophthegm, Apothegm, or Apothem, is a short, sententious, instructive remark, usually in prose, but rarely in verse, uttered on a particular occasion, or by a distinguished character; as that of Cato:

"Men, by doing nothing, soon learn to do mischief."

LXXX.

STYLE.

"For different styles with different subjects sort,
As different garbs with country town and court."

In the Introduction to this volume, it was stated that the most obvious divisions of Composition, with respect to the nature of its subjects, are the Narrative, the Descriptive, the Didactic, the Persuasive, the Pathetic, and the Argumentative. The Narrative division embraces the relation of facts and events, real or fictitious. The Descriptive division includes descriptions of all kinds. The Didactic division comprehends, as its name implies, all kinds of pieces which are designed to convey instruction. The Pathetic division embraces such writings as are calculated to affect the feelings, or excite the passions; and the Argumentative division includes those only which are addressed to the understanding, with the intention of affecting the judgment. These different divisions of composition are not always preserved distinct, but are sometimes united or mixed. With regard to forms of expression, a writer may express his ideas in various ways, thus laying the foundation of a distinction called STYLE.

Style, is defined by Dr. Blair, to be "the peculiar manner in which a writer expresses his thoughts by words."

Various terms are applied to style to express its character, as a harsh style, a dry style, a tumid or bombastic style, a loose style a terse style, a laconic or a verbose style, a flowing style, a lofty style, an elegant style an epistolary style, a formal style, a familiar style, &c.

The divisions of style, as given by Dr. Blair, are as follows: The diffuse and the concise, the nervous and the feeble, the dry, the plain, the neat, the elegant and the florid, the simple, the affected, and the vehement. These terms are altogether arbitrary, and are not uniformly adopted in every treatise on rhetoric. Some writers use the terms barren and luxuriant, forcible and vehement, elevated and dignified, idiomatic, easy and animated, &c., in connexion with the terms, or some of the terms, employed by Dr. Blair.

The character of style, and the term by which it is designated, depends partly on the clearness and fulness with which the idea is expressed, partly on the degree of ornament or of figurative language employed, and partly on the nature of the ideas themselves.

The terms concise, diffuse, nervous, and feeble, refer to the clearness, the fulness, and the force with which the idea is expressed. Dry, plain, neat, and florid, are terms used to express the degree of ornament employed; while the character of the thoughts or ideas themselves is expressed by the names of simple or natural, affected and vehement.

A concise * writer compresses his ideas into the fewest words, and these the most expressive.

A diffuse writer unfolds his idea fully, by placing it in a variety of lights.

A nervous writer gives us a strong idea of his meaning—his words are always expressive—every phrase and every figure renders the picture which he would set before us more striking and complete.

A feeble writer has an indistinct view of his subject; unmeaning words and loose epithets escape him; his expressions are vague and general, his arrangements indistinct, and our conception of his meaning will be faint and confused.

---

* Under the head of Conciseness in style may be noticed what is called the *Laconic Style*, from the inhabitants of Laconia, who were remarkable for using few words. As an instance of that kind of style, may be mentioned the celebrated reply of Leonidas king of Sparta to Xerxes, who, with his army of over a million of men, was opposed by Leonidas, with only three hundred. When Xerxes sent to him with the haughty direction to lay down his arms, the Spartan king replied, with characteristic brevity, "Come and take them."

Another instance of the same is afforded in the celebrated letter of Dr. Franklin to Mr. Strahan, which is in these words:

"Philadelphia, July 5th, 1775.

"Mr. Strahan,

"You are a member of that Parliament, and have formed part of that majority, which has condemned my native country to destruction.

"You have begun to burn our towns, and to destroy their inhabitants.

"Look at your hands, — they are stained with the blood of your relations and your acquaintances.

"You and I were long friends; you are at present my enemy, and I am yours.

"Benjamin Franklin."

A dry writer uses no ornament of any kind, and, content with being understood, aims not to please the fancy or the ear.

A plain writer employs very little ornament; he observes perspicuity, propriety, purity, and precision in his language, but attempts none of the graces of composition. A dry writer is incapable of ornament, — a plain writer goes not in pursuit of it.

A neat writer is careful in the choice of his words, and the graceful collocation of them. His sentences are free from the encumbrances of superfluous words, and his figures are short and accurate, rather than bold and glowing.

An elegant writer possesses all the graces of ornament, — polished periods, figurative language, harmonious expressions, and a great degree of purity in the choice of his words, all characterized by perspicuity and propriety. He is one, in short, who delights the fancy and the ear, while he informs the understanding.

A florid or flowery writer is characterized by excess of ornament; and seems to be more intent on beauty of language than solidity of thought.

A simple or natural writer is distinguished by simplicity of plan; he makes his thoughts appear to rise naturally from his subject; he has no marks of art in his expressions, and although he may be characterized by great richness both of language and imagination, he appears to write in that way not because he had studied it, but because it is the mode of expression most natural to him.

An affected writer is the very reverse of a simple one. He uses words in uncommon meanings — employs pompous expressions — and his whole manner is characterized by singularity rather than by beauty.

A vehement writer uses strong expressions — is characterized by considerable warmth of manner — and presents his ideas clearly and fully before us.*

The following directions are given by Dr. Blair for attaining a good style:

The first direction is, study clear ideas of the subject on which you are to write or speak. What we conceive clearly and feel strongly, we naturally express with clearness and strength.

Secondly, to the acquisition of a good style, frequency of composing is indispensably necessary. But it is not every kind of composition that will improve style. By a careless and hasty habit of writing, a bad style will be acquired. In the beginning, therefore, we ought to write slowly and with much care. Facility and speed are the fruit of experience.

Thirdly, acquaintance with the style of the best authors is peculiarly requisite. Hence a just taste will be formed, and a copious fund of words supplied on every subject. No exercise, perhaps, will be found more useful for acquiring a proper style, than translating some passage from an eminent author in our own words, and then comparing what we have written with the style of the author. Such an exercise will show us our defects, will teach us to correct them, and, from the variety of expression which it will exhibit, will conduct us to that which is most beautiful.

Fourthly, caution must be used against servile imitation of any author whatever. Desire of imitating hampers genius, and generally produces stiffness of expression. They who copy an author closely, commonly copy his faults as well as his beauties. It is much better to have something of our own, though of moderate beauty, than to shine in borrowed ornaments which will at last betray the poverty of our genius.

---

* The student who would see the subject of style treated with great clearness and beauty, will find it treated with much elegance and ability in "*Newman's Rhetorick.*" His remarks on vivacity of style are particularly recommended to the careful study of the learner.

Fifthly, always adapt your* style to the subject, and likewise to the capacity of your hearers or readers. When we are to write or to speak, we should previously fix in our minds a clear idea of the end aimed at; keep this steadily in view, and adapt our style to it. †

Lastly, let not attention to style engross us* so much, as to prevent a higher degree of attention to the thoughts. He is a contemptible writer, who looks not beyond the dress of language; who lays not the chief stress upon his matter, and employs not such ornaments of style as are manly not foppish.

LXXXI.

DIRECTIONS TO STUDENTS IN REVISING AND CORRECTING THEIR COMPOSITIONS, BEFORE THEY ARE PRESENTED TO THE TEACHER.

Read over your exercise to ascertain, 1. whether the words are correctly spelled; 2. the pauses and capital letters are properly used; 3. that the possessive case is correctly written with the apostrophe and the letter *s*; 4. the hyphen placed between the parts of a compound word, and also used at the end of the line when part of the word is in one line and another part in the succeeding line (recollecting, in this case, that *the letters of the same syllable must all be written in the same line*); 5. that the marks of quotation are inserted when you have borrowed a sentence or an expression from any one else; 6. whether the pronouns are all of the same number with their antecedents, and the verbs of the same number with their nominatives; 7. whether you can get rid of some of the "ands" in your exercise, by means of the rules laid down in Lesson XX., and whether some other words may not be omitted without weakening the expression, and also

---

* The change of persons in these rules, if not absolutely faulty, is certainly inelegant. The language is literally taken from the abridgment of Dr. Blair's Rhetorick.

† Two of the greatest faults that can be committed in writing consist in degrading a subject naturally elevated, by low expressions; — and the expressing a mean or trivial idea by high sounding epithets. The former is called *Bathos*; — and the latter *Bombast*.

The student who wishes for specimens of the various kinds of style mentioned above, will find quite a collection of them arranged under their appropriate heads, for examples in rhetoric, in a volume recently prepared by Mrs. L. C. Tuthill and printed and published by S. Babcock, of New Haven, called "The Young Ladies Reader." It was the author's design to insert such specimens in this volume, but he finds it necessary to reserve the space which they would occupy for other matter which he deems more important to the completion of his plan. For the same reason he has omitted the specimens which he intended to present in the respective departments of Narrative, Descriptive, Didactic, Pathetic, and Argumentative writing.

whether you have introduced all the words necessary for the full expression of your ideas; 8. whether you have repeated the same word in the same sentence, or in any sentence near it, and have thus been betrayed into a tautology (See Lesson XXII.); 9. whether you cannot divide some of your long sentences into shorter ones, and thereby better preserve the unity of the sentence (See Lesson XXXI.); and lastly, whether part or parts of your exercise may not be divided into separate paragraphs.

The following rules must also be observed.

1. No abbreviations are allowable in prose, and numbers (except in dates) must be expressed in words, not in figures.
2. In all cases, excepting where despatch is absolutely necessary, the character &, and others of a similar nature, must not be used, but the whole word must be written out.
3. The letters of the same syllable must always be written in the same line. When there is not room in a line for *all* the letters of a syllable, they must *all* be carried into the next line; and when a word is divided by placing one or more of the syllables in one line, and the remainder in the following line, the hyphen must always be placed at the end of the former line.
4. The title of the piece must always be in a line by itself, and should be written in larger letters than the exercise itself.
5. The exercise should be commenced not at the extreme left hand of the line, but a little towards the right. Every separate paragraph should also commence in the same way.
6. The crotchets or brackets which enclose a parenthesis should be used as sparingly as possible. Their place may often be supplied by commas.

Suggestions to Teachers with regard to the written exercises of Students.

1. Examine the exercise in reference to all those points laid down in the directions for students in reviewing and correcting their compositions. (See page 303.)

2. Merits for composition should be predicated on their neatness, correctness, (in the particulars stated in the directions to pupils, page 303), length, style, &c.; but the highest merits should be given for the strongest evidence of intellect in the production of ideas, and original sentiments and forms of expression.

3. Words that are misspelt, should be spelled by the whole class, and those words which are frequently misspelt should

be recorded in a book kept for that purpose, and occasionally spelt on the slate by the class.

4. Keep a book in which the student may have the privilege to record such compositions as are of superior merit. This book should be kept in the hands of the teacher, and remain the permanent property of the institution. This will have an excellent effect, especially if additional merits are given for the recording of a composition.

5. A short lecture on the subject of the composition assigned to a class, showing its bearings, its divisions, and the manner in which it should be treated, will greatly facilitate their progress, and interest them in the exercise.

6. Have a set of arbitrary marks, which should be explained and understood by the class, by which the exercise should be corrected. This is, in fact, nothing less than a method of short hand, and will save the trouble of much writing.

7. *Insist* upon the point, that the exercise should be written in the student's *best hand*, with care, and without haste. For this purpose, ample time should always be allowed for the production of the exercise. A week at least, if not a fortnight, should intervene between the assigning and the requiring of the exercise. Negligence in the mechanical execution, will induce the neglect of the more important qualities.

8. Require the compositions to be written on alternate pages, leaving one page blank, for such remarks as may be suggested by the exercise, or for supplying such words or sentences as may have accidentally been omitted.

9. In correcting the exercises, care should be taken to preserve as much as possible the ideas which the pupil intended to express, making such alterations only as are necessary to give them clearness, unity, strength, and harmony, and a proper connexion with the subject, for it is the student's *own idea* which ought to be "*taught* how to shoot." An idea thus humored will thrive better than one which is not a native of the soil.

10. It is recommended that a uniformity be required in the size and quality of the paper of the exercises of the class — that the name (real or fictitious) of the writer, together with the date and number of the composition, be placed conspicuously on the back of the exercise. The writing should

be plain and without ornament, so that, no room being left for flourish or display, the principal attention of each student may be devoted to the language and the sentiments of his performances. It is also recommended, that the paper on which the exercise is written be a *letter* sheet folded once, or in quarto form, making four leaves or eight pages. This form is of use, especially in the earlier stages of his progress, because it enables him more easily to *fill a page,* and encourages him with the idea that he is making progress in his exercise. In the writing of compositions, a task to which all students address themselves with reluctance, nothing should be omitted by the teacher, however trivial it may at first appear, by which he may stimulate the student to exertion.

11. Accommodate the corrections to the style of the student's own production. An aim at too great correctness may possibly cramp the genius too much, by rendering the student timid and diffident; or perhaps discourage him altogether, by producing absolute despair of arriving at any degree of perfection. For this reason, the teacher should show the student where he has erred, either in the thought, the structure of the sentence, the syntax, or the choice of words. Every alteration, as has already been observed, should differ as little as possible from what the student has written; as giving an entire new cast to the thought and expression will lead him into an unknown path not easy to follow, and divert his mind from that original line of thinking which is natural to him.

12. In large institutions, where a class in composition is numerous, the teacher may avail himself of the assistance of the more advanced students, by requiring them to inspect the exercises of the younger. This must be managed with great delicacy; and no allusion be allowed to be made out of the recitation room, by the inspector, to the errors or mistakes which he has discovered. He should be required to note *in pencil,* his corrections and remarks, and sign his own name (also in pencil) to the exercise under that of the writer, to show that he is responsible for the corrections.*

---

* Instead of a written exercise, the teacher may, with advantage, occasionally present to the student a piece selected from some good writer; requiring him to present a rhetorical analysis of the same. This analysis should comprehend the following operations:

Parsing.

Punctuation.

The preceding exercise is presented merely to show the mode in which, in conformity with the suggestions just made, the student's compositions may be corrected. The exercise is one of a class of very young students By this example, the teacher will become acquainted with a set of arbitrary marks for the correction of errors, which may easily be explained to a class, and when understood will save the teacher much writing.

Thus, when a word is misspelt or incorrectly written, it will be sufficient to draw a horizontal line under it, as in the following exercise. If a capital is incorrectly used, or is wanted instead of a small letter, a short perpendicular mark is used. When entire words or expressions are to be altered, they are surrounded with black lines, and the correct expression is written on the blank page on the left. When merely the order of the words is to be altered, figures are written over the words designating the order in which they are to be read.

Transposition.

Synonymes, collected, applied, defined, distinguished, and illustrated.

Variety of expression, phrases generalized, particularized, translated from Latin to Saxon derivatives, and the reverse, expanded, compressed.

Figures of speech analyzed.

Students of higher grade may also be exercised in the *Logical Analysis* of the same subject, noticing the subject with its scope, topics, method and lastly in a *Critical Analysis*, relating to the choice of words.

Structure of the sentences.
Style.
Eloquence.
Ideas.
Errors.
Beauties.

} Of these he will give the general character, with a particular analysis.

It was a beautiful evening, in the month of August, when I alighted from my carraige, at the house of [my] friend in the picturesque village of M. The broad and beautiful bay lay stretched out with its calm and glossy bosom to the west, while around me, in the distance might be seen little cottages trees, and hills, forming a most beautiful scenery. The setting Sun threw his golden beams upon the water, which did not look now like the grave of human beings.

Tempted by the beauty of the evening, I took a walk along the beach with [my] friend. During the conversation, he [remarked, if you please I will relate] the account of a shipwreck which happened here a short time ago. It was on a night when the [tempests] seemed to be at war with other, [when] one of the vessels belonging to this port [might be] seen approaching the coast, making signals of distress. Soon notwithstanding the severity of the weather a considerable number were gathered on the beach, for there were many expecting friends, and [the] fears [they felt] for their safety together with [their] pity for the sufferers, induced them to use every exertion for the safety of those on board.

The night was such, that it would have been almost instant death to [have] ventured upon the waters in an

carriage a
stretched
west; distance,
Want of Unity.
a
related
elements
each that
was
of people
;

See Grammar, Part II., No. 108.

Corrections	Text
	open boat, and we could render no assistance [to them.]
mingled	The shrieks of the unhappy persons, [mixed] with the roar of the wind and the driving of the rain, seemed more like a frightful dream than [the] dreadful reality.
ship could long survive such a tempest, and we were soon convinced that the vessel before us	But no [vessel could stand such a tempest long, and it was soon evident to us that she] was fast going to pieces.
launched	At length, as the storm abated [a little], four hardy fishermen [got out] their little boat,
determining	[determined] to do their best
though it should endanger	to save the sufferers, even [if it endangered] their own lives, while we stood on the shore to render assistance to any who might be saved. After rowing for some time, and making but slow progress, they finally reached the ship, but
(.)	only to find it fast filling with water, One man was floating near, on a small piece of board, with a little girl lashed to him.
were taken into	These [they placed in] the boat, although but little hope could be entertained of their recovery.
Despairing of saving more, the hardy fishermen reached the shore nearly exhausted with fatigue.	[They at last arrived at the shore, despairing of saving any more, and almost worn out with fatigue.]
them, I assisted others in carrying the survivors	While some attended to [the brave fishermen, I and some others carried the persons who had been saved] to the nearest house. The man was indeed dead, but the little girl recovered, and is
to stay	[now staying] with one of those who were the means of saving her life, until her friends can be found

LXXXII.

MARKS USED BY PRINTERS IN THE CORRECTION OF PROOF-SHEETS.

Many mistakes in printing may be avoided, when the printer and the writer clearly understand one another. It is thought it will be useful to present in this volume a view of the manner in which *proof-sheets* are corrected.

On the opposite page is a specimen of a proof-sheet, with the corrections upon it. A little attention will readily enable the student to understand the object of the various marks which it contains, particularly if taken in connexion with the explanation here given.

An inverted letter is indicated by the character and in the mode represented in No. 2.

When a wrong letter is discovered, a line is drawn through it and the proper letter written in the margin, as in No. 1. The correction is made in the same manner when it is desired to substitute one word for another.

If a letter or word is found to be omitted, a caret (∧) is put under its place, and the letter or word to be supplied is written in the margin; as in Nos. 8 and 19.

If there be an omission of several words, or if it is desired to insert a new clause or sentence, which is too long to admit of being written in the side margin, it is customary to indicate by a caret the place of the omission, or for the insertion of the new matter, and to write on the bottom margin the sentence to be supplied, connecting it with the caret by a line drawn from the one to the other; as in No. 15.

If a superfluous word or letter is detected, it is marked out by drawing a stroke through it, and a character which stands for the Latin word *dele* (expunge) is written against it in the margin; as in No. 4.

The transposition of words or letters is indicated as in the three examples marked No. 12.

If two words are improperly joined together, or there is not sufficient space between them, a caret is to be interposed, and a character denoting separation to be marked in the margin opposite; as in No. 6.

If the parts of a word are improperly separated, they are to be linked together by two marks, resembling parentheses placed horizontally, one above and the other beneath the word, as in the manner indicated in No. 20.

Where the spaces between words are too large, this is to be indicated in a similar manner, excepting that instead of *two* marks, as in the case of a word improperly separated, only *one* is employed; as in No. 9.

Where it is desired to make a new paragraph, the appropriate character (¶) is placed at the beginning of the sentence, and also noted in the margin opposite; as in No. 10.

Where a passage has been improperly broken into two paragraphs, the parts are to be hooked together, and the words "*no break*" written opposite in the margin; as in No. 18.

If a word or clause has been marked out or altered, and it is afterwards

1 a THOUGH a vriety of opinions exists as to
the individual by wqom the art of printing was 2
first discovered; yet all authorities concur in
admitting Peter Schoeffer to be the person 3 Caps
who invented cast metal types, having learned
4 the art of ~~of~~ *cutting* the letters from the Gut-
5 tembergs, he is also supposed to have been
6 # the first whoengraved on copper plates. The 7
following testimony is preseved in the family, 8 r/
9 by Jo. Fred. Faustus of Ascheffenburg:
10 ¶ ¶ "Peter Schoeffer of Gernshiem, perceiving 3 Caps
11 his master Fausts design, and being himself
12 tr. desirous ardently to improve the art, found
out (by the good providence of God) the
method of cutting ~~(incidendi)~~ the characters 13 stet
21 in a *matrix*, that the letters might easily be
, singly *cast*; instead of bieng *cut*. He pri- 12 ei/
14 vately *cut matrices* for the whole alphabet·
15 Faust was so pleased with the contrivance
that he promised Peter to give him his only 17 wf.
daughter Christina in marriage, a promise 3 Ital
which he soon after performed. 18 no break
19 as But there were many difficulties at first
with these *letters*, as there had been before 3 Rom
with wooden ones, the metal being too soft 3 Ital
to support the force of the im pression: but 20
this defect was soon remedied, by mixing
a substance with the metal which sufficiently 12 tr.
6 hardened it,"

and when he showed his master the letters cast from these matrices,

thought best to retain it, it is dotted beneath, and the word *stet* (let it stand) written in the margin; as in No. 13.

The punctuation marks are variously indicated;—the comma and semicolon are noted in the margin with a perpendicular line on the right, as in No. 21; the colon and period have a circle drawn round them, as in the two examples marked No. 5; the apostrophe is placed between two convergent marks like the letter V, as in No. 11; the note of admiration and interrogation, as also the parenthesis, the bracket, and the reference marks, in the same manner as the apostrophe; the hyphen between two perpendicular lines, as in No. 7, and the dash the same as the hyphen.

Capital letters are indicated by three horizontal lines drawn beneath them; small capitals, by two horizontal lines; Italic by a single line; with the words *Cap.*, *S. Cap.*, and *Ital.* written in the margin. When a word is improperly italicised, it should be underscored, and *Rom.* written against it in the margin. Examples, illustrative of all these cases, will be found under No. 3.

A broken line is indicated by a simple stroke of the pen in the margin, drawn either horizontally, or as indicated in No. 16.

A broken letter is indicated by a stroke of the pen drawn under it, and a cross in the margin.

When a letter from a *wrong font*, that is, of a different size from the rest, appears in a word, it is to be noted by passing the pen through it, and writing *wf.* in the margin, as in No. 17.

A space which requires to be depressed is to be marked in the margin by a perpendicular line between two horizontal lines, as in No 14.

Different names are given to the various sizes of types, of which the following are most used in book printing.

Pica.*	Abcdefghijklmnopqrstuvwxyz.
Small Pica.	Abcdefghijklmnopqrstuvwxyz.
Long Primer.	Abcdefghijklmnopqrstuvwxyz.
Bourgeois.	Abcdefghijklmnopqrstuvwxyz.
Brevier.	Abcdefghijklmnopqrstuvwxyz.
Minion.	Abcdefghijklmnopqrstuvwxyz.
Nonpareil.	Abcdefghijklmnopqrstuvwxyz.
Agate.	Abcdefghijklmnopqrstuvwxyz.
Pearl.	Abcdefghijklmnopqrstuvwxyz.
Diamond.	Abcdefghijklmnopqrstuvwxyz.

As it may be interesting to know the frequency with which some of the letters occur, it may here be stated that, in the printer's cases, for every hundred of the letter *q* there are two hundred of the letter *x*, four hundred of *k*, eight hundred of *b*, fifteen hundred of *c*, four thousand each of *i*, *n*, *o*, and *s*, four thousand two hundred and fifty of *a*, four thousand five hundred of *t*, and six thousand of the letter *e*.

---

* The next two sizes of type larger than the above are called English and Great Primer, and all larger than these, Double Pica, two Line Pica, Three Line Pica, Fifteen Line Pica, &c., according as they exceed the Pica in size.

LXXXIII.

TECHNICAL TERMS RELATING TO BOOKS.

A book is said to be in Folio when one sheet of paper makes but two leaves, or four pages. When the sheet makes four leaves or eight pages, it is said to be in Quarto form; eight leaves or sixteen pages, in Octavo; twelve leaves or twenty-four pages, Duodecimo; eighteen leaves, Octodecimo. These terms are thus abbreviated: fol. for folio; 4to for quarto; 8vo for octavo; 12mo for duodecimo; 18mo, 24s, 32s, 64s, signify respectively that the sheet is divided into eighteen, twenty-four, &c., leaves.

The Title-page is the first page, containing the title; and a picture facing it is called the Frontispiece.

Vignette is a French term, used to designate the descriptive or ornamental picture, sometimes placed on the title-page of a book, sometimes at the head of a chapter, &c.

The Running-title is the word or sentence at the top of every page, generally printed in capitals or Italic letters.

When the page is divided into several parts by a blank space, or a line running from the top to the bottom, each division is called a column; as in bibles, dictionaries, spelling-books, newspapers, &c.

The letters A, B, C, &c., and A2, A3, &c., at the bottom of the page, are marks for directing the book-binder in collecting and folding the sheets.

The *catch-word* is the word at the bottom of the page, on the right hand, which is repeated at the beginning of the next, in order to show that the pages succeed one another in proper order. It is seldom inserted in books recently printed.

The Italic words in the Old and New Testaments are those which have no corresponding words in the original Hebrew or Greek, but they were added by the translators to complete or explain the sense.

LXXXIV.

OBITUARY NOTICE.

An Obituary Notice is designed to commemorate the virtues which distinguished an individual recently deceased. Writings of this kind are generally fugitive in their character, and seldom survive the occasion which called them forth. They are not designed to present many of the events of the life of the individual, but rather a general summary of his character. An obituary notice is a kind of writing generally confined to periodical publications, and destitute of the dignity of biography, and the minute detail of memoirs.

Model.

OBITUARY NOTICE OF DR. MATIGNON.

The Rev. Francis A. Matignon, D. D., who died on the 19th of September, 1818, was born in Paris, November 10th, 1753. Devoted to letters and religion from his earliest youth, his progress was rapid and his piety conspicuous. He attracted the notice of the learned faculty, as he passed through the several grades of classical and theological studies; and, having taken the degree of Bachelor of Divinity, he was ordained a Priest, on Saturday, the 19th of September, 1778, the very day of the month and week, which, forty years after, was to be his last. In the year 1782, he was admitted a licentiate, and received the degree of Doctor of Divinity from the college of the Sorbonne in 1785. At this time he was appointed Regius Professor of Divinity in the college of Navarre, in which seminary he performed his duties for several years, although his state of health was not good.

His talents and piety had recommended him to the notice of a Prelate in great credit, (the Cardinal De Brienne,) who obtained for him the grant of an annuity from the king, Louis the Sixteenth, which was sufficient for all his wants, established him in independence, and took away all anxiety for the future. But the ways of Providence are inscrutable to the wisest and best of the children of men. The revolution, which dethroned his beloved monarch, and stained the altar of his God with the blood of holy men, drove Dr. Matignon an exile from his native shores. He fled to England, where he remained several months, and then returned to France, to prepare for a voyage to the United States. He landed in Baltimore, and was appointed by Bishop Carroll Pastor of the Catholic Church in Boston, at which place he arrived August 20th, 1792.

The talents of Dr. Matignon were of the highest order. In him were united a sound understanding, a rich and vigorous imagination, and a logical precision of thought. His learning was extensive, critical, and profound, and all his productions were deeply cast, symmetrically formed, and beautifully colored. The fathers of the church, and the great divines of every age were his familiar friends. His divinity was not merely speculative, nor merely practical; it was the blended influence of thought, feeling, and action. He had learned divinity as a scholar, taught it as a professor, felt it as a worshipper, and diffused it as a faithful pastor. His genius and his virtues were understood; for the wise bowed to his superior knowledge, and the humble caught the spirit of his devotions. With the unbelieving and doubtful, he reasoned with the mental strength of the apostle Paul; and he charmed back the penitential wanderer with the kindness and affection o. John the Evangelist. His love for mankind flowed in the purest current, and his piety caught a glow from the intensity of his feelings. Rigid and scrupulous to himself, he was charitable and indulgent to others. To youth, in a particular manner, he was forgiving and fatherly. With him the tear of penitence washed away the stains of error; for he had gone up to the fountains of human nature, and knew all its weaknesses. Many, retrieved from folly and vice, can bear witness how deeply he was skilled in the science of parental government; that science so little understood, and, for want of which, so many evils arise. It is a proof of a great mind, not to be soured by misfortunes nor narrowed by any particular pursuit. Dr. Matignon, if possible, grew milder and more indulgent, as he advanced in years. The storms of life had broken the heart of the man, but out of its wounds gushed the tide of sympathy and universal Christian charity. The woes of life crush the feeble, make more stupid the dull, and more vindictive the proud; but the great mind and contrite soul are expanded with purer benevolence, and warmed with brighter hopes, by suffering, — knowing, that through tribulation and anguish the diadem of the saint is won.

To him whose heart has sickened at the selfishness of mankind, and who has seen the low and trifling pursuits of the greater proportion of human beings, it is sweet and refreshing to contemplate the philosopher, delighted with the visions of other worlds, and ravished with the harmonies of nature, pursuing his course abstracted from the bustle around him; but how much nobler is the course of the moral and Christian philosopher, who teaches the ways of God to man. He holds a holy communion with Heaven, walks with the Creator in the garden at every hour in the day, without wishing to hide himself. While he muses, the spirit burns within him, and the high influences of the inspiration force him to proclaim to the children of men the deep wonders of divine love.

But this contemplation must give angels pleasure, when they behold this purified and elevated being dedicating his services, not to the mighty, not to the wise, but to the humblest creatures of sorrow and suffering. Have we not seen our friend leaving these sublime contemplations, and entering the habitations of want and woe? relieving their temporal necessities, administering the consolations of religion to the despairing soul in the agonies of dissolution? Yes, the sons of the forest in the most chilling climates, the tenants of the hovel, the erring and the profligate, can bear witness with what patience, earnestness, constancy, and mildness, he labored to make them better.

In manners, Dr. Matignon was an accomplished gentleman, possessing that kindness of heart and delicacy of feeling, which made him study the wants and anticipate the wishes of all he knew. He was well acquainted with the politest courtesies of society, for it must not, in accounting for his accomplishments, be forgotten, that he was born and educated in the bosom of refinement; that he was associated with chevaliers and nobles, and was patronized by cardinals and premiers. In his earlier life, it was not uncommon to see ecclesiastics mingling in society with philosophers and courtiers, and still preserving the most perfect apostolic purity in their lives and conversation. The scrutinizing eye of infidel philosophy was upon them, and these unbelievers would have hailed it as a triumph, to have caught them in the slightest deviation from their professions. But no greater proof of the soundness of their faith, or the ardor of their piety, could be asked, than the fact, that, from all the bishops in France at the commencement of the revolution, amounting to one hundred and thirty-eight, but three only were found wanting in integrity and good faith, when they were put to the test; and it was such a test, too, that it could have been supported by religion only. In passing such an ordeal, pride, fortitude, philosophy, and even insensibility would have failed. The whole strength of human nature was shrunken and blasted, when opposed to the besom of the revolution. Then the bravest bowed in terror, or fled in affright; but then these disciples of the lowly Jesus taught mankind how they could suffer for his sake.

Dr. Matignon loved his native country, and always expressed the deepest interests in her fortunes and fate; yet his patriotism never infringed on his philanthropy. He spoke of England, as a great nation which contained much to admire and imitate; and his gratitude kindled at the remembrance of British munificence and generosity to the exiled priests of a hostile nation of different religious creeds.

When Dr. Matignon came to Boston, new trials awaited him. His predecessors in this place wanted either talents, character, or perseverance; and nothing of consequence had been done towards gathering and directing a flock. The good people of New England were something more than suspicious on the subject of his success; they were suspicious of the Catholic doctrines. Their ancestors, from the settlement of the country, had been preaching against the Church of Rome, and their descendants, even the most enlightened, felt a strong impression of undefined and undefinable dislike, if not hatred, towards every papal relation. Absurd and foolish legends of the Pope and his religion were in common circulation, and the prejudice was too deeply rooted to be suddenly eradicated, or even opposed. It required a thorough acquaintance with the world, to know precisely how to meet those sentiments of a whole people. Violence and indiscretion would have destroyed all hopes of success. Ignorance would have exposed the cause to sarcasm and contempt, and enthusiasm, too manifest, would have produced a reäction, that would have plunged the infant establishment in absolute ruin. Dr. Matignon was exactly fitted to encounter all these difficulties. And he saw them, and knew his task, with the discernment of a shrewd politician. With meekness and humility he disarmed the proud; with prudence, learning, and wisdom, he met the captious and slanderous, and so gentle and so just was his course, that even the censorious forgot to watch him, and the malicious were too cunning to attack one armed so strongly in honesty. For four years he sustained the weight of this charge alone, until Providence sent him a coadjutor in the person of the present excellent Bishop Cheverus, who seemed made by nature, and fitted by education and grace, to soothe his griefs by sympathy, (for he too had suffered,) to cheer him by the blandishments of taste and letters, and all congenial pursuits and habits; and, in fact, they were as far identified as two embodied minds could be. These holy seers pursued their religious pilgrimage together, blessing and being blessed, for more than twenty years; and the young Elisha had received a double portion of the spirit, and worn the mantle of his friend and guide, long before the sons of the prophets heard the cry of, *My father, my father, the chariot of Israel and the horsemen thereof* May the survivor find consolation in the religion he teaches, and long be kept on his journey, to bless the cruise of oil in the dwellings of poverty and widowhood, and to cleanse by the power of God the leprosy of the sinful soul.

Far from the sepulchre of his fathers repose the ashes of the good and great Dr. Matignon; but his grave is not as among strangers, for it was watered by the tears of an affectionate flock, and his memory is cherished by all who value learning, honor genius, or love devotion.

The writer of this brief notice offers it, as a faint and rude memorial only of the virtues of the man whose character he venerated. Time must assuage the wounds of grief before he, who loved him most, and knew him best, can attempt his epitaph

LXXXV.

CRITICAL NOTICE.

Select some biographical work; state any impression you may have received of it as to the age, — the contemporaries, — the influence, — the difficulties and advantages of the author, — the style of his narrative, &c

*Example.**

I have selected the Life of Dr. Benjamin Franklin, written by himself, to a late period. The style of the work is simple and concise, which is the peculiar characteristic of all his writings; indeed, his writing principally for the advantage of the people, (though the most elevated ranks may be benefited by his instructions,) accounts for his desire of expressing himself in plain and simple language. The first part of the book, not being intended for public perusal, is written with more minuteness of particulars, than it otherwise would have been; he even apologizes to his son for the familiarity of the style; observing, that "we do not dress for a private company as for a formal ball."

Dr. Franklin was remarkable from his youth for persevering and indefatigable industry. This, with his prudent and reflecting mind, secured him his fame and importance in the world. He early manifested a love of learning, which his humble birth and narrow circumstances allowed him few opportunities of indulging; but when they did offer, he never suffered them to escape unimproved. He was frugal in his mode of life that he might employ his savings in the purchase of books; and diligent at his work, that he might gain time for his studies. Thus, all obstacles were removed in his pursuit of knowledge. We behold him emerging by degrees from obscurity; then advancing more and more into notice and soon taking a high stand in the estimation of his fellow-citizens.

He was continually before the world in various characters. As a natural philosopher, he surpassed all his contemporaries; as a politician, he adhered to his country during her long struggle for independence, and, throughout his political career, was distinguished for his firm integrity and skilful negotiations; as a citizen, his character shines with peculiar lustre; he seems to have examined every thing, to discover how he might add to the happiness of his friends. Philadelphia shows with delight the many institutions he has founded for her advantage, and boasts of the benefits conferred on her sons by his philanthropic zeal. Indeed, to do good was the grand aim of his life. From the midst of his philosophical researches, he descends to attend to the daily interests of his fellow creatures; after bringing down lightning from the clouds, he invents a stove for the comfort of men. In the midst of the honors paid him for

* This is a genuine college exercise, presented at one of our universities a few years ago.

his discovery of the sameness of lightning with electricity, he rejoices in the thought, that the knowledge of this important fact might contribute to the safety of mankind.

After his death, even, his example is of great use; to the young, his self-acquired learning, which procured for him the honorary distinctions of the European universities and philosophical societies, affords a practical illustration of the value of perseverance and industry; his advanced years offer to the aged an excellent model for the occupation of their time. His private life exhibits a splendid catalogue of virtues; to his temperance he owed his long sojourn upon earth; to his resolution and industry, his wide-spread fame; to his sincerity and moderation, the affection of his friends; to his frugality, the means of benevolence; and to his prudence and integrity, the esteem and approbation of his countrymen. The temptation of courts, and the favors heaped upon him by princes and nobles, robbed him of none of these virtues. These he retained, with a contented mind and a clear conscience. till he was summoned to receive his final reward.

LXXXVI.

CRITICISM.

The following criticism by Dr. Blair is here presented that the student may understand the principles by which literary merit is to be estimated. The subject criticised is No. 411 of the Spectator, written by Mr. Addison; of whom Dr. Johnson has said that all who wish to write the English language with elegance should study the pages of Addison.

"Our sight is the most perfect, and most delightful of all our senses."

This sentence is clear, precise, and simple. The author in a few plain words lays down the proposition, which he is going to illustrate. A first sentence should seldom be long, and never intricate.

He might have said, *our sight is the most perfect and the most delightful* But in omitting to repeat the particle *the*, he has been more judicious; for as between *perfect* and *delightful* there is no contrast, such a repetition is unnecessary. He proceeds:

"It fills the mind with the largest variety of ideas, converses with its objects at the greatest distance, and continues the longest in action, without being tired or satiated with its proper enjoyments."

This sentence is remarkably harmonious, and well constructed. It is entirely perspicuous. It is loaded with no unnecessary words. That quality of a good sentence, which we termed its unity, is here perfectly preserved. The members of it also grow, and rise above each other in sound, till it is conducted to one of the most harmonious closes which our language admits. It is moreover figurative without being too much so for the subject. There is no fault in it whatever, except this, the epithet *large*, which he applies to *variety*, is more commonly applied to extent than to number. It is plain, however, that he employed it to avoid the repetition of the word *great*, which occurs immediately afterward.

"The sense of feeling can, indeed, give us a notion of extension, shape, and all other ideas that enter at the eye, except colors; but, at the same time, it is very much straitened and confined in its operations, to the number, bulk, and distance of its particular objects."

But is not every sense confined as much as the sense of feeling, to the number, bulk, and distance of its own objects? The turn of expression is also very inaccurate, requiring the two words, *with regard*, to be inserted after the word *operations*, in order to make the sense clear and intelligible. The epithet *particular* seems to be used instead of *peculiar;* but these words, though often confounded, are of very different import. *Particular* is opposed to *general; peculiar* stands opposed to what is possessed in *common with others.*

"Our sight seems designed to supply all these defects, and may be considered as a more delicate and diffusive kind of touch, that spreads itself over an infinite multitude of bodies, comprehends the largest figures, and brings into our reach some of the most remote parts of the universe."

This sentence is perspicuous, graceful, well arranged, and highly musical Its construction is so similar to that of the second sentence, that, had it immediately succeeded it, the ear would have been sensible of a faulty monotony. But the interposition of a period prevents this effect.

"It is this sense which furnishes the imagination with its ideas; so that, by the pleasures of the imagination or fancy (which I shall use promiscuously) I here mean such as arise from visible objects, either when we have them actually in our view, or when we call up their ideas into our minds by paintings, statues, descriptions, or any the like occasion."

The parenthesis in the middle of this sentence is not clear. It should have been, *terms which I shall use promiscuously;* since the verb *use* does not relate to the pleasures of the imagination, but to the terms, *fancy* and *imagination*, which were meant to be synonymous. To call a painting or a statue *an occasion*, is not accurate; nor is it very proper to speak of *calling up ideas by occasions.* The common phrase, *any such means*, would have been more natural.

"We cannot indeed have a single image in the fancy, that did not make its first entrance through the sight; but we have the power of retaining, altering, and compounding those images which we have once received, into all the varieties of picture and vision, that are most agreeable to the imagination; for, by this faculty, a man in a dungeon is capable of entertaining himself with scenes and landscapes more beautiful than any that can be found in the whole compass of nature."

In one member of this sentence there is an inaccuracy in syntax. It is proper to say, *altering and compounding those images which we have once received, into all the varieties of picture and vision.* But we cannot with propriety say, *retaining them into all the varieties;* yet the arrangement requires this construction. This error might have been avoided by arranging the passage in the following manner: "We have the power of retaining those images which we have once received; and of altering and compounding them into all the varieties of picture and vision." The latter part of the sentence is clear and elegant.

"There are few words in the English language, which are employed in a more loose and uncircumscribed sense than those of the fancy and the imagination."

Except when some assertion of consequence is advanced, these little words, *it is* and *there are*, ought to be avoided, as redundant and enfeebling. The two first words of this sentence, therefore, should have been omitted. The article prefixed to *fancy and imagination* ought also to have been omitted, since he does not mean the powers of *the fancy and the imagination*, but the words only. The sentence should have run thus: "Few words in the English language are employed in a more loose and uncircumscribed sense than fancy and imagination."

"I therefore thought it necessary to fix and determine the notion of these two words, as I intend to make use of them in the thread of my following speculations, that the reader may conceive rightly what is the subject which I proceed upon.

The words *fix* and *determine*, though they may appear so, are not synonymous. We *fix*, what is loose; we *determine*, what is *uncircumscribed*. They may be viewed, therefore, as applied here with peculiar delicacy.

The *notion of these words*, is rather harsh, and is not so commonly used as *the meaning of these words. As I intend to make use of them in the thread of my speculations*, is evidently faulty. A sort of metaphor is improperly mixed with words in their literal sense. *The subject which I proceed upon* is an ungraceful close of a sentence; it should have been, *the subject upon which I proceed.*

"I must therefore desire him to remember, that, by the pleasures of imagination, I mean only such pleasures as arise originally from sight, and that I divide these pleasures into two kinds."

This sentence begins in a manner too similar to the preceding. *I mean only such pleasures*, the adverb *only* is not in its proper place. It is not intended here to qualify the verb *mean*, but *such pleasures;* and ought therefore to be placed immediately after the latter.

"My design being, first of all, to discourse of those primary pleasures of the imagination, which entirely proceed from such objects as are before our eyes; and, in the next place, to speak of those secondary pleasures of the imagination, which flow from the ideas of visible objects, when the objects are not actually before the eye, but are called up into our memories, or formed into agreeable visions of things, that are either absent or fictitious."

Neatness and brevity are peculiarly requisite in the division of a subject. This sentence is somewhat clogged by a tedious phraseology. *My design being, first of all, to discourse—in the next place to speak of—such objects as are before our eyes—things that are either absent or fictitious.* Several words might have been omitted, and the style made more neat and compact.

"The pleasures of the imagination, taken in their full extent, are not so gross as those of sense, nor so refined as those of the understanding."

This sentence is clear and elegant.

"The last are indeed more preferable, because they are founded on some new knowledge or improvement in the mind of man; yet it must be confessed, that those of the imagination are as great and as transporting as the other."

The phrase, *more preferable*, is so palpable an inaccuracy, that we wonder how it could escape the observation of Mr. Addison. The proposition, contained in the last member of this sentence, is neither clearly nor elegantly expressed. *It must be confessed, that those of the imagination are as great and as transporting as the other.* In the beginning of this sentence he has called the pleasures of the understanding *the last;* and he concludes with observing, that those of the imagination are as great and transporting as *the other*. Beside that *the other* makes not a proper contrast with *the last* it is left doubtful whether by *the other* are meant the pleasures of the understanding, or the pleasures of sense; though without doubt it was intended to refer to the pleasures of the understanding only.

"A beautiful prospect delights the soul as much as a demonstration, and a description in Homer has charmed more readers than a chapter in Aristotle."

This is a good illustration of what he had been asserting, and is expressed with that elegance, by which Mr. Addison is distinguished.

"Besides, the pleasures of the imagination have this advantage above those of the understanding, that they are more obvious and more easy to be acquired."

This sentence is unexceptionable.

"It is but opening the eye, and the scene enters."

Though this is lively and picturesque, yet we must remark a small inaccuracy. A *scene* cannot be said to *enter;* an *actor* enters; but a scene *appears* or *presents itself.*

"The colors paint themselves on the fancy, with very little attention of thought or application of mind in the beholder."

This is beautiful and elegant, and well suited to those pleasures of the imagination of which the author is treating.

"We are struck, we know not how, with the symmetry of any thing we see; and immediately assent to the beauty of an object, without inquiring into the particular causes and occasions of it."

We *assent* to the truth of a proposition; but cannot with propriety be said to *assent to the beauty of an object.* In the conclusion, *particular* and *occasions* are superfluous words; and the pronoun *it* is in some measure ambiguous.

"A man of a polite imagination is let into a great many pleasures that the vulgar are not capable of receiving."

The term *polite* is oftener applied to manners, than to the imagination. The use of *that* instead of *which*, is too common with Mr. Addison. Except in cases where it is necessary to avoid repetition, *which* is preferable to *that*, and is undoubtedly so in the present instance.

"He can converse with a picture, and find an agreeable companion in a statue. He meets with a secret refreshment in a description; and often feels a greater satisfaction in the prospect of fields and meadows, than another does in the possession. It gives him indeed a kind of property in every thing he sees; and makes the most rude uncultivated parts of nature administer to his pleasures: so that he looks upon the world, as it were, in another light, and discovers in it a multitude of charms that conceal themselves from the generality of mankind."

This sentence is easy, flowing, and harmonious. We must, however, observe a slight inaccuracy. *It gives him a kind of property*—to this *it* there is no antecedent in the whole paragraph. To discover its connexion, we must look back to the third sentence preceding, which begins with *a man of a polite imagination.* This phrase, *polite imagination*, is the only antecedent to which *it* can refer; and even this is not a proper antecedent, since it stands in the genitive case as the qualification only of *a man.*

"There are, indeed, but very few who know how to be idle and innocent, or have a relish of any pleasures that are not criminal: every diversion they take is at the expense of some one virtue or another, and their very first step out of business is into vice or folly."

This sentence is truly elegant, musical, and correct.

"A man should endeavor, therefore, to make the sphere of his innocent pleasures as wide as possible, that he may retire into them with safety, and find in them such a satisfaction as a wise man would not blush to take."

This also is a good sentence and exposed to no objection.

"Of this nature are those of the imagination, which do not require such a bent of thought as is necessary to our more serious employments; nor, at the same time, suffer the mind to sink into that indolence and remissness, which are apt to accompany our more sensual delights; but like a gentle exercise to the faculties, awaken from sloth and idleness, without putting them upon any labor or difficulty."

The beginning of this sentence is incorrect. *Of this nature*, says he, *are those of the imagination.* It might be asked, of what nature? For the preceding sentence had not described the nature of any class of pleasures

He had said that it was every man's duty to make the spnere of his innocent pleasures as extensive as possible, that within this sphere he might find a safe retreat and laudable satisfaction. The transition, therefore, is loosely made. It would have been better, if he had said, "this advantage we gain," or "this satisfaction we enjoy," by means of the pleasures of the imagination. The rest of the sentence is correct.

"We might here add, that the pleasures of the fancy are more conducive to health than those of the understanding, which are worked out by dint of thinking, and attended with too violent a labor of the brain.

Worked out by dint of thinking, is a phrase which borders too nearly on the style of common conversation, to be admitted into polished composition.

"Delightful scenes, whether in nature, painting, or poetry, have a kindly influence on the body, as well as the mind, and not only serve to clear and brighten the imagination, but are able to disperse grief and melancholy, and to set the animal spirits in pleasing and agreeable motions. For this reason Sir Francis Bacon, in his Essay upon Health, has not thought it improper to prescribe to his reader a poem or a prospect, where he particularly dissuades him from knotty and subtile disquisitions, and advises him to pursue studies that fill the mind with splendid and illustrious objects, as histories, fables, and contemplations of nature."

In the latter of these two periods a member is out of its place. *Where he particularly dissuades him from knotty and subtile disquisitions*, ought to precede *has not thought it improper to prescribe, &c.*

"I have in this paper, by way to introduction, settled the notion of those pleasures of the imagination, which are the subject of my present undertaking, and endeavored by several considerations to recommend to my readers the pursuit of those pleasures: I shall in my next paper examine the several sources from whence these pleasures are derived."

These two concluding sentences furnish examples of proper collocation of circumstances. We formerly showed that it is difficult so to dispose them, as not to embarrass the principal subject. Had the following incidental circumstances, *by way of introduction—by several considerations—in this paper—in the next paper*, been placed in any other situation, the sentence would have been neither so neat, nor so clear, as it is on the present construction.

LXXXVII.

BIOGRAPHICAL SKETCH.

Example.

BIANCA CAPELLO.

Bianca, descended from the noble house of the Capelli, at Venice, and daughter of Bartolomeo Capello, was born in 1545. Her childhood and early youth passed in the retirement of her father's palace, where, according to the custom of the country, she conversed only with her family and relations.

Opposite to the palace of the Capelli was the house of the Salviati, where, in 1565, Bianca, having entered her twentieth year, attracted, by the charms of her person, the attention of a young Florentine, by the name of Pietro Buonaventuri, whose birth was obscure, and who served in the family of the Salviati in the capacity of a clerk. Indebted more to nature than to fortune, possessing a fine person, insinuating manners, and an aspiring temper, Pietro secured the affections of Bianca, and they were privately married. It is not our present purpose to pursue the narrative of her adventures, which finally led to a separation from her husband, nor the story of her connexion with the house of Medici. Leaving these details to the historian, we propose to present merely those traits of her character by which she was peculiarly distinguished.

On a survey of the life of Bianca Capello, whatever may be thought of the qualities of her heart, which, it must be confessed, are doubtful, it is impossible not to be struck with the powers of her mind, by which, amidst innumerable obstacles, she maintained, undiminished, through life, that ascendancy which her personal charms had first given her over the affections of a capricious prince. The determination and perseverance with which she prosecuted her plans, sufficiently testify her energy and talents: if, in effecting the end proposed, she was little scrupulous respecting the means, the Italian character, the circumstances of the times, the disadvantages attending her entrance into the world, subjected to artifice, and entangled in fraud, must not be forgotten. Brought up in retirement and obscurity, thrown at once into the most trying situations, her prudence, her policy, her self-government, her knowledge of the human mind, and the means of subjecting it, are not less rare than admirable. She possessed singular penetration in discerning characters, and the weaknesses of those with whom she conversed, which she skilfully adapted to her purposes. By an eloquence, soft, insinuating, and powerful, she prevailed over her friends; while, by ensnaring them in their own devices, she made her enemies subservient to her views. Such was the fascination of her manners, that the prejudices of those by whom she was hated, yielded, in her presence, to admiration and delight: nothing seemed too arduous for her talents; inexhaustible in resource, whatever she undertook she found means to accomplish. If she was an impassioned character, she was uniformly animated by ambition. In her first engagement with Buonaventuri, she seems to have been influenced by a restless enterprising temper, disgusted with inactivity, rather than by love: through every scene of her connexion with the duke, her motives are sufficiently obvious. With a disposition like that of Bianca, sensibility and tenderness, the appropriate virtues of the sex, are not to be expected. Real greatness has in it a character of simplicity, with which subtlety and craft are wholly incompatible: the genius of Bianca was such as fitted her to take a part in political intrigues, to succeed in courts, and rise to the pinnacle of power; but, stained with cruelty, and debased by falsehood, if her talents excite admiration, they produce no esteem; and while her accomplishments dazzle the mind, they fail to interest the heart.

Majestic in stature, beautiful in her person, animated, eloquent, and insinuating, she commanded all hearts; a power of which the tranquillity and silence of her own enabled her to avail herself to the utmost. Ill health impaired her beauty at an early period; many portraits of her remain, in all of which she is represented as grand-duchess, when the first bloom of her charms had faded. A beautiful portrait of her, in the ducal robes, is preserved in the palace of the Capelli, at Padua; several are likewise to be found in the Palazzo Pelti, at Florence; and one, also, said to be still superior, in Palazzo Caprara, at Bologna.

LXXXVIII.

COLLEGE EXERCISES.*

The preceding lessons, it is thought, contain most, if not all, of the principles necessary to be understood by the student to prepare him for the performance of such exercises as are generally prescribed in an academic course. The following specimens of the exercises of those to whom academic honors have been awarded, are presented, with the hope that they may be useful to those who may hereafter have similar exer cises to perform.

CONFERENCE, COLLOQUY, AND DIALOGUE.

A Conference is a discoursing between two or more, for the purpose of instruction, consultation, or deliberation; or, it may, in a technical sense, be defined, an examination of a subject by comparison. It is a species of conversation, and is generally confined to particular subjects and des criptions of persons.

A Dialogue signifies a speech between two persons. It is mostly ficti-tious, and is written as if it were spoken. It is always formal and contains an assertion or question with a reply and a rejoinder.

A Colloquy is a species of dialogue. It literally signifies, the act of talking together and is not confined to any particular number of persons nor subjects.

Example of a Theme.

"Est Deus in nobis." OVID, Lib. I.

Metaphysical speculations are, of all others, the most wild and most exposed to error. The relation between volition and action, mind and body,

* The specimens and models here presented, are taken, by the consent of the respective authors, from the files of one of our most respectable uni versities. To the highly respected President of that university, the author is greatly indebted for the kind facilities rendered, by which he was enabled to examine the files of that institution, and to select such as he had been permitted to copy. He does not, however, consider himself authorized more particularly to name the institution nor its presiding officer. It is due, also, to the gentlemen whose juvenile exercises he has been permitted here to present, to state, that their reluctant permission has been given with the understanding that their names will not be mentioned in connexion with the exercises. The question may, perhaps, be asked, why exercises of this kind are presented at all. To this the author replies, that a know-ledge of what has been done on any given occasion cannot be without its use to those who are called upon to exert their talents on any similar occa sion; and if any of the following exercises should be considered as speci mens, rather than models, the author can only say, that he deems examples of this kind, which can be emulated by the student, more encouraging than faultless models. It is the business of the teacher to infuse that spirit which hall adopt as its motto — "*Excelsior*"

the decisive influence of the former on the motions of the latter, and how this intercourse obtains, are subtleties, the investigation of which has ever baffled the ingenuity of philosophers. Nor is reasoning on this subject in any respect conclusive. It sets out from hypothethis, and, instead of leading to any just conclusions, usually leaves the inquirer in a labyrinth of doubt.

In spite of these obstacles, however, there is something in the mind of man that takes a delight in diving into these mysteries; a curiosity which is always alive and restless, grasping at some hidden truth; a fancy that is prone to explore an unknown path, — that loves to float in whimsical reveries. "Est Deus in nobis."

On our first introduction to this world, whether our minds are free from ideas and vacant, "like a piece of white paper," as Mr. Locke quaintly phrases it; and, if this be the fact, whether, as originally cast by the creator, they differ as widely in quality, as the various kinds of white paper from the mill; — are questions which have not yet been determined. When we contemplate society, we are struck with the diversities of character which it discloses. We ask ourselves, how it happens, that such varieties of genius exist; how it is, that one person has a mathematical, another a poetical turn of mind; that one has an imagination, that "bounds from earth to heaven, and sports in the clouds," and another possesses a mind that gropes in the deepest recesses of philosophy, and learns to conceive the most abstruse truth. We wonder for a while, and presently conclude, that all the peculiarities of each mind are coeval with its existence, and impressed by the Deity.

For my own part, although I consider these speculations to be as unimportant, as they are doubtful, they frequently find an indulgence in my mind. Nor are they altogether fruitless. They answer the purpose of a romance. They amuse the imagination, and occupy the vacant thought of a leisure hour. I am inclined to the belief, that, as our minds may be considered to emanate from the same creative spirit, they bear a nearer resemblance to each other than we are apt to imagine. It is probable that our minds are all equally endowed, and, at first, are precisely the same. That they are susceptible of like impressions. And if a case be supposed, where two persons could be brought up in such a manner, that every external circumstance, having the least effect on the senses, could be precisely the same to each, that their dispositions would be in all respects similar; indeed, the men would be perfectly alike. This hypothesis is reconcilable with the maxim (under existing circumstances) that no two persons were ever in every respect alike. For, in the earliest state of the mind, it is so susceptible of impressions, that the slightest circumstances vary its direction and character. Frivolous causes produce the most important and lasting effects. Whence, we may readily account for the numberless shades of character, as resulting, not from an original difference in minds, but from the secret operation of physical causes.

It is curious to observe the relation between the senses of seeing and hearing, and the mind, and how sensibly the imperfections of the former tend to sharpen the faculties of the latter. So uniform has this rule held within the circle of my own acquaintance, that I am apt to conceive one's intellectual powers merely from a knowledge of his faculties of sight. One who is near-sighted, for example, usually possesses mental powers that are clear and nervous. In him, on the contrary, whose vision is bounded only by the horizon, we should look for a mind capable of pleasing in the arts of poetry and fiction; for he embraces at a glance all the beauties of nature. A retentive memory is also naturally associated with one who hears and sees with difficulty. Thus, by a little refinement, (I think reasonably,) we may refer the different faculties of the mind to the construction of the senses. The different bearings of these causes are obvious. They prove the importance of acquiring a habit of close thinking. He who hears and sees with difficulty, treasures up what he learns with care. A partial blindness invites contemplation. A man is not liable to have his attention distracted by frivolous events. They are in some measure shut out. He finds a study everywhere.

*Example of a Conference.**

Public Amusements, Splendid Religious Ceremonies, Warlike Preparations and Display, and a Rigid Police, as means of Despotic Power.

PUBLIC AMUSEMENTS.

Various as are the means by which an individual may acquire despotic power over a nation; none are more easy in their application, or more effectual in their results, than the mere act of providing and supporting what, in such cases, are most erroneously called public amusements. Public amusements! yes, — let but your tyrant, who would lord it with impunity, open his theatres, provide his shows, and procure every thing that can please the fancy, and delight the eyes and ears of the people, then he may rest in security, for those whom he would make slaves are placed upon the broad road that leadeth backward to darkness, but never onwards to light. They may pause at first, but the fatal charm soon overcomes their strength, and, blind to all evil consequences, they plunge madly on in pursuit of present pleasure.

It is easy to show how the people are so readily and so fatally deceived, — it requires few examples and little reasoning to prove that temptations are strong, indulgence ruinous, the truth is written within, legibly upon our hearts.

I cannot, however, pass over this subject without calling your attention to one of the most instructive, the most splendid, and, at the same time, most appalling portions of history, the latter days of the Roman Empire. We have before us a nation that has raised itself from obscurity to grandeur. — that has exchanged the name of exiles and vagabonds for the proud title of conquerors and sovereigns of the world; yet, in this very people, in their proudest day, we can trace the seeds of corruption.

They had early acquired a taste for public amusements, that had ever been gaining strength, and that was soon to be employed as the certain means of working their destruction.

The Roman frame retained as yet too much of its former strength and vigor to be roughly handled. An attempt to force chains upon it would have called forth a third Brutus full of the fire and patriotism of his ancestors. They who aimed at the imperial purple, knew this, and, avoiding all violence, sought to accomplish their designs by craft and subtlety Roman citizens, in their amusements, had already reached the limits, which cannot be passed with impunity; the only work that remained for

* One part only of this Conference is presented.

tyranny was to lead them beyond these limits, and to foster their growing carelessness and inattention to their dearest interests. This step was soon taken. Theatres were opened in all quarters of the city, loaded with every embellishment that the imagination could suggest, or that unbounded wealth could procure. We need not enter into a detail of these amusements; it sufficeth our purpose to point out how readily the people fell into the snare, and how speedily and entire was the ruin that followed. As had been rightly conjectured, the people soon gathered in crowds to these exhibitions, — they passed almost their whole lives within the walls of the circus, utterly regardless of all that was transacted in the world without.

Those who had made this deadly preparation, who had tempted a nation to its ruin, now hastened to improve the opportunities they had acquired. Not in secresy and fear, but openly, and with full confidence they proceeded to fasten their chains upon a slumbering people. And history informs us how complete was their success, — "Rome, Rome imperial, bows her to the shock," — the work of her slavery was finished, — the entrance of the Goth into her gates was a mere change of masters, for she long before had fallen and was conquered.

The case we have just cited is a remarkable one, — few events in history can compare with it, — yet, for all that, it is not to be rejected as an unfair and too highly colored illustration of the truth of our positions. There is nothing in it unnatural, there is nothing improbable, and should the like circumstances at any time occur, I had almost said a child might predict the ruin that would ensue.

When it can be shown how business and pleasure, attention and remissness, can go hand in hand together; in short, when we shall see a nation utterly devoted to amusements, and, at the same time, awake to all its interests, then we may be ready to give our example and positions to the wind.

*Example of a Colloquy.**

Difference of Manners in Ancient Rome and Modern Civilized States

To a careful and attentive observer of human nature, the history of mankind presents an interesting and instructive but mournful picture. It teaches him that man is everywhere the same; but however the picture may be varied by circumstances, however different the light in which it is viewed, the leading features remain ever the same. In no portion of ancient history are we more struck with this important fact than in that of Rome. In considering the manners of that people, great care should be taken that we do not permit the classical associations of our boyhood to give us a too favorable opinion of their character; and again, that we do not run into the opposite, but less probable error, of depreciating their real worth. Cold, indeed, must be the heart, and dull the understanding, that can contemplate unmoved the history of the Eternal City, which, after all, has done its part towards communicating to the world civilization and philosophy. It requires no extraordinary stretch of the imagination to marshal before us, in patriotic array, those venerable magistrates, who, tranquilly seated in their curule chairs defied the fury of Brennus and

* One part only of this Colloquy is presented

his barbarian hordes; or to hear Cicero declaiming with honest indignation against the vices and insolence of Anthony and Verres. Yet, our admiration must gradually subside, when we reflect, that the glory with which they were surrounded, was purchased by the misery and degradation of millions. Did we see the Romans in their true colors, we should perceive that they were in reality a selfish, perfidious, cruel, and superstitious race of barbarians, endued with the scanty and doubtful virtues of savage life, but deformed by more than its ordinary excesses, and whose original purity of manners and good faith among themselves did not endure a moment longer than it enabled them to subdue the rest of mankind. Of the many mistakes which our classical fondness for the Romans have led us into respecting them, there is not a greater or more unfounded one than the high opinion we are apt to entertain of their domestic habits. The Queen of Cities, throned upon her seven hills, in marble majesty, the mistress of a world conquered by the valor of her sons, is a picture of our imagination, which we are unwilling to spoil by filling up all its parts with too curious accuracy. Certain it is that information enough is to be obtained from Roman authors to prepare us for a scene of much more moderate splendor in the capital of Italy. From them we may learn that all the points upon which the imagination reposes with so much complacency and delight, are perfectly consistent with misery, disorder, and filth. We may learn, that though their Venus never attracted public notice in a hooped petticoat, and though their Apollo never dashed in a blue swallow-tailed coat with brass buttons, yet, that the costume of the day, whatever it might be, was pretty generally bestowed upon their deities. We may learn, that the Romans, with all their wealth and power, and ingenious luxury, enjoyed but little real cleanliness and comfort. More of that most desirable and excellent article, comfort, may be had by any one among us, than could have been enjoyed by a Roman noble, who rode in carriages without springs, or on saddles without stirrups, or dined without knives and forks, or lived in rooms without chimneys. And, having duly weighed these and similar points of minute history, we may bring ourselves to adopt more sober views of the magnificence of ancient Rome, and of an ancient Roman. In spite of their admiration for Grecian manners, the Romans were ill-calculated for every elegant pursuit. After abandoning the rigid virtues by which Cincinnatus reached the summit of glory, they gave way to a corruption of manners, and an insatiable rapacity, which would have remained a solitary example of human depravity, had not revolutionary France exhibited scenes still more horrid and revolting. The tyranny of the Romans, and of the French under Bonaparte, is stamped with the same horrid features, the same unbounded and unprincipled lust of dominion rendered both the disturbers of human repose. By the pride and avidity of the descendants of Romulus, Greece was stripped of her pictures and statues; by the rapacity and avidity of the Directorial Government, and that Jacobin General, Italy was robbed of these identical statues, and of paintings more exquisitely beautiful even than those of Zeuxis or Apelles. If to plunder the vanquished of every thing that can contribute to the comfort, instruction, or the ornament of society be an object of merited censure, both nations are equally culpable, both equally tyrants and robbers. The ravager, the exterminator, Verres, was not worse than many others of the Roman Proconsuls. Who can read the Verrine orations and not curse from his heart this cruel and rapacious people? The money of the unhappy Si cilians found its way to his coffers, and their grain, whilst they were starving, into his granaries. The axes of his lictors were blunted on their necks, and the favor of being put to death at a single blow was sold at a heavy price. Turn we from the cruelty, injustice, and rapacity of Verres? As we turn our eyes from the extortions of the Sicilian Prætor, they may perchance light upon the newspapers of the day, and they will there find scenes equally infamous and deplorable. The deeds of Verres stand not alone in the history of the world. What think we of those slaughtered at Vicksburg? "It was in vain that the unhappy men cried out, We are American citizens; the bloodthirsty mob, deaf to all they could urge in their own defence, ordered the infamous punishment to be inflicted. Thus were innocent American citizens publicly murdered, while the only words they uttered amidst their cruel sufferings were, "We are American citizens." "O Liberty! O sound once delightful to every American ear! O sacred privilege of American citizenship! Once sacred, now trampled upon." Tell me not that the storms which now agitate the surface of our institutions are preferable to the calm unruffled sea of despotism in Russia and Austria; give me the despotism of a Nicolas and a Metternich, nay, even the tyranny of a Nero, or a Caligula, any thing but the despotism and tyranny of an infuriated mob.

The taste for gladiatorial murder, prevalent in Rome for centuries, and often indulged to the most extravagant excess, implies so wide a deviation from the common feelings and principles of humanity, that it is to be regarded as an important fact, in the moral history of man. Moralists will tell us that the truly brave are never cruel; but to this the Roman Ampitheatres say, No. There sat the conquerors of the world coolly to enjoy the torture and the death of men who had never offended them. Twice in one day came the matrons and senators of Rome to the butchery; and, when glutted with bloodshed, the Roman ladies sat down in the wet arena, streaming with the blood of their victims, to a luxurious supper. But enough of these humiliating details.

The moral to be derived from Roman history, if properly applied, is most excellent, and cannot be too often, nor too strongly inculcated. It is that the loss of civil liberty involves a destruction of every feeling which distinguishes man from the inferior part of the creation, leaving his faculties to vegetate in indolence or to become brutalized by sensuality; that public opinion, when suffered to waste its energies in wild applause of faction or tyranny, may become one of the most subservient instruments of oppression, and even bow its neck to the ground ere the foot of the tyrant be prepared to tread upon it.

LXXXIX.

ESSAY, TREATISE, TRACT, THESIS

An Essay, literally means nothing more than a trial, or an attempt. It is sometimes used to designate in a specific man ner an author's attempt to illustrate any point. It is commonly applied to small detached pieces, which contain only the general thoughts of a writer on any given subject, and afford room for amplification into details. Some authors modestly used the term for their connected and finished endeavours to elucidate a doctrine.*

A Treatise † is more systematic than an Essay. It treats on the subject in a methodical form, and conveys the idea of something labored, scientific, and instructive.

A Tract † is only a species of small treatise, drawn up upon particular occasions, and published in a separate form.

A Thesis is a position or proposition which a person advances, and offers to maintain, or which is actually maintained by argument.

Essays are either moral, political, philosophical, or literary; they are the crude attempts of the youth to digest his own thoughts, or they are the more mature attempts of the man to communicate his thoughts to others. Of the former description are prize Essays in schools, and of the latter are the Essays innumerable which have been published on every subject since the days of Bacon.

Treatises are mostly written on ethical, political, or speculative subjects, such as Fenelon's, Milton's, or Locke's "Treatise on Education," De Lolme's "Treatise on the Constitution of England."

Tracts are ephemeral productions, mostly on political and religious subjects, which seldom survive the occasion which gave them birth. Of this description are the pamphlets which daily issue from the press for or against the measures of government, or the public measures of any particular party.

The Essay is the most popular mode of writing; it suits the writer who has not talent or inclination to pursue his inquiries farther, and it suits the generality of readers, who are amused with variety and superficiality. The Treatise is adapted for the student, who will not be contented with the superficial Essay, when more ample materials are within his reach.

The Tract is formed for the political or religious partisan, and receives its interest from the occurrence of the motive. The Dissertation interests the disputant. (*See Dissertation, page* 334.)

---

* See Locke's "Essay on the Understanding," and Beattie's "Essay on Truth."

† *Treatise* and *Tract* have both the same derivation, from the Latin *traho* to draw, manage, or handle and its participle, *tractus*.

Example 1st of an Essay.

LITERATURE.

The developement of mind, the exertions of talent, the labors of industry, are all subjects intimately interwoven with the moral character of a rational and accountable being. It is a curious and interesting investigation to trace the history of man, as he emerges from a state of nature, and passes through the successive gradations, from mere animal existence, to a state of refined civilization and moral culture. And it is equally delightful to the man of letters, to behold the effects of learning in its various stages, in amending the inward state of mankind, as the refinements of luxury add to their external convenience.

It is a common remark with the historian, that the discovery of the use of iron is the first step from savage to civilized life. The remark is just, but must be received in a limited sense; for there is an internal as well as external history; a history of mind as well as of matter; an intellectual civilization distinct from the history of nations, and independent of the combinations of beauty of figure and of color. What iron is to the animal nature of man, literature is to his intellectual condition. The former supplies him with the means of defence, enables him to overcome the debility of his organic powers, and endues him with factitious strength, as useful as that which nature has conferred. The latter preserves the acquisitions of the former, guides its operations, concentrates its usefulness, and enables him to avail himself of the achievements of genius struggling with the inertness of matter, or fettered by the restrictions of ignorance and barbarity. The history of literature is the history of the noblest powers of man. There is a sameness in savage life, which affords but little interest to speculation; and confines the investigations of the philosopher and man of observation within narrow limits. The scope of his abilities is narrow and contracted. The construction of rude implements, the provision of the necessaries of life, the strifes, collisions, and bitter feuds of hostile and ambitious chiefs, deficient in interest, because deficient in incidents; the simple tales of love or the sombre stories of licentiousness, these form the material of the history of nations, upon whom science has never beamed, nor literature shed its renovating rays. In the relation of these incidents there is no *history* of *mind*, no account of the progress of intellect, further than what is observed in the ingenuity of mechanical contrivance, limited by the ignorance of the properties of things. But the invention of letters, preceded by the mysticism of hieroglyphic symbols, gave a new face to the world; enlarged the subjects of knowledge, and changed man from a mere animal to an intellectual being. The history of literature, from the invention of letters to the present day, involves all that is interesting in the history of man. To what purpose would the divine gifts of speech and reason have been conferred, unless the monuments of their achievements should have more stability than could exist as they float on the recollections of a single generation. The animal nature of man might, so far as posterity is concerned, be considered the nobler because the more permanent part of his being. The structures which his hands have reared, though still amenable to the laws of decay, would survive the shocks of ages, while no monument would exist of his immortal spirit; no recollection remain of that which distinguishes him from the inferior order of beings. Age would succeed to age without witnessing any accession to the fields of knowledge. Traditionary lore, like the rays of light, would vary in its import as it passed from hand to hand, and one generation could not be enriched by the acquisitions of its predecessor. But the invention of letters has established a chancery by which the acquisitions of one age have been handed down as a rich inheritance to its successor; while the later age, like the posterity of an ancient family, has revelled in the riches entailed by its ancestors. Such are the effects of literature, considered only as it enlarges the fields of knowledge, and gives a wider range to the exercise of the intellectual faculties.

But there is another and a more interesting, because more important, view to be taken of its influence, as it operates on the moral nature of mankind. In the construction of implements of defence, in the arrangement of architectural convenience, in the pursuit of the objects of sense, man is superior to some species of the brute creation, only as his corporeal powers are better adapted to mechanical exertion. The bee, the beaver, the ant, and other inferior orders, rival the most successful efforts of man in the construction of a habitation adapted to the respective exigencies of each. But *they* operate by instinct, — *his* labors are the suggestions of necessity in conference with inventive powers; and it is a curious investigation to trace the gradations from destitution to comfort, from comfort to convenience, and from convenience to ease, and, in its proper connexion, the moral influence of each upon the character of mankind. There it will be found that the vaunted nobleness of savage nature, the magnanimity ascribed by some even of the present day, to the uncultivated states of society, are but the chimeras of prejudice, or at least but erroneous deductions from solitary examples. The history of literature, will abundantly show that such instances are but the taper in the dungeon, which appears the brighter from the darkness by which it is surrounded; while in the improved forms of life, in those ages when the brightness of learning has dispelled the clouds in the minds of men, and day has dawned upon the eyes of all, the aspen flame is eclipsed by brighter light, and is unnoticed, because it is unfavored by the advantages of contrast.

Laws owe their permanency to their consistency; and their consistency is mainly to be attributed to a wise consideration of the exigencies of society, deduced from the operations of cause and effect upon the human mind. When history, therefore, is silent, their deductions must be made from a limited view of society; and, like all conclusions drawn from various views, are likely to be erroneous. It is letters which give a tongue to history, and provide it with a distinct utterance. It is letters which make the past a monitor to the present, and the present a guide to the future.

The view which we have thus taken of literature is narrow and circumscribed. Indeed, the subject is as exhaustless as its objects are innumerable. He must be dead to the most refined pleasures of which his nature is susceptible, who is deaf to the claims of literature to his attention, or is blind to the importance and value of learning

Example 2d of an Essay.

The Pleasure derived from the Fine Arts, by the Artist and Common Spectator.

The pleasure derived from the Fine Arts is doubtless proportioned to our capacity of appreciating them; for they address themselves chiefly to the imagination and the sensibility. The mere pleasures of sense every man may feel; but those derived from intellect and sentiment are more limited, and of a higher order. Hence it is, that the artist feasts on his self-created treasures, and lives on fancy's imagery, whilst the hieroglyphical daub of a sign-painter would be more attractive to the common spectator than the hues of Titian, or the bold master-strokes of a Michael Angelo. Taste is a sentiment of the soul. It is a keen perception of the sublime and beautiful in art and nature. United with genius, it even creates to itself images surpassing human excellence; objects which exist, perhaps, but in the painter's and poet's vision. Guido coveted the wings of an angel, that he might behold the beatified spirits of paradise, and thereby form an archangel such as his imagination was obliged to substitute. How sublime must have been the vision which gave the object his imagination sought for! How intense the feeling which thus transported him from earth to heaven!

To express the passions by outward signs is the artist's aim; and we may add, his envied privilege. What delight to see the cold and gloomy canvas expand with life; the dull void banished by the melting eye, the graceful form, the persuasive suppliant, the conquering hero! Every touch adds something to the soul's expression, till the enraptured painter yields himself up to the delightful contemplation of his new creation. "I, too, am a painter," exclaimed Correggio, with involuntary transport, while contemplating a work of the divine Raphael; "I, too, am a painter." Such was the enraptured feeling which would, otherwise, have been chilled by the cold pressure of his wants and poverty.

To common observers, the most beautiful painting may seem but an assemblage of forms, and the most exquisite poem but doggerel rhyme. The higher efforts of art produce but little effect on uncultivated minds. It is (as Sir Joshua Reynolds observes) only the lowest style of arts, whether of painting, poetry, or music, that may be said, in the vulgar sense, to be naturally pleasing. Taste, and a just discrimination, are the results of education. The concertos of Steibell and Clementi would be jargon to the ear accustomed only to the monotonous tones of "Hob or Nob," and "Yankee Doodle," nor would the admirer of "Punchinello," or "Jack the Giant Killer," be enraptured with the grace and dignity of an Apollo Belvidere, or a Venus de Medicis.

That a susceptibility and love of the sublime and beautiful are a source of happiness, who can doubt, that has seen the "Aurora" of Guido? How rich, how sublime the fancy, which could produce so enchanting an assemblage of all that is graceful and lovely! and how animated, how enraptured, the feelings of him whom a refined taste renders capable of appreciating them! Dupaty's soul melted at the view of Raphael's "Incendia del Borgo." He saw not, in that moment of enraptured feeling, a pictured flame, but the devouring element, raging, enveloping, and consuming the helpless and despairing multitude. To look on such a production with total indifference is impossible. Apelles's critic was a competent judge of the representation of a sandal, and Molière's old woman could decide upon the nature of comic humor; but it is the artist and connoisseur alone, who can judge, appreciate, and feel the highest order of color, modification, and expression.

The portrait painter also claims our attention and gratitude. He who gives to our weeping eyes the form of the beloved and departed friend; whose magic touch arrests beauty in its progress to decay, and whose pencil immortalizes the revered forms of the hero and the statesman; the soul-breathing expression of a Washington, a Franklin, and an Ames.

Painting may, perhaps, be said to be the acme of the arts, since it charms by so many various branches, and admits of such infinite variety of color and expression; but let not the "verba ardentia" of the poet be robbed of their honors. The lyre of a Milton, a Cowper, a Bryant, and a Wordsworth, can never breathe other than harmonious sounds. Their words melt into ideas, as the objects of nature gather light and color from the sun.

Shall we not allow the poet, then, his joys and honors? Shall the emanations of his fancy shine on hearts cold and dead to its rays? No! Through the tear of sensibility we see his power; we feel in the tender accents of the voice that trembles while it reads.

Since the pleasures derived from the Fine Arts are so exquisite, both to the artist and spectator, it cannot be doubted that our sources of happiness might be greatly extended by their liberal cultivation. That arts and morals are materially connected, there is no doubt. Horace observes:

> "Ingenuas didicisse fideliter artes,
> Emollit mores, nec sinit esse feros."

And could this spirit, this admiration of the beautiful, be generously cultivated, the genius of our soil might proudly ascend the summit of Parnassus. Public favor is the most powerful stimulus to talent; exhibitions therefore, of the best productions, both in painting and sculpture, will have a tendency to diffuse a general taste, and to inspire a spirit of emulation, from which the most beneficial results may be anticipated. Let us not suffer the artists who now grace our shores to forsake us, for the want of that patronage which it should be our pride and pleasure to bestow We cannot, indeed, expect to rival the treasures of the Louvre or the Vatican; but from the exercise of native talent, and from the specimens of art we already possess, much may be expected. In the cabinets of private individuals in our city, may be found productions sufficient to form a choice collection for public exhibition, and it is to the liberality and patronage of their possessors that we look for such encouragement as shall stimulate the young artist to immortalize his name, and shed a lustre on his country.

Example 3d.

The Sentiment of Loyalty.

Loyalty, in its primitive signification, implies fidelity to a king. Hence, a loyal subject is one who promotes as far as possible the welfare of the kingdom, who assists in the maintenance of the laws, and in times of danger is ever ready to defend the life and honor of his sovereign, and to sacrifice himself for the good of his country.

This sentiment is natural to the human race. If we analyze our various feelings and emotions, we shall find that the sentiment of love is one of the most powerful passions which nature has implanted in the breast of man; it is the most powerful, because, when excited and kindled, it burns with an ardor almost unquenchable; it warms and spurs the whole man on ward towards the accomplishment of its object; impetuous and irresistible, it overcomes all obstacles which rise before it.

The sentiment of Loyalty is one of the manifestations of this love; springing from that noble source, it flows onward till it meets the waters of other streams, which it deepens and purifies.

Since nature has given to man this sentiment of loyalty, it will always find suitable objects on which to bestow itself. Man was made for love; he must have something to honor, respect, and admire; something usually higher and nobler than himself; consequently, in despotic countries, honor and love are paid by a loyal people to their sovereign, who, being of a higher station, of a more venerated name, or of nobler descent than themselves, is entitled to this respect.

In our own country, we venerate the wisdom and prudence of our ancestors, who, in framing the articles of our constitution, provided for the good of succeeding generations; and, at the present day, when we see a citizen devoting himself to the service of his country with that patriotic spirit which characterized our fathers, our affections are aroused, our lips send forth his praise, we hail him as the defender of the Constitution, and the whole nation rises up to do him homage.

In England, recently, that loyalty, which for two preceding reigns had been slumbering, burst forth with redoubled vigor upon the accession of a female sovereign to the throne.

At the beginning of a new reign, the loyalty of a nation is always openly and warmly exhibited. But on that occasion, there was something in the fact, that their future sovereign was a youthful and accomplished queen, which excited in an unusual degree the hopes and sympathies of the nation. They hailed her accession as emblematical of peace and prosperity.

In the feudal times, in the times of chivalry and the Crusades, the knights were distinguished for their loyalty to the ladies of the court. In those days, the fame and beauty of the lady inspired her champion with courage and strength, and many a battle has been fought and many a vic tory won, under this spirit-stirring influence of loyalty.

Those were brilliant days for Europe, when chivalry stood forth in its might, and first gave birth to loyalty, — loyalty, which taught devotion and reverence to those weak, fair beings, who but in beauty and gentleness have no defence. "It raised love above the passions of the brute, and by dignifying woman, made woman worthy of love. It gave purity to enthu siasm, crushed barbarous selfishness, taught the heart to expand like a flower to the sunshine, beautified glory with generosity, and smoothed even the rugged brow of war." But how have we degenerated? "The age of chivalry is gone; never, never more shall we behold that generous loyalty to rank and sex, that proud submission, that dignified odedience, that sub ordination of the heart, which kept alive, even in servitude itself, the spirit of an exalted freedom!"

But though the sentiment of loyalty has greatly degenerated, it is not wholly extinct; it is now occasionally expressed, but its flame is faint and flickering; should it ever expire, it will go hand in hand with patriotism, and will expire with that faith which gave it life.

To conceive truly what we should then lose, we need only reflect, that loyalty is the bond of society and friendship, it unites all the best affections of the heart in one common cause, it holds a sacred place not to be invaded with impunity, it is respected and honored by the old, and the stories of its valor delight the young, and

> "Though well held, to fools doth make
> Our faith mere folly, yet he that can endure
> To follow with allegiance a fallen lord,
> Doth conquer him, that did his master conquer."

XC.

COLLEGE POEM.

Example.

The Pleasures and Pains of the Student.

When envious time, with unrelenting hand,
Dissolves the union of some little band,
A band connected by those hallowed ties,
That from the birth of lettered friendship rise,
Each lingering soul, before the parting sigh,
One moment waits, to view the years gone by;
Memory still loves to hover o'er the place,
And all our pleasures and our pains retrace.
The Student is the subject of my song,
Few are his pleasures, — yet those few are strong.
Not the gay, transient moment of delight,
Not hurried transports felt but in their flight.
Unlike all else, the Student's joys *endure*,
Intense, expansive, energetic, pure;
Whether o'er classic plains he loves to rove,
'Midst Attic bowers, or through the Mantuan grove, —
Whether, with scientific eye, to trace
The various modes of number, time, and space, —
Whether on wings of heavenly truth to rise,
And penetrate the secrets of the skies,
Or downwards tending, with an humble eye,
Through Nature's laws explore a Deity,
His are the joys no stranger breast can feel,
No wit define, no utterance reveal.
Nor yet, alas! unmixed the joys we boast,
Our pleasures still proportioned labors cost.
An anxious tear oft fills the Student's eye,
And his breast heaves with many a struggling sigh.
His is the task, the long, long task, t' explore
Of every age the lumber and the lore.
Need I describe his struggles and his strife,
The thousand minor miseries of his life,
How Application, never-tiring maid,
Oft mourns an aching, oft a dizzy head?
How the hard toil but slowly makes its way,
One word explained, the labor of a day, —
Here forced to explore some labyrinth without end,
And there some paradox to comprehend?
Here ten hard words fraught with some meaning small,
And there ten folios fraught with none at all.
Or view him meeting out with points and lines
The land of diagrams and mystic signs,

Where forms of spheres "being given" on a plane,
He must transform and bend within his brain.
Or as an author, lost in gloom profound,
When some bright thought demands a period round
Pondering and polishing; ah, what avail
The room oft paced, the anguish-bitten nail?
For see, produced 'mid many a laboring groan,
A sentence much like an inverted cone.
Or should he try his talent at a rhyme,
That waste of patience and that waste of time,
Perchance, like me, he flounders out one line,
Begins the next, — there stops ——.
  Enough, no more unveil the cloister's grief,
Disclose those sources whence it finds relief.
Say how the Student, pausing from his toil,
Forgets his pain 'mid recreation's smile.
Have you not seen, — forgive the ignoble theme, —
The winged tenants of some haunted stream
Feed eager, busy, by its pebbly side,
Then wanton in the cool, luxuriant tide?
So the wise student ends his busy day,
Unbends his mind, and throws his cares away.
To books where science reigns, and toil severe,
Succeeds the alluring tale, or drama dear;
Or haply in that hour his taste might choose
The easy warblings of the modern muse.
Let me but paint him void of every care,
Flung in free attitude across his chair.
From page to page his rapid eye along
Glances and revels through the magic song;
Alternate swells his breast with hope and fear,
Now bursts the unconscious laugh, now falls the pitying tear
Yet more; though lonely joys the bosom warm,
Participation heightens every charm;
And should the happy student chance to know
The warmth of friendship, or some kindlier glow,
What wonder should he swiftly run to share
Some favorite author with some favorite fair!
There, as he cites those treasures of the page
That raise her fancy, or her heart engage,
And listens while her frequent, keen remark
Discerns the brilliant, or illumes the dark,
And doubting much, scarce knows which most to admire,
The critic's judgment, or the writer's fire,
And reading often glances at that face,
Where gently beam intelligence and grace;
And sees each passion in its turn prevail,
Her looks the very echo of the tale;
Sees the descending tear, the swelling breast,
When vice exults, or virtue is distressed;
Or, when the plot assumes an aspect new,
And virtue shares her retribution due,
He sees the grateful smile, th' uplifted eye,

Thread, needle, kerchief, dropt in ecstasy,—
Say, can one social pleasure equal this?
Yet still even here imperfect is the bliss.
For ah! how oft must awkward learning yield
To graceful dulness the unequal field
Of gallantry? What lady can endure
The shrug scholastic, or the bow demure?
Can the poor student hope that heart to gain
Which melts before the flutter of a cane?
Or, of two characters, which shall surpass,
Where one consults his books, and one his glass?
Ye fair, if aught these censures may apply,
'T is yours to effect the surest remedy;
Ne'er should a fop the sacred bond remove
Between the Aonian and the Paphian grove.
'T is yours to strengthen, polish, and secure
The lustre of the mind's rich garniture;
This is the robe that lends you heavenly charms,
And envy of its keenest sting disarms,
A robe whose grace and richness will outvie
The woof of Ormus, or the Tyrian dye.
To count one pleasure more, indulge my muse,—
'T is friendship's self,—what cynic will refuse?
O, I could tell how oft her joys we 've shared,
When mutual cares those mutual joys endeared,
How arm in arm we 've lingered through the vale,
Listening to many a time-beguiling tale.
How oft, relaxing from one common toil,
We 've found repose amid one common smile.
Yes, I could tell, but O, the task how vain!
'T would but increase our fast approaching pain;
The pain so thrilling to a student's heart,
Couched in that talisman of woe, we part.

XCI.

DISSERTATION.

A dissertation is a formal discourse intended to illustrate a subject, and the term is properly applied to performances of an argumentative nature.

Dissertations are principally employed on disputed points of literature and science.*

* See Bentley's "Dissertation upon the Epistles of Phalaris" and De Pau's "Dissertations on the Egyptians and Chinese."

Example.

On the Causes which, independent of their Merit, have contributed to elevate the ancient Classics."

The ancient classics are elevated to a rank in the literature of the world, to which their intrinsic excellence cannot justify their claim. Admitting this position, which their most strenuous supporters will not deny, but unwilling to incur the imputation which a declaimer against classical learning must deservedly hazard among its admirers, I shall attempt to show some of the causes that have united to produce this elevation.

The standard to which every one primarily refers what he examines, is the measure of his own power. That work is not admired which he could equal or surpass. This standard, indeed, is soon extended, and similar efforts of genius of other ages are taken into the comparison. The barbarism in which the world was involved at the revival of learning, made the classics appear to its restorers in an unnaturally strong and dazzling light. Possessing themselves few of the advantages of progressive improvement, and destitute and ignorant of the resources of the ancient authors, they viewed their works as the efforts of transcendent genius, which had completely penetrated and exhausted the mines of nature, — which none could ever after approach, and only the most exalted minds comprehend. They applied themselves to the examination of the treasures they had discovered, and burst forth into unrestrained admiration of authors from whom they had learned to think and to speak.

All who have since justly appreciated the labors of these fathers of modern literature, have concurred in sentiments of gratitude and reverence to their instructors.

For a great part of the time since the revival of letters, those who aimed at the reputation of scholars have been obliged to establish their claim by a knowledge of the classics. The possessor of this knowledge obtained respect, and continued to cultivate it from the pride of displaying learning which was confined to a few, or from the ambition of excelling in what constituted his chief or only distinction. This was necessarily the case when little other than classical learning existed; and it long continued, like the respect for hereditary succession, from the habit of paying honor to what our predecessors deemed honorable. While prejudices were thus strong in favor of the classics, few ventured to appear without their support, and most that was written tended to preserve and strengthen their ascendancy. Regarded as having assisted the first literary efforts of the majority of the learned men of modern times, and being generally, by the nature of their subjects, better suited than most other books to the comprehension of the young, the classics have long been presented to the infant mind of the scholar, when in its most susceptible state. They have thus occupied the most powerful prepossessions, and been allowed to form and constitute the standard of intellectual beauty and excellence. They have intimately insinuated themselves into the mind, at a period when impressions received are most lasting and most forcible. They have been connected with the tenderest and most pleasing associations; with the memory of the sports and enjoyments of childhood, and the more affecting recollections of the attention of instructors and kindness of parents. Those whom the youth was first taught to respect have been men devoted to these studies, and employed to point out their beauties, and to direct the yet unformed taste to their perception and just admiration.

It was under the guidance of such conductors, that the young imagination took its earliest flights. The first scenes of native simplicity and happiness it sketched, were amidst the classical vales of Thessaly. The first popular assemblies it regarded with interest, were those of Athens and Rome. The first battles it pictured to itself were fought under the banners of a Grecian or Roman general. Whenever, in after life and other books, pastoral scenery, or popular commotion, or the tumult of war, presented themselves, they brought back these impressions, were referred to these exemplars, and the justice and elegance of description were determined by the comparison.

To this may be added the undefined sense of the greatness of an object at first imperfectly comprehended, which continues to display beauties and higher excellences the more closely and attentively it is contemplated. This quality, common to every work of merit, must be particularly exhibited in those, which, like the classics, are sufficiently intelligible to interest minds not yet adequate to their complete comprehension.

I insist not on the respect that we pay to antiquity; the records of her wisdom, though for ages deemed sacred, have long since been exposed to the gaze and scrutiny of the profane. Her voice is no longer listened to as speaking the language of inspiration. The charm that riveted attention is dissolved. Men of modern times affect to reverence the dictates of reason alone. But the fact has not always been thus; there were times when the classics were respected merely because they contained the legacies of ancient days.

Inductive philosophy has, indeed, taught other precepts; but to those ignorant of these precepts, or impatient of the long and weary path which this philosophy pointed out, some of the Greek classics offered to show a pleasanter and far shorter way to universal science. Having once embraced the theories of the philosophers, they must have rejected with ridicule the pretensions of other books to competition with the works of such as genius has admitted to the secret councils of nature. The works of the Grecian philosophers constitute, indeed, but a small portion of the classics. But how often are we, by our admiration of a favorite author, prepossessed in favor of the whole nation to which he belongs!

But philosophy cannot boast herself; she is silent and contemplative and must borrow language to communicate her inventions. Philosophical science forms the solid distinction of modern times. Ambitious men may use science as an instrument, but will not pursue it as an end. It is the ostentatious and imposing knowledge of the language, and of the arts which orators and poets have employed to sway the judgment by rousing the passions, and will be sought after by these men; and this knowledge they will find in the classical relics of the days of imagination and enthusiasm.

But if these relics contain more of the fictions of a poetical age, of the playful wanderings of the youth of human society, than of sober reason and thoughtful experience, why do they still delight the wisest of our thinking race?

Our attention, on opening a volume of the classics, is immediately won by the manly and striking manner in which every thing is expressed Thoughts are pursued with ease as they present themselves in language full, forcible, and distinct. We ascribe wholly to intrinsic merit an excellence owing, in a degree, to external circumstances. In a language that has been so many centuries written only, the ideas connected with each word have become long since determinately fixed. The attention is not diverted by the numerous indistinct images with which every word of a living language is necessarily associated; nor is the mind liable to be misled by allusions to subjects foreign to the one in view. The application of each word appears strikingly appropriate and peculiar.

In a living language it cannot be thus. Where philosophy must borrow the garb of ordinary life; when she must converse in the same dialect that is employed in the usual transactions of business, and which must present many images that are low and disgusting, and more that are common, though she may please by her familiarity, she cannot but lose the charm of novelty, and the dignity of elevation. Many of the thoughts that seem admirable in the original of the ancient classics, cease to strike in a modern translation. They lose their simple energy of expression, their innocence and delicacy of sentiment, and are debased by associations with the grossness of sensible, or the meanness of trivial objects Hence it is, that though we may infuse into a translation from the classics all the sense, we cannot the grace and spirit of the original.

These are some of the causes to which the ancient classics owe their elevation. They are esteemed as having assisted the first efforts of reviving literature, and contributed to the highest distinction of modern scholars. They were venerated as the bequest of antiquity; they are still consecrated by their connexion with the pure enjoyments and tender affections of childhood. They are dignified by a lofty freedom from the imperfections of a fluctuating language, and from the analogies and associations that combine obscurity and vulgar coarseness in a language which still continues to be spoken.

XCII.

DISQUISITION.

A Disquisition is a formal or systematic inquiry into any subject by arguments, or discussion of the facts and circumstances that may elucidate truth.

A disquisition differs from a dissertation in its form and extent. A dissertation may be more diffuse in its character, and consequently is generally protracted to a greater length. A disquisition should be characterized by its unity. Nothing should be introduced but what is strictly to the point; while in a dissertation any collateral subjects may be introduced which have a bearing upon the point to be proved, or the subject to be elucidated.

Disquisitions may be ethical, political, scientific, or literary, according to the nature of their subjects.

AN ETHICAL DISQUISITION.

Example.

The strict Application of Moral Rules to the Policy of States.

We all hold to the strict confinement of individuals by the rules of morality; nations are but assemblages of individuals; why, then, should states be exempt from these rules?

Our rules of morality are laid down in the New Testament, as given by Jesus Christ; he appears to have made no distinction between man considered as a single being, or regarded collectively, as existing in states. The spirit, if not the letter, of his sayings, is in favor of the universal application of these principles; and it becomes all, who dispute this position, to take upon themselves the *onus probandi.* Let us spend a few moments in the survey of their objections.

They say, in the first place, that the magnitude of the interest at stake justifies them in resorting to chicanery, the rupture of treaties, the opening of ambassadors' letters, and many other honorable exploits. This interest is the welfare of the community in worldly matters. Can it be obtained by chicanery? No! in the language of a most eloquent writer, "personal and national morality, ever one and the same, dictate the same measures under the same circumstances."

Moreover, the opponents say, that expediency requires the deception commonly practised in national affairs, and laugh at the idea of any other system. "Let those laugh that win!" but remember that derision is no proof of the validity of one position, or the fallacy of another. Long enough has this world grovelled beneath pretended expediency, as if short-sighted man could better frame regulations for the future, than he who holds eternity within his grasp; let us, if no others will, rise as a nation and shake off the chain; let us stand forward in the pursuit of our best interests, for, till the influence of Christianity is combined with that of philosophy, no system of policy can be perfect.

The Holy Alliance is the only instance in which this union has been attempted, and although the title has been branded as deceptive, yet it affords the testimony of the most powerful princes, that its object was just. Having thus done away with the principal objections of our opponents, we come now to a consideration of the benefits to be derived from a strict application of these rules; time will only allow us to touch upon some of the most important, and point out their influence upon our condition.

The laws of the land first claim our attention; not, indeed, as they now are, based upon the narrow views of man, but fixed on the broad and sure foundation of morality. The Saviour has nowhere freed man from his obligation to attend to the interests of his fellow-man; on the contrary, his especial command was, "Do unto others as ye would that men should do unto you." If this precept were observed in all the laws, we should no longer see kings oppressing their subjects, or men of one opinion rising to crush those of an opposite, in defiance of every principle implanted in the human breast.

There is a spirit abroad in the land, which would fain do right, but overdoes in its eagerness; men actuated by it do not wait to see if their fellow-men fully comprehend them, or their object. This is not the spirit of true morality, which makes its path as clear as the perfect day, and leads the good man to consider not merely his own benefit, but also to relieve, as far as possible, the situation of the poorer classes; he would secure their earthly happiness by the only sure means, firm and salutary laws. In these times it becomes every man to consider, that his influence is something; when the wagoner applied his shoulder to the wheel, the cart was dragged from the miry slough. Particularly in this country, where the poorest has an equal interest with the most wealthy, is it necessary for all to coöperate for the support of right views in regard to the power of laws over the governed. We have thus briefly adverted to the policy to be exerted by the state towards its own subjects; there is yet another point of view, the connexion existing between different governments.

In the first place, nations may be regarded as having the same feelings towards one another with individuals. The chicanery and fraud, practised by states towards each other, has already been adverted to; but after a consideration of the relation of state and subject, the matter is again forced upon our attention. Not only are these practices opposed to all morality, but they would not be tolerated between individuals; and the man whose suspicion induced him to open letters, or break the bonds he had voluntarily given to another, would be ejected from the lowest society.

In the whole system of international morality, there is perhaps nothing so unsettled as the rules for the construction of treaties, and yet the way seems clear. A treaty is neither more nor less than a promise between two or more nations, commonly for mutual benefit.

Mankind in a body have no higher interests than they have as individuals; each member of society is anxious only for certain natural rights, and to insure these privileges to posterity; these, we have shown, can best be secured by a strict conformity to moral rules. It is no argument against the introduction of this policy to say, it would not succeed; on the contrary, we have every reason to believe perfect success would crown the effort; the old reasons are vain and futile; let something new be tried; not a diplomatic, but a bold daring, based on the principles of divine justice. When this system of things is adopted, wars will be abolished; in the beautiful language of the prophet, "Men will turn their swords into ploughshares and their spears into pruning-hooks, and learn war no more." These principles, properly carried out, would check the boundless ambition of mankind, and remove those petty jealousies which commonly give rise to the wanton destruction of God's creation; the poet could no longer exclaim with truth, "Devil with devil damned firm concord holds; men only disagree of creatures rational."

The common origin of war is from the pretended or real infringement of a treaty. How can this be remedied? First, by being careful before a treaty is formed. Second, by a firm yet respectful statement of the case when one has been broken. A man of sound common sense, guided by a Christian spirit, is far more likely to frame treaties that will endure, than the wily diplomatist, whose aim is merely to make as much money as he can for his country, regardless of the injuries he may commit Such a man acts for a nation as he does for himself; he carries into practice the precept, "Love thy neighbor as thyself." Many writers have touched upon war, and much has been said, both for and against it; those of the present day are, however, generally opposed; and the Congress of Nations, which, but a few years since, was ridiculed as an emanation from the brains of hot-headed fanatics, is already occupying the attention of the wisest legislators throughout the world.

What a blissful state of things, when all nations shall be at peace! when we shall see each pursuing its own interest with benefit to the rest! This shall be the consequence, and not the cause of the universal spread of Christianity. The situation of our own country is particularly favorable for the application of its rules. It may, indeed, be urged, that they would not yet be appreciated; let us then hasten the period, and not rest in the work of well-doing, till all tribes and nations shall be brought to know their God, and his law. Onward! should then be the cry of every moral man; our time of action here is but short at the most, yet much may be done, and is there one, who, with an immortal's happiness within his grasp, is too indolent to put forth his hand for it? No! that man is unworthy the name of republican, whose sole aim is self, who regards not his country, and his fellow-men throughout the world.

Let us, then, as a nation, stand forward for the introduction of moral precepts to direct our relations with foreign countries. The experiment is new, but does not the interest at stake warrant us in the risk, if there can be danger, in preferring the dictates of conscience and our God, to the precepts of short-sighted man.

XCIII.

A DISCUSSION.

A Discussion is the treating of a subject by argument, to clear it of difficulties, and to separate truth from falsehood. It is generally carried on between two or more persons, who take contrary sides, and defend them by arguments and illustrations.

Discussions are of several kinds, such as philosophical, literary, political, or moral, according to the subjects of which they treat; or colloquial and deliberative, according to the style in which they are written, or the occasion for which they are prepared.

Discussions serve for amusement, rather than for any solid purpose; the cause of truth seldom derives any immediate benefit from them, although the minds of men may become invigorated by a collision of sentiment.

PHILOSOPHICAL DISCUSSION.

Example.

PART I.

On the Expediency of making Authorship a Profession.

In modern civilized communities, a certain opinion or maxim is often prevalent, which, would we strip it of the shroud of conceit and the glitter of cant, would appear unwarrantable prejudice. Of this description is the objection so constantly urged against the profession of the author · a man whom few will call their brother, the laughing-stock of the merchant's clerk, and a laborer poorly paid in the world's coin. The broker seldom meets him on the exchange; the usurer never chaffers with him on the mart; the old man clinks his bags and shrugs his shoulders at his prospects; the schoolmaster takes to trade, and presently rolls by him in his coach, and, perhaps, worst of all, the bright eye is turned away, and the fair hand withheld by one who can never be the wife of an author! This prejudice which I describe, was once common throughout the old world; now it is particularly confined to America. Still everywhere the man whose pen is to be his support is thought a visionary, or an idler The author's garret has long since passed into a by-word, and the gaping elbow has become the escutcheon of his family. His poverty is a kind of general butt, and his sensitiveness a fair subject of caricature. I am aware, that I shall not speak agreeably to the judgment of most who hear me; let us, however, examine fairly some of the errors which have led people to think authorship unprofitable and inexpedient.

There are many persons, who, having neither the vigor nor refinement of mind to distinguish between what is material and intellectaal, would measure poetry by the yard, or fill a library by the bushel! To such, whatever yields the greatest amount of tangible, improvable product is the best producer; unless mind acts openly, as a machine, they suppose it to be dormant. Let such persons first comprehend the purpose of the author whom they censure; let them learn, that there possibly may be higher motives of action than gold or silver, — loftier contemplations than those of the counting-house or factory! And, although this is a working-day world, and man must labor for hire, let them thank God, that there are men, who find times of communion with better thoughts; and, but for whose speculations, and grasps at the infinite, these short-sighted cavillers would be as lifeless as the clods on which they tread! Coleridge says, with the enthusiasm of a genius, — "I expect neither profit nor general fame by my writings, and I consider myself as having been amply repaid without either. Poetry has been to me its own exceeding great reward; it has soothed my afflictions; it has multiplied and refined my enjoyments; it has endeared solitude, and it has given me the habit of wishing to discover the *good* and the *beautiful* in all that meets and surrounds me." Urge such a man, if you can, to convert his "Christabel" into an interest-table, and limit his peace of mind by the rise and fall of stocks!

We of America complain, that we have no established literature; and until more among us are willing to devote themselves to the cause of literature, we must be content to reflect the literary splendor of England Some of the brightest creations, indeed, of modern days, some of the fairest creatures of love, and poetry, and romance, belong to America, but they are not very numerous, and, ten to one, our poet or novelist, like the poor author's garment, which was, "a cap by *night*, a stocking all the *day*," pours forth his strain after completing the routine of a pleader at the bar, a bank officer, or political editor! Among the respectable and vitally important cares of professional life, literature has a poor chance of encouragement; the philosopher's speculations, or the poet's theory, having nothing to do with the brief or the dissecting knife.

"This is the language," says the objector, "of romantic folly; we must live, so let us labor for the readiest recompense; intellect will not support life, nor secure comfort." Such an one, be it observed, mistakes the ambition of the literary man. Without altogether neglecting, he seeks something infinitely better, than pecuniary ease. True, Goldsmith was needy, and Chatterton was driven to despair, and Otway died of starvation. But I do not believe that either would have foregone one sublime conception, or erased from his writings one maxim of sound morality, to gain the wealth of the princes who neglected him! A lying tombstone tells the story of many a rich patron of their time, — their memorials are, "The Deserted Village," and "Venice Preserved."

I am not advocating that sickly, sentimental, "love-in-a-cottage" kind of doctrine, which teaches, that mind is above ordinary necessities, and that the wants of life are not our common inheritance. But I do contend, that the time is coming, and that it should speedily come, in America, when a class of men whose wants are not extravagant, but attainable and refined, will meet with support. The human powers are unfairly and unprofitably employed, if turned to many different subjects; and this truth should be better known in America. The lawyer has an end before him, which only a life can attain; so has the physician, the clergyman, and the author. Unite the duties of either two, and you injure both.

Assuming, what we need not enlarge upon, the importance of a high national literature, let any one observe, who are the supporters of that which adorns England. "Not those, he will find, who united two or three occupations! Goldsmith was a professional man at first, but his patients were few, and he soon became what he was born to be, an author! Scott never figured at the bar, and Shakspeare was an indifferent actor. The problem may be easily solved. Some minds are fitted to investigate by help of the data of others, and apply to God's work their conclusions, and others are designed more exclusively to create; — a distinction rarely sufficiently observed. The author has no common work to perform; he who would instruct others, must untiringly improve himself; presenting no theories undigested, and familiar with the wildest speculations. In America, and everywhere else, we want a race of thinkers; men who will keep aloof from the eddy, which draws in politician and merchant, and even the professional man, and give us the results of long meditation. The mere words are no part of an author's labor; they but represent long previous mental action. The silence of the study is to mature the observations of the world.

Professional men generally appeal to their race only in one capacity; the author, by enlarged views of life, and illustrations of moral truth, may be a great reformer. Vice has long enough run riot; let the author, by moulding passion to his will, make it of service to his race! Is he a philosopher, — the wonders of the past, and the mysteries of the future, are his province. Is he a poet, — the freshness of nature, the fair holiness of woman, and the purity of truth, urge him to a life of thought and meditation. His influence spreads light about him; his pursuits soften his nature; he loves more heartily what is lovely, and is more ready to pity what is frail. The world says truly, he is poor; but what is that poverty which gives wealth to one's contemporaries, and bequeaths an inheritance to posterity!

PART II.

The Expediency of making Authorship a Profession

Almost universal experience proves the pecuniary reward of literary labor to be but trifling. In the throng of authors and men of genius, we find only here and there a solitary instance of well-requited endeavors; and if, at the present day, it is not as formerly quite true, that the idea of an author must be associated with a narrow lane and an obscure garret, it is not because his reward is liberal, or in any degree proportioned to his merits. Individual instances may, indeed, be brought up, to prove the success which sometimes attends literary pursuits; but for every *one* that could be cited, who had basked in the sunshine of prosperity, and enjoyed the smiles of the great and good among his contemporaries, we could marshal a hundred of equal power and genius, depressed by poverty, and treated with indifference and neglect; whose only recompense has been the tribute paid to their memory and writings in after times.

If we judge, then, from the remuneration that has generally attended the labors of the author, we are justified in forming presages little flattering to his future success. And, since fortune and genius are seldom found in companionship, what must be the consequence of making authorship a profession, of individuals devoting themselves to the cause of truth and literature, and relying on the gratitude and favor of the public for support? It is useless to say what *should be* the reward of the author, and to speak of the dignity and importance of the part which he sustains in the public drama, so long as we witness what *is*, and what *has been* the requital of his labors. It is upon facts alone, that we must ground our decision. And with these before our eyes, must we not fear the consequences to literature, if its existence and progress depend upon the exertions of disappointed and ill-requited genius? Consider the situation of that man, who, conscious of his own power, resolves to devote himself to the pursuit of letters, to become an author. Supposing, as has been the case with thousands who have preceded him, that his first attempts at authorship are unsuccessful. His expectations are disappointed; the promise of fame and of support is withered and blighted; the world looks upon him with indifference; a rival regards him with contempt; and the sharp and cold words of the critic ring in his ear the knell of his first literary offspring. If he acquiesces in the decision of his judges, it is only confessing his poor claims to distinction. If not, if he feels that time alone can pronounce the true decision upon his writings, there is yet no resort for him, if he would obtain support from the profession which he has chosen, but to conform his writings to the popular taste. Follow that man to his closet, and witness the struggles of his mind, the contest between inclination and interest. The one prompts him to follow his own genius; to utter the dictates of his own feelings, to be true to his own nature. The other sternly requires him to bow to the critics, to yield to the decision of the public, and in future to lower his aspirations. It is here that we would most deprecate the evils of making authorship a profession; that we would warn the young aspirant for literary distinction, with means inadequate to his support, against trusting to the uncertain reward of his exertions, unless he is willing to degrade his genius, and substitute for his own taste and inclinations, those of the capricious and unthinking multitude. If, instead or relying upon the avails of authorship, he looks to another profession for the means of subsistence, the thoughts of his leisure moments may be given to the world, without being fashioned and moulded by the opinions of other men. How can we expect one to preserve his individuality as a writer, if it must be at the expense of his interests, his only means of support. He that does right only from interested motives, cannot rank among men of the highest moral excellence; nor can the author, who writes mainly with a view to his own support, be considered the most vigilant guardian of the cause of truth and letters.

Nor is this all. When an author has resigned his right of self-guidance, and has taken up the *trade* of writing to suit the public taste; whose desire is to write what may be popular; the kindred desire soon manifests itself of increasing, as fast as possible, the number of his works. Names are not wanting to prove, that this has often been the case, and that, too, with some of the most distinguished authors. We witness it in the thousand ephemeral productions, that appear but to attract the public curiosity for a moment, and then give way to works as worthless and short-lived as themselves; justifying the remark, "that authorship immoderately employed makes the head waste and the heart empty, even were there no other and worse consequences; and that a person who sends away through the pen and the press every thought, the moment it occurs to him, will, in a short time, have sent all away, and will become a mere journeyman of the printing office, a compositor!" The cause of literature is the cause of truth, and it would be as unnecessary as unwise to trust it in the hands of those, who would support its interest, only so far as they coincided with their own.

We would willingly join in the sentiment of Professor Henry, that "we need an order of men of lofty intellectual endowment, an intellectual high priesthood standing within the inner veil of the temple of truth, reverently watching before the holy of holies for its divine revelations, and giving them out to the lower ministers at the altar;" but if this priesthood and their inferior ministers must become the servants and dependents of the multitude, whom it is their great office to guide and direct, their power and their usefulness are at an end. The shrine of truth had better be intrusted to inferior hands, or at once be desecrated and overthrown, than become the sanctuary of hypocrisy and error.

Example.

A LITERARY DISCUSSION.

[One side only.]

The Merits of the Histories of Hume and Lingard.

False opinions in morality, or mistaken notions in philosophy, are not so much to be dreaded, as the wilful misrepresentations of the historian. "Nullius addictus jurare in verba magistri," should be the motto of every honest historian; be his party in the right or wrong, he is to state "the truth, the whole truth, and nothing but the truth." Yet there is no one who has greater inducements to misrepresentations than the historian. Party feelings will lead him, not only to extenuate the guilt and apologize for the measures of his friends, but to exaggerate the misconduct of his adversaries, and attribute every act of theirs to the worst of motives. But, should he have the good fortune to be of no political party, yet the animosities of the church are no less bitter than those of the state, and theological enmities are far more difficult to compose, since each religious sect believes, that the voice of its own partisans is, without doubt, the voice of God.

Almost every historian has been influenced in one or the other of these ways. Hume and Gibbon, professing to be the enemies of all religion, have too often made their writings the channel of their infidelity, and thrown out their doubts and insinuations on every opportunity. Hume, again, was led away by his love of kings; he was too great a favorer of the doctrines of passive obedience and the divine right of kings; too much of a monarchist to feel any of that ardor, which glowed in the breasts of Hampden and Sydney; he consequently views with apathy every attempt of the people to be free, and considers every assertion of popular rights as an invasion of royal prerogative.

Neither is Dr. Lingard free from blame; indeed, we fear that he has wholly forfeited the character of an honest historian; he has erred and greatly erred, from his zeal for his particular religion. Educated in the faith of the Romish church, he must naturally feel a love and a reverence for her institutions; a priest at her altar, and, as we hope, sincerely believing in the doctrines which he teaches, he must feel a desire to defend her from the attacks and calumnies of her enemies. But his zeal has carried him too far; he seems to think himself pledged to support, not only her doctrines, but the means she has used to extend these doctrines, and uphold her temporal as well as her spiritual authority; every thing in the farthest degree related to Holy Mother Church is, in his eyes, sacred and inviolable, and the Popish miracles, the massacre of St. Bartholomew, and the Gunpowder Plot, are as much entitled to defence, as the doctrines of transubstantiation and the infallibility of the Pope.

If the wish to do away the prejudices against his faith, and induce men to look with more charity upon the doctrines of his sect, furnished any motive to Dr. Lingard for writing his history, he has entirely failed of his object by grasping at too much; he has lost the whole, he has weakened his side and exposed himself to the ridicule and attacks of his adversaries.

If he had merely advocated the doctrines of his church, and endeavored by fair argument to convince men of their truth, although we cannot allow an historical work to be the fit place for theological discussions, we should not have so much reason to complain. But when he espouses the cause of error, and virtually by apologizing for, if not openly by vindicating, supports those measures, which every man's conscience must tell him admit of no excuse, – when he defends the characters of those men whom the voice of all ages since their own has condemned to infamy, we must either doubt his sincerity or pity his understanding. People are now too enlightened to justify those means which centuries ago were employed to compel men's consciences. It is idle now to tell a man, that it will be doing God service to assassinate his neighbor, because he will not hear mass, bow to the host, and acknowledge the Pope as his spiritual father.

Dr. Lingard takes every opportunity to exalt the merits of those of his own sect, and to speak in terms of indifference, if not of disparagement, of every distinguished protestant. While Cardinal Pole is the subject of the highest encomiums, Archbishop Cranmer is passed as a man of but little talents, and less strength of character. While he in a manner defends the cruelties of the Marian persecution, and vindicates the characters of Bonner and Gardiner, when scarcely the fires of Smithfield and the piles of Ridley and Latimer, Hooper and Cranmer are extinguished, he complains of the restraints, the fines, and imprisonments, which, under Elizabeth, were imposed on the Popish recusants. While he magnifies every indiscretion of the unfortunate Anne Bolleyn into a crime, and would load her character with the blackest infamy, he extols the virtues and conceals the vices of Mary Stuart, whose only virtue was her weakness, and whose only apology for crime her youth and beauty.

Whatever merit there may be in Dr. Lingard's History, either of originality and deep and extensive research, which he claims, or of beauty of style and pleasing narration, which have been allowed him, all these, however, will by no means make up for the manifest partiality towards the Catholics, and the constant prejudice against the Protestant faith, which prevail through the whole work. It will never be a popular history; it may be read and admired at St. Omer's and Dovay, it may be found in the library of the scholar, but never, like Hume, in every parlor, and in the hands of common readers.

When the historian strays from the truth, his work becomes a mere work of fiction, inheriting all the dulness of narration, without acquiring any of the liveliness of romance; it can neither instruct us like the one, nor amuse us like the other. Facts misrepresented, however they may be skilfully adapted to our particular prejudices, will always be like the flattered portrait, which may gratify our vanity, or please us by the excellence of the coloring, but can never inspire us with that interest that truth alone can impart.

Example.

OF A DELIBERATIVE DISCUSSION.

PART I.

"Liberal Principles as affecting the Strength of Government."

The opinion that the strength of government consists in its being placed as far beyond the influence of popular commotions as possible, is one of long standing, and, when rightly understood, is, without doubt, perfectly correct. But I do very much doubt the correctness of that exposition of it, or rather, of that *perversion* of it, which teaches that the strength of a government consists in crushing the energies of the people, and continuing them in a state of abject mental and moral degradation and darkness. Nay, I conceive such a mode of proceeding to be entirely incompatible with the strength of government. For, let us suppose the existence of such a state of things as has just been alluded to. Let us suppose a people involved in a barbarism the most complete and gloomy that the world ever knew; and that they are ruled with a despotism, compared with which the Ottoman despotism of the present day is very liberty. I allow, that so long as they can be continued in a state of such miserable slavery and darkness, so long will the government stand, and stand firmly. But who will answer for it, that the light shall never break in? Who will vouch that they shall never rouse from this moral lethargy? Who is there that dares affirm that this Samson, though now blinded, and shorn of his strength oppressed, mocked, insulted, will not at some future period, remote it may be, collect the force of his energies, and hurl down the whole fabric of tyranny on the devoted heads of his followers? Station a guard, if you please, in every house,—set a spy over every man's actions; but tell me, of what effect will your guards and your spies be in restraining the current of men's thoughts? Were they possessed of no other means of coming to a sense of their wrongs, the very circumstance that there are in the community those who do not feel these wrongs, (the ministers of despotism,) this very circumstance, I say, would inevitably, though it may be slowly, raise in the minds of the people reflections on their own condition as compared with that of their rulers. It will then be but a short process for them to begin to desire better things; and every one at all conversant with human nature, knows full well that when men once begin to desire in earnest, it is not long ere they make an effort to possess themselves of the object of their wishes. A spirit of insubordination has thus arisen; and now tell me, student of history, tell me, politician, where will it end? Let tyranny, and the illiberal principles which have hitherto prevailed, in haughty assurance of their own might, tremble, for their downfall is at hand. All the experience of all ages shows full well, that when a people are once roused to a sense of injuries, opiates more powerful than man can tell of, are required to lull them to a second sleep.

If, now, there be any need of examples in proof of what I have advanced, I have only to refer you to the revolution which required the best blood of France to wash away the illiberal principles which had hitherto swayed the throne,—to the free states of North America, who owe their independence to the blind and narrow policy which had actuated the British monarchy ever since the days of the first James,—to Greece, the last strong hold, west of the Dardanelles, of those who once spread the terror of their arms from beyond the farthest stretch of the Caucasian range to the most distant shores of remotest Europe; but whose oppressive and impolitic principles are now, we confidently trust, about to force them, a disgraced and despised race, with a weak and irresolute government, into a corner of the earth, a terrible monument to all nations of the insufficiency of intolerance for the support of power.

But, while in a government established on illiberal principles, there are the most formidable springs of ruin, I believe that principles, the opposite of these, contribute, more than any other cause, to the strength and stability of government. It is supposed, of course, that the people are enlightened to the advantages and necessity of government in some shape or other; and to suppose that they would be willing subjects of a power whose constant aim was to oppress and restrain their energies, to reduce their prerogatives, to obstruct their interest, and to hinder their advancement in moral and intellectual improvement; or, to suppose that they would become willing instruments of destruction to a government, which, keeping pace with the progress of civilization, and the spirit of the age, would secure to them every privilege, in as high a degree as would be possible for them to enjoy, would be to deny the very circumstance which has just been taken for granted, namely, an enlightened condition of the people. So far, indeed, from overturning the government, their main solicitude, unless their motives of conduct were strangely at variance with those which usually actuate men in other cases, would be as to the means of supporting it in its fullest strength; — so far from discarding it, their chief anxiety would be lest other powers, jealous of the influence of such an example on their subjects, should endeavor to wrest it from them.

It is, in fact, but the futile imaginings of a disordered brain, which see in the effect of liberal principles any thing approaching to the dissolution of government. For what are liberal principles but a disposition to keep pace with the spirit of improvement which is constantly going on among men? And, can any one, in his sober senses, aver that good government and general civilization are things so entirely incompatible, that the one cannot be enjoyed but at the expense of the other? That vigor and stability in national councils are ever, from their very nature, inconsistent with the progress of the mind? That if men insist on moving onward in the march of intellect, they must be content to sacrifice to this object every thing like a firm and well-regulated state administration? And so, on the contrary, if they wish to be preserved from constant anarchy and civil contention, they must be satisfied to remain in barbarism and degradation? Such doctrines are too monstrous to be harbored for a moment; but yet, I defy any one to deny that they are the doctrines of those who contend that liberal principles are incompatible with the strength of government. For myself, were such my belief, I would utterly discard all allegiance to society. I would betake myself to the obscurest corner of the earth; and there, dwelling aloof from the world, and inaccessible to any of my race, I would prosecute the culture of my understanding and my heart by myself, and undisturbed by that connexion with my species, which would, according to these doctrines, involve my mind in ignorance and darkness. My name should be no more known among all mankind. I would live alone; and none other should rule over me than the Almighty.

PART II.

"*Liberal Principles as affecting the Strength of Government.*"

That the rights which nature has bestowed upon man may be protected and enjoyed, he finds it necessary to subject himself to laws, and to part with some portion of his original freedom, for the maintenance of the rights and freedom of his fellow-men. The social system, of which he is a member, entitles him to other rights, without which, civil liberty is not enjoyed, and the ends for which society was formed are not obtained. Those principles of government are liberal, which secure to man the rights of nature and of society. They are the principles which conduce to the happiness and prosperity of a nation; but it has been observed by political writers, and the observation has been so frequently made that it appears almost an axiom, that those very principles have a powerful effect in weakening government. Reason and experience confirm the remark. Though history has often and clearly proved to us that man is unwilling to be oppressed by man, and will not sacrifice his just rights, when the possession of them will not injure others, he has unfortunately seldom restrained himself from abusing as soon as he begins to enjoy them, till he finally subjects himself to oppression which he endeavored to escape.

It is in their liability to abuse, that the great danger of liberal principles is seen. To enjoy their advantages much precaution must be taken against their evils. They are liable to be carried to excess. To establish the proper security and to mark out the proper limits for them, seem almost impossible. The work will be imperfect. The examples of ancient governments too plainly prove that it was so in them. Faction and corruption were the constant companions of liberty, continually distracting and enfeebling government. They soon exerted their pernicious influence, when Athens began to enjoy that liberal principle, which rendered the voice of the people the law by which they were to be governed. That free principle which declared the proud patricians and humble plebeians of Rome equal, and gave the latter the enjoyment of public offices in company with the former, added not to the strength of government. We find that the interval of tranquillity was but short, and that the tumults of the people, and the oppression of ambitious citizens soon followed. Sylla was the favorite, and became the tyrant of the people.

> "So every scope by the immoderate use
> Leads to restraint."

The principal cause of the fall of the republic of Rome, has been ascribed to the excess of power which the favor of the people too often intrusted to unworthy hands.

As liberal principles allow the people some degree of power, the question may with good reason be asked, whether that power will content them; whether it will not be intentionally abused, or imprudently exercised?

They are forgetful of the relation in which they stand to each other; of the responsibility under which they are placed. Ignorant or thoughtless of the benefit of the whole, which the privileges of each individual enable him to render, they too readily sacrifice the good of the public to their own partiality for some flattering demagogue. They are not sensible of the true value of the liberal principle which is put in their hands, but they are fully aware that they possess power, and will misapply their possession to gratify themselves, at the expense of the public safety, and the public happiness. Such is the abuse of the right of suffrage, an abuse to which the privilege is always exposed, however well informed the people may be of the true design of society, and of the happiness which it is in their power to confer.

We need not examine ancient history, and the imperfect constitutions of old governments, to be convinced that free principles will be dangerous. The history of later times will give us the same information. Will not our own days teach us the same lesson? We have seen the dangers of the press. In the words of one of our own writers, "Its freedom will be abused. It is a precious pest, and necessary mischief, that has spoiled the temper of our liberty, and may shorten its life."

Another effect to be feared from liberal principles, is a want of respect towards those who make and administer the laws. If the people are, directly or indirectly, the makers of the laws, do they the more willingly submit to them! The magistrates whom they have created, they will look upon as their equals, but equality may be forgotten by the magistrates. They will be approved by some, and disapproved by others. There will arise opposition of party to party, and oppression of the one by the other. The purposes of government are forgotten, while each looks with jealousy upon his opponent. There is none of that feeling of awe and reverence which the authority of an hereditary ruler inspires, whose cradle is a throne, of whose oppression it is dangerous to complain, and the success of resistance doubtful.

It is the foundation of the political theory of a distinguished writer, that honor is the support of a monarchy, fear of a despotism, and virtue of a republic. The strongest governments place their security in principles which awe or captivate their subjects. They take advantage of every mode which will excite terror or delight. The will of a despot bows down the victims of ignorance with fear and trembling, who hardly dare to know that nature has bestowed upon them faculties and rights, which were given for their happiness, or the strength of government is derived from a fountain of honor, and consists in ornaments of silver and gold, in the stars and grand crosses of nobility, or in the amusements by which men are charmed into submission. We may, then, say, though in a different sense from the original, "Amusement is the happiness of those who cannot think." But in what does the strength of liberal governments consist? In something of far higher authority than the will of any mortal; in something more ennobling than all other honor; in the only true divine right of sovereignty, the virtue of the people.

This is a strong foundation; but is it not one which is more to be desired than expected? It is little to the honor of human nature that the principle of fear has been found to have a more powerful influence than the principle of virtue. Such has been the case; and liberal principles, from the want of power to preserve them in their purity, have too often produced effects which it seemed contrary to their nature to produce. Though they may be beneficial to themselves, they will be corrupted, unless there is that degree of intellectual and moral cultivation in the community which we are not justified in expecting. It is true, that there is little hope of virtue and learning among a people without liberal principles to encourage and support them. Some portion of freedom is certainly necessary before virtue can be expected to display herself, and exert her influence openly, and before the mind can exercise to advantage the faculties with which it is gifted. But does it follow that this liberty will always reform a community? Liberal principles may be adopted too suddenly, before the character of a people is prepared for them, and then, while they produce not the happiness which they otherwise would produce, will create anarchy or oppression.

Thus it appears that some information and virtue are required for the protection of liberty. But, when free principles are established, and they are producing contentment, virtue may not be secured, may not be preserved. All the effect which fear has over the mind is removed, and the faculties are roused to life and exertion from a state of tranquillity, but a tranquillity like that of the tombs. To escape from the terror of despotism, is a blessing; but there is danger of the slavery of vice. Virtue is, indeed, encouraged by liberty to come forward to the light, and to exercise herself for the benefit of man; but vice meets with like encouragement, and will readily seize its opportunity to gratify itself, and to exert its corrupting influence.

The unfortunate terminations of many revolutions in favor of liberty, are to be found in the want of virtue and knowledge among the people, who are consequently incapable of governing themselves.

Since, then, liberal principles have been so constantly abused, unless the people are, in a high degree, virtuous and enlightened, we must look for strength to the checks provided against the abuse of power in the separate departments of government; not to the agreeable, though poisonous principles of liberty, but to the antidote which is constantly administered against their dangerous effects.

XCIV

DISPUTATIONS.

Disputations are exercises in which parties reason in opposition to each other on some question proposed. They are verbal contests respecting the truth of some fact, opinion, proposition, or argument.

As literary exercises, they are principally of two kinds, Philosophical, and Forensic Disputations.

Philosophical Disputations are those in which some philosophical fact, principle or theory is discussed.

Forensic Disputations are those in which some legal, moral or political subject is argued.

Example 1.

OF A FORENSIC DISPUTATION.

PART I.

Whether Popular Superstitions or Enlightened Opinion, be most favorable to the growth of Poetical Literature.

Fable and superstition form so large a part of the ground-work of ancient poetry, and are so intimately connected with that of all succeeding ages, that a partial investigation of this subject might lead us to very erroneous conclusions. From the bare consideration of this fact, we might be induced to give assent to that opinion, which would make superstition indispensable to the production of poetry, and which would thereby confine its progress to a certain period in the civilization of the world. We might as well, however, consider the dross as a constituent of the virgin gold, as suppose that the imperfections and errors connected with poetry were essential to the divine art.

Homer has left a monument of genius which will be read and admired by remote ages yet to come; but will it be looked upon as one of those prodigies of former times, the history of which alone remains to them, for which, in their time, they can find no parallel or counterpart? Will, then, his poetry be viewed as the production of an art peculiar to former ages, but in those times unknown; a shadow, an illusion, which has vanished before the increasing light of civilization; or will it not rather be admired and venerated, as one of the earliest fountains to which posterity can trace the magnificent stream, which, in their age, may be extending its healthy and invigorating influence through all the channels of society? Yet the idea that superstitious opinions are essentially important to the production of poetry, would exclude the possibility of any great progress in the art. Since error must gradually disappear before knowledge and civilization, and since superstition must vanish wherever Christianity sheds its blessed influence, it follows, that poetry must, some day, in the progress of the world, be seen in the decline. The possibility of this, we should be unwilling for a moment to admit. Poetry is not the peculiar characteristic of a rude and imperfect state of society; it is not a plant which can thrive only in the soil of ignorance; on the contrary, an art, which I do not say, keeps pace with the improvement of society, but is destined rather to precede it; to be, as it were, man's GUIDE to indefinite advancement. In proof of our position, we need only refer to the elevating influence of poetry itself an influence admitted by all, and one which every breast has more or less experienced. The poet's influence is through the feelings, and, as mankind in their nature have been, and always will be, essentially the same the true poet, in the exercise of his profession, has the key to the sensibilities and affections of his fellow-men; when he touches the strings of his lyre, it is only to produce those notes with which every bosom throbs in unison. It becomes, then, an easy task for him to instruct and to elevate, to call man away from the absorbing influence of worldly passions and pursuits, to a view of what is most elevated in his own nature, and most noble in the creation around him, to wean him from the present, and fit him for the future. This exertion of a refining and elevating influence is a prerogative of the poet *admitted by all;* but must, we also believe, that, when he is most successful in his glorious office, he is at the same time diminishing the power and will in his fellow-men to appreciate or countenance his works.

The poet's peculiar liberty and privilege is to give free wing to his imagination; a liberty allowed by every one. In poetry, indeed, we look for fiction, though its legitimate object be truth. Popular superstitions, therefore, afford an easy and ample subject for the poet's pen, and always must, to some degree, enhance the beauty and attraction of his works. For what are popular superstitions but the dreams of the imagination perhaps the fantasies of the poet's own brain? It is asserted by some writers, that the Greeks were indebted for their mythology to the writings of Hesiod and Homer; that their religious notions were vague and unsettled until the fertile imagination of their poets devised for them a system of worship. Indeed, we may safely believe, that a great proportion, if not most of the superstitions, which have prevailed in the world, have sprung into existence at the poet's calling. When this is not the case, they owe their origin to the disordered imagination of some less-gifted mind. From the wonders and beauties of nature, then, one of the poet's most fertile themes, he can no longer receive inspiration, when the floating visions of superstition no longer surround them; when belief in that which ignorance, or the fancy of former poets, has generated, has been resigned for more rational opinions. The genius of poetry forbids such a sentiment. Does the flower which has blossomed and faded from the creation become destitute, in the poet's eye, of poetical associations, because he cannot credit the imaginative belief of ancient bards, that Flora has it in her care, while the sporting Zephyrus fans its petals, parched by the mid-day sun? Is the distant planet less worthy a place in the poet's thought, because its secret influence, whether good or evil, can no more be credited? Does "old ocean" lose any of its sublimity, because it is no longer, even in the poet's mind, peopled by the Tritons, Nereids, and father Neptune? Such, and like notions, were the theme of *ancient* poets and their countrymen gave willing credence to their tales. The *modern* bard might as well stalk the streets in the toga and the buskin, as bring into his lines the dreams of heathen mythology. Yet he is not circumscribed by narrow bounds, because he may not follow, in the regions of imagination, the wild excursions of the ancients, or because his own light fancy may soar no higher than less active reason can accompany her.

The true poet, so far from requiring, will decline the guidance or dictation of his predecessor. It is his office and his pride to present his subject in a novel and interesting view; to shed upon it new light, and invest it with additional attractions. If we admit this, we need have no apprehensions that the muse will be invoked in vain, though she may not be courted, as in former days.

We would not willingly detract from the merits of ancient poetry, or that of any bard that has yet dawned upon the world; but as we would not limit the progress of any art or science by the advancement which they may have reached in former times, so we would not circumscribe the "divinest of all arts" within the narrow boundary of a few centuries in the world's infancy.

PART II.

Whether Popular Superstitions or Enlightened Opinion be most favorable to the growth of Poetical Literature.

"Good sense," says Coleridge, "is the body of poetic genius, fancy its drapery, motion its life, and imagination its soul," — and it is the remark of one who had learned to analyze with exactness the feelings of the poet. Let us see how well examination justifies the definition. We may consider the subject under two heads: — 1st. Do superstition and enlightened opinion united promote poetical literature? 2d. If they are not capable of being thus united, do our ordinary occupations promote that literature?

The first point we shall not strive to establish. Popular superstitions are very few at the present day. Intelligence is widely diffused; books and readers are multiplying, and enlightened opinion is setting up a very wide dominion. It is now thought impossible for superstition and education to exist together. Then are our ordinary occupations, in the second place, favorable to poetical literature? Admitting that enlightened opinion is gaining the ascendency, let us see whether it favors the imagination, — whether a prevailing shrewdness, and the common affairs of life, are sufficient, without the aid of superstition, for poets and novelists.

Life is made up of realities; our wants, though continually supplied, are continually to be supplied. The atmosphere of the world is the chilling atmosphere of reality, exertion, and disappointment. There is little poetry in common life; little poetry in unrewarded exertion, or undeserved oppression, or disappointed ambition. Yet these make an essential part of life, and they are precisely what give such a matter-of-fact, unpoetical tone to most minds. How many feel, as they follow where their duties direct them, any thing of poetry or romance? Are not all disheartened at times by the plain realities of their lot? Notwithstanding many happy connexions, we sometimes feel ourselves, both as individuals and nations, too much fettered, and want something to delight and ennoble, as well as keep us alive. This deficiency is supplied by the emotions springing from popular delusion; which, stealing like a mist over the picture before us, softens the whole landscape. The restraints of society may fetter poetic genius, but the vision and the faculty divine circumstances cannot entirely repress; whenever it is curbed by the world popular superstition frees it from its bondage, and kindles again the trampled spark.

What we degrade as superstition, is, in truth, the very soul of poetry, and no more separable from it than soul from body. It may fail of its object, and make gross what ought to be pure, but the spirit that would condemn superstition on such grounds, would spurn a picture of the Madonna because the same pencil might have delineated a vixen. Superstition springs from the imagination and fancy; poetical literature is directly addressed to these powers of mind, and cannot flourish without them. Philosophy and history are not dependent on them; if they state facts, and draw just conclusions, their ends are attained. Superstition, on the contrary, is an embodying of the grand, the tender, the terrific, as suits the mind, — the creating, as it were, a world of passions and perceptions too spiritual for common life, and yet too natural not to be exercised Now, is not all this poetry in its true sense?

Every imaginative or superstitious nation has abounded in poetical literature. Their peculiarities of thought assist the author, besides cultivating the taste and exercising the imagination of the reader. The success of modern poetic literature, notwithstanding our want of superstition, is not unfavorable to this view. A change has been effected in this kind of writing corresponding to the extension of education. The novelist now draws from human nature rather than superstition; formerly materials were abundant and fanciful, but they were not employed with discretion Perhaps the magnificence of Milton will be adduced as an instance of no superstition in the author, and requiring none in the reader. But Miltons adorn every age. Milton's poetry has been compared to the ocean; and although the ocean is sublime in its own native grandeur, yet the beauty of the inland stream — the lesser poetic strain — is increased when it sounds through the hidden ravine, and is overshadowed by the dark foliage of superstition.

Observe the untutored inhabitants of the mountain, — where the link is shortest between nature and nature's God, — where every cliff is invested with some popular legend, and every valley and lake and hill-top may tell some tale of fancy, some dreaming of speculation, — observe these, as they pay there the vows of a wild superstition, and do you not contemplate the very essence of poetry? Is there no poetry in superstition? Then bid Macbeth and Hamlet be forgotten, and consign "the Wizard of the North" to an unheeded tomb. Call the dreams of his fancy the follies of disease, and pity them. If we deny the poetical nature of superstition, what shall be said of those places where the genius of Scott has revelled till it has hallowed the very traditions of ignorance? Can we make powerless the wand which, in Shakspeare's hand, called the murdered to the banquet, harassed the guilty conscience, and urged the irresolute to revenge?

A good proof that mere enlightenment does little for imaginative writers, may be found in this country. We are wanting in popular legends, and, be it said with deference to wise opponents, wanting in poetical literature. Our poets and novelists are few, and feel too little the inspiration of an American home. Our national character may be the better for this; but our pursuits have made us, as a people, vastly unpo etical. This is readily accounted for. We have been accustomed from childhood, and still continue, to regard chiefly what is necessary in life Interest and thrift are graven on every thing in America; the waves and the winds are unwelcome without the expected gain; and the cliff and stream, however beautiful, are unconnected with superstitious legends Do not the words of one of our poets apply to many of his countrymen?

"The churl who holds it heresy to think,
Who loves no music but the dollar's clink,
Who laughs to scorn the wisdom of the schools,
And deems the first of poets first of fools,
Who never found what good from science grew,
Save the grand truth that one and one are two,
And marvels Bowditch o'er a book should pore,
Unless to make those two turn into four:
Who, placed where Catskill's forehead greets the sky,
Grieves that such quarries all unhewn should lie,
Or, gazing where Niagara's torrents thrill,
Exclaims, 'A monstrous stream to turn a mill!'"

Yes, even at this moment is the demon of utilitarianism throwing his bonds around the cataract of Niagara, — to scoop with a clam-shell the wicked, waste water, and substitute for the torrent's roar, the soul thrilling music of the clapper to a grist-mill! If this is plain common-sense it is not poetry. True, a few of the red man's race remain to wonder at the taste which can so misuse their country; but their spirit has been broken, and they are strangers in the land.

What, then, is the use of popular superstition? Not to bind man to a reverence of folly, nor to exact undeserved admiration, but to soften his nature, by exercising some of his higher powers and sensibilities, and thus make mind minister to happiness.

PHILOSOPHICAL DISPUTATION.

Example.

[One side only is presented.]

Whether Intellectual Improvement be favorable to the Productions of Imagination.

Every age and every nation has its distinguished men. It has had its heroes, poets, orators, philosophers, and statesmen. Whether we go to the abodes of civilization, or to the haunts of savages, we shall find men who are properly the master spirits of their age, and who are destined to give direction to the opinions and actions of their fellow men. This arises from the very constitution of society, and each of the several classes of which it is composed are in some degree dependent on each other. The fame of the hero depends on the historian and poet, and, in return, the achievements of the former afford the most fertile themes for the latter. Some periods, however, are more favorable than others for the developement of a particular kind of talent. The ancients recognized an iron, a bronze, and a golden age, and no impartial reader of history can doubt the justness of such a classification. The golden age was the age when literature and the arts flourished, when civilization had gained the ascendency over barbarism, and when the rights of the individual had begun to be respected.

There is, undoubtedly, an opinion prevalent, that intellectual improvement is unfavorable to the imagination, — that the reasoning power cannot be cultivated without impairing it. But such an opinion has no foundation in fact, and is entitled to no more respect than a thousand other notions that are handed down from age to age, and are regarded as true. The enemies of free government tell us, that learning cannot flourish where all are acknowledged free and equal; that learned men cannot grow up except in the sunshine of royal favor; and that religion cannot work its benign effects except on an ignorant community, and under the guidance of an established church. The different relative progress of the sciences and works of imagination can be accounted for without having recourse to the theory above mentioned. A science is nothing more than the combined experiments and discoveries of men in all ages, while a work of imagination is, to a certain extent, the work of a single person. The philosopher can begin where Bacon and Newton left off: but the poet must begin where Homer began.

There is another cause for the prevalence of this opinion, in the erroneous view taken of the works of an uncultivated people. That wild, figurative language, which arises from its barrenness, is often thought to be conclusive evidence of a lively imagination. As civilization advances, that wildness and extravagance disappear; as language becomes more copious and fixed, those bold figures are no longer used. But does it follow, that the imagination is less lively? That that faculty, on which our happiness so essentially depends, is thus impaired by the very means by which our good is promoted? It cannot be. The God of nature, who made "wisdom's ways ways of pleasantness," did never decree that the improvement of the intellectual should darken that faculty which is truly the mind's eye, and through which the past as well as the future, and the absent as well as the present can be scanned. Imagination does not confine itself to earth, but

"Tired of it
And this diurnal scene, she springs aloft
Through fields of air, pursues the flying storm,
Rides on the volleyed lightning through the heavens,
Or, yoked with whirlwinds and the northern blast,
Sweeps the long track of day."

Should we grant that intellectual improvement was unfavorable to productions of the imagination, then we should no longer look for the best works of that character among a civilized people, but should seek them among our native Indians, or the Tartars of Siberia. We should apply the same rules to individuals as to nations. The least cultivated minds would be the most imaginative. We should look to them for bolder flights than to Milton, Pope, or Byron; the absurdity of which is seen by the mere statement of it, and the principle is unworthy of serious argument. History as well as common sense refutes it. Who of those bards whose works are as immortal as the spirits which produced them had not a cultivated mind? Which of them did not find their imaginative powers increased by intellectual improvement? Though the age of Homer was an age of comparative darkness, yet the sun of literature must have shone on Greece, or the inspired fountains of poetry would have been frozen up. He never would have sung of the heroism of his countrymen had not their feelings responded to his. He never would have written with that correct taste which all succeeding poets have delighted to imitate, had not reason already under her control the wildness and extravagance of the untutored mind.

Our own age bears ample testimony that intellectual improvement does not destroy genius to produce, nor diminish desire to read works of imagination; for there never was a time when so much fiction is written and read as at the present. Poetry is no longer the language of history and oratory, but it is what it ought to be, the language of imagination, clothing in its various dress human passions and affections. In proof of this we need only refer to that giant mind whose powers have been so successfully employed in the world of fiction, making an almost entire revolution in that department of literature. He has shown that the boldest flights of the imagination are not in the darkness of night, but in the clear sunshine of day; that as civilization advances, and the human mind makes progress, so will all its powers be strengthened, and all its faculties be enlarged. Science offers to us new realms, and the astronomer, as well as the poet, may picture to himself worlds moving round in one harmonious whole far beyond the reach of mortal view.

The obscure and the uncertain may be necessary for a full exercise of the imaginative powers, but of this there will always be enough until the whole field of knowledge is explored. In truth, with the advance of knowledge and science, mystery does not diminish. New wonders are continually unfolding themselves, and as the field of vision is enlarged, other views are presented; there still remains beyond the visible and the certain, the invisible and mysterious.

XCV.

ORATION.

An Oration is a speech or discourse composed according to the rules of oratory, and spoken in public; or, it may be defined a popular address on some interesting and important subject. The term is now applied chiefly to speeches or discourses pronounced on special occasions, as a funeral oration, an oration on some anniversary, &c., and to academic declamations.

The term oration is derived from the Latin *oro*, to beg or entreat, and properly signifies that which is said by way of entreaty.

A speech is in general that which is addressed in a formal manner to one person or more. A harangue is a noisy, tumultuous speech, addressed to many; an oration is a solemn speech for any purpose. An address is anything spoken or written from one person or party to another.

A regular oration consists of six parts, namely:

1. The exordium or introduction, which is designed to gain the attention and good will of the hearers, and render them open to persuasion.
2. The stating or division of the subject, in which is expressed what he object of the speaker is, or what he designs to prove or to refute, what doctrine he intends to inculcate, &c.
3. The narration or explication of facts or opinions connected with the subject.
4. The reasoning or arguments.
5. The pathetic part in which an attempt is made to interest the feelings of the hearers.
6. The conclusion, in which a general review may be made of what has been previously said; and the inferences drawn from the arguments may be distinctly stated.

It is by no means necessary that all of these parts should be included in an oration. Much depends on the nature of the subject, and what the speaker has in view. But in listening to a performance of this kind, it is expected that the mind will be informed, the reasoning powers exercised, the imagination excited, and the taste improved. The subject should be one which requires a statement and elucidation of interesting facts and principles; a course of calm, dignified, and persuasive reasoning. At the same time, it should allow of fine writing. There should be opportunity for description and pathos, for historical and classical allusions and illustrations, and for comprehensive and ennobling views. It should admit also of unity of plan. The style should be elevated and elegant, the form of expression manly and dignified, and at the same time characterized by force and vivacity. The ornament should be of a high kind —such as ennobles and exalts the subject. Diffuseness is likewise desirable.

Example 1st.

OF AN ENGLISH ORATION.*

Public Station.

One of the happiest, as well as most useful, improvements which the social system has received, since the earliest congregation of savage life, is the *division of labor.* While it insures to us the greatest profit at the least cost, and enables the labor of each to contribute most effectually to the advantage of the whole, it introduces among men such a variety of classes and conditions — it parts out the business of life into so many and various lots, as may satisfy each peculiar bias, imprinted by nature on the minds of individuals. The great world has many mansions. In one, there are the tools of industry and the bread of care; in another, the insignia of power — the diadem, the mitre, and all the aching luxury

* On taking the First Degree.

of thrones, in a third, is hung up the unfading laurel of the Muse, which, as "it plucks all gaze its way," lets us not behold the cold neglect and starving penury which too often await it; — one looketh out upon the green fields, with their blossoms, their full ears, their bending branches; and another looketh out upon the broad sea, with its tall ships and its cunning merchandise; — all these, and many more, are wide open before us, and it requires but our own *volition*, to decide where we will enter in and abide.

Among the manifold professions and employments of life, however there is much else, beside natural bias, to influence a man's choice. The unyielding necessity of gaining a livelihood, binding upon most of us, is ample security that no one of them will be left vacant. Industry, like wealth, will find its own level. A deficiency in any of its channels will create a demand; and self-interest will ever be at hand, to supply it. But this is not all. We are all, more or less, the slaves of passion. The cold and calculating dictates of prudence are often overruled by the more specious and flattering whispers of pride. The path of reason is too straight-forward and dull for our eager ambition. We cannot bide to toil slowly up her steep and thorny way, for the quiet possession of scanty bread. The echoes of the silver trumpet have reached our ear, and we sigh that it may sound out our own name. The imperial purple has caught our eye, and the plain vestments of an honorable sufficiency seem too mean and common for our wear!

Perhaps there is no prospect, which the imagination can present, so alluring to the mind of a young man as that of public life. The mere fact of being a theme of public interest, and of being exalted by the voice of popular favor to a station above one's fellows, — is of itself a boon, than which, it would seem, the most ardent ambition could desire none greater. But this is but the beginning of good things, — but the portal to the high places of fame. It is in the exercise of this trust, that the full harvest of glory is to be reaped. *Our* mind is to counsel, — *our* voice to direct,—*our* arm to govern all;—the sceptre of power is to be handled, — her royal robes put on — and *we* are to be the gaze of every eye. These are the rich privileges which our eager fancy holds out to us as the rewards of office; and it is not to be wondered at, that the coldest ambition should kindle at the view. It is no longer a strange thing, that popular favor should be courted and public station sought diligently after. It is man's nature to look upward — "*ut aquila, cœlum versus*," — how, then can he but long for this highest heaven of human glory?

But let us strip off the gilded veil of fancy, and look in upon the condition of office when the pomp and parade are over, and the robes are thrown aside. And here, it were a superfluous task to inquire into the comparative happiness and ease of public station. It needs not the eloquent philosophy of the wronged Duke, to tell us, that a life of even undeserved exile is sweeter far than that of painted pomp, — "the inhospitable woods more free from peril than the envious court," — "the icy fang and churlish chiding of the winter's wind," more trusty counsellors than the fawning flattery of court-sycophants. Nor need we the touching examples of Wolsey, of Buckingham, of Mary, and all that host of splendid misery which history supplies, to warn us how sore and galling a burden is "too much honor." We have heard with our ears — our fathers have told us — many of us are in the immediate, sad experience that place and greatness, though fair without, and full of temptation, —

are, like the apples of Asphaltum, but ashes to the taste; and when withdrawn from the excitements of busy life, and left alone to reflection, we are all ready enough to exclaim with the poet:-

"'T is better to be lowly born,
And range with humble livers in content,
Than to be perked up in a glistering grief,
Or wear a golden sorrow."

But this is one of those fireside reflections which are apt to escape us, in the bustle of out-of-door life. Vain hope with all its specious and most plausible cheats, bids us not take upon trust so sad a truth. Ambition, which we strive in vain to "fling away," whispers us, that it is nobler to bide the worst, so *honor* be the stake. To serve one's country, is at least a glorious martyrdom, and we are proud to suffer it. Were such the motive of those who enter the lists of public life, were honor conferred in exact proportion to merit, and trust squared with integrity, this were a sentiment worthy the extremest limit of indulgence. A nobler vocation no one can have, — a more glorious sacrifice was never made, — than to toil and suffer for the public good. Our country's call, as it were the voice of Fate crying out to us, should make "each petty artery in this body, as hardy as the Nemean lion's nerve!" But is it from pure and disinterested patriotism, that so many are daily clothed in the white robe of candidacy? Can we pretend, even in this land of promise, that public honors are never capriciously, nay, are never unjustly, bestowed? We have not, indeed, here, that long line of titled aristocracy, "*state-statues* only," whose rank, dating from the cradle, can be founded, at most, only on a *predestinarian* estimate of future worth! We acknowledge neither "Divine right," nor "original compact," as a claim to supremacy. Much less need we fear that the wise, the virtuous, and the learned should be banished from *our* land, as from Sparta of old, in very fear lest, by the unrestrained exertion of their *pernicious weapons*, they should work out for themselves an extravagant and dangerous influence. The wise, the learned, the good, stand here indeed their chance with the rest; and it is a triumph worthy all rejoicings when they struggle into power. But how often do we see those noble natures, — who, seeking merit rather than fame, would scorn to "flatter Neptune for his trident, or Jove for his power to thunder," — cheated of their rightful inheritance of glory! It cannot be denied, though with shame we confess it, that learning, genius, and virtue, will strive for popular favor, but at fearful and perilous odds, against the supple knee, the flattering tongue, the cringing soul.

What, then, is there in office for which men are thus eagerly striving? What is this highest prize of contention, in pursuit of which, happiness is counted as nothing, and merit is content to be pitted against hypocrisy and intrigue? It is CALLED Power. There are few more ludicrous mistakes, which this erring world exhibits, than those of a false and o'erleaping ambition. The redoubted Knight of la Mancha, though unequalled in story, is not alone in real life. We may, almost daily, behold the brazen basin of the barber, borne proudly along, in all its *soapy lustre*, as if 't were really the golden helmet of Mambrino! In most countries, we may see crowds, and even in our own *practical land* not a few of those dabblers in the pettiness of fame, whose official importance would serve only to remind us of that pretty device of Æsop, — a fly on the axle of a chariot, striving to exclaim "what a dust do *I* raise!" The truth is, that in these times, and especially in our own land, the *power*, which office of itself confers, is most specious and shadowy. Even in the Old World, little else is retained, save the name, the show, the ceremony of power. In the most arbitrary governments of modern times, the popular feeling is respected and obeyed, though it be not directly, and in terms appealed to. But with us, the very boast of our liberty is, that the people are supreme. They indeed do delegate certain of their number, to manage for them their great estate of sovereignty: — but this delegated authority is divided off into so many branches, and so entirely checked by the mutual action of these branches upon each other, that the power of *individual* office is a mere name and a shade. Our governors are in fact but public servants — a most honorable, indeed, and praiseworthy *service*, but containing so much more of burden and care, than of *power*, that we might almost apply to them the old Greek proverb, — "none in the land are so much *slaves*, as its *masters*."

But if public station do not actually *confer* power upon its possessor, it *at least*, affords him the most favorable opportunity for gaining it. If office be not greatness, it *surely* must be the highest vantage-ground for achieving greatness. It was the answer of the Delphic oracle to Cicero, says Plutarch, when he inquired how he should attain to the highest earthly glory, — "by making *his own genius*, and not the will of the people, the guide of his life." To enter into an elaborate discussion of this great question, would far exceed our spare and strict allowance of time; but it may well be doubted, whether that close subjection to popular will, that contracted servitude to party, that unyielding bondage to public opinion, which public officers must necessarily undergo, be not far, very far, from the pure and perfect air of liberty, in which genius exults and thrives. It seems, too, a nobler, as well as freer, task to promote the mental improvement, than the physical welfare, of our race, — to govern *minds*, than to govern men.

I know that history, an honorable mention in whose pages is, perhaps, the proudest reward which mortal merit can aspire to, has hitherto devoted her exclusive praise to those who have led the armies or guided the councils of their nations. It hath now been the diary of princes, and now the "field-book of conquerors," and full rarely hath even the name of a private man, however splendid his talents or exalted his virtues, been deemed worthy of its notice. But the liberty, which has been here worked out, is not confined to the mere form and ceremony of government, — it not only pervades the whole atmosphere, but penetrates the very life-breath, and purifies the very heart's core of society, — and we may confidently hope, that the *Free Historian* of *Free America*, pampered in no court, pensioned by no crown, will pen with the golden pen of Truth, — that *her* history may be, as all history *ought* to be, — philosophy pure, uncompromising philosophy, "teaching by examples," — a history, where crimes may be mentioned only to be condemned, — where virtue, genius, merit, may stand out in their own unfading beauty, the admiration and the model of the world! We would not, indeed, withhold their merited tribute of praise, their proud recompense of glory, from the "patriots who have toiled and in their country's cause bled nobly." The sweet lyre, the sculptured marble, shall have their names in holy keeping! But *they* are not alone *patriots*. This proud title of *patriotism* is no narrow distinction of birth or of fortune. Whoever promotes, or labors to promote, the interest and welfare of his country, be his means never so small, his vocation never so humble, is a patriot. They are patriots who obey and defend, as well as they who make the laws. They are patriots who strive, as they are able, to advance in the land the great cause of religion, of justice, of public improvement. Every good man is a *patriot!* They were patriots, whose names shall hereafter be mentioned as the founders and benefactors of this venerable institution. *He** is a patriot, and worthy a patriot's praise, whose wonted presence at the head of our University, on this high festival of letters, we may no longer look for. If the *youth* of our land be its hope and its promise, as their fathers are its strength and its support, — surely he shall have rendered a goodly and an acceptable service to his country, who by his diligence, his instructions, his example, has trained up so many to her duties and her honor. We would yield him, then, the glory of a *patriot*, as well as the affectionate thanks of grateful hearts, for all that he has done and suffered in the cause of education. His is a glory, "*cui neque profuit quisquam laudando, neque vituperando quisquam nocuit.*" May he live long, to see this ancient abode of science, — the fond object of his care and love, — increased in usefulness and power; standing in all the strength of sound wisdom, in all the majesty of virtue, in all the beauty of holiness, a blessing to the children, and an honor to the fathers of our land; and on its brightest tablet of record, among its best defenders, shall *his* name and *his praise* be ever inscribed. May his years to come be full of comfort, and his end — peace!

It is one of the peculiar features of our republican government, that the doors of office, — which have hitherto been rarely entered, but by those who could produce the passports of high birth or princely patronage, — are here thrown open to all. The natural consequence is, that all are eager to rush in. Imagination has pictured to us this exclusive abode, abundant in all the luxury and splendor of Oriental magnificence; and the prince of Abyssinia felt not more longings, — and, I venture to say *tried not more expedients*, to gain a knowledge and a view of the outer world of man, than we to gain admittance into this favored palace of the Blest. We do not fear, with the enemies of liberty, that this "political ambition" will always prove a canker in the hearts, or engender corruption in the minds of our people, — warring against the interests of literature, and bringing down upon us either the darkness of anarchy or the more gloomy light of despotism. We neither feel, nor feign, any such idle apprehensions. We have seen the flood-gates of ocean suddenly unbarred, and though the dashing waves leaped never so violently in devouring all they met, — it was but for a moment; the waters flowed again into their channel, and the sea was still. But though this temporary evil will ultimately be its own cure, it is well that all means should be employed to diminish its immediate violence. The storm has not yet ceased — we may, even *now*, see it, in all the strength of its rage, fearfully agitating our land. The holy ark of our liberties is, even now, tossed on its angry bosom! It is time that men's eyes were opened to reason. It is time that they looked upon office as it really is; like the other professions of life, a place of honorable labor, conferring on its possessor no absolute superiority, — no exclusive privilege, — no peculiar blessedness; — an elevation where one's failings, as well as excellences, are displayed to a dangerous advantage. We would render to the rulers and counsellors of our land all the respect

* Dr. Kirkland, who had recently retired from the University.

and homage that are their due; but we will not yield up to them the sole possession of that *power* — the only power worth having — the highest power of man — a power which angels from all their glory might stoop to enjoy — the *power* of doing good to mankind — of serving one's country — of improving our race — of ennobling our age! *This* is the power which all may possess — which requires no passport but of Heaven. *This* is the promotion which "cometh neither from the East, from the West, nor yet from the South." *Mind* asks not the seal of office for a sanction of its dictates, "*nec sumit aut ponit secures arbitrio popularis auræ.*" Its course will on, the way it takes, "cracking ten thousand curbs of more strong link asunder," than the slender impediments of artificial society. It will *speak out*, wherever it exists, in tones than which God's thunder is not more audible!

To this power and this greatness let us aspire. Let the education and improvement of mind be the first object of our ambition. Let not the great harvest of our literature lie longer unreaped. Our dizzy mountain-peaks — our green hills — our fertile vales — our thundering cataracts — our pleasant streams, were never made for sealed lips. Our firm hands, our brave hearts, our bright eyes, though eloquent in silence, deserve not a mute lyre. The fair brow of Liberty looks bald and naked without the laurel of the Muse!

Example 2.

THE UTILITARIAN SYSTEM. *

"Cui Bono."

The spirit of the present strongly demands the *useful* in all its objects of pursuit; there is little reason to fear that men will neglect their interests, so far as their judgment enables them to perceive them; for little occupies general attention that does not return some plausible answer to the question, "Of what use is it? what advantage arises from it?" The wild visions conjured up by the heated imaginations of other times, are all viewed through this correcting medium, and stripped of all their bright and deceptive colors, are stamped with that value only to which their utility entitles them. The lance of chivalry rusts in obscurity and neglect, while the ploughshare is bright with honorable use; the venerable castle, moss-covered and shattered by the storms of a thousand years, is of small consequence, as it stands beside the smart, new-built manufactory, its neighbor, whence some of the conveniences and comforts of life are constantly flowing; the mountain, though it be the highest peak of the Alps, or Andes, cloud-capt, and snow-crowned, towering sublime over the domains beneath, the theme of poets, and the resting-place of the imagination, is thought little of in comparison with the dark and gloomy mine at its base, whence are drawn the ore for manufacture, or the coal with which it is prepared.

All things are estimated, not at the price set upon them by the children of poetry and romance, but according to their immediate subserviency in rendering comfortable the condition of the great majority of mankind And shall any one say that there is not much true philosophy in this valuation? Shall any one sigh over the tendency of the age to look with a dispassionate eye on those wild schemes, and false ideas of honor and

* On taking the First Degree

greatness, which in former times caused such a waste of human life and means? Shall any one for this denounce the times as forgetful of all that constitutes excellence or happiness? Shall it be said that this spirit necessarily smothers all the nobler parts of man's nature, and reduces him to a mere pains-taking, money-getting animal? That it is incapable of being turned and guided into any good course, and of forming the groundwork of a better state of things than the world has ever yet seen? Such desponding minds, — such prophets of evil, must have got their ideas of the *summum bonum* from tales of chivalry and romance, from the dreams and longings of a heated imagination, from any thing, in fact, rather than a comparison of the sources of happiness in the present and any former time. Should such an examination be made, that which appears so bright and enchanting when viewed from a distance, will hardly bear a close inspection. Strip these bright visions of all the radiance thrown around them by the charms of an elegant literature, and how meagre do they stand before us, in all the harsh outline of a rude and unpolished nature; the violent passions and harsh impulses of men stand forth, divested of that softening influence thrown upon them by a refined civilization. The courage of the warrior will shrink to the level of mere animal violence; the beauty of the ladies will pall upon the imagination, when it is considered how uninteresting must have been their minds from the want of all those graces and refinements which a more enlightened age only can impart; while throughout all classes the powers of the intellect were but imperfectly developed, and give us no very exalted idea of man and his powers. Let these things be but once thought of in such an abstract way, separated from all the bright associations that are usually wound about them, and the most enthusiastic admirer of antiquity will hardly wish that his lot had been cast in any of those periods that once seemed so delightful.

But though the present estimate of utility be on the whole so correct, is there nothing in it that may be cause of disgust to those of delicate feelings, and at the same time injurious to our truest, best-defined interests? None but the most unhesitating, undiscriminating panegyrist would attempt to deny it. In their endeavors to reduce every thing to the standard of the useful, many have overstepped the limit. In their zeal to do away with all old follies, they cast off with them some of those virtues which are peculiar to no age or state of society, but whose seat is deep in the human heart, and whose free exercise is indispensable to the prosperous continuance of any state or order of things; connecting these with the really worthless objects, with which they are so often associated, with the intention of eradicating all the useless weeds from the soil of humanity, they ruthlessly tear up some of the most beautiful flowers in the gardens of the heart; they crush those buds that would expand, and blossom, and bear good fruit; that would exalt and purify, and refine life, and go far to realize man's imagined perfections.

We may see some signs of such a spirit, in that tone of superior wisdom that would repress all the outbreakings of enthusiasm, and damp the ardor of the grateful heart in its admiration of the beautiful and noble, with a sarcastic and self-conceited manner of asking the question, What use? And if the object of this harsh ridicule cannot show some direct and visible operation of the ideas and sentiments he admires, it warns him to be advised by experience, and to have done with all such foolish and romantic notions, which will only impede his successful progress in the world; that is, drop all that characterizes the man of feeling and sentiment, and retain nothing but the most esteemed maxims of a self-wise and selfish experience. Such a spirit would look upon this fair earth merely as one great farm, intended only to maintain its numberless denizens by its productive powers; it would grudge every acre not devoted to this purpose; it would look with an invidious eye upon lakes and mountains as useless incumbrances; in the pleasant light of heaven, and the blowing of its breezes, it would recog nize only the means to promote vegetation, and bring the harvest to maturity; men it would regard as mere instruments in these great operations as bound to their country, and to each other, by no stronger ties, no better feelings than a low and selfish interest; to it all else seems superfluous: all the glorious and beautiful, and all the touching and delicate, of the natural and moral world, are unvalued and uncared for. Though this false estimate be but too common, the mind that has not been subjected to it must revolt at its dictates. What! must all the refreshing gardens and pleasant walks of life be shut, all its delightful prospects obstructed, and all the gushing streams of the heart be sealed up! Could any one urge this in serious argument, no more concise and appropriate answer could be given him, than the decision of the Creator himself upon the works of his hand, — that they are *good*, *all* good.

But, to such contemners of all that soars above their own limited vision, the use of argument seems altogether superfluous; there are certain epithets to which no definite meaning is attached, but which, when applied with a certain manner of sarcasm or ridicule, do more to injure their object, than the most direct and severe crimination: there is a vagueness about them that gives the imagination room to conjure up a thousand bad qualities, and apply them to whatever is the subject of obloquy. Of this nature is the epithet *romantic*, so frequently and indiscriminately applied to all the impulses which fill the breasts of those who have not lost all the warmth and generosity given them by nature; who are excited with a noble ardor at the mention of great examples of virtue or heroism; who can see and feel the sublime and beautiful in nature and in character; who can kindle with love, swell with pity, or weep in sympathy with another's woes; they are told that all these things *will not do in the world;* that they are only found in silly novels; in fact, that they are all together too romantic. The tendency of this spirit is to make the young distrust their own feelings, and anxious to suppress every word and action that might come within the reach of this far-sweeping romantic; restraint and affected indifference become but too fashionable, even among those who are formed for better things; their fetters, early and long-worn, at length cease to gall, and the man of a once warm heart and strong affections, becomes a frigid and unimpassioned thing, whose impulses are all of the lowest, commonest description. But is it *really so?* Is there any danger in giving way to any of those emotions which are so enchanting in the page of poetry or romance? Are they really incompatible with those necessary duties which are allotted to most men in the common routine of life and occupation? Must we risk all those bright visions of life, enlivened and ennobled by the exercise of those finer feelings we love so to dwell upon? In fine, are they all of *no use?* Let the anxious inquirer look around, and mark the operation of some of those sentiments so harshly condemned as romantic and useless.

Is that feeling *useless* which entwines a love of his native land with every fibre of a man's heart? Which makes him look upon her mountains and plains, her rivers and lakes, or her rock-bound, sea-washed coast, with an indescribable, and almost superstitious veneration? Shall all those associations which make a man look upon his country as something more than so much land inhabited by so many proprietors, whom convenience has led to form themselves into an organized, political body, be laughed at, as the relic of a bygone, barbarous age; as too *romantic* to be indulged even for a moment? Shall that enthusiasm which leads the traveller, weary of wandering, and longing for home, on beholding the rocks and cliffs of his native shore, to exclaim with rapturous joy, — "This is my own, my native land," — be ridiculed as the expression of nothing but a mawkish, and false sensibility? On the contrary, is not such a feeling the foundation of that true and real *patriotism*, which makes a man lay down wealth and comfort, and pour forth blood like water for his country's good? Has it not been the all-pervading sentiment in those martyrs and patriots whom history and fiction equally delight in honoring? Should we make Thermopylæ and Marathon familiar as household words, had there not been some stronger impulse in the breasts of the heroes who fought there than the mere desire to save their lands and property from unjust spoliation? Interest, or fiction, may, for a time, excite men to action in behalf of their country; but, to arouse the undying flame of patriotism, to make such lovers of their country as time has shown, the "caritas ipsius soli," the clinging to all the marks written in memory by affection, the scenes of our youth, the monuments and undying history of our ancestors, our hearthstones, and objects of domestic affection, must all work together in a manner none the less effective, because it cannot be reduced to the cold and exact rules of statesmen or philosophers.

Is that love *useless* which exalts so high in man's judgment the worth of the fairer, softer portion of his race; that takes away so much of the harsh and low from his character, and makes him see every thing in a warmer purer light. Or are any of those other tender feelings, which purify his character, and make him somewhat like the divine original? Equally harsh and false is that estimate that would say so; which would divest life of so much that softens its hard and rugged track; which would stop all those fountains gushing fresh from the heart, which sweeten and quicken the otherwise insipid and sluggish course of duties and labors. And yet such a disposition is but too common; it hears with incredulity of the existence of virtuous enthusiasm, or ardent love; or, if it cannot doubt their existence, it shows its contempt for them by a freezing interrogatory as to their advantage; it would confine all such romantic feelings to the pages of the poet or novelist, who, it thinks, first gave them birth, and insists, that however well they may do to "point a moral, or adorn a tale," they will *never do in real life.*

If such were real life, if none of the holiest and best affections could be indulged with safety, well might the gloomy views of those be entertained, who look upon the pleasant world as a succession of empty nothings, and all our boasted improvements and advancements as only tending to render them lighter and more empty, and to remove us farther from all that makes life worth the having.

Such a feeling of discontent, as it is particularly apt to seize upon minds most delicately tuned by nature, must have an injurious effect upon the age, which has been represented as, on the whole, so discriminating as to what is truly good and useful; since it withdraws from exerting a healthful influence those whose natural impulses would cause them to promote its best interests; but, disgusted by the false. utilitarian spirit just dwelt upon, their minds sink into a morbid and repini g state, which questions if there be any thing pleasant, or excellent, contents itself with railing a all around, and nursing its own misanthropic feelings.

How, then, shall we answer that cold and sarcastic temper, which, in a. the confidence of superior wisdom, thinks to crush all the generous impulses of an ardent nature, the aspirations of genius, or the buddings of an unfeigned love, or strong attachment, by a withering manner of asking the question, *Of what use are all these?* We might answer with another question; Of what use is the pleasant light of the sun? For, not more groping, cold, and melancholy, would be an eternal, sunless night, than life without one ray of those warmer feelings to illumine its dark and tortuous paths, to gild the points of all the sterner, harsher duties, and cast a warm flush of happiness over all its varying scenes. We might tell them, that, banish these, and the world would be a desert of so harsh and uninteresting an aspect, that the most stoical patience could not endure it long; and, if their unsympathizing minds could not comprehend how this might be, we might tell them that to the feelings they so much despise they are indebted for the continuance of that state of things which appears to them so profitable and excellent. That they are the great corner-stones on which society is founded, the bonds that maintain its union; that, but for some of the enthusiasm they so much condemn, civilization would long since have stopped in its progress, the arts and knowledge would have remained undeveloped, and all that tends to exalt and refine man's condition would still have slumbered. If they cannot be induced by this to acknowledge that there are any others but their own beaten highways of life, they must remain in ignorance of all its better part, forfeit all the enjoyments which accrue to those who can rightly estimate its blessings, and plod on in the way they have chosen for themselves; — while, to those who have an undimmed perception of the good and lovely, life spreads itself out like a verdant flowery field, its paths enlivened by the bordering green, the gemming dewdrops not yet dashed from its flowerets, and all beyond a vista of gladness and beauty. Happy those who choose this better portion, and enjoy that *real life* which those only can have, who, in all their estimates of use, are guided by that true philosophy, which, while it hastens the step of improvement, does not prevent the coöperation of our best nature!

Example 3.

*Public Opinion.**

On the return of this ancient anniversary, on this academical jubilee, which borrows all its lustre from the countenance of a great community, I am naturally led to the contemplation of the power of a community. It is public favor which has raised a humble grammar school into the greatest collegiate establishment in our land. And we who are come up this day to make our last obeisance to our venerable parent, cannot consider without interest, that power out of which she sprang, and that power upon whose character our own fortunes must so much depend.

But the growth of a literary seminary is but an exhibition in miniature of that force of which I speak. Compared with some of its greater manifestations, it is the application of the force of steam to the cutting of diamonds, or the enchasing of plate. It is on the spacious stage of history, where ages are the time, and nations the actors, that I find the just examples of the power of public opinion emblazoned. What is the great lesson we learn from the records of our race? What but this? That the true sovereign of the world, the only monarch who is never deposed, and never abridged of his prerogative,

"Who sits on no precarious throne,
Nor borrows leave to be,"

is Public Opinion.

What is a throne? What is a legislature? What is a Congress? What is a constitution? Mere pipes, mere mouth pieces, for the expression of Public Opinion. The moment they cease to give it vent, the moment they resist and set up for original powers, it breaks in pieces these venerable forms, as Daniel broke the gilded images of Babylonish idolatry, and holds up the fragments before the startled nations, with the same dreadful irony, — "Lo, these be the gods ye worship."

One would think, from what has sometimes been advanced, on great authority, that Public Opinion was a new power. I am confident that it is a mistake. Public Opinion is no new creation, no stranger in the world, no child of its old age. It has mingled in the public affairs since man first exchanged his cave in the woods for the arts and alliances of civilized life.

Born in the primeval conventions of uncouth savages, its infant fingers trace that social contract to which the proud monarchies of the Old World

* On taking the first degree.

are not ashamed to go back for the fabulous charter of their legitimacy. And from that hour it has gone about among the kingdoms of the earth, working its pleasure, whether for good or for evil. You may track its lion step across the Syrian sands, when it led the fanatic hosts of Christendom to pour out their libations of blood, and sacrifice their human hecatombs, in pious worship of the Prince of Peace. Or you may find its handiwork in modern England, when it spoiled of its crown the unworthy successor of a line of kings; washed away his balm, and laid his head upon the block; turned loose an incensed people to hunt down the remnant of that old house of tyrants, and purge the realm of their unclean influence. But, by and by, as if in very wantonness, reverting to its ancient faith and affections, it recalls the fugitive princes from their exile, and rebuilds the dynasty it had overturned.

But, if the will of the people has always been the sovereign, under whatever forms it has been disguised, by whatever ministers it has exercised the functions of sovereignty, it will be asked, how are we to explain certain dark passages of the history of man? If the people have been really the master, whence came those odious institutions which have preyed from age to age, like an hereditary disease, on the aggrieved nations? How stole the serpent into the Eden of democracy? In what chamber of the people's deputies, was the order of knighthood created? What bill of rights was it that stipulated for the inviolability of the Canon and Feudal Law? What date do the articles of abdication bear, wherein the major portion of mankind, wearied with the cares of government, resign their irksome state, and sell themselves for slaves to their fellow-men? Where was the popular assembly convened, which followed up the splendid distinctions of chivalry in Europe, with the emoluments and honors of modern aristocracy; "gilding a little that was rich before," and lavishing on an overgrown peerage civil immunities, and injurious monopolies? If Public Opinion is supreme, how came in those abuses which plunder the many of wealth, and honor and freedom, to lay the costly spoils at the feet of a few? Crowns, principalities, and orders of nobility, — are these the trophies with which Public Opinion has strown its path? . . . . . Yes. Even these were called into being by the word of the people. And all those political evils which have plagued the suffering race of men, first sprung into life at the will of the people, and received at its own hand their bloody commission; like fiends raised by the enchanter, whom they will shortly torment. Folly was the disease of which Public Opinion was sorely sick; Ignorance was the deadly charm by which it was bound; and is it strange that it lay powerless along the land, the victim of petty tyranny? It was only Samson submitting his invincible locks to be confined by the fingers of Delilah with the pin of a weaver's beam. And Oh, how faithfully the old patriarch told its history, when he prophesied the fortunes of his unworthy child! "Issachar is a strong ass, couching down between two burdens; and he saw that rest was good, and the land, that it was pleasant, and he bowed his shoulder to bear, and became a servant to tribute."

But these seasons of patient sufferance do not always last. And long periods of torpid quiescence are succeeded by awful reactions. It is this moment when Public Opinion changes, — this turning of the tide, — that is the sublime moment in the annals of nations.

> "Its step is as the tread
> Of a flood that leaves its bed,
> And its march it is rude desolation."

It bursts through the mounds and levées that dammed it up, and strikes terror into ancient societies, and institutions that lie peacefully over the land, by the roar of the inundation. It is when great events are pending, when the scales of human destiny are hung out in heaven, and the eyes of men grow dim with watching the doubtful balance, — when old systems fail, and old principles are a by-word, — when the strong attractions which keep society in its orbit are dissolved, and the winds of Passion go sighing by, — it is then that Public Opinion re-collects itself to meet the solemn emergency; leaving its ancient seats, it shakes off the dust of centuries, and carries the human race forward to the mark they are prepared to reach.

It was in a crisis like this, that the keys of heaven were wrested from the successors of St. Peter, and the light of the Reformation let in upon a mourning church. And when the clearer light of another age revealed the abuses still unreformed, Public Opinion invaded once more the ground that was fenced with ecclesiastical interdictions, continued the heroic work, and finally launched its little fleet of pilgrims on the main, to follow the setting sun, and lodge the floating ark on the mountains of a New World.

And here in the West, it is at the bidding of Public Opinion, that Liberty has unrolled the sky of half the globe, for her star spangled banner. It is at the same high mandate, that Science throws across our rushing streams her triumphant arches; yokes together with a Cyclopean architecture the everlasting hills, and then leads over their giddy summits the peaceful caravans of commerce.

But, with all its splendid triumphs, it is still an unsteadfast and turbulent principle, as inconstant as an individual mind. And the annals of our race are but accusing records, which show how Public Opinion has given its voluntary and omnipotent sanction to every form of crime. It has crossed great enterprises, and broken brave hearts. It has doomed to the faggot and the rack the champions of truth, and the children of God. It is as much the parent of the Holy Inquisition, and the Court of the Star-Chamber, as of Bible Societies, or the Royal Academy.

What, then, is our security? Can we rear no bulwark? Can we dig no trench around our noblest and most venerable establishments of Church and State? Are we all embarked in a frail vessel, and may this blind Polyphemus sink us at pleasure with a swing of his arm? Where is the origin of Public Opinion? It is in private opinion. Each great national feeling, wave after wave, has been first the opinion of a few, the opinion of one. Here, then, is the great check, and safeguard, and regulator, in individual character and influence. Obviously, no external force can act on the all-surrounding energy of a public mind. In vain would we plant sentries, or patrol a watch about this unmastered power. The way to explode a magazine is to apply the match to a kernel. The way to move the public, is to affect individuals. Every honest citizen whom we can enlighten; every mind throughout the nation, by which right views are entertained, and proper feelings cherished, is one more improver of Public Opinion.

Let it be deeply considered by us, since it thus originated, how much every superior understanding is its natural counsellor and guide; and to what extent such men as Swift, Burke, and Mirabeau were the ministers of this real Autocrat; that no longer those titular gentlemen, who, in London and Paris, on solemn days, wear crowns and solemn dresses, but Canning, and Scott, and Malthus, are now the sovereigns of the world. It is in this fact, that Public Opinion has grown wiser, and will continue to become more informed, that I find the superiority and the hope of our times. And the humblest individual, aware that his opinions are a portion of the sovereign law of the land, would do wrong to conceive his influence to be insignificant. It is not insignificant. Not a thought you think, not a syllable you utter, but may, in its consequences, affect the prosperity of your country. Our world is framed like a vast whispering gallery, — one of those curious structures of human skill, where every breath is audible, and the word that at first was faintly spoken, scarce trusted to the silent air, is sent swiftly onward and around the vaulted walls; a thousand babbling echoes repeat and prolong the sound, till it shakes the globe with its thunder.

Come out of your individual shell. Give your thoughts to the interests of your race, and, like the genie in Oriental story, who, creeping out of the casket of a few inches, in which he had been imprisoned, regained his colossal proportions you will grow to the stature of a godlike intelligence. Nor will you fail of your reward. Those who, by their mighty influence, exert a wise control over the will of the people, always receive from the public opinion they have enlightened, their just meed of praise. It is a spectacle we can never behold without emotion, the supremacy of one mind over this concentrated intelligence. It claims our reluctant reverence for characters in which the amiable virtues are wanting. The moral merit of Cromwell is exceedingly questionable; but his astonishing mastery of the public mind, and the energies he wielded in the cause of liberty, have procured him the endless gratitude of freemen.

> "For, if we would speak true,
> Much to the man is due,
> Who from his private gardens, where
> He lived reserved and austere,
> As if his highest plot,
> To plant the Bergamot,
> Could by industrious valor climb
> To ruin the great work of Time,
> And cast the kingdoms old
> Into another mould."

But, where virtues and talents have alike contributed to invest an individual with this authority over his cotemporaries, public opinion rejoices to pay its instructor a hearty tribute of deserved praise. It has lately been signally manifested, in the deep sympathy in our loss, on the resignation of his seat at the head of the university, by one, for so many years, its ornament and pride. I cannot speak of President Kirkland without a crowd of affectionate recollections, which, I am sure, are familiar to all who hear me For he was one of that truly fine genius which identified his character with the institution in which he sat. Whilst he remained here, his elegant mind rained influence on all that harbored in its halls; and it was not easy for dulness to come under his eye without being sweetened and refined. The stranger who saw him, went away glad that there was so much savor in human wit. He was a living refutation of that ancient calumny, that colleges make men morose and unskilful in the science of human nature. He had a countenance that was like a benediction. And what with his liberal heart, his rich conversation, and the grace of his accomplished manners, he reflected a light upon this seminary, which a just community have not failed, and shall not fail to repay with lasting honor.

Example.

OF A VALEDICTORY ENGLISH ORATION.

SECOND DEGREE — *Master's Oration.*

In selecting for our topic, "The Spirit that should accompany our Republican Institutions," let it not be anticipated that we are bringing hither a political tirade to fret and rave about ourselves, or that we mean to run mad at the sound of our own voice, as it pronounces the word "republic." We have not arrayed ourselves, gladiator like, to attack or defend public measures, — to despatch in the few moments allotted us all the political questions that now interest us as a people, — or to set right the executive, legislative and judicial departments of our government, in the short period of twenty minutes. We come not to battle with politicians, whoever they may be and whether they stand on either bank, or in the middle of the Rubicon.

We come not to sweep down regiments of them with a sentence, or to blow up the country with a magazine of words. No; we would dwell upon this spirit, without taking the word "politics" upon our lips. These have entered into and contaminated every other place, — let the house of God, the temple of literature, be sacred a little longer. Let there be one spot left, where rational, thinking man may retreat from political, talking man. We will not be the first to tread it with a sacrilegious step. No; in the spirit in which the prophet of old put off his shoes on Mount Horeb, "because the ground whereon he stood was holy," we would venture in this place to speak of that spirit which should guide and animate us in the enjoyment of our peculiar institutions.

And addressing, as we trust, nay, as we know, a republican assembly, born under the influence, surrounded and supported by the spirit of free institutions, what inquiry can be more important than that which opens to them the way in which they can most safely keep, and most perfectly enjoy these institutions? The work of attaining them is accomplished. The battle is over, the victory is won, and our fathers are at rest. These institutions are now ours. Praise cannot make them more, nor detraction less so. They are ours, bought and paid for. But they are ours under a solemn responsibleness, — under none other than the trust that we will preserve, exalt, and extend them. But we shall discharge this high and honorable trust, only as we hold them in a right spirit, and exercise them upon proper principles. We speak not extravagantly, then, when we say, that in maintaining and holding sacred that spirit which will adorn and perpetuate these institutions, and give them the only thing they want, their free course, consists the whole duty of our generation; and that when this ceases to be important and interesting in our eyes, we cease to deserve them. Honor and gratitude have been to those who attained, — honor and gratitude shall be to those who preserve them.

The spirit, then, in the first place, whose claims we would advocate, is a spirit of national modesty. We use the term in distinction from that national arrogance or vanity which we deem unbecoming and dangerous.

We are aware that the history of our country is a peculiar one, — peculiar in its interest and importance, and not to us only, but to the world. We have read, with a thrilling interest, the story of our father's doings, dwelt upon their glorious anticipations, and hailed the fulfilment of them, as year after year they have been developed. But where, in all this, is the occasion of arrogance to ourselves and denunciation of others, as if we stood on the only elevation, and, what is more, had reached that elevation ourselves? Our duty, we have said, is to adorn our instutions; ostentation is its very opposite, — to diffuse them abroad; detraction of others will defeat us. But who are they who would thus stride the earth like a colossus? Where is the history of their toil, and danger, and suffering? Where are the monuments of their personal valor and heroism, and splendid achievement? Where is the record of their martyrdom? We have seen the conceited descendant of some rich ancestor, decked in the robes which that ancestor has toiled that he might wear, — fluttering about, the puppet of an hour, yet walking, as he imagines, a god amidst the surrounding pigmies, — talking as if the world were made for him alone, because, forsooth, he really cannot conceive, — as certainly no other can, — how he could have been made for the world. We have seen, I say, this poor imitation of humanity, and looked with contempt on what we could not pity. But what do they more, or better, who, in the costume of national vanity, are stalking about amongst the nations of the earth, vainly declaiming about *their* institutions, — theirs, because they happened to be born where these had been planted, — and sweeping down the institutions of others, for the modest yet cogent reason of the Pharisee, that they are not as their own.

But we would see amongst us, as a nation, that modesty which we admire so much in domestic life. Individual modesty, — we have all seen her, —

is a lovely damsel, with simple mien, retiring manners, and chaste array There is nothing about her to remind one of a flower garden in distress, or a rainbow bewitched. What is gaudy, she hates, — display is her abomination. The scene of her glory is at home, acting, not speaking her praises. This is individual modesty, and national modesty is the same damsel grown into a discreet and stately matron. She has changed her robes, it is true, but not their character nor her own. She is still the same, only more perfect in her principles, as she is more extended in her influence, — seen only in the unassuming deportment of her children, — heard only in the voice of their enterprise, — known, as every good tree is, only by her fruits. We would honor the matron, as we courted the damsel. We would hold her fast, for she is our ornament; — we would love her, for she is altogether lovely.

We would not, — for it is the spirit that, in the second place, we would advocate, — we would not, for we dare not, decry that national pride, honest, open, high-minded pride, which originates in self respect, is nurtured by all the generous sympathies that gather round the name of our native land, and which brings forth as its fruits national enterprise and strength and what is more, national virtue. National pride in this sense is patriotism, and who shall decry patriotism? But the vanity that we condemn is opposite in its every look, feature, and gesture, to this honorable virtue, and it is because we think it so, that we do condemn it. Vanity is mean, — patriotism is noble. Vanity is dangerous, — patriotism is our bulwark. Vanity is weakness, — patriotism is power. The organ of the one is the tongue, — that of the other the heart. An old poet has said of a somewhat different passion, — and there are those who hear me who can bear witness to its truth, — that

> "Passions are likened best to floods and streams;
> The shallow murmur, — but the deep are dumb;
> So when affections yield discourse, it seems
> The bottom is but shallow whence they come.
> They that are rich in words must needs discover,
> They are but poor in that which makes a lover."

And there is philosophy as well as poetry in the idea.

Is it asked, then, who is the friend, the firm, true-hearted, ever-to-be-trusted friend of our institutions? We would answer, not he who is perched upon the house-top, shouting hosannas to the four corners of the earth, and proclaiming to the world, "Lo, here, and here alone, perfection has taken up her abode;" but rather he who has placed himself at the bottom, in the most honorable of all attitudes, that of strenuous yet unassuming exertion; — not he who talks, but he who does the most. Is it asked again, where, then, are we to look for the praises of these institutions at home, and their acceptance and diffusion abroad? We would answer again, not to the dangerous sweeping panegyrics of us and ours, or the more dangerous sweeping denunciations of all others and all things else, but to the good they have done, the evil they have prevented, the happiness they have diffused, the misery they have healed or mitigated. Ask of honest industry, why she labors with a strong hand and a smiling face. Ask of commerce, why she dances, like a sailor boy, in the breeze, joyous and impatient. Listen to the busy, gladsome hum of art mingling with the voice of nature on every stream, and the song of contentment blending with and perfecting the melody. Behold education, the inmate of the humblest dwelling, — man enlightened, thinking for himself, and worshipping his maker in the only acceptable way, his own way. Look at yourselves, your children, your homes. And if you see not, hear not, feel not, the praises of these institutions in all these, eloquence cannot varnish them. Let them begone, they are not what they seem to be.

The spirit, again, whose claims we would advocate as an accompaniment of our institutions, is a spirit of national moderation. The theory, and may it ever be the practical effect of these institutions, is this, that every free member of the community, be he high or low, rich or poor, has a right, equal and unquestionable, to think, speak, and act upon every measure originating among and interesting us as a people. And, still further, the full development of these institutions demands the fair and unshackled exertion of this right. Take this single fact in connexion with the history of man. What is the history of man, we mean political man, as he is a member of the community and the subject of government? It is but a history of parties,—of this side and that side of some undefinable line, the direction of which no earthly philosophy can trace. Yes; strange as it may seem, and inconsistent with that rank in creation to which man has laid claim, ever since the time when Abraham and Lot went one to the right hand and the other to the left, men have divided themselves into parties, at the name of which the human tongue falters, and the human understanding shrinks aghast. And this has been the case, while, instead of a general freedom of speech and action, a few only of men, a very few, have been acknowledged to be human beings, and all the rest have been left to make themselves out so. What is to be the consequence now, when all are admitted to be so? Jarring and confusion, and consequent destruction, have made up the story of mankind, while tyranny bridled their tongues, and despotism hung like a dead weight upon their spirits. What is to be the result now, when tyranny and despotism have been hurled "to the moles and the bats," and the tongue and the spirit of every man are admitted, required to be free? The history of our race, we perceive, reads us but a sorry lesson upon the subject. And the history of our own country forms by no means a perfect exception to the rule; for an old Spanish author, not a hundred years ago, declared, "that the air of that country yeleped America, was marvellously infectious, and inclined men's minds to wrangling and contention."

But the spirit which, if any can, must put an end to this hitherto close alliance between freedom and contention, — the spirit which, like our liberties, is nowhere to be found in history, but which must spring up with and protect them, is a spirit of national moderation, — that generous, Christian spirit, which is cool while it thinks, and charitable while it speaks and acts, — that spirit which, if experience does not sanction, reason does, and which, if to be found in no other record, is yet found and enforced in that of the pattern of all institutions — Christianity. Yes; the single consideration, — and we need no other, — the single consideration of the broad extent of our liberties, is in itself the most eloquent advocate of moderation. Perfect freedom must take her for its handmaid, for wherever it has started without her, it has failed. That which, if any thing can, must distinguish the history of the present from that of all past time, is the operation of the true republican principle, that the full enjoyment of liberty by all depends upon the moderate use of it by each.

But why argue an abstract principle? Who are they that oppose it? What is it that impedes its progress? We are not decrying, — God forbid that we ever should, — a spirit of free, open discussion. On the contrary, we advocate it as the life-blood of our institutions, the very promoter of moderation. It is an abandonment of this fair discussion that we condemn as fatal to it, — a willingness to act in obedience to other than our own unbiassed judgment. It is they who would surrender their personal independence for the bondage of patizans, who would sacrifice their sacred birthright of free thought and action, to become the meanest, because the voluntary slaves of another, who must answer for the discord and confusion that result. Who is he that talks of freedom and equality and rights, and yet thinks as another man thinks, acts as he acts, and simply because that other bids him so think and act? If this be liberty, that liberty of which we have heard so much, give us back again the dark ages, for then, at least, we shall not see the chain that binds us to the earth.

Opposed also to this spirit of moderation, is that desire of controversial distinction in the younger members of the community, which, when it has well spiced their tongue and embittered their pen, produces what is called a young politician. I know not a more amusing, were it not so dangerous a specimen of our race, as this class of inexperienced yet fiery combatants. They come into the world, and the first cry you hear is, "We must fight. Our fathers and our grandfathers fought, and why should not we? True, we have nothing very special to fight about, but still we must fight. The old party fires have been burning only half a century; why put them out so soon? And the questions that kindled them, though a little out of date, have still two sides left and what need we more?" And so the battle begins, — would that it might end where it began, — in simple, unattained, and unattainable nothing. We admire their zeal, applaud their ingenuity are astonished at their more than Quixotic valor; but we laugh at their simplicity, we wonder at their folly, we deprecate their effects. We would trust our institutions to cooler heads and safer hands. Experience, — that grey headed old gentleman, who followed time into the world, and who was cotemporary with wisdom, ere the foundations of the earth were laid, is altogether the safest guardian of such precious treasures. True, he may not harangue with quite so much rapidity and fierceness as these fluent usurpers of his place; but the words which drop slowly from his honored lips are full as wise and full as worthy of preservation as theirs. And though he stand leaning upon his staff, and looking with straining eyes, we would trust to his vision quite as implicitly, as to that of the stately, elastic youth, who, with younger and brighter eyes, does not always see. We would call back this venerable seer from his obscurity. He is growing old fashioned. We would array him in a modern costume, and set him in our high places. The free air of our country will renew his youth, and he, in return, will build up our institutions in the spirit of wisdom and moderation.

We would banish from amongst us, then, these and all other dispositions which stand in the way of that national moderation which we deem so essential. And then, behold a contrast! Place yourself upon the highest elevation that overlooks your country. Banish moderation from the multitude beneath you. You may have heard the roar of the thunder, and the lashing of the ocean, but you have heard music, literal music, compared with the roar and lashing of an immoderate, uncharitable, angry, free people. But look again, — she has returned. Behold the sublimest sight which the earth can afford, — ten millions of freemen, different each from the other, yet with a common country, a common interest, and a common hope, meeting, discussing, differing indeed in opinion about common measures, — but the time for action has come, — they have gone up like Christian men to discharge their duty to their country, — it is over, — they have gone, like Christian men, to discharge their duty to themselves. Be the latter picture ours, and freedom will indeed be a goddess; be it ours, and we could almost say that a little vanity would be excusable.

From speaking of the spirit which should animate us as members of our great republic, the occasion naturally brings us for a moment to the spirit with which we meet as members of that smaller republic of letters, whose anniversary has this day brought us together. To those of us who here meet again, where a short time since we parted, the occasion is one of mingled feelings. We have gathered again in this great congregation, and around this sacred altar; but not all. In the little time that has elapsed since our separation, three of our number, and among them one who, in the event which has placed him whom you hear before you, would have so much more ably filled the spot where I am standing, have joined that greater congregation, around a holier altar. The thought is a solemn and melancholy one. But as, in the wisdom of Providence, they were not permitted to enter upon the public stage, the feelings at their loss belong not to the public. It is not here that we should speak of their virtues, which we loved, — or of their talents, which we respected. These feelings belong to us as individuals, and as members of that little circle, their connexion with which we shall always hold in pleasing recollection

But we look round again and behold another wide breach has been made within this short period, in which all of us have a common interest. The venerable head of our institution,* — the guardian, instructor, friend, the father of his pupils, — he under whose benignant auspices we commenced and completed our collegiate career, and who dismissed us from these hospitable walls with a parental blessing, no longer occupies that seat which he filled so long, so honorably, and so usefully. We would mingle our regret with the general feeling that has gone with him to his retirement. We would send to him the grateful remembrance and filial affection of those who will ever be proud to remember their connexion with him. We would bid him farewell on this spot, consecrated by associations which will ever bring him to our remembrance. In the name of that education which he advanced, of that literature which he encouraged, of that religion which he adorned, we would bid him an affectionate farewell. We pray that the old age of that man may be serene and cheerful, whose youth has been so brilliant, and whose manhood so useful. The smiles of a kind Providence be ever with him. The conscience of a faithful steward is his reward here, — his reward hereafter he has learned from higher authority.

With these feelings of regret to sadden this otherwise joyous occasion, may it not have been well for us to have occupied it in dwelling upon the spirit that should accompany those institutions, into the midst of which we are hastening. It is to the young men of our times that the call of our institutions on this subject is the loudest. Be it theirs, then, to cultivate and diffuse this spirit. And then, what if no trumpet-tongued orator shall rise up to proclaim their praises, — what if eloquence be dumb, — the tongue of man silent? They have a heaven-born eloquence, sweeter than music, yet louder than thunder, — the eloquence of truth. They have an argument, which, though it speak not, is heard through the universe, — the argument of a good cause, on a sound bottom. Let the spirit that should accompany them be abroad, — let national modesty, moderation, charity, independence, and, above all, the spirit of Christianity, be their guard, and then, like Christianity, the powers of nature may strive against them, but they will stand, for they are founded upon a rock. Man cannot overthrow them, and the Almighty will not.

Example

OF A VALEDICTORY ORATION IN LATIN.

Omnibus nunc rite et feliciter peractis, restat, auditores spectatissimi, ut vobis pro hac benevolentia gratias agamus, omnia fausta precemur, et pace decedere et valere vos jubeamus. Si spectandi et audiendi vos tædet, ut citissime abeatis præstabimus.

Sed primum, omnibus qui adestis, quod tam frequentes convenistis, tam attente audistis, tam benigne plausistis, gratias bene meritas agimus; — vobis præcipue, virgines dilectæ, matronesque honoratæ, juvenibus virisque spes et solatium. Quid nostra comitia sine vobis? Quid nos disertos, eloquentes denique efficeret, si non ut aribus oculisque vestris nos commenderemus? Etsi nonnullæ

"Spectatum veniunt, veniunt spectentur ut ipsæ," —

et ignoscimus et probamus. Cur venimus nos javenes, nos viri, nisi ut spectemur, audiamur et ipsi? Sed plures, nimirum, ut audiatis, ut oculis, linguis, votis faveatis. Igitur grates, sed

"Grates persolveres dignas
Non opis est nostræ."

---

* Rev. John Thornton Kirkland.

Vir excellentissime, nostræ reipublicæ princeps, te ex animo salutamus, ac virum tantum, bonisque omnibus tam probatum, nostris adesse comitiis gaudemus.

Virum tibi conjunctissimum, patriæque et virtutis fautoribus carissimum, ac, dum vixerit, integritatis, prudentiæ, omnisque virtutis exemplum, in sedes altiores arcessitum, tecum lugemus. Sed bonorum animis, omnium desiderio, "Manet mansurumque est quidquid in eo amavimus, quidquid admirati sumus. Placide quiescat."

Præclara quidem nostræ reipublicæ felicitas videtur, quum inter tam multos virtute eximios nemo ob amorem erga illam insignem se reddere potest; quum omnia prospere pulchreque eveniunt. Florentibus rebus, summâ hujus reipublicæ tranquilitate, summâ concordiâ, respublica mihi quidem et aliis multis ut confido carissima tuis auspiciis evasit nova; * olim quidem terris nunc re et legibus a vobis disjuncta; ut aliam sese libertatis vindicem exhibeat, alium amicitiæ vinculum adjiciat. Perduret atque valeat. Vale, vir excellentissime.

Et tu, honoratissime, cui virticem ætate provecto albentem civiles usque ambiunt honores; et vos, Conciliarii, Curatoresque honorandi, quibus faventibus et adjuvantibus, vigent res summa nostraque Academia, valete.

Vale et tu, Præses reverende et, si mihi liceat, carissime, cujus præsidic lumen veritatis, patrum auspiciis in nostræ Academiæ penetralibus olim accensum, fulsit fulgetque novo semper purioreque splendore. Esto sempiternum.

Valete Professores eruditissimi ac præstantissimi! Quibus eloquemur verbis quantâ observantiâ vos habemus, quam gratis animis vestrûm in nos assiduorum laborum, curæque vigilantis recordamur? Sit vobis hoc excelsum et pene divinum munus et præmium. Omnibus qui merentur certissime eveniet.

Amici sodalesque carissimi, iterum denique, post aliquod temporis intervallum, convenimus, ut his sedibus amatis, quas veluti beatorum insulas dolentes reliquimus, nostræ custodibus juventutis merito honoratis, nobis invicem et illis valedicemus. Quis enim, quum temporis inter camænas et cum amicis acti reminiscitur, dolorem non sentiat quod his omnibus nimium cito sese eripere, marique incerto ac tumultuoso se committere oporteat, nunquam rediturum, nunquam sodalium ora jucunda aspecturum! Interjecto jam nunc brevi tantum triennio, multos optime dilectos oculis animoque frustra requirimus.

Quid ego non audio tantum? Eorum quos inter-lectissimos habuimus, alter morti occubuit, alter in terris externis abest. Quid illos aut alios quos amavimus a me nominari necesse sit? Quisque vestrum eos requirit, quisque desiderat. Valeant omnes qui absunt, et vos, amici fratresque, valete!

Vos quoque valete, omnes qui adestis, — senes atque juvenes, quibus fortuna fida et quibus perfida, — matronæ virginesque, quibus sit decor quibusque desit; — vobis adsint ante omnia virtus,

"Lis nunquam, toga rara, mens quieta,
Vires ingenuæ, salubre corpus;
Quod sitis esse velitis, nihilque malitis."

---

* Anno 1820, resp. Maine a rep. Mass. se separavit.

XCVI.

A BOWDOIN PRIZE DISSERTATION.

Example.

Essay on the Literary Character of Dr. Samuel Johnson.

While an author is living, it is not extraordinary that mankind should form an erroneous estimate of his works. The influence which prejudice and partiality often possess over the minds of his contemporaries, is incompatible with a correct decision of his merits. It is not until time has effaced the recollection of party feelings, when the virtues and foibles of the man are forgotten, and the warm emotions of friendship or resentment are no longer felt, that the merit of an author can be fairly ascertained. So variable is public opinion, which is often formed without examination, and liable to be warped by caprice, that works of real merit are frequently left for posterity to discover and admire, while the pompous efforts of impertinence and folly are the wonders of the age. The gigantic genius of Shakspeare so far surpassed the learning and penetration of his times, that his productions were then little read and less admired. There were few who could understand, and still fewer who could relish the beauties of a writer whose style was as various as his talents were surprising. The immortal Milton suffered the mortification of public neglect, after having enriched the literature of his country with a poem, which has since been esteemed the most beautiful composition in his language; and his poetical talents, which entitled him to a reputation the most extensive and gratifying, could scarcely procure for him, in his own times, a distinction above contemporary authors who are now forgotten. Ignorance and interest, envy and political rancor, have concealed from public notice works, which the enlightened intelligence of after ages have delighted to rescue from oblivion; and it is no less common for posterity to forget ephemeral productions, which were the admiration of the day in which they were produced.

In a retrospect of the literature of any age, the mind views the respective authors as a group of statues, which a cusory glance of the eye discovers at a distance; and although, on a nearer examination, it could admire the features and beauties discoverable in those of a diminutive appearance, yet the energetic expression and lofty attitude of some who overtop the rest, exclusively attract our notice and command attention. Perhaps there has been no age concerning which this remark is more justly applicable, than the eighteenth century. In that period, a most numerous army of authors took the field, greater perhaps in number, but not exceeding in height of stature, excellence of skill, or brilliance of achievement, the great men of the three preceding centuries.

In contemplating this collection of writers, the attention is necessarily withdrawn from those over whom the towering genius of Dr. Johnson seems to bend, and is attracted by the colossal statue which represents the gigantic powers of his mind. Whether we regard the variety of his talents, the soundness of his judgment, the depth of his penetration, the acuteness of his sagacity, the subtleness of his reasoning faculty, or the extent of his knowledge, he is equally the subject of astonishment and admiration.

It will not, perhaps, be hazardous to affirm, that within the range of an cient and modern history, it is difficult, if not impossible, to point out a single individual, in whom was discoverable so various a combination of literary accomplishments. It may also be safely affirmed, that he seemed to possess a mind which actually contained a greater and more variegated mass of knowledge than any other person has been known to possess. It will not, however, be surprising, that his productions excited the wonder and astonishment of mankind, when we reflect, that he had a memory which at any moment could furnish him with all that he had ever read, and a judgment which could exactly combine and compare, analyze and aggregate, the most subtle reasoning, and a love of learning never satiated by indulgence. A clear head and nice discrimination, a logical method and mathematical precision, rendered him one of the most powerful reasoners of his age. A character so eminent, it is not likely could pass his own times without much animadversion and much praise. As he was the most conspicuous literary man of his nation, it is not matter of suprise, that we find written of him more than it would be safe implicitly to credit, and presumption universally to disbelieve. Soon after his death, he was very justly compared to the sick lion in the fable, whom, while living, few had the temerity to attack, but against whom, when in the defenceless state of a corse, all in whom the malignancy of envy, or the voice of prejudice, or the excitement of resentment existed, united their assaults with rancor and bitterness. In many, the gratification of these feelings was like the fury of canine madness. They bit with the mordacity of the viper; but the impassive metal rendered retributive justice to their efforts, and the good sense of mankind reprobated their folly.

It is a delightful employment to trace through the stages of infantine imbecility, the growth of a genius, which, in the progressive gradations of its maturity, expands like the majestic branches of "the Pride of the Forest," by slow degrees, and native hardihood, acquiring strength and enlargement, and becoming at last a sublime emblem of independence, of fortitude, and durability. The development of Dr. Johnson's mind, is a subject, from the contemplation of which, we may derive much pleasure and improvement. It was not like a sickly and tender plant, to be nursed with the most anxious solicitude. It possessed a native vigor and energy, which neither the disadvantages of an unpropitious culture could retard, nor the blasts of adverse fortune could depress. The tempestuous storms, to which a nature less hardy would have yielded, it bore with inflexible firmness; and, like a rock in the midst of the ocean, just protending above the waves, by which it is sometimes overflowed, and at the refluence of the billows, with haughty pride becomes again visible, it withstood the conflict of contending elements. Undaunted by difficulties, from which a mind not underserving of respect would involuntarily have recoiled, we observe it, in the progress of his life, stemming the current of adversity, rather in the pride of triumph, than in the humiliation of despondence. In following him through the dangers and hardships which he too frequently had to encounter, we may observe how wonderfully his mind gained efficiency by resistance; and, like an impetuous torrent, overleaping the barriers of its course, with renovated strength he overwhelmed opposition.

The ninth year of the eighteenth century gave birth to the man, who was afterwards to become the glory of his country, the champion of his language, and the honor and ornament of the literature of his age. Among some of the biographers of Dr. Johnson, we discover a disposition to indulge in tales of absurdity; ascribing to him a jingle of boyish rhymes at the age of three years, and leading readers to suppose him to have mounted his Pegasus before he was entirely out of the cradle. Little appears to have been known respecting his early childhood, and much less with regard to the progress he made in learning under his earliest teachers, both of which were perhaps of no consequence; stories of such strange precocity usually carry with themselves their own refutation. The earliest intelli gence, upon which we may rely, informs us, that Johnson, while at the Litchfield school, had a standing scarcely respectable. The only talent by which he was then in any wise distinguished, was a remarkable tenacity of memory. This, it will be seen, was of the utmost importance to him. After a preparatory course in classical literature, we find him, at the age of nineteen, entered as a commoner in Pembroke College, Oxford, assisting the studies of a young gentleman, by whose aid he was maintained. The performance which first brought him into notice, was the translation of Pope's "Messiah" into Latin, which possessed no other poetical merit than purity of diction. Circumstances occurred, which deprived him of the only support upon which he relied; the gentleman under his charge changing his plan of education. After various discouragements, and embarrassments in his pecuniary resources, he was compelled to quit the university, where his residence, with little interruption, had been continued nearly three years. Having endeavored to obtain the means of living by assisting at a public school, in a short time he relinquished an employment, which yielded him little pleasure, and which became the more irksome from a disgust he had taken with the person by whom it was patronized. It was at this period, that a resort to his pen became necessary for the support of his life. A translation of a voyage to Abyssinia, by Jerome Lobo, a Portuguese missionary, it is believed, was the first literary effort by which he attempted to raise a revenue. In this production, Johnson discovers much of that purity and energy of diction, by which he was afterwards distinguished. An easy flow of language, with a strength of expression, gave a dignity to the translated author he did not naturally possess. The flexibility and harmony of the English tongue added an importance and interest to the performance, to which, for its subsequent reputation, it was much indebted.

In March, 1737, Johnson, in company with David Garrick, made his entry into London, each to try his fortune on the extensive theatre of the metropolis. The former, hitherto the child of disaster and disappontment, determined to enlarge the sphere in which to crowd his way; and both were equally undaunted by the failure of their schemes.

The biographers of Johnson are unable to fix with certainty the period at which the Tragedy of "Irene" was finished. Though there appears some evidence of its completion prior to his arrival in London, it was doomed, if written at that time, to slumber in obscurity, until the fortune and friendship of Garrick, who, in 1747, became one of the managers of Drury Lane Theatre, enabled him to produce it on the stage. With respect to the merits of this production, an observation which was judiciously applied to Addison's "Cato," may, with equal justice, be made: "It wants much of that contrivance and effect, which is best understood by those who are skilled in writing for the stage." It is, in a great measure, destitute of that style, and those incidents, which would render it interesting to an audience; and will much better delight a reader in the retirement of the closet, than the confused assemblage of the theatre. The language is dignified and forcible, and the sentiments worthy of its author. Literary men, who are pleased with "chill philosophy," and "unaffecting elegance," will admire it; readers of taste will be delighted with the beauty of some of its sentiments, and many elegant passages which it contains, which will long preserve it from oblivion. Garrick, upon being asked why he did not produce another tragedy from his Litchfield friend, replied, "when Johnson writes tragedy, passion sleeps, and declamation roars." Johnson himself appears to have been in some degree sensible of the truth of such a remark, as this was his first and only attempt. Having had a run of thirteen nights, Irene was never after revived.

About the year 1738, we find him again invoking his muse, in an imitation of Juvenal's Third Satire, to which he gave the name of "London." It has been thought, that, under the name of Thales, he addresses his friend Savage, whose life he subseqently wrote, and with whom he had previously passed many of his dissipated hours. Savage was a man of very great genius, but of an irregular and dissipated life, from the contamination of which, nothing but good principles, deep rooted which he had early imbibed, could have preserved the morals of Johnson.

If not among the most important of his efforts, this poem, and "The Vanity of Human Wishes," another similar to it, in imitation of the Tenth Satire of Juvenal, may be esteemed among his most happy attempts. The spirit and energy with which he wrote, fully equals the poignancy of the Roman satirist. Juvenal and Johnson were both engaged in the cause of virtue, and the poetic fire and sarcastic severity of the imitation is well worthy of the original. The lines of the English author flow with all that grace and dignity with which the Latin poet abounds. That he should have written with the same ardor and animation, is natural; and the accusatorial strain of invective in which he writes, does ample justice to the censorial department of the satirist. It is related that Mr. Pope, after reading his "London," observed, in allusion to the passage from Terence, which was once applied to Milton, "Ubi, ubi est, diu celari non potest," — a remark which proved truly prophetic.

It is a melancholy reflection, that the superior talents of this eminent writer, at the age of thirty, were scarcely able to provide him with an income adequate to his wants. Being bred to no profession, he was compelled to resort to his pen as a last resource. Many of his schemes in publication failed for want of encouragement, and others, in which he succeeded, proved of little benefit to him. We find some of his fugitive pieces at this time appearing in the "Gentleman's Magazine," and among them several very masterly touches in biographical delineation. In biography, Johnson peculiarly excelled. The "Lives of the Poets," which he at a much later period sent into the world, will remain a lasting monument of his genius, and critical sagacity. Few perhaps, more feelingly illustrated Juvenal's axiom,

> "Haud facile emergunt, quorum virtutibus obstat
> Res angusta domi."

But the independence of his spirit, and the native energy of his mind, rendered him little sensible to the sombre shades by which fortune had surrounded him.

His parliamentary speeches, which appeared about this time, are a model of purity of diction, copiousness of language, and flowing eloquence. In reflecting how scanty were the materials from which they were written, our surprise and admiration are equally excited. His biographers relate, that frequently he was only informed who were the speakers, the order in which they spoke, and the sides they took. At best, the notes which were procured were of but little use to him; and it is well known, he was but once in Parliament-house for this purpose. We are charmed with the dignity and energy which these speeches possess. Without disparagement, some of them may be compared to the ancient specimens of the Grecian and Roman orators. In force of style, harmony of diction, and copiousness of expression, they equal any instances of ancient or modern eloquence.

There is no view in which Johnson appears less advantageous than as a political writer. His warmest friends are ready to acknowledge, that his reputation would have suffered no loss, had he never meddled with politics. His arguments, indeed, were ingenious; but strong prejudices and partialities gave to his pen a direction which his understanding could not approve, and, in moments of cooler reflection, his conscience must have condemned. With the sentiments of a warm tory and rigid high-churchman, his character was frequently exposed to much severity of aspersion; but, possessed with the genius and reputation of the greatest scholar of his age, and the virtues of a man, over whom morality and religion had much influence, he might well defy the attacks of his enemies.

At about the age of forty, he commenced a work which added to his reputation, and gave him, with no inconsiderable degree of justice, the name of the English moralist.

With very little assistance, he completed, in a course of two years, the publication of the "Rambler," giving to the world, on stated days, two papers in a week. It appears, that, though those essays amounted to two hundred and eight, he received but ten numbers from the pens of his friends.

The disadvantages under which an author labors, in periodical publications, whose frequency leaves little time for the interruptions of recreation or necessity, he has most feelingly described. "He that condemns himself to compose on a stated day, will often bring to his task an attention dissipated, a memory embarrassed, an imagination overwhelmed, a mind distracted with anxieties, a body languishing with disease; he will labor on a barren topic till it is too late to change it; or, in the ardor of invention, diffuse his thoughts into wild exuberance, which the present hour cannot suffer judgment to examine or reduce."

For depth of moral reflection, the "Ramblers" of Johnson must ever be preëminent. The ethics of the ancients are not stored with a more valuable mass of moral instruction; and in vain may we search for the principles of the purest philosophy, so beautifully blended with the loveliness of virtue. It was not probable that the frailties or peculiarities of mankind could escape his acute penetration, which was ever on the alert,

> "To mark the age, shoot folly as it flies,
> And catch the manners living as they rise."

From an early period, he had accustomed himself to a habit of close thinking. His active and vigorous mind always first matured what he had to advance, and his confidence in his assertions was owing to deductions which resulted from the deepest reasoning.

The moralizing "Rambler" is always dignified in his sentiments, logical in his inferences, and energetic in his style. Though many of his papers assume a gravity which forbids trifling, his remarks are sententious and forcible. They do not always partake of the sombre shades of melancholy, and seldom seem to participate of a cynical severity. The strain of morality which flows from his pen, discovers a mind at times under the influence of gloomy reflections, and inclined to indulge in the sober feelings of a man prone to look upon the darkest side. Instruction and sublimity may be found in his papers. The majority of mankind will admire them in the retirement of the closet, when the mind is inclined to serious advice; and the friends of virtue will ever rejoice that the great learning of the critic and scholar has so successfully labored in her service. The papers of the "Idler," and those of the "Adventurer," written by Johnson, exhibit the same powers of mind, and fewer of his peculiar faults.

As a Latin poet, he can only be ranked with other admired writers, who attempted metrical excellence in a language that allows no new expressions. The most successful writer can do no more than imitate the flowers which he has discovered on classic ground, and display to the world his acquaintance with its productions. He may heat his mind with the spirit with which the poets of antiquity have written. He may imbibe a portion of their taste, and, as far as he is able, copy their style. His productions, in their language, will still fail of originality, and savor of imitation.

There can be little doubt but that the affair in which Johnson was connected with Lauder, was always to himself a source of regret. His integrity, it may safely be presumed, would have withholden him from giving countenance to an attempt to injure the reputation of the immortal Milton, had he been at first, as he afterwards was, convinced of the injustice of the cause in which he engaged. The recantation he extorted from the person who had thus inveigled him into this infamous plan, made honorable amends to the injured character of the poet. That he had been made a dupe to the duplicity of the enemy of Milton, could, in his own feelings, be but little alleviated by an acknowledgment of his crime. As he harboured no malevolence of feeling towards this sublime writer, posterity have little of which to accuse him; as the best men may at times be deceived, especially when the influence of party feelings fosters their prejudices, and gives to the judgment, for a moment, a bias, which calm reflection, and dispassionate examination, afterwards perceives, acknowledges, and corrects.

His "English Dictionary" will long remain a lasting reccrd of the powerful mind of Dr. Johnson. By it, he has fixed the standard of our language, and, with the most indefatigable labor and acuteness, given precision to the meaning of our words, which, hitherto, had been too much neglected by the lexicographers who precedod him. He has pruned of their excrescences the indeterminate signification of many terms, and placed in appro priate gradations the fluctuating import of many expressions. Until his time there had been no author upon whose judgment the world seemed implicitly to rely; and time has since proved, that the stupendous labor, and powerful talents of Johnson have left nothing for succeeding lexicographers to do in defining the English language.

His benevolent feelings often engaged him in the service of many for whom he had little friendship, and who could lay no claim to the assistance of his pen. The number of dedications, prologues, and recommendatory effusions which issued from it, in behalf of indigent merit, or unaspiring modesty, at once illustrates the kindness of his heart, and the disinterestedness of his motives.

During a season, in which his mind was oppressed with the gloomy reflections of affliction, occasioned by the loss of his aged mother, to whom he was tenderly and affectionately attached, it is related, that he wrote his "Rasselas." This elegant specimen of Oriental imagery, we are told, was written during the evenings of a single week, to enable him to defray the funeral expenses of his deceased parent. Perhaps there is no prosaic effu sion, in which the exuberance and harmony of our language has been more artfully combined, or more fully displayed. It is here that he discovers those surprising powers of imagination, which were the astonishment and admiration of mankind. Though the strain of moralizing reflection, which pervades the whole story, seems to partake of the gloomy shades which oc casionally overshadowed his mind, it may yet be questioned, if the world will again soon be favored with a trifle, from any pen, in which it may be, at the same time, more delighted and improved.

In the poetry of Dr. Johnson, if we do not discover the harmony which delights a musical ear, we are fully compensated by an energy of expression, a lofty style, and a critical elegance of diction. The majesty of his numbers resembles the tones of a powerful instrument, not discordant by the strength of their parts. His versification cannot boast of an unbroken melody, but his measures flow like the slow and solemn progress of a mighty river, rather than like the graceful glidings of a shallow stream. If he does not possess the smoothness of poetical numbers, the ear is not fatigued by the sameness of his style; and we may continue to be delighted with the variety and dignity of his expressions, when we should be glad to be relieved from the monotonous harmony of poets of more musical ears.

Johnson had for some time been solicited by his bookseller to undertake the editorial department in a splendid edition of the British Poets. This was the last great effort of his mind. His reputation needed not, at this period, an accession to give permanency to his fame; yet another laure. was added to grace his brow.

This stupendous publication, which was to be comprised in seventy volumes, in the course of a few years was offered to the world, with the lives of each author prefixed, containing critical observations on their writings. These prefaces were afterwards republished in four separate volumes, to which was given the title of Johnson's "Lives of the Poets." It is here that the philosophical talents of this great man were fully developed. If a vigorous understanding, a sound judgment, a scrutinizing penetration, comprehensive knowledge, and a discriminating sagacity, were qualifications for such an undertaking, it would have been difficult to discover an individual whose native energy of mind, and critical talents, more peculiarly fitted him than Johnson. He possessed the ability to discern, the judgment to commend, and the taste to admire the excellences of his authors, while, at the same time, he had the independence to condemn their failings, even should his animadversions be in opposition to public opinion. The man who would singly dispute the admiration of his contemporaries, chooses for himself a hazardous undertaking. But the mind of Johnson did not deign to stoop to vulgar prejudices, and his nobleness of spirit spurned at opposing the dictates of truth and sound judgment, though error was popular in the best of company. When we compare the decision of his criticisms with the rules of taste, and the learned Institutes of Aristotle and Quintilian, we are irresistibly compelled to revere his opinions. The "Lives of the English Poets" may justly be considered as the noblest specimen of elegant and solid criticism which any age has produced. It is, however, a matter of surprise, that he should have included many in his list of English Poets, who are much less entitled to this distinction, than others, who are omitted. In all his work he gives no excuse for excluding the admired author of the Fairy Queen.

His enemies accuse him of writing, in his life of Milton, with a mind warped by unmanly prejudice, and mingling the feelings of party spirit and bigotry in his delineation of the poet. If he has not bestowed the just meed of panegyric as the biographer of Milton, all must allow that he has done him ample justice as his commentator. His criticism of "Paradise Lost" would have done honor to any pen. As that poem is a production which the genius of Milton only could have produced, so the criticism of Johnson is such as only Johnson could have written.

His "Life of Pope" is a masterly effort of acute judgment and critical skill. He was, perhaps, as justly able to estimate the genius and poetical talents of that English bard, as any man living. Friendship had induced him to write the "Life of Savage," which is prized as one of the finest pieces of biography now extant. His other lives more or less partake of the genius of a writer, who, for nervous elegance and justness of sentiment, has scarcely a competitor. His two prefaces, the one to his "English Dictionary," the other to an edition of Shakspeare, which was published under his superintendence, will long remain the astonishment and admiration of mankind. Few writers have obtained any approach to competition with these pieces. Though entirely different in their subject, the same closeness of thought, purity of diction, nervous strength, and dignity of style, in each are equally conspicuous. Never had an estimate of the genius and merits of Shakspeare been given to the world, to which it would have been safe to yield implicit credence. The truth was, no one had perfectly understood him. He threw light upon parts of his character, which had never before been exposed to view. Learned investigation enabled Johnson to see his author in an aspect which previous commentators had either never noticed, or never had the sagacity to discern. He compares his performances with the rules which the genius of antiquity had discovered and illustrated, and not with the prejudices of modern arrogance and imbecility. He gave the most exalted commendation to a mind, whose intuitive intelligence rendered the laborious acquirement of knowledge, and the culture of study, as but a secondary assistance to its operations; and, though mankind should place but little value upon his commentaries on the text, they may justly feel indebted for his development of the genius of Shakspeare. It is not a matter of wonder, that the exquisitely beautiful preface to the edition of Shakspeare's plays, should lay claim to such superlative merit. Whether we regard the abundance and classical selection of its allusions, the accuracy and justice of the criticisms, or its just appreciation of the excellences and defects of the poet, it is equally the subject of admiration.

The literary character of Dr. Johnson, may, perhaps, receive illustration by examining his life, as well as by criticising his writings. That prejudice should have found no place in a mind of such astonishing energy, would seem as wonderful as it must have been rare. It would seem equally strange, if his antipathies were not sometimes manifested in the heat of passion, or in the ardor of debate. The Scotch and Dissenters, the scholars of Cambridge and the Whigs, were often mentioned with more acrimony than discretion. There was, perhaps, no man who more strenuously advocated the principles of subordination, and few who displayed them less in practice. The tempers of men are more under the influence of external circumstances than moral writers in general are disposed to allow. Dr Johnson too severely felt the weight of disappointment and penury in his early years. At a later period, he was gratified by applause and universal adulation. Can it be wonderful, then, that, with the strong feelings of vigorous passions, and the common failings of human nature, he should, at times, be carried away in conversation, and in hasty compositions, farther than his maturer judgment would sanction, or the better feelings of his heart approve. There were few men whose colloquial powers could give more delight to those around him, and scarcely another whose insulted feelings were more awfully dreaded. Though he might not pass for a scientific scholar, the world can have little reason to doubt the extent of his learning, or the unbounded range of his information. His desultory manner of reading made his knowledge more comprehensive than minute; and his quickness of perception gave him an astonishing facility in grasping the ideas of an author without tiring his patience by perusing a whole book. His extraordinary powers of understanding were much cultivated by study, and still more by reflection. The accuracy of his observations, and the justness of his remarks, were the result of mature deliberation and depth of meditation, before he uttered his sentiments; and his memory furnished him with an inexhaustible fund, from which his reasonings were assisted and enforced. The aptness of his illustrations was a strong evidence of the sagacity of his perceptions, and the soundness of his judgment. His observations received additional weight from the loudness of his voice, and the solemnity with which they were delivered. The sophistry of an antagonist always fell a prey to the piercing glance of his penetration; and he became the more elated by triumph when his opponents had been most decided. The great originality which appeared in his writings, resulted from an activity of mind, which habit had accustomed to reason with precision. His conceptions of things sprang not from idle thought or indolent reflection, but from the keen energies of a vigorous intellect, assisted by the efforts of a soaring imagination. His conversation was striking, interesting, and instructive, and required no exertion to be understood, from the perspicuity and force of his remarks; and his zeal for the interests of religion and virtue was often manifested in his discourse. He was expert at argumentation, and the schools of declamation could not boast of a more subtle reasoner, or a more artful sophist, when his side was a bad one; for he often disputed as much for the sake of victory as of truth. His answers were so powerful, that few dared to engage with him. Universal submission, it is likely, gave an apparent dogmatism which he otherwise might not have possessed. If there was an aspect of harsh severity in his retorts, it should be remembered, how frequently they were provoked by the insults of impertinence and the conceit of ignorance. The specious garb of dissimulation he despised. A noble spirit of indepedence actuated his demeanor. He did not violate the integrity of his feelings by stooping to gratify the pride of rank, when unaccompanied by a superiority of intellect commensurate with its dignity. His utter abhorrence of flattery and adulation lost him that patronage of the great, which he otherwise might probably sooner have acquired; and he rose to eminence rather by the unassisted efforts of his own genius, than the encouragements of the rich and the learned. He was little indebted to the assistance of his friends for his great reputation. The irresistible energy of his character carried him through all his difficulties with an unbroken spirit, and an unblemished fame. If he paid not his court to the noble, it was not from disrespect to the subordinations of rank in society, but a dislike to the arts of dissimulation, and an aversion to the degradation of science at the shrine of patronage. His sarcastic letter to the Earl of Chesterfield is a noble specimen of his independence of spirit, and his contempt of the servile arts of adulation. It is a feeling exposition of the hardships he had endured, until royal munificence placed him beyond the boundaries of want, and smoothed his descent to the grave.

His knowledge of the Greek language, in comparison with his acquaintance with the Latin, was superficial. In his early years, he had devoted himself so closely to the study of the ancient poets, that it may be questioned, if his familiarity with them in his own times could find a superior His decisive denunciations against the genuineness of Ossian's poems, created him many opponents, upon a subject, respecting which, "truth had never been established, or fallacy detected."

It is not a little strange, that, in many instances, the biographers of Johnson have appeared like enemies. It may, however, be observed, that few men could have stood the ordeal to which the minuteness of Boswell exposed him, with so much honor to the reputation of their heart and their head. This mighty Caliban of literature is here stripped of every disguise, and held up to public view. Though the world has been delighted and improved by the record of his converation, in which his learning, his genius, and his undisguised sentiments have so conspicuously shone forth, it cannot but be allowed, that it is informed of much, which it was not important, and, perhaps, was not proper for it to know; and that the coloring which the painter has given to his portrait, will admit of many different shades, from which the partiality of friendship should have guarded his pencil. It is here, however, that we may trace the incredible vastness of an intellect, destined to become the glory of his country, and the pride of English literature.

We may contemplate the gigantic powers of Johnson's mind with feelings similar to those sublime emotions with which we view the boundless expanse of the ocean, fathomless to human measurement, and whose capacity exceeds our conception. In his writings appears more conspicuously than in his conversation the compass and extent of his understanding. His faculties were vigorous, his curiosity and avidity for knowledge insatiable and unlimited, his mind vehement and ardent, the combinations of his fancy various and original, and his imagination neither clouded or depressed by the discipline of study, or the misfortunes of life. His readers are delighted and astonished at the wonderful beauty of his conceptions, and the depth of reflection which his opinions discover. In his style he is dignified and forcible, in his language elegant and copious. He gives to every word its true meaning, and its illustrative purport. His epithets are used with judgment and discrimination. Every thing which he says has a determinate significancy, and his words convey no more than the import of his conceptions. If he introduces hard words, their peculiar adaptation to his meaning should atone for his grandiloquism. It should also be remembered, that Cicero introduced Greek terms, when treating upon learned subjects, to supply the deficiency of the Roman language, and that the "great and comprehensive conceptions of Johnson could not easily be expressed by common words."

Should it be thought that the style of this learned author has injured our language, he must have committed this injury by making it more subor dinate to grammatical rules. Foreigners and future generations will be more capable of understanding it, since he has excluded expressions which are only to be found in colloquial intercourse and vulgar phraseology. From his example, men may learn to give to their style energy, perspicuity, and elegance. They may acquire a habit of close thinking, and become accustomed to express their ideas with force and precision.

His political writings will be read and admired only for the dignity and energy of their style. His compositions are a most valuable addition to the literature of his country, and will confer a lasting reputation on his name. They are replete with "useful instruction, and elegant entertainment," and by perusing them, mankind may advance in knowledge and virtue. The efforts of his mind discover a life of study and meditation. His writings display a genius cultivated with industry, and quickened by exertion. His multifarious productions are an honor to the English nation; and his answer to his sovereign might more fairly be allowed, "that he had written his share," *if he had not written so well.* His mind has been laid open to the public in his printed works, without "reservation or disguise;" and, with all his faults and failings, he is still the admiration of mankind.

XCVII.

ON THE COMPOSITION OF A SERMON.*

On the Choice of Texts.

There are, in general, five parts of a sermon: the exordium, the con nexion, the division, the discussion, and the application; but as connexion and division are parts which ought to be extremely short, we can properly reckon only three parts: exordium, discussion, and application. However, we will just take notice of connexion and division after we have spoken a little on the choice of texts, and a few general rules of discussing them.

1. Never choose such texts as have not complete sense; for only imper tinent and foolish people will attempt to preach from one or two words which signify nothing.

2. Not only words which have a complete sense of themselves must be taken, but they must also include the complete sense of the writer whose words they are; for it is his language, and they are his sentiments, which you explain, For example, should you take these words of 2 Cor. 1: 3. "Blessed be God, the Father of our Lord Jesus Christ, the Father of mercies, and the God of all comfort," and stop here, you will include a complete sense; but it would not be the Apostle's sense. Should you go farther, and add, "who comforteth us in all our tribulation," it would not then be the complete sense of St. Paul, nor would his meaning be wholly taken in, unless you went to the end of the fourth verse. When the complete sense of the sacred writer is taken, you may stop; for there are few texts in Scripture, which do not afford matter sufficient for a sermon, and it is equally inconvenient to take too much text or too little; both extremes must be avoided.

* These directions and remarks are taken from Hannam's "Pulpit Assistant." The student will also find much aid from Gresley's "Treatise on Preaching."

General rules of sermons. 1. A sermon should clearly and purely explain a text, make the sense easily to be comprehended, and place things before the people's eyes, so that they may be understood without difficulty. This rule condemns embarrassment and obscurity, the most disagreeable thing in the world in a gospel pulpit. It ought to be remembered, that the greatest part of the hearers are simple people, whose profit, however, must be aimed at in preaching: but it is impossible to edify them, unless you be very clear. Bishop Burnett says, "a preacher is to fancy himself as in the room of the most unlearned man in the whole parish, and must therefore put such parts of his discourses as he would have all understand, in so plain a form of words, that it may not be beyond the meanest of them. This he will certainly study to do, if his desire be to edify them, rather than to make them admire himself as a learned and high spoken man."

2. A sermon must give the entire sense of the whole text, in order to which it must be considered in every view. This rule condemns dry and barren explications, wherein the preacher discovers neither study nor invention, and leaves unsaid a great number of beautiful things with which his text might have furnished him. In matters of religion and piety, not to edify much is to destroy much; and a sermon cold and poor will do more mischief in an hour, than a hundred rich sermons can do good.

3. The preacher must be wise, in opposition to those impertinent people who utter jests, comical comparisons, quirks, and extravagances; sober, in opposition to those rash spirits who would penetrate all, and curiously dive into mysteries beyond the bounds of modesty; chaste, in opposition to those bold and imprudent geniuses who are not ashamed of saying many things which produce unclean ideas in the mind.

4. A preacher must be simple and grave. Simple, speaking things of good natural sense, without metaphysical speculations; grave, because all sorts of vulgar and proverbial sayings ought to be avoided. The pulpit is the seat of good natural sense, and the good sense of good men.

5. The understanding must be informed, but in a manner, however which affects the heart; either to comfort the hearers, or to excite them to acts of piety, repentance, or holiness.

6. One of the most important precepts for the discussion of a text, and the composition of a sermon, is, above all things, to avoid excess:—

1. There must not be too much genius. I mean, not too many brilliant sparkling, and shining things: for they would produce very bad effects The auditor will never fail to say, "The man preaches himself, aims to display his genius, and is not animated by the spirit of God, but by that of the world."

2. A Sermon must not be overcharged with doctrine, because the hearers' memories cannot retain it all; and by aiming to keep all, they will lose all. Take care, then, not to charge your sermon with too much matter.

3. Care must also be taken never to strain any particular part, either in attempting to exhaust it, or to penetrate too far into it. Frequently in attempting it, you will distil the subject till it evaporates.

4. Figures must not be overstrained. This is done by stretching metaphor into allegory, or by carrying a parallel too far. A metaphor is changed into an allegory when a number of things are heaped up, which agree to the subject in keeping close to the metaphor. Allegories may sometimes be used very agreeably: but they must not be strained: that is, all that can be said of them must not be said.

5. Reasoning must not be carried too far. This may be done many ways; either by long trains of reasons, composed of a number of propositions chained together, or principles and consequences, which way of reasoning is embarrassing and painful to the auditor. The mind of man loves to be conducted in a more smooth and easy way.

Of connexion. The connexion is the relation of your text to the foregoing or following verses. To find this, consider the scope of the discourse and consult commentators; particularly exercise your own good sense

When the coherence will furnish any agreeable considerations for the illustrations of the text, they must be put in the discussion; and they will very often happen. Sometimes, also, you may draw thence an exordium: in such a case, the exordium and connexion will be confounded together.

Of division. Division in general ought to be restrained to a small number of parts; they should never exceed four or five at the most; the most admired sermons have only two or three parts.

There are two sorts of divisions which we may very properly make; the first, which is the most common, is the division of the text into its parts the other is of the discourse, or sermon itself, which is made on the text.

1. This method is proper when a prophecy of the Old Testament is handled; for, generally, the understanding of these prophecies depends on many general considerations, which, by exposing and refuting false senses, open a way to the true explication.

2. This method is also proper on a text taken from a dispute, the understanding of which must depend on the state of the question, the hypothesis of adversaries, and the principles of the inspired writers. All these lights are previously necessary, and they can only be given by general considerations; for example, Rom. iii. 28. "We conclude that a man is justified by faith without the deeds of the law." Some general considerations must precede, which clear up the state of the question between St. Paul and the Jews, touching justification, which mark the hypothesis of the Jews upon that subject, and which discover the true principle which St. Paul would establish; so that, in the end, the text may be clearly understood.

3. This method also is proper in a conclusion drawn from a long preceding discourse; as for example, Rom. v. 1. "Therefore being justified by faith, we have peace with God, through our Lord Jesus Christ." The discourse must be divided into two parts; the first consisting of some general considerations on the doctrine of justification, which St. Paul establishes in the preceding chapters; and the second of his conclusion, that, being thus justified, we have peace with God, &c.

The same may be said of the first verse of the eighth of Romans, "There is, therefore, now no condemnation," &c., for it is a consequence drawn from what he had been establishing before.

4. The same method is proper for texts which are quoted in the New Testament from the Old. You must prove by general considerations that the text is properly produced, and then you may come clearly to its explication. Of this kind are Hebrews i. 5, 6. "I will be to him a Father," &c. "One in a certain place testified," &c., ii. 6. "Wherefore as the Holy Ghost saith," &c., iii. 7. There are many passages of this kind in the New Testament.

5. In this class must be placed divisions into different regards, or different views. These, to speak properly, are not divisions of a text into its parts, but rather different applications which are made of the same texts to divers subjects. Typical texts should be divided thus; and a great number of Passages in the Psalms, which relate not only to David, but also to Jesus Christ. Such should be considered, first, literally, as they relate to David; and then, in the mystical sense, as they refer to the Lord Jesus.

There are also typical passages, which, besides their literal sense, have also figurative meanings, relating not only to Jesus Christ, but also to the church in general, and to every believer in particular.

For example, Dan. ix. 7: "O Lord, righteousness belongeth to thee, but unto us confusion of face, as at this day," must not be divided into parts, but considered in different views: 1. In regard to all men in general. 2. In regard to the Jewish Church in Daniel's time. 3. In regard to ourselves at this present day.

So again, Heb. iii. 7, 8. "To-day, if ye will hear his voice," which is taken from Psalm xcv., cannot be better divided than by referring it — 1 To David's time. 2. St. Paul's. And lastly, to our own.

As to the division of the text itself, sometimes the order of the words is so clear and natural, that no division is necessary, you need only follow simply tne order of the words. As for example, Eph. i. 3. "Blessed be the God and Father of our Lord Jesus Christ, who hath blessed us with all spiritual blessings in heavenly places in Christ." It is not necessary to divide this text, because the words divide themselves, and to explain them, we need only to follow them. Here is a grateful acknowledgment. "Blessed be God." The title under which the Apostle blesses God, "The Father of our Lord Jesus Christ." The reason for which he blesses him, because "he hath blessed us." The plenitude of this blessing, "with all blessings." The nature or kind signified by the term spiritual. The place where he hath blessed us, "in heavenly places." In whom he hath blessed us, "in Christ."

Most texts, however, ought to be formally divided; for which purpose you must principally have regard to the order of nature, and put that division which naturally precedes, in the first place, and the rest must follow, each in its proper order.

There are two natural orders; one natural in regard to subjects themselves; the other natural in regard to us.

And though, in general, you may follow which of the two others you please, yet there are some texts that determine the division; as Phil. ii. 13. "It is God who worketh effectually in you, both to will and to do of his own good pleasure." There are, it is plain, three things to be discussed; the action of God's grace upon men, "God worketh effectually in you;" the effect of this grace, "to will and to do;" and the spring or source of the action, according to "his good pleasure." I think the division would not be proper if we were to treat, 1. Of God's good pleasure; 2. Of his grace; and 3. Of the will and works of men.

Above all things, in divisions, take care of putting any thing in the first part which supposes the understanding of the second; or which obliges you to treat of the second to make the first understood; for, by these means, you will throw yourself into great confusion, and be obliged to Make many tedious repetitions. You must endeavour to disengage the one from the other as well as you can; and when your parts are too closely connected with each other, place the most detached first, and endeavour to make that serve for a foundation to the explication of the second, and the second to the third; so that, at the end of your explication, the hearer may at a glance perceive, as it were, a perfect body, a well finished building; for one of the greatest excellences of a sermon is, the harmony of its component parts; that the first leads to the second, the second serves to introduce the third; that they which go before, excite a desire for those which are to follow.

When, in a text, there are several terms which need a particular explanation, and which cannot be explained without confusion, or without dividing the text into too many parts, then I would not divide the text at all; but I would divide the discourse into two or three parts; and I would propose, first, to explain the terms, and then the subject itself.

There are many texts, in discussing which, it is not necessary to treat of either subject or attribute; but all the discussion depends on the terms, *syncategorematica* (words which, of themselves, signify nothing, but, in conjunction with others, are very significative). For example, John iii. 16, "God so loved the world." The categorical proposition is, God loved the world; yet, it is neither necessary to insist much upon the term *God*, nor to speak in a common-place way of the love of God, but, divide the text into two parts; first, the gift which God in his love hath made of his son; secondly, the end for which he gave him, "that whosoever believeth in him should not perish, but have everlasting life."

There are texts of reasoning, which are composed of an objection and an answer and the division of such is plain; for they naturally divide into the objection and solution. As, Romans vi. 1, 2, "What shall we say then," &c.

There are some texts of reasoning which are extremely difficult to divide because they cannot be reduced into many propositions without confusion. As, John iv. 10, "If thou knewest the gift of God," &c. I think it might not be improper to divide it into two parts, the first including the genera. propositions contained in the words; and the second, the particular application of these to the Samaritan woman.

There are some texts which imply many important truths without ex pressing them; and yet it will be necessary to mention and enlarge upon them, either because they are useful on some important occasion, or because they are important of themselves. Then the text may be divided into two parts, one implied, and the other expressed.

In texts of history, divisions are easy; sometimes an action is related in all its circumstances, and then you may consider the action in itself first, and afterward the circumstances of the action.

To render a division agreeable, and easy to be remembered by the hearer, endeavour to reduce it as often as possible to simple terms.

As to subdivisions, it is always necessary to make them, for they very much assist the composition, and diffuse perspicuity into a discourse; but it is not always necessary to mention them; on the contrary, they must be very seldom mentioned, because it will load the hearer's mind with a mul titude of particulars.

Discussion. There are four methods of discussion. Clear subjects must be discussed by observation, or continued application; difficult and important ones by explication or proposition.

I. *By Explication.* — The difficulty is in regard to the Terms, to the sub ject, or to both.

1. *Explication of Terms.* — The difficulties of these arise from three causes; either the terms do not seem to make any sense, or they are equi vocal, forming different senses; or, the sense they seem to make at first appears perplexed, improper, or contradictory: or, the meaning, though clear, may be controverted, and is exposed to cavil.

Propose the *ratio dubitandi*, which makes the difficulty; then determine it as briefly as you can.

2. *Of Things.* — Difficult things. If the difficulty arise from errors, or false senses, refute and remove them; then establish the truth. If from the intricacy of the subject itself, do not propose difficulties, and raise objections, but enter immediately into the explication of the matter, and take care to arrange your ideas well.

3. Important things, though clear, must be discussed by explication, be cause they are important.

There are two sorts of explications; the one, simple and plain, needs only to be proposed, and agreeably elucidated; the other must be confirmed, if it speak of fact, by proofs of fact; if of right, by proofs of right; if of both, proofs of both. A great and important subject, consisting of many branches, may be reduced to a certain number of propositions or questions, and dis cussed one after the other.

N. B. Sometimes what you will have to explain in a text will consist of one or more simple terms; of ways of speaking peculiar to Scripture; of particles called *syncategorematica;* and sometimes of different propositions.

1. Simple terms are the divine attributes, goodness, &c., man's virtues or vices, faith, hope, &c. Simple terms are either proper or figurative; if figurative, give the meaning of the figure, and, without stopping long, pass on to the thing itself. Some simple terms must only be explained just as they relate to the intention of the sacred author; in a word, explain simple terms as much as possible, in relation to the design of the sacred author. Sometimes the simple terms in a text must be discussed professedly, in order to give a clear and full view of the subject. Sometimes, when there are many, it might be injudicious to treat of them separately, but beauti fully to do it by comparison.

2. Expressions peculiar to Scripture deserve a particular explanation, because they are rich in meaning; such as, "to be *in* Christ," "come *after* Christ," &c.

Particles called *syncategorematica* (such as *none*, *some*, *all*, *now*, *when*, &c.), which augment or limit the meaning of the proposition, should be carefully examined; for often the whole explication depends upon them.

3. When the matter to be explained in a text consists of a proposition, give the sense clearly; if necessary, show its importance; if it require confirmation, confirm it.

In all cases, illustrate by reasons, examples, comparisons of the subject; their relations, conformities, or differences. You may do it by consequences; by the person, his state, &c., who proposes the subject; or the persons to whom it is proposed; by circumstance, time, place, &c. You may illustrate a proposition by its evidence or inevidence. It is discoverable by the light of nature, or only by revelation. Let good sense choose the best topics.

Sometimes a proposition includes many truths which must be distinguished; sometimes a proposition must be discussed in different views; sometimes it has different degrees, which must be remarked; sometimes it is general, and of little importance; then examine whether some of its parts be not more considerable; if so, they must be discussed by a particular application.

II. *By observation;* which is best for clear and historical passages. Some texts require both explication and observation. Sometimes an observation may be made by way of explication. Observations, for the most part, ought to be theological; historical, philosophical, or critical, very seldom. They must not be proposed in a scholastic style, nor common-place form, but in a free, easy, familiar manner.

III. *By continual application.* — This may be done without explaining, or making observations. In this manner we must principally manage texts exhorting to holiness and repentance. In using this method something searching and powerful must be said, or better it should be let alone.

IV. *By proposition.* — The texts must be reduced to two propositions at least, and three or four at most, having a mutual dependence and connexion.

This method opens the most extensive field for discussion. In the former methods you are restrained to your text; but here your subject is the matter contained in your proposition.

The way of explication* is most proper to give the meaning of Scripture; this of systematical divinity; and it has this advantage, it will equally serve either theory or practice.

N. B. Though these four ways are different from each other, for many texts it may be necessary to use two or three, and for some, all the four the discourse has its name from the prevailing method of handling it.

The conclusion. This ought to be lively and animating, full of great and beautiful figures. Aiming to move Christian affections. As the love of God, hope, zeal, repentance, self-condemnation, a desire of self-correction, consolation, admiration of eternal benefits, hope of felicity, courage, and constancy in afflictions, steadiness in temptations, gratitude to God, recourse to him by prayer, and other such dispositions.

There are three sorts of dispositions; the violent, tender, and elevated. To raise these, the conclusion should be violent, tender, or elevated. It may be sometimes mixed, it must always be diversified.

N. B. Let the peroration, or conclusion, be short; let it be bold and lively. Let some one or more striking ideas, not mentioned in the discussion, be reserved for this part, and applied with vigor.

---

* See No. I. on the previous page.

Example.

OF THE SKELETON OF A SERMON.

The existence of God.

"The fool hath said in his heart, there is no God." Psalms **xiv. 1.**

"The fool hath said,"—it is evident that none but a fool would have said it.

The fool, a term in Scripture, signifying a wicked man; one who hath lost his wisdom, and right apprehension of God; one dead in sin, yet one not so much void of rational faculties, as of grace in those faculties; not one that wants reason, but one who abuses his reason.

"Said in his heart;" i. e. he thinks, or he doubts, or he wishes. Thoughts are words in heaven. He dares not openly publish it, though he dares secretly to think it; he doubts, he wishes, and sometimes hopes.

"There is no God,"—no judge, no one to govern, reward, or punish. Those who deny the providence of God. do, in effect, deny his existence; they strip him of that wisdom, goodness, mercy, and justice, which are the glory of the Deity.

Men who desire liberty to commit works of darkness, would not only have the lights in the house dimmed, but extinguished. What men say against Providence, because they would have no check, they would say in their hearts against the very existence of God, because they would have no judge.

The existence of God is the foundation of all religion. The whole building totters, if the foundation be out, of course. We must believe that he is, and that he is what he declared himself, before we can seek him, adore him, and love him.

It is, therefore, necessary we should know why we believe, that our belief be founded on undeniable evidence, and that we may give a better reason for his existence, than that we have heard our parents and teachers tell us so. It is as much as to say, "There is no God," when we have no better arguments than those.

That we may be fully persuaded of, and established in this truth, endeavour,

I. To bring forward a few observations in the defence thereof.

1. All nature shows the existence of its Maker. We cannot open our eyes but we discover this truth shine through all creatures. The whole universe bears the character and stamp of a First Cause, infinitely wise, infinitely powerful. Let us cast our eyes on the earth which bears us, and ask, "Who laid the foundation?" Job xxxviii. 4. Let us look on that vast arch of skies that covers us, and inquire, "Who hath thus stretched it forth?" Isaiah xl. 21, 52. "Who is it also that hath fixed so many luminous bodies, with so much order and regularity?" Job xxvi. 13. The various works of creation proclaim to us "His eternal power and godhead." Romans i. 20; Acts xiv. 16, 17; xvii. 26. Every plant, every atom, as well as every star, bear witness of a Deity. Who ever saw statues, or pictures, but concluded there had been a statuary and limner? Who can behold garments, ships, or houses, and not understand there was a weaver, a carpenter, an architect? All things that are demonstrate something from whence they are. A man may as well doubt whether there be a sun when he sees his beams gilding the earth, as doubt whether there be a God, when he sees his works. Psalms xix. 1–6.

The Atheist is, therefore, a fool, because he denies that which every creature in his constitution asserts; can he behold the spider's net, or the silk-worm's web, the bee's closets, or the ant's granaries, without acknowledging a higher being than a creature, who hath planted that genius in them? Job xxxix.; Psalms civ. 24. "The stars fought against Sisera." Judges v. 20. All the stars in heaven, and the dust on earth, oppose the Atheist. Romans i. 19, 20.

2. The dread of conscience is an argument to convince us of this truth 'Every one that finds me shall slay me," Genesis iv. 14, was the language of Cain; and the like apprehensions are not seldom in those who feel the fury of an enraged conscience. The psalmist tells us concerning those who say in their heart, "There is no God," that "they are in fear, where no fear is," Psalms liii. 5. Their guilty minds invent terrors, and thereby confess "a Deity, whilst they deny it, — that there is a sovereign Being who will punish. Pashur, who wickedly insulted the prophet Jeremiah, had this for his reward, "that his name should be Magor-missabib," i. e. "fear round about," Jeremiah xx. 3, 4. When Belshazzar saw the hand writing, "his countenance was changed," Daniel v. 6. The apostle who tells us, that there is a "law written in the hearts of men," adds, their "consciences also bear witness," Romans ii. 15. The natural sting and horror of conscience are a demonstration that there is a God to judge and punish.

The Atheist is a fool, because he useth violence to his conscience. The operations of conscience are universal. The iron bars upon Pharaoh's conscience at last gave way. Exodus ix. 27.

3. *Universal consent* is another argument. The notion of a God is found among all nations; it is the language of every country and region; the most abominable idolatry argues a Deity. All nations, though ever so barbarous and profligate, have confessed some God. This universal verdict of mankind is no other than the voice of God, the testimony of reason, and the language of nature; there is no speech, nor tongue where this voice is not heard.

Is it not, therefore, folly for any man to deny that which nature has engraven on the minds of all?

4. *Extraordinary judgments.* When a just revenge follows abominable crimes, especially when the judgment is suited to the sin; when the sin is made legible by the inflicted judgments. "The Lord is known by the judgments which he executes," Psalms ix. 16. Herod Agrippa received the flattering applause of the people, and thought himself a God; but was, by the judgment inflicted upon him, forced to confess another. Acts xii. 21 – 23: Judges i. 6, 7; Acts v. 1 – 10.

5. *Accomplishments of prophecies.* To foretell things that are future, as if they did already exist, or had existed long ago, must be the result of a mind infinitely intelligent. "Show the things that are to come hereafter." Isaiah xli. 23. "I am God, declaring the end from the beginning." Isaiah xlvi. 10. Cyrus was prophesied of, Isaiah xliv. 28, and xlv. 1, long before he was born; Alexander's sight of Daniel's prophecy concerning his victories moved him to spare Jerusalem. The four monarchies are plainly deciphered in Daniel, before the fourth rose up. That power, which foretells things beyond the wit of man, and orders all causes to bring about those predictions, must be an infinite power: the same as made, sustains, and governs all things according to his pleasure, and to bring about his own ends; and this being is God. "I am the Lord, and there is none else,' Isaiah xlv. 6, 7.

What folly, then, for any to shut their eyes, and stop their ears; to attribute those things to blind chance, which nothing less than an infinitely wise and infinitely powerful Being could effect!

II. A few observations.

1. If God can be seen in creation, study the creatures; the creatures are the heralds of God's glory. "The glory of the Lord shall endure" Psalms civ. 31.

34

The world is a sacred temple; man is introduced to contemplate it. As grace does not destroy nature, so the book of redemption does not blot out the book of creation. Read nature; nature is a friend to truth.

2. If it be a folly to deny or doubt the being of God, is it not a folly also not to worship God, when we acknowledge his existence? "To fear God, and keep his commandments, is the whole duty of man."

We are not reasonable if we are not religious. "Your reasonable ser vice," Romans xii. 1.

3. If it be a folly to deny the existence of God, will it not be our wisdom since we acknowledge his being, often to think of him? It is the black mark of a fool, "God is not in all his thoughts," Psalms x. 4.

4. If we believe the being of God, let us abhor practical Atheism. Ac tions speak louder than words.

"They professed that they knew God," Titus i. 16. Men's practices are the best indexes to their principles. "Let your light shine before men." Matthew v. 16.

*The following Skeletons are on a different plan.**

1.

Psalm xlvi. 1, "God is our refuge and strength, a very present help in trouble."

Sorrow is our common lot, many seem to know little of it, the widow, fatherless, &c.; text needs no explanation.

I. The wonderful condescension of God in assuming this character to wards man, — not, however, according to the usual reasoning, — man's greatness, — his progressive faculties will equal angels, &c. Surpass all intelligence except God, — but there will still be an infinite distance between God and man, — Man's moral estate; these the reasons.

II. The emphasis of the text, —*present*, *very present*, — our mechanical habits, — the divine presence not *realized*, — a man first awakened or convicted feels it, — but soon is lost, — suppose a pure and holy being were present at your sins, — as an angel, — but God is present! See the Christian in a storm at sea, — hearing the crash, indulging sin. —

Objection to the infinite God's caring for man, — all worlds particles of sand. — How should this thought affect us, — Mother! Jesus stood at the coffin of thy infant child, at the grave of thy parents! He is with thee. Shall we weep and repine even in a garret, when God is with us?

III. Cautiousness of the text. — He is a help, — not sole deliverer, — there is something for us to do, — prayer is one reason of it. — Nothing otherwise. — Farmer. — Mechanic, — health by medicine.

IV. Applicability of the text to all the poor unfortunate, — stranger, — widow, — orphan, — mourner, — Christian in temptation, — quality of all, a guilty conscience.

2.

Rev. vii. 17, "God shall wipe away all tears from their eyes." Context, - Nature and probable design of these prophecies. —

I. Afflictions in the present state of the Christian, an important and ad vantageous part of his moral discipline. 1. The fact that they are per mitted, shows that they are advantageous. — How many instances, — texts.

2. They afford exercise for our Christian virtues, moral, — fortitude patience, resignation.

3. They show us the futility of worldly comforts, — our friends die, — health and beauty fade, — wealth and pleasure must be left behind us.

* They are, in fact, the notes of a distinguished extemporaneous preacher.

II This discipline is preparatory to another which shall be exempt from affliction.

1. The Scriptures assert the existence of such a place called heaven, Kingdom of God, Paradise, New Jerusalem, &c. It is implied in the doctrine of immortality.

2. It is consistent with all rational supposition. — Analogy between this world and other planets. — 3. All causes of sorrow shall cease there. — 4. It is everlasting in its duration. —

APPLICATION.

Do I address the mourner who has lost friends, estate, health? — the aged? — youth declining in early life? &c.

3.

Gal. iii. 18, "But it is good to be zealously affected always in a good thing."

Christianity is designed to call into activity the noblest sentiments of the heart, — firm resolve, — intrepid daring and undaunted perseverance, — zeal. — The Christian's life is a holy warfare, — a holy chivalry. — The Apostle lays down the proposition, that if anything is good, it is good to be zealously affected in that good cause, — Christianity is good considered.

I. In respect to its *orign*, — divine, — bears its marks, -- it is interesting to contemplate nature, — but much more revelation, — the noblest gift of God to man. —

II. In its nature, — its theory of doctrines, — its code of moral rules was never equalled by 1, Philosophy, — 2. Education, — all improvement has failed without it. — Its nature renders it efficient in its effects, — its preservation, — triumph over infidelity. --

III. Its effects, — individual effects. — 1. Benevolence, — 2. Death. — 3. Peace of conscience.

2. General effects, — 1. It prevents crime. — 2. Elevates society. — 3. Sustains good government. — 4. War.

We should be zealous, 1. Because God commands us to be so. 2. The wants of the world call for it. 3. Our happiness hereafter will be proportioned to our zeal, — a philosophical as well as Scriptural fact. — We have high examples to copy, — the apostles, martyrs, and reformers, — Wesley Whitfield, &c.

XCVIII.

SUBJECTS FOR COMPOSITIONS OF ALL SORTS

1. Mythology.
2 Rural happiness.
3 Our native land.
4. Description of a storm.
5. Scene at a summer's noon.
6. A winter landscape.
7. A market day.
8. An evening walk.
9. The entrance of Christ into Jerusalem.
10. Ruins of Rome.
   " Greece.
11. Twilight.
12. A winter evening.
13. Moonlight at sea.
14. Spring.
15. Summer.
16. Autumn.
17. Winter.
18. The equator.

19. The tropics.
20. Mid-summer.
21. Rural scenery.
22. Review of the seasons.
23. Solitude.
24. The love of order.
25. Evils of obstinacy.
26. Firmness.
27. Delicacy of feeling.
28. Delicacy of taste.
29. Novels.
30. Tales of fiction.
31. Contemplation.
32. Correspondence between true politeness and religion.
33. Sympathy.
34. The advantages of a good education.
35. The effects of learning on the countenance.
36. Power of habit.
37. The art of pleasing.
38. Comparison of history and biography.
39. The passions.
40. The difference between beauty and fashion.
41. Enterprise.
42. Exertion.
43. Importance of a good character.
44. Criticism.
45. Religious education.
46. Monumental inscriptions.
47. On forming connexions.
48. Qualifications for the enjoyment of friendship.
49. Duties of hospitality.
50. Moral principles.
51. Moral duties.
52. Civility.
53. Family quarrels, their causes, and mode of preventing them.
54. Early attachments.
55. Taste for the cultivation of flowers.
56. Government of temper.
57. Comedy.
58. Tragedy.
59. Uses of adversity.
60. Poetical taste.
61. Manners.
62. Modesty of merit.
63. Method.
64. Parental indulgence.
65. Parental severity.
66. Profligacy.
67. The study of the Latin language.
68. The study of the French language.
69. Ingenuity.
70. Eloquence.
71. Fancy.
72. Imagination.
73. Classical learning.
74. Taste for simple pleasures.
75. Scepticism.
76. Amusements.
77. Efficacy of moral instruction.
78. A cultivated mind necessary for the enjoyment of retirement.
79. Want of personal beauty as affecting virtue and happiness.
80. Happiness of domestic life.
81. Evils of public life.
82. Modesty a sign of merit.
83. Equanimity the best support under affliction.
84. Ill effects of ridicule.
85. Necessity of temperance to the health of the mind.
86. Moral effects of painting and sculpture.
87. The choice of a profession.
88. Selfishness.
89. Literary genius.
90. Necessity of attention to things as well as to books.
91. Fear of growing old.
92. The butterfly and its changes.
93. Freedom.
94. The rose.
95. The lily.
96. Remorse.
97. The voice.
98. Grace.
99. Gesture.
100. Woman.
101. Man.
102. Youth and manhood.
103. The sacred Scriptures
104. The press.
105. The pulpit.
106. The human frame.
107. Travelling.
108. Language.
109. Liberty.
110. Infidelity.
111. Atheism.
112. Independence.
113. The existence of God.
114. Light.
115. Darkness.
116. Heat.
117. Cold.
118. The rainbow.
119. The wife.
120. The husband.

121. Influence of Christianity.
122. Stability of character.
123. Instability of character
124. Peevishness.
125. Art of pleasing.
126. Local associations.
127. Influence of female character
128. Discretion.
129. New England.
130. Paternal influence.
131. Maternal influence.
132. Intemperance.
133. Fashionable Follies.
134. Emigration.
135. Intellectual dissipation.
136. Intellectual discipline.
137 The warrior.
138. The statesman.
139. The legislator.
140. The judge.
141. A field of battle.
142. A naval engagement.
143. Immortality.
144. Decision of character
145. Romance.
146. Flattery.
147. Industry
148. Temperance.
149. Resentment.
150. Lying.
151. Piety.
152. Anger.
153. Poetry.
154. Envy.
155. Virtue.
156. Justice.
157. Adversity.
158. Pride.
159. Compassion.
160. Avarice
161. Slander.
162. Mercy.
163. Wealth.
164. Prudence.
165. Gratitude.
166. Affectation.
167. Loquacity.
168. Wisdom.
169. Luxury.
170. Health.
171. Pleasure.
172. Gaming.
173 Religion.
174. Study.
175. Experience.
176. Peace and war.
177. Want and plenty.
178. Ignorance and learning
179. Happiness and misery.
180. Virtue and vice.
181. Parsimony and prodigality.
182. Hope and fear.
183. Reward and punishment.
184. Beauty and deformity.
185. Affection and hatred.
186. Arrogance and humility.
187. Order and Confusion.
188. Carelessness and caution
189. Contentment and dissatisfaction.
190. Emulation and sloth.
191. Cleanliness.
192. Religious intolerance.
193. Charity.
194. Contentment.
195. Courage.
196. Hope.
197. Perseverance.
198. Conscience.
199. Death.
200. Life.
201. Sickness.
202. Health.
203. Good humor.
204. Omniscience of God.
205. Omnipresence of God.
206. Truth.
207. Sincerity.
208. Procrastination
209. Trust in God.
210. Pleasures resulting from, proper use of our faculties
211. Modesty.
212. Application.
213. Discretion.
214. Christianity.
215. Suspicion.
216. Fortitude.
217. Forgiveness.
218. The seasons.
219. Filial affection.
220. Harmony of nature.
221. Adversity.
222. Distribution of time.
223. Sources of knowledge.
224. Conjugal affection.
225. Filial piety.
226. Generosity.
227. Heroism.
228. Despair.
229. Government.
230. Dramatic entertainments.
231. Fables and allegories.
232. Figurative language.
233. Commerce.
234. Chivalry.
235. Philosophy.
236. Natural history.

337. Astronomy.
238. The invention of the mariners' compass.
239. The invention of the telescope.
240. The application of steam.
241. The invention of the steam engine.
242. The mathematics.
243. Astrology.
244. Modern discoveries.
245. Architecture.
246. The law.
247. The learned professicns.
248. Curiosity.
249. Nature.
250. Art.
251. The influence and importance of the female character.
252. Is the expectation of reward or the fear of punishment the greater in centive to exertion?
253. The value of time, and the uses to which it should be applied.
254. The character of the Roman Emperor Nero, — of Caligula, — of Augus tus, — of Julius Cæsar, — of Numa Pompilius.
255. The duties we owe to our parents, and the consequences of a neglec of them.
256. How blessings brighten as they take their flight.
257. How dear are all the ties that bind our race in gentleness together.
258. The advantages of early rising; and the arguments which may be ad duced to prove it a duty.
259. Misery is wed to guilt.
260. A soul without reflection, like a pile
Without inhabitant, to ruin runs.
261. Still where rosy pleasure leads
See a kindred grief pursue,
Behind the steps that misery treads
Approaching comforts view.
262. 'T is Providence alone secures,
In every change, both mine and yours.
263. Know then this truth, enough for man to know,
Virtue alone is happiness below.
264. Prayer ardent opens heaven.
Whatever is, is right.
265. Knowledge and plenty vie with each other.
266. When beggars die there are no comets seen;
The heavens themselves blaze forth the death of princes.
267. Friendship is constant in all other things
Save in the office and affairs of love.
268. Man, proud man,
Drest in a little brief authority,
Most ignorant of what he 's most assured.
269. No might nor greatness in mortality
Can censure 'scape; back-wounding calumny
The whitest virtue strikes.
270. They say, best men are moulded out of faults.
271. What we have we prize not to the worth
Whiles we enjoy it; but being lacked and lost,
Why then we rack the value; then we find
The virtue that possession would not show us
Whiles it was ours.
272. All delights are vain; but that most vain
Which, with pain purchased, doth inherit pain.
273 Light, seeking light, doth light of light beguile.

274 Too much to know is to know nought but fame.
275 Where is any author in the world
Teaches such beauty as a woman's eye?
276. The hind that would be mated by the lion
Must die for love.
277. Our remedies oft in ourselves do lie
Which we ascribe to heaven.
278. The web of our life is of mingled yarn,
Good and ill together: our virtues would be
Proud, if our faults whipped them not; and our
Crimes would despair if they were not
Cherished by our virtues.
279. Let 's take the instant by the forward top;
For we are old, and on our quickest decrees
The inaudible and noiseless foot of time
Steals ere we can effect them.
280. They lose the world that do buy it with much care.
281. I can easier teach twenty what were
Good to be done, than be one of the twenty to
Follow mine own teaching.
282. All things that are,
Are with more spirit chased than enjoyed.
283. Love is blind, and lovers cannot see
The petty follies that themselves commit.
284. The world is still deceived with ornament.
285. The man that hath no music in himself,
Nor is not moved with concord of sweet sounds,
Is fit for treason, stratagems and spoils.
286. The nightingale, if she would sing by day,
When every goose is cackling, would be thought
No better a musician than the wren.
How many things by season seasoned are
To their right praise and true perfection.
287. This our life exempt from public haunt,
Finds tongues in trees, books in the running brooks,
Sermons in stones, and good in every thing.
288. Oftentimes, to win us to our harm,
The instruments of darkness tell us truths,
Win us with trifles, to betray us
In deepest consequence.
289. I dare do all that may become a man,
Who dares do more is none.
290. If it were done, when 't is done, then 't were well
It were done quickly.
291. Memory, the warder of the brain.
292. Noughts' had, all 's spent
Where our desire is got without content.
293. Things without remedy
Should be without regard.
294. When our actions do not,
Our fears do make us traitors.
295. Angels are bright still, though the brightest fell.
296. The grief that does not speak
Whispers the o'erfraught heart, and bids it break.
297. Courage mounteth with occasion.
298. When fortune means to men most good,
She looks upon them with a threatening eye.
299 He that stands upon a slippery place
Makes nice of no vile hold to stay him up.

300. Often times excusing of a fault
Doth make the fault the worse by the excuse,
As patches, set upon a little breach
Discredit more in hiding of the fault
Than did the fault before it was so patched.
301. How oft the sight of means to do ill deeds
Makes deeds ill done!
302. That which in mean men we entitle patience,
Is pale, cold cowardice in noble breasts.
303. Woe doth the heavier sit
Where it perceives it is but faintly borne.
304. Gnarling sorrow hath less power to bite
The man that mocks at it and sets it light.
305. O who can hold a fire in his hand
By thinking on the frosty Caucasus?
Or cloy the hungry edge of appetite,
By bare imagination of a feast?
Or wallow naked in December's snow,
By thinking on fantastic summer's heat?
Oh, no! the apprehension of the good,
Gives but the greater feeling to the worse;
Fell sorrow's tooth doth never rankle more
Than when it bites, but lanceth not the sore.
306. If all the year were playing holidays,
To sport would be as tedious as to work.
307. The better part of valor is discretion.
308. See what a ready tongue suspicion hath!
He that but fears the thing he would not know,
Hath, by instinct, knowledge from others' eyes,
That what he feared, is chanced.
309. Nought so vile, that on the earth doth live,
But to the earth some special good doth give;
Nor aught so good, but strained from that fair
Revolts from true birth, stumbling on abuse.
Virtue itself turns vice, being misapplied,
And vice sometimes 's by action dignified.
310. Striving to better, oft we mar what 's well.
311. O reason not the need; our basest beggars
Are in the poorest thing superfluous:
Allow not nature more than nature needs,
Man's life is cheap as beast's.
312. Give thy thoughts no tongue,
Nor any unproportioned thought his act.
313. The friends thou hast and their adoption tried,
Grapple them to thy soul with hooks of steel.
314. Beware
Of entrance to a quarrel: but, being in,
Bear it, that the opposer may beware of thee
315. Give every man thy ear, but few thy voice.
316. The apparel oft proclaims the man.
317. Neither a borrower nor a lender be;
For loan oft loseth both itself and friend,
And borrowing dulls the edge of husbandry
318. To thine own self be true;
And it must follow, as the night the day,
Thou canst not then be false to any man
319. Trifles, light as air,
Are to the jealous confirmations strong
As proofs of holy writ.

320. He that is robbed, not wanting what is stolen,
Let him not know it and he 's not robbed at all.

SUBJECTS FOR CONFERENCES.

1. On the mineral, animal, and vegetable kingdoms, as furnishing subjects of interesting inquiry.
2. On reflection, reading, and observation, as affording a knowledge of human nature.
3. On the present character of the inhabitants of New-England, as resulting from the civil, literary, and religious institutions of our forefathers.
4. The stability of the General Government of the United States as affected by a national literature, common dangers, facility of mutual intercourse, and a general diffusion of knowledge.
5. The obligations of a country to her warriors, her statesmen, her artists, and her authors.
6. Public amusements, splendid religious ceremonies, warlike preparations, and a display of a rigid police, as means of despotic power.
7. The comparative virtue of the enlightened and ignorant classes.
8. On the value to a nation of the abstract sciences, the physical sciences, and literature.
9. The associations excited by visiting Italy, Greece, Egypt, and Palestine, considered with reference to their ancient history.
10. On the fine arts, as affecting the morals, refinement, patriotism, and religion of a country.
11. On architecture, painting, poetry, and music, as tending to produce and perpetuate religious impressions.
12. On the comparative operation in obstructing the progress of truth, of the spirit of controversy, the reverence of antiquity, the passion of novelty, and the acquiescence in authority.
13. On the character of Hume, Robertson, Gibbon, and Mitford, as historians.
14. On the characteristics of man and government, as found in the savage, pastoral, agricultural, and commercial state.
15. On patronage, emulation, and personal necessity, as promotive of literary exertion.
16. On the effect of agriculture and manufactures on the morals of the community.
17. On the influence of Greek, Latin, English, and French literature on taste.
18. On novels formed on fashionable, humble, and sea life.
19. Natural, civil, ecclesiastical, and literary history, considered in relation to the tendency of each to improve and elevate the intellectual faculties.
20. Miss Edgeworth, Hannah More, and Mrs. Hemans.
21. The letters of Lady Mary Wortley Montague, Horace Walpole, and Cowper.
22. Personal merit and powerful friends, as promoting advancement in life.
23. The influence of Young's and Cowper's Poems.
24. The commercial spirit of modern times, considered in its influence on the political, moral, and literary character of a nation.
25. Sterne, Rabelais, and Cervantes.
26. The difference of feeling in the young and the old, with regard to innovation.
27. War, commerce, and missionary enterprises, as means of civilizing barbarous countries.

28. The political reformer, the schoolmaster, and the missionary.
29. The country gentleman and the plebeian.
30. Ancient and modern honors to the dead.
31. Common sense, genius, and learning, — their characteristics, comparative value, and success.
32. The prospects of a scholar, a politician, and an independent gentleman in the United States.
33. Contemporary and subsequent narratives, of historical events.
34. Franklin, Davy, and Fulton. The comparative value of their discoveries and improvements.
35. The comparative influence of natural scenery, the institutions of society, and individual genius on taste.
36. Heraclitus, Democritus, Epicurus, and Diogenes.
37. The ages of Queen Elizabeth, Charles the Second, Queen Anne, and the present age, considered in a literary point of view.
38. Egypt as described by Herodotus, Greece under Pericles, the Augustan age of Rome, Spain under Isabella, Italy in the fifteenth and sixteenth centuries, and France under Louis the Fourteenth.
39. Reading, writing, observation of men and manners, and the study of nature, as means of intellectual development.
40. Popular elections, a free press, and general education.
41. The Roman ceremonies, the system of the Druids, the religion of the Hindoos, and the superstitions of the American Indians.
42. The literature and morals of a country, as affected by the efforts of individual minds, the prevailing religious faith, the established form of government, and the employment most general among the people.
43. Actions, words, manners, and expression of countenance, as indicative of character.
44. The poets of England, Spain, France, and Italy.
45. The military character of Napoleon, Washington, Wellington, Frederick the Great, and Charles the Twelfth.
46. The ages of Augustus, Lorenzo de Medicis, Louis the Fourteenth, and Queen Anne.
47. The religious institutions of Egypt, Greece, and Rome.
48. Politics, war, literature, and science, as a field for the exercise of talents.
49. Astronomy, Anatomy, the instinct of animals, and the moral and intellectual nature of man, as affording proof of an intelligent Creator.
50. History, biography, and fiction.
51. The evils of a life of solitude, of fashion, of business, and of public office.
52. On classical learning, the study of mathematics, and of the science of the human mind, as contributing to intellectual culture.
53. On the operation of climate on the moral, intellectual, and military character.
54. On the power of the oriental, Gothic, and classical superstitions, to affect the imagination and the feelings.
55. On pastoral, epic, and dramatic poetry.
56. On the rank and value of the mental endowments of Shakspeare, Scott, Locke, Newton, and the Earl of Chatham.
57. Roman, Grecian, and Egyptian remains.
58. On the influence of spring, summer, autumn, and winter upon the thoughts, feelings, and imagination.
59. Britain, France, Italy, and Greece, as interesting to an American traveller.
60 On the pleasures of the antiquary, the traveller, the literary recluse and the man of business.
61. On the beneficial effects of mechanics, chemistry, astronomy and agriculture.

62. On the influence of peace upon the condition of the agriculturist, the manufacturer, the merchant, and the professional man.
63. On the views of life taken by Democritus, Heraclitus, Diogenes, and Zeno.
64. On the tendency of poetry, history, and ethical science, to promote improvement in virtue.
65. On the influence on personal happiness, of natural temper, cultivated taste, external condition, and social intercourse.
66. On novelty, sublimity, beauty, and harmony, as sources of gratification.
67. Ancient ethics, considered as pictures of manners, as proofs of genius, or as sources of entertainment.
68. The union which a harmony of motive produces between men of different pursuits, and that which results merely from a similarity of action.
69. The respective claims of poetry, painting, architecture, and sculpture as means of refinement of taste.
70. Personal memoirs and formal histories, as illustrations of national progress.
71. An old and a new country, as fields for enterprise.
72. The superiority of conscience to human laws.
73. Ancient and modern notions of liberty.
74. The scientific traveller and the missionary.
75. A profound philosophy and a wide observation of men, as elements of a statesman.
76. The pastoral and the hunter's life.
77. The war spirit in republics and in monarchies.
78. Modern explorations in Africa and America.
79. The influence of devotion to the person of the Sovereign in monarchies and to that of a popular favorite in republics.
80. Explorations by sea and by land.
81. The study of grammer, logic, and the mathamatics, as contributing to the development of the intellectual powers.
82. Personal beauty, elevation of rank, and the possession of riches, as passports in society.
83. The animal, the mineral, and the vegetable kingdoms, as fields of scientific discovery.
84. The pulpit, the press, and the school room, as efficient agents on the morals of a people.
85. The horse, the cow, and the sheep, as contributing to the comfort and convenience of mankind.
86. The expectation of reward and the fear of punishment, as affecting a moral agent.
87. The pursuits of agriculture, the profession of arms, the business of trade, and the labors of the mechanic, as affecting the taste and morals of a people.
88. Color, form, and size, as elements of physical beauty
89. Quickness of perception, retentiveness of memory, and plodding perseverance, as contributing to mental advancement.
90. The six follies of science. The quadrature of the circle; the multiplication of the cube; perpetual motion; the philosopher's stone magic; and judicial astrology.
91. Skepticism and credulity compared as obstacles to intellectual improvement.
92. Poetry and history considered as sources of amuseme[illegible]

SUBJECTS FOR COLLOQUYS, OR COLLOQUIAL DISCUSSIONS.

1. Attachment to party as a ground of action, for an upright politician.
2. On the defects and advantages of history, as affording a knowledge of the motives and actions of individuals, and of the character of human nature.
3. On the good and bad effects of emulation.
4. On the moral influence of the Christian Sabbath.
5. On the influence of fashion on the judgment of right and wrong.
6. On the influence of the multiplicity of books, on the interests of literature and science.
7. Deference to great names in philosophy, and to high rank in the social state.
8. The enthusiast and the matter of fact man.
9. On the advantages and disadvantages resulting to a scholar, from frequent intercourse with mixed society.
10. On the effects of literary reviews, as at present conducted.
11. On the comparative prevalence and strength of the principles of loyalty and independence in man.
12. On the character of ancient and modern patriotism.
13. Of establishing a University in the country or in a city.
14. Foreign travellers in the United States.
15. On the different views, which literary men take of the world at their first entrance upon it.
16. The difference of manners in Rome and in modern civilized states.
17. On active profession, as injuring or assisting the efforts of a literary man.
18. The comparative influence of governments and of individuals, in effecting great public improvements.
19. The literary influence of a reading public.
20. The views taken of a nation, by itself and others.
21. The moral effects of public, and of domestic amusements.
22. The effects of controversy on partisans, and on the public.
23. The influence of the Roman Gladiatorial shows, and of the Greek games, on the character of the people.
24. The comparative effects of literature and of science, on the progress of civilization.
25. The effect which acquaintance with foreign languages has upon the originality of a nation's literature.
26. The comparative influence of individuals and learned societies in forming the literary character of a nation.
27. The influence of the multiplication of books upon literature.
28. The study of nature, and of man, as affording a proper field for the poet.
29. The standard of taste.
30. The novels of Fielding, Richardson, and the author of Waverley.
31. The comparative importance of the expeditions to ascertain the North West passage, and the source of the Niger.
32. Intellectual, moral, and physical education.
33. The prospects of Christianity in India.
34. The satires of Horace and Juvenal.
35. How far the right should be controlled by the expedient.
36. On the comparative value of contemporaneous and posthumous fame
37. On the evils of anarchy, and of an arbitrary government.
38. Diligent observation of facts and philosophical use of them.
39. On superstition and skepticism.

40. The self-devotion of the Christian martyr and the Roman patriot.
41. Poets and novelists of the poor.
42. Strafford and Sir Henry Vane the Younger.
43. The idea of the beautiful, as developed in Grecian literature and art.
44. The influence of the association of ideas on our practical operations.
45. The moral and intellectual influence of the principle of emulation, on systems of education.
46. Entertaining mysteries, novels of real life, and romantic or supernatu ral fictions, as affording similar species of delight.
47. The Sacred and Profane poets.
48 Milton and Isaiah.
49. Johnson and St. Paul.
50. Moore and David.
51. Addison and St. John.
52. Byron and Ezekiel.
53. Hume and Moses.

SUBJECTS FOR FORENSIC DISPUTATIONS.

1. Whether the increased facilities of intercourse between Europe and the United States be favorable to this country.
2. Whether more evil or good is to be expected from the disposition man ifested, at the present day, to try existing institutions by first prin ciples.
3. Whether voting by ballot should be introduced into all elective and le gislative proceedings.
4. Whether forms of government exert any important influence on the growth and character of national literature.
5. Whether any attempt should be made to preserve severity of manners in a modern republic.
6. Ought Congress to pass an international copy right law.
7. Is there reason to think that the public mind will ever be more settled than at present, about the character of Mary, Queen of Scots.
8. Whether more good than evil has resulted to the world, from the life and religion of Mahomet.
9. Whether popular superstitions, or enlightened opinions, be most favor able to the growth of poetical literature.
10. Whether the literature of America be injured by that of modern foreign countries.
11. Whether a want of reverence be justly chargeable on our age and country.
12. Whether the diversities of individual character be owing more to phys- ical, than to moral causes.
13. Whether the advancement of civil liberty be more indebted to intellect- ual culture, than to physical suffering.
14. Whether the fine or the useful arts afford the better field for the display of originality.
15. Whether prosperity and increase of wealth have a favorable influence upon the manners and morals of a people.
16. Whether modern facilities of testing literary efforts by popular opinion, be unfavorable to the production of great works.
17. Whether the choice of a representative should be restricted to the in habitants af the town or district represented.
18. Whether the sum of human happiness on earth be greater, by a succes sion of generations, than it would have been by one continued race the number of inhabitants being the same.
19. Whether, in a public seminary, the course of study established by rule should be the same for all.
20. Do savage nations possess a full right to the soil.

21 Whether a State have a right to recede from the Union.
22 Whether, in times of political discussion, it is the duty of every citizen to declare his opinion, and attach himself to some party.
23 Whether there were greater facilities, in ancient times for an individual acquiring influence, than there are now.
24 Whether the inequalities of our social condition be favorable to the progress of knowledge.
25. Is it expedient to make colonies of convicts.
26. Is the cause of despotism strengthened by the extermination of the Poles.
27 Whether the inequalities of genius in different countries be owing to moral causes.
28. Whether inflicting capital punishments publicly has any tendency to diminish crime.
29. Whether the personal dependence, incident to a minute division of labor in the arts and sciences, be dangerous to our free institutions.
30. Whether the influences which tend to perpetuate, be stronger than those which tend to dissolve, the union of the United States.
31. Whether we should abstain from publishing the truth, from a fear lest the world be not prepared to receive it.
32. Whether the popularity of a literary work is to be received as an evidence of its real merits.
33. Is there any objection to a man's proposing himself for public office, and using means to obtain it.
34. Does proselytism favor the cause of truth.
35. Whether privateering be incident to the right of war.
36. Whether a written constitution be efficacious in securing civil liberty.
37. Whether the progress of knowledge lessen the estimation of the fine arts.
38. Whether the exclusion of foreign articles, to encourage domestic manufactures, be conducive to public wealth.
39. Whether the world be advancing in moral improvement.
40. Whether the progress of civilization diminish the love of martial glory.
41. Whether personal interest in a subject of investigation be favorable to the discovery of truth.
42. Whether the power of eloquence be diminished by the progress of literature and science.
43. Whether the prevalence of despotism in Asia be occasioned principally by physical causes.
44. Whether the present circumstances of Europe furnish reason to expect an essential amelioration of human affairs.
45. Do facts, or fiction, contribute most to mental enjoyment.
46. Whether writers of fiction be morally responsible for unchaste and profane language in their productions.
47. The policy of requiring property qualifications for office.
48. Ought capital punishments to be inflicted in time of peace.
49. Does the system of modern warfare indicate any advancement in civilization.
50. Is the existence of two great political parties in our country desirable.
51. Has her union with England been detrimental to Ireland.

SUBJECTS FOR DELIBERATIVE, POLITICAL, CRITICAL, PHILOSOPHICAL, AND LITERARY DISCUSSIONS, DISQUISITIONS INQUIRIES, &c.

1. On the right of legislative bodies to provide by law for the support of religion. (Deliberative Discussion.)
2. The character of a philosophical historian. (Philosophical Disquisition.)

3. The effect of prevailing philosophical views on the style of elegant literature. (Disquisition.)
4. On the alleged degeneracy of animals and vegetables in America. (Philosophical Discussion.)
5 Whether works of imagination should be designed to produce a specific moral effect. (Literary Discussion.)
6. The English styles that have attracted the most imitators. (Literary Disquisition.)
7. "Mahomet Ali." (Political Disquisition.)
8. Whether national literature is to be regarded more as a cause or a consequence of national refinement. (Deliberative Discussion.)
9. Originality in literature, as affected by sound criticism. (Literary Disquisition,
10. The influence of superstition on science and literature. (Philosophical Disquisition.)
11. On the materiality of light. (Philosophical Disputation.)
12. Is the preservation of the balance of power a justifiable cause of war (Deliberative Discussion.)
13. On the causes of the variety of complexion and figure in the human species. (Philosophical Disputation.)
14. On the policy of encouraging manufacturing establishments in the United States. (Deliberative Discussion.)
15. The merits of geological systems. (Disquisition.)
16. The comparative interest and importance of Grecian and Roman history. (Literary Discussion.)
17. The causes of the present pecuniary distresses of the commercial world (Disquisition.)
18. The effects of the crusades. (Literary Inquiry.)
19. Changes in English style, since the time of Milton. (Literary Discussion.)
20. Comparative advantages of politics and literature as professions in this country. (Deliberative Discussion.)
21. The influence of the dramatic writers on the age of Elizabeth and Charles the Second. (Literary Discussion.)
22. The restoration of Greece to political independence. (Deliberative Discussion.)
23. The literary influence of the early English prose writers. (Literary Disquisition.)
24. Of presenting literature and science in popular forms. (Literary Discussion.)
25. Manual and intellectual labor. (Philosophical Discussion.)
26. Will the present proposed parliamentary reform endanger the monarchical and aristocratical portion of the British constitution. (Deliberative Discussion.)
27. Importance of independent criticism to the growth of national literature (Literary Disquisition.)
28. Causes of ill health in literary men. (Philosophical Disquisition.)
29. The influence of superstition on science and literature. (Philosophical Discussion.)
30. English biography and French memoirs. (Literary Discussion.)
31. Are political improvements best effected by rulers, or the people (Deliberative Discussion.)
32. The influence of ancient art on ancient literature. (Literary Disquisition.)
33. The poet of an early age, and of a civilized one. (Literary Discussion.
34. Comparative utility of the moral and physical sciences, in the present age. (Philosophical Discussion.)
35. On what does the security of our institutions depend? (Political Disquisition.)

36. The expediency of intervention by one nation in the civil and public contests of others. (Deliberative Discussion.)
37. The evils and benefits of large books. (Literary Discussion.)
38. Skepticism and love of truth, as indications of mental character and vigor. (Philosophical Discussion.)
39. Tendency of free institutions to bring first principles into question. (Deliberative Discussion.)
40. The influence of Lord Bacon's writings on the progress of knowledge (Philosophical Discussion.)
41. An author's writing many books, or resting his fame on a few. (Literary Discussion.)
42. Universal suffrage. (Political Disquisition.)
43. The resources and encouragements of elegant literature in the Old and New World. (Literary Discussion.)
44. The comparative power of moral and physical causes in forming the American character. (Philosophical Discussion.)
45. Are short terms of political office desirable? (Deliberative Discussion.)
46. Modern imitation of the ancient Greek tragedy. (Literary Disquisition.)
47. The real or supposed decline of science, at the present day. (Philosophical Disquisition.)
48. English novels in the reigns of George the Second and George the Third. (Literary Discussion.)
49. The expediency of making authorship a profession. (Philosophical Discussion.)
50. Whether patriotism was inculcated to excesss in the ancient republics (Deliberative Discussion.)
51. The life and services of Linnæus. (Philosophical Disquisition.)
52. The observance of poetical justice in fictitious writings. (Literary Disquisition.)
53. Greek and Roman comedies. (Critical Disquisition.)
54. Education as aiming to develope all the faculties equally, or to foster individual peculiarities of taste and intellect. (Philosophical Discussion.)
55. Utility of chemical knowledge to professional men. (Philosophical Disquisition.)
56, The expediency of religious establishments under any form of civil goverment. (Deliberative Discussion.)
57. On the practicability of reaching the North Pole, and the advantages which would attend such an expedition. (Philosophical Disputation.)
58. Should the right of suffrage in any case depend upon different principles, as it respects different classes or individuals in the same country. (Deliberative Discussion.)
59. On the probability of prolonging the term of human life, by the aid of physical or moral causes. (Philosophical Discussion.)
60. Upon the Huttonian and Wernerian theories of the earth. (Philosophical Disputation.)
61. On the use of heathen mythology in modern poetry. (Literary Discussion.)
62. On the tendency of a legal provision for the support of the poor, to diminish human misery. (Deliberative Discussion.)
63. The moral tendency of the natural sciences. (Philosophical Discussion.)
64. The merits of the histories of Hume and Lingard. (Literary Discussion.)
65. Liberal principles, as affecting the strength of a government. (Deliberative Discussion.)
66. Political patronage in Republics. (Political Disquisitions.)
67. The poet of an early, and of a civilized age. (Literary Discussion; see No. 32.)

68. Are mental resources and moral energy most developed in unprincipled men? (Philosophical Discussion.)
69. Whether heat have an independent existence. (Philosophical Disputations.)
70. On the probable disposition and mutual relation of the fixed stars.
71. On the alleged improvement in the art of composition since the age of Queen Anne.
72. On the expediency of a national university. (Deliberative Discussion.)
73. Whether the climate of any country have undergone any permanent change. (Philosophical Disputation.)
74. Whether extensiveness of territory be favorable to the preservation of a republican form of government.
75. What reasons are there for not expecting another great epic poem (Literary Inquiry.)
76. The probability of the study of the dead languages always being essential to a liberal education.
77. Why are men pleased with imitation, and disgusted with mimicry?
78. What grounds are there distinct from revelation, to believe in the immortality of the soul?
79. On the comparative utility of the moral and physical sciences, in the United States.
80. The views entertained of the duties and objects of public offices by the incumbents.
81. The use of a diversity of languages.
82. The amount and character of crime in an age of barbarism, and an age of laws.
83. An inquiry into the cause of the growth of the power of ancient Rome. The favoring circumstances, — character of the people, — local situation, — early institutions of the republic, — condition of other states.
84. The use of ballads and popular songs in a rude and in a civilized age.
85. The assistance derived from friends, party, and wealth, in a democracy; and from ancestry, court favor, and title, in a despotism.
86. The favorite of nature, and the creature of art.
87. The connexion of religious celebrations with public festivities, as seen both in Pagan and Christian countries.
88. Comparison of Horace's reasons for abandoning irreligion, (See Book 1st, Ode 28th, Parcus Deorum,) with those that might affect a modern skeptic.
89. Comparison of Hume with Sallust in the delineation of character.
90. Sketches of character, as given by the historian, with Shakspeare's (or the dramatist's) mode of acquainting us with men.
91. Spoken and written language, as deceptive or inefficient modes of communication. (*Note.* We are often disappointed in reading, what we much admired in hearing.)
92. The advantages and disadvantages of negative character. (*Note.* "Deficiency of character is oftener taken for positive perfection; want of ardor is exalted into self-command and superior prudence. The cold and indifferent never offend by zealous interference, and never get into difficulties.")
93. The causes which have checked progress, or improvement in moral and physical science, or in arts and government.
94. The triumphs of the soldier and the philosopher, as of Alexander and Aristotle, Bonaparte and Cuvier.
95. Elevation of rank, as affecting turpitude of character.
96. The influence of successive generations, instead of one permanent race on human improvement.
97. The English language as it is spoken, and as it is written.
98. Of what classes of pleasure and gratification are those unfortunate beings susceptible, who are destitute of the senses of sight and hearing, as well as the faculty of speech?

99. Is the loss of sight, or of speech, the greater deprivation ?
100. Of making changes in thé political constitution of free states, easy (Deliberative Discussion.)
101. The history of Astronomy. (Disquisition.)
102. The grounds for thinking that the Malaria will eventually depopulate Rome. (Philosophical Disputation.)
103. The effects on American literature, of a community of language with England. (Literary Discussion.)
104. The comparative advantages of Western Africa and Hayti, for colonizing free blacks. (Deliberative Discussion.)
105. A history of English Literature, in which some notice may be taken of the origin and progress of the language, the influx of different terms; the peculiar styles which from age to age have been predominant; the writers who have contributed to vary, and those who have assisted in fixing its present form, structure and character; the influence of the introduction of scientific terms, — the Latin and Greek style, the French style; the Saxon peculiarities, — an enumeration of the writers who may be considered as of standard authority, — the poets the historians, — the essayists, — the moral, metaphysical, religious philological, philosophical and scientific writers, — the copiousness, precision, force, and elegance of the language; the prospects of its alteration, extinction, or universal prevalence, — the character, style. beauties, defects and influence of the writings of the respective distinguished authors of each age, — the subjects which they treated, and the interest felt by the civilized world in general on these subjects respectively. [These hints will probably furnish subjects for many dissertations, disquisitions, &c., connected wito the history of English Literature.]

SUBJECTS FOR POEMS IN ENGLISH, LATIN, GREEK, &c.

1. Numina Veterum, or the Ancient Divinities.
2. Nature, the source of poetic inspiration.
3. On the discovery of Herculaneum. (Greek.)
4. On the pleasures and pains of the student.
5. On the pursuit of fame.
6. Ode to fancy.
7. Eloquence.
8. Anticipation.
9. A vision of ambition.
10. The missionary.
11. Ad spem. (Latin.) To hope.
12. Novelty. (Greek.) Περι νεοτητος.
13. Ad pacem. (Latin.)
14. Contemplation.
15. On fame.
16. On rank and titles.
17. On civil liberty.
18. Refinement.

SUBJECTS FOR DISSERTATIONS.

1. On diversity of talents among mankind.
2. On the dependence of the mental operations on the condition of the corporeal frame.
3. On the causes of the superiority of character in modern Europe.
4. On the causes, which, independently of their merit, have contributed to elevate the ancient classics.

5. Milton and Homer contrasted and compared.
6. On the literature of the Romans, as affected by their government, religion, and state of society.
7. The influence of the fine arts upon religion.
8. The interest attached to places where distinguished persons have dwelt, or which poets have commemorated.
9. The importance of a popular history, in which the actions of men shall be represented according to the principles of the Christian religion.
10. The peculiar facilities, in modern times, for effecting great purposes in government and in religion.
11. A comparison of the domestic life of the ancient Greeks and Romans and that of our own countrymen.
12. On the influence of Christianity in producing the moral and intellectual revival of Europe, after the dark ages.
13. On the utility of the study of political economy, considered in relation to our own country.
14. On the necessity of public and private patronage, to the advancement of literature in our country.
15. The geological age of the world.
16. Agitation, as a means of effecting reform.
17. The conflict of duties.
18. On the benefit accruing to an individal from a knowledge of the physical sciences.
19. On Christianity, as affecting our domestic habits.
20. Severity of manners in a republic.
21. Heaven lies about us in our infancy.
22. The influence of fashion on our moral judgments.
23. The power of the law in free states.
24. The character of Chief Justice Marshall.
25. Distinctions of rank in the United States.
26. The encouragement to young men to educate themselves, exclusively or chiefly for high political offices.
27. Originality of thought supposed to be necessarily lessened as the world grows older.
28. Modes of publishing, circulating, and perpetuating literary works in different ages and countries.
29. Lafayette.
30. The irresponsibleness of anonymous writings.
31. The respect due from conquerors to works of art.
32. The effect of maritime enterprises on the intellectual character of a nation.
33. The field opened for men of enterprise in the West.
34. Respect for public monuments, whether triumphal or for the dead.
35. Character and writings of Sir James Mackintosh.
36. Literary character of our first settlers.
37. The infirmities of men of genius.
38. The prospects of genuine liberty in Europe.
39. The benefits to be derived from the institution of Lyceums.
40. The benefit accruing to an individual from a knowledge of the exact sciences. (See No. 18.)
41. Prospects of young men in the different learned professions
42. The character of Socrates.
43. Long Life.
44. On the charge of ingratitude made against republics.
45. The effect of the universal diffusion of knowledge on the well being of society.
46. The domestic life of the Romans.
47 The domestic life of the Greeks.
48. The domestic life of the ancient Egyptians.

49. On imagination and sensibility, as affected by the age of the individual.
50. Of making changes in an author's works to adapt them to modern tastes.
51. On the reciprocal influence of literature and morals.
52. On simplicity and ornament in writing.
53. Characteristic defects of modern English poetry.
54. The effects of seclusion and of society upon the literary character.
55. Public opinion, as a standard of right.
56. The moral power of sympathy.
57. The different views which literary men take of the world, at their first entrance upon it. (See Colloquy, No. 15.)
58. The view which a great mind takes of its own productions.
59. The principal charges preferred against the present age, by philosophers and philanthropists.
60. Chaucer and his age.
61. Visits to remarkable places.
62. The contributions of oratory to literature.
63. The influence of the multiplication of books upon literature.
64. The effect of belief in immortality upon literature.
65. The restraints imposed, in modern times, on the warlike spirit.
66. The lyric poetry of Scotland.
67. The fate of reformers.
68. The dread of the prevalence of skepticism.
69. Ages of action and of reflection.
70. The moral tendency of the principles of Malthus.
71. The education of the senses.
72. On the acquisition and use of intellectual power.
73. The literary character of the sacred Scriptures.

SUBJECTS FOR ORATIONS IN ENGLISH, FRENCH, LATIN, GREEK, SPANISH, HEBREW, &c., ESSAYS, &c.

1. The utilitarian system of education.
2. Self sacrifice.
3. Philanthropy.
4. On the names of Deity, in the Hebrew Scriptures. (Hebrew.
5. On the old age of the scholar.
6. On the importance of classical literature.
7. On the durability of our political institutions.
8 The effect of miracles on the character of the Jews. (Hebrew.)
9. On the progress of the exact sciences in France and England. (Essay.)
10. On the progress of literature. (Greek.)
11. On the Roman character and institutions. (Latin.)
12. On the dignity and utility of the philosophy of the human mind.
13. The aspect of revolutions on the advancement of the mind
14. On the decline of poetry.
15. On the cultivation of the taste and imagination
16. On the fallacy of history.
17. On literary evils.
18. On the influence of philosophy on Christianity.
19. On the influence of the arts and sciences on civil liberty.
20. On the different styles of eloquence prevailing at different periods of society.
21. Public opinion.
22. The spirit which should accompany our republican institutions.
23. Public station.
24. A salutary oration.
25. A valedictory oration.

26. On an acquaintance with the Spanish language and literature. (In Spanish.)
27. On the character of Byron.
28. On the progress of refinement.
29. On the condition and prospects of the American people
30. On the sublimity of the Holy Scriptures.
31. De recentioribus cum antiquis collatis; or, ancients and moderns compared. (In Latin.)
32. On American feeling.
33. On national eloquence.
34. The influence of commerce upon letters.
35. A modern canon of criticism.
36. Supposed degeneracy of the age.
37. No good that is possible, but shall one day be real.
38. Public recreations.
39. Empiricism.
40. The literary profession.
41. Moral effort.
42. De virorum illustrium exemplis. (Latin.) The examples of illustrious men.
43. Criticism.
44. The Christian philosophy, its political application.
45. Mental refinement.
46. Popularity.
47. Decision of character, as demanded in our day and country.
48. The character of Lord Bacon.
49. The diversities of character.
50. Literary justice.
51. Superstition.
52. The influence of speculative minds.
53. American aristocracy.
54. The value of the political lessons left us by the founders of our free institutions.
55. Enthusiasm.
56. De mortuis nil nisi bonum. (Latin.) Speak no evil of the dead
57. The spirit of reform.
58. The spirit of ancient and modern education
59. The lot of the portrayer of passion.
60. The love of truth — a practical principl.
61. The progress of man.
62. Radicalism.
63. Ancient veneration for the public.
64. The dangers of intolerance under a popular government.
65. The dangers to which the minds of young men in our country are exposed.
66. The character and prospects of the State of New York.
67. Mutation of taste.
68. Patriotism.
69. Every man a debtor to his profession.
70 Of living in times of great intellectual excitement.
71. The diffusion of scientific knowledge among the people.
72. The importance of efforts and institutions for the diffusion of know ledge.
73. Early prejudices.
74. The advancement of the age.
75. The progress of human nature.
76. Moral sublimity.
77. Home — the American home.
78. The permanence of literary fame.

79. The claims of the age on the young men of America.
80. On Physiognomy. (In Hebrew.)
81. Sur la Révolution Francaise. (French.) On the French Revolution.
82. On decision of character.
83. On innovation.
84. On the restoration of Greece.
85. De institutorum Americanorum eventûs et libertatis causæ conjunctione. (Latin.)
86. The middle ages.
87. De oraculis. (Latin.)
88. The heroic character.
89. The duties of republican citizens.
90. The duties of an American citizen.
91. On republican institutions as affecting private character.
92. On imagination as affecting individual happiness.
93 On war.
94. De Romanæ libertatis et eloquentiæ casu. The decline of Roman liberty and eloquence.
95. Views of happiness.
96. De Caii Marii ævo. (Latin.) The age of Caius Marius.
97. Skepticism.
98. De festis diebus qui nostra in Universitate celebrantur. (Latin.)
99. Modern patriotism.
100. De literis Latinis.
101. The sacrifices and recompense of literary life.
102. Quid de artibus ingenuis in civitatibus Americæ sperandum sit.
103. The American literary character.
104. De Locorum in animum vi.
105. Martyrdom.
106. Socrates. (Greek.)
107. De priscorum diis. (Latin.) The ancient divinities.
108. On the reciprocal influence of genius and knowledge.
109. On the revolutionary spirit of modern times.
110. On the durability of the Federal Union.
111. Present influences on American literature.
112. The return to Palestine.
113. De Græcarum literarum studio. (Latin.)
114. De vitæ in Universitate nostra.
115. Elements of poetry and romance in America.
116. De philosophiæ studio.
117. The pride of scholarship.
118. The physical sciences.
119 The present and former condition of Greece. (Greek.)
120. De oratoribus Americanis.
121. Periodical literature.
122. De hujus temporis indole.
123. The teacher.
124. De eloquentiæ studio in scholis nostris neglecto.
125. American political influences.
126. De literarum scholis nostris.
127. The scholar's hope.
128. De rebus preteritis et presentibus.
129. Pursuit of universal truth.
130. Literæ Americanæ.
131. Revolutions of literature.
132. De linguæ Latinæ hoc tempore usu.
133. The taking of Rome by the Gauls.
134. The progress of human sentiments.
135. The political prospects of Russia.

136. The advantages of speaking in French — in Greek, &c.
137. The moral influence of science.
138. The prospects of America.
139. Literary vanity.
140. The crusades.
141. On artificial aids to memory.
142. On Phrenology.
143. On Mesmerism.
144. On the proneness of genius to theorizing.
145. On intellectual culture.
146. On the prevalence of erroneous views of the value of metaphysical science.
147. The contributions of the fine arts to the pleasures of the domestic circle.
148. The prospects of a universal language.
149. On ancient and modern democracy.
150. On Aristocracy.
151. The future prospects of the United States.

XCIX.

LIST OF WORKS CONSULTED IN THE PREPARATION OF THIS VOLUME.

In presenting a list of authorities which have been consulted in the preparation of this volume, the author makes this general acknowledgment — that, as usefulness, not originality, has been his aim, he has in some instances *copied verbatim* from the pages of those in whom he has found any thing of value subservient to his purpose; in some he has taken the liberty to alter the phraseology, and in others entirely to remodel the principles which he has found scattered throughout these authorities. The works to which he has been most largely indebted, are Booth's Principles of English Composition, Walker's Teacher's Asssistant, Newman's, Blair's, Whately's, and Jamieson's Rhetoric, and Jardine's Principles of English Composition. Other works from which he has gleaned something of value, or hints for the improvement of what he has elsewhere gathered, are as follow:

Rippingham's Rules of English Composition; Rice's Composition; Carey's English Prosody; Roe's Elements of English Metre; Steele's Prosodia Rationalis; Crabbe's Synonymes; Harris's Hermes; Pickbourne on the English Verb; D'Israeli's Curiosities of Modern Literature; Walker's, Johnson's, Sheridan's, Richardson's, and Webster's Dictionaries; Locke's Essay on the Understanding; Watts on the Mind; Dictionary of Quotations; Andrew's and Stoddard's, and Adam's Latin Grammars; Murray's, Brown's, Felton's, Lennie's, Parker's, and Fox's English Grammars; Hedge's Logic; Encyclopædia Americana; Dictionary of Arts and Sciences; Towne's Analysis of Derivative Words; American First Class Book Mayo's Lessons on Objects; Miller's Practice of English Composition Lockhart's Life of Scott; Taylor's Elements of Thought; Hannam's Pulpit Assistant; Claude's Essay on the Composition of a Sermon; The London Quarterly Journal of Education; Beauties of History; The Spectator Inn's Rhetorical Class Book; Lallemand's Artillery Service; Beclard's Physiology; Poole's English Parnassus; The School and the School master; Bentley's Miscellany; Quarles' Books of Emblems; Knox's Essays Hay's Biography.

C.

INDEX OF SUBJECTS NOTICED IN THIS WORK.

www.ingramcontent.com/pod-product-compliance
Lightning Source LLC
LaVergne TN
LVHW021133110826
845150LV00005B/1011

* 9 7 8 1 4 2 5 5 4 9 1 4 5 *